volume one

Understanding the American Experience

Recent Interpretations

VOLUME ONE

Understanding the American Experience

Recent Interpretations

edited by

James M. Banner, Jr.   *Princeton University*

Sheldon Hackney   *Princeton University*

Barton J. Bernstein   *Stanford University*

Under the General Editorship of
John Morton Blum, Yale University

 Harcourt Brace Jovanovich, Inc.

New York   Chicago   San Francisco   Atlanta

ISBN: 0-15-592880-5

Library of Congress Catalog Card Number: 73-75178

Printed in the United States of America

Preface

These volumes present a selection of recent interpretations of major issues in American history from the colonial period to the present. They contain some of the most readable and provocative essays of many of the most thoughtful historians writing today. They also introduce recently developed historical methodologies that have uncovered neglected facts and generated significant interpretations, along with selections on subjects that have increasingly attracted historical concern, such as "inarticulate" classes, women, racial minorities, violence, and war.

We have grouped the readings into topical sections, many of which illustrate controversies among historians. We have provided an introduction for each essay that offers readers factual and historiographical information to assist them in understanding the argument. We have also in some cases raised criticisms that students will wish to consider. A short annotated bibliography of the most important related works follows each group of essays.

We wish to thank Dan T. Carter of the University of Maryland, Robert D. Cuff of York University, George M. Fredrickson of Northwestern University, James M. McPherson of Princeton University, Gary B. Nash of the University of California at Los Angeles, and Gordon S. Wood of Brown University for their advice in the preparation of the manuscript.

James M. Banner, Jr.
Sheldon Hackney
Barton J. Bernstein

Table of Contents

Problems of
Colonial Society

Charles River

No 4

Ferry to Charles=Town

Lee's Ship Yard.
Wall'd W't Still House

Eb N. Mill Dam

N. Water Mill

Gee's Ship Y'd

Hutchins Point

Hunt & White's Ship Y'd

Gooch L
and Sugar Houses

Mill Pond.

Ferry Way

Burying Place

No 4

Water Mill

Margarets

Salem St

Prince's Street

No 6

N G

Hannover St

No 5

Middle Street

North Street

Lyn Street

Union St

Fish Street

Clark's

Ship Street

N Batte

King St

No 3

Wentworth's Wharfe

Burrill's W.
Lee's Ship Y'd

Old Wharfe

Clark's Ship Y'd
Greenwood's Ship Y'd & Wharfe

Scarletts Wharfe

No 6

Marshall's W. Long Wharfe
Pool's Wharf
Olivers Dock

No 5

Clark's Wharfe

Old Wharfe

Wing's Sh'Yd
Olivers Wharfe
Gate's Sh'Yd

Old Wharfe

Battery

HARBOUR

Land, Population and the Evolution of New England Society, 1630-1790

Kenneth Lockridge

In a society of farmers, the relationship—and the ratio —of the land to its inhabitants is a critical one. Land is not only basic to the production of crops but also determines the structure and size of families, the allocation of power and esteem, and the coherence of community. In the following essay, Kenneth Lockridge of the University of Michigan uses some of the most refractory kinds of historical records—registries of births and deaths, recorded wills, and tax rolls—to try to recapture the essence of New England land-holding and population patterns and thus the structure of part of colonial American society.

Lockridge brings together the findings of historians who have recently begun to exploit the vast accumulation of demographic and economic data that for so long was passed by in favor of the more traditional sources used by historians, namely printed and manuscript literary remains. His reexamination of colonial society in the light of this data suggests that we must revise our notion that this society was, throughout its history, expansive, filled with opportunity for all, and, above all, uniquely American.

3

In the author's view, colonial America in fact went through a "Europeanization." At first, population was sparse, land plentiful, opportunity abundant. But as generation succeeded generation in the small towns of the coastal regions, population grew, the available arable lands diminished, land prices rose, wealth became more concentrated, and younger sons and new families faced a reduction of opportunity. Colonial America, like Europe, had become "overcrowded." As for New England,

in terms of land, many "yeomen" or "husbandmen" in this section of late eighteenth-century America were not perceptibly better off as a result of the long-ago emigration of their great-great grandfathers. In terms of the future, in terms of the sons of these American farmers and of the amount of land which each son could hope to inherit, America was no longer the land of opportunity.

Lockridge also concludes, contrary to a long-held belief of American historical scholarship, that, at least during these first generations of settlement, migration beyond the confines of the original towns to the frontier held little appeal. Men and women were reluctant to move. Indeed, it was this combination of a diminishing land-man ratio and the spatial stability of the population that created so many of the social tensions of the eighteenth century. When westering did take place, it was not as a result of the attraction of the interior, as exponents of the "frontier thesis" would have it, but rather because of a desire to escape a society of reduced opportunity and abundance.

Aware of the implications of such findings, Lockridge is careful to qualify his conclusions and ask for further investigation. Surely, too much of the available evidence concerns New England society and will not satisfactorily explain the southern or even middle-colony settlements. In fact, too much colonial history is abstracted from the history of New England, in large part because of the abundance of preserved

Land, Population and the Evolution of New England Society, 1630–1790. World Copyright: The Past and Present Society, Corpus Christi College, Oxford. This article is reprinted with the permission of the Society and the author from *Past and Present, A Journal of Historical Studies*, No. 39, 62–80. Professors Peter Coleman, Jackson T. Main, Darrett Rutman, Philip Greven, Jr., and Van Beck Hall have rendered invaluable assistance in the preparation of this paper. Any remaining errors are, of course, the author's responsibility.

sources. For this reason, new questions and new forms
of research often originate in New England history, as
in Lockridge's essay, which is a fine example of its
type. It remains for other historians to ask equally
critical questions about the Mid-Atlantic settlements
and the colonial South.

Moreover, it remains to be demonstrated conclusively
that the increase in the proportion of landless men led
to a reduction in political participation; official
property qualifications for the vote had often proved
no deterrent to those who failed legally to qualify, and
there is therefore good reason to suppose that even the
landless exercised the suffrage. One also wonders
whether, because colonial society may have been
becoming less economically middle class, its values had
become any less so. One must still account for the
relative absence of class conflict in the American
colonies. To raise such questions is only to join
Lockridge in insisting that students of the past must
now more closely link, rather than separate, social and
political history.

I

*W*as early America an overcrowded society? Though
the idea seems absurd on the face of it, there is evidence in its favour.

American society began with a few men set down in the midst of a vast
and fruitful wilderness. From this beginning until late in the nineteenth century there was no time at which the country was without a frontier in the
literal sense of the word. Whatever it was or whatever it has meant to those
seeking the origins of the American character, the frontier has had one
meaning upon which all men, colonial speculators, genteel visitors from
abroad and modern historians alike, could agree. That meaning is room.
Land was always available. If some did not take it up or if others found
themselves holding bad land, still others, millions and generations of others
who might never have had the opportunity had they lived in another country, did take up acres of good land and throve on those acres.

Yet at first Americans moved only slowly out into the wilderness. For
most of the two hundred years preceding 1800 they clustered near the
eastern coastline. Particularly in the later eighteenth century, even as Daniel
Boone and Ethan Allen led settlers into what were to become the states of
Kentucky and Vermont, a variety of circumstances held most would-be
settlers back of the Appalachian mountains. Behind the mountains, this side

of the war zones of the interior, there had developed by the end of the eighteenth century a society in some respects old, stable, concentrated.

Some historians have been led to reflect on the precocious maturity of late colonial and early national society and to weigh the possibility that the society might have become less than comfortable for some of its inhabitants.[1] But the prevailing tendency has been to treat early American society as a relatively fixed conception, trimmed at either end by periods of "settlement" and "early nationhood," a conception in which the powerful influence of the frontier and the widespread existence of opportunity are not seriously questioned.[2] Certainly no historian has yet come to grips with the quantitative problems posed by the maturation and relative containment of early American society. What does it signify that, by 1790, Americans were not entirely a new or a restless people, or that some counties in Virginia or Maryland and some towns in New England could trace their histories back through a century and a half? How much had the conditions of life changed with time? Was it everywhere, always, necessarily, the America of room and opportunity?

Land and time must be the touchstones of any enquiry into the social evolution of early America: land because the economy was overwhelmingly agricultural and because land has been both the symbol and the essence of American opportunity; time because there was so much of it, so much time in which evolution might have taken place. How much land was available to the typical farmer and how were this and other characteristics of the society changing with time? As a beginning, these questions will be asked of early New England at large and in particular of the agricultural towns of eastern Massachusetts in the years 1630–1790.[3]

II

The only authoritative work on agriculture in colonial New England is a *History of Agriculture in the Northern United States, 1620–1860* by P. W. Bidwell and J. I. Falconer. In discussing the average area of land holdings in early seventeenth century New England they offer a figure of 25 to 50

---

[1] Rowland Berthoff, "The American Social Order: A Conservative Hypothesis," *Amer. Hist. Rev.*, lxv (April, 1960), pp. 495–514, particularly p. 501; see also, Lois Kimball Mathews, *The Expansion of New England* (Boston, 1909), and Percy Wells Bidwell and John I. Falconer, *History of Agriculture in the Northern United States, 1620–1860* (Washington, 1925).

[2] Stuart Bruchey, *The Roots of American Economic Growth, 1607–1861* (New York, 1965); though sensitive to hints of change, Bruchey is forced by sheer lack of evidence to accept the prevailing assumptions of continuity and opportunity. Jackson Turner Main, *The Social Structure of Revolutionary America* (Princeton, 1965), has made the first systematic attempt to study the structure of early American society. Main's conception is fundamentally static, covering only the decades encompassing the Revolution (1760s–1780s), but he is the first to recognize the need for further, long range studies.

[3] The questions at hand could just as well be put to the southern colonies. See Robert E. and B. Katherine Brown, *Virginia 1705–1786: Democracy or Aristocracy?* (East Lansing, 1964). The Browns assert that room and opportunity were prevailing characteristics, but no long-range statistical studies exist which would either support or weaken their view. As will be seen, there are indications that a contrary argument could be offered.

acres. But, as the authors freely admit, the evidence from which this figure is drawn is extremely weak. Nearly every one of the several hundred cases upon which they base their estimate is rendered valueless by the circumstances under which it was recorded.[4] But, if casting doubt on the 25–50 acre figure of Bidwell and Falconer is a simple matter, putting a new estimate in its place is not so simple. The best source of information on landholdings in these years should be the public records of land grants made by the various towns.[5] These would show how much land the typical early settler could expect to receive in his lifetime.[6] The trouble with using New England town records as a source is that few are precise in recording the number and area of dividends granted. In spite of this difficulty, enough bits and pieces of evidence exist to replace Bidwell and Falconer's several hundred suspect cases with several hundred other, better examples. Drawn chiefly from the records of older communities in eastern Massachusetts, these cases show that the usual early settler received a good deal more than 25 to 50 acres.

A thorough investigation has been made of the system of land allotment in Dedham, Massachusetts.[7] Complete records of land acquisitions both public and private can be compiled for thirty-two of the first fifty men to settle in the town. They averaged no less than 210 acres apiece in grants and purchases during lifetimes which ended between 1650 and 1690. From the record of public land divisions alone (of which there were from ten to thirteen between the founding of Dedham in 1636 and the year 1660) it is clear that *any* man in town by 1640 and still alive in 1660 could have expected town grants of between 100 and 200 acres. Some men who died before 1660 and missed the large divisions of the 1650s received less than

---

[4] Percy Wells Bidwell and John I. Falconer, *History of Agriculture in the Northern United States, 1620–1860* (Washington, 1925), pp. 37–8, 53–4. Two major flaws may be noted. In the cases drawn from the towns of Dorchester, Hartford and New Haven, the acreage-per-individual is merely that granted in a single public division of town land. As is well known and as will become evident below, a settler in most early towns could expect roughly three to ten such divisions to be made during his lifetime. Secondly, the figures for several towns on Long Island are only for taxable land. In the Long Island towns the figures "do not include pasture land which was largely held in common" and which was a major component of a man's land-rights. Had this been included, the average acreage would have been "much larger." This circumstance may also have prevailed near Boston; in any event Muddy River was an area assigned to Boston's poor—hardly a fair test-area!

[5] The early estate inventories are unreliable.

[6] He might sell these lands as fast as they were granted him but on the other hand he might buy more land privately. Neither action, given a fairly self-contained local land market, would affect the average area of landholdings per man.

[7] Published town records have been cross-checked against manuscript land records in the Town Hall. Samples of each of the first two generations have been taken and their wills, inventories and deeds co-ordinated with the local records. A full exposition of the methods and results of this work may be found in K. A. Lockridge, *Dedham, 1636–1736: The Anatomy of a Puritan Utopia* (unpublished Ph.D. dissertation, Princeton University, 1965). See also the *Early Records of the Town of Dedham* (Dedham, 1866–1936), i–vi, ed. Don Gleason Hill (i–v) and Julius H. Tuttle (vi). The deeds are in manuscript in the Dedham Historical Society and in the Registry of Deeds in the Suffolk County Courthouse in Boston. There is no indication that more than a very few (if any) landless adult males have escaped inclusion in the averages.

this, but others who lived long and prominent lives were granted public lands up to a total of 400 acres. Since the divisions continued into the first decade of the eighteenth century, the second generation likewise drew large totals of land. Altogether, there were not fewer than 200 individuals each of whom lived for more than three decades as an adult in the town between 1636 and 1690. The typical man among them received an average of 150 acres from the common lands of Dedham.

The records of neighbouring Watertown include land records which give a complete survey of landholdings in the 1630s.[8] For the 160 men listed at this time the average landholding was 126 acres. This average may exclude a few unlisted men who held no land, but it also excludes whatever lands those who were listed held in other towns or were granted in the several subsequent general divisions. Specifically, it does not take cognizance of the fact that the men who held only tiny "homelots" when this record was made were soon after granted farms of respectable acreage. With Dedham, Watertown gives from 300 to 400 cases averaging from 125 to 150 acres.

In six other towns of the immediate region there are indications that the seventeenth-century settlers found that America had plenty of land to offer. Medfield split off from Dedham in 1651; during the first two decades of its existence it made at least six general divisions of land. A man who lived in the town for these two decades would have received roughly 150 acres. The division of 1659 alone ranged from 50 to 150 acres per man.[9] A recent study of Sudbury, Massachusetts implies that any men who lived in that town from its founding in 1638 until 1658 must have been granted approximately 150 acres apiece.[10] The original proprietors of Milford, near Dedham in south-eastern Massachusetts, resolved in 1662 "that the divisions of land . . . shall be by these ensuing rules: that to one hundred pounds estate be granted one hundred and fifty acres of land." Since an estate of twice one hundred pounds was average, the forty original proprietor-settlers must have planned on very large individual holdings.[11] The fifty-five founders of Billerica, north of Cambridge, started off with 115 acres each.[12] A survey of the sixty men living in one section of Concord, Massachusetts in 1665 revealed that each of them held on the average 250 acres.[13] In nearby Andover, "four successive divisions of town land [between 1646 and 1662], together with additional divisions of meadow and swampland, provided each of the inhabitants with at least one hundred acres of land for

[8] *Watertown Records* (Watertown, 1894–1939), i–viii. Volumes i and ii have been used. The editorial warnings on the use of these records have been observed.

[9] William S. Tilden, *History of the Town of Medfield, Massachusetts* (Boston, 1887); and inventories and wills for the period in the Suffolk County Courthouse.

[10] Sumner Chilton Powell, *Puritan Village (Middletown, Connecticut, 1963)*, pp. 118, 122, 191, and Plate xi. The 130-acre farms spoken of on page 191 are the chief component of the total. Sudbury is north of Dedham, a few miles east of Boston. Nearby Marlborough, in deliberately retarding the process of division and keeping most land in common for some time (see Charles Hudson, *History of the Town of Marlborough* [Boston, 1862]) seems to have been the exception to the rule set by Watertown and Sudbury.

[11] A. Ballou, *History of the Town of Milford* (Boston, 1882), pp. 5, 33; also inventories for Suffolk County.

[12] Henry Hazen, *History of Billerica, Massachusetts* (Boston, 1883).

[13] Lemuel Shattuck, *History of the Town of Concord* (Boston, 1835), pp. 36-7.

farming, and as much as six hundred acres."[14] With the information from Dedham and Watertown, these references make it seem that an estimate of 150 acres for the typical early inhabitant of an eastern Massachusetts town is a reasonable figure. Scattered evidence from early communities elsewhere in New England re-enforces this assumption.[15]

In 1786 the Revolution was over. America was now an independent nation. Dedham had been founded exactly a century and a half before; Watertown was older still; Milford, Medfield and the other towns not quite so old. By 1786 Dedham was a town of some 2,000 souls; Watertown had grown more slowly but contained nearly 1,000 inhabitants; there were more than 775 persons in Medfield, close to 1,500 in Billerica, nearly 2,000 in Concord and more than 2,000 in Sudbury.[16] These were no longer tiny villages, but were now towns of a respectable population for an agricultural society. In 1786 the Commonwealth of Massachusetts enacted a law which required every community in the state to complete a detailed questionnaire on the basis of which taxes were to be assessed. Among other items to be filled in were the number of male polls (males over sixteen) and the acreage of every type of land within the town. This last is of the utmost importance. Included under it were "tillage," "English upland and mowing," "fresh meadow," "saltmarsh," "pasture," "woodlands," "other unimproved land," and "unimprovable land." No type of land was left out. By dividing the number of adult males in a given town (polls minus a quarter yields a rough estimate of the number of males over twenty-one)[17] into the total acreage of the town, one may arrive at the average number of acres per man.[18]

<hr />

[14] Philip J. Greven, Jr. "Family Structure in Seventeenth-Century Andover, Massachusetts," *William and Mary Quarterly*, 3rd ser., xxiii (1966), pp. 234–56.

[15] To the evidence of Massachusetts' towns should be added that of Rehoboth, then a part of Plymouth Colony. Here there were some fifteen divisions of land between 1643 and 1713. Richard Le Baron Bowen, *Early Rehoboth* (Rehoboth, 1945–50), 4 vols., iv, pp. 1–21. Another bit of evidence on early land holdings may be drawn from Bidwell and Falconer, one of whose larger samples was based upon the records of New Haven in Connecticut. There 123 persons were found to have averaged a mere 44 acres each. But, as has been pointed out, a single division accounted for the acreage held by these individuals. A few pages later, in another context, the authors reveal that a second division in New Haven in the very same year had the effect of raising the average holding to 110 acres; Bidwell and Falconer, *History of Agriculture*, pp. 37, 54. In nearby Milford, Connecticut, there were four divisions in addition to an initial distribution of homelots between the founding of the town in 1639 and 1657. The process of division continued through the seventeenth century, including a large division ranging from roughly 50 to 200 acres in 1687; Leonard W. Labaree, *Milford, Connecticut, the Early Development of a Town as Shown in its Land Records* (New Haven, 1933), no. 13 in a series of pamphlets sponsored by the Tercentenary Commission of the State of Connecticut.

[16] E. V. Greene and V. Harrington, *American Population before the Federal Census of 1790* (New York, 1932), pp. 19–40.

[17] By comparing information available in volumes i and vi of the *Early records of . . . Dedham*, it is possible to find out how many males included in the typical tax list were not of age; K. A. Lockridge, "The Population of Dedham, Massachusetts, 1636–1736," *Econ. Hist. Rev.*, 2nd ser., xix (1966), pp. 318–44. The estimate that one-fourth of all males over 16 years of age were in the 16–21 group is a conservative one, judging from an article by James A. Henretta on the "Social Structure of Colonial Boston," *William and Mary Quarterly*, 3rd ser., xxii (1965), pp. 75–92.

[18] The discussion which follows is based upon uncatalogued documents in the Ar-

In what had been the "Puritan Village" of Sudbury, there were now 56 acres for each man, and in Medfield and Dedham 44 and 38 acres respectively. Even though town lands and worn lands are indiscriminately included, this represents a shrinkage to less than one-third of the landholdings of the first generation. The shrinkage was greater in Watertown, where the average had fallen to a mere 17 acres per man—less than one-seventh of what it had been in the 1630s! But whether one-third or one-seventh, the change was substantial in each of these old towns. The same might be said of all the towns of the area, almost without exception. The truth is that for the whole of Suffolk County the land area per adult male now averaged no more than 43 acres. If the average rose to 71 acres in Chelsea, it fell to 22 acres next door in Roxbury; if to the south in Wrentham the imaginary "typical" man had 70 acres, to the east in Hingham he had but 32 acres.[19]

If time and the growth that time brought were essential factors in the decrease in the average area of landholdings, the oldest towns in the county should have had the lowest average acreages per man. This was exactly the situation. Twelve towns of Suffolk County were founded between 1630 and

chives of the State of Massachusetts. They are in microfilm in volume clxiii. The resultant figures do not include lands held in other towns, but what evidence exists argues that it was not usual for a man to hold more than trifling amounts of land in towns other than his own. Further, the results make no distinction between good and worn land. Since over a century of rather unsophisticated New World farming must have produced worn land in many towns, an acre in 1786 was likely to have been less productive than an acre in 1636. Lockridge, *Dedham*, chaps. vi and vii; the Suffolk inventories also bear out this assertion. Finally, residual public (town) lands seem to be included in the total, though these were not in the possession of individual farmers. Subsequent computer analysis of the 1786 lists by Professor Van Beck Hall of the University of Pittsburgh indicates that the estimates derived here are in every respect conservative and that the *arable* land per adult male in the older areas of Massachusetts probably fell below five acres. Professor Hall is now engaged in work which will make these revealing documents yield a full picture of the economy and society of Massachusetts at the end of the eighteenth century.

[19] The narrowness of the range from top to bottom is significant. The average of 43 acres for Suffolk County was not produced by a few impossibly crowded towns pulling down the average of a more comfortable, well-endowed majority. The figures for each town begin with Roxbury's 22 acres and rise through averages of 25, 32, 32, 36, 38, 42, 44, 44, 47, 51, 52, 60, 68 and 70 acres to the peak of 71. As the years passed many of the inventories of estates on file in the Suffolk County Courthouse became quite specific as to landholdings. A sample of 300 of these for the years 1765–75 confirms the average-landholding figure derived from the assessment lists of 1786. The average rural estate included 65 acres of land. There are good reasons why this earlier figure is a little above the 43 acres average of 1786. For one thing, these are acreages at death. A man is likely to have held more land at the end of his life than he held on the average throughout that life. There is a second way in which they reflect success. Though there are inventories for men who held no land whatsoever (and 17 per cent of the 300 had no land at death, confirming the indications of the assessment lists that the suffrage could not possibly have been above 90 per cent), inventories for servants and paupers who had virtually no real or personal estate are extremely rare—almost nonexistent. Evidence will be presented below to show that such persons must have existed. Their exclusion from the sample of inventories naturally raises the average landholdings attributed to those who were included. With these adjustments made, it may be seen that the inventories describe much the same situation with regard to landholdings as was described in the town assessment lists of 1786. And, as would be expected, the inventories of estates from the older towns tend to include less land than those based on estates in towns more recently established.

1673.[20] In 1786, their adult males would have had but 37 acres apiece had all the land in these towns been parcelled out equally. The seven newer towns founded between 1705 and 1739 contained in 1786 some 55 acres for every adult male residing within their bounds—an average holding significantly above that found in the older towns, if still substantially below the average of the first generation of New England farmers.[21] Moreover, there is evidence that pressure on the land supply was most severe in the older towns. "Woodlands" and "unimproved" lands totalled 25 acres per man in the towns begun since 1705 but only 13 acres in those begun before 1673. The older towns had half as much uncultivated land per capita because the need for farm land had become most intense in these towns and was pushing men to put poor land under the plough.

More sharply diminished landholdings and a greater cultivation of marginal lands in the older towns are two indications of a mounting pressure on the land supply. A third index is the level of land prices. If there was a disproportionate demand for land, land prices, and probably food prices as well, should have risen more than the prices of most other commodities through the colonial period. A perusal of hundreds of inventories of estates for all of the rural towns of Suffolk County in the years 1660–1760 reveals that land values easily doubled and often tripled over the century throughout the region. By contrast, there was a remarkable long-term stability in items of personal estate, such as furniture, tools, and even clothing. Though a systematic enquiry might refine this contrast, it seems to have been a general phenomenon.

A similar decline in average landholdings may have prevailed elsewhere in New England, and may elsewhere have reached the point at which many towns were becoming "crowded," with waste land turned to crops and the cost of land soaring. A striking study of one particular Connecticut town follows the fortunes of local families through three generations, from 1740 to 1800. Family lands were divided and divided again to accommodate the increasing numbers of young men in the families, young men who did not seem to want to try their fortunes elsewhere. Ultimately, in Kent, Connecticut, "economic opportunity, which had been exceptionally bright from 1740 to 1777, was darkened . . . by the pressure of population . . . against a limited supply of land." [22] Speaking of the whole of late eighteenth century Connecticut, Albert Laverne Olson observed, "Contemporaries were well aware of the decline of Connecticut agriculture and the exhaustion of its soil." It was plain to several of these observers that the population, which had grown fourfold from 1715 to 1756, had become too great for the countryside to support. Land values were rising sharply and marginal lands were being turned into farmland.[23]

<hr>

[20] Watertown is included as one of the twelve, though it later came under the jurisdiction of Middlesex County. As it was only the eleventh largest of the nineteen towns considered, its inclusion does not greatly weight the results.

[21] Brookline, Needham, Medway, Bellingham, Walpole, Stoughton and Chelsea. No towns were incorporated between 1673 and 1705.

[22] Charles S. Grant, *Democracy in the Connecticut Frontier Town of Kent* (New York, 1961), p. 170.

[23] Albert Laverne Olson, *Agricultural Economy and the Population in Eighteenth Century Connecticut* (New Haven, 1935), no. 40 in a series of pamphlets sponsored by the Tercentenary Commission of the State of Connecticut.

The "why" of the process, whether in eastern Massachusetts or in Connecticut, is fairly obvious. In Suffolk County as in Kent, Connecticut the pressure of population against a limited supply of land was the critical mechanism. Boston and a few suburbs aside, Suffolk County was a predominantly agricultural area. Farmers, "yeoman" or "husbandman" or "gentleman" farmers were the solid main stock of inhabitants.[24] Land was the essence of life throughout the region; a sufficiency of land was a vital concern of the great majority of men. Yet, despite the simultaneous settlement of scores of towns to the west, the estimates of the population of eastern Massachusetts reveal the same inexorable growth which was characteristic of Connecticut.[25] Up until 1765, and for most towns even after, an increase of from one to five per cent a year was a normal condition of life. Accompanying this growth, again as in Connecticut, was a pattern of inheritance in which partible descent dominated. Virtually no men left their lands intact to any one son. A double share of the whole estate for the eldest son with equal shares going to all other children (sons and daughters alike) was the standard set by the law for cases of intestacy. Even the minority of men who left wills followed this standard with very few deviations. Since emigration was not sufficient to relieve the situation, the consequence was a process of division and re-division of landholdings.

The process was a product of the fundamental conditions of existence in New England, and its operation could be perceived long before its effects became serious. As early as 1721, "Amicus Patriae" observed that "many of our old towns are too full of inhabitants for husbandry; many of them living upon small shares of land, and generally all are husbandmen. . . . And also many of our people are slow in marrying for want of settlements: . . ."[26] Had "Amicus Patriae" returned in 1790, he might well have redoubled his lamentations.

There is a paradox involved in considering that thousands of farmers in late eighteenth-century New England held on the average little over 40 acres of land apiece. It is the paradox of a land full of opportunity and with room to spare which in practice was coming to support an agricultural society reminiscent of that in the old, more limited nations of Europe. Nor

[24] See Lockridge, *Dedham, 1636–1736*. Also, wills and inventories of estates for all of Suffolk and parts of Middlesex and Essex Counties may be found in the Probate Office of the Suffolk County Courthouse in Boston; several thousand of these have been surveyed. For one example, of 142 men who died in Suffolk County towns outside Boston from 1750 to 1759, 71 per cent were "yeomen" or "husbandmen," and roughly a third of the remaining 29 per cent held over half of their estates in the form of land.

[25] See E. V. Greene and V. Harrington, *American Population Before the Federal Census of 1790*. One of these eastern towns, Dedham, has been studied as a demographic test case, and confirms the broad outlines above. The curve of Dedham's population follows that of the colony as a whole, rising slowly in the seventeenth century, surging and hesitating between 1690 and 1730, rising steadily thereafter—but never declining. Growth of a little less than three per cent a year was average. Natural increase seems to have accounted for the growth, as immigration was negligible until 1736 and probably thereafter. As in Kent, there was no general exodus to new western towns, though the population rose from less than 400 in 1645 to nearly 2,000 in 1765. K. A. Lockridge, "The Population of Dedham, Massachusetts, 1636–1736."

[26] A. P. (John Wise?), *A Word of Comfort to a Melancholy Country* (Boston, 1721), in A. M. Davis, ed., *Colonial Currency Reprints*, ii (Boston, 1911), p. 189.

is this just so much verbiage. The English yeoman of the previous century had farmed lands ranging in area from 25 to 200 acres.[27] In terms of land, many "yeomen" or "husbandmen" in this section of late eighteenth-century America were not perceptibly better off as a result of the long-ago emigration of their great-great-grandfathers.[28] In terms of the future, in terms of the sons of these American farmers and of the amount of land which each son could hope to inherit, America was no longer the land of opportunity.

III

Further evidence drawn from eastern Massachusetts brings to light the possibility that the process which was causing the decrease in average landholdings might have been accompanied by, and perhaps have been leading to, alterations in the structure of the society.

A study of the distribution of estates from the agricultural villages of Suffolk County has been undertaken to see if the pattern in which wealth was distributed in the society could have been changing with time.[29] For the several years on either side of 1660, 300 inventories have been distributed according to their size in £100 increments and the same has been done for 310 inventories from the years adjoining 1765. A process of economic polarization was under way. In 1660 there were only 13 of 300 men whose estates surpassed £900 and only three of these were worth more than £1,500. By 1765 there were 53 out of 310 men worth more than £900 and 19 of them had estates which ranged above £1,500, averaging £2,200. The average estate in 1660 was worth £315; the average in 1765 was £525. This difference came about not because of any long-term inflation or because of any true increase in the individual wealth of most men (land prices went up, but landholdings fell); it is the huge estates of the fifty-four rich men which caused nearly all of the increased size of the "average" estate in the sample of 1765! If there were more very rich men, there were also more distinctly poor individuals among those sampled in 1765. In 1660, fifty-seven men had left estates worth less than £100. In 1765, in spite of the greater aggregate wealth represented in this later sample, seventy-two men had estates in the lowest category. Moreover, the distance between the poor and the rest of society was growing. In 1660 the better-off 80 per cent of the sample had an average wealth 7.6 times as great as the average wealth of the lowest 20 per cent. By 1765 the bulk of society had estates which averaged 13.75 times the size of the estates of the poorest one-fifth. Not only were

[27] Mildred Campbell, *The English Yeoman Under Elizabeth and the Early Stuarts* (New Haven, 1942), pp. 74–100. A remarkably similar process of crowding was experienced in this same period by the English village of Wilston Magna; see W. G. Hoskins, *The Midland Peasant* (London, 1957).

[28] For hints of similar changes in the southern colonies, see V. J. Wyckoff, "The Sizes of Plantations in Seventeenth-Century Maryland," *Maryland Historical Magazine*, xxxii (1937), pp. 331–9; and Jackson T. Main, "The Hundred," *William and Mary Quarterly*, xi (1955), pp. 354–84.

[29] The inventories of these estates may be found in the Probate Office in the Suffolk County Courthouse in Boston. The sample taken represents over 50 per cent of the existing inventories for the towns studied in the years for which the sample was taken.

the rich becoming more numerous and relatively more rich, but the poor were becoming more numerous and relatively poorer.

Before 1700, it had been rare for an inhabitant of a Suffolk County town to call himself "gentleman" or "Esquire" when the time came for him to write his will. This, too, changed as America approached the revolution and in one more small way this change hints at an evolving society. For by the 1750s no less than 12.5 per cent of some 150 men from the farming towns had appropriated these titles of distinction. This becomes more impressive when one considers that the corresponding figure for the great metropolis of Boston was only 13.5 per cent.[30] Perhaps some sort of landed gentry was arising here in the hallowed home of the New England yeoman!

An American pauper class may also have been developing at the same time and for the same reasons. In Dedham the number of vagabonds warned out of town increased sixfold in the first three decades of the eighteenth century, reaching the point where three strangers had to be moved along in the typical year.[31] There was a parallel increase in Watertown.[32] In Rehoboth, the warnings-out increased steadily from one a year (1724–33) to 3.8 (1734–43) to 4.5 (1744–53) to 6.25 (1754–7—where the record ends).[33] In all three towns in the previous century it had been an unusual year which had seen the selectmen have to bestir themselves to ask anyone to move along. By the middle 1700s the wandering poor had become a part of the landscape in this part of New England.

If the town of Dedham has been cited from time to time as an example, it is because this is the only town in the immediate area for which an intensive analysis has been made.[34] Though that analysis has been carried in detail only to 1736, it has uncovered more bits and pieces of evidence indicating social change. Almost every development thus far suggested may be seen in microcosm in Dedham. To run through these quickly. The population grew steadily and few sons emigrated. "Worn land" appears in the inventories of Dedham estates after 1700. In the tax assessment surveys of the 1760s, 70s, and 80s a rich "loaner class" appears in the town, men with large amounts out at interest, men for whom very few seventeenth-century counterparts can be found to have existed. Not only do the numbers of vagabonds warned out increase but the numbers of indigenous poor also rise sharply after 1700. After 1710 the collective and very English term "the poor" comes into use in this town; contributions are taken under this heading almost yearly. As in the 610 Suffolk inventories, so in Dedham the pyramid of wealth derived from tax and proprietors' lists changes in such a way as to put a greater percentage of men in the lower brackets. The numbers of men with no taxable land increase from less than 5 per cent around 1700 to 12 per cent by 1736. Not fully developed in 1736, projected over another half-century these trends must have had a powerful effect on the nature of life

[30] This is based on a study of 350 wills in connection with an investigation into charitable bequests. The wills are in the Suffolk County Probate Office.

[31] Lockridge, *Dedham*, 98; the figures are from the *Early Records of . . . Dedham*, vols. iii–vi.

[32] *Watertown Records*, vols. i and ii.

[33] Bowen, *Rehoboth*, ii, pp. 139 ff.

[34] Lockridge, *Dedham*.

in Dedham. Similar trends most certainly had a great effect on the society of Kent, Connecticut.[35]

In all of this there is (as there is in the study of Kent) an assumption of some degree of cause-and-effect relationship between the process which was causing a shrinkage in landholdings and these indications of social polarization—the two together going to make up what has been labelled an "over-crowded" society. Various linkages are possible. The most obvious would run as follows. In the intensifying competition for land, some men would lose out through ill luck or a lack of business sense. Since competition would be pushing land prices up, a loser would find recovery ever more difficult, a family with little land would have a hard time acquiring more. By the same token those men and families who somehow had acquired large amounts of land would prosper as its value rose with rising demand. In such a process, the pressure would be greater at the lower end of the spectrum. There the continuing division by inheritance would reduce ever greater numbers of young men to dependence upon other sources of income, sources from which to supplement the insufficient profits from their small plots of land, sources which might or might not be available.

IV

Clearly there were evolutionary patterns present within the society of early New England, patterns which reflect most significantly on the direction in which that society was heading. To repeat the hypothesis, the trends which existed in New England were essentially those first isolated in Kent by Charles Grant:[36] "Economic opportunity, bright in 1751, had turned relatively dark by 1796 . . . society, predominantly middle class in 1751, included a growing class of propertyless men by 1796 . . . increased poverty stemmed from the pressure of a population swollen by a fantastic birthrate against a limited amount of land." A finite supply of land and a growing population, a population notably reluctant to emigrate, were combining to fragment and reduce landholdings, bringing marginal lands increasingly into cultivation and raising land prices. Ultimately, the collision of land and population may have been polarizing the structure of society, creating an agricultural "proletariat" and perhaps even a corresponding rural "gentry." As it was in Kent, so, our evidence has suggested, it could have been throughout much of eastern Massachusetts and implicitly throughout much of New England.

What might such a process mean for our understanding of the history of early America? Charles Grant saw one of the major implications of the process which had turned his "frontier town" of Kent into a crowded and poverty-stricken backwater within fifty years. Since 1955 Robert E. Brown has been insisting that colonial society can best be characterized as a "mid-

[35] Grant, in *Kent*, observes that a similar evolutionary process had created an agricultural "proletariat" by 1800: *Kent*, p. 97. Main's *Social Structure of Revolutionary America* confirms these indications. Using tax lists and inventories from many towns, he finds that at least 20 per cent of men in late eighteenth century New England lived a marginal existence, with little, if any, land.

[36] The following excerpts are from Grant, *Kent*, pp. 83–103.

dle-class democracy." He depicts a prosperous, satisfied society in which room and opportunity were available to nearly all, a society in which land and wealth were distributed widely and in which the suffrage was accordingly broad (since the suffrage was tied to a property qualification). The era of the American Revolution, in Brown's view, involved little internal social antagonism. The colonists simply defended their "middle-class democracy," by throwing off British rule and writing the Federal Constitution.[37] Brown musters impressive evidence to support his analysis of the society, yet his critics and other analysts of the society have found scattered evidence to the contrary, evidence which argues for poverty, for a relative lack of opportunity, for a narrower suffrage than he claims prevailed, and for bitter social conflicts in the Revolutionary era.[38] The real issue, as Grant perceived, may not be "who is right?" but "from what period of time does each side draw its evidence?" Thus:

> If Kent were established as typical, then Brown's "middle-class democracy" would be characteristic of the early stages of a new settlement . . . On the other hand, Brown's prosperity would disappear, and the depressed conditions described by a Nettels or an Adams would creep in [together with a reduction in the numbers of men qualified to vote] at a later date. Such conditions . . . would emerge mainly from the pressure of population on a limited supply of land.[39]

In short, as the century wears on Brown's thesis loses validity. In so far as the level of the suffrage is one (and to Brown the chief) element in political democracy, the overcrowding which was becoming a part of the social evolution of so many New England towns must have contributed to a reduction in democratic expression in the society by the time of the American Revolution or shortly after. As the numbers of landless or near-landless men rose, the numbers of men qualified to participate in the political process fell. The men of the Suffolk County town of Dorchester demonstrated their awareness of the political dimensions of the social change which was taking place when, in objecting to the suffrage qualifications written into the Massachusetts Constitution of 1780, they observed that even a low property qualification "infringes upon the Rights and Liberties of a number of useful and Respectable members of Society; which number we believe is daily increasing and possibly may increase in such proportion that one half the people of this Commonwealth will have no choice in any branch of the General Court."[40]

But the most important issue is not whether social changes were reducing the level of the suffrage in early America. Even when *Kent* appeared in 1961, most historians were a bit weary of the battle over Brown's definition

---

[37] Robert E. Brown, *Middle Class Democracy and the Revolution in Massachusetts* (Ithaca, 1955); see also Robert E. and B. Katherine Brown, *Virginia 1705–1786* (cited above, note 3).

[38] See James Truslow Adams, *Provincial Society* (New York, 1948); Curtis P. Nettels, *Roots of American Civilization* (New York, 1940); and Robert Taylor's review of Brown's book on Massachusetts in the *Mississippi Valley Hist. Rev.*, lxiii (1956).

[39] Grant, *Kent*, pp. 102–3.

[40] Massachusetts Archives, cclxxvii, p. 67; quoted in Robert J. Taylor, ed., *Massachusetts, Colony to Commonwealth* (Chapel Hill, 1961), p. 155.

of political "democracy." Most were and are more occupied with political democracy as a matter of social attitudes and political traditions than as the difference between a suffrage of 90 per cent and one of 60 per cent.[41] What is of greatest consequence is not that the society was becoming less "democratic" in the sense of a narrowing suffrage, but that it was becoming less "middle-class." Brown treated eighteenth-century colonial society as relatively static, but the evolutionary hypothesis derived from Kent and from eastern Massachusetts shows the flaw in this conception and points to a society moving from decades of rosy "middle-class" existence toward years of economic polarization and potential class conflict.

Further, the evolutionary patterns which threatened to erode the "middle-class" society described by Brown may have shaped the thinking of many of America's Revolutionary leaders. Recent work suggests that a number of American clergymen and politicians of the later eighteenth century were dissatisfied with the condition of their society. That society was certainly not as stratified, oppressive and corrupt as the society of England had become, but it seemed to some men that it was moving in that direction. The fear of a gradual "Europeanization" of American society, a fear given ground by the tendencies outlined here, probably lent a special energy to their Revolutionary rhetoric. Thus, the leaders of the Revolution adopted Enlightenment ideas with such speed and fervor not merely because these ideas described the egalitarian, "middle-class" society which was the distinctive feature of life in the American colonies, but also because independence and the reforms engendered by Enlightenment ideas would guarantee that happy society against the changes which even then were bringing it closer to the Old World model. The radical ideas of European intellectuals would restore and protect, as well as "complete, formalize, systematize and symbolize," the unique American social order which was the pride of the Revolutionary generation.[42]

If the evolutionary hypothesis advanced here poses problems for one controversialist, it resurrects another. Frederick Jackson Turner was convinced that the frontier—and by this he meant above all the expansive frontier of the nineteenth century—had a great rôle in shaping an energetic, egalitarian and optimistic American character. His speculations have lent

[41] J. R. Pole, "Historians and the Problem of Early American Democracy," *Amer. Hist. Rev.*, lxvii (1962), pp. 626–646. (It might, however, be noted that the reduction in the suffrage caused by "overcrowding" might have been as great as the difference between a suffrage of 90 per cent and one of 60 per cent. The tax surveys of 1786 reveal that at least 20 per cent of the men in the towns of Suffolk County had not enough real or personal property to qualify as voters. See also Grant, *Kent*, p. 140 for evidence of a similar decline.) It is only fair to add that Brown himself has broadened his definition of "democracy" and increased the subtlety of his argument; see Brown, *Virginia*.

[42] The relevant works are Alan Heimert, *Religion and the American Mind from the Great Awakening to the Revolution* (Cambridge, Massachusetts, 1966); and Gordon S. Wood, "Republicanism as Revolutionary Ideology" (paper delivered at the Organization of American Historians meeting in Chicago in April, 1967) and "Rhetoric and Reality in the American Revolution," *William and Mary Quarterly*, 3rd ser., xxiii (1966). The view that Enlightenment ideas served chiefly to "complete, formalize, systematize and symbolize" the American national spirit is that of Bernard Bailyn, "Political Experience and Enlightenment Ideas in Eighteenth Century America," *Amer. Hist. Rev.*, lxvii (1962), p. 351; Bailyn's analysis rests in large part upon an acceptance of Brown's thesis.

energy to several generations of undergraduate lecture courses, but they have most often served as targets for historians who have been more cautious if usually less interesting.[43] Most of these critics have attacked Turner on the basis that conditions on the frontier either were not what he said they were or did not have the effect on men that he claimed they did, or both. A question which might better be asked is: Where would we have been without Turner's frontier? The trend to an overcrowded society sketched in the previous pages throws a new light on this question. Without the emigration that followed 1790, New England society would have become ever more crowded at a rapid rate. If already by 1790 many towns were experiencing an excessive demand for land and the attendant consequences of that demand, what would conditions have been twenty or thirty years later? The most important point to make about the mass exodus to the frontier of the nineteenth century may be that it rescued America as the land of mobility and opportunity at a time when it was beginning to lack both and was beginning to undergo major social changes as a result.[44]

V

Regardless of one's view of the evidence and speculations presented here, it should be clear that historians' understanding of the evolution of early American society is not at all adequate.

For example, a decline in landholdings, even if it was general, need not have meant an overcrowded society. There are at least four interrelated propositions whose validity would render a substantial decline in landholdings meaningless in terms of "negative" social and economic effects. The validity of several of these propositions would open the possibility that any decline in landholdings could actually have been accompanied by an improvement in productivity and in the overall social and economic situation—the evidence offered above notwithstanding. First, agricultural methods might have improved to a substantial degree and, in company with the more favourable man-land ratio which could have resulted from a decrease in the land-area per man, this improvement would have meant that 40-odd acres in 1786 were far more productive than 150-odd acres *circa* 1660. Second, better transportation coupled with the growth of urban areas might have so improved the market situation that a given quantity of agricultural produce in 1786 was worth more than that same quantity *circa* 1660. Third, non-farm occupations (presumably crafts and manufacturing) might have increased in the period under consideration, offering lucrative alternatives to

[43] Among those both cautious and interesting have been Paul W. Gates, "Frontier Estate Builders and Farm Laborers," *The Frontier in Perspective* (Madison, Wisconsin, 1957), pp. 143–63; and Page Smith, *As a City upon a Hill: the Town in American History* (New York, 1966).

[44] The hypothesis likewise reflects on the background of the exodus of 1790–1830. If conditions were tending in the directions depicted, it may be that the waves of New Englanders heading west after 1790 were more "pushed" west by the difficulties of life in Old New England than "pulled" west by the attraction of better land. Lois Mathews felt that this was the case, but even she does not seem to have realized how great the difficulties caused by a dense population might have become by 1790: *Expansion of New England*, pp. 99 ff.

men who chose to or had to leave the land. Finally, 40-odd acres, even though it included "worn" or waste lands, might still have been ample with which to support a large family. The point which must be made is that there is available virtually no evidence in favour of any of these propositions —probably because they are not valid, but also and most significantly because no one has cared to try to find the evidence. What evidence does exist argues that propositions one, two, and probably three are not valid.[45] The only enquiry into the question of subsistence sets the total landholdings required for the support of a farm family at between 40 and 89 acres,[46] indicating that Suffolk County had reached a critical point by 1786.

Papers calling for "further study" have become one of the clichés of the historical profession. Yet the unavoidable conclusion is that the impact of this paper must reside not so much in its evidence and speculations as in a long list of specific questions. Was the decline in landholdings general? Was it always accompanied by the use of marginal lands and by a relative rise in the price of land?[47] How much of the land farmed in the late eighteenth century was "worn" land? Was there an improvement in agricultural techniques and in the man-land ratio? Was there an improvement in access to markets?[48] Did non-farm occupations offer alternate sources of income?[49] Why did sons not leave the crowded towns, towns like Kent, Connecticut and Watertown, Massachusetts, to take advantage of the room which the frontier seemed to offer? Was it fear of Indians or the traditional inertia of rural society or something not yet considered?[50] Was 40 acres enough to support a large family, and exactly how large were families in this period?[51] Was the distribution of wealth in the society changing with time? How reliable are inventories of estates in determining this? Are tax lists better sources for this purpose? Did the numbers of vagabonds and paupers increase with time? Was the increase, if any, greater than the mere rise in population would account for? Did the appropriation of titles of social dis-

[45] Bruchey's basic argument, in his *Roots of American Economic Growth*, rests on the substantial invalidity of propositions one, two, and possibly of proposition three, in the period preceding 1790. Bidwell and Falconer, in their *History of Agriculture*, pp. 84 ff., 142, are skeptical about proposition one and have little to say about propositions two and three.

[46] Grant, *Kent*, pp. 36–8. Only a fraction of this total would be under cultivation—the rest serving as woodlot and pasture or lying fallow, but being nonetheless essential.

[47] For the theoretical basis of the study of differential price increases, see E. Phelps–Brown and S. Hopkins, "Wage-Rates and Prices: Evidence for Population Pressure in the Sixteenth Century," *Economics*, vii (1967).

[48] Inventories of estates could provide answers to these questions, since they list tools, crops as well as debts and credits resulting from commercial transactions. They also list "worn" lands in many instances.

[49] It would be possible to do a long-term census based on records of land transactions in the Registries of Deeds in each county. Men's occupations and ranks are listed with great consistency in these documents.

[50] See Grant, *Kent*, p. 102; Lockridge, "The Population of Dedham"; Greven, "Family Structure in Andover" for various explanations of inertia. This is an essential question, since, as this enquiry shows, the real problem may have been not so much the lack of a viable frontier as the relative failure to take advantage of that frontier.

[51] On the uses of historical demography, American scholars could learn a great deal from the work of their French and English colleagues. See E. A. Wrigley, ed., *An Introduction to English Historical Demography* (London, 1966).

tinction increase similarly? Who appropriated these titles and why? How did all these factors come together in the history of a single town? The studies of Kent, Connecticut and Dedham, Massachusetts are the only long-term local case histories presently available. We need more of them.[52] Finally, what were the attitudes of thoughtful men of the time regarding the state of their society? Was there a universal awareness of change?

Until this work is begun, the irritating hypothesis that much of New England was becoming seriously "overcrowded" by 1790 will have to stand. Instead of being the land of opportunity, this part of America was rapidly becoming more and more an old world society; old world in the sense of the size of farms, old world in the sense of an increasingly wide and articulated social hierarchy, old world in that "the poor" were ever present and in increasing numbers. The word "becoming" is carefully selected. The fact of independence and the egalitarian ideas broadcast by the Revolution, together with the great exodus to the west after 1790, quickly made it ridiculous to speak of this or any part of America as an old world society. Yet this had been the tendency in much of New England for decades. Had it been allowed, by some miraculous suspension of subsequent events, to continue unchecked—who can say what might have been the result? This part of America might soon have come to resemble the Anglicized society dreamed of by some arch-Federalists more than the vigorous, expansive society which has since been a characteristic feature of our national history.

[52] At the Iowa University Conference on Early American History in March of 1967, Professor John M. Bumsted of Simon Fraser University (now of McMaster University) delivered a paper on "Religion, Finance, and Democracy in Massachusetts; the Town of Norton as a Case Study"; Norton, like Kent, Connecticut was a relatively new town which within three generations began to experience many of the characteristic difficulties of overcrowding; here, as elsewhere, there was a reluctance to emigrate. A recent and excellent study of Andover, Massachusetts (Philip Greven, Jr., "Family Structure in . . . Andover," "Four Generations: a Study of Family Structure, Inheritance, and Mobility in Andover, Massachusetts, 1630–1750" [Ph.D. dissertation, Harvard University, 1965]) confirms the trends depicted here, but also supports the possibility that these trends may have called forth a contemporaneous response. Emigration increased during the third and fourth generations, while the use of partible inheritance declined. When and where such responses operated, they could have done much to mitigate the effects of the trend to overcrowding.

Errand into
the Wilderness

Perry Miller

Few American historians of the twentieth century have
had as much impact on historical thought as did the
late Perry Miller of Harvard University. He helped
turn the study of the American mind away from the
examination of the development of "unit ideas" (in
the manner of Arthur O. Lovejoy's *The Great Chain
of Being*, 1936) and toward the study of the total
culture from which ideas emerge. He insisted on
investigating the social psychology of thought and
placed great weight on the collective, as well as the
individual, consciousness. And, as the essay that follows
helps make clear, he always summoned a profound
sympathy for his subjects, even when he was most
critical. Miller, with perhaps two or three others of his
generation (one thinks especially of Clifford K.
Shipton, Samuel Eliot Morison, and Alan Simpson),
rescued the Puritans of New England from both
neglect and ridicule and made the history of their
experience one of the central moments in the life of
the American mind and spirit.

Much like the New Critics of literature (such as
I. A. Richards, Allen Tate, John Crowe Ransom, and
Cleanth Brooks), Miller sought out the tensions and
ironies within ideas and rhetoric. Here he brilliantly
plays on the Reverend Samuel Danforth's conceit of
an "errand" to suggest the ambiguities of the American

experience from the very outset. In our characteristic satisfaction at being Americans, we have long thought that the early colonists, and none more so than the Puritans of Massachusetts Bay, were determined to flee the rotten Old World forever. But Miller reminds us that the aim of the early New England "saints" was to reform the mother country itself, rather than to remain in America permanently, and to do so by returning home in triumph after having created a Zion in the New World. The Old World was their home, spiritually and intellectually.

But when England was rent by civil war after 1640 and by a bitter feud over the type of religious settlement the realm was to enjoy, the mother country became inhospitable to the Puritans beside the Bay. Tragic disappointment resulted. Thus, as had happened in Virginia (see Sigmund Diamond, "From Organization to Society: Virginia in the Seventeenth Century," *American Journal of Sociology*, LXIII [March 1958], 457–75), enduring colonial settlement came almost as an afterthought in Massachusetts. Yet, as Miller suggests, the tragedy of their dashed hopes forced the Puritans to set out on a search for what we like to call "the American way." Their chief problem was to discover a means to make such a sharp and rapid redirection of hope and aspiration psychologically bearable. This they found in the jeremiad, and with it, Miller believes, they found the way to "Americanization." Thus emerged a characteristically American—or is it simply human?—trait of invoking the past in order to justify, and indeed to make possible, what appear to be radical departures in politics and society.

Miller's essay—written in the 1950s, as some of his references make clear—places the critical moment of our colonial history in the 1660s, during the transition from the second to the third generation of settlers. Others, such as Bernard Bailyn, in dealing with the history of colonial Virginia ("Politics and Social Structure in Virginia," in *17th-Century America: Essays in Colonial History*,* James Morton Smith, ed. [1959], pp. 90–115), also agree that the 1660s represented a major turning-point. Still others (such as Oscar Handlin in *The Uprooted** [1951]), writing about entirely different eras and peoples, have

Errand into the Wilderness. Reprinted by permission of the publishers from Perry Miller, *Errand into the Wilderness*, pp. 2–15, Cambridge, Mass., The Belknap Press of Harvard University Press, Copyright, 1956, by the President and Fellows of Harvard College.

suggested that the transit from the second to third generation of any immigrant group marks a moment in which old and new values most sharply clash and in which a redefinition of purpose is most likely to occur. This should not only alert us to the importance of generational change in the history of any modern society but also make us wonder whether in this case the passage from one generation to another created the intellectual crisis or whether the crisis arose from extrinsic causes, as Miller asserts. Were there forces at work at this stage in colonial society—forces such as land and population pressures, changes in local power arrangements, and economic developments, with which Miller does not deal—that might better explain the crisis the author has discovered? To ask this question is to ask about the relationship and priority between intellectual and social forces in any society.

[The title of an election sermon preached in 1670 provided the fitting title for an exhibition of New England imprints at the John Carter Brown Library in Brown University, where I delivered this address on May 16, 1952. Only thereafter did I discover that the Reverend Samuel Danforth had also given me a title.

In his own language, Danforth was trying to do what I too am attempting: to make out some deeper configuration in the story than a mere modification, by obvious and natural necessity, of an imported European culture in adjustment to a frontier. He recognized, as do I, that a basic conditioning factor was the frontier—the wilderness. Even so, the achievement of a personality is not so much the presence of this or that environmental element—no matter how pressing, how terrifying—as the way in which a given personality responds. The real theme is so complex that any simplification does it injustice, though for the sake of communication simplifications are manufactured. Danforth made his simplification by stressing the "errand" more than the "wilderness." So I follow him, and in my context, as in his, "errand" is not a formal thesis but a metaphor.

A metaphor is a vastly different thing from Frederick Jackson Turner's "thesis" that democracy came out of the forest. Happily we no longer are obliged to believe this, although we are ready to recognize, thanks to Turner, that unless we acknowledge the existence of the forest the character of American history is obscure. A newer generation, confessing the importance of Turner's speculations, is concerned with an inherent cultural conflict, in relation to which the forest was, so to speak, as external as the Atlantic Ocean. This ostentatiously simple and monolithic America is in fact a congeries of inner tensions. It has been so from the beginning; it is more so now than at the beginning—as is proved by the frenetic insistence of many Americans that this statement is untrue. Confronted with so gigantic a rid-dle, the analyst becomes wary of generalizations, though incessantly he strives to comprehend.

In this address, then, I am not thinking, nor in any paper of this volume am I thinking, within the framework of interpretation—the "frontier hypothesis"—that Turner bequeathed us. Immense as is the debt that all seekers after national self-knowledge owe to Turner, we have to insist—at least I do —that he did as much to confuse as to clarify the deepest issue. He worked on the premise—which any Puritan logician (being in this regard a scholastic) could have corrected—that the subject matter of a liberal art determines the form, that the content of a discipline automatically supplies the angle of vision. I might even argue that, by remote implication, the struggle of a Protestant culture in America against its weakening hold on the Puritan insight into this law of the mind, namely, that form controls matter, constitutes one theme of the collection. From Turner's conception of the ruling and compulsive power of the frontier no further avenue could be projected to any cultural synthesis. Ideally, this volume might include a study of Turner as being himself an exemplification—I might more accurately say the foremost victim—of his fallacy, rather than the master of it. However, by now it has become rather the mode to point out the romantic prepossessions of Turner; I mention him not only to salute a great name but also, by calling attention to my dissent from him, to underscore my use of the two concepts, both "errand" and "wilderness," as figures of speech.]

*I*t was a happy inspiration that led the staff of the John Carter Brown Library to choose as the title of its New England exhibition of 1952 a phrase from Samuel Danforth's election sermon, delivered on May 11, 1670: *A Brief Recognition of New England's Errand into the Wilderness*. It was of course an inspiration, if not of genius at least of talent, for Danforth to invent his title in the first place. But all the election sermons of this period—that is to say, the major expressions of the second generation, which, delivered on these forensic occasions, were in the fullest sense community expression—have interesting titles; a mere listing tells the story of what was happening to the minds and emotions of the New England people: John Higginson's *The Cause of God and His People In New-England* in 1663, William Stoughton's *New England's True Interest, Not to Lie* in 1668, Thomas Shepard's *Eye-Salve* in 1672, Urian Oakes's *New England Pleaded With* in 1673, and, climactically and most explicitly, Increase Mather's *A Discourse Concerning the Danger of Apostasy* in 1677.

All of these show by their title pages alone—and, as those who have looked into them know, infinitely more by their contents—a deep disquietude. They are troubled utterances, worried, fearful. Something has gone wrong. As in 1662 Wigglesworth already was saying in verse, God has a controversy with New England; He has cause to be angry and to punish it because of its innumerable defections. They say, unanimously, that New England was sent on an errand, and that it has failed.

To our ears these lamentations of the second generation sound strange indeed. We think of the founders as heroic men—of the towering stature of Bradford, Winthrop, and Thomas Hooker—who braved the ocean and the wilderness, who conquered both, and left to their children a goodly heritage. Why then this whimpering?

Some historians suggest that the second and third generations suffered a failure of nerve; they weren't the men their fathers had been, and they knew it. Where the founders could range over the vast body of theology and ecclesiastical polity and produce profound works like the treatises of John Cotton or the subtle psychological analyses of Hooker, or even such a gusty though wrongheaded book as Nathaniel Ward's *Simple Cobler*, let alone such lofty and rightheaded pleas as Roger Williams' *Bloudy Tenent*, all these children could do was tell each other that they were on probation and that their chances of making good did not seem very promising.

Since Puritan intellectuals were thoroughly grounded in grammar and rhetoric, we may be certain that Danforth was fully aware of the ambiguity concealed in his word "errand." It already had taken on the double meaning which it still carries with us. Originally, as the word first took form in English, it meant exclusively a short journey on which an inferior is sent to convey a message or to perform a service for his superior. In that sense we today speak of an "errand boy"; or the husband says that while in town on his lunch hour, he must run an errand for his wife. But by the end of the Middle Ages, errand developed another connotation: it came to mean the actual business on which the actor goes, the purpose itself, the conscious intention in his mind. In this signification, the runner of the errand is working for himself, is his own boss; the wife, while the husband is away at the office, runs her own errands. Now in the 1660's the problem was this: which had New England originally been—an errand boy or a doer of errands? In which sense had it failed? Had it been despatched for a further purpose, or was it an end in itself? Or had it fallen short not only in one or the other, but in both of the meanings? If so, it was indeed a tragedy, in the primitive sense of a fall from a mighty designation.

If the children were in grave doubt about which had been the original errand—if, in fact, those of the founders who lived into the later period and who might have set their progeny to rights found themselves wondering and confused—there is little chance of our answering clearly. Of course, there is no problem about Plymouth Colony. That is the charm about Plymouth: its clarity. The Pilgrims, as we have learned to call them, were reluctant voyagers; they had never wanted to leave England, but had been obliged to depart because the authorities made life impossible for Separatists. They could, naturally, have stayed at home had they given up being Separatists, but that idea simply did not occur to them. Yet they did not go to Holland as though on an errand; neither can we extract the notion of a mission out of the reasons which, as Bradford tells us, persuaded them to leave Leyden for "Virginia." The war with Spain was about to be resumed, and the economic threat was ominous; their migration was not so much an errand as a shrewd forecast, a plan to get out while the getting was good, lest, should they stay, they would be "intrapped or surrounded by their enemies, so as they should neither be able to fight nor flie." True, once the decision was taken, they congratulated themselves that they might become a means for propagating the gospel in remote parts of the world, and thus of serving as steppingstones to others in the performance of this great work; nevertheless, the substance of their decision was that they "thought it better to dislodge betimes to some place of better advantage and less danger, if any such could be found." The great hymn that Bradford, looking back in his old age, chanted about the landfall is one of the greatest passages, if not the very greatest, in all New England's literature; yet it does not resound with the sense of a mission accomplished—instead, it vibrates with the sorrow and exultation of suffering, the sheer endurance, the pain and the anguish, with the somberness of death faced unflinchingly: "May not and ought not the children of these fathers rightly say: Our fathers were Englishmen which came over this great ocean, and were ready to perish in this wilderness; but they cried unto the Lord, and he heard their voyce, and looked on their adversitie . . . ." We are bound, I think, to see in Bradford's account the prototype of the vast majority of subsequent immigrants—of those Oscar Handlin calls "The Uprooted": they came for better advantage and for less danger, and to give their posterity the opportunity of success.

The Great Migration of 1630 is an entirely other story. True, among the reasons John Winthrop drew up in 1629 to persuade himself and his colleagues that they should commit themselves to the enterprise, the economic motive frankly figures. Wise men thought that England was overpopulated and that the poor would have a better chance in the new land. But Massachusetts Bay was not just an organization of immigrants seeking advantage and opportunity. It had a positive sense of mission—either it was sent on an errand or it had its own intention, but in either case the deed was deliberate. It was an act of will, perhaps of willfulness. These Puritans were not driven out of England (thousands of their fellows stayed and fought the Cavaliers) —they went of their own accord.

So, concerning them, we ask the question, why? If we are not altogether clear about precisely how we should phrase the answer, this is not because they themselves were reticent. They spoke as fully as they knew how, and none more magnificently or cogently than John Winthrop in the midst of the passage itself, when he delivered a lay sermon aboard the flagship *Arbella* and called it "A Modell of Christian Charity." It distinguishes the motives of this great enterprise from those of Bradford's forlorn retreat, and especially from those of the masses who later have come in quest of advancement. Hence, for the student of New England and of America, it is a fact demanding incessant brooding that John Winthrop selected as the "doctrine" of his discourse, and so as the basic proposition to which, it then seemed to him, the errand was committed, the thesis that God had disposed mankind in a hierarchy of social classes, so that "in all times some must be rich, some poor, some highe and eminent in power and dignitie; others mean and in subjeccion." It is as though, preternaturally sensing what the promise of America might come to signify for the rank and file, Winthrop took the precaution to drive out of their heads any notion that in the wilderness the poor and the mean were ever so to improve themselves as to mount above the rich or the eminent in dignity. Were there any who had signed up under the mistaken impression that such was the purpose of their errand, Winthrop told them that, although other peoples, lesser breeds, might come for wealth or pelf, this migration was specifically dedicated to an avowed end that had nothing to do with incomes. We have entered into an explicit covenant with God, "we haue professed to enterprise these Accions vpon these and these ends"; we have drawn up indentures with the Almighty, wherefore if we succeed and do not let ourselves get diverted into making money, He will reward us. Whereas if we fail, if we "fall to embrace this present world and prosecute our carnall intencions, seekeing greate things for our selves and our posterity, the Lord will surely breake out in wrathe against us be revenged of such a periured people and make us knowe the price of the breache of such a Covenant."

Well, what terms were agreed upon in this covenant? Winthrop could say precisely—"It is by a mutuall consent through a specially overruleing providence, and a more than ordinary approbation of the Churches of Christ to seeke out a place of Cohabitation and Consorteshipp under a due forme of Government both civill and ecclesiasticall." If it could be said thus concretely, why should there be any ambiguity? There was no doubt whatsover about what Winthrop meant by a due form of ecclesiastical government: he meant the pure Biblical polity set forth in full detail by the New Testament, that method which later generations, in the days of increasing confusion, would settle down to calling Congregational, but which for Winthrop was no denominational peculiarity but the very essence of organized Christianity. What a due form of civil government meant, therefore, became crystal clear: a political regime, possessing power, which would consider its main function to be the erecting, protecting, and preserving of this form of polity. This due form would have, at the very beginning of its list of responsibilities, the duty of suppressing heresy, of subduing or somehow getting rid of dissenters—of being, in short, deliberately, vigorously, and consistently intolerant.

Regarded in this light, the Massachusetts Bay Company came on an errand in the second and later sense of the word: it was, so to speak, on its own business. What it set out to do was the sufficient reason for its setting out. About this Winthrop seems to be perfectly certain, as he declares specifically what the due forms will be attempting: the end is to improve our lives to do more service to the Lord, to increase the body of Christ, and to preserve our posterity from the corruptions of this evil world, so that they in turn shall work out their salvation under the purity and power of Biblical ordinances. Because the errand was so definable in advance, certain conclusions about the method of conducting it were equally evident: one, obviously, was that those sworn to the covenant should not be allowed to turn aside in a lust for mere physical rewards; but another was, in Winthrop's simple but splendid words, "we must be knit togeher in this worke as one man, wee must entertaine each other in brotherly affection." we must actually delight in each other, "always having before our eyes our Commission and community in the worke, our community as members of the same body." This was to say, were the great purpose kept steadily in mind, if all gazed only at it and strove only for it, then social solidarity (within a scheme of fixed and unalterable class distinctions) would be an automatic consequence. A society dispatched upon an errand that is its own reward would want no other rewards: it could go forth to possess a land without ever becoming possessed by it; social gradations would remain eternally what God had originally appointed; there would be no internal contention among groups or interests, and though there would be hard work for everybody, prosperity would be bestowed not as a consequence of labor but as a sign of approval upon the mission itself. For once in the history of humanity (with all its sins), there would be a society so dedicated to a holy cause that success would prove innocent and triumph not raise up sinful pride or arrogant dissension.

Or, at least, this would come about if the people did not deal falsely with God, if they would live up to the articles of their bond. If we do not perform these terms, Winthrop warned, we may expect immediate manifestations of divine wrath; we shall perish out of the land we are crossing the sea to possess. And here in the 1660's and 1670's, all the jeremiads (of which Danforth's is one of the most poignant) are castigations of the people for having defaulted on precisely these articles. They recite the long list of afflictions an angry God had rained upon them, surely enough to prove how abysmally they had deserted the covenant: crop failures, epidemics, grasshoppers, caterpillars, torrid summers, arctic winters, Indian wars, hurricanes, shipwrecks, accidents, and (most grievous of all) unsatisfactory children. The solemn work of the election day, said Stoughton in 1668, is "Foundation-work"—not, that is, to lay a new one, "but to continue, and strengthen, and beautifie, and build upon that which has been laid." It had been laid in the covenant before even a foot was set ashore, and thereon New England should rest. Hence the terms of survival, let alone of prosperity, remained what had first been propounded: "If we should so frustrate and deceive the Lords Expectations, that his Covenant-interest in us, and the Workings of his Salvation be made to cease, then All were lost indeed; Ruine upon Ruine, Destruction upon Destruction would come, until one stone were not left upon another." Since so much of the literature after 1660—in fact, just about all of it—dwells on this theme of declension and apostasy, would not the story of New England seem to be simply that of the failure of a mission? Winthrop's dread was realized: posterity had not found their salvation amid pure ordinances but had, despite the ordinances, yielded to the seductions of the good land. Hence distresses were being piled upon them, the slaughter of King Philip's War and now the attack of a profligate king upon the sacred charter. By about 1680, it did in truth seem that shortly no stone would be left upon another, that history would record of New England that the founders had been great men, but that their children and grandchildren progressively deteriorated.

This would certainly seem to be the impression conveyed by the assembled clergy and lay elders who, in 1679, met at Boston in a formal synod, under the leadership of Increase Mather, and there prepared a report on why the land suffered. The result of their deliberation, published under the title *The Necessity of Reformation*, was the first in what has proved to be a distressingly long succession of investigations into the civic health of Americans, and it is probably the most pessimistic. The land was afflicted, it said, because corruption had proceeded apace; assuredly, if the people did not quickly reform, the last blow would fall and nothing but desolation be left.

Into what a moral quagmire this dedicated community had sunk, the synod did not leave to imagination; it published a long and detailed inventory of sins, crimes, misdemeanors, and nasty habits, which makes, to say the least, interesting reading.

We hear much talk nowadays about corruption, most of it couched in generalized terms. If we ask our current Jeremiahs to descend to particulars, they tell us that the republic is going on the rocks, or to the dogs, because the wives of politicians aspire to wear mink coats and their husbands take a moderate five per cent cut on certain deals to pay for the garments. The Puritans were devotees of logic, and the verb "methodize" ruled their thinking. When the synod went to work, it had before it a succession of sermons, such as that of Danforth and the other election-day or fast-day orators, as well as such works as Increase Mather's *A Brief History of the Warr With the Indians*, wherein the decimating conflict with Philip was presented as a revenge upon the people for their transgressions. When the synod felt obliged to enumerate the enormities of the land so that the people could recognize just how far short of their errand they had fallen, it did not, in the modern manner, assume that regeneration would be accomplished at the next election by turning the rascals out, but it digested this body of literature; it reduced the contents to method. The result is a staggering compendium of iniquity, organized into twelve headings.

First, there was a great and visible decay of godliness. Second, there were several manifestations of pride—contention in the churches, insubordination of inferiors toward superiors, particularly of those inferiors who had, unaccountably, acquired more wealth than their betters, and, astonishingly, a shocking extravagance in attire, especially on the part of these of the meaner sort, who persisted in dressing beyond their means. Third, there were heretics, especially Quakers and Anabaptists. Fourth, a notable increase in swearing and a spreading disposition to sleep at sermons (these two phenomena seemed basically connected). Fifth, the Sabbath was wantonly violated. Sixth, family government had decayed, and fathers no longer kept their sons and daughters from prowling at night. Seventh, instead of people being knit together as one man in mutual love, they were full of contention, so that lawsuits were on the increase and lawyers were thriving. Under the eighth head, the synod described the sins of sex and alcohol, thus producing some of the juiciest prose of the period: militia days had become orgies, taverns were crowded; women threw temptation in the way of befuddled men by wearing false locks and displaying naked necks and arms "or, which is more abominable, naked Breasts"; there were "mixed Dancings," along with light behavior and "Company-keeping" with vain persons, wherefore the bastardy rate was rising. In 1672, there was actually an attempt to supply Boston with a brothel (it was suppressed, but the synod was bearish about the future). Ninth, New Englanders were betraying a marked disposition to tell lies, especially when selling anything. In the tenth place, the business morality of even the most righteous left everything to be desired: the wealthy speculated in land and raised prices excessively; "Day-Labourers and Mechanicks are unreasonable in their demands." In the eleventh place, the people showed no disposition to reform, and in the twelfth, they seemed utterly destitute of civic spirit.

"The things here insisted on," said the synod, "have been oftentimes mentioned and inculcated by those whom the Lord hath set as Watchmen to the house of Israel." Indeed they had been, and thereafter they continued to be even more inculcated. At the end of the century, the synod's report was serving as a kind of handbook for preachers: they would take some verse of Isaiah or Jeremiah, set up the doctrine that God avenges the iniquities of a chosen people, and then run down the twelve heads, merely bringing the list up to date by inserting the new and still more depraved practices an ingenious people kept on devising. I suppose that in the whole literature of the world, including the satirists of imperial Rome, there is hardly such another uninhibited and unrelenting documentation of a people's descent into corruption.

I have elsewhere endeavored to argue[1] that, while the social or economic historian may read this literature for its contents—and so construct from the expanding catalogue of denunciations a record of social progress—the cultural anthropologist will look slightly askance at these jeremaids; he will exercise a methodological caution about taking them at face value. If you read them all through, the total effect, curiously enough, is not at all depressing: you come to the paradoxical realization that they do not bespeak a despairing frame of mind. There is something of a ritualistic incantation about them; whatever they may signify in the realm of theology, in that of psychology they are purgations of soul; they do not discourage but actually encourage the community to persist in its heinous conduct. The exhortation to a reformation which never materializes serves as a token payment upon the obligation, and so liberates the debtors. Changes there had to be: adaptations to environment, expansion of the frontier, mansions constructed, commercial adventures undertaken. These activities were not specifically nominated in the bond Winthrop had framed. They were thrust upon the society by American experience; because they were not only works of necessity but of excitement, they proved irresistible—whether making money, haunting taverns, or committing fornication. Land speculation meant not only wealth but dispersion of the people, and what was to stop the march of settlement? The covenant doctrine preached on the *Arbella* had been formulated in England, where land was not to be had for the taking; its adherents had been utterly oblivious of what the fact of a frontier would do for an imported order, let alone for a European mentality. Hence I suggest that under the guise of this mounting wail of sinfulness, this incessant and never successful cry for repentance, the Puritans launched themselves upon the process of Americanization.

However, there are still more pertinent or more analytical things to be said of this body of expression. If you compare it with the great productions of the founders, you will be struck by the fact that the second and third generations had become oriented toward the social, and only the social, problem; herein they were deeply and profoundly different from their fathers. The finest creations of the founders—the disquisitions of Hooker, Shepard, and Cotton—were written in Europe, or else, if actually penned in the colonies, proceeded from a thoroughly European mentality, upon

---

[1] See *The New England Mind: From Colony to Province* (1952), Chapter II.

which the American scene made no impression whatsoever. The most striking example of this imperviousness is the poetry of Anne Bradstreet: she came to Massachusetts at the age of eighteen, already two years married to Simon Bradstreet; there, she says, "I found a new world and new manners, at which my heart rose" in rebellion, but soon convincing herself that it was the way of God, she submitted and joined the church. She bore Simon eight children, and loved him sincerely, as her most charming poem, addressed to him, reveals:

> If ever two were one, then surely we;
> If ever man were loved by wife, then thee.

After the house burned, she wrote a lament about how her pleasant things in ashes lay and how no more the merriment of guests would sound in the hall; but there is nothing in the poem to suggest that the house stood in North Andover or that the things so tragically consumed were doubly precious because they had been transported across the ocean and were utterly irreplaceable in the wilderness. In between rearing children and keeping house she wrote her poetry; her brother-in-law carried the manuscript to London, and there published it in 1650 under the ambitious title, *The Tenth Muse Lately Sprung Up in America*. But the title is the only thing about the volume which shows any sense of America, and that little merely in order to prove that the plantations had something in the way of European wit and learning, that they had not receded into barbarism. Anne's flowers are English flowers, the birds, English birds, and the landscape is Lincolnshire. So also with the productions of immigrant scholarship: such a learned and acute work as Hooker's *Survey of the Summe of Church Discipline*, which is specifically about the regime set up in America, is written entirely within the logical patterns, and out of the religious experience, of Europe; it makes no concession to new and peculiar circumstances.

The titles alone of productions in the next generation show how concentrated have become emotion and attention upon the interest of New England, and none is more revealing than Samuel Danforth's conception of an errand into the wilderness. Instead of being able to compose abstract treatises like those of Hooker upon the soul's preparation, humiliation, or exultation, or such a collection of wisdom and theology as John Cotton's *The Way of Life* or Shepard's *The Sound Believer*, these later saints must, over and over again, dwell upon the specific sins of New England, and the more they denounce, the more they must narrow their focus to the provincial problem. If they write upon anything else, it must be about the halfway covenant and its manifold consequences—a development enacted wholly in this country—or else upon their wars with the Indians. Their range is sadly constricted, but every effort, no matter how brief, is addressed to the persistent question: what is the meaning of this society in the wilderness? If it does not mean what Winthrop said it must mean, what under Heaven is it? Who, they are forever asking themselves, who are we?—and sometimes they are on the verge of saying, who the Devil are we, anyway?

This brings us back to the fundamental ambiguity concealed in the word "errand," that *double entente* of which I am certain Danforth was aware when he published the words that give point to the exhibition. While it was true that in 1630, the covenant philosophy of a special and peculiar bond lifted the migration out of the ordinary realm of nature, provided it with a definite mission which might in the secondary sense be called its errand, there was always present in Puritan thinking the suspicion that God's saints are at best inferiors, despatched by their Superior upon particular assignments. Anyone who has run errands for other people, particularly for people of great importance with many things on their minds, such as army commanders, knows how real is the peril that, by the time he returns with the report of a message delivered or a bridge blown up, the Superior may be interested in something else; the situation at headquarters may be entirely changed, and the gallant errand boy, or the husband who desperately remembered to buy the ribbon, may be told that he is too late. This tragic pattern appears again and again in modern warfare: an agent is dropped by parachute and, after immense hardships, comes back to find that, in the shifting tactical or strategic situations, his contribution is no longer of value. If he gets home in time and his service proves useful, he receives a medal; otherwise, no matter what prodigies he has performed, he may not even be thanked. He has been sent, as the devastating phrase has it, upon a fool's errand, than which there can be a no more shattering blow to self-esteem.

The Great Migration of 1630 felt insured against such treatment from on high by the covenant; nevertheless, the God of the covenant always remained an unpredictable Jehovah, a *Deus Absconditus*. When God promises to abide by stated terms, His word, of course, is to be trusted; but then, what is man that he dare accuse Omnipotence of tergiversation? But if any such apprehension was in Winthrop's mind as he spoke on the *Arbella*, or in the minds of other apologists for the enterprise, they kept it far back and allowed it no utterance. They could stifle the thought, not only because Winthrop and his colleagues believed fully in the covenant, but because they could see in the pattern of history that their errand was not a mere scouting expedition: it was an essential maneuver in the drama of Christendom. The Bay Company was not a battered remnant of suffering Separatists thrown up on a rocky shore; it was an organized task force of Christians, executing a flank attack on the corruptions of Christendom. These Puritans did not flee to America; they went in order to work out that complete reformation which was not yet accomplished in England and Europe, but which would quickly be accomplished if only the saints back there had a working model to guide them. It is impossible to say that any who sailed from Southampton really expected to lay his bones in the new world; were it to come about—as all in their heart of hearts anticipated—that the forces of righteousness should prevail against Laud and Wentworth, that England after all should turn toward reformation, where else would the distracted country look for leadership except to those who in New England had perfected the ideal polity and who would know how to administer it? This was the large unspoken assumption in the errand of 1630: if the conscious intention were realized, not only would a federated Jehovah bless the new land, but He would bring back these temporary colonials to govern England.

In this respect, therefore, we may say that the migration was running an errand in the earlier and more primitive sense of the word—performing a job not so much for Jehovah as for history, which was the wisdom of

Jehovah expressed through time. Winthrop was aware of this aspect of the mission—fully conscious of it. "For wee must Consider that wee shall be as a Citty upon a Hill, the eies of all people are uppon us." More was at stake than just one little colony. If we deal falsely with God, not only will He descend upon us in wrath, but even more terribly, He will make us "a story and a by-word through the world, wee shall open the mouthes of enemies to speake evill of the wayes of god and all professours for Gods sake." No less than John Milton was New England to justify God's ways to man, though not, like him, in the agony and confusion of defeat but in the confidence of approaching triumph. This errand was being run for the sake of Reformed Christianity; and while the first aim was indeed to realize in America the due form of government, both civil and ecclesiastical, the aim behind that aim was to vindicate the most rigorous ideal of the Reformation, so that ultimately all Europe would imitate New England. If we succeed, Winthrop told his audience, men will say of later plantations, "the lord make it like that of New England." There was an elementary prudence to be observed: Winthrop said that the prayer would arise from subsequent plantations, yet what was England itself but one of God's plantations? In America, he promised, we shall see, or may see, more of God's wisdom, power, and truth "then formerly wee have beene acquainted with." The situation was such that, for the moment, the model had no chance to be exhibited in England; Puritans could talk about it, theorize upon it, but they could not display it, could not prove that it would actually work. But if they had it set up in America—in a bare land, devoid of already established (and corrupt) institutions, empty of bishops and courtiers, where they could start *de novo*, and the eyes of the world were upon it—and if then it performed just as the saints had predicted of it, the Calvinist internationale would know exactly how to go about completing the already begun but temporarily stalled revolution in Europe.[2]

When we look upon the enterprise from this point of view, the psychology of the second and third generations becomes more comprehensible. We realize that the migration was not sent upon its errand in order to found the United States of America, nor even the New England conscience. Actually, it would not perform its errand even when the colonists did erect a due form of government in church and state: what was further required in order for this mission to be a success was that the eyes of the world be kept fixed upon it in rapt attention. If the rest of the world, or at least of Protestantism, looked elsewhere, or turned to another model, or simply got distracted and forgot about New England, if the new land was left with a polity nobody in the great world of Europe wanted—then every success in fulfilling the terms of the covenant would become a diabolical measure of failure. If the due form of government were not everywhere to be saluted, what would New England have upon its hands? How give it a name, this victory nobody could utilize? How provide an identity for something conceived under misapprehensions? How could a universal which turned out

[2] See the perceptive analysis of Alan Heimert (*The New England Quarterly*, XXVI, September 1953) of the ingredients that ultimately went into Puritans' metaphor of the "wilderness," all the more striking a concoction because they attached no significance a priori to their wilderness destination. To begin with, it was simply a void.

to be nothing but a provincial particular be called anything but a blunder
or an abortion?

If an actor, playing the leading role in the greatest dramatic spectacle of
the century, were to attire himself and put on his make-up, rehearse his
lines, take a deep breath, and stride onto the stage, only to find the theater
dark and empty, no spotlight working, and himself entirely alone, he would
feel as did New England around 1650 or 1660. For in the 1640's, during the
Civil Wars, the colonies, so to speak, lost their audience. First of all, there
proved to be, deep in the Puritan movement, an irreconcilable split between
the Presbyterian and Independent wings, wherefore no one system could be
imposed upon England, and so the New England model was unserviceable.
Secondly—most horrible to relate—the Independents, who in polity were
carrying New England's banner and were supposed, in the schedule of
history, to lead England into imitation of the colonial order, betrayed the
sacred cause by yielding to the heresy of toleration. They actually welcomed Roger Williams, whom the leaders of the model had kicked out of
Massachusetts so that his nonsense about liberty of conscience would not
spoil the administrations of charity.

In other words, New England did not lie, did not falter; it made good
everything Winthrop demanded—wonderfully good—and then found that
its lesson was rejected by those choice spirits for whom the exertion had
been made. By casting out Williams, Anne Hutchinson, and the Antino-
mians, along with an assortment of Gortonists and Anabaptists, into that cess-
pool then becoming known as Rhode Island, Winthrop, Dudley, and the
clerical leaders showed Oliver Cromwell how he should go about governing England. Instead, he developed the utterly absurd theory that so
long as a man made a good soldier in the New Model Army, it did not
matter whether he was a Calvinist, an Antinomian, an Armenian, an Ana-
baptist or even—horror of horrors—a Socinian! Year after year, as the circus
tours this country, crowds howl with laughter, no matter how many times
they have seen the stunt, at the bustle that walks by itself: the clown comes
out dressed in a large skirt with a bustle behind; he turns sharply to the left,
and the bustle continues blindly and obstinately straight ahead, on the
original course. It is funny in a circus, but not in history. There is nothing
but tragedy in the realization that one was in the main path of events, and
now is sidetracked and disregarded. One is always able, of course, to stand
firm on his first resolution, and to condemn the clown of history for taking
the wrong turning: yet this is a desolating sort of stoicism, because it
always carries with it the recognition that history will never come back to
the predicted path, and that with one's own demise, righteousness must die
out of the world.

The most humiliating element in the experience was the way the English
brethren turned upon the colonials for precisely their greatest achievement.
It must have seemed, for those who came with Winthrop in 1630 and who
remembered the clarity and brilliance with which he set forth the conditions
of their errand, that the world was turned upside down and inside out
when, in June 1645, thirteen leading Independent divines—such men as
Goodwin, Owen, Nye, Burroughs, formerly friends and allies of Hooker
and Davenport, men who might easily have come to New England and
helped extirpate heretics—wrote the General Court that the colony's law

banishing Anabaptists was an embarrassment to the Independent cause in England. Opponents were declaring, said these worthies, "that persons of our way, principall and spirit cannot beare with Dissentors from them, but Doe correct, fine, imprison and banish them wherever they have power soe to Doe." There were indeed people in England who admired the severities of Massachusetts, but we assure you, said the Independents, these "are utterly your enemyes and Doe seeke your extirpation from the face of the earth: those who now in power are your friends are quite otherwise minded, and doe professe they are much offended with your proceedings." Thus early commenced that chronic weakness in the foreign policy of Americans, an inability to recognize who in truth constitute their best friends abroad.

We have lately accustomed ourselves to the fact that there does exist a mentality which will take advantage of the liberties allowed by society in order to conspire for the ultimate suppression of those same privileges. The government of Charles I and Archbishop Laud had not, where that danger was concerned, been liberal, but it had been conspicuously inefficient; hence, it did not liquidate the Puritans (although it made halfhearted efforts), nor did it herd them into prison camps. Instead, it generously, even lavishly, gave a group of them a charter to Massachusetts Bay, and obligingly left out the standard clause requiring that the document remain in London, that the grantees keep their office within reach of Whitehall. Winthrop's revolutionaries availed themselves of this liberty to get the charter overseas, and thus to set up a regime dedicated to the worship of God in the manner they desired—which meant allowing nobody else to worship any other way, especially adherents of Laud and King Charles. All this was perfectly logical and consistent. But what happened to the thought processes of their fellows in England made no sense whatsoever. Out of the New Model Army came the fantastic notion that a party struggling for power should proclaim that, once it captured the state, it would recognize the right of dissenters to disagree and to have their own worship, to hold their own opinions. Oliver Cromwell was so far gone in this idiocy as to become a dictator, in order to impose toleration by force! Amid this shambles, the errand of New England collapsed. There was nobody left at headquarters to whom reports could be sent.

Many a man has done a brave deed, been hailed as a public hero, had honors and ticker tape heaped upon him—and then had to live, day after day, in the ordinary routine, eating breakfast and brushing his teeth, in what seems protracted anticlimax. A couple may win their way to each other across insuperable obstacles, elope in a blaze of passion and glory—and then have to learn that life is a matter of buying the groceries and getting the laundry done. This sense of the meaning having gone out of life, that all adventures are over, that no great days and no heroism lie ahead, is particularly galling when it falls upon a son whose father once was the public hero or the great lover. He has to put up with the daily routine without ever having known at first hand the thrill of danger or the ecstacy of passion. True, he has his own hardships—clearing rocky pastures, hauling in the cod during a storm, fighting Indians in a swamp—but what are these compared with the magnificence of leading an exodus of saints to found a city on a hill, for the eyes of all the world to behold? He might wage a stout fight against the Indians, and one out of ten of his fellows might perish in the struggle, but the world was no longer interested. He would be reduced to writing accounts of himself and scheming to get a publisher in London, in a desperate effort to tell a heedless world, "Look, I exist!"

His greatest difficulty would not be the stones, storms, and Indians, but the problem of his identity. In something of this sort, I would like to suggest, consists the anxiety and torment that inform productions of the late seventeenth and early eighteenth centuries—and should I say, some thereafter? It appears most clearly in *Magnalia Christi Americana*, the work of that soul most tortured by the problem, Cotton Mather: "I write the Wonders of the Christian Religion, flying from the Depravations of Europe, to the American Strand." Thus he proudly begins, and at once trips over the acknowledgment that the founders had not simply fled from depraved Europe but had intended to redeem it. And so the book is full of lamentations over the declension of the children, who appear, page after page, in contrast to their mighty progenitors, about as profligate a lot as ever squandered a great inheritance.

And yet, the *Magnalia* is not an abject book; neither are the election sermons abject, nor is the inventory of sins offered by the synod of 1679. There is bewilderment, confusion, chagrin, but there is no surrender. A task has been assigned upon which the populace are in fact intensely engaged. But they are not sure any more for just whom they are working; they know they are moving, but they do not know where they are going. They seem still to be on an errand, but if they are no longer inferiors sent by the superior forces of the Reformation, to whom they should report, then their errand must be wholly of the second sort, something with a purpose and an intention sufficient unto itself. If so, what is it? If it be not the due form of government, civil and ecclesiastical, that they brought into being, how otherwise can it be described?

The literature of self-condemnation must be read for meanings far below the surface, for meanings of which, we may be so rash as to surmise, the authors were not fully conscious, but by which they were troubled and goaded. They looked in vain to history for an explanation of themselves; more and more it appeared that the meaning was not to be found in theology, even with the help of the covenantal dialectic. Thereupon, these citizens found that they had no other place to search but within themselves—even though, at first sight, that repository appeared to be nothing but a sink of iniquity. Their errand having failed in the first sense of the term, they were left with the second, and required to fill it with meaning by themselves and out of themselves. Having failed to rivet the eyes of the world upon their city on the hill, they were left alone with America.

Suggested Reading

The nature of English society and politics on the eve of colonization is most successfully captured by Peter Laslett in *The World We Have Lost** (1965), and Carl Bridenbaugh in *Vexed and Troubled Englishmen, 1590–1642* (1968).

An interpretive survey of colonial America, notable for its challenging, if somewhat perverse, views, is Daniel J. Boorstin's *The Americans: The Colonial Experience** (1958). A more judicious appraisal, left unfinished at the time of the author's death, is Richard Hofstadter's *America at 1750: a Social Portrait* (1971). Darrett B. Rutman in *The Morning of America, 1603–1789** (1971) provides another and briefer overview.

W. Frank Craven's *The Southern Colonies in the Seventeenth Century, 1607–1689** (1949) remains the best introduction to its subject. New perspectives on the settlement of Virginia have been provided by Edmund S. Morgan in "The Labor Problem at Jamestown, 1607–18," *American Historical Review*, LXXVI (June 1971), and "The First American Boom: Virginia 1618 to 1630," *William and Mary Quarterly*, 3rd Ser., XXVIII (April 1971).

Samuel Eliot Morison describes the leaders of early Massachusetts in *Builders of the Bay Colony** (1930), which should be supplemented by Edmund S. Morgan's incisive *The Puritan Dilemma: The Story of John Winthrop** (1958). Morison helps dispel false notions of the Puritan's barren spirit and intellect in *The Intellectual Life of Colonial New England,** 2nd ed. (1956).

Perry Miller's works, though often difficult, remain monuments to scholarship and sympathetic understanding. Especially useful are *Orthodoxy in Massachusetts** (1933), on the origins of the Bay Colony; *The New England Mind: From Colony to Province** (1953), on Puritan thought; and his collection of Puritan writings, *The American Puritans: Their Prose and Poetry** (1956), which is, in effect, a shorter version of the more comprehensive volume by Perry Miller and Thomas A. Johnson, eds., *The Puritans** (1938).

Carl Bridenbaugh offers the best introductions to the urban societies of colonial America in *Cities in the Wilderness: The First Century of Urban Life in America, 1625–1742,** 2nd ed. (1955), and *Cities in Revolt: Urban Life in America, 1743–1776** (1955). The cultural life of the early settlers, so much of which was centered in and about the largest towns, is the subject of Louis B. Wright's *The Cultural Life of the American Colonies** (1957).

The most recent strides in the analysis of colonial society have come in detailed investigations of single communities, most of them in New England. The initial studies in this genre were Charles S. Grant's *Democracy in the Connecticut Frontier Town of Kent** (1961) and Sumner Chilton Powell's *Puritan Village** (1963). More recent ones, each dealing in a distinctive fashion with the structure of society and the nature of town life, include John Demos' *A Little Commonwealth: Family Life in Plymouth Colony** (1970); Philip J. Greven, Jr.'s *Four Generations: Population, Land, and Family in Colonial Andover, Massachusetts* (1970); and Kenneth A. Lockridge's *A New England Town: The First Hundred Years, Dedham, Massachusetts** (1970). Richard L. Bushman has written a sensitive study of changes in a province-wide society entitled *From Puritan to Yankee: Character and the Social Order in Connecticut, 1690–1765** (1967).

* Also published in paperback edition.

The Meeting of
Races and
Cultures

Indian Cultural Adjustment to European Civilization

Nancy Oestreich Lurie

Historians are still striving to determine from where, in what manner, and when the Indian tribes first came to the Western hemisphere. But there is no question that when the original Spanish and English settlers landed on the Atlantic shores, they confronted a populous, complex, and mature Indian civilization. In the following essay, Nancy Oestreich Lurie of the University of Michigan examines the responses to the white colonists by one group of these first Americans.

Lurie, an anthropologist, is as concerned as the historian with the past. But more consistently than the historian, the anthropologist concentrates on culture, the entire structure and expression of a society, and is better prepared than most historians to deal with nontextual artifacts and a range of subjects that include language, art, and symbol. The historical anthropologist's approach is exemplified in Lurie's effort to ask what happened when two sharply different cultures met one another.

In her analysis, the Indians' response to the onset of white settlement was quite rational and hardly that of "savage" or "uncivilized" people. If in the end they did not succeed in warding off the whites, they were as capable of trying to exploit the colonists as the

41

colonists were of exploiting them. In fact, the story on both sides is more complex than mere exploitation. Both natives and colonists had problems that at times created a real, if frail, community of interests; the colonists had to survive and, for its part at least, the Powhatan confederacy faced delicate diplomatic and intertribal issues that had to be resolved. Furthermore, Indian culture in what came to be known as Virginia was by no means static. It quite readily adapted to some white ways. And, in turn, a few whites, in the earliest days of settlement, even sought to escape their own culture and to absorb themselves within the Indian communities. In this sense, European culture was adjusting to Indian civilization.

Thus, the admittance that the fate of the American Indian civilization has been a tragic one does not obviate the need for the historian and anthropologist to further clarify the relationship between Indians and whites. Many of the reactions of whites and Indians to each other, as Lurie's account makes clear, depended on such factors as the nature and even the relative location of various white and tribal societies and the point in their own histories when they first encountered each other. The annihilation or assimilation, either partial or total, of Indian culture was thus a function of both its own circumstances and the disposition of the whites it met up with. That the Indian societies were unable in the end to withstand the white threat and to retain their original integrity did not, however, put an end to Indian culture, which has proven its adaptability to European civilization well into the twentieth century. Indeed, recent scholarship forces us to have great respect, not only for the remnants of the Indian civilizations that survive, but also for the cultures the first Americans produced.

Indian Cultural Adjustment to European Civilization. By Nancy Oestreich Lurie from James M. Smith, ed., *17th-Century America: Essays in Colonial History* (Chapel Hill, N.C.: University of North Carolina Press, 1959), pp. 33–60. Reprinted by permission of the University of North Carolina Press and the Institute of Early American History and Culture.

*I*n 1907, on the 300th anniversary of the beginning of English colonization in America, James Mooney made the brief observation that the Jamestown settlers "landed among a people who already knew and hated whites." In effect, this remark summed up the accepted anthropological explanation for the Indians' unpredictable behavior; it indicated why they alternated elaborate expressions and actions of good will with apparent treachery. Mooney implied that the Indians' attitudes and behavior were more than justified by the demonstrated greed and aggressiveness of the whites.[1]

Little work was done in the succeeding years to explore the complete significance of Mooney's remark or to probe more deeply into underlying motivations for the Indians' actions. This neglect was inevitable, since attention had to be devoted to a more fundamental problem. Before achieving an understanding of Indian reaction to the effects of contact with Europeans, it was necessary to establish a valid and cohesive picture of aboriginal culture.[2] Thanks to the labors of such scholars as Mooney, Frank G. Speck, David I. Bushnell, John R. Swanton, Maurice A. Mook, and others, the fragmentary data relating to native life have been gathered into comprehensive and analytical accounts concerned with such problems as Indian demography, the cultural and linguistic identity of given tribes, tribal locations, and the prehistoric diffusion and changes in Indian cultures.

Likewise, in the past fifty years, general theoretical techniques of ethnological interpretation have been refined through field research in observable situations of culture contact. These acculturational studies, which are an invaluable aid in the interpretation of historical data, have investigated the reasons why some groups lose their cultural identity in a situation of culture contact while other groups continue to preserve ethnic integrity despite widespread alterations of purely native patterns.[3] With this backlog of necessary information and analysis, anthropologists have begun a more intensive consideration of the dynamics of culture contact in ethnohistorical terms.

---

[1] James Mooney, "The Powhatan Confederacy, Past and Present," *Amer. Anthropologist*, 9 (1907), 129 and 120–52 *passim*. This Jamestown anniversary issue featured articles dealing with the Virginia Indians.

[2] It must be noted that while the concept of culture can be and often is treated as an abstraction with an existence almost unto itself, this is no more than a semantic devise. Human ideas and reasoning underlie culture and cultural change. Whenever possible, I have devoted attention to the factors of human motivations which give overt expression to observable cultural characteristics. The terms Indian culture and European civilization merely indicate that comparisons are made of two cultures having distinct origins and historical traditions, differing only in the local expressions of certain universal aspects of culture.

[3] Two valuable publications dealing with the general topic of acculturation are: The Social Science Research Council Summer Seminar in Acculturation, 1953, "Acculturation, An Exploratory Formulation," *Amer. Anthropologist*, 56 (1954), 973–1005; and Verne F. Ray, ed., *Proceedings of the 1957 Annual Spring Meeting of the American Ethnological Society* (Seattle, 1957). The latter discusses cultural change and stability.

Turning to Mooney's contention, there is evidence that the Virginia Indians had several opportunities to form opinions about Europeans both in terms of direct experience and of information communicated to them. Direct knowledge of Europeans may have occurred as early as the first quarter of the sixteenth century, when Giovanni de Verrazano and Estevan Gomez are believed to have made observations in the Chesapeake Bay region.[4] Of somewhat greater significance is the alleged founding of a Spanish Jesuit mission on the York River in 1570. According to this theory, the missionaries were killed by Indians under the leadership of a native known as Don Luis de Velasco, who had lived in Spain, where he was educated and converted to Christianity. The Spaniards had hoped that he would act as guide and model in the proselytizing of his people, but it appears that the effects of his early life negated his later training. In 1572 a punitive expedition under Pedro Menendez de Aviles attacked and defeated the Indians responsible for the destruction of the mission; in succeeding years Menendez made other forays into the region. A recent study insists that this area must have been along the Virginia coast.[5]

Whether or not the case for a sixteenth-century mission in Virginia has been proved is problematical. Many details are uncertain: the precise location of the mission on the York River, the tribal affiliations of Don Luis, the extent of his leadership, his age at the time he lived in Spain, and his possible genealogical affiliations with the ruling hierarchy of the Virginia Indians of the seventeenth century. However, historical investigation leaves no doubt of Spanish activity at this time, and these ventures must have occurred between St. Augustine and the Potomac River. The natives of Virginia, who borrowed cultural traits from neighboring tribes along the coast and further inland, could have received news of European explorations to the south and west by the same routes that carried purely native ideas. Generalized impressions of Europeans were doubtless prevalent in the Virginia area long before 1607.

The Spaniards came to America primarily as adventurers and fortune seekers. Although they attempted to found settlements their efforts usually met with failure. They plundered Indian villages but did not remain long in any one region; they were frequently routed by angry Indians or by their own inability to subsist in a strange terrain. After 1520, raids were conducted along the Gulf and southern Atlantic coast to obtain slaves for shipment to the West Indies. News of these incursions may have reached Virginia via the various coast tribes, and similarly Virginia natives may have heard of De Soto's hapless wanderings to the south and west. Even though the Spaniards later achieved success in colonization in Florida through the use of missionaries, the first hostile impressions had been made.

The French entered the scene to the south of Virginia in 1562. Because

---

[4] For a good brief account, see John Bartlett Brebner, *The Explorers of North America, 1492–1806*, reprint edn. (New York, 1955).

[5] Clifford M. Lewis, S. J., and Albert J. Loomie, S. J., *The Spanish Jesuit Mission in Virginia, 1570–1572* (Chapel Hill, 1953), is an exhaustive study, but the Indian data are treated so summarily throughout that they neither help to substantiate the argument nor cast much light on the influence of the mission among the Indians, wherever it was established.

of lack of supplies and Spanish aggression, they failed in their attempts to establish a foothold in the region. However, the interests of France as well as of Britain were served by unknown numbers of piratical freebooters from the Caribbean area who touched along the coast of the Carolinas and intrigued with the Indians. Not until 1580 was Spain able to dislodge foreign intruders and punish recalcitrant Indians. Even then, Spanish dominion remained precarious, although the Spanish Franciscans continued to extend their missions up the coast. Finally, in 1597, a general uprising among the Carolina tribes destroyed these religious outposts and forced Spain again to concentrate most of her forces in Florida.

Thus, during much of the sixteenth century Europeans were active in regions immediately adjacent to Virginia and possibly in Virginia itself. Their activity was often associated with violence, and there was sufficient time for rumors concerning them to have reached the Virginia natives before any direct contacts were made. By the time the English attempted to found colonies on the east coast toward the close of the sixteenth century, they encountered difficulties which may have been more than the simple result of European inexperience in developing techniques for survival in the New World. Raleigh's enterprise, for example, may have been singularly ill-timed. A general unrest in Indian-white relationships marked the period from 1577 to 1597 in the Carolina region where Raleigh's followers chose to remain. Pemisipan, a Secotan chief who attempted to organize opposition to the British in 1585, could hardly have been blamed if he saw a curious similarity to accounts he may have heard concerning the Spanish when, for the trifling matter of the theft of a silver cup, the English burned the corn and destroyed the buildings at his village of Aquascogoc.[6]

The later events at Cape Henry, the first landfall of the Jamestown colonists, suggest that the immediate hostility expressed by the Indians was inspired by fear of reprisals for the fate of Raleigh's colony. The Indians who attacked the English belonged to the Chesapeake tribe, immediately adjacent to the tribes with whom Pemisipan conspired.[7] It is also possible, as Mooney implies, that by 1607 the Virginia Indians evaluated any sudden appearance of Europeans as evil and took immediate measures to repel them. However, this view oversimplifies several important factors. Long before any Europeans arrived at Jamestown, the Indians had been fighting over matters of principle important to them, such as possession of land and tribal leadership. If they were aware of the fate of other Indians at the hands of Europeans, there was no reason for them to assume that their fate would be similar; they were not necessarily allied with the beleaguered tribes, nor did they share a sense of racial kinship. Sharp cultural differences and even sharper linguistic differences separated the various Indian societies. While there was reason to fear and hate the Europeans as invaders who made indiscriminate

[6] Maurice A. Mook, "Algonkian Ethnohistory of the Carolina Sound," *Jour. of The Washington Academy of Sciences*, 34 (1944), 185–86, quotes and discusses the journal of 1585, usually attributed to Sir Richard Grenville, regarding this incident and also establishes the location of Aquascogoc in North Carolina.

[7] [George Percy], "Observations gathered out of *A Discourse of the Plantation of the Southerne Colonie in Virginia by the English, 1606:* written by that Honorable Gentleman, Master George Percy," in Edward Arber, ed., *Captain John Smith . . . Works, 1608–1631* (Birmingham, Eng., 1884), xl–li.

war on all Indians, the fear was only that of being taken unawares and the hate could be modified if the tribes which had falled victim thus far were strangers or even enemies. If the Indians of Virginia had any knowledge of Europeans, they must have been aware that the white men were fundamentally outnumbered, frequently unable to support themselves in an environment which the Indians found eminently satisfactory, and that European settlements were usually short lived. The appearance of the English was probably far less alarming than 350 years of hindsight indicate ought to have been the case.

This is demonstrated by the fact that the Virginia Indians under the leadership of Powhatan seem to have made their first adjustments to Europeans in terms of existing native conditions.[8] Primary among these conditions were Powhatan's efforts to gain firmer control over his subject tribes and to fight tribes traditionally at enmity with his followers. It was expedient to help the settlers stay alive, for they could be useful allies in his established plans; but at the same time he could not allow them to gain ascendancy. The situation was complicated by factionalism in Powhatan's ranks and lack of accord among the settlers. However, recognition of the fundamental aboriginal situation makes the early events at Jamestown understandable on a rational basis. It offers a logical foundation for subsequent developments in Indian-white relationships and Indian adjustments to European civilization as the result of something more than barbaric cupidity and a thirst for the white man's blood.

Certainly a wary sensitivity to any sign of hostility or treachery characterized the behavior of both whites and Indians at the outset of settlement at Jamestown. The Europeans were still seriously concerned about the probable fate of Raleigh's colony and they had already been attacked by the Indians at Cape Henry. The Indians, in turn, may well have possessed information concerning the alarmingly retributive temperament of Europeans, at least in terms of the incident at nearby Aquascogoc, if not through generalized opinions derived from the long history of intermittent European contact along the east coast.

Nevertheless, the party of Europeans that set out on exploration of the country about Jamestown encountered a welcome at the various Indian villages different from the greetings offered at Cape Henry. Except for one cold but not overtly hostile reception in the Weanoc country, the white men were feted, fed, and flattered. At the same time a suggestion of the uncertainty of the next years occurred before the exploring party had even returned to their headquarters—at Jamestown the remaining colonists were attacked by a party of local Indians.[9] Events of this nature as well as the

---

[8] There are many data to indicate that in culture contact situations, generally regular processes of cultural acceptance and rejection can be traced to the formulation of analogies between innovations and existing phenomena on the part of the recipient culture. See Melville J. Herskovits, *Man and His Works* (New York, 1950), 553–58, for a discussion of the processes of reinterpretation and syncretism; Ralph Linton, *The Study of Man* (New York, 1936), 317–18, and Homer G. Barnett, "Cultural Processes," *Amer. Anthropologist*, 42 (1940), 21–48, give similar but independent analyses of analogy formulation on the basis of form, function, meaning, and use or principle of given traits.

[9] [Captain Gabriel Archer], "A Relayton of the Discovery &c. 21 May–22 June, 1607," in Arber, ed., *Works of John Smith*, li–lii. It is worth noting that news of the attack was

general observations recorded during the first two years at Jamestown are particularly instructive in any attempt to understand Indian motivations and policy regarding the British.

The narratives are difficult to follow because of the variety of orthographies employed for Indian words. Certain features remain speculative because initial communication between whites and Indians was limited to the use of signs and the few native words that could be learned readily.[10] However, it is possible to see native culture in terms of regularities and consistencies which were not obvious to the colonists. Likewise, the apparent inconsistencies on the part of the natives, recounted by the settlers as innate savage treachery, indicate that the aboriginal culture was in a process of growth, elaboration, and internal change. These phases of culture, which included both extensive tendencies of intertribal confederation and divisive reactions expressed by individual tribes, were interrupted and redirected but not initiated by the arrival of Europeans in 1607.

From the viewpoint of the twentieth century, it is difficult to realize that the material differences between the Indians and the European colonists, who lived before the full development of the industrial revolution, were equalled if not outweighed by the similarities of culture. This was especially true in Virginia, where a local florescence of culture and a demonstrated ability to prevail over other tribes gave the Indians a sense of strength which blinded them to the enormity of the threat posed by the presence of Europeans. There was actually little in the Europeans' imported bag of tricks which the Indians could not syncretize with their own experience. Metal was not unknown to them: they used native copper, brought in from the West, for decorative purposes. Metal weapons and domestic utensils were simply new and effective forms of familiar objects to accomplish familiar tasks. Even guns were readily mastered after the noise, which evoked astonishment at first, was understood as necessary to their operation. Likewise, fabrics and articles of personal adornment were part of Indian technology. Many utilitarian objects such as nets, weirs, and gardening implements were very similar in both Indian and European culture. European ships were simply larger and different, as was fitting for a people interested in traveling greater distances by open water than the Indians had ever cared to do.

Expansive accounts of the size and permanence of the great European cities could easily have been likened by the natives to the impressive aboriginal developments in the lower Mississippi Valley; archeological evidence suggests that knowledge of this cultural complex was widespread.[11] Even if these Indian models of nascent urbanization are discounted, the statements

---

apparently communicated to the Indians who were entertaining the exploring party, but that Powhatan had either been unable to prevent the attack or had not known of the plan until it was accomplished.

[10] Throughout the present study, spelling of Indian words, apart from direct quotations, has been regularized according to the pattern of Mook's publications.

[11] Paul Martin, George Quimby, and Donald Collier, *Indians Before Columbus* (Chicago, 1947), offer useful illustrations of the far-flung continental diffusion of cultural traits in prehistoric times, although dates assigned have been reassessed during the last ten years.

made by Europeans about their country and king may well have sounded like the exaggerations of outnumbered strangers endeavoring to buttress their weaknesses with talk of powerful but distant brothers. This explanation is admittedly conjectural, although we find ample documentation of the Indians' disinclination to admit any significant superiority in white culture at a somewhat later period. During the early nineteenth century, when the industrial revolution was underway and the eastern United States was heavily populated by whites, Indian visitors were brought from the West in the hope that they would be cowed by the white man's power and cease resistance to the forces of civilization. The Indians remained singularly unimpressed.[12] Furthermore, at the time Jamestown was founded in the seventeenth century, the only knowledge Indians possessed concerning Europeans indicated that Indians were well able to oppose white settlement. Raleigh's ill-fated colony was a clear reminder of the Europeans' mortality.

Although the early accounts tend to take a patronizing view of the Indians, the points on which the Europeans felt superior had little meaning for the aborigines: literacy, different sexual mores, ideas of modesty, good taste in dress and personal adornment, and Christian religious beliefs. The argument of technological superiority at that time was a weak one; despite guns and large ships the Europeans could not wrest a living from a terrain which, by Indian standards, supported an exceptionally large population. Scientific knowledge of generally predictable group reactions thus suggests that the degree of ethnocentrism was probably equal on both sides of the contact between Indians and Europeans in Virginia. Recognition of the Indians' self-appraisal is necessary for a clear understanding of their basis of motivation and consequent behavior in relation to Europeans.

Moreover, it was evident to the colonists that they were dealing with a fairly complex society, exhibiting many characteristics of leadership, social classes, occupational specialization, social control, and economic concepts that were eminently comprehensible in European terms. If the exploring parties overstated the case when they translated *weroance* as "king" and likened tribal territories to European kingdoms, they at least had a truer understanding of the nature of things than did the democratic Jefferson, who first designated the Virginia tribes as the "Powhatan Confederacy."[13] Since the term "Confederacy" is so firmly entrenched in the literature, it will be retained here as a matter of convenience; but, in reality, Powhatan was in the process of building something that approximated an empire. By 1607 it was not an accomplished fact, but the outlines were apparent and the process was sufficiently advanced to allow a geographical description of the extent of Powhatan's domain.

Powhatan's influence, if not his undisputed control, extended over some

[12] See Katherine C. Turner, *Red Men Calling on the Great White Father* (Norman, Okla., 1951), which presents a series of essays on such visits. Although the Indians considered their trips as entertaining educational experiences, their quoted remarks in the main reveal opinions that the white man had an unnecessarily complex and burdensome way of life at the expense of the finer one enjoyed by the Indians.

[13] John Smith observed that "one as Emperour ruleth over many kings or governours." *A Map of Virginia with a Description of the Countrey* . . . and *The General Historie of Virginia* . . . , in Arber, ed., *Works of John Smith*, 79, 375. Mook, "Aboriginal Population of Tidewater Virginia," *Amer. Anthropologist*, 44 (1944), 197, attributes the first use of the term "Powhatan Confederacy" to Jefferson.

thirty Algonkian-speaking tribes along the entire length of the present Virginia coast, including the Accohannoc and Accomac of the Eastern Shore. The nucleus of this domain consisted of six tribes which were centrally located in the region drained by the James, Pamunkey, and Mattaponi rivers. These tribes were the Powhatan, Arrohattoc, Pamunkey, Youghtanund, Appomattoc, and Mattaponi, with Powhatan's own tribe, the Pamunkey, consistently referred to in the early narratives as the largest and most powerful.[14] The Confederacy was bounded to the north and south by other Algonkian tribes. Except on the basis of their declared political allegiance, the uniformity of language and culture in the region makes it difficult to differentiate between the tribes within the Confederacy and even between the Confederacy and neighboring Maryland and Carolina groups.

It is generally accepted that these Algonkian peoples moved into the lower coastal region from the north. According to their own account this had occurred about three hundred years before Jamestown was settled, although recent archeological investigations suggest a longer occupation.[15] Once arrived, the Algonkians acquired numerous cultural traits from the Southeast culture area and developed many similarities to the interior Muskhogean-speaking groups. Some of these new elements were in turn transferred to the more northerly Algonkians, but they never existed there in the cohesive complexity found in the tidelands.[16]

Powhatan inherited the six central tribes as an already unified intertribal organization and extended his domain by conquest from the south bank of the Potomac to the Norfolk region. The Chesapeake Indians are included in the Confederacy, but this southernmost group was not fully under Powhatan's control at the time the settlers arrived. Their attack on the colonists at Cape Henry gave Powhatan the opportunity to gain favor with the English by swiftly avenging the hostile action. Although some historians have implied that Powhatan destroyed the entire tribe, it is far more likely that he simply killed the leaders and placed trusted kinsmen in these positions.[17]

14 Mooney, "Powhatan Confederacy," *Amer. Anthropologist*, 9 (1907), 135–36, notes the possible inclusion of the Werowocomoco and Chiskiac in the nuclear group of tribes inherited by Powhatan. Mook, "Aboriginal Population," *ibid.*, 44 (1944), 194 ff., lists thirty tribes as the largest number in the Confederation at any one time.

15 The Indian informants of the seventeenth century may have referred merely to the period of development of the distinctive social and political characteristics of the region rather than to original occupation. Frank G. Speck, "The Ethnic Position of the Southeastern Algonkian," *Amer. Anthropologist*, 26 (1924), 194, substantially agrees with the Indian accounts. Professor James B. Griffin, University Museum, University of Michigan, stated in a personal communication that unpublished data regarding a site near Washington, D.C., indicate an Algonkian intrusion into the southern area long before 1300.

16 Speck, "Southeastern Algonkian," *Amer. Anthropologist*, 26 (1924), 198, and 184–200 *passim*, sets forth this view of populational migration and cultural diffusion. Alfred L. Kroeber, *Cultural and Natural Areas of Native North America* (Berkeley, Calif., 1939), 94, disagrees with Speck as to the influence of southeastern Muskhogean peoples. Mook, "The Anthropological Position of the Indian Tribes of Tidewater Virginia," *Wm. and Mary College Qtly.*, 2nd ser., 23 (1943), 27–40, defends Speck's reconstruction with further evidence to substantiate the Muskhogean traits, and may be taken as the final word on the matter to date.

17 [Archer], "Relayton," Arber, ed., *Works of John Smith*, xliv; William Strachey, *The Historie of Travaile into Virginia Britannia*, Hakluyt Society edn. (London, 1849), 101, 105; Mooney, "Powhatan Confederacy," *Amer. Anthropologist*, 9 (1907), 130.

Powhatan's method of fighting and his policy of expanding political control combined a reasoned plan of action with quick ferocity and a minimum of bloodshed. Indian warfare was generally limited to surprise attacks and sniping from cover. Constant replacements of fighting men kept the enemy occupied and wore down their resistance, while actual casualties were relatively limited in number. Accounts of Powhatan's conquests and the occurrences observed after 1607 point to a carefully devised method of establishing his control over a wide territory. Entire communities might be killed if they proved exceptionally obstinate in rendering homage and paying tribute, but in most cases Powhatan simply defeated groups of questionable loyalty and upon their surrender moved them to areas where he could keep better watch over them. Trusted members of the Confederacy were then sent to occupy the vacated regions, while Powhatan's relatives were distributed throughout the tribes in positions of leadership.[18] Mook's studies indicate that the degree of Powhatan's leadership decreased in almost direct proportion to the increase in geographical distance between the Pamunkey and the location of a given tribe.[19] Throughout the entire region, however, the combination of ample sustenance, effective techniques of production, provident habits of food storage, and distribution of supplies through exchange offset shortcomings in the political framework connecting the tribes and helped to cement social ties and produce a commonality of culture.

Despite certain internal dissensions the Confederacy can be seen as a unified bloc, distinct from neighboring tribes. To the north were numerous small Algonkian-speaking tribes, either friendly or representing no serious danger to Powhatan. They tended to shade off in cultural characteristics toward the more northern Algonkian types to be found along the coast into New England. The best known of these tribes was the Nanticoke in eastern Maryland and Delaware. North of the Potomac lived the Conoy (Piscataway), Tocwough, Ozinie, and others, about whom little is recorded. At a later date the tribes in this region were known collectively as the "Doeg" Indians. Beyond the Conoy and up into the present state of Pennsylvania were the Susquehanna, in Captain John Smith's judgment a powerful and impressive group, distinguished from the Virginia tribes in both language and culture.[20] However, they seem to have felt closer ties of friendship with the Algonkians than they did with their Iroquoian linguistic affiliates to the north. The Nansemond and Chesapeake tribes formed the southern terminus of the Confederacy, and beyond them in the Carolina region were a number of linguistically and culturally similar tribes extending along the coast to the Neuse River. The Roanoke narratives and particularly the illustrations of John White provide somewhat fuller documentation for the

[18] Mooney, "Powhatan Confederacy," *Amer. Anthropologist*, 9 (1907), 136.

[19] Mook, "Virginia Ethnology from an Early Relation," *Wm. and Mary College Qtly.*, 2nd ser., 23 (1943), 115.

[20] Mooney, "Powhatan Confederacy," *Amer. Anthropologist*, 9 (1907), 140, tentatively identifies the "Doeg" as the Nanticoke. A review of materials relating to Bacon's Rebellion as well as the accounts of the local tribes presented in Kroeber, *Cultural Areas*, 91, 93–94, suggests that "Doeg" was applied to the Nanticoke and other Algonkian groups north of the Potomac. For John Smith's discussion of the Susquehanna, see Arber, ed., *Works of John Smith*, 77, 367.

southerly neighbors of the Confederacy than is available for the northern Algonkian groups.[21]

The western border, formed by the fall line and paralleling the coast, was characterized by greater cultural and linguistic differences than those observed to the north and south of the Confederacy; it also represented a definite danger area for Powhatan. Virtually all Indian occupation ended somewhat east of the falls, however, allowing a strip of land a mile to ten or twelve miles wide as a safe margin between the Powhatan tribes and their nearest neighbors, who were also their deadliest enemies, the tribes of the Virginia piedmont region. These peoples have long been designated as Siouan-speaking but a recent study casts doubt on this identification. It is now suggested that these groups spoke a highly divergent and extremely old dialect of the basic Algonkian language stock.[22] Except for linguistic distinctiveness little is known about these piedmont people. This is most unfortunate, since they appear to figure as a key to much of Powhatan's policy toward the English and helped to influence the course of Indian adjustment to European settlement.[23] A few of these tribes are known by name, but they are usually considered as having comprised two major confederacies, comparable in some measure to the groupings associated with Powhatan. These were the Manahoac on the upper Rappahannock and surrounding region, and the Monacan along the upper James and its tributary streams. Both were aggressive groups, and their incursions were a constant threat to the tidelands Indians. Powhatan's desire to subdue these westerly tribes as a matter of protection was underscored by another consideration: copper, highly prized by the Virginia Confederacy, came from the West, and the enemy tribes formed an obstacle to trade for that commodity.[24]

Thus, at the outset of colonization in 1607 Powhatan's policies can best be understood in relation to circumstances antedating the arrival of the Jamestown settlers. Powhatan saw the whites in his territory as potential allies and as a source of new and deadly weapons to be used in furthering his own

[21] Reproductions of White's original works may be found in David I. Bushnell, "John White—The First English Artist to Visit America, 1585," Va. Mag. of Hist. and Biog., 35 (1927), 419–30, and 36 (1928), 17–26, 124–34. Although less well known, these illustrations are preferable to DeBry's familiar engravings and the work of other copyists in representing the Carolina tribes to augment textual descriptions in the Roanoke accounts.

[22] Carl F. Miller, "Revaluation of the Eastern Siouan Problem with Particular Emphasis on the Virginia Branches—The Occaneechi, the Saponi, and the Tutelo," Bureau of American Ethnology, Smithsonian Institution Bulletin 164, Anthropological Papers, No. 52 (Washington, D.C., 1957), 115–211, discusses the origin of the conjecture that Siouan dialects were spoken in the piedmont area and indicates why such reasoning may be erroneous. However, the traditional view is far from abandoned; see William C. Sturtevant, "Siouan Languages in the East," Amer. Anthropologist, 60 (1958), 138–43, for a specific refutation of Miller's argument.

[23] Ethnologists have long been aware of the significance of the so-called Siouans in Powhatan's actions, although the point is usually mentioned as a side issue in connection with village locations, population size, and tribal distributions. See Bushnell, "The Five Monacan Towns in Virginia," Smithsonian Institution, Miscellaneous Collections, 82 (1930), 1–38; "The Manahoac Tribes in Virginia," ibid., 94 (1935), 1–56; John R. Swanton, "Early History of the Eastern Siouan Tribes," in Essays in Anthropology Presented to A. L. Kroeber (Berkeley, Calif., 1936), 371–81.

[24] John Smith lists the locations and names of subsidiary tribes of the Monacan and Manahoac. Arber, ed., Works of John Smith, 71, 366–67.

plans for maintaining control over his Confederacy and protecting the Confederacy as a whole against the threat posed by the alien tribes of the piedmont region. Likewise, existing concepts of intertribal trade in food-stuffs and other commodities were extended to include trade with the newly arrived whites. It is worth noting that European novelties, apart from weapons, were of far less interest to Powhatan than the fact that the Brtish possessed copper, an object vested with traditional native values and hereto-fore obtained with great difficulty.[25]

In the initial stages of contact between the Indians and the whites, there-fore, it is hardly surprising that Powhatan and his people felt at least equal to the English. The chieftain could appreciate the foreigners as allies in the familiar business of warfare and trade, but in general there seemed little to emulate in European culture and much to dislike about the white men. However, even in the most difficult phases of their early relationship, Pow-hatan did not indulge in a full-scale attack against the settlers. At that time he was still engaged in strengthening his Confederacy and perhaps he could not risk extensive Indian defection to the side of the whites. But there is an equal likelihood that Powhatan's primary motivation was the desire to con-trol and use the whites for his own purposes rather than to annihilate them.

At the time Jamestown was founded, native civilization was enjoying a period of expansion, and Powhatan had ample reason for sometimes considering the English as more an annoyance than a serious danger. The unusually rich natural environment and the security offered by the Confed-eracy stimulated the growth of social institutions and cultural refinements. In addition, the Virginia Indians were exceptionally powerful and, by aboriginal standards, their population was large: the entire Confederacy numbered some 8,500 to 9,000 people, or a density of approximately one person to every square mile.[26] The Indians lived according to a well-ordered and impressively complex system of government. They dwelled in secure villages, had substantial houses and extensive gardens, and had a notable assemblage of artifacts for utilitarian, religious, and decorative purposes.

The Indians won the grudging respect of the colonists for their advanced technology, but the Europeans were contemptuous of their seemingly hope-less commitment to superstition, while their ceremonialism appeared to the whites a ridiculous presumption of dignity.[27] A typical bias of communica-tion between Europeans and Indians is seen in Smith's account of the Quiyoughcohannock chief who begged the settlers to pray to the Christian God for rain because their own deities had not fulfilled the Indians' requests. Smith asserted that the Indians appealed to the whites because they believed the Europeans' God superior to their own, just as the Europeans' guns were

---

[25] "Their manner of trading is for copper, beads, and such like; for which they giue such commodities as they haue, as skins, fowle, fish, flesh, and their country corne." *Ibid.*, 74, 369. Smith reported that Powhatan requested him to abandon the settlement among the Paspehegh and move to his own country: "Hee promised to giue me Corne, Venison, or what I wanted to feede vs: Hatchets and Copper wee should make him, and none should disturb vs." *Ibid.*, 20.

[26] Mook, "Aboriginal Population," *Amer. Anthropologist*, 44 (1944), 201, 208.

[27] [Archer], "Relayton," Arber, ed., *Works of John Smith*, 1, provides a characteristic response of the colonists in his description of Opechancanough, who "so set his Coun-tenance stryving to be be stately, as to our seeming he became a fool."

superior to bows and arrows. Yet Smith notes with some wonder that the Quiyoughcohannock chief, despite his cordiality and interest in the Christian deity, could not be prevailed upon to "forsake his false Gods."[28] Actually this chief of one of the lesser tribes of the Confederacy illustrated the common logic of polytheistic people who often have no objection to adding foreign deities to their pantheon if it seems to assure more efficient control of the natural universe. The chief was not interested in changing his religious customs in emulation of the Europeans; he merely wished to improve his own culture by judicious borrowing—a gun at one time, a supernatural being at another.

Nor would the chief have dared respond to a new religion in its entirety, even if such an unlikely idea had occurred to him. The whole structure of tribal life relied upon controlling the mysterious aspects of the world by a traditional body of beliefs which required the use of religious functionaries, temples, idols, and rituals. These were awesome arrangements and not to be treated lightly, although improvement by minor innovations might be permitted.[29]

The geopolitical sophistication of the Virginia tribes is reflected in the secular hierarchy of leadership which extended in orderly and expanding fashion from the villages, through the separate tribes, up to Powhatan as head of the entire Confederacy. A gauge of the complexity of government is the fact that the Confederacy shared with the Europeans such niceties of civilization as capital punishment.[30] In small societies having a precarious economy, indemnities in goods or services are usually preferred to taking the life of a culprit even in crimes as serious as murder. However, where the life of the offender or one of his kinsmen is exacted for the life of the victim, punishment is the concern of the particular families involved; the rest of the group merely signifies approval of the process as a means of restoring social equilibrium after an offense is committed. Powhatan's government, however, was much closer to that of the English than it was to many of the tribes of North America. Punishment was meted out by a designated executioner for an offense against the society as the society was symbolized in the person of the leader.

Nevertheless, despite its elaborate civil structure, the Confederacy exhibited a universal rule of any society: a complex theory of government does not necessarily assure complete success in application. Powhatan not only had unruly subjects to deal with, but entire tribes in his domain could not be trusted. Relations between whites and Indians therefore were always uncertain, largely because of political developments within the Confederacy. When the colonists were supported by Powhatan, they were in mortal danger from those dissatisfied tribes of the Confederacy which had the foresight to realize that the English might one day assist Powhatan to enforce

[28] Arber, ed., *Works of John Smith*, 79, 374.

[29] For a general account of religion derived from the basic sources, see Charles C. Willoughby, "The Virginia Indians of the Seventeenth Century," *Amer. Anthropologist*, 9 (1907), 61–63. The most complete single account in the early narratives based on first-hand observation is included in Henry Spelman, "Relation of Virginea," 1613, in Arber, ed., *Works of John Smith*, cv–cvi.

[30] Arber, ed., *Works of John Smith*, 81–82, 377–78; Spelman, "Relation," *ibid.*, cxi.

his authority. When Powhatan and his closest associates turned upon the settlers, the less dependable tribes became friendly to the whites.

In view of this morass of political allegiances, it is little wonder that early accounts of the settlers are replete with material which seems to prove the innate treachery of the Indians. Yet the militant phases of Indian activity, as illustrated by the initial attack on Jamestown and Powhatan's vengeance on the offending Chesapeake tribe, must be seen as part of a larger policy involving alternative methods of settling inter-group differences. Although the settlers knew that dissatisfaction among Powhatan's followers offered a means of preventing a coordinated Indian attack, they also discovered that established mechanisms of diplomacy existed among the Indians that could be employed for their benefit. For example, the Jamestown settlement was located in the territory of the Paspehegh tribe, and relations with this tribe frequently became strained. The Powhatan forces represented by the leaders of the Pamunkey, Arrohattoc, Youghtanund, and Mattaponi offered to act as intermediaries in negotiating peace with the Paspehegh and other hostile tribes or, if necessary, to join forces with the settlers in an armed assault on mutual enemies.[31]

If the Europeans found it difficult to live among the Indians, the Europeans seemed equally unpredictable to the Indians. Early in his relationship with the English, Powhatan was promised five hundred men and supplies for a march on the Monacan and Manahoac; but instead of finding wholehearted support among his allies for this campaign, Powhatan discovered that the whites were helpless to support themselves in the New World. As time wore on and they became increasingly desperate for food, the Europeans were less careful in the difficult business of trying to distinguish friends from enemies. They extorted supplies promiscuously, driving hard bargains by the expedient of burning villages and canoes.[32]

It is problematical whether, as Smith implies, Powhatan was actually unable to destroy the handful of English because he could not organize his tribes for a full-scale offensive or whether he was biding his time in the hope of eventually establishing a clear-cut power structure in which the colonists would be allowed to survive but remain subservient to his designs in native warfare. At any rate, after two years of English occupation at Jamestown, Powhatan moved from his traditional home on the Pamunkey River some fifteen miles from the Europeans and settled in a more remote village upstream on the Chickahominy River. Violence flared periodically during these early years: colonists were frequently killed and often captured. Sometimes, being far from united in their allegiance, they fled to the Indian villages, where they were usually well treated. Captives and runaways were exchanged as hostages when one side or the other found it convenient. However, if Powhatan was willing to take advantage of dissident

---

[31] [Archer], "Relayton," *ibid.*, lv.

[32] See Mooney, "Powhatan Confederacy," *Amer. Anthropologist*, 9 (1907), 136–39, for an exhaustive review of instances illustrating the ever harsher measures taken by the colonists in coercing the Indians. In his indignation, Mooney scarcely notes that the Indians took measures of revenge by killing whites so that the process of hostilities increased over a period of time, with each side intent on settling some score with the other side.

feeling among the whites, he was no fool and he finally put to death two colonists who seemed to be traitors to both sides at the same time. The execution was much to Smith's satisfaction, for it saved him from performing the task and assured a far more brutal punishment than he would have been able to inflict upon the renegades.[33]

Throughout the period from 1607 to 1609, the chronicles include a complexity of half-told tales involving alliances and enmities and mutual suspicions, of Indians living among settlers and settlers living among Indians. Although this interaction was of an individual nature, the two groups learned something of each other; yet each side maintained its own values and traditions as a social entity. The Indians were primarily concerned with obtaining new material goods. By theft, trade, and the occupation of European artisans in their villages, they increased their supply of armaments and metal work. With the use of Indian guides and informants, the settlers became familiar with the geography of the region, and they also learned the secrets of exploiting their new environment through techniques of native gardening. For the most part, however, conscious efforts to bridge the cultural gap were unavailing. There was one amusing attempt to syncretize concepts of Indian and European monarchy and thereby bring about closer communication, when Powhatan was treated to an elaborate "coronation." The chief *weroance* was only made more vain by the ceremonies; he was by no means transformed into a loyal subject of the English sovereign, as the white settlers had intended.[34]

An increasing number of settlers arrived in Virginia and, with the help of Indians who by this time had ample reason to let the whites perish, managed to weather the hazards of the "starving time." As the whites became more firmly established, competition between Europeans and Indians took on the familiar form of a struggle for land. Armed clashes occurred frequently, but there were no organized hostilities, and the Indians continued to trade with the English. A peace which was formally established in 1614 and lasted until 1622 is often attributed to a refinement of Powhatan's sensibilities because of the marriage of Pocahontas and John Rolfe. Although Pocahontas was indeed the favorite child of Powhatan, it is likely that the chieftain's interest in her marriage was not entirely paternal. This strengthening of the social bond between Indians and Europeans helped solidify Powhatan's power and prestige among the confederated tribes, as he was thus enduringly allied with the whites.

Continuation of harmony between Indians and whites for a period of eight years was doubtless rendered possible because enough land still remained in Virginia for both settlers and Indians to live according to their accustomed habits. The seriousness of the loss of Indian land along the James River was lessened by the existence of a strip of virtually unoccupied

[33] Smith admitted that Powhatan's move to the village of Orapaks was simply to get away from the settlers. Arber, ed., *Works of John Smith*, 20, 70–71, 366–67; for the execution, see *ibid.*, 487.

[34] *Ibid.*, 124–25, 434–35. Smith's disgust was aroused by the coronation because it not only made Powhatan conceited, but it threatened to disrupt the trade in copper. Powhatan had been willing to exchange huge amounts of corn for a pittance, and Smith feared he would be spoiled by the rich coronation gifts.

territory just east of the fall line which ran the length of the Confederacy's holdings. If properly armed and not disturbed by internal dissensions and skirmishes with the English, the Powhatan tribes could afford to settle at the doorstep of their piedmont neighbors and even hope to expand into enemy territory. Hostilities require weapons, and peaceful trade with the English meant easier access to arms which the Confederacy could turn against the Monacan and Manahoac. It is also possible that by this time Powhatan realized the vast strength of the English across the sea and was persuaded to keep the settlers as friends. Knowledge of Europe would have been available to the chieftain through such Indians as Machumps, described by William Strachey as having spent "somtym in England" as well as moving "to and fro amongst us as he dares and as Powhatan gives him leave."[35]

Whatever were Powhatan's reasons for accepting the peace, it appears that he utilized the lull in hostilities to unify the Confederacy and deal with his traditional enemies. We have no direct evidence of activities against the piedmont tribes, for there is little historical data regarding the western area at this time. However, by the time the fur trade became important in the West the Monacan and Manahoac had lost the power which had once inspired fear among the tribes of the Confederacy. In view of Powhatan's years of scheming and the probable closer proximity of the Confederacy to the piedmont region after 1614, it may be conjectured that the Virginia chieftain and his people took some part in the downfall of the Monacan and Manahoac.[36]

When Powhatan died in 1618, his brother Opechancanough succeeded him as leader of the Confederacy.[37] Opechancanough continued to observe Powhatan's policy of peace for four years, although relations between Indians and Europeans were again degenerating. The Indians' natural resources were threatened as the increasing tobacco crops encroached on land where berries had grown in abundance and game had once been hunted. In the face of European advance, the Indians became restive and complained of the settlers' activities; but these signs went unnoticed by the colonists.[38] Opechancanough was aware that the real danger to the Confederacy arose

---

[35] Strachey, *Historie of Travaile into Virginia*, 54.

[36] Throughout the accounts of 1607–8 there are references to aiding Powhatan in dealing with the piedmont Siouans and Powhatan's satisfaction in the promises, Arber, ed., *Works of John Smith*, 20, 70–71, 366–67; [Archer], "Relayton," *ibid.*, xlvii. As relations between Powhatan and the settlers became strained, Powhatan discouraged the settlers from going to the Monacan, fearing that the whites might ally themselves with his enemies. Smith quotes Powhatan: "As for the *Monacans*, I can revenge my own iniuries." *Ibid.*, 124, and see 482–83. For the subsequent decline of the Monacan, see the journal of Batt's expedition reprinted from the British Museum manuscript in Bushnell, "Discoveries Beyond the Appalachian Mountains in September, 1671," *Amer. Anthropologist*, 9 (1907), 46–53.

[37] Arber, ed., *Works of John Smith*, 451; Robert Beverley, *The History and Present State of Virginia*, ed. by Louis B. Wright (Chapel Hill, 1947), 61.

[38] Edward D. Neill, *History of the Virginia Company of London* (Albany, N.Y., 1869), 317–19, cites references which suggest that the Indians expressed excessive protestations of kindness and friendship in order to lull the settlers' suspicions in 1622. Shortly after Powhatan's death, however, fear of the Indians was so intense that Captain Spelman was harshly dealt with on the belief that he was engaged in inciting the Indians to hostile acts.

from neither internal dissensions nor traditional Indian enemies but from the inexorable growth of European society in Virginia. He was apparently able to convince all the member tribes of this fact, if they had not already drawn their own conclusions. The subsequent uprising of 1622 was a well-planned shock to the English; it was alarming not so much for the destruction wrought, since by that time the Europeans could sustain the loss of several hundred people, but for the fact that the Confederacy could now operate as a unified fighting organization. This was a solidarity which Powhatan either had been unable or was disinclined to achieve.

Doubtless Opechancanough expected reprisals, but he was totally unprepared for the unprecedented and utter devastation of his lands and the wholesale slaughter of his people. The tribes were scattered, some far beyond the traditional boundaries of their lands, and several of the smaller groups simply ceased to exist as definable entities. Gradually as the fury of revenge died down, the remnants of the Confederacy regrouped and began to return to their homelands. However, the settlers were no longer complacent about their Indian neighbors. In addition to campaigning against the natives, they erected a string of fortifications between Chesiac and Jamestown, and they tended to settle Virginia in the south rather than toward the north and west.[39] In effect, therefore, Opechancanough accomplished a limited objective; a line was established between Indians and Europeans, but the line was only temporary and the Indians paid a terrible price.

Moreover, the cultural gap widened during the ensuing years. Following the period of reprisals the Indians were left to make a living and manage their affairs as best they could. Many old grievances seemed to be forgotten, and the natives gave the appearance of accepting their defeat for all time. Opechancanough, who had eluded capture immediately after the attack of 1622, remained at large, but the Europeans attempted to win tribes away from his influence rather than hunt him down at the risk of inflaming his followers. Finally, white settlement once more began to spread beyond the safety of concentrated colonial population. Tensions were re-created on the frontier, and there were minor skirmishes; the Indians complained to the English, but they also continued their trading activities. Thus matters continued for more than twenty years until large-scale hostilities again broke out.[40]

The uprising of 1644 was surprisingly effective. It is generally known that in both the 1622 and the 1644 uprisings the percentage of Indians killed in relation to the total Indian population was far greater than the percentage of settlers killed in relation to the total white population. Yet with far fewer Indians to do the fighting, Opechancanough managed to kill at least as many Europeans in the second attack as he had in the first.[41] The uprising

---

[39] Mook, "Aboriginal Population," *Amer. Anthropologist*, 44 (1944), 204–5, discusses shifts in Indian tribal populations as a response to European movements after 1622.

[40] Edward D. Neill, *Virginia Calororum: The Colony under the Rule of Charles the First and Second, A.D. 1625–A.D. 1685* (Albany, N.Y., 1886), 60–61.

[41] Mooney, "Powhatan Confederacy," *Amer. Anthropologist*, 9 (1907), 138–39, discusses reductions in Indian population. Opechancanough's secrecy inspires wonder, but the success of the attack is indicative of the degree of separation that marked the lives of the colonists and the Indians by 1644.

is another proof that the Indians' method of adjusting to changes wrought by the Europeans continued to be an attempt to prevail over or remove the source of anxiety—the settlers—rather than to adapt themselves to the foreign culture. Certainly the Indians never felt that their difficulties would be resolved by assimilation among the whites, a solution which the colonists at times hoped to effect through the adoption of Indian children, intermarriage, and Indian servitude.[42]

Hopeless though the uprising appears in retrospect, it was entirely logical within Opechancanough's own cultural frame of reasoning. It is impossible to determine whether the Indians were aware of the futility of their action, nor do we know enough about the psychology of these people to ascribe to them such a grim fatalism that they would prefer a quick and honorable death to the indignities of living in subjection to the whites. But there is something impressive about Opechancanough, an old and enfeebled man, being carried on a litter to the scene of battle. Whatever the outcome his days were numbered. His young warriors, however, knew of the horrible reprisals of 1622 and they understood the cost of being defeated by the white man. Yet they too were willing to risk an all-out attack.

There is little doubt that Opechancanough realized the danger inherent in rebellion. He was a shrewd strategist and a respected leader. It is entirely possible that he hoped for assistance from forces outside the Confederacy. Tension had existed between the whites of Virginia and Maryland for a number of years, and in one instance the Virginians had hoped to incite the Confederacy against their neighbors. Maryland had been settled only ten years before the second uprising, and although hostile incidents between whites and Indians had occurred, her Indian policy had been more just and humane than Virginia's. If Opechancanough did expect military assistance from whites for his uprising against whites, he had historical precedent to inspire him. Powhatan had exploited factionalism among the Jamestown settlers, and it may be that the tension between Virginia and Maryland suggested an extension of his policy to Opechancanough. Whatever the motivations behind Opechancanough's design for rebellion, the second uprising attested to the strength of the old Confederacy and indicated clearly the stubborn resistance of the Indians to cultural annihilation.

Although the usual revenge followed the attack of 1644, Virginia's Indian policy was beginning to change. The Powhatan tribes were too seriously reduced in numbers to benefit greatly by the progress, but their treatment at the hands of the colonists following the uprising marked a new development in Indian-white relations, one which eventually culminated in the modern reservation system. In 1646 a formal treaty was signed with the Powhatan Confederacy establishing a line between Indian and white lands and promising the Indians certain rights and protection in their holdings. While their movements were to be strictly regulated, the natives were guaranteed recognition for redress of wrongs before the law. There were two particularly important features of the treaty. First, the Indians were to act as scouts and allies against the possibility of outside tribes' invading the colony; this policy was in contrast to the earlier device of attempting to win the friend-

<hr />

[42] Neill, *Virginia Calororum*, 74.

ship of peripheral tribes to enforce order among the local Indians.[43] Second, and consistent with the growing importance of the fur trade in colonial economics, the Indians were to pay a tribute each year in beaver skins. During the following years various legislative acts were adopted to protect the Indians in their rights and establish mutual responsibilities with the tribes.[44]

As the treaty of 1646 symbolized the establishment of new policies in dealing with the Indians, so did the circumstances surrounding Bacon's Rebellion afford a glimpse of other future developments. Within the tangled events of the Rebellion was an indication of the later effects of the frontier on many Indian groups. The Rebellion reflected the heretofore traditional rivalry between Indians and whites; its outcome marked the final defeat of the Virginia Indians and the complete demise of some tribes. But in the records of Bacon's Rebellion appears a new element which was to have continuing influence in Indian adjustment to Europeans. By 1675 Indian-white relations were no longer highly localized. The English began to appreciate the need for greater unity among their scattered colonies—the struggle of European countries to establish sovereignty over all of North America had begun—and they recognized the value of the Indians as allies rather than opponents in the design of empire.

The turmoil of international rivalry delayed the movement of settlement inland, and the development of the fur trade also promoted isolation of the West. The fur traders strongly opposed pioneer settlement, in order to protect the natural habitat of the beaver—and incidentally the status quo of the Indians who engaged in the actual business of hunting and trapping the animals. Thus circumstances combined to give the Indians of the inland tribes a vital delay. From the beginning of contact, the western natives had an opportunity to meet the white man on equal terms, and they came to accept the presence of Europeans as a permanent and in many ways a desirable phenomenon. They developed policies of negotiation, diplomacy, and warfare, and distinguished one European group from another as ally or enemy as seemed most expedient to their own interests. This was in sharp contrast to the coastal situation, where hostilities represented a more clear-cut contest between Indians and whites for supremacy.[45]

[43] As early as 1609, the instructions given Thomas Gates as acting governor of the colony indicate the initial policy decided upon: "If you make friendship with any of thiese nations as you must doe, choose to do it with those that are farthest from you & enemies unto those amongst whom you dwell for you shall have least occasion to have differences with them, and by that means a surer league of amity." The entire text of Gates's instructions as they related to the Indians is quoted in Bushnell, "Virginia From Early Records," *Amer. Anthropologist*, 9 (1907), 35.

[44] See Wesley Frank Craven, *The Southern Colonies in the Seventeenth Century, 1607–1689* (Baton Rouge, La., 1949), 361–66, for a discussion of changes in Virginia's Indian policy.

[45] These facts, central to the theoretical propositions underlying the initial research in the present study, doubtless contributed to continuing adaptability of the more inland tribes. It is possible to see striking destruction of coastal or peripheral tribes along both the Atlantic and the Pacific oceans in North America, while the groups somewhat inland have been able to preserve a greater degree of cultural integrity. The Plains area, however, represents a third zone in the effects of the frontier on Indian cultures; the absence of white allies and of a social symbiosis between whites and Indians based on the fur trade explains in large part the rapid cultural disorganization when the tide turned against the Indians.

The events of Bacon's Rebellion in Virginia contributed to the final ruin of both the tidelands and the piedmont tribes, but the complications of alliances of interest groups illustrate the changing situation of the frontier as it affected the Indians. Initially the Rebellion involved the border settlers of Virginia and Maryland, and the Susquehanna, Seneca, and "Doeg" Indians. The Susquehanna had enjoyed friendly relations with the French as early as 1615, but, living on the Susquehanna River, they were too far removed from French outposts to benefit by the association.[46] To the north were their traditional enemies, the Seneca, a member tribe of the powerful league of the Iroquois. The Seneca, however, appeared as a threat to the colonists of Maryland, and the settlers in that area therefore allied themselves with the Susquehanna and supplied the tribe with arms. Later Maryland, an English colony, arranged a pact of peace with the Seneca in accordance with the general alliance of the Iroquois league with the English at that time. The Susquehanna, nominally allied with the French, were left without arms or nearby allies and were thus forced by the new alliance to retreat from their homeland. In the face of armed action they took up residence north of the Potomac among the Algonkian-speaking tribes, although they were themselves of Iroquoian linguistic affiliation. Shifts of tribal residence and inter-Indian campaigns involved Iroquoian tribes of the Carolina region as well as certain so-called Siouan groups such as the Tutelo and Occaneechi, who were enemies of the Seneca.

Meanwhile white settlement had penetrated west and north to the extent that skirmishes between whites and the Indians occurred. The memories of the uprisings of 1622 and 1644 had not died easily among the English, and when protection furnished by Governor Berkeley seemed inadequate, an unofficial campaign against the natives was initiated by the border settlers of the once competitive Virginia and Maryland. Although the causes of Bacon's Rebellion were also deeply rooted in internal disputes among the colonists, its results were catastrophic for the Virginia Indians. Bacon's followers showed no disposition to distinguish Indians as friends or enemies; they made indiscriminate war on all natives. After Bacon's forces had decimated the Susquehanna and Algonkians, they turned upon the Occaneechi, who had long been allied with the English as middlemen in the fur trade between the coastal settlements and the tribes located farther inland. The final action was against the Pamunkey, peacefully residing on lands secured to them by the treaty of 1646.[47] The Pamunkey king had been killed some ten years after the treaty of 1646 while serving with the colonists against a presumed invasion of the colony by a group of strange Indians known as Richeharians.[48] Thus his people were considered doubly wronged, for they

[46] Brebner, *Explorers*, 144–49, discusses the "Andastes" Indians, but they are easily identified by internal evidence as the Susquehanna.

[47] See Wilcomb E. Washburn, *The Governor and the Rebel, A History of Bacon's Rebellion in Virginia* (Chapel Hill, 1957), for a recent analysis of Bacon's Rebellion which devotes special attention to the complications of the Indian problem. Washburn notes that there is no evidence that Bacon's followers killed any really hostile Indians; instead, they attacked tribes which were neutral in the border disputes or nominally friendly to the whites.

[48] Mooney, "Powhatan Confederacy," *Amer. Anthropologist*, 9 (1907), 141, tentatively

were not only at peace with the colonists, but they had made common cause with the English against Indian enemies.[49]

Peace was finally affirmed officially with the Virginia tribes in a treaty signed in 1677. However, the effects of the Rebellion had been devastating, and after their long history of war and defeat, the Indians of the tidelands and piedmont regions found it increasingly difficult to preserve their accustomed habits of existence. This was equally true of the Susquehanna and Algonkian tribes north of the Potomac.

Nevertheless, several tribes of the Powhatan Confederacy are represented today by groups preserving a sense of social distinctiveness, based largely on historical and racial origins rather than any cultural characteristics. These tribes are the Pamunkey, Rappahannock, Mattaponi, Chickahominy, and Nansemond.[50] The story of their survival is uncertain in its details. Often it appeared that these tribes had been swept away by the rush of history, but each time after an interval the names reappeared on contemporary documents. For example, the signatory tribes of the Confederacy in the treaty of 1677 included the Pamunkey, Appomattoc, Weanoc, Nansemond, Nantaughtacund, and Portobacco—the last a collective term for the tribes of the Eastern Shore. Also signatory to the treaty were the Iroquoian-speaking tribes of the piedmont, the Nottaway and Meherrin, as well as Powhatan's old enemies, the Monacan. Undoubtedly the Pamunkey, the largest tribe of the Confederacy, had temporarily subsumed the unlisted Chickahominy, Mattaponi, and Rappahannock.[51]

In a similarly complex process of development, many of the piedmont tribes which were still extant in the latter seventeenth century regrouped permanently under different names. The Nottaway, Meherrin, and Monacan, for example, were signatory to the treaty of 1677, but only the Nottaway and Meherrin signed the Treaty of Albany in 1722. However, the Christanna were named in the 1722 treaty, and this group had come to include remnant Monacan and other piedmont tribes as well as recent migrants from the Algonkian, Iroquoian, and Siouan groups of North Carolina. Governor Spotswood of Virginia gathered these tribes together in 1715 and set-

---

identifies the Richeharians as Cherokee. Although this view has been questioned by other scholars, there is no agreement on any alternative identification. The Richeharians defeated the attacking party of whites and allied Indians, and the incident is worthy of notice in regard to the later events of Bacon's Rebellion as a gauge of the insecurity felt by the border settlers as early as 1656. An investigation of the affair indicated that the Richeharians probably only wanted to trade but that hostilities began before the intensions of these strange Indians were determined.

[49] [The Royal Commissioners], "A True Narrative of the Late Rebellion in Virginia," in Charles M. Andrews, ed., *Narratives of the Insurrections, 1675–1690* (New York, 1915), 123 and 127; [Thomas Mathew], "The Beginning, Progress and Conclusion of Bacon's Rebellion, 1675–1676," *ibid.*, 26.

[50] William H. Gilbert, "Surviving Indian Groups in the Eastern United States," in Smithsonian Institution, *Annual Reports of the Board of Regents* (Washington, D.C., 1948), 417–18.

[51] Mooney, "Powhatan Confederacy," *Amer. Anthropologist,* 9 (1907), 141–47, traces the course of affiliations and residence of piedmont and tidelands Indians between 1677–1722 on the basis of the two treaties and intervening documents.

tled them at Fort Christanna near the Carolina border in southwestern Virginia.[52]

The condition of the Indians toward the end of the sevententh century is illustrated in many contemporary documents. A letter from the Reverend Mr. Clayton provides a detailed and well-organized summary.[53] It is worth special attention for its factual data and as an illustration that both whites and Indians continued to view each other from their own culture's frame of logic, without any real understanding. Describing the populational degeneration which had resulted largely from disease, deprivation, and malnutrition, the letter states: "This is very certain that the Indian inhabitants of Virginia are now very inconsiderable as to their numbers and seem insensibly to decay though they live under the English protection and have no violence offered them. They are undoubtedly no great breeders."

Clayton, like many white observers imbued with Christian concepts of proselytization, appeared surprised that one of the most striking retentions of native patterns was the cultural aspect of religion. He noted that special structures were still set aside for temples and that the shaman or *wichiost* enjoyed a degree of prestige which was secondary only to that accorded to their "King and to their great War-Captain." The retention of this prestige illustrates secular authority distinguished from the sacred sway of the *wichiost* and shows a continuity of concepts regarding social structure. The king remained the center of authority and continued to receive homage and tribute in the form of personal services performed by other members of the tribe. Apparently the ruling position was still hereditary within a line of descent recognized as that of the chief family. None of the records are clear on this point, for lines of chieftainship are confused in the documents by the indiscriminate use of such titles as "King" and "Queen." Hereditary leadership occasionally did devolve on women, and Archer noted such a case in 1607 when he described the Queen of Appomattoc, who held her rank by virtue of some now obscure genealogical reckoning. Leadership was inherited first by the surviving male siblings and then the female siblings, and evidently passed on to the next generation only with the death of all members of the preceding generation.[54] In later years the Queen of Pamunkey was so designated by the whites because her husband, the hereditary Pamunkey ruler, had been killed in 1656 while fighting for the British. The settlers paid his widow the honor of the title, but it is questionable whether she exercised any traditional authority within her own group, although she was their recognized representative in dealings with the colonists.

The role of the ordinary Indian woman generally receives little notice in acculturational descriptions by untrained observers, and the Clayton letter is no exception. A brief sentence notes gardening, cooking, pottery making, and the weaving of mats. The domestic phase of Indian life was easily over-

[52] *Ibid.*, 144–52; see also J. C. Householder, "Virginia's Indian Neighbors in 1712," Indiana Academy of Science, *Proceedings*, 55 (1946), 23–25, for a discussion of Governor Spotswood's administration of Indian affairs.

[53] Bushnell, "Virginia From Early Records," *Amer. Anthropologist*, 9 (1907), 41–44, prints the entire text of the letter from the original in the records of the British Museum, "A Letter from the Rev. Mr. John Clayton, afterwards Dean of Kildare in Ireland, to Dr. Green in answer to several qurys sent to him . . . A.D. 1687. . . ." All references to the condition of the Indians in this period are from Clayton unless otherwise noted.

[54] Arber, ed., *Works of John Smith*, 451.

looked although it changed less than other aspects. Actually, the domesticity of the whites and Indians differed only slightly. Kingdoms might rise and fall, but housekeeping, child care, cooking, and garment making had to be regularly performed in both cultures. Like many European observers, Clayton describes hunting, a principal occupation of the Indian male, as "Exercise." This error probably contributed to an early and persistent stereotype of the Indian: the industrious, overburdened woman, the slothful, pleasure-seeking man. Like all stereotypes, it is worthy of examination and it is an especially interesting example of adjustment to change. The traditional division of labor was approximately equal, the men hunting, the women gardening. These two activities supplied the principal subsistence. The English depended on the hunt in the early stages of settlement, but as soon as it ceased to have great economic importance they reverted to the European tradition of categorizing it as sport. The Indians also had their tradition: both men and women considered agriculture to be an unmanly task. When game diminished and gardening became the primary productive activity, they found it extremely difficult to make appropriate changes in the socio-economic role of the male.

Clayton's references to the material culture of the Indians may be augmented from many sources, as this was the most easily discerned aspect of Indian life. The natives frequently observed traditional habits of dress. They continued to use indigenous material such as deerskin of clothing, but they prized European textiles, being especially fond of linen goods and a heavy woolen cloth, called a "matchcoat," which they often used instead of fur or feather mantles. Certain changes in style, if not modesty, may be noted in the matter of dress. When the Queen of Appomattoc greeted the Europeans in 1607, she wore only a skirt and a great amount of jewelry, but "all ells was naked";[55] but the Queen of Pamunkey was clad in Indian finery from neck to ankles for an occasion of state in 1677.[56]

Although the blue and white shell beads known as "wampum" probably originated as a currency through the trade with the New England tribes, they were manufactured in great quantities by Europeans for use in the fur trade and by 1687 figured as a quasi currency as far south as Virginia. The Indian shaman who also acted in the capacity of physician was paid by the natives in wampum as well as in skins and other commodities. When he treated English settlers, the *wichiost* usually received his remuneration in matchcoats or rum. Further details from Clayton's letter reveal that metal armaments, tools, and utensils were in common usage by the end of the century, although the bow and arrow and native pottery continued to be available.

From Clayton's observations and comparable data it is evident that Indian adjustment to European civilization in the late seventeenth century continued to take the form of resistance whenever there remained any possibility of retaining essential elements of the old culture. Specific items were accepted, as they fitted into existing patterns and represented elaboration or improvement of familiar features. In-group recognition of the danger posed for their traditional ways is illustrated in a fragment of folklore included in

[55] [Archer], "Relayton," *ibid.*, 1.
[56] [Mathew], "Bacon's Rebellion," Andrews, ed., *Narratives of the Insurrections, 1675–1690*, 25–26; [Royal Commissioners], "Late Rebellion," *ibid.*, 126–27.

Clayton's account. There was supposedly an ancient prophecy, made long before the Europeans arrived, that "bearded men . . . should come and take away their country and that there should none of the original Indians be left within a certain number of years, I think it was an hundred and fifty." This rationalization of history is a recurrent myth found among many Indian groups. It helps to preserve a degree of dignity and pride by saying in effect, "We knew it all along, but we put up an admirable fight anyway."

The cultural disorganization noted in 1687 was to be a continuing process. The prophecy of destruction has now been fulfilled, to the extent that the Indians have ceased to exist as a culturally definable entity, although remnant groups maintain their social identities and tribal names. Throughout the seventeenth and eighteenth centuries the tribes which had temporarily resided with the Pamunkey wandered back to their original territories, leaving only the Pamunkey and part of the Mattaponi on lands secured to them by colonial treaties and guaranteed today by the state of Virginia. Traditional habits were generally abandoned as it became ever more difficult to exist in the white man's world. Eventually, the only effective economic system was that practiced by the surrounding Europeans; the Indians who were not located on reservations tended to settle in neighborhoods and acquire land on an individual basis. The destruction of the native social and religious mores, almost a predictable consequence of the disastrous wars and scattering of tribes, was virtually accomplished. A civil and religious structure which had been designed to accommodate the needs and activities of thirty tribes, almost nine thousand people, was impossibly cumbersome when the population had dwindled to one thousand people who were not in regular communication with one another and who were at any rate overwhelmingly occupied with the problem of sheer physical survival. The Indians in time found social and religious satisfaction in the traditions of their white neighbors; but they remained socially distinct from them.

Despite the loss of their own culture, many Indians remain aware of their historical origins. Beginning in 1908 with the Chickahominy, the various non-reservation natives of Virginia obtained official recognition as Indian tribes from the state government. In 1923 they formed an organization known as the "Powhatan Confederacy" and included the Nanticoke, recognized by Delaware as non-reservation Indians but otherwise not historically eligible for inclusion in the Confederacy. Showing Caucasoid and Negroid ancestry, the Nanticoke are the most racially heterogeneous of the modern confederated tribes, although a blending of racial characteristics may be seen to a lesser extent in the reservation Pamunkey and Mattaponi and the non-reservation Mattaponi, Rappahannock, Chickahominy, and Nansemond. In cultural terms the modern Virginia Indians retain little more of their heritage than tribal names and a sense of common origin.[57] The value of Indian identity has been increased by the social isolation of dark-skinned peoples in American life, since Indians in contrast to other racial minorities have generally enjoyed a degree of prestige in the opinion of the dominant group. In the tidewater region this may well be due to the influence of socially prominent Virginians who trace their ancestry to Pocahontas; she was, after all, a "Princess."

[57] Gilbert, "Surviving Indian Groups," Smithsonian Institution, *Annual Reports of the Board of Regents*, 418–19.

The end result of European contact in the piedmont region presents a somewhat different picture. Along the western border of Virginia and in the adjoining regions there are well-defined groups who claim Indian descent but no longer recall any particular tribal affiliations. They are known locally as Ramps, Melungeons, Brown People, Issues, and other terms. In order to avoid the social disabilities of classification with Negroes, they cling to their unofficial classification as Indians and remain rooted in regions where their peculiar status is known.[58] Some of these people may very well be descendants of the historic piedmont tribes of Virginia which vanished as identifiable tribal entities. Although much research remains to be done on this point, it is probable that their almost complete loss of identity, in contrast to the tidelands tribes, which at least recall their tribal origins, may be traced to the fact that they experienced disorganizing defeats at the hands of other Indians before the tidelands groups were ultimately conquered by the Europeans. The coastal Indians were in possession of European weapons at an earlier date and in all likelihood turned them against traditional enemies in the piedmont region before they found the need to use them primarily in forays against the white settlers. Thus the piedmont groups suffered a military disadvantage almost at the outset of European contact. By the time the whites penetrated to the piedmont region these tribes had already lost much of their former power. Furthermore, by the late seventeenth century they were also harassed by native enemies to the rear.[59] Unlike the tribes further inland, the piedmont peoples did not have time to regroup effectively and take advantage of the fur trade as a means of survival by adaptation to the presence of whites. Throughout the latter part of the seventeenth century they were in the path of westward movement by the whites, northward migrations of dispossessed Carolina tribes, and southern invasions by the Seneca on warlike campaigns. Their only hope for survival was in intertribal mixture and intermarriage with racially alien populations, both Negro and white.

Although the Virginia Indians were utterly defeated by the close of the seventeenth century, the experience of that period laid the foundations for modern adjustment to the white man's culture. As a result of stubborn opposition to amalgamation, some tribes have survived into the mid-twentieth century as populational entities, although they have been unable to retain a distinctive culture. Their primary technique of adjustment to European civilization, at least as documented in the Virginia tidelands region, was, with few exceptions, one of rigid resistance to alien ways which held no particular attractions, except for disparate items. Their culture simply disintegrated under the strain of continued pressure placed upon it. In contrast, the tribes further inland, by their more flexible adaptation to Europeans, achieved a social and cultural continuity which is still impressive despite many material innovations from European and American civilization.

[58] *Ibid.*, 419.

[59] Mooney, "Siouan Tribes of The East," Bureau of American Ethnology, Smithsonian Institution, *Bulletin 22* (Washington, D.C., 1894), 28, notes that the Monacan were "directly in the path of the Richahecrian (Rickohockan, Cherokee)," who ostensibly invaded the Virginia area in 1656. Thus, Mooney suggested that the Monacan may have been victims of attacks by tribes to their west.

Unthinking Decision: Enslavement of Negroes in America to 1700

Winthrop D. Jordan

Slavery, in one form or another, has existed throughout the recorded history of human life. Where it differed in the New World was that it was race slavery. It would be satisfying if its origins were to be found simply in prejudice and if slavery had been the same in all the colonies of North and South America, but it would not be the truth. Like all human institutions, slavery had its own particular history, governed by time and place and culture, and its historians must analyze why it came about where, when, and how it did. Winthrop D. Jordan of the University of California at Berkeley has provided the most complete and subtle explanation of the origins and structure of American slavery and whites' response to it in his Pulitzer Prize–winning study *White Over Black** (1968), from which the following selection has been taken.

Jordan's argument is too encompassing to compress. Its critical tenet, however—in contrast to the arguments of historians such as Oscar and Mary Handlin ("Origins of the Southern Labor System," *William and Mary Quarterly*, 3rd Ser., VII [April 1950], 199–222) that slavery preceded prejudice, and in closer agreement with that of Carl Degler ("Slavery and the Genesis of American Race Prejudice,"

Comparative Studies in Society and History, II
[October 1959], 49–66) that prejudice antedated
slavery—is that slavery and prejudice were dynamically
related, constantly reinforcing each other and snaring
black people in a situation from which they could not
escape. The strains and necessities of white settlement
created the initial conditions for enslavement. Then
the change in the value of labor in the wilderness made
the early colonists cast about for cheap and dependable
sources of labor. This they found initially in the
institution of indenture—a form of contract labor to
which, in the beginning, thousands of whites and
blacks alike were bound. All the while, Jordan
emphasizes, cultural influences common to most whites
—such factors as the definitions they attached to such
key concepts as freedom and bondage, the heritage of
common law institutions and practices, and the mark
of "strangeness" on blacks in a white society—worked
to make it possible to distinguish and then to separate
the status of white and black laborers. The skimpiness
of evidence, Jordan believes, will always prevent us
from knowing conclusively when life-long slavery
became the normal condition of black Africans in
America from generation to generation. But by the
end of the first century of settlement, and despite the
absence of any satisfactory model of slavery in
England, slavery had become institutionalized and by
and large had taken on the form it would possess for
another hundred and fifty years. Indeed, Jordan
concludes, nineteenth-century Americans would have
found slavery as it was in 1705 a familiar condition of
Southern life.

Whether chattel slavery after the early eighteenth
century was a dynamic or static institution, whether it
underwent growth and change, is only one of the
many questions that students of American race
relations must ask. The very title of this selection raises
another central issue, namely, the role of human
agency in the development of the "peculiar institution."
To write that the enslavement of black Africans was
an "unthinking decision" is to offer a judgment with
normative as well as descriptive implications. If the
apportionment of responsibility for so fateful and

Unthinking Decision: Enslavement of Negroes in America to 1700. By Winthrop D. Jordan from *White Over Black: American Attitudes Toward the Negro, 1550–1812* (Chapel Hill, N.C.: University of North Carolina Press, 1968), pp. 44–56, 66–82, 91–98. Reprinted by permission of the University of North Carolina Press and the Institute of Early American History and Culture.

tragic a series of actions as those that led to mass bond servitude falls within the tasks of the responsible historian, then we must consider the implications of such a term as *unthinking*. Does Jordan's account of the history of slavery's genesis mean to suggest that the course from freedom to slavery was inevitable? Does the author deal satisfactorily with the alternatives that were open to whites and blacks alike in the seventeenth century? And does he convince us that cultural and economic factors played the proportional role he assigns them?

*A*t the start of English settlement in America, no one had in mind to establish the institution of Negro slavery. Yet in less than a century the foundations of a peculiar institution had been laid. The first Negroes landed in Virginia in 1619, though very, very little is known about their precise status during the next twenty years. Between 1640 and 1660 there is evidence of enslavement, and after 1660 slavery crystallized on the statute books of Maryland, Virginia, and other colonies. By 1700 when African Negroes began flooding into English America they were treated as somehow deserving a life and status radically different from English and other European settlers. The Negro had been debased to a condition of chattel slavery; at some point, Englishmen in America had created a legal status which ran counter to English law.

Unfortunately the details of this process can never be completely reconstructed; there is simply not enough evidence (and very little chance of more to come) to show precisely when and how and why Negroes came to be treated so differently from white men, though there is just enough to make historians differ as to its meaning. Concerning the first years of contact especially we have very little information as to what impression Negroes made upon English settlers: accordingly, we are left knowing less about the formative years than about later periods of American slavery. That those early years were crucial ones is obvious, for it was then that the cycle of Negro debasement began; once the Negro became fully the slave it is not hard to see why white men looked down upon him. Yet precisely because understanding the dynamics of these early years is so important to understanding the centuries which followed, it is necessary to bear with the less than satisfactory data and to attempt to reconstruct the course of debasement undergone by Negroes in seventeenth-century America. In order to comprehend it, we need first of all to examine certain social pressures generated by the American environment and how these pressures interacted with certain qualities of English social thought and law that existed on the eve of settlement, qualities that even then were being modified by examples set by England's rivals for empire in the New World.

1. The Necessities of a New World

When Englishmen crossed the Atlantic to settle in America, they were immediately subject to novel strains. In some settlements, notably Jamestown and Plymouth, the survival of the community was in question. An appalling proportion of people were dead within a year, from malnutrition, starvation, unconquerable diseases, bitter cold, oppressive heat, Indian attacks, murder, and suicide. The survivors were isolated from the world as they had known it, cut off from friends and family and the familiar sights and sounds and smells which have always told men who and where they are. A similar sense of isolation and disorientation was inevitable even in the settlements that did not suffer through a starving time. English settlers were surrounded by savages. They had to perform a round of daily tasks to which most were unaccustomed. They had undergone the shock of detachment from home in order to set forth upon a dangerous voyage of from ten to thirteen weeks that ranged from unpleasant to fatal and that seared into every passenger's memory the ceaselessly tossing distance that separated him from his old way of life.[1]

Life in America put great pressure upon the traditional social and economic controls that Englishmen assumed were to be exercised by civil and often ecclesiastical authority. Somehow the empty woods seemed to lead much more toward license than restraint. At the same time, by reaction, this unfettering resulted in an almost pathetic social conservatism, a yearning for the forms and symbols of the old familiar social order. When in 1618, for example, the Virginia Company wangled a knighthood for a newly apponted governor of the colony the objection from the settlers was not that this artificial elevation was inappropriate to wilderness conditions but that it did not go far enough to meet them; several planters petitioned that a governor of higher rank be sent, since some settlers had "only Reverence of the Comanders Eminence, or Nobillitye (whereunto by Nature everye man subordinate is ready to yeild a willing submission without contempt, or repyning)."[2] English social forms were transplanted to America not simply because they were nice to have around but because without them the new settlements would have fallen apart and English settlers would have become men of the forest, savage men devoid of civilization.

For the same reason, the communal goals that animated the settlement of the colonies acquired great functional importance in the wilderness; they served as antidotes to social and individual disintegration. The physical hardships of settlement could never have been surmounted without the stiffened nerve and will engendered by commonly recognized if sometimes unarticulated purposes. In New England lack of articulation was no problem. The Puritans knew precisely who they were (the chosen of God, many of them) and that they were seeking to erect a Godly community. Though that community (eventually) eluded them, they retained their conviction that they manned a significant outpost of English civilization. As Cotton

---

[1] There is an eloquent revivification by William Bradford, *Of Plymouth Plantation, 1620–1647*, ed. Samuel Eliot Morison (N.Y., 1952), 61–63.

[2] Susan M. Kingsbury, ed., *Records of the Virginia Company of London*, 4 vols. (Washington, D.C., 1906–35), III, 216–19, 231–32.

Mather grandly told the Massachusetts governor and General Court in 1700, "It is no Little Blessing of God, that we are a part of the *English nation*."[3] A similar deep sense of self-transplantation buttressed the settlements in Virginia and Maryland. While there was less talk than in New England about God's special endorsement, virtually every settler knew that Englishmen were serving His greater glory by removing to Virginia and by making a prosperous success of the project. They recognized also that their efforts at western planting aggrandized English wealth and power and the cause of reformed Christianity. As Richard Hakluyt summarized these purposes, "This enterprise may staye the spanishe kinge ["the supporter of the greate Antechriste of Rome"] from flowinge over all the face of that waste firme of America, yf wee seate and plante there in time."[4] For Englishmen planting in America, then, it was of the utmost importance to know that they were Englishmen, which was to say that they were educated (to a degree suitable to their station), Christian (of an appropriate Protestant variety), civilized, and (again to an appropriate degree) free men.

It was with personal freedom, of course, that wilderness conditions most suddenly reshaped English laws, assumptions, and practices. In America land was plentiful, labor scarce, and, as in all new colonies, a cash crop desperately needed. These economic conditions were to remain important for centuries; in general they tended to encourage greater geographical mobility, less specialization, higher rewards, and fewer restraints on the processes and products of labor. Supporting traditional assumptions and practices, however, was the need to retain them simply because they were familiar and because they served the vital function of maintaining and advancing orderly settlement. Throughout the seventeenth century there were pressures on traditional practices which similarly told in opposite directions.

In general men who invested capital in agriculture in America came under fewer customary and legal restraints than in England concerning what they did with their land and with the people who worked on it. On the other hand their activities were constrained by the economic necessity of producing cash crops for export, which narrowed their choice of how they could treat it. Men without capital could obtain land relatively easily: hence the shortage of labor and the notably blurred line between men who had capital and men who did not. Men and women in England faced a different situation. A significant amount of capital was required in order to get to America, and the greatest barrier to material advancement in America was the Atlantic Ocean.

Three major systems of labor emerged amid the interplay of these social and economic conditions in America. One, which was present from the beginning, was free wage labor, in which contractual arrangements rested upon a monetary nexus. Another, which was the last to appear, was chattel slavery, in which there were no contractual arrangements (except among

[3] Cotton Mather, *A Pillar of Gratitude* . . . (Boston, 1700), 32–33.

[4] From his own "Discourse on Western Planting" (1584), in E. G. R. Taylor, ed., *The Original Writings and Correspondence of the Two Richard Hakluyts (Works Issued by the Hakluyt Soc.*, 2d Ser., 76–77 [1935]), II, 314–15. See Perry Miller, "Religion and Society in the Early Literature of Virginia," in his *Errand into the Wilderness* (Cambridge, Mass., 1956), 99–140.

owners). The third, which virtually coincided with first settlement in America, was temporary servitude, in which complex contractual arrangements gave shape to the entire system. It was this third system, indentured servitude, which permitted so many English settlers to cross the Atlantic barrier. Indentured servitude was linked to the development of chattel slavery in America, and its operation deserves closer examination.

A very sizable proportion of settlers in the English colonies came as indentured servants bound by contract to serve a master for a specified number of years, usually from four to seven or until age twenty-one, as repayment for their ocean passage. The time of service to which the servant bound himself was negotiable property, and he might be sold or conveyed from one master to another at any time up to the expiration of his indenture, at which point he became a free man. (Actually it was his *labor* which was owned and sold, not his *person*, though this distinction was neither important nor obvious at the time.) Custom and statute law regulated the relationship between servant and master. Obligation was reciprocal: the master undertook to feed and clothe and sometimes to educate his servant and to refrain from abusing him, while the servant was obliged to perform such work as his master set him and to obey his master in all things. This typical pattern, with a multitude of variations, was firmly established by mid-seventeenth century. In Virginia and Maryland, both the legal and actual conditions of servants seem to have improved considerably from the early years when servants had often been outrageously abused and sometimes forced to serve long terms. Beginning about 1640 the legislative assemblies of the two colonies passed numerous acts prescribing maximum terms of service and requiring masters to pay the customary "freedom dues" (clothing, provisions, and so forth) at the end of the servant's time.[5] This legislation may have been actuated partly by the need to attract more immigrants with guarantees of good treatment, in which case underpopulation in relation to level of technology and to natural resources in the English colonies may be said to have made for greater personal freedom. On the other hand, it may also have been a matter of protecting traditional freedoms threatened by this same fact of underpopulation which generated so powerful a need for labor which would not be transient and temporary. In this instance, very clearly, the imperatives enjoined by settlement in the wilderness interacted with previously acquired ideas concerning personal freedom. Indeed without some inquiry into Elizabethan thinking on that subject, it will remain impossible to comprehend why Englishmen became servants in the plantations, and Negroes slaves.

2. Freedom and Bondage in the English Tradition

Thinking about freedom and bondage in Tudor England was confused and self-contradictory. In a period of social dislocation there was considerable disagreement among contemporary observers as to what actually was going

[5] William Waller Hening, ed., *The Statutes at Large Being a Collection of All the Laws of Virginia*, 13 vols. (Richmond, N.Y., and Phila., 1809–23), I, 257, 435, 439–42, II, 113–14, 240, 388, III, 447–62; *Archives of Maryland*, 69 vols. (Baltimore, 1883–), I, 53, 80, 352–53, 409–10, 428, 443–44, 453–54, 464, 469, II, 147–48, 335–36, 527.

on and even as to what ought to be. Ideas about personal freedom tended to run both ahead of and behind actual social conditions. Both statute and common law were sometimes considerably more than a century out of phase with actual practice and with commonly held notions about servitude. Finally, ideas and practices were changing rapidly. It is possible, however, to identify certain important tenets of social thought that served as anchor points amid this chaos.

Englishmen lacked accurate methods of ascertaining what actually was happening to their social institutions, but they were not wrong in supposing that villenage, or "bondage" as they more often called it, had virtually disappeared in England. William Harrison put the matter most strenuously in 1577:

> As for slaves and bondmen we have none, naie such is the privilege of our countrie by the especiall grace of God, and bountie of our princes, that if anie come hither from other realms, so soone as they set foot on land they become so free of condition as their masters, whereby all note of servile bondage is utterlie remooved from them.[6]

Other observers were of the (correct) opinion that a few lingering vestiges —bondmen whom the progress of freedom had passed by—might still be found in the crannies of the decayed manorial system, but everyone agreed that such vestiges were anachronistic. In fact there were English men and women who were still "bond" in the mid-sixteenth century, but they were few in number and their status was much more a technicality than a condition. In the middle ages, being a villein had meant dependence upon the will of a feudal lord but by no means deprivation of all social and legal rights. In the thirteenth and fourteenth centuries villenage had decayed markedly, and it may be said not to have existed as a viable social institution in the second half of the sixteenth century.[7] Personal freedom had become the normal status of Englishmen. Most contemporaries welcomed this fact; indeed it was after about 1550 that there began to develop in England that preening consciousness of the peculiar glories of English liberties.

How had it all happened? Among those observers who tried to explain, there was agreement that Christianity was primarily responsible. They thought of villenage as a mitigation of ancient bond slavery and that the continuing trend to liberty was animated, as Sir Thomas Smith said in a famous passage, by the "perswasion . . . of Christians not to make nor keepe his brother in Christ, servile, bond and underling for ever unto him, as a beast rather than as a man."[8] They agreed also that the trend had been

---

6 [Harrison], *Historicall Description of Britaine*, in *Holinshed's Chronicles*, I, 275.

7 The best place to start on this complicated subject is Paul Vinagradof, *Villainage in England: Essays in English Mediaeval History* (Oxford, 1892). The least unsatisfactory studies of vestiges seem to be Alexander Savine, "Bondmen under the Tudors," Royal Historical Society, *Transactions*, 2d Ser., 17 (1903), 235–89; I. S. Leadam, "The Last Days of Bondage in England," *Law Quarterly Review*, 9 (1893), 348–65. William S. Holdsworth, *A History of English Law*, 3d ed., 12 vols. (Boston, 1923), III, 491–510, explodes the supposed distinction between villeins *regardant* and *gross*.

8 Thomas Smith, *De Republica Anglorum: A Discourse on the Commonwealth of England*, ed. L. Alston (Cambridge, Eng., 1906), 133.

forwarded by the common law, in which the disposition was always, as the phrase went, *in favorem libertatis*, "in favor of liberty." Probably they were correct in both these suppositions, but the common law harbored certain inconsistencies as to freedom which may have had an important though imponderable effect upon the reappearance of slavery in English communities in the seventeenth century.

The accreted structure of the common law sometimes resulted in imperviousness to changing conditions. The first book of Lord Coke's great *Institutes of the Laws of England* (1628), for example, was an extended gloss upon Littleton's fifteenth-century treatise on *Tenures* and it repeatedly quoted the opinions of such famous authorities as Bracton, who had died in 1268. When Bracton had described villenage, English law had not yet fully diverged from the civil or Roman law, and villenage actually existed. Almost four hundred years later some legal authorities were still citing Bracton on villenage without even alluding to the fact that villenage no longer existed. The widely used legal dictionary, Cowell's *Interpreter* (1607 and later editions), quoted Bracton at length and declared that his words "expresse the nature of our villenage something aptly."[9] Anyone relying solely on Cowell's *Interpreter* would suppose that some Englishmen in the early seventeenth century were hereditary serfs. Thus while villenage was actually extinct, it lay unmistakenly fossilized in the common law. Its survival in that rigid form must have reminded Englishmen that there existed a sharply differing alternative to personal liberty. It was in this vague way that villenage seems to have been related to the development of chattel slavery in America. Certainly villenage was not the forerunner of slavery, but its survival in the law books meant that a possibility which might have been foreclosed was not. Later, after Negro slavery had clearly emerged, English lawyers were inclined to think of slavery as being a New World version of the ancient tenure described by Bracton and Cowell and Coke.

That the common law was running centuries behind social practice was only one of several important factors complicating Tudor thought about the proper status of individuals in society. The social ferment of the sixteenth century resulted not only in the impalpable mood of control and subordination which seems to have affected English perception of Africans but also in the well-known strenuous efforts of Tudor governments to lay restrictions on elements in English society which seemed badly out of control. From at least the 1530's the countryside swarmed with vagrants, sturdy beggars, rogues, and vagabonds, with men who could but would not work. They committed all manner of crimes, the worst of which was remaining idle. It was an article of faith among Tudor commentators (before there were "Puritans" to help propound it) that idleness was the mother of all vice and the chief danger to a well-ordered state. Tudor statesmen valiantly attempted to suppress idleness by means of the famous vagrancy laws which provided for houses of correction and (finally) for whipping the vagrant from constable to constable until he reached his home parish. They assumed

[9] Coke's section on villenage is Lib. II, cap. XI; see John Cowell, *The Interpreter: Or Booke Containing the Signification of Words . . .* (Cambridge, Eng., 1607), "villein."

that everyone belonged in a specific social niche and that anyone failing to labor in the niche assigned to him by Providence must be compelled to do so by authority.

Some experiments in compulsion ran counter to the trend toward personal liberty. In 1547, shortly after the death of Henry VIII, a parliamentary statute provided that any able-bodied person adjudged a vagabond upon presentment to two justices of the peace should be branded with a "V" on the chest and made a "slave" for two years to the presenter who was urged to give "the saide Slave breade and water or small dryncke and such refuse of meate as he shall thincke mete [and] cause the said Slave to worke by beating cheyninge or otherwise in such worke and Labor how vyle so ever it be." Masters could "putt a rynge of Iron about his Necke Arme or his Legge for a more knowledge and suretie of the keepinge of him." A runaway "slave" convicted by a court was to be branded on the cheek or forehead and adjudged "to be the saide Masters Slave for ever." These provisions reflected desperation. Fully as significant as their passage was their repeal three years later by a statute which frankly asserted in the preamble that their "extremitie" had "byn occacion that they have not ben putt in ure [use]."[10]

Englishmen generally were unwilling to submit or subscribe to such debasement. Despite a brief statutory experiment with banishment "beyond the Seas" and with judgment "perpetually to the Gallyes of this Realme" in 1598,[11] Tudor authorities gradually hammered out the legal framework of a labor system which permitted compulsion but which did not permit so total a loss of freedom as lifetime hereditary slavery. Apprenticeship seemed to them the ideal status, for apprenticeship provided a means of regulating the economy and of guiding youth into acceptable paths of honest industry. By 1600, many writers had come to think of other kinds of bound labor as inferior forms of apprenticeship, involving less of an educative function, less permanence, and a less rigidly contractual basis. This tendency to reason from apprenticeship downward, rather than from penal service up, had the important effect of imparting some of the very strong contractualism in the master-apprentice relationship to less formal varieties of servitude. There were "indentured" servants in England prior to English settlement in America. Their written "indentures" gave visible evidence of the strong element of mutual obligation between master and servant: each retained a copy of the contract which was "indented" at the top so as to match the other.

As things turned out, it was indentured servitude which best met the requirements for settling in America. Of course there were other forms of bound labor which contributed to the process of settlement: many convicts were sent and many children abducted.[12] Yet among all the numerous varieties and degrees of non-freedom which existed in England, there was none

10 *The Statutes of the Realm*, 11 vols. ([London], 1810–28), 1 Edw. VI. c. 3; 3 and 4 Edw. VI. c. 16. A standard treatment is Frank Aydelotte, *Elizabethan Rogues and Vagabonds* (Oxford, 1913).

11 *Statutes of the Realm*, 39 Eliz. c. 4.

12 The "standard" work on this subject unfortunately does not address itself to the problem of origins: Abbot Emerson Smith, *Colonists in Bondage: White Servitude and Convict Labor in America, 1607–1776* (Chapel Hill, 1947).

which could have served as a well-formed model for the chattel slavery which developed in America. This is not to say, though, that slavery was an unheard-of novelty in Tudor England. On the contrary, "bond slavery" was a memory trace of long standing. Vague and confused as the concept of slavery was in the minds of Englishmen, it possessed certain fairly consistent connotations which were to help shape English perceptions of the way Europeans should properly treat the newly discovered peoples overseas.

3. The Concept of Slavery

At first glance, one is likely to see merely a fog of inconsistency and vagueness enveloping the terms *servant* and *slave* as they were used both in England and in seventeenth-century America. When Hamlet declaims "O what a rogue and peasant slave am I," the term seems to have a certain elasticity. When Peter Heylyn defines it in 1627 as "that ignominious word, *Slave;* whereby we use to call ignoble fellowes, and the more base sort of people,"[13] the term seems useless as a key to a specific social status. And when we find in the American colonies a reference in 1665 to "Jacob a negro slave and servant to Nathaniel Utye,"[14] it is tempting to regard slavery as having been in the first half of the seventeenth century merely a not very elevated sort of servitude.

In one sense it was, since the concept embodied in the terms *servitude, service*, and *servant* was widely embracive. *Servant* was more a generic term than *slave*. Slaves could be "servants"—as they were eventually and ironically to become in the ante-bellum South—but servants *should not* be "slaves." This injunction, which was common in England, suggests a measure of precision in the concept of slavery. In fact there was a large measure which merits closer inspection.

First of all, the "slave's" loss of freedom was complete. "Of all men which be destitute of libertie or freedome," explained Henry Swinburne in his *Briefe Treatise of Testaments and Last Willes* (1590), "the slave is in greatest subjection, for a slave is that person which is in servitude or bondage to an other, even against nature." "Even his children," moreover, ". . . are infected with the Leprosie of his father's bondage." Swinburne was at pains to distinguish this condition from that of the villein, whom he likened to the *Ascriptitius Glebae* of the civil law, "one that is ascrited or assigned to a ground or farme, for the perpetuall tilling or manuring thereof." "A villeine," he insisted, "howsoever he may seeme like unto a slave, yet his bondage is not so great."[15] Swinburne's was the prevailing view of bond slavery; only the preciseness of emphasis was unusual. At law, much more clearly than in literary usage, "bond slavery" implied utter deprivation of liberty.

Slavery was also thought of as a perpetual condition. While it had not yet come invariably to mean lifetime labor, it was frequently thought of in those terms. Except sometimes in instances of punishment for crime, slavery was

[13] Hamlet, II, ii; Heylyn, ΜΙΚΡόΚΟΣΜΟΣ, 175.
[14] *Archives of Maryland*, XLIX, 489.
[15] Henry Swinburne, *A Briefe Treatise of Testaments and Last Willes* . . . (London, 1590), 43.

open ended; in contrast to servitude, it did not involve a definite term of years. Slavery was perpetual also in the sense that it was often thought of as hereditary. It was these dual aspects of perpetuity which were to assume such importance in America.

So much was slavery a complete loss of liberty that it seemed to Englishmen somehow akin to loss of humanity. No theme was more persistent than the claim that to treat a man as a slave was to treat him as a beast. Almost half a century after Sir Thomas Smith had made this connection a Puritan divine was condemning masters who used "their servants as slaves, or rather as beasts" while Captain John Smith was moaning about being captured by the Turks and "all sold for slaves, like beasts in a market-place."[16] No analogy could have better demonstrated how strongly Englishmen felt about total loss of personal freedom.

Certain prevalent assumptions about the origins of slavery paralleled this analogy at a different level of intellectual construction. Lawyers and divines alike assumed that slavery was impossible before the Fall, that it violated natural law, that it was instituted by positive human laws, and, more generally, that in various ways it was connected with sin. These ideas were as old as the church fathers and the Roman writers on natural law. In the social atmosphere of pre-Restoration England it was virtually inevitable that they should have been capsulated in the story of Ham. The Reverend Jeremy Taylor (an opponent of the Puritans) explained what it was "that brought servitude or slavery into the world": God had "consigned a sad example that for ever children should be afraid to dishonour their parents, and discover their nakedness, or reveal their turpitude, their follies and dishonours." Sir Edward Coke (himself scarcely a Puritan) declared, "This is assured, That Bondage or Servitude was first inflicted for dishonouring of Parents: For Cham the Father of Canaan . . . seeing the Nakedness of his Father Noah, and shewing it in Derision to his Brethren, was therefore punished in his Son Canaan with Bondage."[17]

The great jurist wrote this in earnest, but at least he did offer another description of slavery's genesis. In it he established what was perhaps the most important and widely acknowledged attribute of slavery: at the time of the Flood "all Things were common to all," but afterward, with the emergence of private property, there "arose battles";

> then it was ordained by Constitution of Nations . . . that he that was taken in Battle should remain Bond to his taker for ever, and he to do with him, all that should come of him, his Will and Pleasure, as with his Beast, or any other Cattle, to give, or to sell, or to kill.

This final power, Coke noted, had since been taken away (owing to "the

[16] William Gouge, *Of Domesticall Duties Eight Treatises* (London, 1622), 690; Edward Arber, ed., *Travels and Works of Captain John Smith* . . . , 2 vols. (Edinburgh, 1910), II, 853.

[17] *The Whole Works of the Right Rev. Jeremy Taylor* . . . , 10 vols. (London, 1850–54), X, 453; Sir Edward Coke, *The First Part of the Institutes of the Laws of England: or, a Commentary upon Littleton* . . . , 12th ed. (London, 1738), Lib. II, Cap. XI. For the long-standing assumption that slavery was brought about by man's sinfulness see R. W. and A. J. Carlyle, *A History of Medieval Political Theory in the West*, 6 vols. (Edinburgh and London, 1903–36), I, 116–24, II, 119–20.

Cruelty of some Lords") and placed in the hands only of kings.[18] The animating rationale here was that captivity in war meant an end to a person's claim to life as a human being; by sparing the captive's life, the captor acquired virtually absolute power over the life of the man who had lost the power to control his own.

More than any other single quality, *captivity* differentiated slavery from servitude. Although there were other, subsidiary ways of becoming a slave, such as being born of slave parents, selling oneself into slavery, or being adjudged to slavery for crime, none of these were considered to explain the way slavery had originated. Slavery was a power relationship; servitude was a relationship of service. Men were "slaves" to the devil but "servants" of God. Men were "galley-slaves," not galley servants. Bondage had never existed in the county of Kent because Kent was "never vanquished by [William] the Conquerour, but yeelded it selfe by composition."[19]

This tendency to equate slavery with captivity had important ramifications. Warfare was usually waged against other people; captives were usually foreigners—"strangers" as they were termed. Until the emergence of nation-states in Europe, by far the most important category of strangers was the non-Christian. International warfare seemed above all a ceaseless struggle between Christians and Turks. Slavery, therefore, frequently appeared to rest upon the "perpetual enmity" which existed between Christians on the one hand and "infidels" and "pagans" on the other.[20] In the sixteenth and seventeenth centuries Englishmen at home could read scores of accounts concerning the miserable fate of Englishmen and other Christians taken into "captivity" by Turks and Moors and oppressed by the "verie worst manner of bondmanship and slaverie."[21] Clearly slavery was tinged by the religious disjunction.

Just as many commentators thought that the spirit of Christianity was responsible for the demise of bondage in England, many divines distinguished between ownership of Christian and of non-Christian servants. The Reverend William Gouge referred to "such servants as being strangers were bond-slaves, over whom masters had a more absolute power than others." The Reverend Henry Smith declared, "He which counteth his servant a slave, is in error: for there is difference betweene beleeving servants and infidell servants."[22] Implicit in every clerical discourse was the assumption that common brotherhood in Christ imparted a special quality to the master-servant relationship.

Slavery did not possess that quality, which made it fortunate that English-

---

[18] Coke, *Institutes*, Lib. II, Cap. XI.

[19] William Lambard[e], *A Perambulation of Kent* . . . (London, 1576), 11. The notion of selling oneself into slavery was very much subsidiary and probably derived from the Old Testament. Isaac Mendelsohn, *Slavery in the Ancient Near East* . . . (N.Y., 1949), 18, points out that the Old Testament was the only ancient law code to mention voluntary slavery and self-sale.

[20] The phrases are from Michael Dalton, *The Countrey Justice* . . . (London, 1655), 191.

[21] *The Estate of Christians, Living under the Subjection of the Turke* . . . (London, 1595), 5.

[22] Gouge, *Domesticall Duties*, 663; *The Sermons of Master Henry Smith* . . . (London, 1607), 40.

men did not enslave one another. As we have seen, however, Englishmen did possess a *concept* of slavery, formed by the clustering of several rough but not illogical equations. The slave was treated like a beast. Slavery was inseparable from the evil in men; it was God's punishment upon Ham's prurient disobedience. Enslavement was captivity, the loser's lot in a contest of power. Slaves were infidels or heathens.

On every count, Negroes qualified.

.   .   .

6. *Enslavement: New England*

Negro slavery never really flourished in New England. It never became so important or so rigorous as in the plantation colonies to the southwards. There were relatively few Negroes, only a few hundred in 1680 and not more than 3 per cent of the population in the eighteenth century; no one thought that Negroes were about to rise and overwhelm the white community.[23] Treatment of slaves in New England was milder even than the laws allowed: Negroes were not employed in gangs except occasionally in the Narragansett region of Rhode Island, and the established codes of family, congregation, and community mitigated the condition of servitude generally. Negroes were not treated very differently from white servants —except that somehow they and their children served for life.

The question with New England slavery is not why it was weakly rooted, but why it existed at all. No staple crop demanded regiments of raw labor. That there was no compelling economic demand for Negroes is evident in the numbers actually imported: economic exigencies scarcely required establishment of a distinct status for only 3 per cent of the labor force. Indentured servitude was adequate to New England's needs, and in fact some Negroes became free servants rather than slaves. Why, then, did New Englanders enslave Negroes, probably as early as 1638? Why was it that the Puritans rather mindlessly (which was not their way) accepted slavery for Negroes and Indians but not for white men?

The early appearance of slavery in New England may in part be explained by the provenance of the first Negroes imported. They were brought by Captain William Peirce of the Salem ship *Desire* in 1638 from the Providence Island colony where Negroes were already being kept as perpetual servants.[24] A minor traffic in Negroes and other products developed between the two Puritan colonies, though evidently some of the Negroes proved less than satisfactory, for Governor Butler was cautioned by the Providence Company to take special care of "the cannibal negroes brought from New England."[25] After 1640 a brisk trade got under way between New England and the other English islands, and Massachusetts vessels

[23] Lorenzo J. Greene, *The Negro in Colonial New England, 1620–1776* (N.Y., 1942); report by the Massachusetts governor, Box 4, bundle: The Royal African Co. of England, MS. relating to the Company's trade in Negroes (1672–1734/35), 13, Parish Transcripts, N.-Y. Hist. Soc.

[24] John Winthrop, *Winthrop's Journal: "History of New England," 1634–1649*, ed. James K. Hosmer, 2 vols. (N.Y., 1908), I, 260.

[25] Newton, *Colonising Activities of the English Puritans*, 260–61.

sometimes touched upon the West African coast before heading for the Caribbean. Trade with Barbados was particularly lively, and Massachusetts vessels carried Negroes to that bustling colony from Africa and the Cape Verde Islands. As John Winthrop gratefully described the salvation of New England's economy, "it pleased the Lord to open to us a trade with Barbados and other Islands in the West Indies."[26] These strange Negroes from the West Indies must surely have been accompanied by prevailing notions about their usual status. Ship masters who purchased perpetual service in Barbados would not have been likely to sell service for term in Boston. Then too, white settlers from the crowded islands migrated to New England, 1,200 from Barbados alone in the years 1643–47.[27]

No amount of contact with the West Indies could have by itself created Negro slavery in New England; settlers there had to be willing to accept the proposition. Because they were Englishmen, they were so prepared—and at the same time they were not. Characteristically, as Puritans, they officially codified this ambivalence in 1641 as follows:

> there shall never be any bond-slavery, villenage or captivitie amongst us; unless it be lawfull captives taken in just warrs, and such strangers as willingly sell themselves, or are solde to us: and such shall have the libertyes and christian usages which the law of God established in Israell concerning such persons doth morally require, provided, this exempts none from servitude who shall be judged thereto by Authoritie.[28]

Here were the wishes of the General Court as expressed in the Massachusetts Body of Liberties, which is to say that as early as 1641 the Puritan settlers were seeking to guarantee in writing their own liberty without closing off the opportunity of taking it from others whom they identified with the Biblical term, "strangers." It was under the aegis of this concept that Theophilus Eaton, one of the founders of New Haven, seems to have owned Negroes before 1658 who were "servants forever or during his pleasure, according to Leviticus, 25:45 and 46."[29] ("Of the children of the strangers that do sojourn among you, of them shall ye buy, and of their families . . . · and they shall be your possession. And ye shall take them as an inheritance for your children . . . ; they shall be your bondmen for ever: but over your brethren the children of Israel, ye shall not rule one over another with rigor.") Apart from this implication that bond slavery was reserved to those not partaking of true religion nor possessing proper nationality, the Body of Liberties expressly reserved the colony's right to enslave convicted criminals. For reasons not clear, this endorsement of an existing practice was followed almost immediately by discontinuance of its application to white men. The first instance of penal "slavery" in Massachusetts came in 1636, when an Indian was sentenced to "bee kept as a slave

[26] Winthrop, *Journal*, ed. Hosmer, II, 73–74, 328; Donnan, ed., *Documents of the Slave Trade*, III, 4–5, 6, 9, 10, 11–14.

[27] Harlow, *Barbados*, 340.

[28] Max Farrand, ed., *The Laws and Liberties of Massachusetts* (Cambridge, Mass., 1929), 4. See the very good discussion in George H. Moore, *Notes on the History of Slavery in Massachusetts* (N.Y., 1866).

[29] Simeon E. Baldwin, "Theophilus Eaton, First Governor of the Colony of New Haven," New Haven Colony Historical Society, *Papers*, 7 (1908), 31.

for life to worke, unles wee see further cause." Then in December 1638, ten months after the first Negroes arrived, the Quarter Court for the first time sentenced three white offenders to be "slaves"—a suggestive but perhaps meaningless coincidence. Having by June 1642 sentenced altogether some half dozen white men to "slavery" (and explicitly releasing several after less than a year) the Court stopped.[30] Slavery, as had been announced in the Body of Liberties, was to be only for "strangers."

The Body of Liberties made equally clear that captivity in a just war constituted legitimate grounds for slavery. The practice had begun during the first major conflict with the Indians, the Pequot War of 1637. Some of the Pequot captives had been shipped aboard the *Desire*, to Providence Island; accordingly, the first Negroes in New England arrived in exchange for men taken captive in a just war! That this provenance played an important role in shaping views about Negroes is suggested by the first recorded plea by an Englishman on the North American continent for the establishment of an African slave trade. Emanuel Downing, in a letter to his brother-in-law John Winthrop in 1645, described the advantages:

> If upon a Just warre [with the Narragansett Indians] the Lord should deliver them into our hands, wee might easily have men woemen and children enough to exchange for Moores, which wilbe more gaynefull pilladge for us then wee conceive, for I doe not see how wee can thrive untill wee get into a stock of slaves sufficient to doe all our buisiness, for our children's children will hardly see this great Continent filled with people, soe that our servants will still desire freedome to plant for themselves, and not stay but for verie great wages. And I suppose you know verie well how wee shall mayneteyne 20 Moores cheaper than one Englishe servant.[31]

These two facets of justifiable enslavement—punishment for crime and captivity in war—were closely related. Slavery as punishment probably derived from analogy with captivity, since presumably a king or magistrates could mercifully spare and enslave a man whose crime had forfeited his right to life. The analogy had not been worked out by commentators in England, but a fairly clear linkage between crime and captivity seems to have existed in the minds of New Englanders concerning Indian slavery. In 1644 the commissioners of the United Colonies meeting at New Haven decided, in light of the Indians' "proud affronts," "hostile practices," and "protectinge or rescuinge of offenders," that magistrates might "send some convenient strength of English and, . . . seise and bring away" Indians from any "plantation of Indians" which persisted in this practice and, if no satisfaction was forthcoming, could deliver the "Indians seased . . . either to serve or be shipped out and exchanged for Negroes."[32] Captivity and criminal justice seemed to mean the same thing, slavery.

[30] Nathaniel B. Shurtleff, ed., *Records of the Governor and Company of the Massachusetts Bay in New England*, 5 vols. in 6 (Boston, 1853–54), I, 181, 246; John Noble and John F. Cronin, eds., *Records of the Court of Assistants of the Colony of the Massachusetts Bay, 1630–1692*, 3 vols. (Boston, 1901–28), II, 78–79, 86, 90, 94, 97, 118.

[31] Donnan, ed., *Documents of the Slave Trade*, III, 8.

[32] Nathaniel B. Shurtleff and David Pulsifer, eds., *Records of the Colony of New Plymouth in New England*, 12 vols. (Boston, 1855–61), IX, 70–71. See also Ebenezer Hazard, comp., *Historical Collections; Consisting of State Papers, and Other Authentic Documents* . . . , 2 vols. (Phila., 1792–94), II, 63–64.

It would be wrong to suppose that all the Puritans' preconceived ideas about freedom and bondage worked in the same direction. While the concepts of difference in religion and of captivity worked against Indians and Negroes, certain Scriptural injunctions and English pride in liberty told in the opposite direction. In Massachusetts the magistrates demonstrated that they were not about to tolerate glaring breaches of "the Law of God established in Israel" even when the victims were Negroes. In 1646 the authorities arrested two mariners, James Smith and Thomas Keyser, who had carried two Negroes directly from Africa and sold them in Massachusetts. What distressed the General Court was that the Negroes had been obtained during a raid on an African village and that this "haynos and crying sinn of man stealing" had transpired on the Lord's Day. The General Court decided to free the unfortunate victims and ship them back to Africa, though the death penalty for the crime (clearly mandatory in Scripture) was not imposed.[33] More quietly than in this dramatic incident, Puritan authorities extended the same protections against maltreatment to Negroes and Indians as to white servants.

Only once before the eighteenth century was New England slavery challenged directly, and in that instance the tone was as much bafflement as indignation. This famous Rhode Island protest perhaps derived from a diffuse Christian equalitarianism which operated to extend the English presumption of liberty to non-Englishmen. The Rhode Island law of 1652 actually forbade enslavement.

> Whereas, there is a common course practised amongst English men to buy negers, to that end they may have them for service or slaves forever; for the preventigge of such practices among us, let it be ordered, that no blacke mankind or white being forced by covenent bond, or otherwise, to serve any man or his assighnes longer than ten yeares, or untill they come to bee twentie four yeares of age, if they bee taken in under fourteen, from the time of thier cominge within the liberties of this Collonie. And at the end or terme of ten yeares to sett them free, as the manner is with the English servants. And that man that will not let them goe free, or shall sell them away elsewhere, to that end that they may bee enslaved to others for a long time, hee or they shall forfeit to the Collonie forty pounds.

Perhaps it was Rhode Island's tolerance of religious diversity and relatively high standard of justice for the Indian which led to this attempt to prevent Englishmen from taking advantage of a different people.[34]

The law remained a dead letter. The need for labor, the example set in

---

[33] Donnan, ed., *Documents of the Slave Trade*, III, 6–9. Exodus 21:16: "And he that stealeth a man, and selleth him, or if he be found in his hand, he shall surely be put to death." Compare with Deuteronomy 24:7: "If a man be found stealing any of his brethren of the children of Israel, and maketh merchandise of him, or selleth him; then that thief shall die; and thou shalt put evil away from among you."

[34] John R. Bartlett, ed., *Records of the Colony of Rhode Island and Providence Plantations, in New England*, 10 vols. (Providence, 1856–65), I, 243. The act passed during the Coddington secession; only two of the four towns, Providence and Warwick, were represented. Roger Williams was in England, and it seems likely Samuel Gorton pressed passage. The absence of the two southern towns (where trading in Negroes must have centered) suggests a strangely prophetic division of opinion. See Charles M. Andrews, *The Colonial Period of American History*, 4 vols. (New Haven, 1934–38), II, 29–30.

the West Indies, the condition of Negroes as "strangers," and their initial connection with captive Indians combined to override any hesitation about introducing Negro bond slavery into New England. Laws regulating the conduct of Negroes specifically did not appear until the 1690's.[35] From the first, however, there were scattered signs that Negroes were regarded as different from English people not merely in their status as slaves. In 1639 Samuel Maverick of Noddles Island attempted, apparently rather clumsily, to breed two of his Negroes, or so an English visitor reported:

> Mr. Maverick was desirous to have a breed of Negroes, and therefore seeing [that his "Negro woman"] would not yield by persuasions to company with a Negro young man he had in his house; he commanded him will'd she nill'd she to go to bed to her which was no sooner done but she kickt him out again, this she took in high disdain beyond her slavery.

In 1652 the Massachusetts General Court ordered that Scotsmen, Indians, and Negroes should train with the English in the militia, but four years later abruptly excluded Negroes, as did Connecticut in 1660.[36] Evidently Negroes, even free Negroes, were regarded as distinct from the English. They were, in New England where economic necessities were not sufficiently pressing to determine the decision, treated differently from other men.

7. Enslavement: Virginia and Maryland

In Virginia and Maryland the development of Negro slavery followed a very different course, for several reasons. Most obviously, geographic conditions and the intentions of the settlers quickly combined to produce a successful agricultural staple. The deep tidal rivers, the long growing season, the fertile soil, and the absence of strong communal spirit among the settlers opened the way. Ten years after settlers first landed at Jamestown they were on the way to proving, in the face of assertions to the contrary, that it was possible "to found an empire upon smoke." More than the miscellaneous productions of New England, tobacco required labor which was cheap but not temporary, mobile but not independent, and tireless rather than skilled. In the Chesapeake area more than anywhere to the northward, the shortage of labor and the abundance of land—the "frontier" —placed a premium on involuntary labor.

This need for labor played more directly upon these settlers' ideas about freedom and bondage than it did either in the West Indies or in New England. Perhaps it would be more accurate to say that settlers in Virginia (and in Maryland after settlement in 1634) made their decisions concerning

---

[35] The Acts and Resolves, Public and Private, of the Province of the Massachusetts Bay . . . , 21 vols. (Boston, 1869–1922), I, 130, 154, 156, 325, 327; J. Hammond Trumbull and Charles J. Hoadly, eds., The Public Records of the Colony of Connecticut, 15 vols. (Hartford, 1850–90), IV, 40. For treatment of servants see Lawrence W. Towner, " 'A Fondness for Freedom': Servant Protest in Puritan Society," Wm. and Mary Qtly., 3d Ser., 19 (1962), 201–19.

[36] John Josselyn, An Account of Two Voyages to New-England . . . , 2d ed. (London, 1675), reprinted in Massachusetts Historical Society, Collections, 3d Ser., 3 (1833), 231; Shurtleff, ed., Records of Massachusetts Bay, III, 268, 397, IV, Pt. i, 86, 257; Acts and Resolves Mass., I, 130; Trumbull and Hoadly, eds., Recs. Col. Conn., I, 349.

Negroes while relatively virginal, relatively free from external influences and from firm preconceptions. Of all the important early English settlements, Virginia had the least contact with the Spanish, Portuguese, Dutch, and other English colonies. At the same time, the settlers of Virginia did not possess either the legal or Scriptural learning of the New England Puritans whose conception of the just war had opened the way to the enslavement of Indians. Slavery in the tobacco colonies did not begin as an adjunct of captivity; in marked contrast to the Puritan response to the Pequot War the settlers of Virginia did *not* generally react to the Indian massacre of 1622 with propositions for taking captives and selling them as "slaves." It was perhaps a correct measure of the conceptual atmosphere in Virginia that there was only one such proposition after the 1622 disaster and that that one was defective in precision as to how exactly one treated captive Indians.[37]

In the absence, then, of these influences which obtained in other English colonies, slavery as it developed in Virginia and Maryland assumes a special interest and importance over and above the fact that Negro slavery was to become a vitally important institution there and, later, to the southwards. In the tobacco colonies it is possible to watch Negro slavery *develop*, not pop up full-grown overnight, and it is therefore possible to trace, very imperfectly, the development of the shadowy, unexamined rationale which supported it. The concept of Negro slavery there was neither borrowed from foreigners, nor extracted from books, nor invented out of whole cloth, nor extrapolated from servitude, nor generated by English reaction to Negroes as such, nor necessitated by the exigencies of the New World. Not any one of these made the Negro a slave, but all.

In rough outline, slavery's development in the tobacco colonies seems to have undergone three stages. Negroes first arrived in 1619, only a few days late for the meeting of the first representative assembly in America. John Rolfe described the event with the utmost concern: "About the last of August came in a dutch man of warre that sold us twenty Negars."[38] Negroes continued to trickle in slowly for the next half century; one report in 1649 estimated that there were three hundred among Virginia's population of fifteen thousand—about 2 per cent.[39] Long before there were more appreciable numbers, the development of slavery had, so far as we can tell, shifted gears. Prior to about 1640, there is very little evidence to show how Negroes were treated—though we will need to return to those first twenty years in a moment. After 1640 there is mounting evidence that some Negroes were in fact being treated as slaves, at least that they were being held in hereditary lifetime service. This is to say that the twin essences of slavery—the two kinds of perpetuity—first become evident during the twenty years prior to the beginning of legal formulation. After 1660 slavery was written into statute law. Negroes began to flood into the two colonies at the end of the seventeenth century. In 1705 Virginia produced a codification of laws applying to slaves.

Concerning the first of these stages, there is only one major historical

[37] Kingsbury, ed., *Recs. Virginia Company*, III, 672–73, 704–7.

[38] Arber, ed., *Travels of John Smith*, II, 541.

[39] *A Perfect Description of Virginia* . . . (London, 1649), reprinted in Peter Force, ed., *Tracts* . . . , 4 vols. (N.Y., 1947), II, no. 8.

certainty, and unfortunately it is the sort which historians find hardest to bear. There simply is not enough evidence to indicate with any certainty whether Negroes were treated like white servants or not. At least we can be confident, therefore, that the two most common assertions about the first Negroes—that they were slaves and that they were servants—are *unfounded*, though not necessarily incorrect. And what of the positive evidence?

Some of the first group bore Spanish names and presumably had been baptized, which would mean they were at least nominally Christian, though of the Papist sort. They had been "sold" to the English; so had other Englishmen but not by the Dutch. Certainly these Negroes were not fully free, but many Englishmen were not. It can be said, though, that from the first in Virginia Negroes were set apart from white men by the word *Negroes*. The earliest Virginia census reports plainly distinguished Negroes from white men, often giving Negroes no personal name; in 1629 every commander of the several plantations was ordered to "take a generall muster of all the inhabitants men woemen and Children as well *Englishe* as Negroes."[40] A distinct name is not attached to a group unless it is regarded as distinct. It seems logical to suppose that this perception of the Negro as being distinct from the Englishman must have operated to debase his status rather than to raise it, for in the absence of countervailing social factors, the need for labor in the colonies usually told in the direction of non-freedom. There were few countervailing factors present, surely, in such instances as in 1629 when a group of Negroes were brought to Virginia freshly captured from a Portuguese vessel which had snatched them from Angola a few weeks earlier.[41] Given the context of English thought and experience sketched in this chapter, it seems probable that the Negro's status was not ever the same as that accorded the white servant. But we do not know for sure.

When the first fragmentary evidence appears about 1640 it becomes clear that *some* Negroes in both Virginia and Maryland were serving for life and some Negro children inheriting the same obligation.[42] Not all Negroes, certainly, for Nathaniel Littleton had released a Negro named Anthony Longoe from all service whatsoever in 1635, and after the mid-1640's the court records show that other Negroes were incontestably free and were accumulating property of their own. At least one Negro freeman, Anthony Johnson, himself owned a Negro. Some Negroes served only terms of usual length, but others were held for terms far longer than custom and statute permitted with white servants.[43] The first fairly clear indication that slavery

[40] Henry R. McIlwaine, ed., *Minutes of the Council and General Court of Colonial Virginia, 1622–1632, 1670–1676* (Richmond, 1924), 196. Lists and musters of 1624 and 1625 are in John C. Hotten, ed., *The Original Lists of Persons of Quality . . .* (N.Y., 1880), 169–265.

[41] Philip A. Bruce, *Economic History of Virginia in the Seventeenth Century . . .*, 2 vols. (N.Y., 1896), II, 73.

[42] Further details are in Winthrop D. Jordan, "Modern Tensions and the Origins of American Slavery," *Journal of Southern History*, 28 (1962), 18–30.

[43] Susie M. Ames, *Studies of the Virginia Eastern Shore in the Seventeenth Century* (Richmond, 1940), 99; John H. Russell, *The Free Negro in Virginia, 1619–1865* (Baltimore, 1913), 23–39; and his "Colored Freemen As Slave Owners in Virginia," *Journal of Negro History*, 1 (1916), 234–37.

was practiced in the tobacco colonies appears in 1639, when a Maryland statute declared that "all inhabitants of this Province being Christians (Slaves excepted) Shall have and enjoy all such rights liberties immunities priviledges and free customs within this Province as any naturall born subject of England." Another Maryland law passed the same year provided that "all persons being Christians (Slaves excepted)" over eighteen who were imported without indentures would serve for four years.[44] These laws make very little sense unless the term *slaves* meant Negroes and perhaps Indians.

The next year, 1640, the first definite indication of outright enslavement appears in Virginia. The General Court pronounced sentence on three servants who had been retaken after absconding to Maryland. Two of them, a Dutchman and a Scot, were ordered to serve their masters for one additional year and then the colony for three more, but "the third being a negro named John Punch shall serve his said master or his assigns for the time of his natural life here or else where." No white servant in any English colony, so far as is known, ever received a like sentence. Later the same month a Negro (possibly the same enterprising fellow) was again singled out from a group of recaptured runaways; six of the seven culprits were assigned additional time while the Negro was given none, presumably because he was already serving for life.[45]

After 1640, when surviving Virginia county court records began to mention Negroes, sales for life, often including any future progeny, were recorded in unmistakable language. In 1646 Francis Pott sold a Negro woman and boy to Stephen Charlton "to the use of him . . . forever." Similarly, six years later William Whittington sold to John Pott "one Negro girle named Jowan; aged about Ten yeares and with her Issue and produce duringe her (or either of them) for their Life tyme. And their Successors forever"; and a Maryland man in 1649 deeded two Negro men and a woman "and all their issue both male and Female." The executors of a York County estate in 1647 disposed of eight Negroes—four men, two women, and two children—to Captain John Chisman "to have hold occupy posesse and injoy and every one of the afforementioned Negroes forever."[46] The will of Rowland Burnham of "Rapahanocke," made in 1657, dispensed his considerable number of Negroes and white servants in language which clearly differentiated between the two by specifying that the whites were to serve for their "full terme of tyme" and the Negroes "for ever."[47] Nothing in the will indicated that this distinction was exceptional or novel.

Further evidence that some Negroes were serving for life in this period lies in the prices paid for them. In many instances the valuations placed on Negroes (in estate inventories and bills of sale) were far higher than for white servants, even those servants with full terms yet to serve. Higher

[44] *Archives Md.*, I, 41, 80, also 409, 453–54.

[45] "Decisions of the General Court," *Virginia Magazine of History and Biography*, 5 (1898), 236–37.

[46] For these four cases, Northampton County Deeds, Wills, etc., no. 4 (1651–54), 28 (misnumbered 29), 124, Virginia State Library, Richmond; *Archives Md.*, XLI, 261–62; York County Records, no. 2 (transcribed Wills and Deeds, 1645–49), 256–57, Va. State Lib.

[47] Lancaster County Loose Papers, Box of Wills, 1650–1719, Folder 1656–1659, Va. State Lib.

prices must have meant that Negroes were more highly valued because of their greater length of service. Negro women may have been especially prized, moreover, because their progeny could also be held perpetually. In 1643, for example, William Burdett's inventory listed eight servants, with the time each still had to serve, at valuations ranging from 400 to 1,100 pounds of tobacco, while a "very anntient" Negro was valued at 3,000 and an eight-year-old Negro girl at 2,000 pounds, with no time remaining indicated for either. In the late 1650's an inventory of Thomas Ludlow's estate evaluated a white servant with six years to serve at less than an elderly Negro man and only one half of a Negro woman.[48] Similarly, the labor owned by James Stone in 1648 was evaluated as follows:

	lb tobo
Thomas Groves, 4 yeares to serve	1300
Francis Bomley for 6 yeares	1500
John Thackstone for 3 yeares	1300
Susan Davis for 3 yeares	1000
Emaniell a Negro man	2000
Roger Stone 3 yeares	1300
Mingo a Negro man	2000[49]

The 1655 inventory of Argoll Yeardley's estate provides clear evidence of a distinction between perpetual and limited service for Negroes. Under the heading "Servants" were listed "Towe Negro men, towe Negro women (their wifes) one Negro girle aged 15 yeares, Item One Negro girle aged about teen yeares and one Negro child aged about sixe moneths," valued at 12,000 pounds, and under the heading "Corne" were "Servants, towe men their tyme three months," valued at 300 pounds, and "one Negro boye ["about three yeares old"] (which by witness of his godfather) is to bee free att twenty foure yeares of age and then to have towe cowes given him," valued at 600 pounds.[50] Besides setting a higher value on Negroes, these inventories failed to indicate the number of years they had still to serve, presumably because their service was for an unlimited time.

Where Negro women were involved, higher valuations probably reflected the facts that their issue were valuable and that they could be used for field work while white women generally were not. This latter discrimination between Negro and white women did not necessarily involve perpetual service, but it meant that Negroes were set apart in a way clearly not to their advantage. This was not the only instance in which Negroes were subjected to degrading distinctions not immediately and necessarily attached to the concept of slavery. Negroes were singled out for special treatment in several ways which suggest a generalized debasement of Negroes as a

[48] Northampton County Orders, Deeds, Wills, etc., no. 2 (1640–45), 224; York County Deeds, Orders, Wills, etc. (1657–62), 108–9; in 1645 two Negro women and a boy sold for 5,500 lbs. of tobacco, York County Records, no. 2, 63; all Va. State Lib.

[49] York County Records, no. 2, 390, Va. State Lib.

[50] Nora Miller Turman and Mark C. Lewis, eds., "Inventory of the Estate of Argoll Yeardley of Northampton County, Virginia, in 1655," Va. Mag. of Hist. and Biog., 70 (1962), 410–19.

group. Significantly, the first indications of this debasement appeared at about the same time as the first indications of actual enslavement.

The distinction concerning field work is a case in point. It first appears on the written record in 1643, when Virginia almost pointedly endorsed it in a tax law. Previously, in 1629, tithable persons had been defined as "all those that worke in the ground of what qualitie or condition soever." The new law provided that *all* adult men were tithable and, in addition, *Negro* women. The same distinction was made twice again before 1660. Maryland adopted a similar policy beginning in 1654.[51] This official discrimination between Negro and other women was made by men who were accustomed to thinking of field work as being ordinarily the work of men rather than women. As John Hammond wrote in a 1656 tract defending the tobacco colonies, servant women were not put to work in the fields but in domestic employments, "yet som wenches that are nasty, and beastly and not fit to be so employed are put into the ground."[52] The essentially racial character of this discrimination stood out clearly in a law passed in 1668 at the time slavery was taking shape in the statute books:

> Whereas some doubts, have arisen whether negro women set free were still to be accompted tithable according to a former act, *It is declared by this grand assembly* that negro women, though permitted to enjoy their Freedome yet ought not in all respects to be admitted to a full fruition of the exemptions and impunities of the English, and are still lyable to payment of taxes.[53]

Virginia law set Negroes apart from all other groups in a second way by denying them the important right and obligation to bear arms. Few restraints could indicate more clearly the denial to Negroes of membership in the white community. The first foreshadowing of the slave codes came in 1640, at just the time when other indications first appeared that Negroes were subject to special treatment.[54]

[51] Hening, ed., *Statutes Va.*, I, 144, 242, 292, 454; *Archives Md.*, I, 342, II, 136, 399, 538–39, XIII, 538–39.

[52] John Hammond, *Leah and Rachel, or, the Two Fruitfull Sisters Virginia, and Mary-land: Their Present Condition, Impartially Stated and Related . . .* (London, 1656), 9.

[53] Hening, ed., *Statutes Va.*, II, 267.

[54] *Ibid.*, I, 226; for the same act in more detail, "Acts of General Assembly, Jan. 6, 1639–40," *Wm. and Mary Qtly.*, 2d Ser., 4 (1924), 147. In Bermuda, always closely connected with Virginia, the first prohibition of weapons to Negroes came in 1623, only seven years after the first Negro landed. The 1623 law was the first law anywhere in English specifically dealing with Negroes. After stressing the insolence of Negroes secretly carrying "cudgells and other weapons and working tools, very dangerous and not meete to be suffered to be carried by such vassalls," it prohibited (in addition to arms) Negroes going abroad at night, trespassing on other people's lands, and trading in tobacco without permission of their masters. Unfortunately the evidence concerning lifetime service for Negroes is much less definite in the scanty Bermuda sources than in those for Maryland and Virginia; the first known incident suggestive of the practice might reasonably be placed anywhere from 1631 to 1656. Later evidence shows Bermuda's slavery and proportion of Negroes similar to Virginia's, and it seems unlikely that the two colonies' early experience was radically different. Henry C. Wilkinson, *The Adventurers of Bermuda; A History of the Island from Its Discovery until the Dissolution of the Somers Island Company in 1684* (London, 1933), 114; J. H. Lefroy, comp., *Memorials of the Discovery and Early Settlement of the Bermudas or Somers Islands,*

Finally, an even more compelling sense of the separateness of Negroes was revealed in early reactions to sexual union between the races. Prior to 1660 the evidence concerning these reactions is equivocal, and it is not possible to tell whether repugnance for intermixture preceded legislative enactment of slavery. In 1630 an angry Virginia court sentenced "Hugh Davis to be soundly whipped, before an assembly of Negroes and others for abusing himself to the dishonor of God and shame of Christians, by defiling his body in lying with a negro," but it is possible that the "negro" may not have been female. With other instances of punishment for interracial union in the ensuing years, fornication rather than miscegenation may well have been the primary offense, though in 1651 a Maryland man sued someone who he claimed had said "that he had a black bastard in Virginia." (The court recognized the legitimacy of his complaint, but thought his claim for £20,000 sterling somewhat overvalued his reputation and awarded him 1500 pounds "of Tobacco and Cask.")[55] There may have been no racial feeling involved when in 1640 Robert Sweet, a gentleman, was compelled "to do penance in church according to laws of England, for getting a negroe woman with child and the woman whipt."[56] About 1650 a white man and a Negro woman were required to stand clad in white sheets before a congregation in lower Norfolk County for having had relations, but this punishment was sometimes used in cases of fornication between two whites.[57] A quarter century later in 1676, however, the emergence of distaste for racial intermixture was unmistakable. A contemporary account of Bacon's Rebellion caustically described one of the ringleaders, Richard Lawrence, as a person who had eclipsed his learning and abilities "in the darke imbraces of a Blackamoore, his slave: And that in so fond a Maner, . . . to the noe meane Scandle and affrunt of all the Vottrisses in or about towne."[58]

Such condemnation was not confined to polemics. In the early 1660's when slavery was gaining statutory recognition, the assemblies acted with full-throated indignation against miscegenation. These acts aimed at more than merely avoiding confusion of status. In 1662 Virginia declared that "if any christian shall committ Fornication with a negro man or woman, hee or shee soe offending" should pay double the usual fine. (The next year Bermuda prohibited all sexual relations between whites and Negroes.) Two years later Maryland banned interracial marriages:

> forasmuch as divers freeborne English women forgettfull of their free Condicion and to the disgrace of our Nation doe intermarry with Negro Slaves

1515–1685 . . . , 2 vols. (London, 1877–79), I, 308–9, 505, 526–27, 633, 645, II, 34–35, 70. But Negroes were to be armed at times of alarm (*ibid.*, II, 242, 366, 380 [1666–73]): Bermuda was exposed to foreign attack.

55 Hening, ed., *Statutes Va.*, I, 146. (The term "negro woman" was in very common use.) *Archives Md.*, X, 114–15.

56 Hening, ed., *Statutes Va.*, I, 552; McIlwaine, ed., *Minutes Council Va.*, 477.

57 Bruce, *Economic History of Va.*, II, 110.

58 "The History of Bacon's and Ingram's Rebellion, 1676," in Charles M. Andrews, ed., *Narratives of the Insurrections, 1675–1690* (N.Y., 1915), 96. Cf. the will of John Fenwick (1683), *Documents Relating to the Colonial, Revolutionary and Post-Revolutionary History of the State of New Jersey* . . . [New Jersey Archives], 1st Ser. (Newark, etc., 1880–1949), XXIII, 162.

by which alsoe divers suites may arise touching the Issue of such woemen and a great damage doth befall the Masters of such Negroes for prevention whereof for deterring such freeborne women from such shamefull Matches,

strong language indeed if "divers suites" had been the only problem. A Maryland act of 1681 described marriages of white women with Negroes as, among other things, "always to the Satisfaccion of theire Lascivious and Lustfull desires, and to the disgrace not only of the English butt allso of many other Christian Nations." When Virginia finally prohibited all inter-racial liaisons in 1691, the Assembly vigorously denounced miscegenation and its fruits as "that abominable mixture and spurious issue."[59]

From the surviving evidence, it appears that outright enslavement and these other forms of debasement appeared at about the same time in Mary-land and Virginia. Indications of perpetual service, the very nub of slavery, coincided with indications that English settlers discriminated against Negro women, withheld arms from Negroes, and—though the timing is far less certain—reacted unfavorably to interracial sexual union. The coincidence suggests a mutual relationship between slavery and unfavorable assessment of Negroes. Rather than slavery causing "prejudice," or vice versa, they seem rather to have generated each other. Both were, after all, twin aspects of a general debasement of the Negro. Slavery and "prejudice" may have been equally cause and effect, continuously reacting upon each other, dynamically joining hands to hustle the Negro down the road to complete degradation. Much more than with the other English colonies, where the enslavement of Negroes was to some extent a borrowed practice, the avail-able evidence for Maryland and Virginia points to less borrowing and to this kind of process: a mutually interactive growth of slavery and unfavor-able assessment, with no cause for either which did not cause the other as well. If slavery caused prejudice, then invidious distinctions concerning working in the fields, bearing arms, and sexual union should have appeared *after* slavery's firm establishment. If prejudice caused slavery, then one would expect to find these lesser discriminations preceding the greater dis-crimination of outright enslavement. Taken as a whole, the evidence reveals a process of debasement of which hereditary lifetime service was an im-portant but not the only part.

White servants did not suffer this debasement. Rather, their position im-proved, partly for the reason that they were not Negroes. By the early 1660's white men were loudly protesting against being made "slaves" in terms which strongly suggest that they considered slavery not as wrong but as inapplicable to themselves. The father of a Maryland apprentice petitioned in 1663 that "he Craves that his daughter may not be made a Slave a tearme soe Scandalous that if admitted to be the Condicion or tytle of the Apprentices in this Province will be soe distructive as noe free borne Christians will ever be induced to come over servants."[60] An Irish youth complained to a Maryland court in 1661 that he had been kidnapped and

---

[59] Hening, ed., *Statutes Va.*, II, 170, III, 86–87; *Archives Md.*, I, 533–34, VII, 204; Lefroy, comp., *Memorials Bermudas*, II, 190 (a resolution, not a statute). Some evidence suggests miscegenation was not taken as seriously in 17th-century Bermuda as on the mainland: *ibid.*, I, 550, II, 30, 103, 141, 161, 228, 314.

[60] *Archives Md.*, I, 464.

forced to sign for fifteen years, that he had already served six and a half years and was now twenty-one, and that eight and a half more years of service was "contrary to the lawes of God and man that a Christian Subject should be made a Slave." (The jury blandly compromised the dispute by deciding that he should serve only until age twenty-one, but that he was now only nineteen.) Free Negro servants were generally increasingly less able to defend themselves against this insidious kind of encroachment.[61] Increasingly, white men were more clearly free because Negroes had become so clearly slave.

Certainly it was the case in Maryland and Virginia that the legal enactment of Negro slavery followed social practice, rather than vice versa, and also that the assemblies were slower than in other English colonies to declare how Negroes could or should be treated. These two patterns in themselves suggest that slavery was less a matter of previous conception or external example in Maryland and Virginia than elsewhere.

The Virginia Assembly first showed itself incontrovertibly aware that Negroes were not serving in the same manner as English servants in 1660 when it declared "that for the future no servant comeing into the country without indentures, of what christian nation soever, shall serve longer then those of our own country, of the like age." In 1661 the Assembly indirectly provided statutory recognition that some Negroes served for life: "That in case any English servant shall run away in company with any negroes who are incapable of making satisfaction by addition of time," he must serve for the Negroes' lost time as well as his own. Maryland enacted a closely similar law in 1663 (possibly modeled on Virginia's) and in the following year, on the initiative of the lower house, came out with the categorical declaration that Negroes were to serve "Durante Vita."[62] During the next twenty-odd years a succession of acts in both colonies defined with increasing precision what sorts of persons might be treated as slaves.[63] Other acts dealt with the growing problem of slave control, and especially after 1690 slavery began to assume its now familiar character as a complete deprivation of all rights.[64] As early as 1669 the Virginia Assembly unabashedly enacted a brutal law which showed where the logic of perpetual servitude was inevitably tending. Unruly servants could be chastened by sentences to additional terms, but "WHEREAS the only law in force for the punishment of refractory servants resisting their master, mistris or overseer cannot be inflicted upon negroes, nor the obstinacy of many of them by other then violent meanes supprest," if a slave "by the extremity of the correction

[61] *Ibid.*, XLI, 476–78, XLIX, 123–24. Compare the contemporary difficulties of a Negro servant: William P. Palmer *et al.*, eds., *Calendar of Virginia State Papers* . . . , 11 vols. (Richmond, 1875–93), I, 9–10.

[62] Hening, ed., *Statutes Va.*, I, 539, II, 26; *Archives Md.*, I, 449, 489, 526, 533–34. The "any negroes who are incapable" suggests explicit recognition that some were free, but in several sources the law as re-enacted the next year included a comma between "negroes" and "who," as did the Maryland act of 1663. See *The Lawes of Virginia Now in Force: Collected out of the Assembly Records* . . . (London, 1662), 59.

[63] Hening, ed., *Statutes Va.*, II, 170, 270, 283, 490–91, III, 137–40, 447-48; *Archives Md.*, VII, 203–5, XIII, 546–49, XXII, 551–52.

[64] Especially Hening, ed., *Statutes Va.*, II, 270–71, 481–82, 493, III, 86, 102–3; *Archives Md.*, XIII, 451–53, XIX, 167, 193, XXII, 546–48, XXVI, 254–56.

should chance to die" his master was not to be adjudged guilty of felony "since it cannot be presumed that prepensed malice (which alone makes murther Felony) should induce any man to destroy his owne estate."[65] Virginia planters felt they acted out of mounting necessity: there were disturbances among slaves in several areas in the early 1670's.[66]

By about 1700 the slave ships began spilling forth their black cargoes in greater and greater numbers. By that time, racial slavery and the necessary police powers had been written into law. By that time, too, slavery had lost all resemblance to a perpetual and hereditary version of English servitude, though service for life still seemed to contemporaries its most essential feature.[67] In the last quarter of the seventeenth century the trend was to treat Negroes more like property and less like men, to send them to the fields at younger ages, to deny them automatic existence as inherent members of the community, to tighten the bonds on their personal and civil freedom, and correspondingly to loosen the traditional restraints on the master's freedom to deal with his human property as he saw fit.[68] In 1705 Virginia gathered up the random statutes of a whole generation and baled them into a "slave code" which would not have been out of place in the nineteenth century.[69]

· · ·

10. Racial Slavery: From Reasons to Rationale

And *difference*, surely, was the indispensable key to the degradation of Negroes in English America. In scanning the problem of *why* Negroes were enslaved in America, certain constant elements in a complex situation can be readily, if roughly, identified. It may be taken as given that there would have been no enslavement without economic need, that is, without persistent demand for labor in underpopulated colonies. Of crucial importance, too, was the fact that for cultural reasons Negroes were relatively helpless in the face of European aggressiveness and technology. In themselves, however, these two elements will not explain the enslavement of Indians and Negroes. The pressing exigency in America was labor, and Irish and English servants were available. Most of them would have been helpless to ward off outright enslavement if their masters had thought themselves privileged and able to enslave them. As a group, though, masters did not think themselves so empowered. Only with Indians and Negroes did Englishmen attempt so radical a deprivation of liberty—which brings the matter abruptly to the most difficult and imponderable question of all: what was it about Indians and Negroes which set them apart, which rendered them *different* from Englishmen, which made them special candidates for degradation?

To ask such questions is to inquire into the *content* of English attitudes,

---

[65] Hening, ed., *Statutes Va.*, II, 270; compare law for servants, I, 538, II, 118.

[66] *Ibid.*, II, 299.

[67] Robert Beverley, *The History and Present State of Virginia*, ed., Louis B. Wright (Chapel Hill, 1947), 271–72.

[68] For illustration, Hening, ed., *Statutes Va.*, II, 288, 479–80 (Negro *children* taxed from age 12, white *boys* from 14), III, 102–3; *Archives Md.*, VII, 76 (county courts required to register births, marriages, burials of all "Except Negroes Indians and Molottos").

[69] Hening, ed., *Statutes Va.*, III, 447–62.

and unfortunately there is little evidence with which to build an answer. It may be said, however, that the heathen condition of the Negroes seemed of considerable importance to English settlers in America—more so than to English voyagers upon the coasts of Africa—and that heathenism was associated in some settlers' minds with the condition of slavery.[70] This is not to say that the colonists enslaved Negroes because they were heathens. The most clear-cut positive trace of such reasoning was probably unique and certainly far from being a forceful statement: in 1660 John Hathorne declared, before a Massachusetts court in partial support of his contention that an Indian girl should not be compelled to return to her master, that "first the law is undeniable that the indian may have the same distribusion of Justice with our selves: ther is as I humbly conceive not the same argument as amongst the negroes[,] for the light of the gospell is a begineing to appeare amongst them—that is the indians."[71]

The importance and persistence of the tradition which attached slavery to heathenism did not become evident in any positive assertions that heathens might be enslaved. It was not until the period of legal establishment of slavery after 1660 that the tradition became manifest at all, and even then there was no effort to place heathenism and slavery on a one-for-one relationship. Virginia's second statutory definition of a slave (1682), for example, awkwardly attempted to rest enslavement on religious difference while excluding from possible enslavement all heathens who were not Indian or Negro.[72] Despite such logical difficulties, the old European equation of slavery and religious difference did not rapidly vanish in America, for it cropped up repeatedly after 1660 in assertions that slaves by becoming Christian did not automatically become free. By about the end of the seventeenth century, Maryland, New York, Virginia, North and South Carolina, and New Jersey had all passed laws reassuring masters that conversion of their slaves did not necessitate manumission.[73] These acts were passed in

[70] See above, chap. 1, sec. 3. Also John C. Hurd, *The Law of Freedom and Bondage in the United States*, 2 vols. (Boston, 1858–62), I, 159–60; Horne, *The Mirror of Justices*, ed. Robinson, 124; Marcus W. Jernegan, *Laboring and Dependent Classes in Colonial America, 1607–1783; Studies of the Economic, Educational, and Social Significance of Slaves, Servants, Apprentices, and Poor Folk* (Chicago, 1931), 24–26; Helen T. Catterall, ed., *Judicial Cases Concerning American Slavery and the Negro*, 5 vols. (Washington, 1926–37), I, 55*n*. Data in the following pages suggest this. The implication that slavery could last only during the heathen state is in Providence Company to Gov. Philip Bell, London, Apr. 20, 1635, Box 9, bundle: List no. 7, 2d portion, MS. relating to the Royal African Co. and Slavery matters, 43, Parish Transcripts, N.-Y. Hist. Soc.: ". . . a Groundless opinion that Christians may not lawfully keepe such persons in a state of Servitude during their strangeness from Christianity." In 1695 Gov. John Archdale of South Carolina prohibited sale of some Indians, captured by his own Indian allies, as slaves to the West Indies and freed them because they were Christians: John Archdale, *A New Description of That Fertile and Pleasant Province of Carolina . . .* (London, 1707), in Alexander S. Salley, Jr., ed., *Narratives of Early Carolina, 1650–1708* (N.Y., 1911), 300.

[71] *Records and Files of the Quarterly Courts of Essex County Massachusetts, 1636–1683*, 8 vols. (Salem, 1911–21), II, 240–42.

[72] Hening, ed., *Statutes Va.*, II, 490–92.

[73] *Archives Md.*, I, 526, 533 (1664), II, 272; "Duke's Laws," C. O. 5/1142, f. 33v., P. R. O., a portion of the section of "Bondslavery" omitted from the standard New York printed sources which reads "And also provided that This Law shall not extend to sett

response to occasional pleas that Christianity created a claim to freedom and to much more frequent assertions by men interested in converting Negroes that nothing could be accomplished if masters thought their slaves were about to be snatched from them by meddling missionaries.[74] This decision that the slave's religious condition had no relevance to his status as a slave (the only one possible if an already valuable economic institution was to be retained) strongly suggests that heathenism was an important component in the colonists' initial reaction to Negroes early in the century.

Yet its importance can easily be overstressed. For one thing, some of the first Negroes in Virginia had been baptized before arrival. In the early years others were baptized in various colonies and became more than nominally Christian; a Negro woman joined the church in Dorchester, Massachusetts, as a full member in 1641.[75] With some Negroes becoming Christian and others not, there might have developed a caste differentiation along religious lines, yet there is no evidence to suggest that the colonists distinguished consistently between the Negroes they converted and those they did not. It was racial, not religious, slavery which developed in America.

Still, in the early years, the English settlers most frequently contrasted themselves with Negroes by the term *Christian*, though they also sometimes described themselves as *English*;[76] here the explicit religious distinction would seem to have lain at the core of English reaction. Yet the concept embodied by the term *Christian* embraced so much more meaning than was contained in specific doctrinal affirmations that it is scarcely possible to assume on the basis of this linguistic contrast that the colonists set Negroes apart because they were heathen. The historical experience of the English people in the sixteenth century had made for fusion of religion and nationality; the qualities of being English and Christian had become so inseparably blended that it seemed perfectly consistent to the Virginia Assembly in 1670 to declare that "noe negroe or Indian though baptised and enjoyned their owne Freedome shall be capable of any such purchase of christians, but yet not debarred from buying any of their owne nation." Similarly, an order of the Virginia Assembly in 1662 revealed a well-knit sense of self-identity of which Englishness and Christianity were interrelated parts: "METAPPIN

---

at Liberty Any Negroe or Indian Servant who shall turne Christian after he shall have been bought by Any Person." (This unpublished Crown Copyright material is reproduced by permission of the Controller of H. M. Stationery Office.) *The Colonial Laws of New York from the Year 1664 to the Revolution . . .* , 5 vols. (Albany, 1894–96), I, 597–98 (1706); Hening, ed., *Statutes Va.,* II, 260 (1667); Saunders, ed., *Col. Recs. N. C.,* I, 204 (1670), II, 857; Cooper and McCord, eds., *Statutes S. C.,* VII, 343 (1691), 364–65; *Anno Regni Reginae Annae . . . Tertio; [The Acts Passed by the Second Assembly of New Jersey in December, 1704]* ([N.Y., 1704]), 20, an act which was disallowed for other reasons.

[74] For example, in 1652 a mulatto girl pleaded Christianity as the reason why she should not be "a perpetuall slave" (Lefroy, comp., *Memorials Bermudas,* II, 34–35, also 293–94), and in 1694 some Massachusetts ministers asked the governor and legislature to remove that "wel-knowne Discouragement" to conversion of slaves with a law denying that baptism necessitated freedom (*Acts and Resolves Mass.,* VII, 537).

[75] Winthrop, *Journal,* ed. Hosmer, II, 26.

[76] These statements on prevailing word usage are based on a wide variety of sources, many of them cited in this chapter; some passages already quoted may serve to amplify the illustrations in the following paragraphs.

a Powhatan Indian being sold for life time to one Elizabeth Short by the king of Wainoake Indians who had no power to sell him being of another nation, *it is ordered* that the said Indian be free, he speaking perfectly the English tongue and desiring baptism."[77]

From the first, then, vis-à-vis the Negro the concept embedded in the term *Christian* seems to have conveyed much of the idea and feeling of *we* as against *they:* to be Christian was to be civilized rather than barbarous, English rather than African, white rather than black. The term *Christian* itself proved to have remarkable elasticity, for by the end of the seventeenth century it was being used to define a species of slavery which had altogether lost any connection with explicit religious difference. In the Virginia code of 1705, for example, the term sounded much more like a definition of race than of religion:

> And for a further christian care and usage of all christian servants, *Be it also enacted, by the authority aforesaid, and it is hereby enacted*, That no negroes, mulattos, or Indians, although christians, or Jews, Moors, Mahometans, or other infidels, shall, at any time, purchase any christian servant, nor any other, except of their own complexion, or such as are declared slaves by this act.

By this time "Christianity" had somehow become intimately and explicitly linked with "complexion." The 1705 statute declared

> That all servants imported and brought into this country, by sea or land, who were not christians in their native country (except Turks and Moors in amity with her majesty, and others that can make due proof of their being free in England, or any other christian country, before they were shipped, in order to transportation hither), shall be accounted and be slaves, and as such be here bought and sold notwithstanding a conversion to christianity afterwards.[78]

As late as 1753 the Virginia slave code anachronistically defined slavery in terms of religion when everyone knew that slavery had for generations been based on the racial and not the religious difference.[79]

It is worth making still closer scrutiny of the terminology which Englishmen employed when referring both to themselves and to the two peoples they enslaved, for this terminology affords the best single means of probing the content of their sense of difference. The terms *Indian* and *Negro* were both borrowed from the Hispanic languages, the one originally deriving from (mistaken) geographical locality and the other from human complexion. When referring to the Indians the English colonists either used that proper name or called them *savages*, a term which reflected primarily their view of Indians as uncivilized, or occasionally (in Maryland especially) *pagans*, which gave more explicit expression to the missionary urge. When

[77] Hening, ed., *Statutes Va.*, II, 281 (1670), 155 (1662).

[78] *Ibid.*, III, 447–48 (1705), also 283, V, 547–48, VI, 356–57. Lingering aftereffects of the old concept cropped up as late as 1791, when *Negro* was still contradistinguished by *Christian:* Certificate of character of Negro Phill, Feb. 20, 1791, Character Certificates of Negroes, Papers of the Pennsylvania Abolition Society, Historical Society of Pennsylvania, Philadelphia.

[79] Hening, ed., *Statutes Va.*, VI, 356–57.

they had reference to Indians the colonists occasionally spoke of themselves as *Christians* but after the early years almost always as *English*.

In significant contrast, the colonists referred to *Negroes* and by the eighteenth century to *blacks* and to *Africans*, but almost never to Negro *heathens* or *pagans* or *savages*. Most suggestive of all, there seems to have been something of a shift during the seventeenth century in the terminology which Englishmen in the colonies applied to themselves. From the initially most common term *Christian*, at mid-century there was a marked drift toward *English* and *free*. After about 1680, taking the colonies as a whole, a new term appeared—*white*.

So far as the weight of analysis may be imposed upon such terms, diminishing reliance upon *Christian* suggests a gradual muting of the specifically religious element in the Christian-Negro disjunction in favor of secular nationality: Negroes were, in 1667, "not in all respects to be admitted to a full fruition of the exemptions and impunities of the English."[80] As time went on, as some Negroes became assimilated to the English colonial culture, as more "raw Africans" arrived, and as increasing numbers of non-English Europeans were attracted to the colonies, the colonists turned increasingly to the striking physiognomic difference. By 1676 it was possible in Virginia to assail a man for "eclipsing" himself in the "darke imbraces of a Blackamoore" as if "Buty consisted all together in the Antiphety of Complections." In Maryland a revised law prohibiting miscegenation (1692) retained *white* and *English* but dropped the term *Christian*—a symptomatic modification. As early as 1664 a Bermuda statute (aimed, ironically, at protecting Negroes from brutal abandonment) required that the "last Master" of senile Negroes "provide for them such accomodations as shall be convenient for Creatures of that hue and colour untill their death." By the end of the seventeenth century dark complexion had become an independent rationale for enslavement: in 1709 Samuel Sewall noted in his diary that a "Spaniard" had petitioned the Massachusetts Council for freedom but that "Capt. Teat alledg'd that all of that Color were Slaves."[81] Here was a barrier between "we" and "they" which was visible and permanent: the Negro could not become a white man. Not, at least, as yet.

What had occurred was not a change in the justification of slavery from religion to race. No such justifications were made. There seems to have

[80] *Ibid.*, II, 267.
[81] "History of Bacon's and Ingram's Rebellion," Andrews, ed., *Narratives of the Insurrections*, 96; *Archives Md.*, XIII, 546–49; Lefroy, comp., *Memorials Bermudas*, II, 216; *Diary of Samuel Sewall, 1674–1729* (Mass. Hist. Soc., *Collections*, 5th Ser. 5–7 [1878–82]), II, 248. In 1698 Gov. Francis Nicholson informed the Board of Trade that the "major part" of Negroes in Maryland spoke English: *Archives Md.*, XXIII, 499. For first use of "white" in statutes of various colonies, Bartlett, ed., *Recs. Col. R. I.*, 1, 243 (1652); *Archives Md.*, VII, 204–5 (1681); Aaron Leaming and Jacob Spicer, eds., *The Grants, Concessions, and Original Constitutions of the Province of New Jersey* . . . , 2d ed. (Somerville, N.J., 1881), 236 (1683); *Col. Laws N.Y.*, I, 148 (1684); Cooper and McCord, eds., *Statutes S. C.*, VII, 343 (1691); Hening, ed., *Statutes Va.*, III, 86–87 (1691); *Acts of Assembly, Made and Enacted in the Bermuda or Summer-Islands, from 1690, to 1713–14* (London, 1719), 12–13 (1690 or 1691). West Indian assemblies used the term in the 1680's and 1690's, possibly earlier. Officials in England were using "whites" and "blacks" as early as 1670 in questionnaires to colonial governors: Hening, ed., *Statutes Va.*, II, 515; Trumbull and Hoadly, eds., *Recs. Col. Conn.*, III, 293.

been, within the unarticulated concept of the Negro as a different sort of person, a subtle but highly significant shift in emphasis. Consciousness of the Negro's heathenism remained through the eighteenth and into the nineteenth and even the twentieth century, and an awareness, at very least, of his different appearance was present from the beginning. The shift was an alteration in emphasis within a single concept of difference rather than a development of a novel conceptualization. The amorphousness and subtlety of such a change is evident, for instance, in the famous tract, *The Negro's and Indians Advocate*, published in 1680 by the Reverend Morgan Godwyn. Baffled and frustrated by the disinterest of planters in converting their slaves, Godwyn declared at one point that "their *Complexion*, which being most obvious to the sight, by which the *Notion* of things doth seem to be most certainly conveyed to the Understanding, is apt to make no *slight* impressions upon rude Minds, already prepared to admit of any thing for *Truth* which shall make for Interest." Altering his emphasis a few pages later, Godwyn complained that "these two words, *Negro* and *Slave*" are "by custom grown Homogeneous and Convertible; even as *Negro* and *Christian, Englishman* and *Heathen*, are by the like corrupt Custom and Partiality made Opposites."[82] Most arresting of all, throughout the colonies the terms *Christian, free, English*, and *white* were for many years employed indiscriminately as metonyms. A Maryland law of 1681 used all four terms in one short paragraph![83]

Whatever the limitations of terminology as an index to thought and feeling, it seems likely that the colonists' initial sense of difference from the Negro was founded not on a single characteristic but on a congeries of qualities which, taken as a whole, seemed to set the Negro apart. Virtually every quality in the Negro invited pejorative feelings. What may have been his two most striking characteristics, his heathenism and his appearance, were probably prerequisite to his complete debasement. His heathenism alone could never have led to permanent enslavement since conversion easily wiped out that failing. If his appearance, his racial characteristics, meant nothing to the English settlers, it is difficult to see how slavery based on race ever emerged, how the concept of complexion as the mark of slavery ever entered the colonists' minds. Even if the colonists were most unfavorably struck by the Negro's color, though, blackness itself did not urge the complete debasement of slavery. Other qualities—the utter strangeness of his language, gestures, eating habits, and so on—certainly must have contributed to the colonists' sense that he was very different, perhaps disturbingly so. In Africa these qualities had for Englishmen added up to *savagery;* they were major components in that sense of *difference* which provided the mental margin absolutely requisite for placing the European on the deck of the slave ship and the Negro in the hold.

The available evidence (what little there is) suggests that for Englishmen settling in America, the specific religious difference was initially of greater importance than color, certainly of much greater relative importance than for the Englishmen who confronted Negroes in their African homeland.

[82] Godwyn, *The Negro's and Indians Advocate*, 20, 36.
[83] *Archives Md.*, VII, 204.

Perhaps Englishmen in Virginia, living uncomfortably close to nature under a hot sun and in almost daily contact with tawny Indians, found the Negro's color less arresting than they might have in other circumstances. Perhaps, too, these first Virginians sensed how inadequately they had reconstructed the institutions and practices of Christian piety in the wilderness; they would perhaps appear less as failures to themselves in this respect if compared to persons who as Christians were *totally* defective. In this connection they may be compared to their brethren in New England, where godliness appeared (at first) triumphantly to hold full sway; in New England there was distinctly less contrasting of Negroes on the basis of the religious disjunction and much more militant discussion of just wars. Perhaps, though, the Jamestown settlers were told in 1619 by the Dutch shipmaster that these "negars" were heathens and could be treated as such. We do not know. The available data will not bear all the weight that the really crucial questions impose.

Of course once the cycle of degradation was fully under way, once slavery and racial discrimination were completely linked together, once the engine of oppression was in full operation, then there is no need to plead *ignoramus.* By the end of the seventeenth century in all the colonies of the English empire there was chattel racial slavery of a kind which would have seemed familiar to men living in the nineteenth century. No Elizabethan Englishman would have found it familiar, though certain strands of thought and feeling in Elizabethan England had intertwined with reports about the Spanish and Portuguese to engender a willingness on the part of English settlers in the New World to treat some men as suitable for private exploitation. During the seventeenth century New World conditions had exploited this predisposition and vastly enlarged it, so much so that English colonials of the eighteenth century were faced with full-blown slavery—something they thought of not as an institution but as a host of ever present problems, dangers, and opportunities.

Suggested Reading

The African civilization from which black settlers came and the slave trade by which they were transported are surveyed by Basil Davidson in *Black Mother: The Years of the African Slave Trade** (1961; retitled in the paper edition *The African Slave Trade*), and James Pope-Hennessy in *Sins of the Fathers: A Study of the Atlantic Slave Traders, 1441–1807** (1968). A difficult but path-breaking study is Philip D. Curtin's *The Atlantic Slave Trade: A Census* (1969).

In addition to Jordan's extensive work, the magisterial study of David Brion Davis, *The Problem of Slavery in Western Culture** (1966), compels reading for its effort to examine in comparative terms the origins and nature of slavery at different times and places. Two important works that deal with the problem of the indentured servants and of colonial labor generally are Richard B. Morris' *Government and Labor in Early America** (1946), and Abbot Emerson Smith's *Colonists in Bondage: White Servitude and Convict Labor in America, 1607–1776** (1947). The standard work on the role of black Americans in the revolu-

tionary struggle is Benjamin Quarles' *The Negro in the American Revolution**
(1961).

The best introductions to the Indian civilizations of North America are Alvin
M.' Josephy, Jr.'s *The Indian Heritage of America** (1968), and Peter Farb's
*Man's Rise to Civilization as Shown by the Indians of North America from Pro-
vincial Times to the Coming of the Industrial State** (1968). The place of the
Indian in the white mind is the subject of Roy Harvey Pearce in *The Savages of
America: A Study of the Indian and the Idea of Civilization** (1953). The re-
sistance of the Indians to settlement is conveyed by Alden T. Vaughan in *New
England Frontier: Puritans and Indians, 1620–1675** (1965).

* Also published in paperback edition.

The Problem of
Democracy in
Colonial America

The Social Context
of Democracy
in Massachusetts

Michael Zuckerman

By asking to what degree any society is democratic,
one immediately raises the problem of defining
democracy. And whether we conclude that democracy
has to do with participation or opportunity or consent,
we still must determine what the function of
democracy is to begin with. Michael Zuckerman of
the University of Pennsylvania addresses himself to
these questions in the following essay and, though his
arguments concern eighteenth-century Massachusetts,
he also asks us to consider how the meanings and uses
of democracy may differ in time and place.

  The eighteenth century, Zuckerman reminds us,
possessed a different notion of democracy than does
the twentieth century. Indeed, if there was democracy
at all in the towns of the old Bay Colony, it was a
"democracy without democrats." The town meeting,
so often taken to be the very hallmark of democracy,
was in fact a "school for enforcement" of collective
decisions rather than a "school for democracy," that is,
of open debate and majority rule. The widespread
participation in the town meetings of Massachusetts
was not due to the triumph of an ideal but rather grew
from the "exigencies of the situation." In Zuckerman's
view, the inclusiveness of participation did not

Pilgrim meeting house (The Bettmann Archive)

function so as to satisfy appeals for greater influence or to co-opt the fractious and dissenters. Instead, it was intended to help maintain peace and harmony by legitimizing decisions taken in the name of the entire community.

Zuckerman's argument absorbs two opposing views of colonial democracy that have for some time engaged historians. One view, best represented by Robert E. Brown (*Middle-Class Democracy and the Revolution in Massachusetts, 1691–1780** [1955]), is that the franchise in town affairs was widely available to adult white males in colonial Massachusetts and elsewhere. Although there is now little dissent to this argument, others have argued persuasively that the possession of the franchise means little unless accompanied by a sense of efficacy, unless the habit of deference to others is absent. Zuckerman's achievement has been to concede the availability of the vote without assuming its usefulness. He is at considerable pains to demonstrate precisely what the vote gained both the elector and the community.

This he accomplishes by use of the notion of consensus. Where for others consensus has been a category of interpretation (used for example to determine whether a society is marked by concord or discord), Zuckerman employs it as an analytical method, acknowledging that a consensus of views was generally achieved in Massachusetts towns and then going on to ask how consensus was engineered. Democracy thus becomes a means to an end—that of community solidarity—and not an end in itself. As for majority rule, it was not even conceived at the time; in fact, it was considered divisive and illegitimate.

Such an interpretation is provocative in that it allows us to understand the many implications of participation in a society. It also suggests that what is important is not merely the possession of the vote but also the context in which it is registered. Ironically, a democracy in political terms need not be democratic, a fact to which the political history of the Massachusetts towns attests.

But is Zuckerman's description of towns with so little conflict itself accurate? Might it not be that conflict could be surreptitious or take other forms, such as suits in court or debates over religious and

The Social Context of Democracy in Massachusetts. From *William and Mary Quarterly,* 3rd Ser., XXV (October 1968), 523–44. Reprinted by permission of the William and Mary Quarterly and Michael Zuckerman.

theological matters? Even if there was so little conflict, was the placidity due only to the success of the open town meeting in gaining consent through the vote? Does Zuckerman perhaps exclude too thoroughly the impact of common values and ideals from his explanation? And what of the notion of democracy itself? Contemporaries had not yet accepted the term; when, some decades later, it came into more common usage, it was used as a term of condemnation. Perhaps Zuckerman would do better to avoid an anachronistic term altogether and to write more simply of "the social context of voting in Massachusetts."

Yet, for all these difficulties, the essay decidedly advances our understanding of colonial political culture. It makes clear the departure later achieved by the revolutionary generation in accepting the notion of majority rule in such situations as the constitutional ratifying conventions of the 1780s. It also enables us to understand more clearly the resistance after the Revolution to the advent of new-style democracy, where the vote did not mean consensus but rather strife and contention. Nor, by that time, was the vote conceived as a device for achieving unity; rather it had become a device for allowing a choice between conflicting alternatives. By the nineteenth century, harmony had to be achieved by means other than democracy.

*F*or at least a decade now, a debate has passed through these pages on the extent of democracy in the old New England town. It began, of course, with Robert E. Brown, and it did not begin badly: Brown's work was a breath of fresh air in a stale discussion, substituting statistics for cynicism and adding figures to filiopietism. But what was begun decently has degenerated since, and findings that should have provoked larger questions have only produced quibbles and counterquibbles over methodology and quantification. The discussion has not been entirely futile —few would now maintain the old claim that the franchise was very closely confined in provincial Massachusetts—but neither has its apparent potential been realized. We are, ultimately, as far from agreement as we ever were about whether eighteenth-century Massachusetts was democratic. Somehow, the discussion has stalled at the starting point; a promising avenue of inquiry has not developed beyond its initial promise.

Perhaps a part of that failure was implicit in Brown's initial formulation of the problem; but one man cannot do everything, and Brown did advance our consideration of the New England town as far as any one man ever has. If he did not answer, or even ask, all the questions which might have been raised, other students could have done so. Brown's work made that possible. But since *Middle-Class Democracy and the Revolution in Massachusetts* (Ithaca, 1955) no comparable advances have been made. Indeed, the discussion seems to have stopped conceptually where Brown stopped, and one is forced to wonder not merely whether the right questions are being asked but whether any significant questions at all are being asked, other than those of how better to compute voting percentages. Certainly the terms of the debate have been, and are, inadequate to its resolution. Most obviously, figures on the franchise simply cannot serve to establish democracy. In our own time we have seen too many travesties on universal suffrage in too many non-democratic regimes to continue to take seriously in and of itself such an abstract calculus. Yet on both sides the discussion of New England town-meeting democracy has often assumed that the franchise is a satisfactory index of democracy, and the recourse to the seeming solidity of the voting statistics has depended, if only implicitly, upon that dubious premise.

Even those few critics who have challenged the contention that the issue of eighteenth-century democracy could be settled by counting heads have generally acquiesced in the far more fundamental assumption that in one way or another the issue of the eighteenth century was what the Browns have declared it to be: "democracy or aristocracy?" But democracy and aristocracy are probably false alternatives in any case for provincial Massachusetts; and in this case they are surely so, because they have been made initial tools of inquiry instead of end terms.

Of course, the Browns have hardly been alone in their strategy of frontal assault. On the contrary, it is indicative of how thoroughly their work established the contours of subsequent study that others have also rushed right into the issue of democracy without even a pause to ponder whether that issue was quite so readily accessible. Yet it would be admitted on most sides that democracy was hardly a value of such supreme salience to the men of provincial Massachusetts that it governed their conscious motives and aspirations; nor, after all, did it provide the framework for social structure in the towns of the province. In application to such a society, then, a concept such as democracy must always be recognized for just that: a concept of our own devising. It is not a datum that can be directly apprehended in all its immediacy; it is an abstraction—a rather elevated abstraction —which represents a covering judgment of the general tenor or tendency of social relations and institutions. As such, it can carry its own assurance of validity only if it proceeds out of, rather than precedes, analysis of the society to which it is applied. To rip it out of its social context is to risk exactly the disembodied discussion of democracy we have witnessed over the past decade.

If we would study democracy in provincial Massachusetts, we cannot plunge headlong into that issue without sacrificing the context which conferred meaning on whatever degree of democracy did exist. Since democracy was incidental to the prime purposes of provincial society, we must first confront that society. Democracy, to the extent that it existed, was no isolated element in the organization of the political community, and problems of political participation and inclusion cannot be considered apart from the entire question of the nature of the provincial community. Even if most men in eighteenth-century Massachusetts could vote, that is only the beginning, not the end, of inquiry. What, then, was the *function* of a widely extended suffrage, and what was the function of voting itself in the conduct of the community? Who specifically was admitted to the franchise, and who was denied that privilege, and on what grounds? For ultimately, if we are to understand the towns that made the Revolution in Massachusetts, we must find out not only *whether* most men could vote but also *why*.

It is particularly imperative that we place provincial democracy in its social context because nothing else can plausibly account for its development. The founders of the settlement at Massachusetts Bay came with neither an inclusive ethos nor any larger notions of middle-class democracy. In 1630 a band of true believers had entered upon the wilderness, possessed of a conviction of absolute and invincible righteousness. Their leaders, in that first generation, proudly proclaimed that they "abhorred democracy," and, as Perry Miller maintained, "theirs was not an idle boast."[1] The spirit of the founders was set firmly against inclusion, with the very meaning of the migration dependent for many on an extension of the sphere of ecclesiastical exclusivity. The right of every church to keep out the unworthy was precisely the point of the Congregationalists' difference with the established church, and it was a right which could not be realized in England.[2] Yet, without any English prodding and within about a decade of the first settlements, the original ideals of exclusion had begun to break down at the local level. Until 1692 the colonial suffrage extended only to freemen, but by that time non-freemen had been voting in town affairs for almost half a century.[3] The ability of the settlers to sustain suffrage restrictions at the colonial level so long after they were abandoned in the towns not only indicates the incomplete coincidence of intellectual currents and local conduct in early New England but also contradicts any contention that the pressures for democratic participation derived from Puritan theology or thought. The New England Puritans were pressed to the popularization of political authority only in grudging adjustment to the exigencies of their situation.

Their situation, quite simply, was one that left them stripped of any *other* sanctions than those of the group. The sea passage had cut the new settlement off from the full force of traditional authority, so that even the maintenance of law and order had to be managed in the absence of any customarily accepted agencies for its establishment or enforcement. Furthermore, as the seventeenth century waned and settlement dispersed, the preservation of public order devolved increasingly upon the local community. What was reluctantly admitted in the seventeenth century was openly

---

[1] Perry Miller, *Orthodoxy in Massachusetts* (Boston, 1959), 37.

[2] Edmund S. Morgan, *Visible Saints* (New York, 1963), esp. 10–12, 21.

[3] The first break occurred in 1641 when the Body of Liberties made all men free to attend town meetings; an enactment of 1647 allowed them to vote. On the other hand, some restrictions on non-freemen did remain. See Joel Parker, "The Origin, Organization, and Influence of the Towns of New England," Massachusetts Historical Society, *Proceedings*, IX (Boston, 1866), 46.

acknowledged in the eighteenth, after the arrival of the new charter: the public peace could not be entrusted to Boston, but would have to be separately secured in each town in the province. And though this devolution of effective authority to the local level resolved other difficulties, it only aggravated the problem of order, because the towns even more than the central government were without institutions and authorities sanctioned by tradition. Moreover, the towns had relatively limited instruments of enforcement, and they were demonstrably loath to use the coercive power they did possess.[4]

Nonetheless, order was obtained in the eighteenth-century town, and it was obtained by concord far more than by compulsion. Consensus governed the communities of provincial Massachusetts, and harmony and homogeneity were the regular—and required—realities of local life. Effective action necessitated a public opinion approaching if not attaining unanimity, and public policy was accordingly bent toward securing such unanimity. The result was, to be sure, a kind of government by common consent, but government by consent in eighteenth-century Massachusetts did not imply democracy in any more modern sense because it required far more than mere majoritarianism. Such majoritarianism implied a minority, and the towns could no more condone a competing minority by their norms and values than they could have constrained it by their police power. Neither conflict, dissent, nor any other structured pluralism ever obtained legitimacy in the towns of the Bay before the Revolution.[5]

Thus, authority found another form in provincial Massachusetts. Its instrument was the town meeting, which was no mere forum but the essential element in the delicate equipoise of peace and propriety which governed the New England town. In the absence of any satisfactory means of traditional or institutional coercion, the recalcitrant could not be compelled to adhere to the common course of action. Therefore, the common course of action had to be so shaped as to leave none recalcitrant—that was the vital function of the New England town meeting. To oversimplify perhaps, the town meeting solved the problem of enforcement by evading it. The meeting gave

[4] Difficulties of enforcement are not easy to demonstrate in a few sentences, but they can be suggested, perhaps, by the ease of mob mobilization and by the extensive evasion of the office of constable, especially by the middling and upper classes of the community, which was both symptomatic of and contributory to the structural weakness of the constabulary. There was, in other words, a formal legal system in the province without an autonomous instrument for its own enforcement. A more elaborate development of the general theme is in Michael Zuckerman, The Massachusetts Town in the Eighteenth Century (unpubl. Ph.D. diss., Harvard University, 1967), esp. 118–126.

[5] The import of the argument sketched here and developed below must be understood. No full-scale defense of the consensus hypothesis will be attempted here, nor would one be possible in such a piece as this: an examination of such a narrow matter as electoral eligibility can hardly *prove* a set of propositions about so substantial a subject as the social organization of the New England town. A full-scale defense of the hypothesis assumed here is found in Zuckerman, Massachusetts Town in the Eighteenth Century. What is in fact claimed here is, first, that this hypothesis in particular does illuminate many aspects of political "democracy" in the Massachusetts town of the eighteenth century and, second, that whatever failings may be found in this particular hypothesis, *some* kind of hypothesis is surely necessary to ground the discussion of democracy in the colony and establish it in a social context.

institutional expression to the imperatives of peace. In the meetings consensus was reached, and individual consent and group opinion were placed in the service of social conformity. There the men of the province established their agreements on policies and places, and there they legitimized those agreements so that subsequent deviation from those accords became socially illegitimate and personally immoral as well, meaning as it did the violation of a covenant or the breaking of a promise. In the town meetings men talked of politics, bult ultimately they sought to establish moral community.

In the context of such a community, the significance of an extended franchise becomes quite clear: governance by concord and concurrence required inclusiveness. In communities in which effective enforcement depended on the moral binding of decisions upon the men who made them, it was essential that most men be parties to such decisions. Not the principled notions of the New Englanders but the stern necessities of enforcement sustained town-meeting democracy in Massachusetts. The politics of consensus made a degree of democracy functional, even made it a functional imperative. Men were allowed to vote not out of any overweening attachment to democratic principles *per se* but simply because a wide canvass was convenient, if not indeed critical, in consolidating a consensus in the community.

Under this incentive to inclusion, most towns did set their suffrage almost as liberally as Brown claimed. To seek the social context of the suffrage, then, necessitates no major quarrel with Brown's figures on franchise democracy; what it may provide is an explanation for them. It also offers the possibility of accounting for more than just the figures. As soon as we see that the high degree of participation permitted in the politics of the provincial town was not an isolated phenomenon but rather an integral aspect of the conduct of the community, we are in a position to go beyond a disembodied study of electoral eligibility and a simple celebration of middle-class democracy in Massachusetts. We are in a position to convert polemics into problems, and to press for answers.

In many communities, for example, a substantial and sometimes an overwhelming proportion of the people were *not* technically entitled to vote. Brown did not discuss some of these places, and the ones he did discuss were added to his evidence only with the special explanation that sometimes even the ineligible were admitted to the ballot box. But in the context of community such lapses would not necessarily invalidate his larger conclusions, nor would such *ad hoc* expedients be required; for the same imperatives impinged on towns where few were legally qualified as on the others, and the same results of wide political participation obtained because of the same sense that inclusiveness promoted peace while more rigorous methods threatened it. The town of Douglas, with only five qualified voters in its first years, flatly refused to be bound by a determination confined to those five, declaring its conviction "that the intent of no law can bind them to such ill consequences." Mendon, in its "infant state" in 1742, voted "to permit a considerable number of persons not qualified by law to vote . . . being induced thereto by an apprehension that it would be a means of preserving peace and unity amongst ourselves." Princeton, incorporated in

1760 with forty-three settlers but only fourteen eligible to vote according to provincial regulations, established a formal "agreement among themselves to overlook" those regulations, and the General Court upheld that agreement. "The poor freeholders" in the early days of Upton were also "allowed liberty to vote in town meeting," and it had produced "an encouraging harmony" in local affairs until 1746, when a few of the qualified voters, momentarily possessed of a majority of the ten in town, sought to upset the customary arrangements and limit the franchise as the law required. The rest of the town at once protested that "such a strenuous method of proceeding would endanger the peace of the town" and begged the General Court "to prevent the dismal damages that may follow" therefrom. The Court did exactly as it was asked, and at the new meeting the town reverted to its old form: "everyone was admitted to vote, qualified or not."[6]

The principle which governed such universalism was not deliberate democracy; it was merely a recognition that the community could not be governed solely by the qualified voters if they were too few in number. Such a situation was most likely to occur in new communities, but it was not limited to them. Middleton had been established for almost a quarter of a century when it was conceded that in the local elections of 1752 "there was double the number of votes to the lawful voters." In a variety of towns and at other times, requirements for the franchise were also ignored and admission of the unqualified acknowledged explicitly.[7] Thomas Hutchinson's wry lament that "anything with the appearance of a man" was allowed the vote may have been excessive, but it was not wholly fabricated.[8] And even towns whose political procedures were more regular resorted to universalism in cases of conflict or of major issues. Fitchburg, for instance, voted in 1767 that "every freholder be a votter in Chusing of a minestr," while twenty years earlier, in a bitterly contested election in Haverhill, "there was not any list of valuation read nor any list of non-voters nor any weighting of what name or nature whatsoever by which the selectmen did pretend to show who was qualified to vote in town affairs."[9]

The question of inclusiveness itself sometimes came before a town, not always without challenge but generally with a democratic outcome. Dudley, more than a decade after the incorporation of the town, voted "that all the freeholder of sd town should be voters by a graet majorytie and all agreed to it." In Needham in 1750 it was also "put to vote whether it be the mind of the town to allow all freeholders in town to vote for a moderator," and there too the vote carried in the affirmative. And that verdict for inclusion was not even as revealing as the method by which that verdict was reached, for in voting *whether* to include all in the election, Needham *did* include

[6] Massachusetts Archives, CXV, 168, 169, 316–317, 319–320, 469–471, 864–865; CXVII, 647–649, 652; CXVIII, 734–735a, 762, State House, Boston; Francis E. Blake, *History of the Town of Princeton* (Princeton, Mass., 1915), I, 76–77.

[7] Mass. Archives, VIII, 279, for others see *ibid.*, 278; XLIX, 398–400; L, 20–22, 25–26, 85–88, 89–90; CXIII, 270; CXV, 36–37, 291; CXVI, 373–374; CXVII, 291–293, 302–305; CLXXXI, 23–24a.

[8] Brown, *Middle-Class Democracy*, 60.

[9] Walter A. Davis, comp., *The Old Records of the Town of Fitchburg Massachusetts 1764–1789* (Fitchburg, Mass., 1898), 39; Mass. Archives, VIII, 273.

all in the procedural issue. Every man did vote on the question of whether every man was to be allowed to vote.[10]

Of course, absolute inclusiveness never prevailed in provincial Massachusetts—women could not vote at all, and neither could anyone under 21—and property and residence qualifications, introduced in 1692, were probably adhered to as often as they were ignored, so that even the participation of adult males was something less than universal. It was an important part of Brown's achievement to show that, in general, it was not *very much* less than universal, but, by the nature of his research strategy, he could go no further than that. If we are to penetrate to particulars—if we are to ask who was excluded, and why, and why the suffrage standards were what they were—we must consider not only numbers but also the conditions of community.

The men who were not allowed legitimately to vote with their fellow townsmen were commonly tenants or the sons of voters; as Brown discovered, it was these two groups against which the property requirement primarily operated. But where the controversialists seek to *excuse* these exclusions, or to magnify them, a broader perspective allows one to *explain* them, for against these two groups sanctions were available that were far more effective than those of the generalized community. Stringent property qualifications were clearly self-defeating in a society where consensus was the engine of enforcement, but overly generous qualifications were equally unnecessary. Where some men, such as tenants and dependent sons, could be privately coerced, liberality on their behalf, from the standpoint of social control, would have meant the commission of a sin of superfluity.

Similarly, almost nothing but disadvantage could have accrued from a loose residence requirement enabling men not truly members of the community to participate in its decision-making process, since voting qualifications in provincial Massachusetts were connected to the concept of community, not the concept of democracy. The extensions and contractions of the franchise were significant to the townsmen of the eighteenth century primarily as a means of consolidating communal consensus. All those whose acquiescence in public action was necessary were included, and all those whose concurrence could be compelled otherwise or dispensed with were excluded, often very emphatically. Sixty-six citizens of Watertown, for example, petitioned against the allowance of a single unqualified voter in a 1757 election because he was "well known to belong to the town of Lincoln." In many towns such as Sudbury the town clerk "very carefully warned those that were not legally qualified not to vote and prayed the selectmen to be very careful and watchful that nobody voted that was not legally qualified."[11] Even in disputes over specific qualifications, both sides often agreed on the principle of exclusion of the unqualified; contention occurred only over the application of that principle.[12]

Consciousness of voting qualifications colored the conduct of other town

[10] *Town Records of Dudley, Massachusetts, 1732–1754,* I (Pawtucket, R.I., 1893), 106; Mass. Archives, CXV, 616–617.

[11] Mass. Archives, CXVII, 302–305; XLIX, 361–362; see also *ibid.,* CXVII, 300, 306–307, 647–649; Jeremiah L. Hanaford, *History of Princeton* (Worcester, Mass., 1852), 23.

[12] See for example, Mass. Archives, CXV, 412–413, 463.

affairs as well as elections, as indeed was natural since the meaning of the franchise went so far beyond mere electoral democracy. Protests by men recently arrived in a town could be discredited, as they were in Haverhill in 1748, without any reference to the justice of the protest itself, simply by stating that "many of their petitioners are not qualified to vote in town affairs as may be seen by the selectmen's list of voters, and some of them were never known to reside in town or did we ever hear of them before we saw their petition." Similarly, in the creation of new communities qualification for the franchise could be crucial. Inhabitants of Bridgewater resisted their own inclusion in a precinct proposed by thirty-seven men dwelling in their vicinity by pointing out that "there is not above eleven or twelve that are qualified to vote in town meetings as the law directs." Many towns in their corporate capacity made much the same plea when confronted with an appeal for separation from the community. As Worcester once noted in such a case, more than half the petitioners were "not voters and one is a single Indian."[13]

Such consciousness of qualifications sometimes appeared to be nothing more than an insistence on a "stake in society" in order to participate in the society's deliberations and decisions, but the stake-in-society concept, despite its popularity in the West and its convergence with certain conditions of public life in the province, was not precisely the notion which controlled those restrictions of the franchise which did persist after 1692. It was not out of any intrinsic attachment to that concept, but simply out of a fear that those without property were overly amenable to bribery or other such suasion, that the men of Massachusetts clung to their voting qualifications. As the Essex Result was to state the principle in 1778, "all the members of the state are qualified to make the election, unless they have not sufficient discretion, or are so situated as to have no wills of their own."[14] Participation in community decisions was the prerogative of independent men, of *all* a town's independent men, but, ideally, *only* of those. Indeed, it was precisely because of their independence that they had to be accorded a vote, since only by their participation did they bind themselves to concur in the community's chosen course of action. The town meeting was an instrument for enforcement, not—at least not intentionally—a school for democracy.

This logic of competence governed the exclusion of women and children and also accounted for the antipathy to voting by tenants. The basis of the prohibitions which were insisted upon was never so much an objection to poverty *per se*—the stake-in-society argument—as to the tenant's concomitant status of dependence, the pervasive assumption of which emerged clearly in a contested election in Haverhill in 1748. There the petitioners charged that a man had been "refused as a voter under pretense that he was a tenant and so not qualified, when the full reason was that he was a tenant to one of their [the selectmen's] opposers and so at all hazards to be sup-

[13] *Ibid.*, 305–308, 144; "Early Records of the Town of Worcester," Worcester Society of Antiquity, *Collections* (Worcester, 1881–1882), II, no. 8, 42–43. See also, Mass. Archives, CXV, 392.

[14] [Theophilus Parsons], *Result of the Convention of Delegates Holden at Ipswich* . . . (Newburyport, 1778), 28–29.

pressed," while another man, a tenant to one of the selectmen themselves, had been received as a voter though "rated at much less in the last year's taxes than he whom they refused." The protest was thus directed primarily against the abuses of the selectmen: that tenants would do as their landlords desired was simply taken for granted.[15] And naturally the same sort of assumption controlled the exclusion of sons still living with their parents. The voting age of twenty-one was the most rudimentary expression of this requirement of a will of one's own, but the legal age was not very firm at the edges. Like other laws of the province, it could not stand when it came up against local desires, and the age qualifications were often abrogated when unusual dependence or independence was demonstrable, as in the case of the eighteen-year-old who voted in a Sheffield election of 1751 because his father had died and he had become head of his family. As the town's elected representative could declare on that occasion, quite ignoring the legal age requirement, the lad "had a good right to vote, for his estate rested in him and that he was a town-born child and so was an inhabitant."[16]

Of course, the townsmen of the eighteenth century placed no premium on independence as such. Massachusetts townsmen were expected to be independent but not too independent; ultimately, they were supposed on their own to arrive at the same actions and commitments as their neighbors. Any *genuine* independence, excessive *or* insufficient, was denigrated if not altogether denied a place in the community. Thus, when a number of inhabitants of a gore of land near Charlton faced the threat of incorporation with the town, they submitted "one word of information" about the townsmen who had asked for that incorporation. The note said only:

Baptist signers	— 7
Churchmen	— 3
Tenants	— 4
Neither tenants nor freeholders but intruders upon other men's property	—15

The whole of the petitioners in Charlton consisting of 35 in number.

In other words, tenants were tainted, but so too were all others who were their own men, such as squatters and those who dared to differ in religion. In denigrating them, the inhabitants of the gore drew no distinctions: tenant and Baptist were equally offensive because equally outside of orthodoxy, beyond the confines of consensus.[17]

Ultimately almost *any* taint on membership in the homogeneous community was a potential basis for derogation. Some inhabitants of Rutland once even attempted to deny the validity of a town decision merely because many of its supporters were "such as were and are dissenters from the public worship of God in the old meeting-house." And though Rutland's religious orthodoxy was a bit exquisite even for eighteenth-century New England,

[15] Mass. Archives, CXV, 330–334, 412–413; CXVI, 276–277; CXVII, 84–86, 306–307; "Early Records of Worcester," Worc. Soc. Ant., *Coll.*, II, no. 6, 63.

[16] Mass. Archives, VIII, 278; for a comparable case in the opposite direction see *ibid.*, CXVI, 668–669. Another basis for exclusion was insanity. For a revealing contretemps see *ibid.*, L, 85–88; CXVII, 295–297, 302–305.

[17] *Ibid.*, CXVII, 86, and see 84–85.

it was so only in degree. For example, when Sutton opposed the erection of a new district out of parts of itself and several other towns in 1772, the town actually deducted the Anabaptists from the number of signatories to the application—Baptists simply did not count as full citizens. Worcester did the same thing and indeed went even further. Several of the signers of the petition for separation were not heads of families but mere "single persons, some of them transient ones," and so, said the town, were not to be "accounted as part of the number of families the petitioners say are within the limits of the proposed district." Whereas excessively reliable bonds confined the tenant, no reliable bonds at all attached a single man to the community, and either alternative evoked suspicion.[18]

Ultimately, however, the insistence on orthodoxy did not directly exclude any excessive number, and neither did the property and residence requirements disqualify any great proportion of the province's adult males. In the perspective of the English villages from which the New Englanders came, these very dimensions of disqualification may be better seen, in fact, as defining a broader qualification than had previously prevailed in English practice. Far more fundamentally, the criteria of exclusion were measures of the inclusiveness of the communities of early Massachusetts.

The most fundamental shift that had occurred was the one from property to residence as the irreducible basis of town citizenship. In England, several classes of property-holders were "technically termed inhabitants even though they dwelt in another town"; property defined political citizenship, and only those who held the requisite property in the community directed its affairs. In provincial Massachusetts such stake-in-society notions never prevailed for reasons that had little to do with any abstract attachment to democracy or antipathy to absentee ownership. They never prevailed because the point of the town meeting was not so much the raising of a revenue as it was political government, especially the maintenance of law and order. In Massachusetts it was necessary to act only on the individuals living in each town, and it was imperative to act upon all of them. Of course, taxation as well as residence provided the basis for the ballot in Massachusetts, but that was of a piece with the residence requirement. As early as 1638 "every inhabitant of a town was declared liable for his proportion of the town's charges," in sharp contrast to the towns of England where only a few were so taxed.[19]

The democracy of the Massachusetts towns was, then, a democracy despite itself, a democracy without democrats. But it was still, so far as anything yet said is concerned, a democracy, at least in the simple sense of a widely diffused franchise. Such democracy is admitted—indeed, required—in the analysis advanced above; the objection urged against the defenders of

---

[18] *Ibid.*, CXV, 741–742; CXVIII, 613–616, 619; see also *ibid.*, CXVI, 276–277. And others found more reasons to discredit any who stood outside communal orthodoxy. See *ibid.*, CXV, 393–396, 412–413, 596.

[19] Edward Channing, "Town and County Government in the English Colonies of North America," *Johns Hopkins University Studies in Historical and Political Science,* 2d Ser., II, no. 10 (1884), 12, 32.

that democracy is not that they are wrong but that they are right for the wrong reasons, or for no reasons at all. When they examine electoral eligibility apart from its social setting and when they place franchise democracy at the center of provincial social organization instead of in the peripheral position it actually occupied, they do not condemn their findings to invalidity, only to sterility. They may be correct about the degree of diffusion of the vote, but they can go no further. Within their original terms, they cannot systematically study the purposes of participation, the relative importance of inclusiveness when it confronted competing values, the limits of eligibility and the reasons for them, or, more broadly, the particular texture of the electorate as against abstract statistics.

But if the analysis urged thus far has basically buttressed Brown's position by extending and explaining his statistics, that analysis also has another side. For when we see franchise democracy as a mere incident in the central quest for concord and concurrence among neighbors, we must also observe that the same concern for consensus which promoted wide participation also imposed very significant limitations on the democracy of the provincial community, limitations sufficiently serious to suggest that the democratic appellation itself may be anachronistic when applied to such a society.

For one thing, the ideal of "townsmen together"[20] implied the power of each town to control its own affairs, and that control not only extended to but also depended upon communal control of its membership. From the founding of the first towns communities retained the right to accept only those whom they wished, and that right persisted without challenge to the time of the Revolution. "Such whose dispositions do not suit us, whose society will be hurtful to us," were simply refused admission as enemies of harmony and homogeneity. Dedham's first covenant, "to keepe of from us all such, as ar contrarye minded. And receave onely such unto us as be such as may be probably of one harte," was typical. For inhabitancy was a matter of public rather than private concern, and among the original settlers it scarcely had to be argued that "if the place of our cohabitation be our own, then no man hath right to come in to us without our consent."[21] Consent meant the formal vote of the town or its selectmen, and none were admitted without one or the other. Not even inhabitants themselves could entertain outsiders—"strangers," they were called—without the permission of the town, and any who violated the rule were subject to penalties.[22] And of course the original thrust of congregational Puritanism to lodge disciplinary

[20] The phrase is from Conrad M. Arensberg, "American Communities," *American Anthropologist*, LVII (1955), 1150. For affirmations of that ideal as a consummatory value see Mass. Archives, CXIII, 616–617; CIV, 645; CXV, 282–283; CXVI, 527–528; CXVII, 563–565; CLXXXI, 122b–122d.

[21] Sumner C. Powell, *Puritan Village* (Middletown, Conn., 1963), xviii; George L. Haskins, *Law and Authority in Early Massachusetts* (New York, 1960), 70; Josiah Benton, *Warning Out in New England* (Boston, 1911), 8. The early towns also forbade inhabitants to "sell or let their land or houses to strangers without the consent of the town"; see *ibid.*, 18, 19, 23, 87, and William Weeden, *Economic and Social History of New England, 1620–1789* (Boston, 1891), 57.

[22] Benton, *Warning Out*, 18, 33. And the fines were indeed established and enforced in the towns. See Myron Allen, *The History of Wenham* (Boston, 1860), 26, and Weeden, *Economic and Social History*, 79–80.

powers with the individual churches rather than with bishops also aimed at more local control of the membership of the local community.[23]

Most of these practices continued unabated into the eighteenth century. Swansea's "foundation settlement" of 1677 provided that "if any person denied any particular in the said agreement they should not be admitted an inhabitant in said town," and half a century later seventy-eight townsmen reaffirmed their commitment to the ancestral covenant. Cotton Mather's manual of 1726, *Ratio Disciplinae Fratum Nov-Anglorum* (Boston, 1726), described a process of "mutual Conferences" by which men came to "a good understanding" which might be subscribed to by any applicant. And even in the crisis of the dissolution of a church, as at Bellingham in 1747, the congregation could not simply disperse to the nearest convenient towns. Each of the congregants, for all that he had already met the tests of church membership and partaken of communion, had to be accepted anew into the nearby churches and approved by their towns, and in 1754 Sunderland claimed that this right of prior approval was "always customary."[24]

Another customary instrument for the stringent control of access to the town which was also sustained throughout the provincial era was the practice of "warning out." Under this aegis, anyone who did secure entry to the town and was then deemed undesirable could be warned and, if necessary, lawfully ejected from the community. Such a policy was, in some part, a device to escape undue expenses in the support of paupers, but it was also, and more importantly, the product of the powerful communitarian assumptions of the early settlers, and those assumptions did not decline in the eighteenth century. William Weeden found the invocation of warning procedures so common that "the actual occurrences hardly need particular mention," and he concluded that "the old restrictions on the admission of freemen to the municipality, and on the sale of land to outsiders, do not appear to have been relaxed generally" as late as the era immediately preceding the imperial crisis. Town records such as Worcester's were studded with such warnings, from the time of the town's founding to the time of the Revolution itself. In other towns, too, penalties were still imposed for violation of the rules of inhabitancy.[25]

The result was that fundamental differences in values were rarely admitted within a town, while differences of race, nationality, or culture scarcely appeared east of the Hudson River before the Revolution. Massachusetts was more nearly restricted to white Anglo-Saxon Protestants than any other province in English America, with the possible exception of its New England neighbors, Connecticut and New Hampshire. Less than 1 per

---

[23] Morgan, *Visible Saints*, 10–12, 21.

[24] Mass. Archives, CXIII, 613–615; CXV, 268, 272, 276; XLIX, 380–383; Mather, *Ratio Disciplinae*, Pt. iii, 2. See also Mass. Archives, CXVI, 392–393; CXVII, 15–16. In one case, that of Medway, *ibid.*, XLIX, 380–383, such consideration was not accorded.

[25] Weeden, *Economic and Social History*, 519, 673; "Early Records of Worcester," Worc. Soc. Ant., *Coll.*, II, no. 6, 22–23, 102, 122–123; II, no. 8, 19, 27, 57–58, 128; IV, 28, 47, 67, 85, 99, 137, 147, 148, 202, 223. For penalties in other towns, see *Town of Weston: Records of the First Precinct, 1746–1754 and of the Town, 1754–1803* (Boston, 1893), 61, 101, 108, 115, 126; Herman Mann, *Historical Annals of Dedham, from its Settlement in 1635 to 1847* (Dedham, Mass., 1847), 23, 25; Allen, *History of Wenham*, 26.

cent of the quarter of a million Germans who came to the English colonies between 1690 and 1770 came to New England, and the proportion of Irish, Scotch, and Scotch-Irish was little larger. There was no welcome whatsoever for French Catholics and very little encouragement, according to Governor Bellomont, even for the Huguenots.[26] Negroes never attained significant numbers at the Bay—by 1780 they accounted for only 2 per cent of the population of the province and a bare 1 per cent of all the Negroes in the Confederation—and the Indians, who once were significant, were on their way to extinction well before the Revolution broke out.[27] Committed to a conception of the social order that precluded pluralism, the townsmen of Massachusetts never made a place for those who were not of their own kind. The community they desired was an enclave of common believers, and to the best of their ability they secured such a society, rooted not only in ethnic and cultural homogeneity but also in common moral and economic ideas and practices. Thus, the character of the community became a critical—and non-democratic—condition of provincial democracy; for a wide franchise could be ventured only after a society that sought harmony had been made safe for such democracy. In that society it was possible to let men vote precisely because so many men were not allowed entry in the first place.

Thus we can maintain the appearance of democracy only so long as we dwell on elections and elections alone, instead of the entire electoral process. As soon as we depart from that focus, the town meetings of Massachusetts fall short of any decent democratic standard. Wide participation did obtain, but it was premised on stringently controlled access to eligibility, so that open elections presupposed anterior constriction of the electorate. Similarly, most men could vote, but their voting was not designed to contribute to a decision among meaningful alternatives. The town meeting had one prime purpose, and it was not the provision of a neutral battleground for the clash of contending parties or interest groups. In fact, nothing could have been more remote from the minds of men who repeatedly affirmed, to the very end of the provincial period, that "harmony and unanimity" were what "they most heartily wish to enjoy in all their public concerns." Conflict occurred only rarely in these communities, where "prudent and amicable composition and agreement" were urged as preventives for "great and sharp disputes and contentions." When it did appear it was seen as an unnatural and undesirable deviation from the norm. Protests and contested elections almost invariably appealed to unity and concord as the values which had been violated; and in the absence of any socially sanctioned role for dissent, contention was generally surreptitious and scarcely ever sustained for long. The town meeting accordingly aimed at unanimity. Its function was the

[26] On the Germans and Scotch-Irish see Clarence Ver Steeg, *The Formative Years, 1607–1763* (New York, 1964), 167–168. On the Huguenots see Charles W. Baird, *History of the Huguenot Emigration to America* (New York, 1885), II, 251–253; G. Elmore Reaman, *The Trail of the Huguenots* . . . (London, 1964), 129.

[27] On the Negro, Marvin Harris, *Patterns of Race in the Americas* (New York, 1964), 84. For some of the story of the extinction of the last Indian town in the province see Mass. Archives, CXVII, 690–691, 733–735.

arrangement of agreement or, more often, the endorsement of agreements already arranged, and it existed for accommodation, not disputation.[28]

Yet democracy devoid of legitimate difference, dissent, and conflict is something less than democracy; and men who are finally to vote only as their neighbors vote have something less than the full range of democratic options. Government by mutual consent may have been a step in the direction of a deeper-going democracy, but it should not be confused with the real article. Democratic consent is predicated upon legitimate choice, while the town meetings of Massachusetts in the provincial era, called as they were to reach and register accords, were still in transition from assent to such consent. The evidence for such a conclusion exists in an abundance of votes from all over the province on all manner of matters "by the free and united consent of the whole" or "by a full and Unanimous Vote that they are Easie and satisfied With What they have Done."[29] Most men may have been eligible to vote, but their voting did not settle differences unless most men voted together. In fact, differences had no defined place in the society that voting could have settled, for that was not in the nature of town politics. Unanimity was expected ethically as well as empirically. Indeed, it was demanded as a matter of social decency, so that even the occasional cases of conflict were shaped by the canons of concord and consensus, with towns pleading for the preservation of "peace and unanimity" as "the only occasion of our petitioning."[30]

This demand for unanimity found its ultimate expression in rather frequent denials of one of the most elementary axioms of democratic theory, the principle of majority rule. A mere majority often commanded scant authority at the local level and scarcely even certified decisions as legitimate. In communities which provided no regular place for minorities a simple majority was not necessarily sufficient to dictate social policy, and many men such as the petitioners from the old part of Berwick were prepared to say so quite explicitly. Since its settlement some eighty or ninety years earlier, that town had grown until by 1748 the inhabitants of the new parts easily outnumbered the "ancient settlers" and wished to establish a new meetinghouse in a place which the inhabitants of the older parts conceived injurious to their interest. Those who lived in the newer parts of town had the votes, but the "ancient settlers" were icily unimpressed nonetheless. Injury could not be justified "merely because a major vote of the town is or may be obtained to do it," the petitioners protested. They would suffer "great hurt and grievance," and "for no other reason that this: a major vote to do it, which is all the reason they have for the same." Equity, on the other hand, required a "just regard" for the old part of town and its inhabitants. They "ought" to retain their privileges despite their loss of numerical preponderance. And that principle was no mere moral fabrication of a

---

[28] Mass. Archives, CXVIII, 707–712, 715–717. The theme is omnipresent in the records of the towns and of such conflicts as did occur. See Zuckerman, Massachusetts Town in the Eighteenth Century, especially chap. 3.

[29] Mass. Archives, CXVIII, 388–390; *Weston Records*, 11. See also Mass. Archives, CXVI, 446–447; CXVIII, 715–717; "Records of Worcester," Worc. Soc. Ant., *Coll.*, II, no. 8, 43, 75; IV, 18, 173, 264–266.

[30] Mass. Archives, L, 30–31; CXV, 479–480; CXVI, 709–710.

desperate minority. Six years earlier the Massachusetts General Court had endorsed exactly the same position in a similar challenge to the prerogatives of numerical power by the "ancient part" of another town, and in the Berwick controversy the town majority itself tacitly conceded the principle upon which the old quarter depended. Accusing the old quarter of "gross mis-representation," the rest of the town now maintained that there had been a disingenuous confusion of geography and population. There could be no question as to the physical location of the old town, but, as to its inhabitants, "the greatest part of the ancient settlers and maintainers of the ministry do live to the northward of the old meetinghouse and have always kept the same in times of difficulty and danger." The newer townsmen, then, did not deny that ancient settlers were entitled to special consideration; they simply denied that the inhabitants of the old quarter were in fact the ancient settlers.[31]

Antiquity restricted majoritarianism elsewhere as well in demands of old settlers and in determinations of the General Court. In Lancaster as in Berwick, for example, a "standing part" could cite efforts to disrupt the old order which had been rejected by the Court as unreasonable, "and now though they have obtained a vote from the town the case still remains equally unreasonable." In other towns, too, a majority changed nothing.[32] Consensus comprehended justice and history as well as the counting of a vote. In such a society a case could not be considered solely in its present aspects, as the original inhabitants of Lunenburg made quite clear. "What great discouragement must it needs give to any new settler," those old ones inquired,

> to begin a settlement and go through the difficulties thereof, which are well known to such as have ever engaged in such service, if when, so soon as ever they shall through the blessing of heaven upon their diligence and industry have arrived to live in some measure peaceably and comfortably, if then, after all fatigues and hardships undergone, to be cut to pieces and deprived of charter privileges and rights, and instead of peace and good harmony, contention and confusion introduced, there will be no telling what to trust to.[33]

Nor was history the only resort for the repudiation of a majority. Other men offered other arguments, and some scarcely deigned to argue at all. In a contested election in Haverhill, for example, one side simply denied any authority at all to a majority of the moment. It was, they said, nothing but the creature of "a few designing men who have artfully drawn in the multitude and engaged them in their own cause." That, they argued, was simply "oppression." The merchants of Salem similarly refused to accept the hazards of populistic politics, though their refusal was rather more articulate. The town meeting had enacted a tax schedule more advantageous to the farmers than to themselves, and the merchants answered that they felt no force in that action, because "the major part of those who were present

---

[31] Ibid., CXV, 368–375, 377–378, 393–396.

[32] Ibid., CXIV, 613–614; CXIII, 275–276; CXVI, 736–738.

[33] Ibid., CXVII, 165–169. In this case, nonetheless, the General Court declined to accept the argument and thus afforded no special safeguard to the original settlers. For similar cases without the adverse action of the Court see ibid., CXIV, 286–288; CXV, 729–730.

were [farmers], and the vote then passed was properly their vote and not the vote of the whole body of the town." That legitimacy and obligation attached only to a vote of the whole community was simply assumed by the merchants, as they sought a subtle separation of a town ballot—sheer majoritarianism—from a "vote of the whole body of the town"—a notion akin to the general will—for which the consent of every part of the population was requisite.[34]

Disdain for direct democracy emerged even more explicitly and sweepingly in a petition from the west precinct of Bridgewater in 1738. The precinct faced the prospect of the loss of its northern part due to a town vote authorizing the northern inhabitants to seek separation as an independent town, and the precinct feared that the loss would be fatal. Accordingly, the parishioners prayed the General Court's intervention, and after briefly disputing the majority itself, the precinct allowed that, whether or not a majority in the town *had* been obtained, such a majority *could* be contrived. "We own it is easy for the two neighboring parishes joining with the petitioners to vote away our just rights and privileges and to lay heavy burdens upon us, which they would not be willing to touch with the ends of their fingers." Yet for all the formal validity of such a vote, the precinct would not have assented to it or felt it to be legitimate, "for we trust that your Excellency and Honors will not be governed by numbers but by reason and justice." Other men elsewhere urged the same argument; perhaps none caught the provincial paradox of legality without legitimacy any better than the precinct of Salem Village, soon to become the independent town of Danvers. After a recitation of the imposition it had suffered from the town of Salem for no reason but superior numbers, the village came to its indictment of the town: "we don't say but you have had a legal right to treat us so, but all judgment without mercy is tedious to the flesh."[35]

Typically in such cases, the defense against this indictment was not an invocation of majority rights but rather a denial of having employed them oppressively. Both sides, therefore, operated upon an identical assumption. One accused the other of taking advantage of its majority, the other retorted that it had done no such thing, but neither disputed the principle that majority disregard of a minority was indefensible.[36]

This principle was no mere pious protestation. In Kittery, for instance, the parent parish complained that the men who later became the third parish had "long kept us in very unhappy circumstances . . . counter-acting us in all our proceedings" until finally "we were obliged to come into an agreement with them for dividing the then-lower parish of Kittery into two separate parishes," yet it was conceded on both sides that the old inhabitants enjoyed an easy numerical supremacy. Had they been disposed to employ it, almost any amount of "counteracting" could have been contained and ultimately quashed, so far as votes in public meeting were concerned. But the parish clearly did not rely upon simple majoritarian procedures. It was more than morality that made consensus imperative; it was also the incapacity for

[34] *Ibid.*, 330–334, 596.
[35] *Ibid.*, CXIV, 244–246, 244a, 786–788; also CXVII, 463–465.
[36] *Ibid.*, CXV, 866, 872–875; CXVIII, 388–390; CLXXXI, 133–134, 139.

coercion without widespread consent. It was the same incapacity which shaped a hundred other accommodations and abnegations across the province, which enabled some "aggrieved brethern" in Rehoboth to force the resignation of a minister, which paralyzed the town of Upton in the relocation of its meetinghouse. "All are agreed that it should be removed or a new one built," a town petition explained, "but cannot agree upon the place." In the absence of agreement they could see no way to act at all on their own account; there was never any thought of constructing a coalition within the town or contending for a majority.[37]

Ultimately almost every community in the province shared Upton's determination "to unite the people." Disputes, when they arose at all, were commonly concluded by "a full and amicable agreement" in which all parties "were in peace and fully satisfied," and the conflicts that did occur evoked no efforts at resolution in a majoritarian manner. "Mutual and general advantage" was the condition of town continuance in "one entire corporate body."[38] But that corporate ethos was something distant indeed from democracy, and electoral eligibility is, therefore, an unsatisfactory index even of political participation, let alone of any more meaningful democracy. Most men may have been able to vote in the eighteenth-century town, but the town's true politics were not transacted at the ballot box so much as at the tavern and all the other places, including the meeting itself, where men met and negotiated so that the vote might be a mere ratification, rather than a decision among significant alternatives. Alternatives were antithetical to the safe conduct of the community as it was conceived at the Bay, and so to cast a vote was only to participate in the consolidation of the community, not to make a choice among competing interests or ideals.

Accordingly, the claim for middle-class democracy in provincial Massachusetts simply cannot be sustained from the figures on electoral eligibility; relevant participation resided elsewhere than in the final, formal vote. And yet, ironically, local politics may have been democratic indeed, at least in the limited terms of political participation, since a politics of consensus required consultation with most of the inhabitants in order to assure accord. In little towns of two or three hundred adult males living in close, continuing contact, men may very well have shared widely a sense of the amenability of the political process to their own actions and attitudes, and the feeling of involvement may well have been quite general. But to find out we will have to go beyond counting heads or tallying the town treasurers' lists.

[37] *Ibid.*, CXV, 872–875; CXVI, 276–277; CXVIII, 207; George H. Tilton, *A History of Rehoboth, Massachusetts* (Boston, 1918), 106–107, 102.

[38] Mass. Archives, CXV, 461–462; CXVIII, 526, 707–712; see also Samuel A. Bates, ed., *Records of the Town of Braintree, 1640 to 1793* (Randolph, Mass., 1886), 69–70.

Jack Tar in the Streets: Merchant Seamen in the Politics of Revolutionary America

Jesse Lemisch

During the past two decades, American historians have begun to examine the history of the "inarticulate." Patterning themselves after the pioneering historians of French and British society, these students of marginal and "lower "class peoples have broadened the very conception of social history, as well as deepening our understanding of the inarticulate subjects themselves. Where American social historians, especially those of a radical or Marxian bent, have long examined the unfortunate and "losing" members of society (such as the small farmers), many recent historians, particularly younger scholars associated with the so-called New Left, have turned their attention to those whose histories are even more hidden—those, such as sailors and tramps, who were marginal even within the marginal groups, who had few spokesmen such as labor leaders, and whose mark on life was rarely left in written documents. The following essay by Jesse Lemisch of Roosevelt University is one of the outstanding achievements of this kind of history.

As Lemisch makes clear, merchant seamen in the eighteenth century were deprived and endangered as much as any group of people—save perhaps the chattel slaves, to whose condition Lemisch finds some reason to compare that of seamen. Among the most vulnerable of the vulnerable classes, these seamen had real grievances against their "betters" and especially against the seafaring agents of the mother country who hounded and impressed them. In fact, Lemisch increases our understanding of the American Revolution (without making the conflict out to be a radical revolution on the model of the French or Russian revolutions) by adding impressment to the list of causes that brought the large majority of American colonists to seek independence.

In Lemisch's reckoning, the merchant seamen found few avenues of participation in society open to them. But, insists the author, they did not react irrationally to their plight. Their responses to danger and hardship were in all ways purposeful, extending from armed opposition to flight. Moreover, these seamen partook of a common seafaring culture and possessed the solidarity of a common cause. Therefore, writes Lemisch, it cannot be said that this portion of the laboring classes of colonial America was inert, nor that its activity in the cause of revolution dated from the Stamp Act of 1765. In the case of the merchant seamen at least, the entire eighteenth century was marked by a constant succession of threat and agitation.

Lemisch's footnotes reveal both the strategic and didactic intentions of this kind of social history. The density of citation is meant to make clear that the history of the inarticulate can be written by means of a thorough exploitation of sources often overlooked by historians, especially obscure court and admiralty records. The wealth of citation is furthermore meant to answer those who might be inclined to believe that the inarticulate can have no historian.

Lemisch successfully establishes the legitimacy of the history of the underclasses and the integrity of the lives of the vulnerable. The history of society, he believes, must include the history of the inarticulate as well as that of the elites. But granting that a complete history must incorporate the powerless and defeated, one must still ask if Lemisch's merchant seamen in fact come out too responsible, too unblemished, and too unified. Other historians of other oppressed peoples—such as black slaves or common

Jack Tar in the Streets: Merchant Seamen in the Politics of Revolutionary America. From *William and Mary Quarterly*, 3rd Ser., XXV (July 1968), 371–407. Copyright © 1968 by Jesse Lemisch and reprinted with his permission.

laborers—suggest the effectiveness with which the dominant classes have been able to divide and control them.

*H*ere comes Jack Tar, his bowed legs bracing him as if the very Broadway beneath his feet might begin to pitch and roll.[1] In his dress he is, in the words of a superior, "very nasty and negligent," his black stockings ragged, his long, baggy trousers tarred to make them waterproof.[2] Bred in "that very shambles of language," the merchant marine, he is foul-mouthed, his talk alien and suspect.[3] He is Jolly Jack, a bull in a china shop, always, in his words, "for a Short Life and a Merry one," and, in the concurring words of his superiors, "concerned only for the present . . . incapable of thinking of, or inattentive to, future welfare," "like froward Childeren not knowing how to judge for themselves."[4]

Clothes don't make the man, nor does language; surely we can do better

[1] His walk was sometimes described as a "waddle," *New-York Gazette; or the Weekly Post-Boy,* Sept. 3, 1759. Seamen were often called Jack Tar in England and in the colonies, for example, *ibid.,* Oct. 15, 1770. The term was used more or less interchangeably along with "seaman," "sailor," and "mariner," with the latter frequently connoting "master" (as in Panel of Jurors [n.d.], New York Supreme Court, Pleadings P-2689, Office of County Clerk, Hall of Records, New York City, where seven of ten "mariners" are identifiable as captains by comparison with such sources as *The Burghers of New Amsterdam and the Freemen of New York, 1675–1866* [New-York Historical Society, *Collections,* XVIII (New York, 1886)], *passim; N.-Y. Gaz.; Weekly Post-Boy, passim;* and the especially valuable list of privateer captains in Stuyvesant Fish, *The New York Privateers, 1756–1763* [New York, 1945], 83–90). In this article Jack Tar is a merchant seaman, a "sailor" is in the Royal Navy, and a "mariner" is the captain of a merchant vessel. If a source calls a man a "mariner" or a "sailor" I have had to have evidence that he was in fact a merchant seaman before I would count him as one. For a useful discussion of terms see I. M. V., "Note," *Mariner's Mirror,* VII (1921), 351.

[2] [George Balfour], "Memorandum," *Mariner's Mirror,* VIII (1922), 248. For the seaman's dress see *Abstracts of Wills on File in the Surrogate's Office, City of New York* (N.-Y. Hist. Soc., *Coll.,* XXV–XLI [New York, 1893–1909]), VI, iii; descriptions of dress scattered throughout Admiralty Group, Class 98, Piece 11–14, Public Record Office. Hereafter cited as Adm. 98/11–14; *N.-Y. Gaz.; Weekly Post-Boy,* Dec. 10, 1759, Oct. 14, Dec. 16, 1762, Nov. 3, 1763, Mar. 6, June 26, 1766, Oct. 1, 1767, Jan. 29, 1770, July 6, 1772; Samuel Eliot Morison, *John Paul Jones* (Boston, 1959), 72. A pair of useful illustrations appears in *Mariner's Mirror,* IX (1923), 128.

[3] J. R. Hutchinson, *The Press-Gang, Afloat and Ashore* (New York, 1913), 29. See *The Acts and Resolves . . . of the Province of Massachusetts Bay . . .* (Boston, 1869–1922), III, 318–319, for an act of Feb. 10, 1747, prescribing the stocks and whipping for seamen guilty of "profane cursing or swearing." For a landsman's version of some seamen's dialogue, see *N.-Y. Gaz.; Weekly Post-Boy,* Dec. 10, 1767.

[4] Robert E. Peabody, "The Naval Career of Captain John Manley of Marblehead," Essex Institute, *Historical Collections,* XLV (1909), 25; Ralph D. Paine, *The Ships and Sailors of Old Salem* (New York, 1909), 23; John Cremer, *Ramblin' Jack . . . ,* ed. R. Reynell Bellamy (London, 1936), 38–39; Congressman Edward Livingston, Apr. 10, 1798, United States, Congress, *Debates and Proceedings in the Congress of the United States . . .* (Washington, D. C., 1834–1856), 5th Cong., 2d sess., 1388. Hereafter cited as *Annals of Congress;* Colvill to Admiralty, Nov. 12, 1765, Adm. 1/482.

than these stereotypes. Few have tried. Maritime history, as it has been written, has had as little to do with the common seaman as business history has had to do with the laborer. In that *mischianza* of mystique and elitism, "seaman" has meant Sir Francis Drake, not Jack Tar; the focus has been on trade, exploration, the great navigators, but rarely on the men who sailed the ships.[5] Thus we know very little about Jack. Samuel Eliot Morison is one of the few who have tried to portray the common seaman. In an influential anecdote in *The Maritime History of Massachusetts* Morison has described a "frequent occurrence" in early New England. A farmer's boy, called by the smell or the sight of the sea, suddenly runs off; three years later he returns as a man, marries the hired girl, and lives "happily ever after." This experience, Morison tells us, was "typical of the Massachusetts merchant marine," where the "old salt" was almost non-existent and where there never was "a native deep-sea proletariat." The ships were sailed by wave after wave of "adventure-seeking boys," drawn by high wages and *wanderlust*. If they recovered, they took their earnings, married, and bought a farm; if not, these "young, ambitious seamen culled from the most active element of a pushing race" stayed on and rose to become masters in a merchant marine distinguished from its class-ridden European counterparts by easy mobility.[6]

There is much to support Morison's *tableau*. Even if the mystique of the sea has been no more than mystique, still it has existed and exerted a powerful force. Washington, Franklin, and thousands of others did suffer attacks of "sea fever."[7] Seamen were, as Morison says, young men, averaging in one sample slightly over twenty-four, with many like John Paul Jones who went to sea at thirteen and even some who went at eight.[8] Many of them "hove in hard at the Hause-hole"[9] and became masters of their own vessels; later, while their sons and grandsons added to their wealth, they retired, perhaps to their farms, and wrote proud histories of their successes.[10] Some,

[5] The bibliography is endless: a typical recent instance is Edmund O. Sawyer, *America's Sea Saga* (New York, 1962), foreword, 185, "a tale of unending courage" by a retired lieutenant colonel who now lives in Hollywood where he "plays an active role in the relentless crusade against the Communist conspiracy." Although there is much of use in *American Neptune*, the magazine's definition of maritime history has been too genteel, dwelling too often on such matters as ship design and construction, yachting, reminiscences, and model-building. On the other hand, even the W. P. A. Writer's Program neglected the seamen in *Boston Looks Seaward* (Boston, 1941) and in *A Maritime History of New York* (Garden City, N.Y., 1941).

[6] Samuel Eliot Morison, *The Maritime History of Massachusetts* (Boston, 1921), 105–107, 111; see also Morison, *John Paul Jones*, 22–23.

[7] Mason L. Weems, *The Life of Washington*, ed. Marcus Cunliffe (Cambridge, Mass., 1962), xxxv, 27; Douglas S. Freeman, *George Washington* (New York, 1948–1957), I, 190–199; Jesse Lemisch, ed., *Benjamin Franklin: The Autobiography and Other Writings* (New York, 1961), 23; Elmo Paul Hohman, *Seamen Ashore* (New Haven, 1952), 217, calls this kind of motivation "positive"; see *ibid.*, for "negative" motives.

[8] Morison, *John Paul Jones*, 11; sixty-one American seamen of ascertainable age listed in *Muster Rolls of New York Provincial Troops: 1755–1764* (N.-Y. Hist. Soc., *Coll.*, XXIV [New York, 1892]), *passim*, average 24.3 years; Cremer, *Ramblin' Jack*, ed. Bellamy, 38.

[9] The phrase appears in Cremer, *Ramblin' Jack*, ed. Bellamy, 31–32, and in Morison, *Maritime History*, 107.

[10] See for example, Mary Barney, ed., *A Biographical Memoir of the Late Commodore*

like Nicholas Biddle, found the navy a better outlet for their ambitions than the merchant service.[11] Others, following Morison's pattern, quit the sea early and turned to farming.[12] For many there was mobility between generations and between trades.[13] Seamen and landsmen might be distinct classes in Europe, but in America, men such as Albert Gallatin who knew both the Old World and the New found no "material distinction."[14] So Jack Tar seems to have been simply the landsman gone to sea, indistinguishable from his fellows ashore, and, together with them, on his way to prosperity.

If the seaman was a clean young farm-boy on the make—and likely to succeed—why was Josiah Franklin so apprehensive lest young Benjamin "break loose and go to sea"? Why did Josiah fight his son's "strong inclination to go to sea" by frantically trying to make of him a joiner, a bricklayer, a turner, a brazier, a tallow-chandler, a cutler, a printer—anything, so long as it would keep him on land?[15] Why did Washington's uncle suggest that young George would better become a planter or even an apprentice to a tinker, while explicitly urging that he not become a seaman?[16]

"All masters of vessels are warned not to harbor, conceal, or employ him, as they will answer for it, as the law directs."[17] To a fleeing apprentice, dissatisfied with the "bondage" of work ashore,[18] to a runaway slave, the sea might appear the only real shelter. Men with no experience at sea tried to pass for seamen and before long discovered that they had indeed become

---

Joshua Barney (Boston, 1832); Thomas Dring, Recollections of the Jersey Prison-Ship, ed. Albert G. Greene (Providence, 1829); Ebenezer Fox, The Adventures of Ebenezer Fox in the Revolutionary War (Boston, 1847 ?); Christopher Hawkins, The Adventures of Christopher Hawkins (New York, 1864); Paine, Ships and Sailors of Salem, 100, 117–119; James A. Henretta, "Economic Development and Social Structure in Colonial Boston," William and Mary Quarterly, 3d Ser., XXII (1965), 76.

[11] Joseph Galloway to Benjamin Franklin, Apr. 23, 1771, Franklin Papers, III, 50, American Philosophical Society, Philadelphia.

[12] "In America . . . all sorts of people turn farmers—where no mechanic or artizan—sailor—soldier—servant, etc. but what, if they get money, take land, and turn farmers." Harry J. Carman, ed., American Husbandry (New York, 1939), 124.

[13] The sons of captains might find themselves apprenticed to gentlemen or to butchers or barbers as well as to other mariners. See, for example, Burghers of New Amsterdam, 577–578, 617, 620; Indentures of Apprentices, 1718–1727 (N.-Y. Hist. Soc., Coll., XLII [New York, 1910]), 122–123, 140, 142–143, 150, 155, 166, 169, 181, 188, 189, 193, 195.

[14] Albert Gallatin, Apr. 10, 1798, Annals of Congress, 5th Cong., 2d sess., 1392; J. Hector St. John de Crevecoeur, Letters from an American Farmer (New York, 1957), 122, has similar observations about American "sea-faring men," but he seems to be describing only whalers.

[15] Lemisch, ed., Franklin, 23, 25–26. History apparently repeated itself in the next generation. Franklin's son William "left my house unknown to us all, and got on board a privateer, from whence I fetched him." Benjamin Franklin to Jane Mecom [June ? 1748], Leonard W. Labaree et al., eds., The Papers of Benjamin Franklin (New Haven, 1959–), III, 303.

[16] Freeman, Washington, I, 198–199. For some other instances of opposition by families of young men who expressed the intention of going to sea, see Barney, ed., Memoir, 3–4, and Fox, Adventures, 29, 36, 40.

[17] This is a composite of advertisements appearing in almost every colonial newspaper. See, for example, N.-Y. Gaz.; Weekly Post-Boy, May 17, 24, 1764, June 27, 1765.

[18] The term is used by Fox, Adventures, 18, describing his situation in 1775. In an interesting passage ibid., 17–19, he sees in the movement for independence a cause of a general "spirit of insubordination" among American youth at the time. For another runaway, see Bushnell, Adventures of Hawkins, 10, 60–61.

seamen. Others *were* seamen, apprenticed in one vessel and fled to another. Still others, deserted soldiers, bail-jumpers, thieves, and murderers, had gotten into trouble with the law.[19] And others went to sea entirely unwillingly, originally impressed—perhaps from jail—into the navy, or tricked into the merchant service by crimps.[20] These were the floaters who drifted and slipped their moorings, the suicides, the men whose wives—if they had wives —ran off with other men; the beneficiaries in their wills—when they left wills—were innkeepers.[21] Hitherto, argued a proponent of a United States navy in 1782, the merchant marine had been "the resource of necessity, accident or indulgence."[22]

The merchant marine was a place full of forces beyond the seaman's control: death and disease, storms, and fluctuations in employment. Indeed, the lack of "old salts" in Morison's merchant marine might reflect a sombre irony: was the average seaman young because mobility rapidly brought him to another trade or because seamen died young?[23] A man in jail, said Dr. Johnson, was at least safe from drowning, and he had more room, better food, and better company. The Quaker John Woolman was one of the few sensitive enough to see that if the "poor bewildered sailors" drank and cursed, the fault lay not so much in themselves as in the harsh environment

[19] See *N.-Y. Gaz.; Weekly Post Boy*, Sept. 3, Dec. 10, 1759, Oct. 14, Dec. 16, 1762, July 21, Oct. 6, Nov. 3, 1763, Mar. 29, May 10, 24, July 19, Sept. 6, 20, 1764, Apr. 4, 18, June 27, 1765, June 29, July 6, 1772; *New-York Journal: or the General Advertiser*, May 13, 1773. For a Negro seaman see log of *Hunter*, Sept. 8, 1758, Adm. 51/465. Some Negro seamen were free and some received their freedom as a reward for service in warships. Benjamin Quarles, *The Negro in the American Revolution* (Chapel Hill, 1961), 84; Robert McColley, *Slavery and Jeffersonian Virginia* (Urbana, 1964), 89. But Negroes also served at sea and in related maritime trades as part of their bondage and were sometimes advertised as "brought up from his Infancy to the sea." William Waller Hening, *The Statutes at Large . . . of Virginia* (Richmond, 1809–1823), XI, 404; *N.-Y. Gaz.; Weekly Post-Boy*, Mar. 26, 1761, July 7, Aug. 18, Nov. 17, 1763; Samuel Hallett in American Loyalists: Transcripts of the Commission of Enquiry into the Losses and Services of the American Loyalists . . . 1783–1790, XIX, 207, New York Public Library; George William Edwards, *New York as an Eighteenth Century Municipality, 1731–1776* (New York, 1917), 178.

[20] For crimps, see Hutchinson, *Press-Gang*, 48–49. Hohman, *Seamen Ashore*, 273–274, dates the development of crimping in America between 1830 and 1845, but there were crimps in Norfolk in 1767. See Captain Jeremiah Morgan to Governor Francis Fauquier, Sept. 11, 1767, Adm. 1/2116, Library of Congress transcript.

[21] *N.-Y. Gaz.; Weekly Post-Boy*, Sept. 30, 1773; *The King. v. Jane the Wife of Thomas Dun*, Indictment for Bigamy, filed Oct. 26, 1763, N.Y. Supreme Court, Pleadings K-41. Although no statistical conclusions are possible, to a surprising extent the beneficiaries in a sample of seamen's wills are not wives but rather brothers and sisters, friends and innkeepers, *Abstracts of Wills*, VI, 111, 226; VII, 12, 38, 148, 397; VIII, 98; XI, 194.

[22] *Independent Chronicle* (Boston), Sept. 5, 1782.

[23] For some reflections on mortality in the merchant marine see Ralph Davis, *The Rise of the English Shipping Industry in the Seventeenth and Eighteenth Centuries* (London, 1962), 156. As late as the 1840's Massachusetts seamen, with an average age at death of 42.47 years, died younger than farmers, clergymen, lawyers, physicians, blacksmiths, carpenters, merchants, and laborers. Only painters, fishermen, manufacturers, mechanics, and printers are listed as having shorter lives in Lemuel Shattuck *et al.*, *Report of the Sanitary Commission of Massachusetts, 1850* (Cambridge, Mass., 1948), 87. For employment see *N. Y. Journal or Gen. Adv.*, Oct. 5, 1775; Thomas Paine, *The Complete Writings*, ed. Philip S. Foner (New York, 1945), I, 33; in addition, a kind of unemployment is built into the profession; a seaman ashore is generally unemployed. See Hohman, *Seamen Ashore*, 209.

and the greed of employers. Nor was the road up through the hawse-hole so easy as Morison asserts. That the few succeeded tells us nothing of the many; only the successful left autobiographies.[24] Perhaps the sons of merchants and ship-masters made it, along with the captain's brother-in-law[25] and those who attended schools of navigation,[26] but what of the "poor lads bound apprentice" who troubled Woolman, those whose wages went to their masters? What of the seamen in Morison's own Boston who died too poor to pay taxes and who were a part of what James Henretta has called "the bottom" of Boston society?[27] What of those who went bankrupt with such frequency in Rhode Island?[28] Why, at the other end of the colonies, did Washington's uncle warn that it would be "very difficult" to become master of a Virginia vessel and not worth trying?[29]

The presence of such men, fugitives and floaters, powerless in a tough environment, makes *wanderlust* appear an ironic parody of the motives which made at least some men go to sea. Catch the seaman when he is not pandering to your romanticism, said former seaman Frederick Law Olmsted a century later, and he will tell you that he hates the sight of blue water, he hates his ship, his officers, and his messmates—and he despises himself. Melville's Ishmael went to sea when he felt grim, hostile, and suicidal: "It is a way I have of driving off the spleen." No matter what we make of Ishmael, we cannot possibly make him into one of Morison's "adventure-seeking boys." Others, perhaps, but not Ishmael. The feelings of eighteenth-century Americans toward seafaring and seamen, and what evidence we have of the reasons men had for going to sea indicate that there were many like Ishmael in the colonial period, too, who left the land in flight and fear, outcasts, men with little hope of success ashore. These were the dissenters from the American mood. Their goals differed from their fellows ashore; these were the rebels, the men who stayed on to become old salts.[30]

[24] Quoted in Davis, *Rise of English Shipping*, 154; John Woolman, *The Journal of John Woolman and A Plea for the Poor* (New York, 1961), 206, 192–193, 196. For comments on elitism in the writings of Morison and of other historians of early America, see Jesse Lemisch, "The American Revolution Seen from the Bottom Up," in Barton J. Bernstein, ed., *Towards a New Past: Dissenting Essays in American History* (New York, 1968), 3–45.

[25] Barney, ed., *Memoir*, 10. For the relative prospects of the sons of merchants and masters as opposed to others in the English merchant marine, see Davis, *Rise of English Shipping*, 117.

[26] For such schools see Boston Registry Department, *Records Relating to the Early History of Boston* (Boston, 1876–1909), XIII, 2, 204; Carl Bridenbaugh, *Cities in Revolt* (New York, 1955), 377.

[27] Woolman, *Journal*, 195; *Bethune* v. *Warner*, May 27, 1724, Admiralty Court, Boston, Minute Book II (1718–1726), 177, Office of Clerk, Supreme Judicial Court, Suffolk County, Mass.; Boston Reg. Dept., *Records of Boston*, XIV, 88–89, 94–95; Henretta, "Economic Development," 85; see also Jackson T. Main, *The Social Structure of Revolutionary America* (Princeton, 1965), 74.

[28] Only three occupational groups exceeded "mariners" in the number of insolvency petitions filed with the Rhode Island legislature from 1756 to 1828. See Peter J. Coleman, "The Insolvent Debtor in Rhode Island, 1745–1828," *Wm. and Mary Qtly.*, 3d Ser., XXII (1965), 422n. Mr. Coleman has stated in conversation with the author that the "mariners" appear to be predominantly common seamen.

[29] Freeman, *Washington*, I, 199.

[30] Frederick Law Olmsted, *A Journey in the Back Country . . .* (New York, 1860), 287. Morison, *Maritime History*, offers no evidence for the assertion that his anecdote of

Admiralty law treated seamen in a special way, as "wards." Carl Ubbelohde says that seamen favored the colonial Vice Admiralty Courts as "particular tribunals in case of trouble," and Charles M. Andrews and Richard B. Morris agreed that these courts were "guardians of the rights of the seamen." The benefits of being classified as a "ward" are dubious, but, regardless of the quality of treatment which admiralty law accorded to seamen, it certainly does not follow that, all in all, the colonial seaman was well treated by the law. Indeed, if we broaden our scope to include colonial law generally, we find an extraordinarily harsh collection of laws, all justifying Olmsted's later claim that American seamen "are more wretched, and are governed more by threats of force than any other civilized laborers of the world."[31] There are laws providing for the whipping of disobedient seamen and in one case for their punishment as "seditious"; laws prohibiting seamen in port from leaving their vessels after sundown and from travelling on land without certificates of discharge from their last job; laws empowering "every free white person" to catch runaway seamen.[32] We find other laws, less harsh, some seeming to protect the seaman: laws against extending credit to seamen and against arresting them for debt, and against entertaining them in taverns for more than one hour per day; laws against selling them liquor and prohibiting them from playing with cards or dice; laws waiving imprisonment for seamen convicted of cursing; laws requiring masters to give discharge certificates to their seamen and laws prohibiting hiring without such certificates.[33] Finally, there are laws which clearly do help the seaman:

---

the adventurous farm-boy is "typical" and that Massachusetts "has never had a native deep-sea proletariat." In the absence of such evidence and in the light of the evidence offered above for the existence of a very different type there is no basis for a claim that either group was "typical." My contention about the nature of the merchant marine is limited and negative. The presence of runaway slaves, thieves, murderers, fugitives, and floaters, *in addition to* Morison's adventure-seekers prevents any statement about typicality until we can offer quantitative evidence. Meanwhile all that we can say is that both types existed and that it is misleading to view the colonial merchant marine as a homogeneous entity.

[31] Carl Ubbelohde, *The Vice-Admiralty Courts and the American Revolution* (Chapel Hill, 1960), 20, 159–160, Charles M. Andrews, introduction to Dorothy S. Towle, ed., *The Records of the Vice Admiralty Court of Rhode Island, 1716–1752* (Washington, 1936), 60; Richard B. Morris, *Government and Labor in Early America* (New York, 1946), 232, 256; Olmsted, *Journey*, 287. Ubbelohde, Morris, and Andrews do not contend that the seaman was well treated by the law in an overall sense. Ubbelohde and Morris show that the seaman was better treated in Vice Admiralty Courts than in courts of common law; but when the focus moves to colonial legislation the hostility of the law emerges as the central fact for the seaman.

[32] Hening, *Statutes of Virginia*, IV, 107–108; VI, 26; E. B. O'Callaghan, ed., *Laws and Ordinances of New Netherland, 1638–1674* (Albany, 1868), 11–12. This law also prevented landsmen from going aboard vessels without authorization from the director of the West India Company. On June 13, 1647, two seamen convicted of tearing down a copy of this law attached to their vessel's mainmast were sentenced to be chained to a wheelbarrow and employed at hard labor on bread and water for three months. I. N. P. Stokes, *The Iconography of Manhattan Island, 1498–1909* (New York, 1915–1928), IV, 87. Thomas Cooper, ed., *The Statutes at Large of South Carolina* (Columbia, 1836–1841), III, 736.

[33] See the laws cited in Morris, *Government and Labor*, 230, n. 2; *Minutes of the Common Council of the City of New York, 1675–1776* (New York, 1905), I, 223, 372; *Acts and Resolves*, I, 142, 560; III, 318–319; IV, 73; James T. Mitchell and Henry Flan-

laws requiring masters to provide "good and sufficient diet and accommodation" and providing for redress if the master refused; laws providing punishment for masters who "immoderately beat, wound, or maim" their seamen; laws providing that seamen's contracts be written.[34]

These harsh or at best paternalistic laws[35] add up to a structure whose purpose is to assure a ready supply of cheap, docile labor.[36] Obedience, both at sea and ashore, is the keystone.[37] Charles Beard at his most rigidly mechanistic would doubtless have found the Constitution merely mild stuff alongside this blatantly one-sided class legislation. Today's historians of the classless society would do well to examine the preambles of these laws, written in a more candid age, by legislatures for which, even by Robert Brown's evidence, most seamen could not vote.[38] Again and again these laws aim to inhibit acts of seamen which may do "prejudice to masters and owners of vessels" or constitute a "manifest detriment of . . . trade."[39] The seamen's interests are sacrificed to the merchants', and even the laws which

---

ders, eds., *Statutes at Large of Pennsylvania from 1682 to 1801* (Harrisburg, 1896–1908), II, 239–240; Albert S. Batchellor and Henry H. Metcalf, *Laws of New Hampshire* (Manchester, 1904–1922), I, 691; J. Hammond Trumbull and C. J. Hoadly, eds., *The Public Records of the Colony of Connecticut (1636–1776)* (Hartford, 1850–1890), III, 54; *Charters and General Laws of the Colony and Province of Massachusetts* (Boston, 1814), 185; Cooper, ed., *Statutes of South Carolina*, III, 735, 736; Hening, *Statutes of Virginia*, IV, 108–110; VI, 25, 28.

[34] Hening, *Statutes of Virginia*, IV, 109–110, VI, 27. *Colonial Laws of New York from the year 1664 to the Revolution* . . . (Albany, 1894–1896), IV, 484–485; Morris, *Government and Labor*, 230, n. 5 and 7.

[35] Eugene T. Jackman, "Efforts Made Before 1825 to Ameliorate the Lot of the American Seaman: With Emphasis on his Moral Regeneration," *American Neptune*, XXIV (1964), 109, describes legislation for seamen after the Revolution as "paternalistic." As late as 1897 the Supreme Court declared that "seamen are treated by Congress, as well as by the Parliament of Great Britain, as deficient in that full and intelligent responsibility for their acts which is accredited to ordinary adults." Hohman, *Seamen Ashore*, 214.

[36] Morris, *Government and Labor*, 230, agrees with this statement in a somewhat more limited form.

[37] See Deposition of Commander Arthur Tough [1742], Gertrude MacKinney, ed., *Pennsylvania Archives*, 8th Ser. (Harrisburg, 1931–1935), IV, 2993.

[38] Robert E. Brown, *Middle-Class Democracy and the Revolution in Massachusetts, 1691–1780* (Ithaca, 1955), 27–30, acknowledges that the "city proletariat" constituted "the largest disfranchised group" and strongly implies that itinerant seamen could not vote. Even so, Brown has stated the case too optimistically. By including propertied captains under the ambiguous label "mariner," he has disguised the fact, legible in his own evidence, that the "mariners" who could vote were captains and the common seamen could not. See John Cary, "Statistical Method and the Brown Thesis on Colonial Democracy, With a Rebuttal by Robert E. Brown," *Wm. and Mary Qtly.*, 3d Ser., XX (1963), 257. For Brown's acknowledgement of the error see *ibid.*, 272. Arthur M. Schlesinger, *The Colonial Merchants and the American Revolution, 1763–1776* (New York, 1918), 28, includes seamen in a list of those who were "for the most part, unenfranchised." For an assertion that "sailors" could vote based on evidence that *masters* could compare Jacob R. Marcus, *Early American Jewry* (Philadelphia, 1953), II, 231, and B. R. Carroll, ed., *Historical Collections of South Carolina* (New York, 1836), II, 441.

[39] Trumbull and Hoadly, *Public Records of Connecticut*, III, 54; Cooper, ed., *Statutes of South Carolina*, II, 54; III, 735; for other legislation containing similar phrases see Batchellor and Metcalf, *Laws of New Hampshire*, I, 691; *Minutes of the Common Council of New York*, I, 223; *Colonial Laws of New York*, IV, 483; Hening, *Statutes of Virginia*, IV, 107.

seem friendly to the seaman benefit the master. Laws against giving credit, arresting, and suing aim to keep the seaman available rather than involved in a lawsuit or imprisoned, the certificates and written contracts seek to prevent desertion and to protect the master against what would today be called a "strike";[40] the laws protecting seamen against immoderate punishment and requiring adequate food and accommodation are implicitly weak in that they require that dependents make open complaint against their superiors.[41] Sometimes this limitation is made explicit, as in a South Carolina law of 1751 whose stated purpose is "TO DISCOURAGE FRIVOLOUS AND VEXATIOUS ACTIONS AT LAW BEING BROUGHT BY SEAMEN AGAINST MASTERS AND COMMANDERS."[42]

Thus if we think of Jack Tar as jolly, childlike, irresponsible, and in many ways surprisingly like the Negro stereotype, it is because he was treated so much like a child, a servant, and a slave. What the employer saw as the necessities of an authoritarian profession were written into law and culture: the society that wanted Jack dependent made him that way and then concluded that that was the way he really was.[43]

II

Constantly plagued by short complements, the Royal Navy attempted to solve its manning problems in America, as in England, by impressment.[44]

[40] For instance, *Colonial Laws of New York*, IV, 484 (later disallowed), required a written contract in order to end such practices as this: "very often when Ships and vessels come to be cleared out . . . the Seamen refuse to proceed with them, without coming to new agreements for increasing their wages and many of them will Leave their Ships and Vessels and not proceed on their voyages which puts the owners of such ships and vessels to Great Trouble and Charges." The act also mentions subterfuges of seamen but fails to acknowledge the possibility that masters might also use subterfuge. For a "mutiny" which clearly expressed a labor grievance see below, 406.

[41] See the procedure provided in Hening, *Statutes of Virginia*, IV, 109–110. See also Morris, *Government and Labor*, 268.

[42] Cooper, ed., *Statutes of South Carolina*, III, 735.

[43] For examples of the similarity between life at sea and life on the plantation compare Morris, *Government and Labor*, 230, 247, 256, 262, 274, and McColley, *Slavery and Jeffersonian Virginia*, 103. For Frederick Olmsted's comments on the similarity, based on his own experience at sea in 1843–1844, see *The Cotton Kingdom*, ed. Arthur M. Schlesinger (New York, 1953), 453. For the image of the seaman in literature see Harold F. Watson, *The Sailor in English Fiction and Drama, 1550–1880* (New York, 1931), 159–160, and *passim*.

[44] For shortages which led to impressment see, for example, Capt. Thos. Miles to Admiralty, Jan. 31, 1705/6, Adm. 1/2093; Lord Cornbury to Lords of Trade, Oct. 3, 1706, E. B. O'Callaghan, ed., *Documents Relative to the Colonial History of the State of New York* (Albany, 1853–1887), IV, 1183–1185; Captain A. Forrest to Lt. Gov. Spencer Phips, Oct. 26, 1745, Adm. 1/1782. For a detailed record of such shortages see items headed "The State and Condition of His Majesty's Ships and Sloops" appearing frequently, scattered throughout Admirals' Dispatches, Adm. 1/480–486. For impressment in the colonies see Neil R. Stout, "Manning the Royal Navy in North America, 1763–1775," *American Neptune*, XXIII (1963), 174–185, and Neil R. Stout, The Royal Navy in American Waters, 1760–1775 (unpubl. Ph.D. diss., University of Wisconsin, 1962), 359–395; R. Pares, "The Manning of the Navy in the West Indies, 1702–63," Royal Historical Society, *Transactions*, 4th Ser., XX (1937), 31–60; Dora Mae Clark, "The Impressment of Seamen in the American Colonies," in *Essays in Colonial History Presented to Charles McLean Andrews by his Students* (New Haven, 1931), 198–224; Jesse Lemisch,

Neil Stout has recently attributed these shortages to "death, illness, crime, and desertion" which were in turn caused largely by rum and by the deliberate enticements of American merchants.[45] Rum and inveiglement certainly took a high toll, but to focus on these two causes of shortages is unfairly to shift the blame for impressment onto its victims. The navy itself caused shortages. Impressment, said Thomas Hutchinson, caused desertion, rather than the other way around.[46] Jack Tar had good reasons for avoiding the navy. It would, a young Virginian was warned, "cut him and staple him and use him like a Negro, or rather, like a dog"; James Otis grieved at the loss of the "flower" of Massachusetts's youth "by ten thousands" to a service which treated them little better than "hewers of wood and drawers of water." Discipline was harsh and sometimes irrational, and punishments were cruel.[47] Water poured into sailors' beds, they went mad, and died of fevers and scurvy.[48] Sickness, Benjamin Franklin noted, was more common in the navy than in the merchant service and more frequently fatal.[49] In a fruitless attempt to prevent desertion, wages were withheld and men shunted about from ship to ship without being paid.[50] But the accumulation of even

---

Jack Tar vs. John Bull: The Role of New York's Seamen in precipitating the Revolution (unpubl. Ph.D. diss., Yale University, 1962), 12–51. Two useful accounts primarily dealing with impressment in England may be found in Hutchinson, *Press-Gang, passim,* and Daniel A. Baugh, *British Naval Administration in the Age of Walpole* (Princeton, 1965), 147–240.

[45] Stout, "Manning the Royal Navy," 176–177, suggests the possibility of other causes when he notes that desertion was high "whatever the causes," but he mentions no cause other than rum and inveiglement. The Admiralty made the seamen's "natural Levity" another possible reason for desertion. Admiralty to Gov. Thomas on Impressments, 1743, *Pennsylvania Archives,* 1st Ser. (Philadelphia, 1852–1856), I, 639; see also Massachusetts Historical Society, *Journals of the House of Representatives of Massachusetts* (Boston, 1919–), XX, 84, 98; Colvill to Admiralty, Aug. 8, 1765, Adm. 1/482; Pares, "Manning the Navy," 31, 33–34.

[46] Hutchinson to Richard Jackson, June 16, 1768, G. G. Wolkins, "The Seizure of John Hancock's Sloop 'Liberty,'" Massachusetts Historical Society, *Proceedings,* LV (Boston, 1923), 283.

[47] Freeman, *Washington,* I, 199; James Otis, *The Rights of the British Colonies Asserted and Proved* (Boston, 1764) in Bernard Bailyn, ed., *Pamphlets of the American Revolution, 1750–1776* (Cambridge, Mass., 1965), I, 464. Flogging was universal and men received as many as 600 and 700 lashes. Colvill to Admiralty, Nov. 12, 1765, Adm. 1/482. For obscenity the tongue was scraped with hoop-iron. There were punishments for smiling in the presence of an officer. One captain put his sailors' heads in bags for trivial offenses. Hutchinson, *Press-Gang,* 31–36. And, of course, the captain might go mad, as did Captain Robert Bond of *Gibraltar.* Admiral Gambier to Admiralty, Oct. 10, 1771, Adm. 1/483, log of *Gibraltar,* Feb. 10, 14, 1771, Adm. 51/394.

[48] Log of *Arethusa,* Dec. 28, 1771, Adm. 51/59; Petition of Jeremiah Raven, [fall 1756], Letters as to Admission of Pensioners to Greenwich Hospital, 1756–1770, Adm. 65/81, an excellent source for the discovery of the effects of service in the navy on health. See also the items headed "Weekly Account of Sick and Wounded Seamen" in Admirals' Dispatches, for example, Admiral Gambier to Admiralty, May 6, June 10, July 20, 27, 1771, Adm. 1/483; Nov. 9, 1771, Aug. 29, 1772, Adm. 1/484.

[49] Remarks on Judge Foster's Argument in Favor of . . . Impressing Seamen, Jared Sparks, ed., *The Works of Benjamin Franklin,* II, (Boston, 1844), 333. Sparks gives this no date; John Bigelow, ed., *The Complete Works of Benjamin Franklin* (New York, 1887–1888), IV, 70, dates it 1767; Helen C. Boatfield of the Papers of Benjamin Franklin, Yale University, dates it post-1776.

[50] Pares, "Manning the Navy," 31–38; Roland G. Usher, Jr., "Royal Navy Impressment during the American Revolution," *Mississippi Valley Historical Review,* XXXVII

three or four years' back wages could not keep a man from running.[51] And why should it have? Privateering paid better in wartime, and wages were higher in the merchant service; even laborers ashore were better paid.[52] Thus Stout's claim that the navy was "forced" to press is only as accurate as the claim that the South was forced to enslave Negroes. Those whose sympathies lie with the thousands of victims of this barbaric practice—rather than with naval administrators—will see that the navy pressed because to be in the navy was in some sense to be a slave, and for this we must blame the slaveowners rather than the slaves.[53]

Impressment angered and frightened the seamen, but it pervaded and disrupted all society, giving other classes and groups cause to share a common grievance with the press-gang's more direct victims: just about everyone had a relative at sea.[54] Whole cities were crippled. A night-time operation in New York in 1757 took in eight hundred men, the equivalent of more than one-quarter of the city's adult male population.[55] Impressment and the attendant shortage of men may have been a critical factor in the stagnancy of "the once cherished now depressed, once flourishing now sinking Town of Boston."[56] H.M.S. Shirley's log lists at least ninety-two men

---

(1950–1951), 686. At the time of the Mutiny at the Nore the crew of one ship had not been paid in 15 years, Hutchinson, Press-Gang, 44.

51 Mr. William Polhampton to Lords of Trade, Mar. 6, 1711, O'Callaghan, ed., Docs. Rel. Col. Hist. N.Y. V, 194. A seaman who deserted his ship would leave an "R"—for "run"—written against his name in the ship's book. See Hutchinson, Press-Gang, 151, for a song which urges seamen to flee the press-gang and "leave 'em an R in pawn!"

52 Peter Warren to Admiralty, Sept. 8, 1744, Adm. 1/2654; Mr. William Polhampton to Lords of Trade, Mar. 6, 1711, O'Callaghan, ed., Docs. Rel. Col. Hist. N. Y., V, 194; Admiralty to Thomas, 1743, Pa. Arch., 1st Ser., I, 638–639; Morris, Government and Labor, 247–248. The navy's most imaginative response to the problem was sporadic and abortive attempts to limit the wages given to merchant seamen, but the inviting differential remained. When the navy offered bounties for enlistment, this merely served to induce additional desertions by men who could pick up a month's pay simply by signing up. Pares, "Manning the Navy," 33–34; Hutchinson, Press-Gang, 22, 48–49; Remarks on Judge Foster's Argument, Sparks, ed., Works of Franklin, II, 333; N.-Y. Gaz.; Weekly Post-Boy, Mar. 31, Apr. 21, 1755, Mar. 11, 1771.

53 Stout, "Manning the Royal Navy," 182. England abolished the press-gang in 1833, Hutchinson, Press-Gang, 311. Parliament abolished slavery in the British colonies in the same year.

54 At least in Pennsylvania and New Jersey, according to the Independent Chronicle (Boston), Sept. 5, 1782.

55 Three thousand men participated in this massive operation. Three or four hundred of those seized were released. Lord Loudoun to Pitt, May 30, 1757, Gertrude S. Kimball, ed., Correspondence of William Pitt (New York, 1906), I, 69; Paul L. Ford, ed., The Journals of Hugh Gaine, Printer (New York, 1902), II, 8–9; May 20, 1757, The Montresor Journals (N.-Y. Hist. Soc., Coll., XIV [New York, 1882]), Benjamin Cutter, History of the Cutter Family of New England (Boston, 1871), 67; Evarts B. Greene and Virginia D. Harrington, American Population before the Federal Census of 1790 (New York, 1932), 101, 1756 census.

56 Boston is so described in a petition of the town meeting to the House of Representatives, Mar. 11, 1745/6, Mass. Hist. Soc., Mass. House Journals, XXII, 204. This petition is but one of many attributing the depletion of Boston's population in part to impressment. For a table indicating a downward trend in Boston's population after 1743 see Stuart Bruchey, ed., The Colonial Merchant: Sources and Readings (New York, 1966), 11. I am indebted to Joel Shufro, a graduate student at the University of Chicago, for the suggestion of a connection between impressment and the decline of Boston.

pressed off Boston in five months of 1745–1746; *Gramont* received seventy-three pressed men in New York in three days in 1758; *Arethusa* took thirty-one in two days off Virginia in 1771.[57] Binges such as these left the communities where they occurred seriously harmed. Preachers' congregations took flight, and merchants complained loudly about the "many Thousands of Pounds of Damage."[58] "Kiss my arse, you dog," shouted the captain as he made off with their men, leaving vessels with their fires still burning, unmanned, finally to be wrecked.[59] They took legislators and slaves, fishermen and servants.[60] Seamen took to the woods or fled town altogether, dreading the appearance of a man-of-war's boat—in the words of one—as a flock of sheep dreaded a wolf's appearance.[61] If they offered to work at all, they demanded inflated wages and refused to sail to ports where there was danger of impressment.[62] "New York and Boston," Benjamin Franklin commented during the French and Indian War, "have so often found the inconvenience of . . . Station Ships that they are very indifferent about having them: The Pressing of their Men and thereby disappointing Voyages, often hurting their Trade more than the Enemy hurts it." Even a

[57] Log of *Shirley*, Dec. 25, 1745–May 17, 1746, Adm. 51/4341; log of *Gramont*, Apr. 25–27, 1758, Adm. 51/413; log of *Arethusa*, Mar. 19–20, 1771, Adm. 51/59. *Shirley's* haul was not mentioned in the *Boston Evening Post* or in the records of any American governmental body. Here is but one instance in which the serious grievance of 92 Americans has previously gone unnoticed. Such grievances are nonetheless real and play a causal role despite their invisibility to historians. On the other hand, overdependence on British sources is apt to be extremely misleading. Either because of sloppiness or because of the clouded legality of impressment, official records seem more often to ignore the practice or to distort it than to complement information from American sources. Admiral Charles Hardy neglected to mention the massive press in New York in 1757 in his correspondence with the Admiralty. See May–June 1757, Adm. 1/481. The absence of impressment in *Triton's Prize's* log in 1706, Adm. 51/1014, is contradicted in Lord Cornbury to Lords of Trade, Oct. 3, 1706, O'Callaghan, ed., *Docs. Rel. Col. Hist. N. Y.*, IV, 1183–1185. Sometimes logs show what seems to be purposeful distortion: *Diana*, whose log, Apr. 15, 1758, Adm. 51/4162, reveals only that she "saluted with 9 Guns" *Prince of Orange* privateer, in fact pressed her hands, *Montresor Journal*, 152. In another instance *St. John* "received on board a Boat Load of Ballast," log, July 16, 1764, Adm. 51/3961, which seems in fact to have consisted of hogs, sheep, and poultry stolen from the people of Martha's Vineyard, *Newport Mercury*, July 23, 1764. See below n. 69.

[58] *Boston Evening Post*, Sept. 3, 1739, July 6, 1741.

[59] Deposition of Nathaniel Holmes, July 18, 1702, Deposition of John Gullison, July 17, 1702, Lt. Gov. Thomas Povey to Lords Commissioners for Trade and Plantations, July 20, 1702, Colonial Office Group, Class 5, Piece 862, Public Record Office. Hereafter cited as C.O. 5/862; *Boston Evening Post*, Dec. 14, 1747; *N.-Y. Gaz.; Weekly Post-Boy*, Jan. 14, 1771.

[60] Peter Woodbery and John Tomson to Governor William Phips, July 1, 2, 1692, C.O. 5/751; James and Drinker to [?], Oct. 29, 1756, James and Drinker Letterbook 1, Historical Society of Pennsylvania, Philadelphia; *Boston Evening Post*, Dec. 9, 1745; Mass. Hist. Soc., *Mass. House Journals*, II, 300–301, XXXIII, Pt. ii, 433; *N.-Y. Gaz.; Weekly Post-Boy*, July 12, 1764.

[61] Mass. Hist. Soc., *Mass. House Journals*, XXXV, 267; William Shirley to Gideon Wanton, June 6, 1745, Charles H. Lincoln, ed., *Correspondence of William Shirley* (New York, 1912), I, 227; Mr. Colden to Lords of Trade, Aug. 30, 1760, O'Callaghan, ed., *Docs. Rel. Col. Hist. N. Y.*, VII, 446; Andrew Sherburne, *Memoirs of Andrew Sherburne* (Utica, 1828), 68.

[62] Mass. Hist. Soc., *Mass. House Journals*, XXXV, 267; James and Drinker to Nehemiah Champion, July 13, 1757, James and Drinker Letterbook, I, 145.

ferryboat operator complained as people shunned the city during a press; food and fuel grew short and their prices rose.[63]

From the very beginning the history of impressment in America is a tale of venality, deceit, and vindictiveness. Captains kept deserters and dead men on ships' books, pocketing their provision allowances. In 1706 a captain pressed men and literally sold them to short-handed vessels; his midshipman learned the business so well that after his dismissal he became a veritable entrepreneur of impressment, setting up shop in a private sloop. Another commander waited until New York's governor was away to break a no-press agreement and when the governor returned he seriously considered firing on the Queen's ship.[64] In Boston in 1702 the lieutenant-governor *did* fire, responding to merchants' complaints. "Fire and be damn'd," shouted the impressing captain as the shots whistled through his sails. The merchants had complained that the press was illegal under 1697 instructions which required captains and commanders to apply to colonial governors for permission to press.[65] These instructions, a response to complaints of "irregular proceedings of the captains of some of our ships of war in the impressing of seamen," had clearly not put an end to irregularities.[66] In 1708 a Parliament fearful of the disruptive effect of impressment on trade forbade the practice in America. In the sixty-seven years until the repeal in 1775 of this "Act for the Encouragement of the trade to America" there was great disagreement as to its meaning and indeed as to its very existence. Did the Sixth of Anne, as the act was called, merely prohibit the navy from impressing and leave governors free to do so? At least one governor, feeling "pinioned" under the law, continued impressing while calling it "borrowing."[67] Was the act simply a wartime measure, which expired with the re-

---

[63] Franklin to Joseph Galloway, Apr. 7, 1759, Labaree *et al.*, eds., *Papers of Benjamin Franklin*, VIII, 315–316; Morris, *Government and Labor*, 274; Mr. Colden to Lords of Trade, Aug. 30, 1760, O'Callaghan, ed., *Docs. Rel. Col. Hist. N. Y.*, VII, 446; Mass. Hist. Soc., *Mass. House Journals*, XVIII, 202; XX, 84; Boston Reg. Dept., *Records of Boston*, XVII, 125. See also Gerard G. Beekman to William Beekman, July 3, 1764, Philip L. White, ed., *The Beekman Mercantile Papers, 1746–1749* (New York, 1956), I, 469.

[64] William Polhampton to the Lords of Trade, Mar. 6, 1711, Lord Cornbury to Lords of Trade, Oct. 3, Dec. 14, 1706, O'Callaghan, ed., *Docs. Rel. Col. Hist. N. Y.*, V, 194; IV, 1183–1184, 1190–1191. The captain later publicly declared that he hated the whole province and would not help a New York vessel in distress at sea if he met one, Lord Cornbury to Lords of Trade, July 1, 1708, *ibid.*, V, 60. It seems increasingly to have become common practice to press after a public declaration that there would be no press, for example, *Boston Evening Post*, Dec. 9, 23, 1745; log of *Shirley*, Dec. 25, 1745–May 17, 1746, Adm. 51/4341.

[65] Lieutenant Governor Thomas Povey to Lords Commissioners for Trade and Plantations, July 20, 1702, Memorial of Thomas Povey, [July, 1702], Deposition of Nathaniel Holmes, July 18, 1702, Deposition of John Arnold and John Roberts, July 18, 1702, C.O. 5/862.

[66] For instructions to royal governors giving them sole power to press in their province see Leonard W. Labaree, ed., *Royal Instructions to British Colonial Governors, 1670–1776* (New York, 1935), I, 442–443; Instructions for the Earl of Bellomont, Aug. 31, 1697, Copy of . . . Lovelace's Instructions, n.d., O'Callaghan, ed., *Docs. Rel. Col. Hist. N. Y.*, IV, 287; V, 101. See also Clark, "Impressment of Seamen," in *Essays to Andrews*, 202–205.

[67] *Calendar of Council Minutes, 1668–1783* (New York State Library, *Bulletin 58* [Mar. 1902]), 229, 230; Stokes, *Iconography of Manhattan*, IV, 465, 973; V, 99–101; Chief

turn of peace in 1713?[68] Regardless of the dispute, impressment continued, routine in its regularity, but often spectacular in its effects.[69]

Boston was especially hard-hit by impressment in the 1740's, with frequent incidents throughout the decade and major explosions in 1745 and 1747. Again and again the town meeting and the House of Representatives protested, drumming away at the same themes: impressment was harmful to maritime commerce and to the economic life of the city in general and illegal if not properly authorized.[70] In all this the seaman himself becomes all but invisible. The attitude towards him in the protests is at best neutral and often sharply antagonistic. In 1747 the House of Representatives condemned the violent response of hundreds of seamen to a large-scale press as "a tumultuous riotous assembling of armed Seamen, Servants, Negroes, and others . . . tending to the Destruction of all Government and Order." While acknowledging that the people had reason to protest, the House chose to level *its* protest against "the most audacious Insult" to the governor, Council, and House. And the town meeting, that stronghold of democracy, offered its support to those who took "orderly" steps while expressing its "Abhorence of such Illegal Criminal Proceedings" as those undertaken by the seamen "and other persons of mean and Vile Condition."[71]

Protests such as these reflect at the same time both unity and division in colonial society. All kinds of Americans—both merchants and seamen—opposed impressment, but the town meeting and the House spoke for the merchant, not the seaman. They opposed impressment not for its effect on the seaman but for its effect on commerce. Thus their protests express antagonism to British policy at the same time that they express class division.

Justice . . . Opinion, June 30, 1709, Report of the Councill, July 3, 1709, Governor Hunter to Secretary St. John, Sept. 12, 1711, O'Callaghan, ed., *Docs. Rel. Col. Hist. N. Y.*, V, 100, 102, 254–255.

[68] In 1716 the attorney-general declared, "I am of Opinion, that the whole American Act was intended . . . only for the War," *Massachusetts Gazette* (Boston), June 17, 1768. Governor Shirley of Massachusetts agreed in 1747, despite the fact that, along with other colonial governors, he was still instructed to enforce the Sixth of Anne and had indeed sworn to do so, The Lords Justices to William Shirley, Sept. 10, 1741, Lincoln, ed., *Correspondence of Shirley*, I, 74–76; Stout, *Royal Navy*, 391. Twenty-two years later Governor Hutchinson feared that John Adams might publicize the act. The Admiralty continued to instruct American commanders to obey the act after Queen Anne's War, for example, see Admiralty to Captain Balcher, Mar. 9, 1714, Adm. 2/48, but ceased so to instruct them in 1723, Clark, "Impressment of Seamen," in *Essays to Andrews*, 211. Of course, the act's repeal in 1775 indicated that it had been on the books, if no place else, all that time.

[69] Stout's claim in *Royal Navy*, 366, that the navy began pressing again only in 1723 illustrates the dangers of over-reliance on British sources in such controversial matters. That the Admiralty continued to instruct commanders not to press does not mean that they did not in fact press. *Shark* pressed in Boston in 1720, Mass. Hist. Soc., *Mass. House Journals*, II, 300–301; interestingly, her log for Oct.–Nov. 1720, Adm. 51/892, contains no mention of the fact.

[70] See, for example, Mass. Hist. Soc., *Mass. House Journals*, XVIII, 202; XX, 98–99; XXII, 76–77, 204–205.

[71] *Ibid.*, XXIV, 212; Boston Reg. Dept., *Records of Boston*, XIV, 127. Bridenbaugh, *Cities in Revolt*, 117, sees the law of 1751 for suppressing riots as in part a response to the Knowles Riots; he calls the law "brutal" even for its own day and a "triumph for the reactionaries."

These two themes continue and develop in American opposition to impressment in the three decades between the Knowles Riots of 1747 and the
Declaration of Independence.

During the French and Indian War the navy competed with privateers for
seamen.[72] Boston again protested against impressment, and then considered
authorizing the governor to press, "provided said Men be impressed from
inward-bound Vessels from Foreign Parts only, and that none of them be
Inhabitants of this Province."[73] In 1760 New York's mayor had a naval
captain arrested on the complaint of two shipmasters who claimed that he
had welched on a deal to exchange two men he had pressed for two others
they were willing to furnish.[74] With the return of peace in 1763 admirals
and Americans alike had reason to suppose that there would be no more
impressment.[75] But the Admiralty's plans for a large new American fleet
required otherwise, and impressment began again in the spring of 1764
in New York, where a seven-week hot press was brought to a partial stop
by the arrest of one of the two offending captains.[76] In the spring and summer a hunt for men between Maine and Virginia by four naval vessels
brought violent responses, including the killing of a marine at New York;
another fort, at Newport, fired on another naval vessel.[77]

Along with the divisions there was a certain amount of unity. Seamen
who fled after violently resisting impressment could not be found—probably
because others sheltered them—and juries would not indict them. Captains
were prevented from impressing by the threat of prosecution.[78] And in 1769
lawyer John Adams used the threat of displaying the statute book contain-

[72] See, for example, Lord Loudoun to Pitt, Mar. 10, May 30, 1757, Kimball, ed., *Correspondence of Pitt*, I, 19, 69; Lieutenant-Governor De Lancey to Secretary Pitt, Mar.
17, 1758, O'Callaghan, ed., *Docs. Rel. Col. Hist. N. Y.*, VII, 343.

[73] Mass. Hist. Soc., *Mass. House Journals*, XXXIII, Pt. ii, 434; XXXIV, Pt. i, 134; Boston Reg Dept., *Records of Boston*, XIX, 96–97; log of *Hunter*, Aug. 31, 1758, Adm.
51/465. The Council voted such authorization, but the House did not concur.

[74] Capt. George Ant. Tonyn to Admiralty, Mar. 1, 1760, Depositions of Peter Vail
and Singleton Church, Jan. 15, 16, 1760, Adm. 1/2588.

[75] Admiral Colvill, Journal, Mar. 19, 1764, Adm. 50/4; Colvill to Admiralty, May 19,
1764, Adm. 1/482; *N.-Y. Gaz.; Weekly Post-Boy*, July 18, 1765.

[76] Stout, Royal Navy, 72–73, citing Admiralty to Egremont, Jan. 5, 1763, State Papers
Group, Class 42, Piece 43, Public Record Office. Hereafter cited as S.P. 42/43; Captain
Jno. Brown to Admiralty, May 16, 1764, Adm. 1/1494; log of *Coventry*, Mar. 31, 1764,
Adm. 51/213, indicates impressment on that date; compare Stout, Royal Navy, 379,
393*n*.

[77] Admiral Colvill, Journal, June 4, 1764, Adm. 50/4; Colvill to Admiralty, June 18,
1764, Adm. 1/482. On the violence at New York see log of *Jamaica*, June 8, 1764, Adm.
51/3874; *N.-Y. Gaz.; Weekly Post-Boy*, July 12, 1764; Report of the Grand Jury, Aug.
2, 1764, New York Supreme Court Minute Book (July 31, 1764–Oct. 28, 1764), 7. On
the violence at Newport see log of *St. John*, July 10, 1764, Adm. 51/3961; Captain Smith
to Colvill, July 12, 1764, in Colvill to Admiralty, Aug. 24, 1764, Adm. 1/482; John
Temple to Treasury, Sept. 9, 1765, Treasury Group, Class 1, Piece 442, Library of Congress transcript.

[78] *The King v. Osborn Greatrakes* and *The King v. Josiah Moore*, Oct. 24, 28, 30,
Nov. 11–17, 1760, New York Supreme Court Minute Book (1756–1761), 1–6, 200, 209,
215; Henry B. Dawson, *The Sons of Liberty in New York* (New York, 1859), 53; *N.-Y.
Gaz.; Weekly Post-Boy*, July 12, 1764; Report of Grand Jury, Aug. 2, 1764, New York
Supreme Court Minute Book (July 31, 1764–Oct. 28, 1767), 7; Colvill to Admiralty, Aug.
5, 1766, Adm. 1/482.

ing the Sixth of Anne to frighten a special court of Admiralty into declaring the killing of an impressing lieutenant justifiable homicide in necessary self-defense.[79]

There were two kinds of impressment incidents: those in which there was immediate self-defense against impressment, usually at sea, and those in which crowds ashore, consisting in large part of seamen, demonstrated generalized opposition to impressment. This is what the first kind of incident sounded like: a volley of musketry and the air full of langrage, grapeshot, round shot, hammered shot, double-headed shot, even rocks. "Come into the boat and be damned, you Sorry Son of a Whore or else Ile breake your head, and hold your tongue." Small arms, swords and cutlasses, blunderbusses, clubs and pistols, axes, harpoons, fishgigs, twelve-pounders, six-pounders, half-pounders. "You are a parsill of Raskills." Fired five shots to bring to a snow from North Carolina, pressed four. "You have no right to impress me . . . If you step over that line . . . by the eternal God of Heaven, you are a dead man." "Aye, my lad, I have seen many a brave fellow before now."[80]

Here is hostility and bloodshed, a tradition of antagonism. From the beginning, impressment's most direct victims—the seamen—were its most active opponents. Bernard Bailyn's contention that "not a single murder resulted from the activities of the Revolutionary mobs in America" does not hold up if extended to cover resistance to impressment; there were murders on both sides. Perhaps the great bulk of incidents of this sort must remain forever invisible to the historian, for they often took place out of sight of friendly observers, and the only witness, the navy, kept records which are demonstrably biased and faulty, omitting the taking of thousands of men.[81] But

[79] Charles Francis Adams, ed., *The Works of John Adams* (Boston, 1850–1856), II, 225*n*–226*n*, and "The Inadmissible Principles of the King of England's Proclamation of October 16, 1807, Considered" [1809], IX, 317–318; Thomas Hutchinson, *The History of the Colony and Province of Massachusetts-Bay*, ed. Lawrence S. Mayo (Cambridge, Mass., 1936), III, 167*n*; log of *Rose*, Apr. 22, 1769, Adm. 51/804; Admiral Hood to Admiralty, May 5, 1769, Adm. 1/483.

[80] *The King* v. *Ship Sampson*, Examination of Hugh Mode, Pilot, taken Aug. 19, 1760, N.Y. Supreme Court, Pleadings K-304; *N.-Y. Gaz.; Weekly Post-Boy*, May 1, 1758, Aug. 7, 1760; Captain J. Hale to Admiralty, Aug. 28, 1760, Adm. 1/1895; William McCleverty to Admiralty, July 31, 1760, Adm. 1/2172; Howard Thomas, *Marinus Willett* (Prospect, N.Y., 1954), 3–4; Deposition of John Gullison, July 17, 1702, Deposition of Woodward Fay, July 17, 1702, C.O. 5/862; log of *Magdelen*, Apr. 6, 1771, Adm. 51/3984, describing the loss during a press "by Accident" of a sword and musquet—apparently a common accident; see also log of *Arethusa*, Apr. 18, 1772, Adm. 51/59; Weyman's *New-York Gazette*, Aug. 25, 1760; Admiral Hood to Admiralty, May 5, 1769, Adm. 1/483; paraphrase of log of *Shirley*, Jan. 17, 1746, Adm. 51/4341; "Inadmissable Principles" [1809], Adams, ed., *Works of Adams*, IX, 318.

[81] Bailyn, ed., *Pamphlets*, I, 581. Six Englishmen of varying ranks were killed while pressing in the 1760's. In addition to the incidents just discussed in which a lieutenant of marines was murdered on June 8, 1764, while pressing at New York and in which John Adams's clients-to-be, accused of murdering a lieutenant off Cape Ann Apr. 22, 1769, got off with justifiable homicide in self-defense, four sailors were shot to death at New York, Aug. 18, 1760. Cadwallader Colden to Lords of Trade, Aug. 30, 1760, O'Callaghan, ed., *Docs. Rel. Col. Hist. N. Y.*, VII, 446; *The King* v. *Osborn Greatrakes* and the *King* v. *Josiah Moore*, Oct. 24, 28, 30, Nov. 11–17, 1760, New York Supreme Court Minute Book (1756–1761), 1–16, 200, 209, 215; *The King* v. *Ship Sampson*, Examination of Hugh Mode, Pilot, taken Aug. 19, 1760, N.Y. Supeme Court, Pleadings K-304; Capt. J. Hale to

even the visible records provide a great deal of information. This much we know without doubt: seamen did not go peacefully. Their violence was purposeful, and sometimes they were articulate. "I know who you are," said one, as reported by John Adams and supported by Thomas Hutchinson.

> You are the lieutenant of a man-of-war, come with a press-gang to deprive me of my liberty. You have no right to impress me. I have retreated from you as far as I can. I can go no farther. I and my companions are determined to stand upon our defence. Stand off.[82]

(It was difficult for Englishmen to fail to see impressment in such terms—even a sailor *doing* the pressing could feel shame over "fighting with honest sailors, to deprive them of their liberty.")[83]

Ashore, seamen and others demonstrated their opposition to impressment with the only weapon which the unrepresentative politics of the day offered them—riot. In Boston several thousand people responded to a nighttime impressment sweep of the harbor and docks with three days of rioting beginning in the early hours of November 17, 1747. Thomas Hutchinson reported that "the lower class were beyond measure enraged." Negroes, servants, and hundreds of seamen seized a naval lieutenant, assaulted a sheriff and put his deputy in the stocks, surrounded the governor's house, and stormed the Town House where the General Court was sitting. The rioters demanded the seizure of the impressing officers, the release of the men they had pressed, and execution of a death sentence which had been levied against a member of an earlier press-gang who had been convicted of murder. When the governor fled to Castle William—some called it "abdication"—Commodore Knowles threatened to put down what he called "arrant rebellion" by bombarding the town. The governor, who, for his part, thought the rioting was a secret plot of the upper class, was happily surprised when the town meeting expressed its "Abhorence" of the seamen's riot.[84]

After the French and Indian War press riots increased in frequency. Armed mobs of whites and Negroes repeatedly manhandled captains, of-

---

Admiralty, Aug. 28, 1760, Adm. 1/1895; Weyman's *N.-Y. Gaz.*, Aug. 25, 1760, Dawson, *Sons of Liberty*, 51–54. Governor Cadwallader Colden called the last incident murder, but the jury refused to indict. For some instances of Americans killed while resisting impressment see deposition of William Thwing, Nathaniel Vaill, and Thomas Hals, July 15, 1702, C.O. 5/862; Governor Hunter to Secretary St. John, Sept. 12, 1711, O'Callaghan, ed., *Docs. Rel. Col. Hist. N. Y.*, V, 254–255 (conviction of murder); Bridenbaugh, *Cities in Revolt*, 114–115; *N.-Y. Gaz.*; *Weekly Post-Boy*, Aug. 7, 1760. There is every reason to suppose that this list is partial. See above n. 57.

82 "Inadmissable Principles" [1809], Adams, ed., *Works of Adams*, IX, 318, quotes Michael Corbet, commenting that Corbet displayed "the cool intrepidity of a Nelson, reasoned, remonstrated, and laid down the law with the precision of a Mansfield." Hutchinson, *History of Massachusetts-Bay*, ed. Mayo, III, 167n, notes that Corbet and his companions "swore they would die before they would be taken, and that they preferred death to slavery."

83 "Inadmissable Principles" [1809], Adams, ed., *Works of Adams*, IX, 317–318.

84 Hutchinson, *History of Massachusetts-Bay*, ed. Mayo, II, 330–331, 333; Mass. Hist. Soc., *Mass. House Journals*, XXIV, 212; Bridenbaugh, *Cities in Revolt*, 115–117; Boston Reg. Dept., *Records of Boston*, XIV, 127; William Shirley to Lords of Trade, Dec. 1, 1747, Lincoln, ed., *Correspondence of Shirley*, I, 412–419, is the best single account. Shirley says that only the officers responded to his call for the militia.

ficers and crews, threatened their lives, and held them hostage for the men they pressed. Mobs fired at pressing vessels and tried to board them; they threatened to burn one, and they regularly dragged ships' boats to the center of town for ceremonial bonfires. In Newport in June 1765, five hundred seamen, boys, and Negroes rioted after five weeks of impressment. "Sensible" Newporters opposed impressment but nonetheless condemned this "Rabble." In Norfolk in 1767 Captain Jeremiah Morgan retreated, sword in hand, before a mob of armed whites and Negroes. "Good God," he wrote to the governor, "was your Honour and I to prosecute all the Rioters that attacked us belonging to Norfolk there would not be twenty left unhang'd belonging to the Toun."[85] According to Thomas Hutchinson, the *Liberty* Riot in Boston in 1768 may have been as much against impressment as against the seizure of Hancock's sloop: *Romney* had pressed before June 10, and on that day three officers were forced by an angry crowd "arm'd with Stones" to release a man newly pressed from the Boston packet.[86] *Romney* pressed another man, and on June 14, after warding off "many wild and violent proposals," the town meeting petitioned the governor against both the seizure and impressment; the instructions to their representatives (written by John Adams) quoted the Sixth of Anne at length. On June 18 two councilors pleaded with the governor to procure the release of a man pressed by *Romney* "as the peace of the Town seems in a great measure to depend upon it."[87]

[85] *Newport Mercury*, June 10, 1765; Captain Jeremiah Morgan to Governor Francis Fauquier, Sept. 11, 1767, Adm. 1/2116; log of *St. John*, July 10, 1764, Adm. 51/3961; Remarks of Thomas Hill in Colvill to Admiralty, July 26, 1764, Colvill to Admiralty, Jan. 12, Sept. 21, 1765, Adm. 1/482; log of *Maidstone*, June 5, 1765, Adm. 51/3897; Captain Smith to Colvill, July 12, 1764 (extract) in Colvill to Admiralty, Aug. 24, 1764, Adm. 1/482; *N.-Y. Gaz.; Weekly Post-Boy*, July 12, 1764; Thomas Laugharne to Admiral Colvill, Aug. 11, 1764 (extract) in Colvill to Admiralty, Aug. 24, 1764, Adm. 1/482; Stout's contention, "Manning the Royal Navy," 185, that "there is no recorded case of impressment on shore during the 1760's and 1770's, although the Navy did capture some deserters on land" is inaccurate. See Captain Jeremiah Morgan to Governor Francis Fauquier, Sept. 11, 1767, Adm. 1/2116, and *Pennsylvania Chronicle and Universal Advertiser* (Philadelphia), Oct. 26, 1767.
[86] For impressment by *Romney*, see log, June 10, 1768, Adm. 51/793; Mayo, ed., *Hist.*, III, 139. Oliver M. Dickerson, *The Navigation Acts and the American Revolution* (Philadelphia, 1951), 238, sees the riot as growing out of the seizure and has the support of most sources. Massachusetts Council to Governor Gage, Oct. 27, 1768, Bowdoin-Temple Papers, I, 120, Massachusetts Historical Society, Boston; Admiral Hood to Admiralty, July 11, 1768, Adm. 1/483; Hutchinson, *History of Massachusetts-Bay*, III, 136. On the other hand Thomas Hutchinson also spoke of impressment as adding "more fewel to the great stock among us before." Mass. Hist. Soc., *Proceedings, 1921–1922* (Boston, 1923), 283. Clark, "Impressment of Seamen," in *Essays to Andrews*, 219, describes the rioting as a response to impressment alone by a mob "which seemed to be always ready to resent any infringement of American liberties." Dickerson, *Navigation Acts*, 219–220, attributes the burning of a boat belonging to the customs collector to the mob's failure to locate *Romney's* press boat. In 1922 G. G. Wolkins, "Seizure of Liberty," 250, speculated that "impressment of seamen, rather than the seizure of John Hancock's goods, was perhaps the genesis of what happened." L. Kinvin Wroth and Hiller B. Zobel, eds., *Legal Papers of John Adams* (Cambridge, Mass., 1965), II, 179n, summarize: "Boston's position was that the employment of the *Romney*, already despised for the impressment activities of her captain, brought on the riot of 10 June." The riot seems to have been caused by a combination of factors among which impressment has been given too little attention.
[87] Boston Reg. Dept., *Records of Boston*, XX, 296; [Thomas Hutchinson], State of the Disorders, Confusion and Misgovernment, which have lately prevailed . . . in . . .

There were other impressment riots at New York in July of 1764 and July of 1765;[88] at Newport in July of 1764;[89] at Casco Bay, Maine, in December 1764.[90] Incidents continued during the decade following, and impressment flowered on the very eve of the Revolution. Early in 1775 the practice began to be used in a frankly vindictive and political way—because a town had inconvenienced an admiral, or because a town supported the Continental Congress.[91] Impresses were ordered and took place from Maine to Virginia.[92] In September a bundle of press warrants arrived from the Admiralty, along with word of the repeal of the Sixth of Anne. What had been dubious was now legal. Up and down the coast, officers rejoiced and went to work.[93]

Long before 1765 Americans had developed beliefs about impressment, and they had expressed those beliefs in words and deeds. Impressment was bad for trade and it was illegal. As such, it was, in the words of the Massachusetts House in 1720, "a great Breach on the Rights of His Majesties Subjects." In 1747 it was a violation of "the common Liberty of the Subject," and in 1754 "inconsistent with Civil Liberty, and the Natural Rights of Mankind."[94] Some felt in 1757 that it was even "abhorrent to the English Constitution."[95] In fact, the claim that impressment was unconstitutional was wrong. (Even *Magna Charta* was no protection. *Nullus liber homo capiatur* did not apply to seamen.)[96] Instead impressment indicated to Benjamin Franklin "that the constitution is yet imperfect, since in so general a case it doth not secure liberty, but destroys it." "If impressing seamen

---

Massachusetts, June 21, 1770, C.O. 5/759, Pt. 4; Report of Resolves Relating to Riot of June 10, June 14, 1768, James Bowdoin and Royall Tyler to Jno. Corner, June 18, 1768, Bowdoin-Temple Papers, I, 102, 104; *Mass. Gaz.* (Boston), Nov. 10, 1768. For Adams's authorship, see L. H. Butterfield *et al.*, eds., *Diary and Autobiography of John Adams* (New York, 1964), III, 291; Adams, ed., *Works of Adams*, III, 501.

88 *N.-Y. Gaz.; Weekly Post-Boy*, July 12, 1764, July 18, 1765; Thos. Laugharne to Admiral Colvill, Aug. 11, 1764 (extract) in Colvill to Admiralty, July 26, Aug. 24, 1764, Adm. 1/482; Weyman's *N. Y. Gaz.*, July 18, 1765.

89 Captain Smith to Colvill, July 12, 1764 (extract) in Colvill to Admiralty, Aug. 24, 1764, Adm. 1/482; Remarks of Thomas Hill in Colvill to Admiralty, July 26, 1764, Adm. 1/482; log of *Squirrel*, July 10, 1764, Adm. 51/929, log of *St. John*, July 10, 1764, Adm. 51/3961; *Newport Mercury*, July 16, 1764.

90 Colvill to Admiralty, Jan. 12, 1765, Adm. 1/482; log of *Gaspee*, Dec. 8, 10, 12, 1764, Adm. 51/3856.

91 Graves to Admiralty, Feb. 20, 1775, Adm. 1/485; *N. Y. Journal or Gen. Adv.*, Feb. 23, 1775; Margaret Wheeler Willard, ed., *Letters on the American Revolution, 1774–1776* (Boston, 1925), 65–66.

92 Graves to Admiralty, Apr. 11, 1775, Mowat to Graves, May 4, 1775, in Graves to Admiralty, May 13, 1775, Barkley to Graves, June 5, 1775, in Graves to Admiralty, June 22, 1775, Montagu to Graves, June 17, 1775, in Graves to Admiralty, July 17, 1775, Adm. 1/485; log of *Scarborough*, May 14, 1775, Adm. 51/867; log of *Fowey*, July 16, 1775, Adm. 51/375. Despite the troubles at Marblehead in February, *Lively* was still pressing there in May, Graves to Admiralty, May 13, 1775, Adm. 1/485.

93 Admiralty to Graves, June 24, Sept. 29, 1775, Adm. 2/549, 550; Graves to Admiralty, Sept. 12, 1775, List of . . . Press Warrants, Jan. 27, 1776, in Graves to Admiralty, Jan. 1776, Adm. 1/486; Shuldham to Arbuthnot, June 5, 1776, in Shuldham to Admiralty, July 24, 1776, Adm. 1/484.

94 Mass. Hist. Soc., *Mass. House Journals*, II, 300–301; Freeman, *Washington*, I, 199; *N.-Y. Gaz.; Weekly Post-Boy*, Aug. 12, 1754.

95 Mass. Hist. Soc., *Mass. House Journals*, XXXIII, Pt. ii, 434.

96 Hutchinson, *Press-Gang*, 5–7.

is of right by common law in Britain," he also remarked, "slavery is then of right by common law there; there being no slavery worse than that sailors are subjected to."[97]

For Franklin, impressment was a symptom of injustice built into the British Constitution. In *Common Sense* Tom Paine saw in impressment a reason for rejecting monarchy. In the Declaration of Independence Thomas Jefferson included impressment among the "Oppressions" of George III; later he likened the practice to the capture of Africans for slavery. Both "reduced [the victim] to . . . bondage by force, in flagrant violation of his own consent, and of his natural right in his own person."[98]

Despite all this, and all that went before, we have thought little of impressment as an element in explaining the conduct of the common man in the American Revolution.[99] Contemporaries knew better. John Adams felt that a tactical mistake by Thomas Hutchinson on the question of impressment in 1769 would have "accelerated the revolution. . . . It would have spread a wider flame than Otis's ever did, or could have done."[100] Ten years later American seamen were being impressed by *American* officers. The United States Navy had no better solution for "public Necessities" than had the Royal Navy. Joseph Reed, President of Pennsylvania, complained to Congress of "Oppressions" and in so doing offered testimony to the role of *British* impressment in bringing on revolution.

> We cannot help observing how similar this Conduct is to that of the British Officers during our Subjection to Great Brittain and are persuaded it will

[97] Sparks, ed., *Works of Franklin*, II, 338, 334. For opposition to impressment on the part of the Genevan democrat, Jean Louis De Lolme, and by the British radical John Wilkes, see Robert R. Palmer, *The Age of the Democratic Revolution* (Princeton, 1959), 148. *N.-Y. Gaz.; Weekly Post-Boy*, Dec. 31, 1770; *Annual Register . . . for 1771* (London, 1772), 67, 68, 70–71; R. W. Postgate, *That Devil Wilkes* (New York, 1929), 182; Percy Fitzgerald, *The Life and Times of John Wilkes* (London, 1888), II, 120.

[98] Paine, *Writings*, ed. Foner, I, 11. For later attacks on impressment by Paine see *ibid.*, I, 449, II, 476. The complaint in the Declaration of Independence alludes to impressment after the outbreak of fighting: "He has constrained our fellow Citizens taken Captive on the high Seas to bear Arms against their Country, to become the executioners of their friends and Brethren, or to fall themselves by their Hands." Carl L. Becker, *The Declaration of Independence* (New York, 1958), 190, 156, 166. Thomas Jefferson to Dr. Thomas Cooper, Sept. 10, 1814, Andrew A. Lipscomb and Albert Ellery Bergh, eds., *The Writings of Thomas Jefferson*, XIV (Washington, 1907), 183.

[99] James Fulton Zimmerman, *Impressment of American Seamen* (New York, 1925), esp. 11–17, treats the practice as almost non-existent before the Revolution, giving the pre-revolutionary phenomenon only the briefest consideration, and concluding, on the basis of speculative evidence, that impressment was rare in the colonies. The author does not understand the Sixth of Anne and thinks it was repealed in 1769. Clark, "Impressment of Seamen," in *Essays to Andrews*, 202; Paine, *Ships and Sailors of Salem*, 65; George Athan Billias, *General John Glover and his Marblehead Mariners* (New York, 1960), 31; Bridenbaugh, *Cities in Revolt*, 114–117, 308–310; Bernhard Knollenberg, *Origin of the American Revolution: 1759–1766* (New York, 1961), 12, 179–181, all see impressment as contributing in some way to the revolutionary spirit.

[100] Adams, ed., *Works of Adams*, II, 226*n*. Neil Stout, "Manning the Royal Navy," 182–184; suggests that impressment did not become a "great issue" of the American Revolution because American "radicals" did not *make* an issue of it and especially because of the failure of John Adams's attempt to make a "*cause celebre*" in 1769. Stout's approach sides with the navy and minimizes the *reality* of impressment as a grievance. Its implication is that the seaman had in fact no genuine grievance and that he acted in response to manipulation.

have the same unhappy effects viz., an estrangement of the Affections of the People from the Authority under which they act which by an easy Progression will proceed to open Opposition to the immediate Actors and Bloodshed.[101]

Impressment had played a role in the estrangement of the American people from the British government. It had produced "Odium" against the navy, and even six-year-olds had not been too young to have learned to detest it.[102] The anger of thousands of victims did not vanish. Almost four decades after the Declaration of Independence an orator could still arouse his audience by tapping a folk-memory of impressment by the same "haughty, cruel, and gasconading nation" which was once again trying to enslave free Americans.[103]

III

The seamen's conduct in the 1760's and 1770's makes more sense in the light of previous and continued impressment. What may have seemed irrational violence can now be seen as purposeful and radical. The pattern of rioting as political expression, established as a response to impressment, was now adapted and broadened as a response to the Stamp Act. In New York General Gage described the "insurrection" of October 31, 1765, and following as "composed of great numbers of Sailors." The seamen, he said, were "the only People who may be properly Stiled Mob," and estimates indicate that between a fifth and a fourth of New York's rioters were seamen. The disturbances began among the seamen—especially former privateersmen—on October 31. On November 1 they had marched, led primarily by their former captains; later they rioted, led by no one but themselves. Why? Because they had been duped by merchants, or, if not by merchants, then certainly by lawyers. So British officials believed—aroused by these men who meant to use them, the seamen themselves had nothing more than plunder on their minds. In fact, at that point in New York's rioting when the leaders lost control, the seamen, who were then in the center of town, in an area rich for plunder, chose instead to march in an orderly and disciplined way

---

[101] Pres. Reed to Pres. of Congress, 1779, Oct. 21, 1779, *Pa. Archives*, 1st Ser., VII, 762. Reed renewed his complaint of these "Oppressions" in the following year, Reed to Pennsylvania Delegates in Congress, 1780, *ibid.*, 1st Ser., VIII, 643.

[102] Colvill to Admiralty, Aug. 8, 1765, Adm. 1/482; Sherburne, *Memoirs*, 68.

[103] William M. Willett, *A Narrative of the Military Actions of Colonel Marinus Willett, Taken Chiefly from his own Manuscript* (New York, 1831), 149–151. On the level of leadership impressment was not a major cause of the American Revolution. But the extent to which the articulate voice a grievance is rarely an adequate measure of the suffering of the inarticulate. Since it is unrealistic to suppose that the victims of impressment forgot their anger, the question becomes not, why was impressment irrelevant to the American Revolution—for it had to be relevant, in this sense—but, rather, why were the articulate not *more* articulate about the seamen's anger? In part, perhaps, because much impressment took place offshore and was invisible to all but the seamen directly involved. But the leaders had always perceived even visible impressment more as an interference with commerce than as a form of slavery. As the Revolution approached, impressment as human slavery interested them even less than Negro slavery did; the gap between Jack Tar and the men who made laws for him continued. The failure of the elite to see impressment more clearly as a political issue means only that they failed, as we have, to listen to the seamen.

clear across town to do violence to the home and possessions of an English major whose provocative conduct had made him the obvious political enemy. Thus the "rioting" was actually very discriminating.[104]

Seamen and non-seamen alike joined to oppose the Stamp Act for many reasons,[105] but the seamen had two special grievances: impressment and the effect of England's new attitude toward colonial trade. To those discharged by the navy at the end of the war and others thrown out of work by the death of privateering were added perhaps twenty thousand more seamen and fishermen who were thought to be the direct victims of the post-1763 trade regulations.[106] This problem came to the fore in the weeks following

[104] General Gage to Secretary Conway, Nov. 4, Dec. 21, 1765, Clarence Edwin Carter, ed., *The Correspondence of General Thomas Gage . . . 1763–1775* (New Haven, 1931), I, 70–71, 79; *N.-Y. Gaz.; Weekly Post-Boy*, Nov. 7, 1765, estimates that there were four to five hundred seamen in the mob; Nov. 1, 7, 1765, *Montresor Journal*, 336, 339, estimates the total mob at "about 2000" and is the only source describing the participation of a professional group other than seamen, estimating 300 carpenters; R. R. Livingston to General Monckton, Nov. 8, 1765, Chalmers Manuscripts, IV, New York Public Library, for a note signed "Sons of Neptune"; Lieutenant-Governor Colden to Secretary Conway, Nov. 5, 9, 1765, O'Callaghan, ed., *Docs. Rel. Col. Hist. N. Y.*, VII, 771–774; *New York Mercury*, Nov. 4, 1765. For additional information on the leadership of privateer captains, especially Isaac Sears, see William Gordon, *History of the Rise, Progress, and Establishment of the United States of America* (London, 1788), I, 185–186. The navy continued to press during the crisis. See log of *Guarland*, Apr. 22, 1766, Adm. 51/386; Apr. 21, 1766, *Montresor Journal*, 361. Impressment also limited the navy's activities against the rioting. "As most of our men are imprest," wrote a captain in answer to a governor's request for men to put down a mob, "there is a great risque of their deserting." Marines were needed as sentries to keep the men from deserting. Archibald Kennedy to Cadwallader Colden, Nov. 1, 1765, *The Letters and Papers of Cadwallader Colden* (N.-Y. Hist. Soc., *Coll*. L–LVI [New York, 1918–1923]), VII, 85–86.

[105] For a fuller account of the seamen's opposition to the Stamp Act see Lemisch, "Jack Tar vs. John Bull," 76–128.

[106] *N.-Y. Gaz.; Weekly Post-Boy*, May 19, 1763; "Essay on the trade of the Northern Colonies," *ibid.*, Feb. 9, 1764. Even admirals were worried about the prospects of postwar unemployment, Colvill to Admiralty, Nov. 9, 1762, Adm. 1/482. During the French and Indian War 18,000 American seamen had served in the Royal Navy, *Annual Register . . . for 1778* (London, 1779), 201, and a large additional number had been privateersmen. Fifteen to twenty thousand had sailed in 224 privateers out of New York alone, 5670 of them in 1759, Fish, *New York Privateers*, 4, 54–82; Bridenbaugh, *Cities in Revolt*, 62. A New York merchants' petition of Apr. 20, 1764, expressed the fear that seamen thrown out of work by the Sugar Act might drift into foreign merchant fleets, *Journal of the Votes and Proceedings of the General Assembly of the Colony of New York* (New York, 1764–1766), II, 742–743. On the eve of the Revolution maritime commerce employed approximately 30,000–35,000 American seamen, Carman, ed., *American Husbandry*, 495–496; John Adams to the President of Congress, June 16, 1780, Francis Wharton, ed., *The Revolutionary Diplomatic Correspondence of the United States* (Washington, 1889), III, 789. I am presently assembling data which will allow more detailed statements on various demographic matters involving seamen, such as their numbers, comparisons with other occupations, their origins and permanence. For some further quantitative information on seamen in various colonial ports, see in addition to the sources cited immediately above, Evarts B. Greene and Richard B. Morris, *A Guide to the Principal Sources for Early American History (1600–1800) in the City of New York*, 2d ed., rev. (New York, 1953), 265; E. B. O'Callaghan, ed., *The Documentary History of the State of New York*, I (Albany, 1849), 493; Governor Clinton's Report on the Province of New York, May 23, 1749, Report of Governor Tryon on the Province of New York, June 11, 1774, O'Callaghan, ed., *Docs. Rel. Col. Hist. N. Y.*, VI, 511, VIII, 446; Main, *Social Structure*, 38–39; Benjamin W. Labaree, *Patriots and Partisans* (Cambridge, Mass., 1962), 5; John R. Bartlett, ed., *Records of the Colony of Rhode Island and Providence Plantations . . .* (Providence, 1856–1865), VI, 379.

November 1, 1765, when the Stamp Act went into effect. The strategy of opposition chosen by the colonial leadership was to cease all activities which required the use of stamps. Thus maritime trade came to a halt in the cities.[107] Some said that this was a cowardly strategy. If the Americans opposed the Stamp Act, let them go on with business as usual, refusing outright to use the stamps.[108] The leaders' strategy was especially harmful to the seamen, and the latter took the more radical position—otherwise the ships would not sail. And this time the seamen's radicalism triumphed over both colonial leadership and British officials. Within little more than a month the act had been largely nullified. Customs officers were allowing ships to sail without stamps, offering as the reason the fear that the seamen, "who are the people that are most dangerous on these occasions, as their whole dependance for a subsistence is upon Trade," would certainly "commit some terrible Mischief." Philadelphia's customs officers feared that the seamen would soon "compel" them to let ships pass without stamps. Customs officers at New York yielded when they heard that the seamen were about to have a meeting.[109]

Customs officers had worse luck on other days. Seamen battled them throughout the 1760's and 1770's. In October 1769 a Philadelphia customs officer was attacked by a mob of seamen who also tarred, feathered, and nearly drowned a man who had furnished him with information about illegally imported goods. A year later a New Jersey customs officer who approached an incoming vessel in Delaware Bay had *his* boat boarded by armed seamen who threatened to murder him and came close to doing so. When the officer's son came to Philadelphia, he was similarly treated by a mob of seamen; there were one thousand seamen in Philadelphia at the time, and according to the customs collector there, they were "always ready" to do such "mischief."[110] This old antagonism had been further politicized in

---

[107] See, for example, James and Drinker to William Starkey, Oct. 30, 1765, James and Drinker Letterbook; *N.-Y. Gaz.; Weekly Post-Boy*, Dec. 19, 1765.

[108] See, for example, *N.-Y. Gaz.; Weekly Post-Boy*, Nov. 28, Dec. 5, 1765. For a fuller account of this dispute, see Jesse Lemisch, "New York's Petitions and Resolves of December 1765: Liberals vs. Radicals," New-York Historical Society, *Quarterly*, XLIX (1965), 313–326.

[109] Edmund S. and Helen M. Morgan, *The Stamp Act Crisis* (Chapel Hill, 1953), 162. For a fuller account of the nullification of the Stamp Act, see *ibid.*, 159–179. The seamen's strategy may have been more effective in bringing about repeal than was the strategy of the leaders. Commenting on Parliament's secret debates, Lawrence Henry Gipson, "The Great Debate in the Committee of the Whole House of Commons on the Stamp Act, 1766, as Reported by Nathaniel Ryder," *Pennsylvania Magazine of History and Biography*, LXXXVI (1962), 10–41, notes that merchant pressure was only the "ostensible cause" of repeal and that many members were influenced by the violent resistance in America. I am indebted to E. S. Morgan for calling Ryder's notes to my attention.

[110] John Swift to Commissioners of Customs, Oct. 13, 1769, Customs Commissioners to Collector and Comptroller at Philadelphia, Oct. 23, 1769, John Hatton, A State of the Case, Nov. 8, 1770, John Hatton to John Swift, Nov. 9, 1770, Customs Commissioners at Boston to Collector and Comptroller at Philadelphia, Jan. 1771, John Swift to Customs Commissioners, Feb. 11, 1772, John Swift to Customs Commissioners, Nov. 15, 1770, Collector and Comptroller at Philadelphia to Customs Commissioners, Dec. 20, 1770, Philadelphia Custom House Papers, X, 1205, 1209, 1286, 1288; XI; XII; X, 1291–1292; XI, Hist. Soc. Pa. Swift made the customary contention that the seamen rioted because their captains told them to. For a qualification of this contention see Arthur L.

1768 when, under the American Board of Customs Commissioners, searchers began to break into sea chests and confiscate those items not covered by cockets, thus breaking an old custom of the sea which allowed seamen to import small items for their own profit. Oliver M. Dickerson has described this new "Invasion of Seamen's Rights" as a part of "customs racketeering" and a cause of animosity between seamen and customs officers.[111]

Many of these animosities flared in the Boston Massacre. What John Adams described as "a motley rabble of saucy boys, negroes and molattoes, Irish teagues and out landish jack tarrs," including twenty or thirty of the latter, armed with clubs and sticks, did battle with the soldiers. Their leader was Crispus Attucks, a mulatto seaman; he was shot to death in front of the Custom House.[112] One of the seamen's reasons for being there has been too little explored. The Massacre grew out of a fight between workers and off-duty soldiers at a ropewalk two days before.[113] That fight, in turn, grew out of the long-standing practice in the British army of allowing off-duty soldiers to take civilian employment. They did so, in Boston and elsewhere, often at wages which undercut those offered to Americans—including unemployed seamen who sought work ashore—by as much as 50 per cent.[114] In hard times this led to intense competition for work, and the Boston Massacre was in part a product of this competition. Less well known is the Battle of Golden Hill, which arose from similar causes and took place in New York six weeks before. In January 1770 a gang of seamen went from house to house and from dock to dock, using clubs to drive away the soldiers employed there and threatening anyone who might rehire them.[115] In the days of rioting which followed and which came to be called the Battle of Golden Hill, the only fatality was a seaman, although many other seamen were

---

Jensen, *The Maritime Commerce of Colonial Philadelphia* (Madison, 1963), 152. For a mob which attacked a collector of customs and others at the time of the Stamp Act and which may have been led by a seaman, see Morgan and Morgan, *Stamp Act Crisis*, 191–194; log of *Cygnet*, Aug. 29, 30, 1765, Adm. 51/223; Captain Leslie to Admiral Colvill, Aug. 30, 31, 1765, Adm. 1/482.

[111] Dickerson, *Navigation Acts*, 218–219. On seamen's right to import, see Morris, *Government and Labor*, 238–239.

[112] On the participation of seamen in the Boston Massacre see testimony of Robert Goddard, Oct. 25, 1770; Ebenezer Bridgham, Nov. 27, 1770; James Bailey, Nov. 28, Dec. 4, 1770; James Thompson, Nov. 30, 1770; all in Wroth and Zobel, eds., *Legal Papers of Adams*, III, 57–58, 103–106, 114–115, 115n–120n, 188, 189n, 268–269; also Frederick Kidder, *History of the Boston Massacre, March 5, 1770* (Albany, 1870), 288. For Adams's description, see Wroth and Zobel, eds., *Legal Papers of Adams*, III, 266. For Attucks see testimony of James Bailey, Nov. 28, 1770, of Patrick Keeton, Nov. 30, 1770, *ibid.*, III, 114–115, 115n–120n, 191–192, 262, 268–269; Kidder, *Boston Massacre*, 29n–30n, 287; Hutchinson, *History of Massachusetts-Bay*, ed. Mayo, III, 196; *Boston Herald*, Nov. 19, 1890 [sic.]; John Hope Franklin, *From Slavery to Freedom* (New York, 1956), 127.

[113] Lt. Col. W. Dalrymple to Hillsborough, Mar. 13, 1770, C.O. 5/759, Pt. 3, Library of Congress photostat; Capt. Thos. Rich to Admiralty, Mar. 11, 1770, Adm. 1/2388; Morris, *Government and Labor*, 190–192.

[114] *The Times*, Broadsides, 1770–21, New-York Historical Society, New York City; Morris, *Government and Labor*, 190n.

[115] *N.-Y. Gaz., Weekly Post-Boy*, Feb. 5, 1770, reports on the gang of seamen which went from dock to dock turning out soldiers. *The Times*. N.-Y. Hist. Soc. Broadsides, 1770–21 describes what could only be the same group and adds the threat of vengeance.

wounded in the attempt to take vengeance for the killing.[116] The antipathy between soldiers and seamen was so great, said John Adams, "that they fight as naturally when they meet, as the elephant and Rhinoceros."[117]

IV

To wealthy Loyalist Judge Peter Oliver of Massachusetts, the common people were only "Rabble"—like the "Mobility of all Countries, perfect Machines, wound up by any Hand who might first take the Winch." The people were "duped," "deceived," and "deluded" by cynical leaders who could "turn the Minds of the great Vulgar." Had they been less ignorant, Americans would have spurned their leaders, and there would have been no Revolution.[118] I have tested this generalization and found it unacceptable, at least in its application to colonial seamen. Obviously the seamen did not cause the American Revolution. But neither were they simply irrational fellows who moved only when others manipulated them. I have attempted to show that the seaman had a mind of his own and genuine reasons to act, and that he did act—purposefully. The final test of this purposefulness must be the Revolution itself. Here we find situations in which the seamen are separated from those who might manipulate them and thrown into great physical danger; if they were manipulated or duped into rebellion, on their own we might expect them to show little understanding of or enthusiasm for the war.

To a surprising extent American seamen remained Americans during the Revolution. Beaumarchais heard from an American in 1775 that seamen, fishermen, and harbor workers had become an "army of furious men, whose actions are all animated by a spirit of vengeance and hatred" against the English, who had destroyed their livelihood "and the liberty of their country."[119] The recent study of loyalist claimants by Wallace Brown confirms Oliver Dickerson's earlier contention that "the volumes dealing with loyalists and their claims discloses an amazing absence of names" of seamen. From a total of 2786 loyalist claimants whose occupations are known Brown found only 39, 1.4 per cent, who were seamen (or pilots). (It is possible to exclude fishermen and masters but not pilots from his figures.) In contrast, farmers numbered 49.1 per cent, artisans 9.8 per cent, merchants and shopkeepers 18.6 per cent, professionals 9.1 per cent, and officeholders 10.1 per cent. Although as Brown states, the poor may be underrepresented among

116 *N.-Y. Gaz.*, *Weekly Post-Boy*, Jan. 22, Feb. 5, 1770; Dawson, *Sons of Liberty*, 117n; William J. Davis, "The Old Bridewell," in Henry B. Dawson, *Reminiscences of the Park and its Vicinity* (New York, 1855), 61. Thomas Hutchinson noted the death of the seaman and believed that the Battle of Golden Hill "encouraged" Boston, thus leading to the Boston Massacre, Hutchinson, *History of Massachusetts-Bay*, ed. Mayo, III, 194.

117 Wroth and Zobel, eds., *Legal Papers of Adams*, III, 262. See also John Shy, *Toward Lexington* (Princeton, 1965), 309.

118 Douglass Adair and John A. Schutz, eds., *Peter Oliver's Origin and Progress of the American Rebellion: A Tory View* (San Marino, Calif., 1961), 65, 94–95, 48, 158, 39, 162, 165.

119 Louis de Loménie, *Beaumarchais and His Times*, trans. Henry S. Edwards (London, 1856), III, 110. See also Paine, *Writings*, ed. Foner, I, 33.

the claimants, "the large number of claims by poor people, and even Negroes, suggests that this is not necessarily true."[120]

An especially revealing way of examining the seamen's loyalties under pressure is to follow them into British prisons.[121] Thousands of them were imprisoned in such places as the ship *Jersey*, anchored in New York harbor, and Mill and Forton prisons in England. Conditions were abominable. Administration was corrupt, and in America disease was rife and thousands died.[122] If physical discomfort was less in the English prisons than in *Jersey*, the totality of misery may have been as great, with prisoners more distant from the war and worse informed about the progress of the American cause. Lost in a no-man's land between British refusal to consider them prisoners of war and Washington's unwillingness in America to trade trained soldiers for captured seamen, these men had limited opportunities for exchange. Trapped in this very desperate situation, the men were offered a choice: they could defect and join the Royal Navy. To a striking extent the prisoners remained patriots,[123] and very self-consciously so. "Like brave men, they resisted, and swore that they would never lift a hand to do any thing on

[120] Dickerson, *Navigation Acts*, 219, offers no explanation of the extent or method of his search. Wallace Brown, *The King's Friends* (Providence, 1965), 263, 287–344. Although Brown states that those listed pages 261–263 "make up 100 per cent of the claimants," he has excluded those whose occupations are unknown without noting the exclusion. He has also made some minor errors in his calculations, *ibid.*, 261–263, 295, 300, 313. The figures given in the text are my own computations based on corrected totals. I would like to thank Mr. Brown for his assistance in clearing up some of these errors. My own examination of New York materials in Loyalist Transcripts, I–VIII, XLI–XLVIII, and Lorenzo Sabine, *Biographical Sketches of Loyalists of the American Revolution with an Historical Essay* (Boston, 1864), turned up very few loyalist seamen, some of whom were obviously captains. See for example, Alpheus Avery and Richard Jenkins, Loyalist Transcripts, XVIII, 11–15, XLIII, 495–504. Brown, *King's Friends*, 307–308, also finds five out of a total of nine New York loyalist "seamen" are masters.

[121] See Morison, *John Paul Jones*, 165–166. "The unpleasant subject of the treatment of American naval prisoners during the war afforded fuel for American Anglophobes for a century or more, and there is no point in stirring it up again." For a plea that the horrors of the prisons not be forgotten see *New Hampshire Gazette* (Portsmouth), Feb. 9, 1779. The following brief account of the prisons in England and America summarizes my full-length study, "Jack Tar in the Darbies: American Seamen in British Prisons during the Revolution," to be completed shortly.

[122] On the prison ships the standard work at present is James Lenox Banks, *David Sproat and Naval Prisoners in the War of the Revolution with Mention of William Lenox, of Charlestown* (New York, 1909). This contains many useful documents, but the commentary is a one-sided whitewash written by a descendant who was not above ignoring evidence that Sproat elicited favorable accounts of conditions in *Jersey* through threats and bribery. Compare *ibid.*, 12–14, 81–84, with Danske Dandridge, *American Prisoners of the Revolution* (Charlottesville, 1911), 419–423.

[123] For instance, computations based on a list of prisoners in Mill Prison from May 27, 1777, to Jan. 21, 1782, from the *Boston Gaz.*, June 24, July 1, 8, 1782, indicate that 7.7% of 1013 men entered the king's service. This figure may be slightly distorted by the presence of a small number of non-Americans, but there is almost precise confirmation in Adm. 98/11–14 which lists only 190 out of a total of 2579 Americans, 7.4%, entered from all English prisons. This figure is slightly inflated. See Adm. 98/13, 108. See also, John Howard, *The State of the Prisons in England and Wales*, 3d ed. (Warrington, Eng., 1784), 185, 187, 188, 192, 194. I am indebted to John K. Alexander, a graduate student at the University of Chicago, for these figures and for valuable assistance in connection with the prisons.

board of King George's ships."[124] The many who stayed understood the political significance of their choice as well as the few who went. "What business had he to sell his Country, and go to the worst of Enemies?"[125] Instead of defecting they engaged in an active resistance movement. Although inexperienced in self-government and segregated from their captains, on their own these men experienced no great difficulties in organizing themselves into disciplined groups. "Notwithstanding they were located within the absolute dominions of his Britanic majesty," commented one, the men "adventured to form themselves into a republic, framed a constitution and enacted wholesome laws, with suitable penalties."[126] Organized, they resisted, celebrating the Fourth of July under British bayonets, burning their prisons, and escaping. Under these intolerable conditions, seamen from all over the colonies discovered that they shared a common conception of the cause for which they fought.[127]

At the Constitutional Convention Benjamin Franklin spoke for the seamen:

> It is of great consequence that we shd. not depress the virtue and public spirit of our common people; of which they displayed a great deal during the war, and which contributed principally to the favorable issue of it. He related the honorable refusal of the American seamen who were carried in great numbers into the British prisons during the war, to redeem themselves from misery or to seek their fortunes, by entering on board of the Ships of the Enemies to their Country; contrasting their patriotism with a contemporary instance in which the British seamen made prisoners by the Americans, readily entered on the ships of the latter on being promised a share of the prizes that might be made out of their own Country.[128]

Franklin spoke *against limiting* the franchise, not for *broadening* it: he praised the seamen, but with a hint of condescension, suggesting that it would be prudent to grant them a few privileges. A decade later a French traveller noticed that "except the laborer in ports, and the common sailor,

---

[124] Charles Herbert, *A Relic of the Revolution* (Boston, 1847), 157. See also entry for Aug. 19, 1778, in Marion S. Coan, "A Revolutionary Prison Diary: the Journal of Dr. Jonathan Haskins," *New England Quarterly*, XVII (1944), 430. Clearly there is plagiarism here, as there is in many other, but by no means all, entries in the two journals. For a contention that Haskins is the plagiarist, see John K. Alexander, "Jonathan Haskins' Mill Prison 'Diary': Can it be Accepted at Face Value?" *ibid.*, XL (1967), 561–564.

[125] William Russell, "Journal," Dec. 31, 1781, Paine, *Ships and Sailors of Salem*, 155.

[126] Sherburne, *Memoirs*, 81. For a prisoners' committee in Forton Prison see Jan. 27, 1779, Adm. 98/11, 442–444; for a trial in Mill Prison for "the crime of profanely damning of the Honrbl. Continental Congress," see Mar. 4, 1778, in Coan, "Revolutionary Prison Diary," 305. For self-government in *Jersey*, see Dring, *Recollections*, ed. Greene, 84–86.

[127] For example, Dring, *Recollections*, ed. Greene, 97–116; Herbert, *Relic of the Revolution*, 142; Russell, July 4, 1781, Paine, *Ships and Sailors of Salem*, 142. For a celebration of the British defeat at Yorktown, see Benjamin Golden to Benjamin Franklin, Dec. 2, 1781, Franklin Papers, XXIII, 94.

[128] Max Farrand, ed., *The Records of the Federal Convention of 1787*, rev. ed. (New Haven, 1937), II, 204–205.

148   JESSE LEMISCH

everyone calls himself, and is called by others, a *gentleman*."[129] Government was still gentleman's government: more people were defined as gentlemen, but Jack Tar was not yet among them.

V

Bernard Bailyn has recently added needed illumination to our understanding of pre-Revolutionary crowd action. Bailyn has disagreed with Peter Oliver and with modern historians who have concurred in describing pre-Revolutionary rioters as mindless, passive, and manipulated: "far from being empty vessels," rioters in the decade before the outbreak of fighting were "politically effective" and "shared actively the attitudes and fears" of their leaders; theirs was a " 'fully-fledged political movement.' "[130] Thus it would seem that Bailyn has freed himself from the influential grasp of Gustave Le Bon.[131] But Bailyn stopped short of total rejection. Only in 1765, he says, was the colonial crowd "transformed" into a political phenomenon. Before then it was "conservative"—like crowds in seventeenth- and eighteenth-century England, aiming neither at social revolution nor at social reform, but only at immediate revenge. Impressment riots and other "demonstrations by transient sailors and dock workers," Bailyn says, expressed no "deeply-lying social distress" but only a "diffuse and indeliberate antiauthoritarianism"; they were "ideologically inert."[132]

[129] Duke de la Rochefoucauld Liancourt, *Travels through the United States of North America . . .* , trans. H. Neuman (London, 1799), II, 672, quoted in Staughton Lynd and Alfred Young, "After Carl Becker: The Mechanics and New York City Politics, 1774–1801," *Labor History*, V (1964), 220.

[130] Bailyn, ed., *Pamphlets*, 581–583, 740, n. 10; Bailyn quotes the last phrase from George Rudé, "The London 'Mob' of the Eighteenth Century," *Historical Journal*, II (1959), 17. Bailyn is here contending that the post-1765 crowd was more highly developed than its English counterpart which was, according to Rudé, not yet "a fully-fledged political movement." See also Gordon S. Wood, "A Note on Mobs in the American Revolution," *Wm. and Mary Qtly.*, 3d Ser., XXIII (1966), 635–642.

[131] See Gustave Le Bon, *The Crowd* (New York, 1960). For a critique of interpretations of the American Revolution which seem to echo Le Bon, see Lemisch, "American Revolution," in Bernstein, ed., *Towards a New Past, passim.* Two useful discussions which place Le Bon and those he has influenced in the context of the history of social psychology (and of history) are George Rudé, *The Crowd in History* (New York, 1964), 3–15, and Roger W. Brown, "Mass Phenomena," in Gardner Lindzey, ed., *Handbook of Social Psychology* (Cambridge, Mass., 1954), II, 833–873. Both Rudé and Brown describe Le Bon's bias as "aristocratic." Also relevant are some of the studies in Duane P. Schultz, ed., *Panic Behavior* (New York, 1964), especially Alexander Mintz, "Non-Adaptive Group Behavior," 84–107.

[132] Bailyn, ed., *Pamphlets*, 581–583, citing Max Beloff, *Public Order and Popular Disturbances, 1660–1714* (London, 1938), 33, 153, 155, calls Beloff "the historian of popular disturbances in pre-industrial England," thus bypassing at least one other candidate for the title, George Rudé, whom he describes as "an English historian of eighteenth-century crowd phenomena." Rudé has shown in *The Crowd in History* and elsewhere that the crowd was purposeful, disciplined, and discriminating, that "in the eighteenth century the typical and ever recurring form of social protest was the riot." Rudé finds in Beloff echoes of Burke and Taine. Thus, the European foundation for Bailyn's interpretation of the pre-1765 American crowd is somewhat one-sided. Compare with Bailyn R. S. Longley's extremely manipulative "Mob Activities in Revolutionary Massachusetts," *New Eng. Qtly.*, VI (1933), 108: "Up to 1765, the Massachusetts mob was not political. Even after this date, its political organization was gradual, but it began with the Stamp Act."

Other historians have seen the colonial seamen—and the rest of the lower class—as mindless and manipulated, both before and after 1765.[133] The seeming implication behind this is that the seamen who demonstrated in colonial streets did so as much out of simple vindictiveness or undisciplined violence as out of love of liberty. Certainly such motivation would blend well with the traditional picture of the seaman as rough and ready. For along with the stereotype of Jolly Jack—and in part belying that stereotype—is bold and reckless Jack, the exotic and violent.[134] Jack *was* violent; the conditions of his existence were violent. Was his violence non-political? Sometimes. The mob of seventy to eighty yelling, club-swinging, out-of-town seamen who tried to break up a Philadelphia election in 1742 had no interest in the election; they had been bought off with money and liquor.[135]

Other violence is not so clear-cut. Edward Thompson has seen the fighting out of significant social conflict in eighteenth-century England "in terms of Tyburn, the hulks and the Bridewells on the one hand; and crime, riot, and mob action on the other."[136] Crime and violence among eighteenth-century American seamen needs reexamination from such a perspective. Does "mutiny" adequately describe the act of the crew which seized *Black Prince*, re-named it *Liberty*, and chose their course and a new captain by voting? What shall we call the conduct of 150 seamen who demanded higher wages by marching along the streets of Philadelphia with clubs, un-rigging vessels, and forcing workmen ashore? If "mutiny" is often the captain's name for what we have come to call a "strike," perhaps we might also detect some significance broader than mere criminality in the seamen's frequent assaults on captains and thefts from them.[137] Is it not in some sense a political act for a seaman to tear off the mast a copy of a law which says this disobedient seamen will be punished as "seditious"?

Impressment meant the loss of freedom, both personal and economic, and, sometimes, the loss of life itself. The seaman who defended himself

[133] For a further discussion see Lemisch, "American Revolution," in Bernstein, ed., *Towards a New Past, passim*. Bailyn, ed., *Pamphlets*, 581, is not entirely clear on the situation *after* 1765. He denies that "Revolutionary mobs" in America were in fact "revolutionary" and questions their "meliorist aspirations."

[134] For rough and ready Jack see Watson, *Sailor in English Fiction*, 45, 159–160; Hohman, *Seamen Ashore*, 217.

[135] *Pa. Archives*, 8th Ser., IV, 2971, 2987, 2995–2998, 3009; "Extracts from the Gazette, 1742," Labaree *et al.*, eds., *Papers of Benjamin Franklin*, II, 363–364. Yet even these men can be shown to have had some ideas; their shouts, which included attacks on "Broad-brims," "Dutch dogs," and "You damned Quakers, . . . Enemies to King GEORGE," are similar to those of the European "Church and King" rioters. See Rudé, *Crowd in History*, 135–148; E. J. Hobsbawm, *Primitive Rebels* (New York, 1965), 110, 118, 120–123.

[136] E. P. Thompson, *The Making of the English Working Class* (New York, 1964), 60.

[137] Deposition of Thomas Austin, Dec. 10, 1769, in Hutchinson to Hillsborough, Dec. 20, 1769, C.O. 5/759, Pt. 2, Library of Congress Transcript; *Pennsylvania Packet* (Philadelphia), Jan. 16, 1779; *Colonial Records of Pennsylvania 1683–1790* (Harrisburg, 1852–1853), XI, 664–665; J. Thomas Scharf and Thompson Westcott, *History of Philadelphia, 1609–1884* (Philadelphia, 1884), I, 403. For some crimes of seamen against masters see *The King v. John Forster*, Indictment for Petty Larceny, filed Oct. 23, 1772, N. Y. Supreme Court, Pleadings K-495; Deposition of Cap. Elder and Examination of John Forster, sworn Oct. 20, 1772, N. Y. Supreme Court, Pleadings K-457; *N.-Y. Gaz.; Weekly Post-Boy*, Feb. 2, 1764.

against impressment felt that he was fighting to defend his "liberty," and he justified his resistance on grounds of "right."[138] It is in the concern for liberty and right that the seaman rises from vindictiveness to a somewhat more complex awareness that certain values larger than himself exist and that he is the victim not only of cruelty and hardship but also, in the light of those values, of injustice. The riots ashore, whether they be against impressment, the Stamp Act, or competition for work express that same sense of injustice. And here, thousands of men took positive and effective steps to demonstrate their opposition to both acts and policies.

Two of England's most exciting historians have immensely broadened our knowledge of past and present by examining phenomena strikingly like the conduct and thought of the seamen in America. These historians have described such manifestations as "sub-political" or "pre-political," and one of them has urged that such movements be "seriously considered not simply as an unconnected series of individual curiosities, as footnotes to history, but as a phenomenon of general importance and considerable weight in modern history."[139] When Jack Tar went to sea in the American Revolution, he fought, as he had for many years before, quite literally, to protect his life, liberty, and property. It might be extravagant to call the seamen's conduct and the sense of injustice which underlay it in any fully developed sense ideological or political; on the other hand, it makes little sense to describe their ideological content as zero. There are many worlds and much of human history in that vast area between ideology and inertness.

Suggested Reading

The focus of historical argument about the extent of democracy in colonial America is provided by Robert E. and B. Katherine Brown in *Middle-class Democracy and the Revolution in Massachusetts, 1691–1780** (1955), which shows conclusively how widely available was the franchise, at least in the Bay Colony. The Browns have supplemented this work with *Virginia, 1705–1786: Democracy or Aristocracy?* (1964). As Zuckerman indicates—and as he argues at greater length in *Peaceable Kingdoms: New England Towns in the Eighteenth Century* (1970)—democracy must be defined in larger terms than the vote. Zuckerman has been challenged by David G. Allen and has rejoined in an exchange in *William and Mary Quarterly*, 3rd Ser., XXIX (July 1972), 443–68. Two important and useful essays that examine the entire debate and offer judicious arguments of their own are J. R. Pole's "Historians and the Problem of Early American Democracy," *American Historical Review*, LXVII (April 1962); and Richard Buel, Jr.'s "Democracy and the American Revolution: A Frame of Reference," *William and Mary Quarterly*, 3rd Ser., XXI (April 1964). Suffrage requirements and opportunities from the colonial period to the Civil War are evaluated in Chilton Williamson's *American Suffrage from Property to Democracy** (1960). An important work that relates the franchise, representation, and political thought is J. R. Pole's *Political Representation and the Origins of the American Republic**

---

[138] See above, 390.
[139] Thompson, *Making of the English Working Class*, 55, 59, 78; Hobsbawm, *Primitive Rebels*, 2, 7, 10.

(1966). Charles S. Sydnor's *American Revolutionaries in the Making: Political Practices in Washington's Virginia** (originally published as *Gentlemen Freeholders*, 1952) is a delightful study of late colonial politics, which may be supplemented by the relevant portions of Richard P. McCormick's case study, *The History of Voting in New Jersey: A Study of the Development of Election Machinery, 1664–1911* (1953), which introduces, as all studies of voting in the modern era must, the problem of the link between electoral democracy and partisan organization. Elisha P. Douglass in *Rebels and Democrats** (1955) examines the debates over democracy during the revolutionary era.

Democracy, of course, is more than an electoral condition. It is also a social circumstance, having to do with opportunity and social mobility. The principal attempt to examine social structure generally in late colonial America is Jackson Turner Main's *The Social Structure of Revolutionary America** (1965), which finds a high rate of social mobility and wide opportunity in a loose class structure. These conditions, Main argues in *The Upper House in Revolutionary America, 1765–1788* (1967), were reflected in the democratization of the upper chambers of the legislatures. Social conditions in an outlying New England town are portrayed in Charles S. Grant's fine *Democracy in the Connecticut Frontier Town of Kent** (1961).

The social structure of an urban setting, in which Lemisch's sailors lived and worked, is the subject of James A. Henretta's "Economic Development and Social Structure in Colonial Boston," *Wililam and Mary Quarterly*, 3rd Ser., XXII (January 1965). In a critique of Lemisch's general assumptions about the underclasses, James H. Hutson in "An Investigation of the Inarticulate: Philadelphia's White Oaks," *William and Mary Quarterly*, 3rd Ser., XXVIII (January 1971), argues that the proletariat was divided in its politics and loyalties, to which Lemisch has rejoined in *William and Mary Quarterly*, 3rd Ser., XXIX (January 1972).

* Also published in paperback edition.

The American Revolution

The Logic of Rebellion

Bernard Bailyn

When one thinks of the causes of the American
Revolution, one usually calls to mind a series of revenue
and punitive acts, restrictions on colonial government,
the long and "salutary" neglect by the mother country
of thirteen mature colonies, the needs of the British
in governing an empire, and the failure of repeated
colonial pleas for redress, most of which have to do
with political events and institutions. But what we so
easily identify as "causes" must first have had meaning
to the participants; something must have made them
seem part of a pattern and have given them a general
significance. Such a means of understanding was
provided the American colonists by a powerful
revolutionary ideology, about which Bernard Bailyn
of Harvard University has written in his Pulitzer
Prize–winning *Ideological Origins of the American
Revolution* (1967), from which the following selection
is taken.

  Bailyn's achievement has been to demonstrate that
the ideas that provided the terms in which the
colonists understood the events of the eighteenth
century derived from the writings of members of
the British opposition. Since the late seventeenth
century, such men as John Trenchard and Thomas
Gordon (authors of *Cato's Letters*, so popular in the
colonies), Viscount Bolingbroke, and Benjamin
Hoadley had been assailing the growing power and
pretensions of the Whig ministries of Britain. They

155

and others like them were the product of a tradition of religious dissent that had long arrayed itself against the great influence of the Church of England and against the worship and theology of High Church Anglicanism. Their writings became so influential in the colonies as the century wore on, Bailyn argues, precisely because they helped make sense of the circumstances faced by rapidly maturing colonial societies governed by a distant authority.

One of the modes of thought transmitted by these critics was the conspiracy explanation. Conspiracy theories are often viewed as the products of anxious and disordered minds. But Bailyn, without trying to determine whether or not a real conspiracy existed, implies that the colonists' belief in a "conspiracy against liberty" on the part of the church, the ministry, the army, the courts, the moneyed interests, the colonial governors, and some individuals was a rational response to a series of events that seemed to run counter to the traditions of British law and government. At any rate, according to Bailyn, this conspiracy theory was transformed under the press of events into constitutional arguments which, by 1776, had become a "world regenerative creed," an ideology of republicanism with its characteristic notes of optimism, moralism, and exclusivism.

Bailyn has succeeded, where no one else has, in placing the intellectual and cultural history of the Revolution within the context of British and American thought. But in placing so much emphasis on the intellectual setting of events, is he able to explain why the American Revolution occurred when it did? After all, it should make a difference to our understanding of the Revolution whether the conspiracy seen by contemporaries did or did not exist. Even if a conscious and purposeful conspiracy can reasonably be deduced from events by reasonable men, are we to conclude that the Revolution sprang from misunderstanding among mistaken men—and was thus perhaps unnecessary?

A further problem posed by Bailyn's approach concerns the relationship of ideas and actions. Ideas seem to require events to give them meaning and relevance; this is an argument that at least prevents us from viewing ideas as mere rationalizations of action. But then, in explaining such an occurrence as a revolution, must we not then give far more explanatory weight to events than Bailyn does?

Lord Chancellor Camden . . . *declared . . . that for some time he had beheld with silent indignation the arbitrary measures which were pursuing by the ministry; . . . that, however, he would do so no longer, but would openly and boldly speak his sentiments . . . In a word, he accused the ministry . . . of having formed a conspiracy against the liberties of their country.*
                        —Report of Speech in the House of Lords, 1770

A series of occurrences, many recent events, . . . afford great reason to believe that a deep-laid and desperate plan of imperial despotism has been laid, and partly executed, for the extinction of all civil liberty . . . The august and once revered fortress of English freedom—the admirable work of ages—the BRITISH CONSTITUTION *seems fast tottering into fatal and inevitable ruin. The dreadful catastrophe threatens universal havoc, and presents an awful warning to hazard all if, peradventure, we in these distant confines of the earth may prevent being totally overwhelmed and buried under the ruins of our most established rights.*
                        —Boston Town Meeting to its Assembly
                        Representatives, 1770

*T*he colonists believed they saw emerging from the welter of events during the decade after the Stamp Act a pattern whose meaning was unmistakable. They saw in the measures taken by the British government and in the actions of officials in the colonies something for which their peculiar inheritance of thought had prepared them only too well, something they had long conceived to be a possibility in view of the known tendencies of history and of the present state of affairs in England. They saw about them, with increasing clarity, not merely mistaken, or even evil, policies violating the principles upon which freedom rested, but what appeared to be evidence of nothing less than a deliberate assault launched surreptitiously by plotters against liberty both in England and in America. The danger to America, it was believed, was in fact only the small, immediately visible part of the greater whole whose ultimate manifestation would be the destruction of the English constitution, with all the rights and privileges embedded in it.

This belief transformed the meaning of the colonists' struggle, and it added an inner accelerator to the movement of opposition. For, once assumed, it could not be easily dispelled: denial only confirmed it, since what conspirators profess is not what they believe; the ostensible is not the real; and the real is deliberately malign.

It was this—the overwhelming evidence, as they saw it, that they were faced with conspirators against liberty determined at all costs to gain ends which their words dissembled—that was signaled to the colonists after 1763, and it was this above all else that in the end propelled them into Revolution.

Suspicion that the ever-present, latent danger of an active conspiracy of power against liberty was becoming manifest within the British Empire, assuming specific form and developing in coordinated phases, rose in the consciousness of a large segment of the American population before any of the famous political events of the struggle with England took place. No adherent of a nonconformist church or sect in the eighteenth century was free from suspicion that the Church of England, an arm of the English state, was working to bring all subjects of the crown into the community of the Church; and since toleration was official and nonconformist influence in English politics formidable, it was doing so by stealth, disguising its efforts, turning to improper uses devices that had been created for benign purposes. In particular, the Society for the Propagation of the Gospel in Foreign Parts, an arm of the Church created in 1701 to aid in bringing the Gospel to the pagan Indians, was said by 1763 to have "long had a formal design to root out Presbyterianism, etc., and to establish both episcopacy and bishops."[1]

. . .

Fear of an ecclesiastical conspiracy against American liberties, latent among nonconformists through all of colonial history, thus erupted into public controversy at the very same time that the first impact of new British policies in civil affairs was being felt. And though it was, in an obvious sense, a limited fear (for large parts of the population identified themselves with the Anglican Church and were not easily convinced that liberty was being threatened by a plot of Churchmen) it nevertheless had a profound indirect effect everywhere, for it drew into public discussion— evoked in specific form—the general conviction of eighteenth-century Englishmen that the conjoining of "temporal and spiritual tyranny" was, in John Adams' words, an event totally "calamitous to human liberty" yet an event that in the mere nature of things perpetually threatened. For, as David Hume had explained,

> in all ages of the world priests have been enemies to liberty . . . Liberty of thinking and of expressing our thoughts is always fatal to priestly power . . . and, by an infallible connection which prevails among all kinds of liberty,

---

[1] Jonathan Mayhew, *Observations on the Charter and Conduct of the Society for the Propagation of the Gospel in Foreign Parts* . . . (Boston, 1763), pp. 103–108.

this privilege can never be enjoyed . . . but in a free government. Hence
. . . all princes that have aimed at despotic power have known of what
importance it was to gain the established clergy; as the clergy, on their part,
have shown a great facility in entering into the views of such princes.

Fear of the imposition of an Anglican episcopate thus brought into focus a
cluster of ideas, attitudes, and responses alive with century-old Popish-
Stuart-Jacobite associations that would enter directly into the Revolutionary
controversy in such writings as John Adams' *Dissertation on the Canon and
Feudal Law* (1765) and Samuel Adams' "A Puritan" pieces published in the
Boston Gazette in 1768. And more than that, it stimulated among highly
articulate leaders of public opinion, who would soon be called upon to
interpret the tendency of civil affairs, a general sense that they lived in a
conspiratorial world in which what the highest officials professed was not
what they in fact intended, and that their words masked a malevolent design.[2]

Reinforcement for this belief came quickly. Even for those who had in no
way been concerned with the threat of an episcopal establishment, the
passage of the Stamp Act was not merely an impolitic and unjust law that
threatened the priceless right of the individual to retain possession of his
property until he or his chosen representative voluntarily gave it up to
another; it was to many, also, a danger signal indicating that a more general
threat existed. For though it could be argued, and in a sense proved by the
swift repeal of the act, that nothing more was involved than ignorance or

---

[2] Adams, *Dissertation, in Works*, III, 450, 451; Hume, "Of the Parties of Great
Britain," in Charles W. Hendel, ed., *David Hume's Political Essays* (New York, 1953),
pp. 86, 87; Henry A. Cushing, ed., *The Writings of Samuel Adams* (New York, 1904–
1908), I, 201–212. Fear of the conjunction of civil and ecclesiastical tyrannies was central
to John Adams' understanding of American history as well as of the Revolutionary
crisis. It had been, he wrote, "a hatred, a dread, a horror, of the infernal confederacy before described that projected, conducted, and accomplished the settlement of America,"
and it was this same confederacy that confronted Americans in 1765; "There seems to be
a direct and formal design on foot to enslave all America. This, however, must be done
by degrees. The first step that is intended seems to be an entire subversion of the whole
system of our fathers by the introduction of the canon and feudal law into America
(*Works*, III, 464). "Popery," the conjunction of the Church of Rome with aggressive
civil authority, was felt to be the greatest threat, the classic threat; but "popery" was
only a special case, though the superlative one, of the more general phenomenon: "it has
been a general mistake," Molesworth had pointed out, to think "that the popish religion
is the only one of all the Christian sects proper to introduce and establish slavery in a
nation insomuch that popery and slavery have been thought inseparable . . . Other
religions, and particularly the *Lutheran*, has [sic] succeeded as effectually in this design
as ever popery did . . . It is not popery as such but the doctrine of a blind obedience,
in what religion soever it be found, that is the destruction of the liberty and consequently of all the happiness of any nation." *An Account of Denmark* . . . (London,
1694), pp. 258–259. Fear of the association of priesthood and magistracy in arbitrary rule
runs through Eliot's and Mayhew's correspondences with Thomas Hollis; Mayhew contributed to the fear not only indirectly in his attacks on the Society for the Propagation
of the Gospel but directly in his Dudleian lecture, *Popish Idolatry* . . . (Boston, 1765).
On the persistence of the fear of episcopacy and its spillover into secular problems, see,
for example, Eliot to Hollis, January 26, 1771, MHS *Colls.*, 4th ser., IV, 255: "The design
will never be abandoned—we fear a *coup de main*"; and, in general, Bridenbaugh, *Mitre
and Sceptre*, chap. ix: "Bishops and Stamps, 1764–1766." For John Adams' final summary
of the Mayhew-Apthorp affair, see below, pp. 256–257.

confusion on the part of people in power who really knew better and who, once warned by the reaction of the colonists, would not repeat the mistake —though this could be, and by many was, concluded, there nevertheless appeared to be good reason to suspect that more was involved. For from whom had the false information and evil advice come that had so misled the English government? From officials in the colonies, said John Adams, said Oxenbridge Thacher, James Otis, and Stephen Hopkins—from officials bent on overthrowing the constituted forms of government in order to satisfy their own lust for power, and not likely to relent in their passion. Some of these local plotters were easily identified. To John Adams, Josiah Quincy, and others the key figure in Massachusetts from the beginning to the end was Thomas Hutchinson who by "serpentine wiles" was befuddling and victimizing the weak, the avaricious, and the incautious in order to increase his notorious engrossment of public office. In Rhode Island it was, to James Otis, that "little, dirty, drinking, drabbing, contaminated knot of thieves, beggars, and transports . . . made up of Turks, Jews, and other infidels, with a few renegado Christians and Catholics"—the Newport junto, led by Martin Howard, Jr., which had already been accused by Stephen Hopkins and others in Providence of "conspiring against the liberties of the colony."[3]

But even if local leaders associated with power elements in England had not been so suspect, there were grounds for seeing more behind the Stamp Act than its ostensible purpose. The official aim of the act was, of course, to bring in revenue to the English treasury. But the sums involved were in fact quite small, and "some persons . . . may be inclined to acquiesce under it." But that would be to fall directly into the trap, for the smaller the taxes, John Dickinson wrote in the most influential pamphlet published in America before 1776, the more dangerous they were, since they would the more easily be found acceptable by the incautious, with the result that a precedent would be established for making still greater inroads on liberty and property.

> Nothing is wanted at home but a PRECEDENT, the force of which shall be established by the tacit submission of the colonies . . . If the Parliament

[3] For a succinct explanation of the manifest threat of the Stamp Act, see Stephen Hopkins, *The Rights of Colonies Examined* (Providence, 1765: JHL Pamphlet 9), pp. 16–17. Adams' almost paranoiac suspicions of Hutchinson's hidden motives run through his *Diary and Autobiography;* e.g., I, 306; II, 39; III, 430. See also his "Novanglus" papers, in *Works*, IV, esp. pp. 62–63, 67–71, 87; and references in his correspondence: *Works*, X, 285–286, 298. It is the generality of such suspicions that accounts for the furor caused by the publication in 1773 of Hutchinson's innocuous letters of 1768—letters in which, the publishers wrote in the pamphlet's title, "*the Judicious Reader Will Discover the Fatal Source of the Confusion and Bloodshed*" (JHL Pamphlet 40). Josiah Quincy thought he saw the final proof of Hutchinson's conspiratorial efforts in his maneuverings with the North administration in London in 1774 and 1775: "Journal of Josiah Quincy Jun. . . . in England . . . ," MHS *Procs.*, 50 (1916–17), 444, 446, 447, 450, 452. Thacher's suspicions of Hutchinson (whom he called "Summa Potestatis," or "Summa" for short) are traced in the Introduction to his *Sentiments of a British American* (Boston, 1764; JHL Pamphlet 8), in Bailyn, *Pamphlets*, I. Otis' phrase is quoted from his abusive pamphlet, *Brief Remarks on the Defence of the Halifax Libel . . .* (Boston, 1765), p. 5. The charge against Howard appeared in the *Providence Gazette*, September 15, 1764, and is part of the intense antipathy that built up in Providence against the royalist group in Newport. See, in general, Edmund S. Morgan and Helen M. Morgan, *The Stamp Act Crisis* (Chapel Hill, 1953), chap. iv; and Introduction to Howard's *Letter from a Gentleman at Halifax* (Newport, 1765: JHL Pamphlet 10).

succeeds in this attempt, other statutes will impose other duties . . . and thus the Parliament will levy upon us such sums of money as they choose to take, *without any other* LIMITATION *than their* PLEASURE.

Others saw more drastic hidden meanings and implications in the passage of the Stamp Act. "If the real and only motive of the minister was to raise money from the colonies," Joseph Warren wrote in 1766, "that method should undoubtedly have been adopted which was least grievous to the people." Choice of so blatantly obnoxious a measure as the Stamp Act, consequently, "has induced some to imagine that the minister designed by this act to force the colonies into a rebellion, and from thence to take occasion to treat them with severity, and, by military power, to reduce them to servitude." Such a supposition was perhaps excessive: "charity forbids us to conclude [the ministry] guilty of so black a villainy. But . . . it is known that tyrannical ministers have, at some time, embraced even this hellish measure to accomplish their cursed designs," and speculation based on "admitting this to have been his aim" seemed well worth pursuing. To John Adams it seemed "very manifest" that the ultimate design behind the Stamp Act was an effort to forge the fatal link between ecclesiastical and civil despotism, the first by stripping the colonists "in a great measure of the means of knowledge, by loading the press, the colleges, and even an almanac and a newspaper with restraints and duties," the second, by recreating the inequalities and dependencies of feudalism "by taking from the poorer sort of people all their little subsistence, and conferring it on a set of stamp officers, distributors, and their deputies." This last point was the most obvious: "as the influence of money and places generally procures to the minister a majority in Parliament," Arthur Lee wrote, so an income from unchecked taxation would lead to a total corruption of free government in America, with the result that the colonies would "experience the fate of the *Roman* people in the deplorable times of their slavery."[4]

. . .

. . . During the same years the independence of the judiciary, so crucial a part of the constitution, was suddenly seen to be under heavy attack, and by the mid-1760's to have succumbed in many places.[5]

This too was not a new problem. The status of the colonial judiciary had been a controversial question throughout the century. The Parliamentary statute of 1701 which guaranteed judges in England life tenure in their posts had been denied to the colonies, in part because properly trained lawyers were scarce in the colonies, especially in the early years, and appoint-

[4] *Letters from a Farmer in Pennsylvania* . . . (Philadelphia, 1768: JHL Pamphlets 23), p. 55; Warren to Edmund Dana, Boston, March 19, 1766, in Richard Frothingham, *Life and Times of Joseph Warren* (Boston, 1865), pp. 21–22; Adams, *Dissertation,* in *Works,* III, 464; [Arthur Lee], "Monitor VI," in *Virginia Gazette* (R), March 31, 1768. For an elaboration of Dickinson's argument on the special dangers of "imperceptible" taxes, see Mercy Otis Warren, *History of the . . . American Revolution* . . . (Boston, 1805), I, 45.

[5] For further details on the problem of the judiciary—which had been discussed in terms indistinguishable from those of the Revolutionary era probably as early as 1701 (Louis B. Wright, ed., *An Essay upon the Government of the English Plantations* . . . , San Marino, 1945, p. 40), certainly as early as 1707 (Roy N. Lokken, *David Lloyd,* Seattle, 1959, pp. 173–175)—and for documentation of the paragraphs that follow, see the Introduction and notes to *A Letter to the People of Pennsylvania* (Philadelphia, 1760: JHL Pamphlet 2), in Bailyn, *Pamphlets,* I.

ments for life would prevent the replacment of ill-qualified judges by their betters, when they appeared; and in part because, judicial salaries being provided for by temporary legislative appropriations, the removal of all executive control from the judiciary, it was feared, would result in the hopeless subordination of the courts to popular influences. The status of the judiciary in the eighteenth century was therefore left open to political maneuvering in which, more often than not, the home government managed to carry its point and to make the tenure of judges as temporary as their salaries. Then suddenly, in the early 1760's, the whole issue exploded. In 1759 the Pennsylvania Assembly declared that the judges of that province would thereafter hold their offices by the same permanence of tenure that had been guaranteed English judges after the Glorious Revolution. But the law was disallowed forthwith by the crown. Opposition newspapers boiled with resentment; angry speeches were made in the Assembly; and a pamphlet appeared explaining in the fullest detail the bearing of judicial independence on constitutional freedom.

In New York the issue was even more inflamed and had wider repercussions. There, the judges of the Supreme Court, by a political maneuver of 1750, had managed to secure their appointments for life. But this tenure was interrupted by the death of George II in 1760 which required the reissuance of all crown commissions. An unpopular and politically weak lieutenant governor, determined to prevent his enemies from controlling the courts, refused to recommission the judges on life tenure. The result was a ferocious battle in which the opposition asserted New York's "*undoubted right* of having the judges of our courts on a constitutional basis," and demanded the "liberties and privileges" of Englishmen in this connection as in all others. But they were defeated, though not by the governor. In December 1761 orders were sent out from the King in Council to all the colonies, permanently forbidding the issuance of judges' commissions anywhere on any tenure but that of "the pleasure of the crown."[6]

All the colonies were affected. In some, like New Jersey, where the governor's incautious violation of the new royal order led to his removal from office, or like North Carolina, where opposition forces refused to concede and managed to keep up the fight for permanent judicial tenure throughout the entire period from 1760 to 1776, the issue was directly joined. In others, as in Massachusetts, where specific Supreme Court appointments were vehemently opposed by anti-administration interests, the force of the policy was indirect. But everywhere there was bitterness at the decree and fear of its implications, for everywhere it was known that judicial tenure "at the will of the crown" was "dangerous to the liberty and property of the subject," and that if the bench were occupied by "men who depended upon the smiles of the crown for their daily bread," the possibility of having an independent judiciary as an effective check upon executive power would be wholly lost.[7]

[6] Milton M. Klein, "Prelude to Revolution in New York: Jury Trials and Judicial Tenure," *W.M.Q.*, 3d ser., 17 (1960), 452.

[7] [William H. Drayton], *A Letter from Freeman of South-Carolina* . . . (Charleston, 1774: JHL Pamphlet 45), pp. 10, 20. For other characteristic expressions of the fear of a corrupt judiciary, see [John Allen], *An Oration upon the Beauties of Liberty* . . . (Boston, 1773; JHL Pamphlet 38), pp. 21 ff.; *The Conduct of Cadwallader Colden* . . .

This fear was magnified by the rumor, which was circulating vigorously as early as 1768, that it was part of the administration's policy to have the salaries of the colonial judges "appointed for them by the crown, independent of the people." If this ever happened, the Boston Town Meeting asserted when the rumor was becoming actuality, it would "complete our slavery." The reasoning was simple and straightforward:

> if taxes are to be raised from us by the Parliament of Great Britain without our consent, and the men on whose opinions and decisions our properties, liberties, and lives in a great measure depend receive their support from the revenues arising from these taxes, we cannot, when we think of the depravity of mankind, avoid looking with horror on the danger to which we are exposed!

"More and more," as the people contemplated the significance of crown salaries for a judiciary that served "at pleasure," was it clear that "the designs of administration [were] totally to subvert the constitution." Any judge, the House in Massachusetts ultimately stated, who accepted such salaries would thereby declare "that he has not a due sense of the importance of an impartial administration of justice, that he is an enemy to the constitution, and has it in his heart to promote the establishment of an arbitrary government in the province."[8]

Long before this, however, another aspect of the judicial system was believed also to have come under deliberate attack. The jury system, it was said, in New York particularly but elsewhere as well, was being systematically undermined. In New York the same executive who had fought the permanent tenure of judges insisted on the legality of allowing jury decisions, on matters of fact as well as of law, to be appealed to the governor and Council. This effort, though defeated within a year by action of the Board of Trade in England, had a lasting impact on the political consciousness of New Yorkers. It was publicly assailed, in the year of the Stamp Act, as "arbitrary" and "scandalous" in its deliberate subversion of the British constitution.[9]

Associated with this but more important because more widespread in its effect was the extension and enforcement of the jurisdiction of the vice-admiralty courts—"prerogative" courts composed not of juries but of single judges whose posts were "political offices in the hands of the royal governors, to be bestowed upon deserving friends and supporters." Since these courts had jurisdiction over the enforcement of all laws of trade and navigation as well as over ordinary marine matters, they had always been potentially threatening to the interests of the colonists. But in the past, by one

([New York], 1767), reprinted in *Collections of the New-York Historical Society*, X (New York, 1877), 433–467; [John Allen], *The American Alarm . . . for the Rights, and Liberties, of the People . . .* (Boston, 1773: JHL Pamphlet 39), 1st sec., pp. 17, 20, 27, 28; *Votes and Proceedings of Boston* (JHL 36), pp. 37–38; Adams, *Diary and Autobiography*, II, 36, 65–67; III, 297 ff.

[8] *Votes and Proceedings of Boston* (JHL 36), p. 20; Thomas Hutchinson, *The History of . . . Massachusetts-Bay* (Lawrence S. Mayo, ed., Cambridge, 1936), III, 278, 279. See also, Gipson, *British Empire*, XII, 47, 139 ff., and Hutchinson, *History*, III, Appendices V, W.

[9] Klein, "Prelude to Revolution in New York," pp. 453–459.

means or another, they had been curtailed in their effect, and much of their business had been shunted off to common law courts dominated by juries. Suddenly in the 1760's they acquired a great new importance, for it was into their hands that the burden of judicial enforcement of the new Parliamentary legislation fell. It was upon them, consequently, and upon the whole principle of "prerogative" courts that abuse was hurled as the effect of their enhanced power was felt. "What has America done," victims of the decisions of these courts asked, "to be thus particularized, to be disfranchised and stripped of so invaluable a privilege as the trial by jury?" The operations of the vice-admiralty courts, it was felt, especially after their administrative reorganization in 1767, denied Americans a crucial measure of the protection of the British constitution. "However respectable the judge may be, it is however an hardship and severity which distinguishes [defendants before this court] from the rest of Englishmen." The evils of such prerogative invasion of the judiciary could hardly be exaggerated: their "enormous created powers . . . threatens future generations in America with a curse tenfold worse than the Stamp Act."[10]

The more one looked the more one found evidences of deliberate malevolence. In Massachusetts, Thomas Hutchinson's elaborate patronage machine, long in existence but fully organized only after the arrival of Governor Francis Bernard in 1760, appeared to suspicious tribunes like Oxenbridge Thacher and John Adams to constitute a serious threat to liberty. The Hutchinsons and the Olivers and their ambitious allies, it was said (and the view was widely circulated through the colonies), had managed, by accumulating a massive plurality of offices, to engross the power of all branches of the Massachusetts government thereby building a "foundation sufficient on which to erect a tyranny."

> Bernard had all the executive, and a negative of the legislative; Hutchinson and Oliver, by their popular arts and secret intrigues, had elevated to the [Council] such a collection of crown officers and their own relations as to have too much influence there; and they had three of a family on the superior bench . . . This junto, therefore, had the legislative and executive in their control, and more natural influence over the judicial than is ever to be trusted to any set of men in the world.

With encouragement, no doubt, from England, they were stretching their power beyond all proper bounds, becoming "conspirators against the public liberty."[11]

The same evil of plural officeholding, tending to destroy the protective mechanism of the separation of powers, was observed to be at work in

---

[10] Carl Ubbelohde, *The Vice-Admiralty Courts and the American Revolution* (Chapel Hill, 1960), pp. 125–126, 112. For further expressions of antipathy to the admiralty courts, see especially the Laurens pamphlet cited in note 7 above, and also, besides the references indexed in Bailyn, *Pamphlets*, I, Adams, *Works*, III, 466–467; *Votes and Proceedings of Boston* (JHL 36), p. 24; and Oliver M. Dickerson, comp., *Boston under Military Rule, 1768–1769* . . . (Boston, 1936), pp. 46, 54, 56, 68, 72, which documents the popular comparison of vice-admiralty courts and the Court of Star Chamber.

[11] John Adams ("Novanglus"), *Works*, IV, 53 ff., 63, and citations in note 29 below; Ellen E. Brennan, *Plural Office-Holding in Massachusetts, 1760–1780* (Chapel Hill, 1945), chaps. i, ii. See also references to Hutchinson, above, note 4.

South Carolina. In both cases the filiation between the engrossing of offices in England and in America could be said to be direct. The self-seeking monopolists of office in the colonies, advancing themselves and their faithful adherents "to the exclusion of much better men," Adams wrote somewhat plaintively, were as cravenly obedient to their masters in power in England as their own despicable "creatures" were to them.[12] How deep this issue ran, how powerful its threat, could be seen best when one noted the degree to which it paralleled cognate developments in England.

John Wilkes's career was crucial to the colonists' understanding of what was happening to them; his fate, the colonists came to believe, was intimately involved with their own.[13] Not only was he associated in their minds with general opposition to the government that passed the Stamp Act and the Townshend Duties, that was flooding the colonies with parasitic placemen, and that appeared to be making inroads into the constitution by weakening the judiciary and bestowing monopolies of public offices on pliant puppets—not only was he believed to be a national leader of opposition to such a government, but he had entered the public arena first as a victim and then as the successful antagonist of general warrants, which, in the form of writs of assistance, the colonists too had fought in heroic episodes known throughout the land. He had, moreover, defended the sanctity of private property against confiscation by the government. His cause was their cause. His *Number 45 North Briton* was as celebrated in the colonies as it was in England, and more generally approved of; its symbolism became part of the iconography of liberty in the colonies. His return from exile in 1768 and subsequent election to Parliament were major events to Americans. Toasts were offered to him throughout the colonies, and substantial contributions to his cause as well as adulatory letters were sent by Sons of Liberty in Virginia, Maryland, and South Carolina. A stalwart, independent opponent of encroaching government power and a believer in the true principles of the constitution, he was expected to do much in Parliament for the good of all: so the Bostonians wrote him in June 1768

> your perseverance in the *good old cause* may still prevent the great system from dashing to pieces. 'Tis from your endeavors we hope for a royal 'Pascite, ut ante, boves,' and from our attachment to 'peace and good order' we wait for a constitutional redress: being determined that the King of Great Britain shall have subjects but not slaves in these remote parts of his dominions.[14]

By February 1769 it was well known that "*the fate of Wilkes and America must stand or fall together*."[15] The news, therefore, that by the maneuvers of the court party Wilkes had been denied the seat in Parliament to

[12] Drayton, *Letter from Freeman* (JHL 45), pp. 9, 18–19, 32–33; Edward McCrady, *The History of South Carolina under the Royal Government, 1719–1776* (New York, 1899), pp. 533–535, 710–713; Adams, *Diary and Autobiography*, I, 306; II, 39.

[13] For a detailed discussion of the Wilkes affair in the context of the present discussion, see Pauline Maier, "John Wilkes and American Disillusionment with Britain," *W.M.Q.*, 3d ser., 20 (1963), 373–395.

[14] Boston Sons of Liberty to Wilkes, June 6, 1768, MHS *Procs.*, 47 (1913–14), 191. The quotation is from Vergil, *Eclogues*, i, 45; "pasture your cattle as of old."

[15] William Palfrey to Wilkes, February 21, 1769, MHS *Procs.*, 47 (1913–14), 197.

which he had been duly elected came as a profound shock to Americans. It shattered the hopes of many that the evils they saw around them had been the result not of design but of inadvertence, and it portended darker days ahead. When again, and then for a second, a third, and a fourth time Wilkes was re-elected to Parliament and still denied his seat, Americans could only watch with horror and agree with him that the rights of the Commons, like those of the colonial Houses, were being denied by a power-hungry government that assumed to itself the privilege of deciding who should speak for the people in their own branch of the legislature. Power had reached directly and brutally into the main agency of liberty. Surely Wilkes was right: the constitution was being deliberately, not inadvertently, torn up by its roots.

Meanwhile an event even more sinister in its implications had taken place in the colonies themselves. On October 1, 1768, two regiments of regular infantry, with artillery, disembarked in Boston. For many months the harassed Governor Bernard had sought some legal means or excuse for summoning military help in his vain efforts to maintain if not an effective administration then at least order in the face of Stamp Act riots, circular letters, tumultuous town meetings, and assaults on customs officials. But the arrival of troops in Boston increased rather than decreased his troubles. For to a populace steeped in the literature of eighteenth-century English politics the presence of troops in a peaceful town had such portentous meaning that resistance instantly stiffened. It was not so much the physical threat of the troops that affected the attitudes of the Bostonians; it was the bearing their arrival had on the likely tendency of events. Viewed in the perspective of Trenchard's famous tracts on standing armies and of the vast derivative literature on the subject that flowed from the English debates of the 1690's, these were not simply soldiers assembled for police duties; they were precisely what history had proved over and over again to be prime movers of the process by which unwary nations lose "that precious jewel *liberty*." The mere rumor of possible troop arrivals had evoked the age-old apprehensions. "The raising or keeping a standing army within the kingdom in time of peace, unless it be with the consent of Parliament, is against the law," the alarmed Boston Town Meeting had resolved. It is, they said,

> the indefeasible right of [British] subjects to be *consulted* and to give their *free consent in person* or by representatives of their own free election to the raising and keeping a standing army among them; and the inhabitants of this town, being free subjects, have the same right derived from nature and confirmed by the British constitution as well as the said royal charter; and therefore the raising or keeping a standing army without their consent in person or by representatives of their own free election would be an infringement of their natural, constitutional, and charter rights; and the employing such army for the enforcing of laws made without the consent of the people, in person or by their representatives, would be a grievance.[16]

But the troops arrived, four regiments in all: in bold, stark actuality a standing army—just such a standing army as had snuffed out freedom in Denmark, classically, and elsewhere throughout the world. True, British

[16] *Sixteenth Report of the Boston Record Commissioners*, p. 263.

regulars had been introduced into the colonies on a permanent basis at the end of the Seven Years' War; that in itself had been disquieting. But it had then been argued that troops were needed to police the newly acquired territories, and that they were not in any case to be regularly garrisoned in peaceful, populous towns.[17] No such defense could be made of the troops sent to Boston in 1768. No simple, ingenuous explanation would suffice. The true motive was only too apparent for those with eyes to see. One of the classic stages in the process of destroying free constitutions of government had been reached.

To those most sensitive to the ideological currents of the day, the danger could scarcely have been greater. "To have a standing army!" Andrew Eliot wrote from Boston to Thomas Hollis in September, 1768,

> Good God! What can be worse to a people who have tasted the sweets of liberty! Things are come to an unhappy crisis; there will never be that harmony between Great Britain and her colonies that there hath been; all confidence is at an end; and the moment there is any blood shed all affection will cease.

He was convinced, he wrote, that if the English government "had not had their hands full at home they would have crushed the colonies." As it was, England's most recent actions tended only "to hasten that independency which at present the warmest among us deprecate." "I fear for the nation," he concluded, and his fears were shared not only by all liberty-minded Bostonians but also, through the stimulation of the "Journal of the Times," a day-by-day account of Boston "under military rule" that was, in effect, syndicated throughout the colonies, it was shared by politically and ideologically sensitive Americans everywhere. Time did not ease these anxieties; it merely complicated them. Fear and hatred became edged with contempt. "Our people begin to despise a military force," Eliot observed a year after the troops had first appeared; they coolly woo away the soldiers and drag offending officers before the courts—which, he grimly added, continue to function "notwithstanding all their efforts." But "things cannot long remain in the state they are now in; they are hastening to a crisis. What will be the event, God knows."[18]

And again significant corroboration for America's fears could be found in developments in England, and support furnished for the belief that events in America were only part of a larger whole. On May 10, 1768, a mob, assembled in St. George's Fields, London, in support of the imprisoned Wilkes, was fired upon by the regiment of Foot Guards that had been summoned

[17] Gipson, *British Empire*, X, 200–201, 328–329, 408; cf. Bernhard Knollenberg, *Origin of the American Revolution, 1759–1766* (New York, 1960), pp. 87–96.

[18] Eliot to Hollis, Boston, September 27, 1768; July 10, September 7, 1769, in MHS *Colls.*, 4th ser., IV, 428, 442, 444. The "Journal of the Times" was a series of newspaper articles published from October 13, 1768, to November 30, 1769. The pieces, dilating on day-by-day offenses of the military in Boston, were apparently written in Boston but were sent to New York for weekly publication in the *New York Journal* and to Pennsylvania for reprinting in the *Pennsylvania Chronicle*. After these two initial appearances the articles were again reprinted in the *Boston Evening Post*, and thereafter generally copied in American and English publications. The series has been collected by Oliver M. Dickerson as *Boston under Military Rule, 1768–1769.*

by the nervous magistrates. Several deaths resulted, the most dramatic being that of a boy, wrongly identified as a leader of the mob, who was tracked down and shot to death on orders of the commander. The political capital made of this episode by the Wilkesites and other anti-government groups in London, who declared it to have been a deliberately planned "massacre," was echoed loudly in the colonies, the more so when it appeared that convictions of the guilty soldiers by normal processes of law were being quashed by the government. Could it be believed to be a coincidence that in February 1770 an eleven-year-old boy was also shot to death in a Boston riot by a suspected customs informer? This was more than a parallel to what had happened in London: the two events were two effects of the same cause.[19]

And then, a few weeks later, came the Boston Massacre. Doubts that the troops in Boston constituted a standing army and that it was the purpose of standing armies to terrify a populace into compliance with tyrannical wills were silenced by that event, which, Eliot assured Hollis, had obviously been coming. It "serves to show the impossibility of our living in peace with a standing army. A free people will sometimes carry things too far, but this remedy will always be found worse than the disease. Trenchard's *History of Standing Armies*, with which you formerly obliged me, is excellent . . . Unless there is some great alteration in the state of things the era of the independence of the colonies is much nearer than I once thought it, or now wish it."[20] The same response was generally broadcast in the narrative of the Massacre, written by James Bowdoin and others for the Boston Town Meeting, which was distributed everywhere in the English-speaking world. This famous pamphlet stressed the deliberateness of the shooting and the clarity of the design that lay behind the lurid event; nor was the parallel to the St. George's Fields murders neglected. The acquittal of the indicted soldiers did not alter the conviction that the Massacre was the logical work of a standing army, for it accentuated the parallel with the English case which also had concluded with acquittal; and in Boston too there was suspicion of judicial irregularities. How the murderers managed to escape was known to some, it was said, but was "too dark to explain."[21]

.   .   .

---

[19] George Rudé *Wilkes and Liberty* (Oxford, 1962), pp. 49 ff.; Maier, "Wilkes and American Disillusionment," pp. 386–387; Gipson, *British Empire*, XI, 275, 281. For an example of the currency in personal correspondence of the St. George's Fields "massacre," see William Strahan to David Hall, London, December 30, 1768, *Pa. Mag.* 10 (1886), 468–469. On the role of the shooting of the Snider boy in the Revolutionary movement in Boston, see John Cary, *Joseph Warren* (Urbana, 1961), pp. 91–92.

[20] Eliot to Hollis, June 28, 1770, MHS *Colls.*, 4th ser., N, 452.

[21] Allen, *Oration upon the Beauties of Liberty* (JHL 38), p. xiii; [Bowdoin, *et al.*], *A Short Narrative of the Horrid Massacre in Boston* . . . (Boston, 1770: JHL Pamphlet 32), reprinted within the year three times in Boston, three times in London and once (retitled) in Dublin; for the association of the Massacre with the problem of standing armies, see *Short Narrative*, p. 8. The annual Massacre Day orators played up this association in lurid detail: see, for example, Joseph Warren, *An Oration* . . . (Boston, 1772; JHL Pamphlet 35), pp. 11–12; John Hancock, *An Oration* . . . (Boston, 1774; JHL Pamphlet 41), pp. 13–15. The view of the Massacre held by John Adams and Josiah Quincy, Jr., the lawyers who successfully defended the soldiers in court, is especially im-

The turning point was the passage of the Tea Act[22] and the resulting Tea Party in Boston in December 1773. Faced with this defiant resistance to intimidation, the powers at work in England, it was believed, gave up all pretense of legality—"threw off the mask," John Adams said in a phrase that for a century had been used to describe just such climactic disclosures[23]— and moved swiftly to complete their design. In a period of two months in the spring of 1774 Parliament took its revenge in a series of coercive actions no liberty-loving people could tolerate: the Boston Port Act, intended, it was believed, to snuff out the economic life of the Massachusetts metropolis; the Administration of Justice Act, aimed at crippling judicial processes once and for all by permitting trials to be held in England for offenses committed in Massachusetts; the Massachusetts Government Act, which stripped from the people of Massachusetts the protection of the British constitution by giving over all the "democratic" elements of the province's government— even popularly elected juries and town meetings—into the hands of the executive power; the Quebec Act, which, while not devised as a part of the coercive program, fitted it nicely, in the eyes of the colonists, by extending the boundaries of a "papist" province, and one governed wholly by preroga- tive, south into territory claimed by Virginia, Connecticut, and Massachu- setts; finally, the Quartering Act, which permitted the seizure of unoccupied buildings for the use of troops on orders of the governors alone even in situations, such as Boston's, where barracks were available in the vicinity.

Once these coercive acts were passed there could be little doubt that "the

---

portant. Both thought the Massacre was "the strongest of proofs of the danger of stand- ing armies" despite their efforts on the soldiers' behalf; Adams saw nothing incompatible between the verdict of the jury and his being invited to deliver one of the orations com- memorating the Massacre, and Quincy publicly urged continued discussion of the "fatal effects of the policy of standing armies and . . . quartering troops in populous cities in time of peace." Josiah Quincy, *Memoir of the Life of Josiah Quincy Jun*. . . . (Boston, 1825), p. 67; Adams, *Diary and Autobiography*, II, 74, 79; Gipson, *British Empire*, XI, 281. For the complete documentation and an excellent analysis of the trial, see L. Kinvin Wroth and Hiller B. Zobel, eds., *Legal Papers of John Adams* (Cambridge, 1965), III.

[22] For an analysis of the motivation behind the opposition to the Tea Act on the part of the merchant community, explicitly contradicting the interpretation of A. M. Schlesinger's *Colonial Merchants and the American Revolution* (1918), see Arthur L. Jensen, *The Maritime Commerce of Colonial Philadelphia* (Madison, Wis., 1963), pp. 193 ff. Jensen concludes that "it is difficult to see how the constitutional question can be lightly dismissed as mere window dressing for the more fundamental economic questions when there is an impressive amount of contemporary testimony, private as well as public, to the contrary."

[23] Thus the commonwealthman and regicide Edmund Ludlow described in his *Memoirs* (written 1663–1673) how Charles I, fatally attracted to French and Spanish despotism, "immediately after his ascent to the throne pulled off the mask, and openly discovered his intentions to make the crown absolute and independent" (C. H. Firth, ed., Oxford, 1894, I, 10). Similarly—or perhaps conversely—Governor Hunter of New York, who had for months been seething with indignation at the arrogance of the New York Assembly, finally wrote the Secretary of State in 1712 that "now the mask is thrown off; they have called in question the Council's share in the legislation . . . and have but one short step to make towards what I am unwilling to name [i.e., indepen- dence]." E. B. O'Callaghan and Berthold Fernow, eds., *Documents Relative to the Colonial History of the State of New-York* . . . (Albany, 1856–1887), V, 296; cf. pp. 255–256. The Secretary of State involved was Bolingbroke, who himself used the phrase in similar circumstances: e.g., *Works* (Philadelphia, 1841), I, 116.

system of slavery fabricated against America . . . is the offspring of mature deliberation." To the leaders of the Revolutionary movement there was, beyond question, "a settled, fixed plan for *enslaving* the colonies, or bringing them under arbitrary government, and indeed the nation too." By 1774 the idea "that the British government—the *King, Lords,* and *Commons*—have laid a regular plan to enslave America, and that they are now deliberately putting it in execution" had been asserted, Samuel Seabury wrote wearily but accurately, "over, and over, and over again." The less inhibited of the colonial orators were quick to point out that "the MONSTER of a standing ARMY" had sprung directly from "a PLAN . . . *systematically* laid, and pursued by the British *ministry,* near twelve years, for enslaving America"; the Boston Massacre, it was claimed, had been "planned by Hillsborough and a knot of treacherous knaves in Boston." Careful analysts like Jefferson agreed on the major point; in one of the most closely reasoned of the pamphlets of 1774 the Virginian stated unambiguously that though "single acts of tyranny may be ascribed to the accidental opinion of a day . . . a series of oppressions, begun at a distinguished period and pursued unalterably through every change of ministers, too plainly prove a deliberate and systematical plan of reducing us to slavery." So too the fastidious and scholarly John Dickinson, though in 1774 he still clung to the hope that inadvertence, at least on the part of the King, was involved, believed that "a plan had been deliberately framed and pertinaciously adhered to, unchanged even by frequent changes of ministers, unchecked by any intervening gleam of humanity, to sacrifice to a passion for arbitrary dominion the universal property, liberty, safety, honor, happiness, and prosperity of us unoffending yet devoted Americans." So too Washington, collaborating with George Mason in writing the Fairfax Resolves of 1774, agreed that the trouble had arisen from a "regular, systematic plan" of oppression, the English government "endeavoring by every piece of art and despotism to fix the shackles of slavery upon us"; he was convinced "beyond the smallest doubt," he wrote privately, "that these measures are the result of deliberation . . . I am as fully convinced as I am of my own existence that there has been a regular, systematic plan formed to enforce them." The more sensitive observers were to ideological issues—the more practiced in theoretical discourse—the more likely they were to find irrefutable evidence of what Richard Henry Lee called "designs for destroying our constitutional liberties." In 1766 Andrew Eliot had been unsure; the Stamp Act, he wrote, had been "calculated (I do not say designed) to enslave the colonies." By 1768 things had worsened, and the distinction between "calculation" and "design" disappeared from his correspondence. "We have everything to fear and scarce any room to hope," he then wrote to Hollis; "I am sure this will put you in mind of 1641." He was convinced that the English government "had a design to new-model our constitution, at least in this province," and they would already have succeeded had they not been so occupied with other business at home. His friends in Boston concurred, and, beginning in 1770 wrote out in a series of town resolutions, instructions to representatives, and House declarations their conviction that "a deep-laid and desperate plan of imperial despotism had been laid, and partly executed, for the extinction of all civil liberty . . . The august and once revered fortress of

English freedom—the admirable work of ages—the BRITISH CONSTITUTION seems fast tottering into fatal and inevitable ruin."[24]

Specifics were sought, especially as to the date of the origins of the plot. Josiah Quincy—"Wilkes Quincy," Hutchinson called him—found it in the Restoration of Charles II; others traced it to the administration of Robert Walpole; and though John Adams, with one eye on Hutchinson, wrote in 1774 that "the conspiracy was first regularly formed and begun to be executed in 1763 or 4," later he traced it back to the 1750's and 1740's and the administration of Governor Shirley of Massachusetts. Nor were the specific stages of its development neglected. They could be traced, if in no other place, in the notorious Hutchinson letters in 1768–69, those "profoundly secret, dark, and deep" letters which, published in 1773, totally exposed Hutchinson's "machiavellian dissimulation," John Adams wrote, and convicted him of "junto conspiracy"; they gave proof, the Boston Committee of Correspondence wrote, that God had "wonderfully interposed to bring to light the plot that has been laid for us by our malicious and invidious enemies."[25]

But who, specifically, were these enemies, and what were their goals? Josiah Quincy, at the center of affairs in London in the winter of 1774–75, was convinced "that all the measures against America were planned and pushed on by Bernard and Hutchinson." But most observers believed that local plotters like Hutchinson were only "creatures" of greater figures in England coordinating and impelling forward the whole effort. There were a number of specific identifications of these master influences. One of the most common was the claim that at the root of the evil stood the venerable John Stuart, Lord Bute, whose apparent absence from politics since 1763 could be seen as one of his more successful dissimulations: "he has been

[24] [Alexander Hamilton], *A Full Vindication of the Measures of the Congress . . .* (New York, 1774), in Harold C. Syrett, *et al.,* eds., *Papers of Alexander Hamilton* (New York and London, 1961–), I, 50; Baldwin, *Appendix* (JHL 52), p. 67; [Samuel Seabury], *A View of the Controversy . . .* (New York, 1774), in Clarence H. Vance, ed., *Letters of a Westchester Farmer (1774–1775)* (*Publications of the Westchester County Historical Society,* VIII, White Plains, 1930), p. 123; Oliver Noble, *Some Strictures upon the . . . Book of Esther . . .* (Newburyport, 1775: JHL Pamphlet 58), pp. 28, 26; Hancock, *Oration* (JHL 41), p. 9; [Jefferson], *A Summary View of the Rights of British America . . .* (Williamsburg, [1774]: JHL Pamphlet 43), p. 11; on the development of Dickinson's understanding of the cause of the crisis, see the Introduction to his *Late Regulations* (Philadelphia, 1765: JHL Pamphlet 14), in Bailyn, *Pamphlets,* I; Colbourn, *Lamp of Experience,* p. 155; Washington to Bryan Fairfax, August 27, 1774, in John C. Fitzpatrick, ed., *Writings of George Washington . . .* (Washington, D.C., 1931–1944), III, 241, 242; Gipson, *British Empire,* XII, 36n; MHS *Colls.,* 4th ser., IV, 400, 429, 444; [*Eighteenth*] *Report of the Record Commissioners of the City of Boston . . .* (Boston, 1887), p. 26 (cf. pp. 83–86).

[25] Quincy, *Observations on the . . . Boston Port-Bill; with Thoughts on . . . Standing Armies* (Boston, 1774), in Quincy, *Memoir,* p. 446 (cf. pp. 464–465); Adams, *Works,* X, 242–243 (for Adams' full elaboration of the ministry's "dark intrigues and wicked machinations" so clearly dovetailed with the Hutchinson clique's maneuverings, see *Works,* IV, 18 ff., 62–64, 70, 91–92; *Diary and Autobiography,* II, 80, 90, 119); John C. Miller, *Origins of the American Revolution* (Boston, 1943), p. 332. For other expressions of the fear of "a constant, unremitted, uniform aim to enslave us," see *Votes and Proceedings of Boston* (JHL 36), pp. 30, 37; Allen, *American Alarm* (JHL 39), 1st sec., pp. 8–9, 17, 18, 33; Edmund S. Morgan, *The Gentle Puritan* (New Haven, 1962), pp. 263–265.

aiming for years . . . to destroy the ancient right of the subjects," and now was finally taking steps to "overthrow both . . . King and state; to bring on a revolution, and to place another whom he [is] more nearly allied to upon the throne." Believing the people to "have too much liberty," he intended to reduce them to the "spiritless SLAVES" they had been "in the reign of the *Stuarts*." So it had seemed to Arthur Lee, who had written from London at the beginning of the period that "Lord Bute, though seemingly retired from the affairs of court, too plainly influences all the operations of government"; the hard facts, he said, lead one to condemn "the unprincipled ambition and partiality of the Scots lord as having produced all the mischiefs of the present period." Eliot too feared "this mysterious THANE," declaring in 1769 that "he has too much influence in the public measures." Five years later John Dickinson still lumped together "the Butes, Mansfields, Norths, Bernards, and Hutchinsons" as the people "whose falsehoods and misrepresentations have enflamed the people," and as late as 1775 an informed American could write confidently from London that "this plan you may be assured was devised by Lords North, Bute, and Jenkinson only."[26] A more general version of this view was that a Stuart-Tory party, the "corrupt, Frenchified party in the nation," as it was described in 1766—"evil-minded individuals," Jonathan Mayhew believed, "not improbably in the interests of the houses of Bourbon and the Pretender"—was at work seeking to reverse the consequences of the Glorious Revolution. It was a similar notion that in all probability accounts for the republication of Rapin's *Dissertation on . . . the Whigs and Tories* in Boston in 1773; and it was this notion that furnished Jefferson with his ultimate understanding of the "system" that sought to destroy liberty in America. Still another explanation, drawing no less directly on fears that had lain at the root of opposition ideology in England since the turn of the century, emphasized the greed of a "monied interest" created by the crown's financial necessities and the power of a newly risen, arrogant, and irresponsible capitalist group, that battened on wars and stock manipulation. The creation of this group was accompanied

> by levying of taxes, by a host of tax gatherers, and a long train of dependents of the crown. The practice grew into system, till at length the crown found means to break down those barriers which the constitution had assigned to each branch of the legislature, and effectually destroyed the independence of both Lords and Commons.[27]

---

[26] Allen, *American Alarm* (JHL 39), 1st sec., pp. 18–19 (cf. the same author's reference to "*Scotch-barbarian troops*" at the St. George's Fields riot, in *Oration upon the Beauties of Liberty* [JHL 38], p. xiii); Arthur Lee Papers (MSS in Houghton Library, Harvard University), I, 2; II, 26, 33; Eliot to Hollis, December 25, 1769, MHS *Colls.*, 4th ser., IV, 445.

[27] [Stephen Johnson], *Some Important Observations . . .* (Newport, 1766: JHL Pamphlet 19), p. 15; Jonathan Mayhew, *The Snare Broken . . .* (Boston, 1766: JHL Pamphlet 20), p. 9; [Carter Braxton], *An Address to . . . Virginia; on the Subject of Government . . .* (Philadelphia, 1776: JHL Pamphlet 66), p. 10. Jefferson's explanation appeared first as notes he jotted down on reading François Soulé's *Histoire des troubles de l'Amérique anglaise* (London, 1785) at the point where George III's education is mentioned: "The education of the present King was Tory. He gave decisive victories to the Tories. To these were added sundry rich persons sprung up in the E. I. America

The most common explanation, however—an explanation that rose from the deepest sources of British political culture, that was a part of the very structure of British political thought—located "the spring and cause of all the distresses and complaints of the people in England or in America" in "a kind of fourth power that the constitution knows nothing of, or has not provided against." This "overruling arbitrary power, which absolutely controls the King, Lords, and Commons," was composed, it was said, of the "ministers and favorites" of the King, who, in defiance of God and man alike, "extend their usurped authority infinitely too far," and, throwing off the balance of the constitution, make their "despotic will" the authority of the nation.

> For their power and interest is so great that they can and do procure whatever laws they please, having (by power, interest, and the application of the people's money to *placemen* and *pensioners*) the whole legislative authority at their command. So that it is plain (not to say a word of a particular reigning arbitrary *Stuarchal* power among them) that the rights of the people are ruined and destroyed by ministerial *tyrannical* authority, and thereby . . . become a kind of slaves to the ministers of state.

This "junto of courtiers and state-jobbers," these "court-locusts," whispering in the royal ear, "instill in the King's mind a divine right of authority to command his subjects" at the same time as they advance their "detestable scheme" by misinforming and misleading the people.[28]

. . .

The fact that the ministerial conspiracy against liberty had risen from corruption was of the utmost importance to the colonists. It gave a radical new meaning to their claims: it transformed them from constitutional arguments to expressions of a world regenerative creed. For they had long known—it had been known everywhere in the English-speaking world in the eighteenth century—that England was one of the last refuges of the ancient gothic constitution that had once flourished everywhere in the civilized world. And now, in the outpourings of colonial protest, it was again repeated, but with new point and urgency, that by far "the greatest part of the human race" already lies in "total subjection to their rulers." Through-

---

would have been too formidable a weight in the scale of the Whigs. It was necessary therefore to reduce them by force to concur with the Tories." Later he wrote more formally to Soulé: "The seeds of the war are here traced to their true source. The Tory education of the King was the first preparation for that change in the British government which that party never ceases to wish. This naturally ensured Tory administrations during his life. At the moment he came to the throne and cleared his hands of his enemies by the peace of Paris, the assumptions of unwarrantable right over America commenced; they were so signal, and followed one another so close as to prove they were part of a system either to reduce it under absolute subjection and thereby make it an instrument for attempts on Britain itself, or to sever it from Britain so that it might not be a weight in the Whig scale. This latter alternative however was not considered as the one which would take place. They knew so little of America that they thought it unable to encounter the little finger of Great Britain." *The Papers of Thomas Jefferson* (Julian P. Boyd, ed., Princeton, 1950–), X, 373n2, 369.

[28] Allen, *American Alarm* (JHL 39), 1st sec., pp. 8–9; Noble, *Some Strictures* (JHL 58), p. 6; Allen, *Oration upon the Beauties of Liberty* (JHL 38), p. 29.

out the whole continent of Asia people are reduced "to such a degree of abusement and degradation"

> that the very idea of liberty is unknown among them. In *Africa*, scarce any human beings are to be found but barbarians, tyrants, and slaves: all equally remote from the true dignity of human nature and from a well-regulated state of society. Nor is *Europe* free from the curse. Most of her nations are forced to drink deep of the bitter cup. And in those in which freedom seem to have been established, the vital flame is going out. Two kingdoms, those of *Sweden* and *Poland*, have been betrayed and enslaved in the course of one year. The free towns of *Germany* can remain free no longer than their potent neighbors shall please to let them. *Holland* has got the forms if she has lost the spirit of a free country. *Switzerland* alone is in the full and safe possession of her freedom.

And if now, in this deepening gloom, the light of liberty went out in Britain too—in Britain, where next to "self-preservation, political liberty is the main aim and end of her constitution"—if, as events clearly portended and as "senators and historians are repeatedly predicting . . . continued corruption and standing armies will prove mortal distempers in her constitution"—what then? What refuge will liberty find?
"To our own country," it was answered,

> must we look for the biggest part of that liberty and freedom that yet remains, or is to be expected, among mankind . . . For while the greatest part of the nations of the earth are held together under the yoke of universal slavery, the North American provinces yet remain *the country of free men:* the *asylum*, and the last, to which such may yet flee from the common deluge.

More than that: "our native country . . . bids the fairest of any to promote *the perfection and happiness of mankind.*" No one, of course, can predict "the state of mankind in future ages." But insofar as one can judge the ultimate "designs of providence by the number and power of the causes that are already at work, we shall be led to think that the perfection and happiness of mankind is to be carried further in America than it has ever yet been in any place." Consider the growth the colonies had enjoyed in so short a time—growth in all ways, but especially in population: a great natural increase it had been, supplemented by multitudes from Europe, "tired out with the miseries they are doomed to at home," migrating to America "as the only country in which they can find food, raiment, and rest." Consider also the physical vigor of the people. But above all consider the moral health of the people and of the body politic.

> The fatal arts of luxury and corruption are but comparatively beginning among us . . . Nor is corruption yet established as the common principle in public affairs. Our representatives are not chosen by bribing, corrupting, or buying the votes of the electors. Nor does it take one half of the revenue of a province to manage her house of commons . . . We have been free also from the burden and danger of standing armies . . . Our defense has been our *militia* . . . the general operation of things among ourselves indicate strong tendencies towards a state of greater perfection and happiness than mankind has yet seen.

No one, therefore, can conceive of the cause of America as "the cause of a mob, of a party, or a faction." The cause of America "is the cause of self-defense, of public faith, and of the liberties of mankind . . . 'In our destruction, liberty itself expires, and human nature will despair of evermore regaining its first and original dignity.' "[29]

This theme, elaborately orchestrated by the colonial writers, marked the fulfillment of the ancient idea, deeply embedded in the colonists' awareness, that America had from the start been destined to play a special role in history. The controversy with England, from its beginning in the early 1760's, had lent support to that belief, so long nourished by so many different sources: the covenant theories of the Puritans, certain strands of Enlightenment thought, the arguments of the English radicals, the condition of life in the colonies, even the conquest of Canada. It had been the Stamp Act that had led John Adams to see in the original settlement of the colonies "the opening of a grand scene and design in providence for the illumination of the ignorant and the emancipation of the slavish part of mankind all over the earth." And Jonathan Mayhew, celebrating the conclusion of the same episode, had envisioned future streams of refugees escaping from a Europe sunk in "luxury, debauchery, venality, intestine quarrels, or other vices." It was even possible, Mayhew had added, "who knows?" that "our liberties being thus established, . . . on some future occasion . . . we or our posterity may even have the great felicity and honor to . . . keep Britain herself from ruin."[30]

Now, in 1774, that "future occasion" was believed to be at hand. After the passage of the Coercive Acts it could be said that "all the spirit of patriotism or of liberty now left in England" was no more than "the last snuff of an expiring lamp," while "the same sacred flame . . . which once showed forth such wonders in Greece and in Rome . . . burns brightly and strongly in America." Who ought then to suppress as "whimsical and enthusiastical" the belief that the colonies were to become "the foundation of a great and

[29] Samuel Williams, A Discourse on the Love of Our Country . . . (Salem, 1775: JHL Pamphlet 55), pp. 21, 22, 23, 25, 26. Cf., e.g., Thomas Coombe, A Sermon Preached . . . (Philadelphia, 1775), pp. 19–20; [Richard Wells], A Few Political Reflections . . . (Philadelphia, 1774), pp. 38–40, 50.

[30] Adams, Dissertation, in Works, III, 452n; Mayhew, Snare Broken (JHL 20), pp. 36, 38. The concept of America as a refuge for liberty was by no means an exclusively American notion. As early as 1735 James Thomson had celebrated the idea in his book-length poem Liberty (the relevant passage is quoted, and the secondary literature cited, in Bailyn, Pamphlets, I, 730). The idea that liberty was drifting steadily westward was commonly accepted; Thomas Pownall invoked the notion explicitly in the opening section of his Administration of the Colonies: he had long assumed, he wrote, "from the spirit and genius of the people" that the colonies would "become in some future and perhaps not very distant age an asylum to that liberty of mankind which, as it hath been driven by corruption and the consequent tyranny of government, hath been constantly retiring westward" (4th ed., 1768, pp. 44–45). Beyond these specific references to America was the more abstract and general notion that overseas territories were the natural sanctuaries for liberty and virtue bedeviled by domestic corruption and authoritarianism. See, e.g., Andrew Eliot's confession of his thrill in reading of the regicide "honest General [Edmund] Ludlow's account of the generous protection afforded him by the magistrates of Berne, and felt a secret pleasure in the thought that there was such a land of liberty to be an asylum to patriots and virtue in distress." To Hollis, January 29, 1769, MHS Colls., 4th ser., IV, 436.

mighty empire, the largest the world ever saw to be founded on such principles of liberty and freedom, both civil and religious . . . [and] which shall be the principal seat of that glorious kingdom which Christ shall erect upon earth in the latter days?" America "ere long will build an empire upon the ruins of Great Britain; will adopt its constitution purged of its impurities, and from an experience of its defects will guard against those evils which have wasted its vigor and brought it to an untimely end." The hand of God was "in America now giving a new epocha to the history of the world."[31]

In the invigorating atmosphere of such thoughts, the final conclusion of the colonists' logic could be drawn not with regret but with joy. For while everyone knew that when tyranny is abroad "submission is a crime"; while they readily acknowledged that "no obedience is due to arbitrary, unconstitutional edicts calculated to enslave a free people"; and while they knew that the invasion of the liberties of the people "constitutes a state of war with the people" who may properly use "all the power which God has given them" to protect themselves—nevertheless they hesitated to come to a final separation even after Lexington and Bunker Hill. They hesitated, moving slowly and reluctantly, protesting "before God and the world that the utmost of [our] wish is that things may return to their old channel." They hesitated because their *sentiments of duty and affection* were sincere; they hesitated because their respect for constituted authority was great; and they hesitated too because their future as an independent people was a matter of doubt, full of the fear of the unknown.[32]

What would an independent American nation be? A republic, necessarily —and properly, considering the character and circumstances of the people. But history clearly taught that republics were delicate polities, quickly degenerating into anarchy and tyranny; it was impossible, some said, to "recollect a single instance of a nation who supported this form of government for any length of time or with any degree of greatness." Others felt that independence might "split and divide the empire into a number of petty, insignificant states" that would easily fall subject to the will of "some foreign tyrant, or the more intolerable despotism of a few American demagogues"; the colonies might end by being "parceled out, Poland-like."

But if what the faint-hearted called "the ill-shapen, diminutive brat, INDEPENDENCY" contained within it all that remained of freedom; if it gave promise of growing great and strong and becoming the protector and propagator of liberty everywhere; if it were indeed true that "the cause of America is in a great measure the cause of all mankind"; if " 'Tis not the concern of a day, a year, or an age; posterity are virtually involved in the contest, and will be more or less affected even to the end of time by our proceedings now"—if all of this were true, ways would be found by men

[31] Rokeby, *Considerations*, p. 148; Ebenezer Baldwin, *The Duty of Rejoicing under Calamities and Afflictions* . . . (New York, 1776), p. 38; Hooper to Iredell, cited in note 40 above, pp. 985, 986.

[32] Johnson, *Some Important Observations* (JHL 19), pp. 21, 23; [Robert Carter Nicholas], *Considerations on the Present State of Virginia Examined* ([Williamsburg], 1774), in the Earl G. Swem edition (New York, 1919), pp. 68, 42.

inspired by such prospects to solve the problems of a new society and government. And so let every lover of mankind, every hater of tyranny,

> stand forth! Every spot of the old world is overrun with oppression. Freedom hath been hunted round the globe. Asia and Africa have long expelled her. Europe regards her like a stranger, and England hath given her warning to depart. O! receive the fugitive, and prepare in time an asylum for mankind.[33]

[33] Braxton, *Address* (JHL 66), p. 19; Seabury, *A View*, in Vance, *Letters of a West-chester Farmer*, pp. 12, 117; [Daniel Leonard] ("Massachusettensis"), *The Origin of the American Contest with Great-Britain* . . . (New York, 1775; JHL Pamphlet 56), p. 84; [Joseph Galloway], *A Candid Examination of the Mutual Claims of Great-Britain and the Colonies* . . . (New York, 1775), p. 31; [Thomas Paine], *Common Sense* . . . (Philadelphia, 1776: JHL Pamphlet 63), pp. [ii], 30, 60.

The American Revolution: The People as Constituent Power

R. R. Palmer

What was revolutionary about the American Revolution? This question has compelled attention from the time of Lexington and Concord to our own. Differing over both the meaning and desirability of revolution, Americans have long wondered in what ways the American Revolution altered the shape of American society and the structure of American government and contributed to the process of revolution elsewhere. In the following essay, R. R. Palmer of Yale University, in a selection from his magisterial two-volume *Age of the Democratic Revolution: A Political History of Europe and America, 1769–1800* (1959), argues that the American revolutionaries broke new ground in the matter of political institutions and that what was revolutionary in the years between 1776 and 1788 was not ideas but their implementation.

In the larger study from which the selection is taken, Palmer sets the revolution of the thirteen English colonies within the context of the entire series of interrelated, late-eighteenth-century Western revolutions. All of them, Palmer argues, were affected to some degree by notions of republican government and all of them aimed to increase the authority of the people in government. Of these, the American Revolution was one of the earliest and, in the realm of political science, one of the most venturesome. Events during the long struggle for independence and government gave birth to the idea that sovereignty resides in the people of a nation and that it is the people who must "ordain and establish" a new government. After the Philadelphia Convention of 1787, no other revolutionary nation, and least of all revolutionary France, would be unaffected by the American example.

As important as Palmer's emphasis is his method. His interpretation of what he calls "the age of the democratic revolution" is above all an exercise in comparative history, in which he determines what was distinctive about each of the late-eighteenth-century revolutions and what was characteristic of all by comparing them and attempting to understand how each built on previous examples or departed from them. For one thing, this perspective allows us to see the American Revolution as only one incident in a half-century-long revolutionary age. For another, it moves debate about the Revolution from a parochial stage—in which we argue whether John Adams was more or less radical than Thomas Jefferson—to a more universal level, in which we can see more clearly the achievement of the Massachusetts constitution of 1780, the contributions made to the Western science of politics by such institutions as federalism, and the impact on Western political thought of such concepts, now universalized, as the rights of man.

As for the general relevance of the Revolution, Palmer finds it "ambivalent." In this conclusion he is in partial agreement with scholarly commentators who, like Samuel P. Huntington ("Political Modernization: America vs. Europe," *World Politics*, XVIII [April 1966], 378–414), believe that it is American society, not its political institutions, that has always seemed revolutionary to others and those who, like Louis Hartz (*The Liberal Tradition in America** [1955]), believe that American political culture became fossilized at the time of the Revolution and therefore held little continuing inspiration to other

The American Revolution: The People as Constituent Power. In Vol. I, *The Challenge* (copyright © 1959 by Princeton University Press; Princeton Paperback, 1969) of R. R. Palmer, *The Age of Democratic Revolution: A Political History of Europe and America, 1769–1800*, pp. 213–35. Reprinted by permission of Princeton University Press.

nations. But Palmer differs fom Huntington in arguing that if American political institutions now seem so quaint, at one time they were path-breaking, and from Hartz in seeing the American Revolution not simply as a quite predictable stage in the evolution of a "fragment" culture derived from a mother county, but as a major episode in a great age of revolutions everywhere.

*I*f it be asked what the American Revolution distinctively contributed to the world's stock of ideas, the answer might go somewhat along these lines. It did not contribute primarily a social doctrine—for although a certain skepticism toward social rank was an old American attitude, and possibly even a gift to mankind, it long antedated the Revolution, which did not so much cut down, as prevent the growth of, an aristocracy of European type. It did not especially contribute economic ideas—for the Revolution had nothing to teach on the production or distribution of goods, and the most advanced parties objected to private wealth only when it became too closely associated with government. They aimed at a separation of economic and political spheres, by which men of wealth, while free to get rich, should not have a disproportionate influence on government, and, on the other hand, government and public emoluments should not be used as a means of livelihood for an otherwise impecunious and unproductive upper class.

The American Revolution was a political movement, concerned with liberty, and with power. Most of the ideas involved were by no means distinctively American. There was nothing peculiarly American in the concepts, purely as concepts, of natural liberty and equality. They were admitted by conservatives, and were taught in the theological faculty at the Sorbonne.[1] Nor could Americans claim any exclusive understanding of the ideas of government by contract or consent, or the sovereignty of the people, or political representation, or the desirability of independence from foreign rule, or natural rights, or the difference between natural law and positive law, or between certain fundamental laws and ordinary legislation, or the separation of powers, or the federal union of separate states. All these

---

[1] See on Réal de Curban Chapter III above, and my *Catholics and Unbelievers in Eighteenth Century France* (Princeton, 1939), 126, quoting L. J. Hooke, *Religionis naturalis et moralis philosophiae principia, methodo scholastica digesta* (Paris, 1752–1754), 1, 623–24: "Status is a permanent condition of man, involving various rights and a long series of obligations. It is either *natural*, constituted by nature itself, or *adventitious*, arising from some human act or institution. . . . By the *status of nature* we understand that in which men would be who were subject to no government but joined only by similarity of nature or by private pacts. . . . In the status of nature all men are equal and enjoy the same rights. For in that state they are distinguished only by the gifts of mind or body by which some excel others." Italics are the Abbé Hooke's.

ideas were perfectly familiar in Europe, and that is why the American Revolution was of such interest to Europeans.

The Distinctiveness of American Political Ideas

The most distinctive work of the Revolution was in finding a method, and furnishing a model, for putting these ideas into practical effect. It was in the implementation of similar ideas that Americans were more successful than Europeans. "In the last fifty years," wrote General Bonaparte to Citizen Talleyrand in 1797, "there is only one thing that I can see that we have really defined, and that is the sovereignty of the people. But we have had no more success in determining what is constitutional, than in allocating the different powers of government." And he said more peremptorily, on becoming Emperor in 1804, that the time had come "to constitute the Nation." He added: "I am the constituent power."[2]

The problem throughout much of America and Europe, for half a century, was to "constitute" new government, and in a measure new societies. The problem was to find a constituent power. Napoleon offered himself to Europe in this guise. The Americans solved the problem by the device of the constitutional convention, which, revolutionary in origin, soon became institutionalized in the public law of the United States.[3]

The constitutional convention in theory embodied the sovereignty of the people. The people chose it for a specific purpose, not to govern, but to set up institutions of government. The convention, acting as the sovereign people, proceeded to draft a constitution and a declaration of rights. Certain "natural" or "inalienable" rights of the citizen were thus laid down at the same time as the powers of government. It was the constitution that created the powers of government, defined their scope, gave them legality, and balanced them one against another. The constitution was written and comprised in a single document. The constitution and accompanying declaration, drafted by the convention, must, in the developed theory, be ratified by the people. The convention thereupon disbanded and disappeared, lest its members have a vested interest in the offices they created. The constituent power went into abeyance, leaving the work of government to the authorities now constituted. The people, having exercised sovereignty, now came under government. Having made law, they came under law. They put themselves voluntarily under restraint. At the same time, they put restraint upon government. All government was limited government; all public authority must keep within the bounds of the constitution and of the declared rights. There were two levels of law, a higher law or constitution that only the people could make or amend, through constitutional conventions or bodies similarly empowered; and a statutory law, to be made and unmade, within the assigned limits, by legislators to whom the constitution gave this function.

[2] *Correspondence de Napoleon I*, III (Paris, 1859), 314; R. M. Johnston, *The Corsican* (N.Y., 1910), 182.

[3] See, for example, J. A. Jameson, *The Constitutional Convention: Its History, Powers and Modes of Proceeding* (N.Y., 1867); H. C. Hockett, *The Constitutional History of the United States, 1776–1826* (N.Y., 1939).

Such was the theory, and it was a distinctively American one. European thinkers, in all their discussion of a political or social contract, of government by consent and of sovereignty of the people, had not clearly imagined the people as actually contriving a constitution and creating the organs of government. They lacked the idea of the people as a constituent power. Even in the French Revolution the idea developed slowly; members of the French National Assembly, long after the Tennis Court oath, continued to feel that the constitution which they were writing, to be valid, had to be accepted by the King as a kind of equal with whom the nation had to negotiate. Nor, indeed, would the King tolerate any other view. On the other hand, we have seen how at Geneva in 1767 the democrats advanced an extreme version of citizen sovereignty, holding that the people created the constitution and the public offices by an act of will; but they failed to get beyond a simple direct democracy; they had no idea of two levels of law, or of limited government, or of a delegated and representative legislative authority, or of a sovereign people, which, after acting as a god from the machine in a constituent convention, retired to the more modest status of an electorate, and let its theoretical sovereignty become inactive.

The difficulty with the theory was that the conditions under which it could work were seldom present. No people really starts *de novo;* some political institutions always already exist; there is never a *tabula rasa,* or state of nature, or Chart Blanche as Galloway posited for conservative purposes. Also, it is difficult for a convention engaged in writing a constitution not to be embroiled in daily politics and problems of government. And it is hard to live voluntarily under restraint. In complex societies, or in times of crisis, either government or people or some part of the people may feel obliged to go beyond the limits that a constitution has laid down.

In reality, the idea of the people as a constituent power, with its corollaries, developed unclearly, gradually, and sporadically during the American Revolution. It was adumbrated in the Declaration of Independence: the people may "institute new government." Jefferson, among the leaders, perhaps conceived the idea most clearly. It is of especial interest, however, to see how the "people" themselves, that is, certain lesser and unknown or poorer or unsatisfied persons, contributed to these distinctive American ideas by their opposition to the Revolutionary elite.

There were naturally many Americans who felt that no change was needed except expulsion of the British. With the disappearance of the British governors, and collapse of the old governor's councils, the kind of men who had been active in the colonial assemblies, and who now sat as provincial congresses or other *de facto* revolutionary bodies, were easily inclined to think that they should keep the management of affairs in their own hands. Some parallel can be seen with what happened in Europe. There was a revolution, or protest, of constituted bodies against authorities set above them, and a more popular form of revolution, or protest, which aimed at changing the character or membership of these constituted bodies themselves. As at Geneva the General Council rebelled against the patriciate, without wishing to admit new citizens to the General Council; as in Britain the Whigs asserted the powers of Parliament against the King, without wishing to change the composition of Parliament; as in

Belgium, in 1789, the Estates party declared independence from the Emperor, while maintaining the preexisting estates; as in France, also in 1789, the nobility insisted that the King govern through the Estates-General, but objected to the transformation of the three estates into a new kind of national body; as in the Dutch provinces in 1795 the Estates-General, after expelling the Prince of Orange, tried to remain itself unchanged, and resisted the election of a "convention"; so, in America in 1776, the assemblies that drove out the officers of the King, and governed their respective states under revolutionary conditions, sought to keep control of affairs in their own hands, and to avoid reconstitution at the hands of the "people."

Ten states gave themselves new constitutions in 1776 and 1777. In nine of these states, however, it was the ordinary assembly, that is, the revolutionary government of the day, that drafted and proclaimed the constitution. In the tenth, Pennsylvania, a constituent convention met, but it soon had to take on the burden of daily government in addition. In Connecticut and Rhode Island the colonial charters remained in force, and the authorities constituted in colonial times (when governors and councils had already been elected) remained unchanged in principle for half a century. In Massachusetts the colonial charter remained in effect until 1780.

Thus in no state, when independence was declared, did a true constituent convention meet, and, as it were, calmly and rationally devise government out of a state of nature. There was already, however, some recognition of the principle that constitutions cannot be made merely by governments, that a more fundamental power is needed to produce a constitution than to pass ordinary laws or carry on ordinary executive duties. Thus, in New Hampshire, New York, Delaware, Maryland, North Carolina, and Georgia, the assemblies drew up constitutions only after soliciting authority for that purpose from the voters. In Maryland and North Carolina there was a measure of popular ratification.

Constitution-making in North Carolina, Pennsylvania, and Massachusetts

The popular pressures that helped to form American political doctrine are best illustrated from North Carolina, Pennsylvania, and Massachusetts.[4]

In North Carolina class lines had been sharply drawn by the Regulator movement and its suppression. The people of the back-country even inclined to be loyalist, not eager for an independence that might only throw them into the hands of the county gentry. In the turbulent election of October 1776 the voters knew that the assembly which they elected would draft a state constitution. There was no demand for a convention to act exclusively and temporarily as a constituent power. But several counties drew up instructions for the deputies, in which the emerging doctrine was set forth clearly.

Orange and Mecklenburg counties used identical language. This is a sign, as in the case of identical phrasing in the French *cahiers* of 1789, where the matter has been carefully studied, that some person of influence and educa-

---

[4] Here I am indebted, without sharing all his conclusions, to E. P. Douglass, *Rebels and Democrats: the Struggle for Equal Political Rights and Majority Rule during the American Revolution* (Chapel Hill, 1955).

tion, and not some poor farmer ruminating in his cabin, had probably written out a draft. Still, the public meetings of both counties found it to their taste. "Political power," they said,

> is of two kinds, one principal and superior, the other derived and inferior. . . . The principal supreme power is possessed only by the people at large. . . . The derived and inferior power by the servants which they employ. . . . The rules by which the inferior power is exercised are to be constituted by the principal supreme power. . . .[5]

In other words, government was not a form of guardianship. Office was to be no longer a perquisite of the gentry, or "an aristocracy of power in the hands of the rich," to use their own language, but a form of employment by the people, whom they did not hesitate to call "the poor." Mecklenburg favored a unicameral legislature, Orange a bicameral one, but both called for a separation of powers. It was not that any organ of government should enjoy independence from the electorate (the essence of balance-of-power theory in the European, British, and loyalist view), but rather that the various functions of government should be defined and distributed among different men, to prevent what had happened in colonial times. The fact that before 1776 the council had possessed executive, legislative, and judicial functions, and that members of the assembly had served as justices of the peace, or had their relatives appointed judges and sheriffs, was the basis on which North Carolina had been dominated by small groups of gentry. It was popular objection to this situation, probably more than a reading of European books, that made the separation of powers a principal American doctrine.

The North Carolina constitution, as written and adopted, enlarged the electorate by granting all taxpayers the right to vote for members of the lower house. It equalized the representation by giving more deputies to the western counties. It required a freehold of 100 acres for members of the lower house, and of 300 acres for those of the upper house, who were to be elected only by voters possessing 50 acres. The governor, elected by the two houses, had to have a freehold worth £1,000. The constitution was a compromise between populace and landed gentry. It lasted until the Civil War.[6]

The situation in Pennsylvania was complex. The Quaker colony, idealized by European intellectuals as the haven of innocent equality and idyllic peace, had long been plagued by some of the most acrimonious politics in America. Quaker bigwigs had long clashed with the non-Quaker lesser orders of Philadelphia and the West. In the spring of 1776 Pennsylvania was the only colony in which the assembly was still legal under the old law. It still showed a desire for reconciliation with England, and, with it, maintenance of the old social and political system. This persistence of conservatism in high places made a great many people all the more radical. A year of open war with Britain had aroused the determination for independence, and in May 1776 a mass meeting of 4,000 people in Philadelphia demanded the

[5] *Ibid.*, 126.
[6] For the text of the constitutions, see F. N. Thorpe, *Federal and State Constitutions, Colonial Charters and Other Organic Laws of the . . . United States of America* (Washington, 7 vols., 1909).

calling of a constitutional convention. Various local committees got to work, and a convention was elected by irregular methods. Where the three eastern counties had formerly been heavily over represented, the situation was now not equalized, but reversed. The West, with the same population as the three eastern counties, had 64 delegates in the convention to only 24 for the East. "The Convention in Pennsylvania was a political expedient, and not, as in Massachusetts, the cornerstone of constitutional government."[7] Its real function was to promote the Revolution, and assure independence from England, by circumventing the assembly and all other opposition. Like the more famous French Convention elected in 1792, it rested on a kind of popular mandate which did not reflect an actual majority of the population; like it, it became the government of the country during war and revolution; like it, it behaved dictatorially. The constitutions drafted in Pennsylvania in 1776, and in France in 1793, were, in their formal provisions, by far the most democratic of any produced in the eighteenth century. The Pennsylvania constitution of 1776, unlike the French constitution of the Year I, was never submitted even to the formalities of popular ratification. But the two constitutions became a symbol of what democrats meant by democracy.

The Pennsylvania constitution vested legislative power in a single house. For the executive it avoided the name and office of governor, entrusting executive power to a council and "president," a word which then meant no more than chairman. All male taxpayers twenty-one years of age had the vote, and were eligible for any office. To sit in the assembly, however, it was necessary publicly to acknowledge the divine inspiration of the Old and New Testaments. Voters elected the legislators, the executive councillors, sheriffs, coroners, tax-assessors, and justices of the peace. Voting was by ballot. The president was chosen by the legislature and the executive council; he had no veto or appointive powers, and what powers he did have he could exercise only in agreement with his council. All officers were elected for one year, except that councillors served for three. Rotation of office was provided for; legislators, councillors, president, and sheriffs could be re-elected only a certain number of times. Doors of the legislative assembly must always be open to the public. There was a kind of referendum, in that no bill passed by the assembly, short of emergency, became law until submitted for public consideration and enacted in the assembly of the following year, if there was no public objection. Officeholders received pay, but if revenues of any office became too large the assembly could reduce them. All officers and judges could be impeached by the assembly. Judges of the Supreme Court could be removed by the assembly for "misbehavior." There was an elected council of censors, or board of review, which every seven years ascertained whether the constitution had been preserved inviolate, and called a convention if amendment seemed necessary.

The Pennsylvania constitution represented the doctrine of a single party, namely the democrats, people of the kind who had formerly had little to do with government, and whose main principle was that government should never become a separate or vested interest within the state. This was indeed an understandable principle, at a time when government, in all countries

---

[7] Douglass, *op.cit.*, 260.

in varying degree, had in fact become the entrenched interest of a largely
hereditary governing class. The Pennsylvania constitution substituted almost
a direct democracy, in which no one government could carry any responsibility or pursue any sustained program of his own. Many people in
Pennsylvania objected to it from the beginning. It must be remembered that
the democratic constitution did not signify that Pennsylvania was really
more democratic than some of the other states; it signified, rather, that
Pennsylvania was more divided, and that conservatism was stronger, certain
upper-class and politically experienced elements, which elsewhere took a
leading part in the Revolution, being in Pennsylvania tainted with Anglo-
philism. Whether the constitution of 1776 was workable or not, these people
soon put an end to it. It lasted only until 1790.[8]

The most interesting case is that of Massachusetts. Here the great political
thinker was John Adams, who became the main author of the Massachusetts
constitution of 1780, which in turn had an influence on the Constitution of
the United States. In his own time Adams was denounced as an Anglo-
maniac and a Monocrat. In our own time some sympathizers with the
eighteenth-century democrats have considered him very conservative, while
on the other hand theorists of the "new conservatism" would persuade us
that John Adams was in truth the American Edmund Burke. I confess that
I see very little in any of these allegations.

Adams in 1776 published some *Thoughts on Government*, for the guidance of those in the various colonies who were soon to declare independence
and begin to govern themselves. This was in some ways a conservative
tract. Adams thought it best, during the war, for the new states simply to
keep the forms of government that they had. He obviously approved the
arrangement under the Massachusetts charter of 1691, by which the popular
assembly elected an upper house or council. In other ways he was not very
conservative. He declared, like Jefferson, that the aim of government is
welfare or happiness, that republican institutions must rest on "virtue," and
that the people should support a universal system of public schools. He
wanted one-year terms for governors and officials (the alternative would be
"slavery"), and he favored rotation of office. He quite agreed that someday
the state governors and councillors might be popularly elected, as they
were in Connecticut already. He gave six reasons for having a bicameral
legislature, but in none of these six reasons did he show any fear of the
people, or belief that, with a unicameral legislature, the people would
plunder property or degenerate into anarchy. He was afraid of the one-
house legislature itself. He never committed the folly of identifying the
deputies with the deputizers. He was afraid that a single house would be
arbitrary or capricious, or make itself perpetual, or "make laws for their
own interest, and adjudge all controversies in their own favor."[9] He himself
cited the cases of Holland and the Long Parliament. The fear of a self-perpetuating political body, gathering privileges to itself, was certainly better
grounded in common observation than vague alarms about anarchy or
pillage.

[8] *Ibid.*, 214–86; J. P. Selsam, *The Pennsylvania Constitution of 1776: a Study in Revolutionary Democracy* (Philadelphia, 1936).
[9] *Works* (1851), IV, 196.

The *Thoughts* of 1776 were conservative in another way, if conservatism be the word. Adams had not yet conceived the idea of a constitutional convention. He lacked the notion of the people as constituent power. He had in mind that existing assemblies would draft the new constitutions, when and if any were drafted. Adams was familiar with all the high-level political theory of England and Europe. But the idea of the people as the constituent power arose locally, from the grass roots.

The revolutionary leadership in Massachusetts, including both Adamses, was quite satisfied to be rid of the British, and otherwise to keep the Bay State as it had always been. They therefore "resumed" the charter of 1691. They simply undid the Massachusetts Government Act of 1774. Some of the commonality of Boston, and farmers of Concord and the western towns, envisaged further changes. It is hard to say what they wanted, except that they wanted a new constitution. Experts in Massachusetts history contradict each other flatly; some say that debtors, poor men, and Baptists were dissatisfied; others that all kinds of diverse people naturally owed money anyway, that practically no one was too poor to vote, and that Baptists were an infinitesimal splinter group in a solidly Congregationalist population. It may be that the trouble was basically psychological; that many people of fairly low station, even though they had long had the right to vote, had never until the Revolution participated in politics, were aroused by the Revolution, the war, and excitement of soldiering, and, feeling that affairs had always been managed by people socially above them, wanted now to act politically on their own.

Demands were heard for a new constitution. It was said that the charter of 1691 was of no force, since the royal power that had issued it was no longer valid. It was said that no one could be governed without his consent, and that no living person had really consented to this charter. Some Berkshire towns even hinted that they did not belong to Massachusetts at all until they shared in constituting the new commonwealth. They talked of "setting themselves apart," or being welcomed by a neighboring state. Echoes of the social contract floated through the western air. "The law to bind all must be assented to by all," declared the farmers of Sutton. "The Great Secret of Government is governing all by all," said those of Spencer.[10] It began to seem that a constitution was necessary not only to secure liberty but to establish authority, not only to protect the individual but to found the state.

The house of representatives proposed that it and the council, that is, the two houses of legislation sitting together, should be authorized by the people to draw up a constitution. All adult males were to vote on the granting of this authorization, not merely those possessing the customary property qualification. In a sense, this was to recognize Rousseau's principle that there must be "unanimity at least once": that everyone must consent to the law under which he was to live, even if later, when constitutional arrangements were made, a qualification was required for ordinary voting. The council objected to a plan whereby it would lose its identity by merging with the house. A little dispute occurred, not unlike that in France in 1789 between "vote by head" and "vote by order." The plan nevertheless went

[10] Douglass, *op. cit.*, 178.

through. The two houses, sitting as one, and authorized by the people, produced a constitution in 1778. It was submitted for popular ratification. The voters repudiated it. Apparently both democrats and conservatives were dissatisfied. This is precisely what happened in Holland in 1797, when the first constitution of the Dutch revolution was rejected by a coalition of opposite-minded voters.

A special election was therefore held, in which all towns chose delegates to a state convention, "for the sole purpose of forming a new Constitution." John Adams, delegate from Braintree, was put on the drafting committee. He wrote a draft, which the convention modified only in detail. The resulting document reflected many influences. It is worth while to suggest a few.

There is a modern fashion for believing that Rousseau had little influence in America, particularly on such sensible characters as John Adams. I do not think that he had very much. Adams, however, had read the *Social Contract* as early as 1765, and ultimately had four copies of it in his library. I suspect that, like others, he found much of it unintelligible or fantastic, and some of it a brilliant expression of his own beliefs. He himself said of the Massachusetts constitution: "It is Locke, Sidney, Rousseau, and de Mably reduced to practice."[11]

Adams wrote in the preamble: "The body politic is formed by a voluntary association of individuals. It is a social compact, by which the whole people covenants with each citizen, and each citizen with the whole people, that all shall be governed by certain laws for the common good."[12] The thought here, and the use of the word "covenant," go back to the Mayflower compact. But whence comes the "social" in *social* compact? And whence comes the word "citizen"? There were no "citizens" under the British constitution, except in the sense of freemen of the few towns known as cities. In the English language the word "citizen" in its modern sense is an Americanism, dating from the American Revolution.[13] It is entirely possible that Jean-Jacques Rousseau had deposited these terms in Adams' mind. The whole passage suggests Chapter vi, Book 1, of the *Social Contract*. The convention adopted this part of Adams' preamble without change.

In the enacting clause of the preamble Adams wrote: "We, therefore, the delegates of the people of Massachusetts . . . agree upon the following . . . Constitution of the Commonwealth of Massachusetts." The convention made a significant emendation: "We, therefore, the people of Massachusetts . . . agree upon, ordain and establish. . . ." The formula, *We the people ordain and establish*, expressing the developed theory of the people as constituent power, was used for the first time in the Massachusetts constitu-

---

[11] *Works* (1851), IV, 216. Adams also, in 1787, cited Rousseau's *Discourse on Inequality* and *Considerations on Poland* with approval, recommending the former for its picture of the evil in civilized men, the latter for its view that Poland was dominated exclusively by nobles. *Works*, IV, 409 and 367.

[12] *Ibid.*, 219; Thorpe, *op. cit.*, III, 1889.

[13] This may be readily confirmed from the Oxford Dictionary, or by comparison of definitions of "citizen" in British and American dictionaries, or by tracing the article "citizen" through successive editions of the Encyclopaedia Britannica, where the modern meaning does not appear until the eleventh edition in 1910.

tion of 1780, whence it passed into the preamble of the United States constitution of 1787 and the new Pennsylvania constitution of 1790, after which it became common in the constitutions of the new states, and in new constitutions of the old states. Adams did not invent the formula. He was content with the matter-of-fact or purely empirical statement that the "delegates" had "agreed." It was the popularly elected convention that rose to more abstract heights. Providing in advance for popular ratification, it imputed the creation of government to the people.

Adams wrote, as the first article of the Declaration of Rights: "All men are born equally free and independent, and have certain natural, essential and unalienable rights," which included defense of their lives, liberties, and property, and the seeking of "safety and happiness." The Virginia Declaration of Rights, drafted by George Mason in June 1776, was almost identical, and Adams certainly had it in mind. The Massachusetts convention made only one change in this sentence. It declared: "All men are born free and equal." The convention, obviously, was thinking of the Declaration of Independence, that is, Jefferson's more incisive rewording of Mason's Virginia declaration.

The convention had been elected by a true universal male suffrage, but it adopted, following Adams' draft, a restriction on the franchise. To vote, under the constitution, it was necessary to own real estate worth £3 a year, or real and personal property of a value of £60. The charter of 1691 had specified only £2 and £40 respectively. The state constitution was thus in this respect more conservative than the charter. How much more conservative? Here we run into the difference between experts already mentioned.[14] A whole school of thought, pointing to a 50 per cent increase in the voting qualification, has seen a reaction of property-owners against dangers from below. Closer examination of the values of money reveals that the £3 and £60 of 1780 represent an increase of only one-eighth over the figures of 1691. Even if half the people of Boston were unfranchised, all Boston then had only a twentieth of the population of the state. In the rural areas, where farm ownership was usual, it was mainly grown sons living for a few years with their parents who lacked the vote. There seems to have been only sporadic objection to the suffrage provision.

Adams put into the constitution, and the convention retained it, that ghost of King, Lords, and Commons that now assumed the form of governor, senate, and house of representatives. Partisans of the British system, in England or America, would surely find this ghost highly attenuated. The point about King and Lords, in the British system, was precisely that they were not elected by anyone, that they were immune to popular pressure, or any pressure, through their enjoyment of life tenure and hereditary personal rights to political position. Governor and senators in Massachusetts, like representatives, both in Adams' draft and in the final document, were all elected, all by the same electorate, and all for one-year terms. To Adams (as, for example, to Delolme), it was of the utmost importance to prevent

[14] For emphasis on the conservative or reactionary character of the Massachusetts constitution, see Douglass, op. cit., 189–213, and more specialized writers cited there; for the opposite view, which I follow in part, see R. E. Brown, Middle-Class Democracy and the Revolution in Massachusetts, 1691–1780 (Ithaca, 1955), 384–400.

the executive from becoming the mere creature of the legislature. He even wished the governor to have an absolute veto, which the convention changed to a veto that could be overridden by a two-thirds majority of both houses. Adams continued to prefer a final veto. Jeffersonians and their numerous progeny found this highly undemocratic. In all states south of New York, at the end of the Revolution, governors were elected by the legislative houses, and none had any veto. Adams justified the veto as a means "to preserve the independence of the executive and judicial departments."[15] And since governors could no longer be appointed by the crown, an obvious way to prevent their dependence on legislatures was to have them issue, like legislators, from the new sovereign, the people. It was legislative oligarchy that Adams thought the most imminent danger. As he wrote to Jefferson in 1787: "You are afraid of the one—I, of the few."[16]

As for the phantom "lords," or senators, though they were directly elected by the ordinary voters for one-year terms, they were in a way supposed to represent property rather than numbers. They were apportioned among the counties of Massachusetts not according to population but according to taxes paid, that is, according to assessed value of taxable wealth. Suffolk County, which included Boston, thus received 6 senators out of 40, where on a purely numerical basis it would have received only four. The Maine districts, Cape Cod, and the western counties were numerically somewhat underrepresented. The three central and western counties received 11 senators, where a representation in proportion to numbers would have given them 12 or 13. Inequalities in wealth in Massachusetts, as between individuals or as between city and country, were not yet great enough to make a senate apportioned according to "property" (which included the small man's property as well as the rich man's) very different from a senate apportioned according to numbers.[17]

The Massachusetts constitution prescribed certain qualifications for eligibility. The governor was required to have a freehold worth at least £1,000, senators a freehold of £300 or £600 total estate, representatives a freehold of £100 or £200 total estate. (British law at this time required £300 or £600 *annual income* from land to qualify for the House of Commons.) These Massachusetts requirements resembled those in North Carolina, where the governor had to have a £1,000 freehold, and members of the upper and lower houses freeholds of 300 or 100 acres respectively. In the absence of comparative statistics on land values and distribution of land ownership in the two states, it is impossible to compare the real impact of these legal qualifications for office. In Massachusetts, however, whatever may have been true in North Carolina, the average 100-acre one-family farm was worth well over £300, and there were a great many such farms, so that the

---

[15] Adams, *Works* (1851), IV, 231 and 232 note.

[16] *Papers of Thomas Jefferson*, XII (Princeton, 1955), 396.

[17] Compare the apportionment of senators in the Massachusetts constitution with the population of counties in the census of 1790. The fact the senate represented property rather than numbers is stressed by those who see the Massachusetts constitution of 1780 as a very conservative or reactionary document. I confess to sharing the impatience of Professor Brown at academic theories which dissolve under a little grade-school computation.

ordinary successful farmer could qualify for either house of the legislature, and a few well-to-do ones in almost every village might if they chose have aspired to the office of governor.[18] The requirements in Massachusetts, as set forth by John Adams, were, if anything, Jeffersonian or agrarian in their tendency, since they favored the farm population, and made it even harder for middle-class townspeople, who might own no land, to occupy public office. The aim was clearly to limit office to the substantial segment of the population, but the substantial segment was broadly defined. Still, there were people who by this definition were not "substantial," and some of them objected to these provisions, though not many would in any case have ventured to run for office or been elected if they did, in the Massachusetts of 1780.

It was Article III of the Declaration of Rights, both in Adams' draft and in the finished constitution, that caused most debate in the convention and most disagreement among the voters during ratification. This article, declaring religion to be the foundation of morality and of the state, authorized the legislature to "enjoin" people to go to church, and required the use of public funds to maintain the churches, while allowing any "subject" to have his own contribution paid to the denomination of his choice. While it received a large majority of the popular vote, 8,885 to 6,225, it was the one article which most clearly failed to obtain a two-thirds majority, and the one which may have never been legally ratified, though declared so by the convention. Those voting against it expressed a desire to separate church and state. These, in turn, included perhaps a few Baptists who favored such separation on religious principle, a great many Protestants who feared that the article might legalize Roman Catholicism, and an unknown number of people, one suspects, who were no longer very regular in attending any church at all.

The Massachusetts constitution of 1780 was adopted by a two-thirds majority in a popular referendum from which no free adult male was excluded. The vote was light, for opinion on the matter seems not to have been excited.[19] It was six years since the rebellion against King George, and four years since the British army had left Massachusetts; doubtless many people wished to be bothered no longer. The action of the people as constituent power is, after all, a legal concept, or even a necessary legal fiction where the sovereignty of any concrete person or government is denied. It does not signify that everyone is actually engrossed in the fabrication of constitu-

[18] Brown, op. cit., 18, 394.

[19] About 23 per cent of adult males voted on ratification of the constitution of 1780, a figure which may be compared with 30 per cent of adult males voting on ratification of the French constitution of 1793, with the difference that in the France of 1793 only those voting "yes" took the trouble to vote at all (1,801,918 "ayes" to 11,610 "no's" with some 4,300,000 abstentions). It is a question whether a vote by 23 per cent of the population should be considered "light." This percentage may have been a good measure of the politically interested population; in the annual elections of the governor the ratio of persons actually casting a vote to the total of adult white males ranged between 9 per cent and 28 per cent until it began to rise with the election of 1800. See J. R. Pole, "Suffrage and Representation in Massachusetts: A Statistical Note," in *William and Mary Quarterly*, xvi (October 1957), 590–92, and J. Godechot, *Les institutions de la France sous la Révolution et l'Empire* (Paris, 1951), 252.

tions. On the other hand, it does not seem necessary to believe that the convention, when it declared the constitution ratified, put something over on an innocent or apathetic or reluctant people. The people of Massachusetts had rejected the constitution proposed in 1778. They could have rejected the one proposed in 1780. It was adopted, not because it was thought perfect or final by everyone, but because it offered a frame of government, or basis of agreement, within which people could still lawfully disagree. It has lasted, with many amendments, until the present day.

A Word on the Constitution of the United States

The idea that sovereignty lay with the people, and not with states or their governments, made possible in America a new kind of federal structure unknown in Europe. The Dutch and Swiss federations were unions of component parts, close permanent alliances between disparate corporate members. For them no other structure was possible, because there was as yet no Dutch or Swiss people except in a cultural sense. It was in the Dutch revolution of 1795 and the Swiss revolution of 1798 that these two bundles of provinces or cantons were first proclaimed as political nations. In America it was easier to make the transition from a league of states, set up during the Revolution, to a more integral union set up in the United States constitution of 1787. The new idea was that, instead of the central government drawing its powers from the states, both central and state governments should draw their powers from the same source; the question was the limit between these two sets of derived powers. The citizen, contrariwise, was simultaneously a citizen both of the United States and of his own state. He was the sovereign, not they. He chose to live under two constitutions, two sets of laws, two sets of courts and officials; theoretically, he had created them all, reserving to himself, under each set, certain liberties specified in declarations of rights.

It has been widely believed, since the publication in 1913 of Charles A. Beard's *Economic Interpretation of the Constitution*, that the federal constitution of 1787 marked a reaction against democratic impulses of the Revolution, and was a device by which men of property, particularly those holding securities of the state or continental governments, sought to protect themselves and their financial holdings against the dangers of popular rule. The Philadelphia convention has been represented as an almost clandestine body, which exceeded its powers, and which managed (as has also been said of the Massachusetts convention of 1780) to impose a conservative constitution on a confused or apathetic people. Recently the flimsiness of the evidence for this famous thesis has been shown by Professor Robert Brown.[20] The thesis takes its place in the history of historical writing, as a product of that Progressive and post-Progressive era in which the common man could be viewed as the dupe or plaything of private interests.

It seems likely enough that there was a conservative reaction after the American Revolution, and even a movement among the upper class (minus

---

[20] R. E. Brown, *Charles Beard and the Constitution: a Critical Analysis of "An Economic Interpretation of the Constitution"* (Princeton, 1956). The critique of Beard is carried even further in a more recent work, Forrest McDonald, *We the People: The Economic Origins of the Constitution* (Chicago, 1958).

the old loyalists) not wholly unlike the "aristocratic resurgence" which I shall soon describe in the Europe of the 1780's. The difference is that these neo-aristocrats of America were less obstinate and less caste-conscious than in Europe. They did not agree with each other, and they knew they could not rule alone. The men at Philadelphia in 1787 were too accomplished as politicians to be motivated by anything so impractical as ideology or mere self-interest. They hoped, while solving concrete problems, to arouse as little opposition as possible. They lacked also the European sense of the permanency of class status. Thinking of an upper class as something that individuals might move into or out of, they allowed for social mobility both upward and downward. The wealthy Virginian, George Mason, at the Philadelphia convention, on urging that the upper class should take care to give adequate representation to the lower, offered it as one of his reasons that, however affluent they might be now, "the course of a few years not only might, but certainly would, distribute their posterity through the lowest classes of society."[21] No one seems to have disputed this prognostication. Such acceptance of future downward mobility for one's own grandchildren, if by no means universal in America, was far more common than in Europe. Without such downward mobility there could not long remain much room for newcomers at the top, or much assurance of a fluid society. With it, there could not be a permanent aristocracy in the European sense.

It was the state legislatures that chose the delegates to the Philadelphia convention, in answer to a widely expressed demand for strengthening the federal government under the Articles of Confederation. The Philadelphia convention proceeded, not to amend the Articles, but to ignore and discard them. It repudiated the union which the thirteen states had made. Beard in 1913 found it satisfying to call this operation a revolution, a revolution from above to be sure, which he compared to a *coup d'état* of Napoleon. His critic, Professor Brown, in 1956, found it satisfying and important to deny any revolutionary action in what happened.

What did really happen? The men at Philadelphia did circumvent the state governments, and in a sense they betrayed those who sent them. They did so by adopting the revolutionary principle of the American Revolution, which had already become less purely revolutionary and more institutionalized as an accepted routine, as shown in the Massachusetts convention of 1780, which had been followed by a New Hampshire convention, and new constitution for New Hampshire in 1784. The Philadelphia convention went beyond the existing constituted bodies, that is, the state governments and the Congress under the Articles, by appealing for support directly to the people, who in each state elected, for this purpose only, conventions to discuss, ratify, or refuse to ratify the document proposed by the convention at Philadelphia. The authors of the proposed federal constitution needed a principle of authority; they conceived that "the people were the fountain of all power," and that if popularly chosen conventions ratified their work "all disputes and doubts concerning [its] legitimacy" would be removed.[22] In each state, in voting for ratifying conventions, the voters voted according

---

[21] *Writings* of James Madison, 9 vols. (N.Y., 1902–1910), III, 47.
[22] Quoted by Brown, *op. cit.*, 140.

to the franchise as given by their state constitutions. No use was made of the more truly revolutionary idea, still alive in Massachusetts in 1780, that on the acceptance of a government *every* man should have a vote. In some states the authorized voters were a great majority; in none were they a small minority. The actual vote for the ratifying conventions was light, despite protracted public discussion, because most people lost interest, or never had any, in abstract debates concerning governmental structure at the distant federal level. Eleven states ratified within a few months, and the constitution went into effect for the people of those eleven states. The remaining two states came in within three years. The whole procedure was revolutionary in a sense, but revolution had already become domesticated in America. The idea of the people as the constituent power, acting through special conventions, was so generally accepted and understood that a mere mention of the word "convention," in the final article of the proposed constitution, was thought sufficient explanation of the process of popular endorsement.

Nevertheless, men of popular principles, those who would soon be called democrats, and who preferred the arrangements of the Pennsylvania constitution, with its single-house legislature to which the executive was subordinated, found much in the new federal constitution not to their liking, at least at first sight. The new instrument reproduced the main features of the Massachusetts constitution of 1780: the strong president, the senate, the house of representatives, the partial executive veto, the independent judiciary, the separation and balance of powers. In fact, the longer tenure of offices—four years for the president, six for senators, two for representatives, in place of the annual terms for corresponding functionaries in Massachusetts—shows a reaction away from revolutionary democracy and toward the giving of more adequate authority to those entrusted with public power. The president was not popularly elected, like the governor in Massachusetts; but neither was he designated by the legislative assembly, like the president in Pennsylvania and governors in the Southern states. He was elected by an electoral college, with each state free to determine how its own share of these electors should be chosen. Although as early as 1788 almost half the states provided for popular election of presidential electors, it was not until 1828 that this became the general and permanent rule. In the federal constitution the unique feature, and key to the main compromise, was the senate. Not only did large and small states have the same number of senators, but it was the state legislatures that chose them. Since it was the state legislatures that conservative or hard-money men mainly feared in the 1780's, this provision can hardly have been introduced in the hope of assuring economic conservatism. It was introduced to mollify the states as states. In the senate the new union was a league of preexisting corporate entities. In the house of representatives it rested more directly on the people. Anyone who had the right to vote in his state could vote for a member of the lower house of Congress. In one respect the federal constitution, by its silence, was more democratic in a modern sense than any of the state constitutions. No pecuniary or religious qualifications was specified for any office.

The new constitution was a compromise, but that it produced a less popular federal government, less close to the people, than that of the Articles of Confederation, seems actually contrary to the facts. It created a national arena for political controversy. There were now, for the first time, national elections in which voters could dispute over national issues. One result was the rise, on a national scale, of the Jeffersonian democratic movement in the 1790's.

Ambivalence of the American Revolution

In conclusion, the American Revolution was really a revolution, in that certain Americans subverted their legitimate government, ousted the contrary-minded and confiscated their property, and set the example of a revolutionary program, through mechanisms by which the people was deemed to act as the constituent power. This much being said, it must be admitted that the Americans, when they constituted their new states, tended to reconstitute much of what they already had. They were as fortunate and satisfied a people as any the world has known. They thus offered both the best and the worst example, the most successful and the least pertinent precedent, for less fortunate or more dissatisfied peoples who in other parts of the world might hope to realize the same principles.

Pennsylvania and Georgia gave themselves one-chamber legislatures, but both had had one-chamber legislatures before the Revolution. All states set up weak governors; they had been undermining the authority of royal governors for generations. South Carolina remained a planter oligarchy before and after independence, but even in South Carolina fifty-acre freeholders had a vote. New York set up one of the most conservative of the state constitutions, but this was the first constitution under which Jews received equality of civil rights—not a very revolutionary departure, since Jews had been prospering in New York since 1654.[23] The Anglican Church was disestablished, but it had had few roots in the colonies anyway. In New England the sects obtained a little more recognition, but Congregationalism remained favored by law. The American revolutionaries made no change in the laws of indentured servitude. They deplored, but avoided, the matter of Negro slavery. Quitrents were generally abolished, but they had been nominal anyway, and a kind of manorial system remained long after the Revolution in New York. Laws favoring primogeniture and entail were done away with, but apparently they had been little used by landowners in any case. No general or statistical estimate is yet possible on the disposition of loyalist property. Some of the confiscated estates went to strengthen a new propertied class, some passed through the hands of speculators, and some either immediately or eventually came into the possession of small owners. There was enough change of ownership to create a material interest in the Revolution, but obviously no such upheaval in property relations as in France after 1789.

Even the apparently simple question of how many people received the right to vote because of the Revolution cannot be satisfactorily answered. There was some extension of democracy in this sense, but the more we examine colonial voting practices the smaller the change appears. The Virginia constitution of 1776 simply gave the vote to those "at present" qualified. By one estimate the number of persons voting in Virginia actually

[23] J. R. Marcus, *Early American Jewry* (Philadelphia, 1953), II, 530.

declined from 1741 to 1843, and those casting a vote in the 1780's were about a quarter of the free male population over twenty-one years of age.[24] The advance of political democracy, at the time of the Revolution, was most evident in the range of officers for whom voters could vote. In the South the voters generally voted only for members of the state legislatures; in Pennsylvania and New England they voted also for local officials, and in New England for governors as well.

In 1796, at the time of the revolution in Europe, and when the movement of Jeffersonian democracy was gathering strength in America, seven of the sixteen states then in the union had no property qualification for voters in the choice of the lower legislative house, and half of them provided for popular election of governors, only the seaboard South, and New Jersey, persisting in legislative designation of the executive.[25] The best European historians underestimate the extent of political democracy in America at this time. They stress the restrictions on voting rights in America, as in the French constitution of 1791.[26] They do so because they have read the best American historians on the subject and have in particular followed the school of Charles Beard and others. The truth seems to be that America was a good deal more democratic than Europe in the 1790's. It had been so, within limits, long before the revolutionary era began.

Nor in broad political philosophy did the American Revolution require a violent break with customary ideas. For Englishmen it was impossible to maintain, in the eighteenth century or after, that the British constitution placed any limits on the powers of Parliament. Not so for Americans; they constantly appealed, to block the authority of Parliament or other agencies of the British government, to their rights as Englishmen under the British constitution. The idea of limited government, the habit of thinking in terms of two levels of law, of an ordinary law checked by a higher constitutional law, thus came out of the realities of colonial experience. The colonial Americans believed also, like Blackstone for that matter, that the rights of Englishmen were somehow the rights of all mankind. When the highest English authorities disagreed on what Americans claimed as English rights, and when the Americans ceased to be English by abjuring their King, they were obliged to find another and less ethnocentric or merely historical principle of justification. They now called their rights the rights of man. Apart from abstract assertions of natural liberty and equality, which were not so much new and alarming as conceptual statements as in the use to which they were applied, the rights claimed by Americans were the old rights of Englishmen—trial by jury, *habeas corpus*, freedom of the press, freedom of religion, freedom of elections, no taxation without representation. The content of rights was broadened, but the content changed less than the form,

---

[24] C. S. Sydnor, *Gentlemen Freeholders: Political practices in Washington's Virginia* (Williamsburg, 1952), 138–39, 143.

[25] W. L. Smith, *A Comparative View of the Several States with Each Other . . .* (Philadelphia, 1796). There are six tables showing comparisons.

[26] See, for example, G. Lefebvre, *La Révolution française* (Paris, 1951), 99, and *Coming of the French Revolution*, Eng. trans. (Princeton, 1947), 180–81; P. Sagnac, *La fin de l'ancien régime et al Révolution américaine 1763–1789* (Paris, 1947), 386–93, where the Beard view of issues involved in the writing and ratification of the federal constitution is clearly expounded.

for the form now became universal.[27] Rights were demanded for human being as such. It was not necessary to be English, or even American, to have an ethical claim to them. The form also became more concrete, less speculative and metaphysical, more positive and merely legal. Natural rights were numbered, listed, written down, and embodied in or annexed to constitutions, in the foundations of the state itself.

So the American Revolution remains ambivalent. If it was conservative, it was also revolutionary, and vice versa. It was conservative because colonial Americans had long been radical by general standards of Western Civilization. It was, or appeared, conservative because the deepest conservatives, those most attached to King and empire, conveniently left the scene. It was conservative because the colonies had never known oppression, excepting always for slavery—because, as human institutions go, America had always been free. It was revolutionary because the colonists took the risks of rebellion, because they could not avoid a conflict among themselves, and because they checkmated those Americans who, as the country developed, most admired the aristocratic society of England and Europe. Henceforth the United States, in Louis Hartz's phrase, would be the land of the frustrated aristocrat, not of the frustrated democrat; for to be an aristocrat it is not enough to think of oneself as such, it is necessary to be thought so by others; and never again would deference for social rank be a characteristic American attitude. Elites, for better or for worse, would henceforth be on the defensive against popular values. Moreover the Americans in the 1770's, not content merely to throw off an outside authority, insisted on transmuting the theory of their political institutions. Their revolution was revolutionary because it showed how certain abstract doctrines, such as the rights of man and the sovereignty of the people, could be "reduced to practice," as Adams put it, by assemblages of fairly levelheaded gentlemen exercising constituent power in the name of the people. And, quite apart from its more distant repercussions, it was certainly revolutionary in its impact on the contemporary world across the Atlantic.

Suggested Reading

A good review of various analytical approaches to revolution is Lawrence Stone's "Theories of Revolution," *World Politics*, XVIII (January 1966). The best introduction to the vast literature on the American Revolution itself is the opening essay by Jack P. Greene in his collection *The Reinterpretation of the American Revolution, 1763–1789** (1968), which also contains many of the leading historical essays on the causes and consequences of the conflict. A good overview of the entire revolutionary era that emphasizes the colonists' early commitment to principles is Edmund S. Morgan's *The Birth of the Republic, 1763–1789** (1956). Bernard Bailyn, ed., *Pamphlets of the American Revolution, 1750–1776*, Vol. I (1965), and Henry Steele Commager and Richard B. Morris, eds., *The Spirit of 'Seventy-Six: The Story of the American Revolution as Told by*

---

[27] For a European view, see O. Vossler, "Studien zur Erklärung der Menschenrechte," *Historische Zeitschrift*, vol. 142 (1930), 536–39.

Participants (2 vols., 1958) are the most valuable collections of original source material, albeit of different kinds.

Books that deal with the major events and issues of the prerevolutionary years include Edmund S. and Helen S. Morgan's *The Stamp Act Crisis: Prologue to Revolution** (1953), which lays great stress on the continuity of views of the revolutionaries; Benjamin W. Labaree's *The Boston Tea Party** (1964); Carl L. Becker's classic *The Declaration of Independence: A Study in the History of Ideas** (1922); and Carl Bridenbaugh's *Mitre and Scepter: Trans-Atlantic Faiths, Ideas, Personalities, and Politics, 1689–1775** (1962), which takes up currents within colonial religion and especially the struggle over the appointment of an Anglican bishop for the colonies. Two important studies that explore colonial politics and political institutions before Independence from different perspectives are Bernard Bailyn's *The Origins of American Politics** (1968), which amplifies arguments presented in his *Ideological Origins of the American Revolution** (1967), and Jack P. Greene's "The Role of the Lower Houses of Assembly in Eighteenth-Century Politics," *Journal of Southern History*, XXVII (November 1961), which demonstrates the maturity of the provincial legislatures. The coming of the Revolution is spelled out in detail in Pauline Maier's *From Resistance to Revolution: Colonial Radicals and the Development of American Opposition to Britain, 1765–1776* (1972), which explores the interrelationships of thought and action. Clinton Rossiter's *The Seedtime of the Republic** (1953) encompasses the entire colonial period and emphasizes the growth of American nationalism.

The literature on the imperial background of the Revolution grows larger each year. Jack P. Greene's introduction to *The Reinterpretation of the American Revolution** provides a good overview of works on trade and administration. Charles McLean Andrews' *The Colonial Background of the American Revolution: An Interpretation,** rev. ed. (1931) remains a brilliant presentation of the so-called imperial interpretation. More sympathetic to the British and also challenging is Lawrence H. Gipson's *The Coming of the Revolution, 1763–1775** (1954).

The Revolutionary War itself has had many historians. The best analysis of military affairs is Don Higginbotham's recent *The War of American Independence: Military Attitudes, Policies, and Practices, 1763–1789* (1971). The critical international relations of the war were examined some time ago by Samuel Flagg Bemis in *The Diplomacy of the American Revolution,** rev. ed. (1957). The conclusion of the war is the principal emphasis of Richard B. Morris's more recent *The Peacemakers: The Great Powers and American Independence* (1965).

William H. Nelson, in *The American Tory** (1961), examines the too-often forgotten losers of the conflict. A still challenging early effort to assess the social consequences of the Revolution is J. Franklin Jameson's *The American Revolution Considered as a Social Movement** (1926), which has been revised by Frederick B. Tolles in "The American Revolution Considered as a Social Movement: A Re-Evaluation," *American Historical Review*, LIX (October 1954). Much of the literature on the Revolution and the Constitution touches in one way or another on this subject.

* Also published in paperback edition.

The Fulfillment
of Revolution:
Confederation and
Constitution

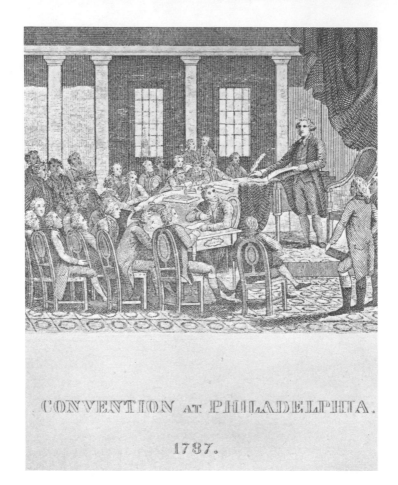

CONVENTION at PHILADELPHIA.

1787.

The Worthy Against
the Licentious

Gordon S. Wood

The historiography of the Constitution defies brief
summary. Historians have long debated whether the
product of the Philadelphia Convention of 1787
marked a culmination of the American Revolution or
whether it was a conservative reaction against that
revolution. Did the framers intend to subvert the will
of the people or did they design a government
through which the people's voice could be better
heard? Was the Constitution a radical departure in
the history of American governments, or did it absorb
and enshrine the principles and devices of the state
constitutions? Was the decade of the 1780's a time of
real economic and civic crisis which the Constitution
helped end? Or was the crisis illusory, a good excuse
for a constitutional reaction? Or perhaps did the
average citizens demand redress for real grievances and
find in the new constitutional settlement a device to
help resolve them?

Gordon S. Wood of Brown University, from whose
influential and exhaustive work *The Creation of the
American Republic** (1970) the following selections are
taken, has succeeded as few recent historians have in
recapturing the terms and tone of contemporary
debate surrounding the movement for a stronger
government. In his judgment, the Constitution was on
the one hand an "intrinsically aristocratic document

201

designed to check the democratic tendencies of the period." On the other hand, its purpose was radical: it was designed to create an unprecedented republican government over an extended territory. According to Wood, both backers and opponents of the Constitution —Federalists (not to be confused with partisans of the political party of Hamilton and John Adams) and Antifederalists—shared a fondness for elite rule. All feared disorder and faction. But they differed, believes Wood, in both their social location and in the boldness of their thought.

The Federalists possessed a national perspective, favored rule by a cultured aristocracy, were wary of the people, had confidence in the capacity of institutions to create social harmony and good order, were better stationed by wealth and social status, and were the best politicians. The Antifederalists, by contrast, tended to be localists, had little faith in institutions, preferred a greater voice for the average citizen, were of lower wealth and station, and were less able politicians. And yet, Wood emphasizes, the divisions were by no means only economic or social. The contending parties had different conceptions of society and political life. Their differences were as much ideological as anything else.

Wood therefore goes beyond the older perimeters of historical interpretations to show how complex and genuine was the constitutional debate. For him, contemporaries were seeking to define the very nature of the good republican society. In this, his interpretation differs from that of Charles A. Beard (to whom he nevertheless owes a great intellectual debt), who saw, in his *An Economic Interpretation of the Constitution of the United States** (1913), the constitutional struggle as a battle between men of different propertied interests in which the antidemocratic conservatives were triumphant. Wood, on the contrary, argues that the Federalist victors absorbed the lessons of the 1770s and 1780s; they adjusted themselves to the idea of democracy and worked both to legitimize and to curb the voice of the people.

Wood's view is by and large that of the Revolution's contemporaries—and of articulate and literate contemporaries at that. One wonders, however, to

The Worthy Against the Licentious. By Gordon S. Wood from *The Creation of the American Republic* (Chapel Hill, N.C.: University of North Carolina Press, 1970), pp. 471, 474–80, 483–92, 496–506, 513–18. Reprinted by permission of the University of North Carolina Press and the Institute of Early American History and Culture.

what degree the writings of the time illuminate social reality. Wood carefully presents evidence from all sides, as if to suggest that what so many thought to be true must have been so. He also insists that what men think to be so is critical in determining their actions. But what if their fears were misplaced? What if the people were more orderly, society less in crisis, than they supposed? The answers to these questions remain shrouded, and historians are only now beginning to examine late eighteenth-century American society with the same care with which they have investigated the preceding two centuries. Until we know more about revolutionary society, however, Wood's treatment is likely to remain the most intelligent and most satisfactory.

1. The Federalist Revolution

Nearly everyone in 1787 conceded "the weakness of the Confederation." All "men of reflection," even "the most orthodox republicans," said Madison, were alarmed by "the existing embarrassments and mortal diseases of the Confederacy." "It is on all hands acknowledged," said Thomas Tredwell, a New York opponent of the Constitution, "that the federal government is not adequate to the purpose of the Union." It had become, said Samuel Bryan, "the universal wish of America to grant further powers" to Congress, "so as to make the federal government adequate to the ends of its institution." But what men like Madison had in mind for America "was not," as the Antifederalists soon perceived, "a mere revision and amendment of our first Confederation, but a compleat System for the future government of the United States." "All parties" had admitted "the propriety of some material change" in the federal government, but they had hardly expected what they got—a virtual revolution in American politics, promising a serious weakening, if not a destruction, of the power of the states.[1]

. . .

[1] James Galloway (N.C.), in Elliot, ed., *Debates*, IV, 25; Madison to Edmund Pendleton, Feb. 24, 1787, to Jefferson, Mar. 18, 1787, to James Madison, Apr. 1, 1787, Hunt, ed., *Writings of Madison*, II, 318, 326, 335; Tredwell (N.Y.), in Elliot, ed., *Debates*, II, 358; [Samuel Bryan], "Letters of Centinel, No. III," Nov. 8, 1787, McMaster and Stone, eds., *Pennsylvania and the Federal Constitution*, 594; "Letters of John De Witt," Oct. 27, 1787, Cecelia M. Kenyon, ed., *The Antifederalists* (Indianapolis, 1966), 96; James Monroe to Thomas Jefferson, July 12, 1788, Hamilton, ed., *Writings of Monroe*, I, 186. On the willingness of the Antifederalists to reform the Confederation see Main, *Antifederalists*, 113–14, and Linda G. De Pauw, *The Eleventh Pillar: New York State and the Federal Constitution* (Ithaca, N.Y., 1966), esp. pp. 58–60, 69, 173, 176, 201, 264.

Like the reformers of the state constitutions in the decade after 1776 the Federalists were filled with "an enlightened zeal for energy and efficiency of government" to set against "the turbulence and follies of democracy" as expressed by the lower houses of the state legislatures, "the democratic parts of our constitutions." If the proposed central government that Madison and other nationalists had in mind in the spring of 1787 were to play the impartial role of neutralizer of interested majorities within the states, something more than simple amendment of the Articles was required. No longer would the granting of "*any* further degree of power to Congress do the business." The people of America, as John Jay said, had to become "one nation in every respect," and their separate state legislatures had to stand in relation to the Confederacy "in the same light in which counties stand to the State, of which they are parts, viz., merely as districts to facilitate the purposes of domestic order and good government." Thus the new general government could not remain a confederation of independent republics but had to be in its own right "a stable and firm Government organized in the republican form," divided into three distinct departments and somehow superimposed on the state republics, "a government," declared Oliver Ellsworth, "capable of controlling the whole, and bringing its force to a point," in order to enable, in James Iredell's words, "justice, order and dignity" to take the place "of the present anarchical confusion prevailing almost everywhere."[2]

Such a government had to be founded "on different principles" and "have a different operation" from the Articles because its purpose was truly radical. The new national government was not simply a response to the domestic problems of credit, commerce, and interstate rivalries, or to the foreign problems of a confederated republic in a hostile monarchical world. It was not, in short, meant merely to save the Union, for strengthening the Confederation along the lines of the New Jersey plan could have done that. The Federalists of the late eighties wanted and believed they needed much more than the nationalists of the early eighties had sought. Their focus was not so much on the politics of the Congress as it was on the politics of the states. To the Federalists the move for the new central government became the ultimate act of the entire Revolutionary era; it was both a progressive attempt to salvage the Revolution in the face of its imminent failure and a reactionary effort to restrain its excesses. Only a new continental republic that cut through the structure of the states to the people themselves and yet was not dependent on the character of that people could save America's experiment in republicanism. In some way or other this new republican government had to accommodate itself to the manners and habits of a people which experience in the past few years had demonstrated were incapable of supporting republican government. Believing with Washington that virtue had "in a great degree taken its departure from our land" and

[2] *The Federalist*, No. 1; Randolph, in Farrand, ed., *Records of the Federal Convention*, I, 51, 26; Jay to Washington, Jan. 7, 1787, Jay to John Adams, May 4, 1786, Johnston, ed., *Papers of Jay*, III, 226, 195; Madison, in Farrand, ed., *Records of the Federal Convention*, I, 219; [Oliver Ellsworth], "A Landholder, No. III," Nov. 19, 1787, Ford, ed., *Essays on the Constitution*, 146–47; James Iredell, *Answers to Mr. Mason's Objections to the New Constitution . . .* (Newburn, N.C., 1788), in Paul L. Ford, ed., *Pamphlets on the Constitution of the United States . . .* (Brooklyn, 1888), 370.

was not to be easily restored, the Federalists hoped to create an entirely new and original sort of republican government—a republic which did not require a virtuous people for its sustenance. If they could not, as they thought, really reform the character of American society, then they would somehow have to influence the operation of the society and moderate the effects of its viciousness. The supporters of the new federal Constitution thus aimed to succeed where the states, not the Confederation, had failed, in protecting, in John Dickinson's phrase, "the worthy against the licentious."[3]

2. The Separation of Social and Political Authority

How the Federalists expected a new central government to remedy the vices the individual states had been unable to remedy is the central question, the answer to which lies at the heart of their understanding of what was happening in the critical period. In the minds of the Federalists and of "men of reflection" generally, most of the evils of American society—the atmosphere of mistrust, the breakdown of authority, the increase of debt, the depravity of manners, and the decline of virtue—could be reduced to a fundamental problem of social disarrangement. Even the difficulties of the United States in foreign affairs and its weakness as a nation in the world, as Jay argued in The Federalist, Number 3, could be primarily explained by what the Revolution had done to America's political and social hierarchy. More than anything else the Federalists' obsession with disorder in American society and politics accounts for the revolutionary nature of the nationalist proposals offered by men like Madison in 1787 and for the resultant Federalist Constitution. Only an examination of the Federalists' social perspective, their fears and anxieties about the disarray in American society, can fully explain how they conceived of the Constitution as a political device designed to control the social forces the Revolution had released.

The most pronounced social effect of the Revolution was not harmony or stability but the sudden appearance of new men everywhere in politics and business. "When the pot boils, the scum will rise," James Otis had warned in 1776; but few Revolutionary leaders had realized just how much it would rise. By the end of the war men like Governor James Bowdoin of Massachusetts could "scarcely see any other than new faces," a change almost "as remarkable as the revolution itself." The emigration of thousands of Tories, the intensification of interest in politics, the enlargement of the legislatures and the increase in elections, the organization of new militia and political groups, the breakup of old mercantile combinations and trade circuits, the inflation and profiteering caused by the war—all offered new opportunities for hitherto unknown but ambitious persons to find new places for themselves. As John Adams noted, his own deep resentment of his supposed social superiors was being echoed throughout various levels of the society. For every brilliant provincial lawyer ready to challenge the supremacy of the imperial clique in the colonial metropolis, there were dozens of lesser men,

---

[3] Madison to Jefferson, Oct. 24, 1787, Boyd, ed., *Jefferson Papers*, XII, 274; Washington to Jay, May 18, 1786, Johnston, ed., *Papers of Jay*, III, 196; [John Dickinson], *The Letters of Fabius, in 1788, on the Federal Constitution* . . . (Wilmington, Del., 1797), in Ford, ed., *Pamphlets*, 188.

not so brilliant but equally desirous of securing a local magistracy, a captaincy of the militia, some place, however small, of honor and distinction. With the elimination of Crown privilege and appointment men were prepared to take the republican emphasis on equality seriously. The result, as one Baltimore printer declared as early as 1777, was "Whiggism run mad." "When a man, who is only fit 'to patch a shoe,' attempts 'to patch the State,' fancies himself a *Solon* or *Lycurgus*, . . . he cannot fail to meet with contempt." But contempt was no longer enough to keep such men in their place.[4]

Everywhere *"Specious, interested designing* men," "men, respectable neither for their property, their virtue, nor their abilities," were taking a lead in public affairs that they had never quite had before, courting "the suffrages of the people by tantalizing them with improper indulgences." Thousands of the most respectable people "who obtained their possessions by the hard industry, continued sobriety and economy of themselves or their virtuous ancestors" were now witnessing, so the writings of nearly all the states proclaimed over and over, many men *"whose fathers they would have disdained to have sat with the dogs of their flocks,* raised to immense wealth, or at least to carry the appearance of a haughty, supercilious and luxurious spendthrift." "Effrontery and arrogance, even in our virtuous and enlightened days," said John Jay, "are giving rank and Importance to men whom Wisdom would have left in obscurity."[5] Since "every new election in the States," as Madison pointed out in *The Federalist*, Number 62, "is found to change one half of the representatives," the newly enlarged state legislatures were being filled and yearly refilled with different faces, often with "men without reading, experience, or principle." The Revolution, it was repeatedly charged (and the evidence seems to give substance to the charges), was allowing government to fall "into the Hands of those whose ability or situation in Life does not intitle them to it."[6] Everywhere in the 1780's the press and the correspondence of those kinds of men whose letters are apt to be preserved complained that "a set of unprincipled men, who sacrifice everything to their popularity and private views, seem to have acquired too much influence in all our Assemblies." The Revolution was acquiring a degree of social turbulence that many, for all of their knowledge of revolutions, had not anticipated. Given the Revolutionary leaders' conventional eighteenth-century assumption of a necessary coincidence be-

[4] Otis quoted by John Eliot to Jeremy Belknap, Jan. 12, 1777, *Belknap Papers,* 104; James Bowdoin to Thomas Pownall, Nov. 20, 1783, quoted in Paul Goodman, *The Democratic-Republicans of Massachusetts: Politics in a Young Republic* (Cambridge, Mass., 1964), 8; John Adams, entry, Feb. 4, 1772, Butterfield, ed., *Diary of Adams,* II, 53; William Goddard, *The Prowess of the Whig Club* . . . (Baltimore, 1777), 7, 12.

[5] Charleston *Columbian Herald,* Sept. 23, 1785; "Sober Citizen," *To the Inhabitants of the City and County of New-York, Apr. 16, 1776* (N.Y., 1776); Baltimore *Md. Journal,* Mar. 30, 1787; Phila. *Pa. Gazette,* Mar. 31, 1779; Jay to Hamilton, May 8, 1778, Syrett and Cooke, eds., *Hamilton Papers,* I, 483.

[6] *The Federalist,* No. 62; Samuel Johnston to James Iredell, Dec. 9, 1776, quoted in Jones, *Defense of North Carolina,* 288; Coleman, *Revolution in Georgia,* 85. For the infusion of new men in the Revolutionary legislatures see Main, "Government by the People," *Wm. and Mary Qtly.,* 3d Ser., 23 (1966), 391–407.

tween social and political authority, many could actually believe that their world was being "turned upside down."[7]

Beginning well before the Revolution but increasing to a fever pitch by the mid-eighties were fears of what this kind of intensifying social mobility signified for the traditional conception of a hierarchical society ("In due gradation ev'ry rank must be, Some high, some low, but all in their degree") —a conception which the Revolution had unsettled but by no means repudiated. In reaction to the excessive social movement accelerated by the Revolution some Americans, although good republicans, attempted to confine mobility within prescribed channels. Men could rise, but only within the social ranks in which they were born. Their aim in life must be to learn to perform their inherited position with "industry, economy, and good conduct." A man, wrote Enos Hitchcock in his didactic tale of 1793, must not be "elevated above his employment." In this respect republicanism with its emphasis on spartan adversity and simplicity became an ideology of social stratification and control.[8] Over and over writers urged that "the crosses of life improve by retrenching our enjoyments," by moderating "our expectations," and by giving "the heart a mortal disgust to all the gaudy blandishments of sense." Luxury was such a great evil because it confounded "every Distinction between the Poor and the Rich" and allowed "people of the very meanest parentages, or office, if fortune be but a little favourable to them" to "vie to make themselves equal in apparel with the principal people of the place." "Dissipation and extravagance" encouraged even "country-girls in their market carts, and upon their panniered horses," to ride "through our streets with their heads deformed with the plumes of the ostrich and the feathers of other exotick birds." Although many, especially in the South, had expected the Revolution to lessen this kind of social chaos, republicanism actually seemed only to have aggravated it.[9]

---

[7] James Hogg to Iredell, May 17, 1783, McRee, *Life of Iredell*, II, 46; *Providence Gazette*, Mar. 3, 1787. The Tory, Jonathan Boucher, writing in 1797, reflected in an insightful passage on what he thought was happening in both England and America to the political and social structure. What alarmed Boucher was the growing tendency for "those persons who are probably the least qualified, and certainly (as far as having much at stake in the welfare of a State can make it proper for any persons to take a lead in the direction of it's public affairs) the least proper exclusively to become public man. . . . O that the people, seeing their error, and their misfortune in thus submitting to be dupes of those who in general are their superiors only in confidence, would at length have the resolution (the ability they already have) to assert their undoubted right—and no longer bear to be the marketable property of a new species of public men, who study the arts of debate, and pursue politics merely as a gainful occupation!" The emergence of this "new species of public men," and not the extension of the suffrage, was to Boucher the essence of democratic politics. Boucher, *View of the Causes*, lxxvi.

[8] Robert Proud, "On the Violation of Established and Lawful Order, Rule or Government—Applied to the Present Times in Penna in 1776," quoted in Selsam, *Pennsylvania Constitution*, 210; Enos Hitchcock, *The Farmer's Friend, or the History of Mr. Charles Worthy. Who, from Being a Poor Orphan, Rose, through Various Scenes of Distress and Misfortune, to Wealth and Eminence, by Industry, Economy and Good Conduct . . .* (Boston, 1793), 40.

[9] *Providence Gazette*, Nov. 12, 1785; Samuel Adams to John Adams, July 2, 1785, Cushing, ed., *Writings of Samuel Adams*, IV, 316; Charleston *Columbian Herald*, Oct. 7, 1785; Gardiner, *Oration, Delivered July 4, 1785*, 33.

Most American leaders, however, were not opposed to the idea of social movement, for mobility, however one may have decried its abuses, lay at the heart of republicanism. Indeed, many like John Adams had entered the Revolution in order to make mobility a reality, to free American society from the artificial constraints Britain had imposed on it, and to allow "Persons of obscure Birth, and Station, and narrow Fortunes" to make their mark in the world. Republicanism represented equality of opportunity and careers open to talent. Even "the reins of state," David Ramsay had said at the outset, "may be held by the son of the poorest man, if possessed of abilities equal to that important station." Ramsay's qualification, however, was crucial to his endorsement of mobility. For all of its emphasis on equality, republicanism was still not considered by most to be incompatible with the conception of a hierarchical society of different gradations and a unitary authority to which deference from lower to higher should be paid. Movement must necessarily exist in a republic, if talent alone were to dominate, if the natural aristocracy were to rule. But such inevitable movement must be into and out of clearly discernible ranks. Those who rose in a republic, it was assumed, must first acquire the attributes of social superiority—wealth, education, experience, and connections—before they could be considered eligible for political leadership. Most Revolutionary leaders clung tightly to the concept of a ruling elite, presumably based on merit, but an elite nonetheless—a natural aristocracy embodied in the eighteenth-century ideal of an educated and cultivated gentleman. The rising self-made man could be accepted into this natural aristocracy only if he had assimilated through education or experience its attitudes, refinements, and style. For all of their earlier criticism of "the better sort of People" in the name of "real Merit," few of the Revolutionary leaders were prepared to repudiate the idea of a dominating elite and the requisite identity of social and political authority.[10]

. . .

3. Aristocracy and Democracy

The division over the Constitution in 1787–88 is not easily analyzed. It is difficult, as historians have recently demonstrated, to equate the supporters or opponents of the Constitution with particular economic groupings. The Antifederalist politicians in the ratifying conventions often possessed wealth, including public securities, equal to that of the Federalists.[11] While the relative youth of the Federalist leaders, compared to the ages of the prominent Antifederalists, was important, especially in accounting for the Federalists' ability to think freshly and creatively about politics, it can hardly be used

[10] John Adams, entry, Nov. 5, 1760, Butterfield, ed., Diary of Adams, I, 167; Ramsay, Oration on the Advantages of American Independence, in Niles, ed., Principles, 375; Adams, entry, Dec. 24, 1766, Butterfield, ed., Diary of Adams, I, 326. For explicit avowals of the compatibility of social distinctions and republicanism see Observations on "Considerations upon the Cincinnati," 21; Elizur Goodrich, The Principles of Civil Union and Happiness Considered and Recommended . . . (Hartford, 1787), 20–22. See also John G. Cawelti, Apostles of the Self-Made Man (Chicago, 1965), 34.

[11] See especially Forrest McDonald, We the People: The Economic Origins of the Constitution (Chicago, 1958).

to explain the division throughout the country.[12] Moreover, the concern of the 1780's with America's moral character was not confined to the proponents of the Constitution. That rabid republican and Antifederalist, Benjamin Austin, was as convinced as any Federalist that "the luxurious living of all ranks and degrees" was "the principal cause of all the evils we now experience." Some leading Antifederalist intellectuals expressed as much fear of "the injustice, folly, and wickedness of the State Legislatures" and of "the usurpation and tyranny of the majority" against the minority as did Madison. In the Philadelphia Convention both Mason and Elbridge Gerry, later prominent Antifederalists, admitted "the danger of the levelling spirit" flowing from "the excess of democracy" in the American republics.[13] There were many diverse reasons in each state why men supported or opposed the Constitution that cut through any sort of class division. The Constitution was a single issue in a complicated situation, and its acceptance or rejection in many states was often dictated by peculiar circumstances—the prevalence of Indians, the desire for western lands, the special interests of commerce—that defy generalization. Nevertheless, despite all of this confusion and complexity, the struggle over the Constitution, as the debate if nothing else makes clear, can best be understood as a social one. Whatever the particular constituency of the antagonists may have been, men in 1787–88 talked as if they were representing distinct and opposing social elements. Both the proponents and opponents of the Constitution focused throughout the debates on an essential point of political sociology that ultimately must be used to distinguish a Federalist from an Antifederalist. The quarrel was fundamentally one between aristocracy and democracy.

Because of its essentially social base, this quarrel, as George Minot of Massachusetts said, was "extremely unequal." To be sure, many Antifederalists, especially in Virginia, were as socially and intellectually formidable as any Federalist. Richard Henry Lee was undoubtedly the strongest mind the Antifederalists possessed, and he sympathized with the Antifederalist cause. Like Austin and other Antifederalists he believed that moral regeneration of America's character, rather than any legalistic manipulation of the constitutions of government, was the proper remedy for America's problems. "I fear," he wrote to George Mason in May 1787, "it is more in vicious manners, than mistakes in form, that we must seek for the causes of the present discontent."[14] Still, such "aristocrats" as Lee or Mason did not truly represent Antifederalism. Not only did they reject the vicious state politics of the 1780's which Antifederalism, by the very purpose of the Constitution, was implicitly if not always explicitly committed to defend, but they could

[12] On the relative youth of the Federalists see Charles Warren, "Elbridge Gerry, James Warren, Mercy Warren and the Ratification of the Federal Constitution in Massachusetts," Mass. Hist. Soc., *Proceedings*, 64 (1930–32), 146; Stanley Elkins and Eric McKitrick, "The Founding Fathers: Young Men of the Revolution," *Pol. Sci. Qtly.*, 76 (1961), 203; but cf. Main, *Antifederalists*, 259.

[13] Boston *Independent Chronicle*, Dec. 6, 1787; R. H. Lee to Francis Lightfoot Lee, July 14, 1787, Ballagh, ed., *Letters of R. H. Lee*, II, 424; [James Winthrop], "Letters of Agrippa, XVIII," Feb. 5, 1788, Ford, ed., *Essays on the Constitution*, 117; Farrand, ed., *Records of the Federal Convention*, I, 48, II, 647.

[14] Minot, quoted in Rutland, *Ordeal of the Constitution*, 113; Lee to Mason, May 15, 1787, Ballagh, ed., *Letters of R. H. Lee*, II, 419.

have no real identity, try as they might, with those for whom they sought to speak. Because, as Lee pointed out, "we must recollect how disproportionately the democratic and aristocratic parts of the community were represented" not only in the Philadelphia Convention but also in the ratifying conventions, many of the real Antifederalists, those intimately involved in the democratic politics of the 1780's and consequently with an emotional as well as an intellectual commitment to Antifederalism, were never clearly heard in the formal debates of 1787-88.[15]

The disorganization and inertia of the Antifederalists, especially in contrast with the energy and effectiveness of the Federalists, has been repeatedly emphasized.[16] The opponents of the Constitution lacked both coordination and unified leadership; "their principles," wrote Oliver Ellsworth, "are totally opposite to each other, and their objections discordant and irreconcilable." The Federalist victory, it appears, was actually more of an Antifederalist default. "We had no principle of concert or union," lamented the South Carolina Antifederalist, Aedanus Burke, while the supporters of the Constitution "left no expedient untried to push it forward." Madison's description of the Massachusetts Antifederalists was applicable to nearly all the states: "There was not a single character capable of uniting their wills or directing their measures. . . . They had no plan whatever. They looked no farther than to put a negative on the Constitution and return home." They were not, as one Federalist put it, "good politicians."[17]

But the Antifederalists were not simply poorer politicians than the Federalists; they were actually different kinds of politicians. Too many of them were state-centered men with local interests and loyalties only, politicians without influence and connections, and ultimately politicians without social and intellectual confidence. In South Carolina the up-country opponents of the Constitution shied from debate and when they did occasionally rise to speak apologized effusively for their inability to say what they felt had to be said, thus leaving most of the opposition to the Constitution to be voiced by Rawlins Lowndes, a low-country planter who scarcely represented their interests and soon retired from the struggle. Elsewhere, in New Hampshire, Connecticut, Massachusetts, Pennsylvania, and North Carolina, the situation was similar: the Federalists had the bulk of talent and influence on their side "together with all the Speakers in the State great and small." In convention after convention the Antifederalists, as in Connecticut, tried to speak, but "they were browbeaten by many of those Cicero'es as they think

[15] [Richard Henry Lee], *Observations Leading to a Fair Examination of the System of Government, Proposed by the Late Convention . . . in a Number of Letters from the Federal Farmer . . .* ([N.Y.], 1787), in Ford, ed., *Pamphlets*, 285; Main, *Antifederalists*, 172-73, 177.

[16] On the political effectiveness of the Federalists in contrast to the ineptness of the Antifederalists see John P. Roche, "The Founding Fathers: A Reform Caucus in Action," *Amer. Pol. Sci. Rev.*, 55 (1961), 799-816; Main, *Antifederalists*, 252-53; and above all, Rutland, *Ordeal of the Constitution*, 66, 76-77, 113, 165, 210, 236, 243-44, 309, 313.

[17] [Ellsworth], "The Landholder, VIII," Dec. 24, 1787, Ford, ed., *Essays on the Constitution*, 176; Aedanus Burke to John Lamb, June 23, 1788, quoted in Rutland, *Ordeal of the Constitution*, 165; Madison to Jefferson, Feb. 19, 1788, Hunt, ed., *Writings of Madison*, V, 101-02; Tobias Lear to Washington, June 2, 1788, in *Documentary History of the Constitution* (Washington, 1894-1905), IV, 676.

themselves and others of Superior rank." "The presses are in a great measure secured to *their* side," the Antifederalists complained with justice: out of a hundred or more newspapers printed in the late eighties only a dozen supported the Antifederalists, as editors, "afraid to offend the great men, or Merchants, who could work their ruin," closed their columns to the opposition. The Antifederalists were not so much beaten as overawed.[18] In Massachusetts the two leading socially established Antifederalists, Elbridge Gerry and James Warren, were defeated as delegates to the Ratifying Convention, and Antifederalist leadership consequently fell into the hands of newer, self-made men, of whom Samuel Nasson was perhaps typical—a Maine shopkeeper who was accused of delivering ghostwritten speeches in the Convention. Nasson had previously sat in the General Court but had declined reelection because he had been too keenly made aware of "the want of a proper Education I feel my Self So Small on many occasions that I all most Scrink into Nothing Besides I am often obliged to Borrow from Gentlemen that had advantages which I have not." Now, however, he had become the stoutest of Antifederalists, "full charged with Gass," one of those grumblers who, as Rufus King told Madison, were more afraid of the proponents of the Constitution than the Constitution itself, frightened that "some injury is plotted against them" because of "the extraordinary Union in favor of the Constitution in this State of the Wealthy and sensible part of it."[19]

This fear of a plot by men who "talk so finely and gloss over matters so smoothly" ran through the Antifederalist mind. Because the many "new men" of the 1780's, men like Melancthon Smith and Abraham Yates of New York or John Smilie and William Findley of Pennsylvania, had bypassed the social hierarchy in their rise to political leadership, they lacked those attributes of social distinction and dignity that went beyond mere wealth. Since these kinds of men were never assimilated to the gentlemanly cast of the Livingstons or the Morrises, they, like Americans earlier in confrontation with the British court, tended to view with suspicion and hostility the high-flying world of style and connections that they were barred by their language and tastes, if by nothing else, from sharing in. In the minds of these socially inferior politicians the movement for the strengthening of the central government could only be a "conspiracy" "planned and set to work" by a few aristocrats, who were at first, said Abraham Yates, no larger in number in any one state than the cabal which sought to undermine English liberty at the beginning of the eighteenth century. Since men like Yates could not quite comprehend what they were sure were the inner maneuverings of the elite, they were convinced that in the aristocrats' program, "what was their view in the beginning" or how "far it was Intended to be carried Must be Collected from facts that Afterwards have happened." Like American Whigs in the sixties and seventies forced to delve into the dark and complicated workings of English court politics, they could judge motives

[18] Rogers, *William Loughton Smith*, 150; Rutland, *Ordeal of the Constitution*, 211, 55, 98, 118–19, 212, 253, 85, 211, 165. Rutland's book is particularly important in demonstrating the political and social inferiority of the Antifederalists.

[19] Harding, *Ratification in Massachusetts*, 64; Rufus King to James Madison, Jan. 20, 27, 1788, King, *Life of King*, I, 314, 316–17. See also John Brown Cutting to Jefferson, July 11, 1788, Boyd, ed., *Jefferson Papers*, XIII, 331; Welch, *Sedgwick*, 64–65.

and plans "but by the Event."[20] And they could only conclude that the events of the eighties, "the treasury, the Cincinnati, and other public creditors, with all their concomitants," were "somehow or other, . . . inseparably connected," were all parts of a grand design "concerted by a few *tyrants*" to undo the Revolution and to establish an aristocracy in order "to lord it over the rest of their fellow citizens, to trample the poorer part of the people under their feet, that they may be rendered their servants and slaves." In this climate all the major issues of the Confederation period—the impost, commutation, and the return of the Loyalists—possessed a political and social significance that transcended economic concerns. All seemed to be devices by which a ruling few, like the ministers of the English Crown, would attach a corps of pensioners and dependents to the government and spread their influence and connections throughout the states in order "to dissolve our present Happy and Benevolent Constitution and to erect on the Ruins, a proper Aristocracy."[21]

Nothing was more characteristic of Antifederalist thinking than this obsession with aristocracy. Although to a European, American society may have appeared remarkably egalitarian, to many Americans, especially to those who aspired to places of consequence but were made to feel their inferiority in innumerable, often subtle, ways, American society was distinguished by its inequality. "It is true," said Melancthon Smith in the New York Ratifying Convention, "it is our singular felicity that we have no legal or hereditary distinctions . . . ; but still there are real differences." "Every society naturally divides itself into classes. . . . Birth, education, talents, and wealth, create distinctions among men as visible, and of as much influence, as titles, stars, and garters." Everyone knew those "whom nature hath destined to rule," declared one sardonic Antifederalist pamphlet. Their "qualifications of authority" were obvious: "such as the dictatorial air, the magisterial voice, the imperious tone, the haughty countenance, the lofty look, the majestic mien." In all communities, "even in those of the most democratic kind," wrote George Clinton (whose "family and connections" in the minds of those like Philip Schuyler did not "entitle him to so distinguished a predominance" as the governorship of New York), there were pressures—"superior talents, fortunes and public employments"—demarcating an aristocracy whose influence was difficult to resist.[22]

Such influence was difficult to resist because, to the continual annoyance of the Antifederalists, the great body of the people willingly submitted to it. The "authority of names" and "the influence of the great" among ordinary

[20] Amos Singletary (Mass.), in Elliot, ed., *Debates*, II, 102; Staughton Lynd, ed., "Abraham Yates's History of the Movement for the United States Constitution," *Wm. and Mary Qtly.*, 3d Ser., 20 (1963), 232, 231.

[21] Samuel Osgood to Stephen Higginson, Feb. 2, 1784, Burnett, ed., *Letters of Congress*, VII, 435; Phila. *Independent Gazetteer*, Feb. 7, 1788, in Kenyon, ed., *Antifederalists*, 71; Farmington Records, May 6, 1783, quoted in Main, *Antifederalists*, 108–09, see also 76–77.

[22] Smith (N.Y.), in Elliot, ed., *Debates*, II, 246; *The Government of Nature Delineated; Or an Exact Picture of the New Federal Constitution* (Carlisle, Pa., 1788), 7; [George Clinton], "Cato, VI," Dec. 16, 1787, Ford, ed., *Essays on the Constitution*, 273; Philip Schuyler to John Jay, July 14, 1777, Johnston, ed., *Papers of Jay*, I, 147. De Pauw, *Eleventh Pillar*, 283–92, questions Clinton's authorship of the "Cato" letters and suggests that Abraham Yates may have written them.

people were too evident to be denied. "Will any one say that there does not exist in this country the pride of family, of wealth, of talents, and that they do not command influence and respect among the common people?"

> The people are too apt to yield an implicit assent to the opinions of those characters whose abilities are held in the highest esteem, and to those in whose integrity and patriotism they can confide; not considering that the love of domination is generally in proportion to talents, abilities and superior requirements.

Because of this habit of deference in the people, it was "in the power of the enlightened and aspiring few, if they should combine, at any time to destroy the best establishments, and even make the people the instruments of their own subjugation." Hence, the Antifederalist-minded declared, the people must be awakened to the consequences of their self-ensnarement; they must be warned over and over by popular tribunes, by "those who are competent to the task of developing the principles of government," of the dangers involved in paying obeisance to those who they thought were their superiors. The people must "not be permitted to consider themselves as a grovelling, distinct species, uninterested in the general welfare."[23]

Such constant admonitions to the people of the perils flowing from their too easy deference to the *"natural aristocracy"* were necessary because the Antifederalists were convinced that these "men that had been delicately bred, and who were in affluent circumstances," these "men of the most exalted rank in life," were by their very conspicuousness irreparably cut off from the great body of the people and hence could never share in its concerns nor look after its interests. It was not that these "certain men exalted above the rest" were necessarily "destitute of morality or virtue" or that they were inherently different from other men. "The same passions and prejudices govern all men." It was only that circumstances in their particular environment had made them different. There was "a charm in politicks"; men in high office become habituated with power, "grow fond of it, and are loath to resign it"; "they feel themselves flattered and elevated," enthralled by the attractions of high living, and thus they easily forget the interests of the common people, from which many of them once sprang. By dwelling so vividly on the allurements of prestige and power, by emphasizing again and again how the "human soul is affected by wealth, in all its faculties, . . . by its present interest, by its expectations, and by its fears," these ambitious Antifederalist politicians may have revealed as much about themselves as they did about the "aristocratic" elite they sought to displace.[24] Yet at the same time by such language they contributed to a new appreciation of the nature of society.

[23] [Bryan], "Centinel, No. I," Oct. 5, 1787, McMaster and Stone, eds., *Pennsylvania and the Federal Constitution*, 566–67; Smith (N.Y.), in Elliot, ed., *Debates*, II, 246–47; *Rudiments of Law and Government*, 26; Main, *Antifederalists*, 203.
[24] *Government of Nature Delineated*, 8; Smith (N.Y.), in Elliot, ed., *Debates*, II, 246; Bernard Steiner, "Connecticut's Ratification of the Federal Constitution," Amer. Antiq. Soc., *Proceedings*, 25 (1915), 77; "Address and Reasons of Dissent of the Minority of the Convention of the State of Pennsylvania," Dec. 18, 1787, McMaster and Stone, eds., *Pennsylvania and the Federal Constitution*, 472; Smith (N.Y.) and Patrick Henry (Va.), in Elliot, ed., *Debates*, II, 260, 247, III, 54; "John De Witt," Nov. 5, 1787, Kenyon, ed., *Antifederalists*, 105; Carey, ed., *Debates of the General Assembly of Pennsylvania*, 66; Robert Lansing and Smith (N.Y.), in Elliot, ed., *Debates*, II, 293, 13, 247, 260.

In these repeated attacks on deference and the capacity of a conspicuous few to speak for the whole society—which was to become in time the distinguishing feature of American democratic politics—the Antifederalists struck at the roots of the traditional conception of political society. If the natural elite, whether its distinctions were ascribed or acquired, was not in any organic way connected to the "feelings, circumstances, and interests" of the people and was incapable of feeling "sympathetically the wants of the people," then it followed that only ordinary men, men not distinguished by the characteristics of aristocratic wealth and taste, men "in middling circumstances" untempted by the attractions of a cosmopolitan world and thus "more temperate, of better morals, and less ambitious, than the great," could be trusted to speak for the great body of the people, for those who were coming more and more to be referred to as "the middling and lower classes of people."[25] The differentiating influence of the environment was such that men in various ranks and classes now seemed to be broken apart from one another, separated by their peculiar circumstances into distinct, unconnected, and often incompatible interests. With their indictment of aristocracy the Antifederalists were saying, whether they realized it or not, that the people of America even in their several states were not homogeneous entities each with a basic similarity of interest for which an empathic elite could speak. Society was not an organic hierarchy composed of ranks and degrees indissolubly linked one to another; rather it was a heterogeneous mixture of "many different classes or orders of people, Merchants, Farmers, Planter Mechanics and Gentry or wealthy Men." In such a society men from one class or group, however educated and respectable they may have been, could never be acquainted with the "*Situation* and Wants" of those of another class or group. Lawyers and planters could never be "adequate judges of tradesmens concerns." If men were truly to represent the people in government, it was not enough for them to be for the people; they had to be actually of the people. "Farmers, traders and mechanics . . . all ought to have a competent number of their best informed members in the legislature."[26]

Thus the Antifederalists were not only directly challenging the conventional belief that only a gentlemanly few, even though now in America naturally and not artificially qualified, were best equipped through learning and experience to represent and to govern the society, but they were as well indirectly denying the assumption of organic social homogeneity on which republicanism rested. Without fully comprehending the consequences of their arguments the Antifederalists were destroying the great chain of being, thus undermining the social basis of republicanism and shattering that unity and harmony of social and political authority which the eighteenth century generally and indeed most Revolutionary leaders had considered essential to the maintenance of order.

[25] William Heath (Mass.), Lansing (N.Y.), Smith (N.Y.), and Henry (Va.), in Elliot, ed., *Debates*, II, 13, 293, 247, 260.

[26] Samuel Chase quoted in Philip A. Crowl, "Anti-Federalism in Maryland, 1787–1788," *Wm. and Mary Qtly.*, 3d Ser., 4 (1947), 464; Walsh, *Charleston's Sons of Liberty*, 131–32; "Dissent of the Minority," McMaster and Stone, eds., *Pennsylvania and the Federal Constitution*, 472.

Confronted with such a fundamental challenge the Federalists initially backed away. They had no desire to argue the merits of the Constitution in terms of its social implications and were understandably reluctant to open up the character of American society as the central issue of the debate. But in the end they could not resist defending those beliefs in elitism that lay at the heart of their conception of politics and of their constitutional program. All of the Federalists' desires to establish a strong and respectable nation in the world, all of their plans to create a flourishing commerical economy, in short, all of what the Federalists wanted out of the new central government seemed in the final analysis dependent upon the prerequisite maintenance of aristocratic politics.

. . .

In refuting the Antifederalists' contention "that all classes of citizens should have some of their own number in the representative body, in order that their feelings and interests may be the better understood and attended to," Hamilton in *The Federalist*, Number 35, put into words the Federalists' often unspoken and vaguely held assumption about the organic and the hierarchical nature of society. Such explicit class or occupational representation as the Antifederalists advocated, wrote Hamilton, was not only impractical but unnecessary, since the society was not as fragmented or heterogeneous as the Antifederalists implied. The various groups in the landed interest, for example, were "perfectly united, from the wealthiest landlord down to the poorest tenant," and this "common interest may always be reckoned upon as the surest bond of sympathy" linking the landed representative, however rich, to his constituents. In a like way, the members of the commercial community were "immediately connected" and most naturally represented by the merchants.

> Mechanics and manufacturers will always be inclined, with few exceptions, to give their votes to merchants, in preference to persons of their own professions or trades. . . . They know that the merchant is their natural patron and friend; and . . . they are sensible that their habits in life have not been such as to give them those acquired endowments, without which in a deliberative assembly, the greatest natural abilities, are for the most part useless.

However much many Federalists may have doubted the substance of Hamilton's analysis of American society, they could not doubt the truth of his conclusion. That the people were represented better by one of the natural aristocracy "whose situation leads to extensive inquiry and information" than by one "whose observation does not travel beyond the circle of his neighbors and acquaintances" was the defining element of the Federalist philosophy.

It was not simply the number of public securities, or credit outstanding, or the number of ships, or the amount of money possessed that made a man think of himself as one of the natural elite. It was much more subtle than the mere possession of wealth: it was a deeper social feeling, a sense of being socially established, of possessing attributes—family, education, and refinement—that others lacked, above all, of being accepted by and being able to move easily among those who considered themselves to be the respectable and cultivated. It is perhaps anachronistic to describe this social sense as a class interest, for it often transcended immediate political or economic concerns, and, as Hamilton's argument indicates, was designed to cut through narrow occupational categories. The Republicans of Philadelphia, for example, repeatedly denied that they represented an aristocracy with a united class interest. "We are of different occupations; of different sects of religion; and have different views of life. No factions or private system can comprehend us all." Yet with all their assertions of diversified interests the Republicans were not without a social consciousness in their quarrel with the supporters of the Pennsylvania Constitution. If there were any of us ambitious for power, their apology continued, then there would be no need to change the Constitution, for we surely could attain power under the present Constitution. "We have already seen how easy the task is for *any character* to rise into power and consequence under it. And there are some of us, who think not so meanly of ourselves, as to dread any rivalship from those who are now in office."[27]

In 1787 this kind of elitist social consciousness was brought into play as perhaps never before in eighteenth-century America, as gentlemen up and down the continent submerged their sectional and economic differences in the face of what seemed to be a threat to the very foundations of society. Despite his earlier opposition to the Order of the Cincinnati, Theodore Sedgwick, like other frightened New Englanders, now welcomed the organization as a source of strength in the battle for the Constitution. The fear of social disruption that had run through much of the writing of the eighties was brought to a head to eclipse all other fears. Although state politics in the eighties remains to be analyzed, the evidence from Federalist correspondence indicates clearly a belief that never had there occurred "so great a change in the opinion of the best people" as was occurring in the last few years of the decade. The Federalists were astonished at the outpouring in 1787 of influential and respectable people who had earlier remained quiescent. Too many of "the better sort of people," it was repeatedly said, had withdrawn at the end of the war "from the theatre of public action, to scenes of retirement and ease," and thus "demagogues of desperate fortunes, mere adventurers in fraud, were left to act unopposed."[28] After all, it was explained, "when the wicked rise, men hide themselves." Even the problems of Massachusetts in 1786, noted General Benjamin Lincoln, the repressor of the Shaysites, were not caused by the rebels, but by the laxity of "the good people of the state." But the lesson of this laxity was rapidly being learned. Everywhere, it seemed, men of virtue, good sense, and property, "almost the whole body of our enlighten'd and leading characters in every state," were awakened in support of stronger government. "The scum which was thrown upon the surface by the fermentation of the war is daily sinking," Benjamin Rush told Richard Price in 1786, "while a pure spirit is occupying its place." "Men are brought into action who had consigned

[27] *The Federalist*, No. 35; Phila. *Pa. Gazette*, Mar. 24, 1779.
[28] Welch, *Sedgwick*, 56; St. John de Crèvecoeur to Jefferson, Oct. 20, 1788, Boyd, ed., *Jefferson Papers*, XIV, 30; Edward Rutledge to Jay, Nov. 12, 1786, Johnston, ed., *Papers to Jay*, III, 216–19; Edward Carrington to Jefferson, June 9, 1787, Boyd, ed., *Jefferson Papers*, XI, 408–09.

themselves to an eve of rest," Edward Carrington wrote to Jefferson in June 1787, "and the Convention, as a Beacon, is rousing the attention of the Empire." The Antifederalists could only stand amazed at this "weight of talents" being gathered in support of the Constitution. "What must the individual be who could thus oppose them united?"[29]

Still, in the face of this preponderance of wealth and respectability in support of the Constitution, what remains extraordinary about 1787–88 is not the weakness and disunity but the political strength of Antifederalism. That large numbers of Americans could actually reject a plan of government created by a body "composed of the first characters in the Continent" and backed by Washington and nearly the whole of the natural aristocracy of the country said more about the changing character of American politics and society in the eighties than did the Constitution's eventual acceptance.[30] It was indeed a portent of what was to come.

4. The Extended Sphere of Government

Actually the confrontation of sociologies between Federalists and Antifederalists that emerged in 1787 was not as sharp as it logically might have been. By challenging the right of an elite to represent the common people, the Antifederalists without being quite aware of what they were doing had brought into question the traditional hierarchical and organic nature of society that made such elitism comprehensible to the eighteenth century. For, as Hamilton's social analysis in *The Federalist*, Number 35, suggested, what justified elite rule, together with the notion of virtual representation and the idea of the homogeneity and unity of the people's interest, was the sense that all parts of the society were of a piece, that all ranks and degrees were organically connected through a great chain in such a way that those on the top were necessarily involved in the welfare of those below them. Although the Antifederalists were presumably committed by their actual and class-based conception of representation to a quite different view of the nature of society, nevertheless they did not follow out the implications of their attack on elitism. Indeed, in the end they became fervent defenders of the traditional assumption that the state was a cohesive organic entity with a single homogeneous interest at the very time they were denying the consequences of this assumption. Given the extensive size of the proposed national republic, they perhaps had no other choice.

To the Antifederalists the Constitution was "so essentially differing from the principles of the revolution and from freedom" that it was unbelievable that it could have been proposed. The best political science of the century, as expressed most pointedly but hardly exclusively by Montesquieu, had told them "that so extensive a territory as that of the United States, includ-

[29] Parsons, *Sermon Preached May 28, 1788*, 22–23; Taylor, *Western Massachusetts*, 164; John Brown Cutting to Jefferson, July 11, 1788, Boyd, ed., *Jefferson Papers*, XIII, 332; Rush to Richard Price, Apr. 22, 1786, Butterfield, ed., *Rush Letters*, I, 386; Carrington to Jefferson, June 9, 1787, Boyd, ed., *Jefferson Papers*, XI, 408–09; William Nelson to William Short, July 12, 1788, quoted in Rutland, *Ordeal of the Constitution*, 253.
[30] Rutland, *Ordeal of the Constitution*, 39.

ing such a variety of climates, productions, interests; and so great differences of manners, habits, and customs" could never be a single republican state. "No government formed on the principles of freedom can pervade all North America." An extended republic, such as the Federalists proposed, could never be "so competent to attend to the various local concerns and wants, of every particular district, as well as the peculiar governments, who are nearer the scene, and possessed of superior means of information." Southerners and northerners were different peoples with different cultures, and therefore could never constitute a single organic society with a similarity of interest. "It is impossible for one code of laws to suit Georgia and Massachusetts." The idea of a single republic, "on an average one thousand miles in length, and eight hundred in breadth, and containing six millions of white inhabitants all reduced to the same standard of morals, of habits, and of laws, is," said the Antifederalists, "in itself an absurdity, and contrary to the whole experience of mankind." "Nothing would support government, in such a case as that, but military coercion."[31]

It was a very powerful argument, resting as it did on the republican assumptions of 1776. For what gave such an argument force was the belief that a republic, wholly based as it was on the suffrage of the people, had to possess a population homogeneous in its customs and concerns. Otherwise the unitary public good, the collective welfare of the people that made a republic what it was, would be lost in the clashing of "interests opposite and dissimilar in their nature."[32] While the Antifederalists had unwittingly shaken the foundations of this belief with their denial of elite rule, it was actually left to the Federalists, or the most perceptive of them, to expose fully the flimsiness of this assumption and to grasp and exploit the significance of a new conception of society. In doing so, however, they ultimately destroyed whatever remained of the traditional social justification for aristocratic politics.

In the minds of many observers the relatively hierarchical society of the eighteenth century seemed at last to be breaking up, as more and more groups with broadly based social, economic, and religious interests were emerging in politics, led by obscure men who stimulated and courted their concerns. Farmers, merchants, mechanics, manufacturers, debtors, creditors, Baptists, Presbyterians—all seemed more self-conscious of their special interests than ever before. "Every one must take care of himself—Necessity requires that political opinions should be squared to private views." Not only had "the great objects of the nation" been "sacrificed constantly to local views," but "the general interests of the States had been sacrificed to those of the Coun-

[31] "Philadelphiensis," Mar. 8, 1788, Kenyon, ed., *Antifederalists*, 84; Lee to ?, Apr. 28, 1788, Ballagh, ed., *Letters of R. H. Lee*, II, 464; John Dawson (Va.), in Elliot, ed., *Debates*, III, 608; [Bryan], "Centinel, No. I," Oct. 5, 1787, McMaster and Stone, eds., *Pennsylvania and the Federal Constitution*, 573; Joseph Taylor (N.C.), in Elliot, ed., *Debates*, IV, 24; [Winthrop] "Agrippa, IV," Dec. 3, 1787, Ford, ed., *Essays on the Constitution*, 64–65; Samuel Spencer (N.C.), Elliot, ed., *Debates*, IV, 52. See Cecelia M. Kenyon, "Men of Little Faith: The Anti-Federalists on the Nature of Representative Government," *Wm. and Mary Qtly.*, 3d Ser., 12 (1955), 7–8.

[32] [George Clinton], "Cato, III," Oct. 25, 1787, Ford, ed., *Essays on the Constitution*, 256; Phila. *Independent Gazetteer*, Apr. 15, 1788, McMaster and Stone, eds., *Pennsylvania and the Federal Constitution*, 536.

ties," lost in the scramble for private advantages and local favors.[33] Such developments had occurred precisely because "the best people" had lost control of politics. "Instead of choosing men for their abilities, integrity and patriotism," the people seemed too prone to "act from some mean, interested, or capricious motive." They

> choose a man, because he will vote for a new town, or a new county, or in favour of a memorial; because he is noisy in blaming those who are in office, has confidence enough to suppose that he could do better, and impudence enough to tell the people so, or because he possesses in a supereminent degree, the all-prevailing popular talent of coaxing and flattering.

The bulging and fluctuating state assemblies were filled with such narrowminded politicians who constantly mistook "the particular circle" in which they moved for "the general voice" of the society. Under such circumstances men could ask whether the principles of "the spirit of '75 . . . a glorious spirit for *that period*" still applied "at the present day?"[34]

The Americans of 1776, convinced that a republic could only exist in a small area, wrote Madison from the perspective of a decade, had assumed "that the people composing the Society enjoy not only an equality of political rights; but that they have all precisely the same interests and the same feelings in every respect." The narrow limits of the state were necessary to maintain this social homogeneity and to prevent factionalism. In such an organic republic

> the interest of the majority would be that of the minority also; the decisions could only turn on mere opinion concerning the good of the whole of which the major voice would be the safest criterion; and within a small sphere, this voice could be most easily collected and the public affairs most accurately managed.

Now, however, such an assumption seemed "altogether fictitious." No society, no matter how small (Rhode Island was an object lesson), "ever did or can consist of so homogeneous a mass of Citizens." "In all civilized Societies, distinctions are various and unavoidable." There were "rich and poor; creditors and debtors; a landed interest, a monied interest, a mercantile interest, a manufacturing interest," together with numerous subdivisions of these economic interests and interests based on differing religious and political opinions. All of this heterogeneity, it had become increasingly evident, was responsible for the "instability" in the states. "Labouring parties, differing views and jarring Interests," said James Sullivan of Massachusetts, "were the sum of our politicks." Many were now prepared to conclude that the great danger to republicanism was not magisterial tyranny or aristocratic dominance but "faction, dissension, and consequent subjection of

[33] Taylor, *Western Massachusetts*, 167; Hartford *Conn. Courant*, Aug. 6, 1787; Gouverneur Morris, in Farrand, ed., *Records of the Federal Convention*, I, 552. See *The Federalist*, No. 46.

[34] Hartford *Conn. Courant*, Nov. 27, 1786, Feb. 5, 1787; James Wilson, in Farrand, ed., *Records of the Federal Convention*, I, 253; [Monroe], *Observations upon the Proposed Plan of Federal Government* . . . (Petersburg, Va., 1788), in Hamilton, ed., *Writings of Monroe*, I, 357, 365; Boston *Mass. Centinel*, May 10, 1788, quoted in John C. Miller, *Sam Adams: Pioneer in Propaganda* (Boston, 1936), 387.

the minority to the caprice and arbitrary decisions of the majority, who instead of consulting the interest of the whole community collectively, attend sometimes to partial and local advantages."[35]

Indeed, it was this factious majoritarianism, an anomalous and frightening conception for republican government, grounded as it was on majority rule, that was at the center of the Federalist perception of politics. In the minds of the Federalists the measure of a free government had become its ability to control factions, not, as used to be thought, those of a minority, but rather those of "an interested and overbearing majority." "To secure the public good and private rights against the danger of such a faction, and at the same time to preserve the spirit and form of popular government," said Madison, was the "great *desideratum* of republican wisdom."[36]

From the moment, often at the very beginning of the Revolution, that various Americans realized that their separate states were not to be homogeneous units, they sought to adjust their thoughts and their institutions to the diversity. By the 1780's the most common conception used to describe the society was the dichotomy between aristocracy and democracy, the few and the many. The essential struggle of politics was not between the magistracy and the people, as the Whigs had thought, but between two social groups of the people themselves. "All political societies have two contending parties—the majority, whose interest it is to be free, and who have the power to be so—and the minority, whose interest it is to oppress, but who can never succeed, till they have blinded their opponents." As early as the seventies men talked publicly of the struggle between the few and the many, and in some states, particularly in Massachusetts, came to see this struggle embodied in the two houses of the legislature. Instead of merely allowing the natural aristocracy of wisdom and talent a special voice to promote the welfare of the people equally with the lower house, the senates had become for some blatantly self-interested bodies representing the distinct concerns of the propertied or rich of the community set in opposition to the common good of the ordinary people. While most Americans shied away from the implications of what some now saw as an inevitable social division, others were even going so far as to argue that such factions of rich and poor were "the materials of which the most perfect societies are formed. . . . The most opposite interests rightly blended, make the harmony of the State."[37]

By 1787 it seemed evident to Madison and to others that property and persons, the few and the many, were rapidly becoming distinct elements in the society. "In future times," said Madison in the Philadelphia Convention, "a great majority of the people will not only be without landed, but any

[35] Madison to Jefferson, Oct. 24, 1787, Boyd, ed., *Jefferson Papers*, XII, 277–78; Madison, in Farrand, ed., *Records of the Federal Convention*, I, 214; James Sullivan to Rufus King, June 14, 1787, King, *Life of King*, I, 222; Francis Corbin (Va.), in Elliot, ed., *Debates*, III, 107.

[36] *The Federalist*, No. 10. See Gottfried Dietze, *The Federalist: A Classic on Federalism and Free Government* (Baltimore, 1960), 150.

[37] Phila. *Pa. Journal*, Nov. 8, 1783; Boston *Independent Chronicle*, Oct. 18, 1787. On the celebration of the "diversity of tempers and constitutions among men" as "both a spur and check to one another" see Henry Cumings, *A Sermon Preached at Lexington on the 19th of April, 1781* (Boston, 1781), 28–29; Adams, *Sermon Preached May 29, 1782*, 42.

other sort of, property." Since persons and property were "both essential objects of Government," both should be embodied in and protected by the structure of the government. This could most obviously be done through the bicameral system, in particular by "confining to the holders of property, the object deemed least secure in popular Governments, the right of suffrage for one of the two Legislative branches," as had been attempted in several states, most conspicuously in Massachusetts. Yet this bicameral solution had not really worked in the United States, admitted Madison. Since the senates had too often been composed of the self-same elements as the lower houses, they were ineffectual checks to the thrusts of the common people. America, said Madison, had not yet "reached the stage of Society in which conflicting feelings of the Class with, and the Class without property, have the operation natural to them in Countries fully peopled." But although the revised theory of mixed government made famous by the Massachusetts Constitution was as yet inapplicable to America's immature society, still, said Madison, the difficult problem remained "of so adjusting the claims of the Two Classes as to give security to each, and to promote the welfare of all." If bicameralism could not yet work, then some other constitutional solution would have to be found.[38]

What Madison and other Federalists did was turn all the old assumptions about republicanism around in order to create and justify their enlarged federal republic with its new kind of "mixed character." Seizing on David Hume's radical suggestion that a republican government operated better in a large territory than in a small one, several Federalists and Madison in particular ingeniously developed it. Since experience in America had demonstrated that no republic could be made small enough to contain a homogeneous interest that the people could express through the voice of the majority, the republican state, said Madison, must be so enlarged, "without departing from the elective basis of it," that "the propensity in small republics to rash measures and the facility of forming and executing them" would be stifled. Religion and exhortation had proved ineffective in restraining the rash and overbearing majorities of small republics. "What remedy can be found in a republican Government, where the majority must ultimately decide," argued Madison, "but that of giving such an extent to its sphere, that no one common interest or passion will be likely to unite a majority of the whole number in an unjust pursuit." Another Federalist put it more bluntly. "The ambition of the poor, and the avarice of the rich demagogue can never be restrained upon the narrow scale of state government." Only in the "extensive reservoir of power" of the federal government "will it be impossible for them to excite storms of sedition or oppression." Thus the Antifederalist objection to the extended territory of the new national republic was actually its greatest source of strength. "In a large Society," concluded Madison, "the people are broken into so many interests and parties, that a common sentiment is less likely to be felt, and the requisite concert less likely to be formed, by a majority of the whole."[39]

[38] Madison, in Farrand, ed., *Records of the Federal Convention*, II, 204.
[39] *The Federalist*, No. 39; Madison, in Farrand, ed., *Records of the Federal Convention*, II, 204; Madison to Jefferson, Oct. 24, 1787, Boyd, ed., *Jefferson Papers*, XII, 277–78; *The Federalist*, No. 10; "To the Freemen of the United States," *American Museum*,

But Madison did not want to be misunderstood. "I mean not by these remarks," he warned Jefferson, "to insinuate that an esprit de corps will not exist in the national Government." Although an impassioned and factious majority could not be formed in the new federal government, Madison had by no means abandoned the idea that the public good was the goal of government, a goal that should be positively promoted. He did not expect the new federal government to be neutralized into inactivity by the pressure of numerous conflicting interests. Nor did he conceive of politics as simply a consensus of the various groups that made up the society. The peculiar advantage of the new expanded national republic for Madison lay not in its inability to find a common interest for such an enlarged territory, but rather "in the substitution of representatives whose enlightened views and virtuous sentiments render them superior to local prejudices and to schemes of injustice." In the new federal scheme power would be "more likely to centre in men who possess the most attractive merit and the most diffusive and established characters," men who would be able to pursue vigorously what they saw to be the true interest of the country free from the turbulence and clamors of "men of factious tempers, of local prejudices, or of sinister designs."[40] Beneath his sophisticated analysis of American society and politics, Madison grounded the success of the new Constitution on a common assumption about the social character of the federal government that lay at the heart of the Federalist program.

5. The Filtration of Talent

.   .   .

In short, through the artificial contrivance of the Constitution overlying an expanded society, the Federalists meant to restore and to prolong the traditional kind of elitist influence in politics that social developments, especially since the Revolution, were undermining. As the defenders if not always the perpetrators of these developments—the "disorder" of the 1780's —the Antifederalists could scarcely have missed the social implications of the Federalist program. The Constitution was intrinsically an aristocratic document designed to check the democratic tendencies of the period, and as such it dictated the character of the Antifederalist response. It was therefore inevitable that the Antifederalists should have charged that the new govern-

1, (1787), 431. On the advantages of an extensive republic see also [Jonathan Jackson], *Thoughts upon the Political Situation of the United States . . .* (Worcester, 1788), 88–90. For Hume's influence on Madison see Douglass Adair, " 'That Politics May Be Reduced to a Science': David Hume, James Madison and the Tenth *Federalist,*" *Huntington Lib. Qtly.,* 20 (1956–57), 343–60. On Madison as a "Republican Savior" see the articles by Neal Riemer, "The Republicanism of James Madison," *Pol. Sci. Qtly.,* 69 (1954), 45–64; and especially "James Madison's Theory of the Self-Destructive Features of Republican Government," *Ethics,* 65 (1954–55), 34–43. Much of the recent interest in Madison has been stimulated or anticipated by the work of Douglass Adair; see his unpublished doctoral dissertation, The Intellectual Origins of Jeffersonian Democracy (Yale, 1943).

[40] Madison to Jefferson, Oct. 24, 1787, Boyd, ed., *Jefferson Papers,* XII, 275; *The Federalist,* No. 10, No. 27.

ment was "dangerously adapted to the purposes of an immediate *aristocratic tyranny.*" In state after state the Antifederalists reduced the issue to those social terms predetermined by the Federalists themselves: the Constitution was a plan intended to "raise the fortunes and respectability of the *well-born few,* and oppress the plebians"; it was "a continental exertion of the *well-born* of America to obtain that darling domination, which they have not been able to accomplish in their respective states"; it "will lead to an aristocratical government, and establish tyranny over us." Whatever their own particular social standing, the Antifederalist spokesmen spread the warning that the new government either would be "in practice a *permanent* ARISTOCRACY" or would soon "degenerate to a compleat Aristocracy."[41] Both George Mason and Richard Henry Lee, speaking not out of the concerns of the social elite to which they belonged but out of a complicated sense of alienation from that elite, expressed as much fear of a "consolidating aristocracy" resulting from the new Constitution as any uncultivated Scotch-Irish upstart. While Lee privately revealed his deep dislike of "the hasty, unpersevering, aristocratic genius of the south" which "suits not my disposition," Mason throughout the duration of the Philadelphia Convention acted as the conscience of an old republicanism he thought his Virginia colleagues had forgotten and continually reminded them of what the Revolution had been about. "Whatever inconveniency may attend the democratic principle," said Mason repeatedly, "it must actuate one part of the Government. It is the only security for the rights of the people." As the Constitution seemed to demonstrate, the "superior classes of society" were becoming too indifferent to the "lowest classes." Remember, he warned his fellow delegates pointedly, "our own children will in a short time be among the general mass." The Constitution seemed obviously "calculated," as even young John Quincy Adams declared, "to increase the influence, power and wealth of those who have it already." Its adoption would undoubtedly be "a grand point gained in favor of the aristocratic party."[42]

Aristocratic principles were in fact "interwoven" in the very fabric of the proposed government. If a government was "so constituted as to admit but few to exercise the powers of it," then it would "according to the natural course of things" end up in the hands of "the natural aristocracy." It went almost without saying that the awesome president and the exalted Senate, "a compound of *monarchy* and *aristocracy*," would be dangerously far removed from the people. But even the House of Representatives, the very body that "should be a true picture of the people, possess a knowledge of their circumstances and their wants, sympathize in all their distresses, and disposed to seek their true interest," was without "a tincture of democracy."

[41] [Mercy Warren], *Observations on the New Constitution* . . . ([Boston, 1788]), in Ford, ed., *Pamphlets*, 6; *Providence Gazette*, Jan. 5, 1788; [Bryan], "Centinel, No. IX," Jan. 8, 1788, "Centinel, No. I," Oct. 5, 1787, McMaster and Stone, eds., *Pennsylvania and the Federal Constitution*, 627, 575; William Goudy (N.C.), in Elliot, ed., *Debates*, IV, 56; "John De Witt," Nov. 5, 1787, Kenyon, ed., *Antifederalists*, 104.

[42] [Lee], *Letters from the Federal Farmer*, Ford, ed., *Pamphlets*, 285, 295; George Mason, *Objections . . . to the Proposed Federal Constitution* (n.p., n.d.), *ibid.*, 332; Lee to John Adams, Oct. 8, 1779, Ballagh, ed., *Letters of R. H. Lee*, II, 155; Mason, in Farrand, ed., *Records of the Federal Convention*, I, 359, 49, 56; John Quincy Adams, *Life in a New England Town: 1787-1788* . . . (Boston, 1903), 46.

Since it could never collect "the interests, feelings, and opinions of three or four millions of people," it was better understood as "an Assistant Aristo-cratical Branch" to the Senate than as a real representation of the people.[43] When the number of representatives was "so small, the office will be highly elevated and distinguished; the style in which the members live will prob-ably be high; circumstances of this kind will render the place of a represen-tative not a desirable one to sensible, substantial men, who have been used to walk in the plain and frugal paths of life." While the ordinary people in extensive electoral districts of thirty or forty thousand inhabitants would remain "divided," those few extraordinary men with "conspicuous military, popular, civil or legal talents" could more easily form broader associations to dominate elections; they had family and other connections to "unite their interests." If only a half-dozen congressmen were to be selected to repre-sent a large state, then rarely, argued the Antifederalists in terms that were essentially no different from those used by the Federalists in the Constitu-tion's defense, would persons from "the great body of the people, the mid-dle and lower classes," be elected to the House of Representatives. "The Station is too high and exalted to be filled out [by] the *first Men* in the State in point of Fortune and Influence. In fact no order or class of the people will be represented in the House of Representatives called the Demo-cratic Branch but the rich and wealthy."[44] The Antifederalists thus came to oppose the new national government for the same reason the Federalists favored it: because its very structure and detachment from the people would work to exclude any kind of actual and local interest representation and prevent those who were not rich, well born, or prominent from exercis-ing political power. Both sides fully appreciated the central issue the Consti-tution posed and grappled with it throughout the debates: whether a professedly popular government should actually be in the hands of, rather than simply derived from, common ordinary people.

Out of the division in 1787–88 over this issue, an issue which was as con-spicuously social as any in American history, the Antifederalists emerged as the spokesmen for the growing American antagonism to aristocracy and as the defenders of the most intimate participation in politics of the widest variety of people possible. It was not from lack of vision that the Anti-federalists feared the new government. Although their viewpoint was in-tensely localist, it was grounded in as perceptive an understanding of the social basis of American politics as that of the Federalists. Most of the Antifederalists were majoritarians with respect to the state legislatures but not with respect to the national legislature, because they presumed as well as the Federalists did that different sorts of people from those who sat in the state assemblies would occupy the Congress. Whatever else may be said

[43] [Clinton], "Cato, VI," Dec. 16, 1787, Ford, ed., *Essays on the Constitution*, 273; Smith (N.Y.), in Elliot, ed., *Debates*, II, 246, 245; "Philadelphiensis," Feb. 7, 1788, Ken-yon, ed., *Antifederalists*, 72; [Lee], *Letters from the Federal Farmer*, Ford, ed., *Pam-phlets*, 295; "John De Witt," Nov. 5, 1787, Kenyon, ed., *Antifederalists*, 108.

[44] "Dissent of the Minority," McMaster and Stone, eds., *Pennsylvania and the Federal Constitution*, 471; Smith (N.Y.), in Elliot, ed., *Debates*, II, 246; Boston *Independent Chronicle*, Dec. 13, 1787; Samuel Chase, quoted in Crowl, "Anti-Federalism in Mary-land," *Wm. and Mary Qtly.*, 3d Ser., 4 (1947), 464.

about the Antifederalists, their populism cannot be impugned. They were true champions of the most extreme kind of democratic and egalitarian politics expressed in the Revolutionary era. Convinced that "it has been the principal care of free governments to guard against the encroachments of the great," the Antifederalists believed that popular government itself, as defined by the principles of 1776, was endangered by the new national government. If the Revolution had been a transfer of power from the few to the many, then the federal Constitution clearly represented an abnegation of the Revolution. For, as Richard Henry Lee wrote in his *Letters from the Federal Farmer*, "every man of reflection must see, that the change now proposed, is a transfer of power from the many to the few."[45]

Although Lee's analysis contained the essential truth, the Federalist program was not quite so simply summed up. It was true that through the new Constitution the Federalists hoped to resist and eventually to avert what they saw to be the rapid decline of the influence and authority of the natural aristocracy in America. At the very time that the organic conception of society that made elite rule comprehensible was finally and avowedly dissolving, and the members of the elite were developing distinct professional, social, or economic interests, the Federalists found elite rule more imperative than ever before. To the Federalists the greatest dangers to republicanism were flowing not, as the old Whigs had thought, from the rulers or from any distinctive minority in the community, but from the widespread participation of the people in the government. It now seemed increasingly evident that if the public good not only of the United States as a whole but even of the separate states were to be truly perceived and promoted, the American people must abandon their Revolutionary reliance on their representative state legislatures and place their confidence in the high-mindedness of the natural leaders of the society, which ideally everyone had the opportunity of becoming. Since the Federalists presumed that only such a self-conscious elite could transcend the many narrow and contradictory interests inevitable in any society, however small, the measure of a good government became its capacity for insuring the predominance of these kinds of natural leaders who knew better than the people as a whole what was good for the society.

The result was an amazing display of confidence in constitutionalism, in the efficacy of institutional devices for solving social and political problems. Through the proper arrangement of new institutional structures the Federalists aimed to turn the political and social developments that were weakening the place of "the better sort of people" in government back upon themselves and to make these developments the very source of the perpetuation of the natural aristocracy's dominance of politics. Thus the Federalists did not directly reject democratic politics as it had manifested itself in the 1780's; rather they attempted to adjust to this politics in order to control and mitigate its effects. In short they offered the country an elitist theory of democracy. They did not see themselves as repudiating either the Revolution or popular government, but saw themselves as saving both from their excesses. If the Constitution were not established, they told themselves and

[45] Smith (N.Y.), in Elliot, ed., *Debates*, II, 247; [Lee], *Letters from the Federal Farmer*, Ford, ed., *Pamphlets*, 317.

the country over and over, then republicanism was doomed, the grand experiment was over, and a division of the confederacy, monarchy, or worse would result.

Despite all the examples of popular vice in the eighties, the Federalist confidence in the people remained strong. The letters of "Caesar," with their frank and violent denigration of the people, were anomalies in the Federalist literature.[46] The Federalists had by no means lost faith in the people, at least in the people's ability to discern their true leaders. In fact many of the social elite who comprised the Federalist leadership were confident of popular election if the constituency could be made broad enough, and crass electioneering be curbed, so that the people's choice would be undisturbed by ambitious demagogues. "For if not blind to their own interest, they choose men of the first character for wisdom and integrity." Despite prodding by so-called designing and unprincipled men, the bulk of the people remained deferential to the established social leadership—for some aspiring politicians frustratingly so. Even if they had wanted to, the Federalists could not turn their backs on republicanism. For it was evident to even the most pessimistic "that no other form would be reconcilable with the genius of the people of America; with the fundamental principles of the Revolution; or with that honorable determination which animates every votary of freedom, to rest all our political experiments on the capacity of mankind for self-government." Whatever government the Federalists established had to be "strictly republican" and "deducible from the only source of just authority—the People."[47]

[46] The "Caesar" letters are reprinted in Ford, ed., *Essays on the Constitution*, 283–91. It now appears that Hamilton did not write them. See Jacob E. Cooke, "Alexander Hamilton's Authorship of the 'Caesar' Letters," *Wm. and Mary Qtly.*, 3d Ser., 17 (1960), 78–85.

[47] Hartford, *Conn. Courant*, Feb. 5, 1787; *The Federalist*, No. 39; Jay to Washington, Jan. 7, 1787, Johnston, ed., *Papers of Jay*, III, 229. See Martin Diamond, "Democracy and *The Federalist*: A Reconsideration of the Framers' Intent," *Amer. Pol. Sci. Rev.*, 53 (1959), 52–68.

The Founding Fathers:
A Reform Caucus
in Action

John P. Roche

In this witty and cogent essay, John P. Roche of
Brandeis University asks us to acknowledge the
political skills that went into the drafting and
ratification of the federal Constitution. We must
disabuse ourselves, he argues, of the idea that the
Founding Fathers were aristocratic ideologues, bent
on putting into practice a shared theory of political
science; or scheming Machiavellis, determined to put a
national and centralized government over on the
people without their assent; or men who had no
concern for the principles of the Declaration of
Independence and willfully signed away the rights of
millions of black slaves in order to achieve the goal
of effective government. Rather, writes Roche, they
are to be understood best as "superb democratic
politicians." Given the political realities of the 1780s,
they achieved just about all that reasonable men might
then have asked of them—and, by implication, all that
historians have any right today to expect.

Reflecting a trend toward interpretation that plays
down the role and efficacy of ideals, Roche—himself
a political scientist and sometime practitioner of the
political arts—suggests that it is only at considerable
cost to our understanding that we ignore the political

dynamics of a situation in favor of the political ideologies of participants. The danger inherent in this viewpoint, he believes, is especially great when considering the Constitutional period, for he places the Founding Fathers among the great "realists" of our history, who were motivated more by the critical need to fashion the best possible government through compromise than by unswerving fidelity to plans and principles. The alternatives open to the Founding Fathers, if they were to gain the government they sought to replace the ineffective Confederation, were few. And we would do best, Roche suggests, not to debate whether the sacrifices made to gain that end were worth it, but whether the federalists possessed a realistic appraisal of their resources and responsibilities.

In addition to putting forth this argument, Roche subtly introduces perspectives derived from the sociology of small group behavior. We shall not understand the outcome of the Convention of 1787, he suggests, without coming to grips with the internal structure and interrelationships of the group that framed it. Roche's approach is very much that of the "structural-functional" school of interpretation which has so influenced American social science since the Second World War. Its practitioners emphasize group norms, place a high value on solidarity, consensus, and social equilibrium, and tend to depreciate the independent role and importance of ideas and ideals.

In following these lines of analysis, Roche illuminates dimensions of the work of the Constitutional Convention that, as he justly argues, are usually overlooked. We must ask, however, if Roche is sufficiently clear about his definition of a "democratic politician." Should we agree that political wizards who always seek the assent of the voters and "mobilize public opinion" are thereby "democrats"? To claim the title of "democrat" in 1787 surely required more than membership in a "reform caucus"; it had equally to do with an acceptance of the spread of popular participation in social and political life and an acquiescence in the lessening of deference toward the "better sort." Moreover, although there were a few genuine "democrats" in the United States in 1787, most of the members of the Convention were

The Founding Fathers: A Reform Caucus in Action. From *American Political Science Review*, LV (December 1961), 799–816. Reprinted by permission of the American Political Science Association and John P. Roche.

"democrats" more by necessity than by choice—and then in the political sector alone. Recent research does indeed reveal that by the time of the Revolution the mass of white American male freeholders possessed the right to vote. But we have also learned the deficiencies in a narrowly political definition of "democracy": many who possessed the right to vote did not do so, and many more deferred to a continued system of government by the educated and wealthy elite. While society was far more democratized in the early republic than, say, in England or France, social democracy had by no means yet arrived.

More importantly, since Roche originally published his essay in 1961, we have gained a much greater appreciation of the role of political ideas in the great debate over the making of the constitution. If the Founding Fathers were not political philosophers in the formal sense, they were nevertheless men of great learning who possessed a deep appreciation and knowledge of the traditions of Western political thought. They adapted their intellectual experience to the native conditions of the 1780s, but they were not mere pragmatists as a result. What is more, the Philadelphia and state ratifying conventions, as well as the periodical press of the time, were arenas of genuine debate over first principles of government. Roche's high estimation of the Founding Fathers arises in part from his judgment that they outmaneuvered their antifederalist opponents. One might better argue that the backers of the new constitution outargued its detractors—an interpretation that incorporates the pragmatism of the federalists whom Roche praises into a larger analytical scheme that gives the ideological content of the federal and state conventions its due.

*O*ver the last century and a half, the work of the Constitutional Convention and the motives of the Founding Fathers have been analyzed under a number of different ideological auspices. To one generation of historians, the hand of God was moving in the assembly; under a later dispensation, the dialectic (at various levels of philosophical sophistication) replaced the Deity: "relationships of production" moved into the niche previously reserved for Love of Country. Thus in counterpoint to the Zeitgeist, the Framers have undergone miraculous metamorphoses: at one time acclaimed as liberals and bold social engineers, today they appear in the guise of sound Burkean conservatives, men who in our time would subscribe to *Fortune,* look to Walter Lippmann for political theory, and chuckle patronizingly at the antics of Barry Goldwater. The implicit assumption is that if James Madison were among us, he would be President of the Ford Foundation, while Alexander Hamilton would chair the Committee for Economic Development.

The "Fathers" have thus been admitted to our best circles; the revolutionary ferocity which confiscated all Tory property in reach and populated New Brunswick with outlaws has been converted by the "Miltown School" of American historians into a benign dedication to "consensus" and "prescriptive rights." The Daughters of the American Revolution have, through the ministrations of Professors Boorstin, Hartz, and Rossiter, at last found ancestors worthy of their descendants. It is not my purpose here to argue that the "Fathers" were, in fact, radical revolutionaries; that proposition has been brilliantly demonstrated by Robert R. Palmer in his *Age of the Democratic Revolution.* My concern is with the further position that not only were they revolutionaries, but also they were democrats. Indeed, in my view, there is one fundamental truth about the Founding Fathers that *every* generation of Zeitgeisters has done its best to obscure: they were first and foremost superb democratic politicians. I suspect that in a contemporary setting, James Madison would be Speaker of the House of Representatives and Hamilton would be the *eminence grise* dominating (*pace* Theodore Sorenson or Sherman Adams) the Executive Office of the President. They were, with their colleagues, *political men*—not metaphysicians, disembodied conservatives or Agents of History—and as recent research into the nature of American politics in the 1780s confirms,[1] they were committed (perhaps willy-nilly) to working within the democratic framework, within a universe of public approval. Charles Beard *and* the filiopietists to the contrary notwithstanding, the Philadelphia Convention was not a College of Cardinals or a council of Platonic guardians working within a manipulative, pre-democratic framework; it was a *nationalist* reform caucus which had to operate with great delicacy and skill in a political cosmos full of enemies to achieve the one definitive goal—popular approbation.

Perhaps the time has come, to borrow Walton Hamilton's fine phrase, to raise the Framers from immortality to mortality, to give them credit for their magnificent demonstration of the art of democratic politics. The point must be reemphasized; they *made* history and did it within the limits of consensus. There was nothing inevitable about the future in 1787; the *Zeitgeist,* that fine Hegelian technique of begging causal questions, could only be discerned in retrospect. What they did was to hammer out a pragmatic com-

---

[1] The view that the right to vote in the states was severely circumscribed by property qualifications has been thoroughly discredited in recent years. See Chilton Williamson, *American Suffrage from Property to Democracy, 1760–1860* (Princeton, 1960). The contemporary position is that John Dickinson actually knew what he was talking about when he argued that there would be little opposition to vesting the right of suffrage in freeholders since "The great mass of our Citizens is composed at this time of freeholders, and will be pleased with it." Max Farrand, *Records of the Federal Convention,* Vol. 2, p. 202 (New Haven, 1911). (Henceforth cited as *Farrand.*)

promise which would bolster the "National interest" and be acceptable to the people. What inspiration they got came from their collective experience as professional politicians in a democratic society. As John Dickinson put it to his fellow delegates on August 13, "Experience must be our guide. Reason may mislead us."

In this context, let us examine the problems they confronted and the solutions they evolved. The Convention has been described picturesquely as a counter-revolutionary junta and the Constitution as a *coup d'etat*,[2] but this has been accomplished by withdrawing the whole history of the movement for constitutional reform from its true context. No doubt the goals of the constitutional elite were "subversive" to the existing political order, but it is overlooked that their subversion could only have succeeded if the people of the United States endorsed it by regularized procedures. Indubitably they were "plotting" to establish a much stronger central government than existed under the Articles, but only in the sense in which one could argue equally well that John F. Kennedy was, from 1956 to 1960, "plotting" to become President. In short, on the fundamental *procedural* level, the Constitutionalists had to work according to the prevailing rules of the game. Whether they liked it or not is a topic for spiritualists—and is irrelevant: one may be quite certain that had Washington agreed to play the De Gaulle (as the Cincinnati once urged), Hamilton would willingly have held his horse, but such fertile speculation in no way alters the actual context in which events took place.

I

When the Constitutionalists went forth to subvert the Confederation, they utilized the mechanisms of political legitimacy. And the roadblocks which confronted them were formidable. At the same time, they were endowed with certain potent political assets. The history of the United States from 1786 to 1790 was largely one of a masterful employment of political expertise by the Constitutionalists as against bumbling, erratic behavior by the opponents of reform. Effectively, the Constitutionalists had to induce the states, by democratic techniques of coercion, to emasculate themselves. To be specific, if New York had refused to join the new Union, the project was doomed; yet before New York was safely in, the reluctant state legislature had *sua sponte* to take the following steps: (1) agree to send delegates to the Philadelphia Convention; (2) provide maintenance for these delegates (these were distinct stages: New Hampshire was early in naming delegates, but did not provide for their maintenance until July); (3) set up the special *ad hoc* convention to decide on ratification; and (4) concede to the decision of the *ad hoc* convention that New York should participate. New York ad-

---

[2] The classic statement of the *coup d'etat* theory is, of course, Charles A. Beard, *An Economic Interpretation of the Constitution of the United States* (New York, 1913), and this theme was echoed by Vernon L. Parrington, Merrill Jensen and others in "populist" historiographical tradition. For a sharp critique of this thesis see Robert E. Brown, *Charles Beard and the Constitution* (Princeton, 1956). See also Forrest McDonald, *We the People* (Chicago, 1958); the trailblazing work in this genre was Douglas Adair, "The Tenth Federalist Revisited," *William and Mary Quarterly*, Third Series, Vol. VIII (1951), pp. 48-67.

mittedly was a tricky state, with a strong interest in a *status quo* which permitted her to exploit New Jersey and Connecticut, but the same legal hurdles existed in every state. And at the risk of becoming boring, it must be reiterated that the *only* weapon in the Constitutionalist arsenal was an effective mobilization of public opinion.

The group which undertook this struggle was an interesting amalgam of a few dedicated nationalists with the self-interested spokesmen of various parochial bailiwicks. The Georgians, for example, wanted a strong central authority to provide military protection for their huge, underpopulated state against the Creek Confederacy; Jerseymen and Connecticuters wanted to escape from economic bondage to New York; the Virginians hoped to establish a system which would give that great state its rightful place in the councils of the republic. The dominant figures in the politics of these states therefore cooperated in the call for the Convention.[3] In other states, the thrust towards national reform was taken up by opposition groups who added the "national interest" to their weapons system; in Pennsylvania, for instance, the group fighting to revise the Constitution of 1776 came out four-square behind the Constitutionalists, and in New York, Hamilton and the Schuyler *ambiance* took the same tack against George Clinton.[4] There was, of course, a large element of personality in the affair: there is reason to suspect that Patrick Henry's opposition to the Convention and the Constitution was founded on his conviction that Jefferson was behind both, and a close study of local politics elsewhere would surely reveal that others supported the Constitution for the simple (and politically quite sufficient) reason that the "wrong" people were against it.

To say this is not to suggest that the Constitution rested on a foundation of impure or base motives. It is rather to argue that in politics there are no immaculate conceptions, and that in the drive for a stronger general government, motives of all sorts played a part. Few men in the history of mankind have espoused a view of the "common good" or "public interest" that militated against their private status; even Plato with all his reverence for disembodied reason managed to put philosophers on top of the pile. Thus it is not surprising that a number of diversified private interests joined to push the nationalist public interest; what would have been surprising was the absence of such a pragmatic united front. And the fact remains that, however motivated, these men did demonstrate a willingness to compromise their parochial interests in behalf of an ideal which took shape before their eyes and under their ministrations.

As Stanley Elkins and Eric McKitrick have suggested in a perceptive essay,[5] what distinguished the leaders of the Constitutionalist caucus from

---

[3] A basic volume, which, like other works by Warren, provides evidence with which one can evaluate the author's own opinions, is Charles Warren, *The Making of the Constitution* (Boston, 1928). The best brief summary of the forces behind the movement for centralization is Chapter 1 of *Warren* (as it will be cited hereafter).

[4] On Pennsylvania see Robert L. Brunhouse, *Counter-Revolution in Pennsylvania* (Harrisburg, 1942) and Charles P. Smith, *James Wilson* (Chapel Hill, 1956), ch. 15; for New York, which needs the same sort of microanalysis Pennsylvania has received, the best study is E. Wilder Spaulding, *New York in the Critical Period, 1783–1789* (New York, 1932).

[5] Stanley Elkins and Eric McKitrick, "The Founding Fathers: Young Men of the Revolution," *Political Science Quarterly*, Vol. 76, p. 181 (1961).

their enemies was a "Continental" approach to political, economic and military issues. To the extent that they shared an institutional base of operations, it was the Continental Congress (thirty-nine of the delegates to the Federal Convention had served in Congress[6]), and this was hardly a locale which inspired respect for the state governments. Robert de Jouvenal observed French politics half a century ago and noted that a revolutionary Deputy had more in common with a non-revolutionary Deputy than he had with a revolutionary non-Deputy;[7] similarly one can surmise that membership in the Congress under the Articles of Confederation worked to establish a continental frame of reference, that a Congressman from Pennsylvania and one from South Carolina would share a universe of discourse which provided them with a conceptual common denominator *vis à vis* their respective state legislatures. This was particularly true with respect to external affairs: the average state legislator was probably about as concerned with foreign policy then as he is today, but Congressmen were constantly forced to take the broad view of American prestige, were compelled to listen to the reports of Secretary John Jay and to the dispatches and pleas from their frustrated envoys in Britain, France and Spain.[8] From considerations such as these, a "Continental" ideology developed which seems to have demanded a revision of our domestic institutions primarily on the ground that only by invigorating our general government could we assume our rightful place in the international arena. Indeed, an argument with great force—particularly since Washington was its incarnation—urged that our very survival in the Hobbesian jungle of world politics depended upon a reordering and strengthening of our national sovereignty.[9]

Note that I am not endorsing the "Critical Period" thesis; on the contrary, Merrill Jensen seems to me quite sound in his view that for most Americans, engaged as they were in self-sustaining agriculture, the "Critical Period" was not particularly critical.[10] In fact, the great achievement of the Constitutionalists was their ultimate success in convincing the elected representatives of a majority of the white male population that change was imperative. A small group of political leaders with a Continental vision and essentially a consciousness of the United States' international importance, provided the matrix of the movement. To their standard other leaders rallied with their own parallel ambitions. Their great assets were (1) the presence in their caucus of the one authentic American "father figure," George Washington, whose prestige was enormous;[11] (2) the energy and talent of their leadership (in which one must include the towering intellectuals of the time, John Adams and Thomas Jefferson, despite their absence abroad),

---

[6] *Warren*, p. 55.

[7] In *La Republique des Camarades* (Paris, 1914).

[8] See Frank Monaghan, *John Jay* (New York, 1935), ch. 13.

[9] "[T]he situation of the general government, if it can be called a government, is shaken to its foundation, and liable to be overturned by every blast. In a word, it is at an end; and, unless a remedy is soon applied, anarchy and confusion will inevitably ensue." Washington to Jefferson, May 30, 1787, *Farrand*, III, 31. See also Irving Brant, *James Madison, The Nationalist* (New York, 1948), ch. 25.

[10] Merrill Jensen, *The New Nation* (New York, 1950). Interestingly enough, Prof. Jensen virtually ignores international relations in his laudatory treatment of the government under the Articles of Confederation.

[11] The story of James Madison's cultivation of Washington is told by Brant, *op. cit.*, pp. 394–97.

and their communications "network," which was far superior to anything on the opposition side;[12] (3) the preemptive skill which made "their" issue The Issue and kept the locally oriented opposition permanently on the defensive; and (4) the subjective consideration that these men were spokesmen of a new and compelling credo: *American* nationalism, that ill-defined but nonetheless potent sense of collective purpose that emerged from the American Revolution.

Despite great institutional handicaps, the Constitutionalists managed in the mid-1780s to mount an offensive which gained momentum as years went by. Their greatest problem was lethargy, and paradoxically, the number of barriers in their path may have proved an advantage in the long run. Beginning with the initial battle to get the Constitutional Convention called and delegates appointed, they could never relax, never let up the pressure. In practical terms, this meant that the local "organizations" created by the Constitutionalists were perpetually in movement building up their cadres for the next fight. (The word organization has to be used with great caution: a political organization in the United States—as in contemporary England[13]—generally consisted of a magnate and his following, or a coalition of magnates. This did not necessarily mean that it was "undemocratic" or "aristocratic," in the Aristotelian sense of the word: while a few magnates such as the Livingstons could draft their followings, most exercised their leadership without coercion on the basis of popular endorsement. The absence of organized opposition did not imply the impossibility of competition any more than low public participation in elections necessarily indicated an undemocratic suffrage.)

The Constitutionalists got the jump on the "opposition" (a collective noun: opposition*s* would be more correct) at the outset with the demand for a Convention. Their opponents were caught in an old political trap: they were not being asked to approve any specific program of reform, but only to endorse a meeting to discuss and recommend needed reforms. If they took a hard line at the first stage, they were put in the position of glorifying the *status quo* and of denying the need for *any* changes. Moreover, the Constitutionalists could go to the people with a persuasive argument for "fair play"—"How can you condemn reform before you know precisely what is involved?" Since the state legislatures obviously would have the final say on any proposals that might emerge from the Convention, the Constitutionalists were merely reasonable men asking for a chance. Besides, since they did not make any concrete proposals at that stage, they were in a position to capitalize on every sort of generalized discontent with the Confederation.

Perhaps because of their poor intelligence system, perhaps because of over-confidence generated by the failure of all previous efforts to alter the

[12] The "message center" being the Congress; nineteen members of Congress were simultaneously delegates to the Convention. One gets a sense of this coordination of effort from Broadus Mitchell, *Alexander Hamilton, Youth to Maturity* (New York, 1957), ch. 22.

[13] See Sir Lewis Namier, *The Structure of Politics at the Accession of George III*, 2d ed. (New York, 1957); *England in the Age of the American Revolution* (London, 1930).

Articles,[14] the opposition awoke too late to the dangers that confronted them in 1787. Not only did the Constitutionalists manage to get every state but Rhode Island (where politics was enlivened by a party system reminiscent of the "Blues" and the "Greens" in the Byzantine Empire)[15] to appoint delegates to Philadelphia, but when the results were in, it appeared that they dominated the delegations. Given the apathy of the opposition, this was a natural phenomenon: in an ideologically non-polarized political atmosphere those who get appointed to a special committee are likely to be the men who supported the movement for its creation. Even George Clinton, who seems to have been the first opposition leader to awake to the possibility of trouble, could not prevent the New York legislature from appointing Alexander Hamilton—though he did have the foresight to send two of his henchmen to dominate the delegation. Incidentally, much has been made of the fact that the delegates to Philadelphia were not elected by the people; some have adduced this fact as evidence of the "undemocratic" character of the gathering. But put in the context of the time, this argument is wholly specious: the central government under the Articles was considered a creature of the component states and in all the states but Rhode Island, Connecticut and New Hampshire, members of the national Congress were chosen by the state legislatures. This was not a consequence of elitism or fear of the mob; it was a logical extension of states'-rights doctrine to guarantee that the national institution did not end-run the state legislatures and make direct contact with the people.[16]

II

With delegations safely named, the focus shifted to Philadelphia. While waiting for a quorum to assemble, James Madison got busy and drafted the so-called Randolph or Virginia Plan with the aid of the Virginia delegation. This was a political master-stroke. Its consequence was that once business got underway, the framework of discussion was established on Madison's

[14] The Annapolis Convention, called for the previous year, turned into a shambles: only five states sent commissioners, only three states were legally represented, and the instructions to delegates named varied quite widely from state to state. Clinton and others of his persuasion may have thought this disaster would put an end to the drive for reform. See Mitchell, *op. cit.*, pp. 362–67; Brant, *op. cit.*, pp. 375–87.

[15] See Hamilton M. Bishop, *Why Rhode Island Opposed the Federal Constitution* (Providence, 1950) for a careful analysis of the labyrinthine political course of Rhode Island. For background see David S. Lovejoy, *Rhode Island Politics and the American Revolution* (Providence, 1958).

[16] The terms "radical" and "conservative" have been bandied about a good deal in connection with the Constitution. This usage is nonsense if it is employed to distinguish between two economic "classes"—e.g., radical debtors versus conservative creditors, radical farmers versus conservative capitalists, etc.—because there was no polarization along this line of division; the same types of people turned up on both sides. And many were hard to place in these terms: does one treat Robert Morris as a debtor or a creditor? or James Wilson? See Brown, *op. cit.*, *passim*. The one line of division that holds up is between those deeply attached to states'-rights and those who felt that the Confederation was bankrupt. Thus, curiously, some of the most narrow-minded, parochial spokesmen of the time have earned the designation "radical" while those most willing to experiment and alter the *status quo* have been dubbed "conservative"! See Cecelia Kenyon, "Men of Little Faith," *William and Mary Quarterly*, Vol. 12, p. 3 (1955).

terms. There was no interminable argument over agenda; instead the delegates took the Virginia Resolutions—"just for purposes of discussion"—as their point of departure. And along with Madison's proposals, many of which were buried in the course of the summer, went his major premise: a new start on a Constitution rather than piecemeal amendment. This was not necessarily revolutionary—a little exegesis could demonstrate that a new Constitution might be formulated as "amendments" to the Articles of Confederation—but Madison's proposal that this "lump sum" amendment go into effect after approval by nine states (the Articles required unanimous state approval for any amendment) was thoroughly subversive.[17]

Standard treatments of the Convention divide the delegates into "nationalists" and "states'-righters" with various improvised shadings ("moderate nationalists," etc.), but these are *a posteriori* categories which obfuscate more than they clarify. What is striking to one who analyzes the Convention as a case-study in democratic politics is the lack of clear-cut ideological divisions in the Convention. Indeed, I submit that the evidence—Madison's *Notes*, the correspondence of the delegates, and debates on ratification—indicates that this was a remarkably homogeneous body on the ideological level. Yates and Lansing, Clinton's two chaperones for Hamilton, left in disgust on July 10. (Is there anything more tedious than sitting through endless disputes on matters one deems fundamentally misconceived? It takes an iron will to spend a hot summer as an ideological *agent provocateur*.) Luther Martin, Maryland's bibulous narcissist, left on September 4 in a huff when he discovered that others did not share his self-esteem; others went home for personal reasons. But the hard core of delegates accepted a grinding regimen throughout the attrition of a Philadelphia summer precisely because they shared the Constitutionalist goal.

Basic differences of opinion emerged, of course, but these were not ideological; they were *structural*. If the so-called "states'-rights" group had not accepted the fundamental purposes of the Convention, they could simply have pulled out and by doing so have aborted the whole enterprise. Instead of bolting, they returned day after day to argue and to compromise. An interesting symbol of this basic homogeneity was the initial agreement on secrecy: these professional politicians did not want to become prisoners of publicity; they wanted to retain that freedom of maneuver which is only possible when men are not forced to take public stands in the preliminary stages of negotiation.[18] There was no legal means of binding the tongues of the delegates: at any stage in the game a delegate with basic principled objections to the emerging project could have taken the stump (as Luther Martin did after his exit) and denounced the convention to the skies. Yet Madison did not even inform Thomas Jefferson in Paris of the course of the

[17] Yet, there was little objection to this crucial modification from any quarter—there almost seems to have been a gentlemen's agreement that Rhode Island's *liberum veto* had to be destroyed.

[18] See Mason's letter to his son, May 27, 1787, in which he endorsed secrecy as "a proper precaution to prevent mistakes and misrepresentation until the business shall have been completed, when the whole may have a very different complexion from that in which the several crude and indigested parts might in their first shape appear if submitted to the public eye." *Farrand*, III, 28.

deliberations[19] and available correspondence indicates that the delegates generally observed the injunction. Secrecy is certainly uncharacteristic of any assembly marked by strong ideological polarization. This was noted at the time: the *New York Daily Advertiser*, August 14, 1787, commented that the ". . . profound secrecy hitherto observed by the Convention [we consider] a happy omen, as it demonstrates that the spirit of party on any great and essential point cannot have arisen to any height."[20]

Commentators on the Constitution who have read *The Federalist* in lieu of reading the actual debates have credited the Fathers with the invention of a sublime concept called "Federalism."[21] Unfortunately *The Federalist* is probative evidence for only one proposition: that Hamilton and Madison were inspired propagandists with a genius for retrospective symmetry. Federalism, as the theory is generally defined, was an improvisation which was later promoted into a political theory. Experts on "federalism" should take to heart the advice of David Hume, who warned in his *Of the Rise and Progress of the Arts and Sciences* that ". . . there is no subject in which we must proceed with more caution than in [history], lest we assign causes which never existed and reduce what is merely contingent to stable and universal principles." In any event, the final balance in the Constitution between the states and the nation must have come as a great disappointment to Madison, while Hamilton's unitary views are too well known to need elucidation.

It is indeed astonishing how those who have glibly designated James Madison the "father" of Federalism have overlooked the solid body of fact which indicates that he shared Hamilton's quest for a unitary central government. To be specific, they have avoided examining the clear import of the Madison-Virginia Plan,[22] and have disregarded Madison's dogged inch-by-inch retreat from the bastions of centralization. The Virginia Plan envisioned a unitary national government effectively freed from and dominant over the states. The lower house of the national legislature was to be elected directly by the people of the states with membership proportional to population. The upper house was to be selected by the lower and the two chambers would elect the executive and choose the judges. The national government would be thus cut completely loose from the states.[23]

---

[19] See Madison to Jefferson, June 6, 1787, *Farrand*, III, 35.

[20] Cited in *Warren*, p. 138.

[21] See, *e.g.*, Gottfried Dietze, *The Federalist, A Classic on Federalism and Free Government* (Baltimore, 1960); Richard Hofstadter, *The American Political Tradition* (New York, 1948); and John P. Roche, "American Liberty," in M. Konvitz and C. Rossiter, eds., *Aspects of Liberty* (Ithaca, 1958).

[22] "I hold it for a fundamental point, that an individual independence of the states is utterly irreconcilable with the idea of an aggregate sovereignty," Madison to Randolph, cited in Brant, *op. cit.*, p. 416.

[23] The Randolph Plan was presented on May 29, see *Farrand*, I, 18–23; the state legislatures retained only the power to *nominate* candidates for the upper chamber. Madison's view of the appropriate position of the states emerged even more strikingly in Yates' record of his speech on June 29: "Some contend that states are sovereign when in fact they are only political societies. There is a gradation of power in all societies, from the lowest corporation to the highest sovereign. The states never possessed the essential rights of sovereignty . . . . The states, at present, are only great corporations, having the power of making by-laws, and these are effectual only if they are not con-

The structure of the general government was freed from state control in a truly radical fashion, but the scope of the authority of the national sovereign as Madison initially formulated it was breathtaking—it was a formulation worthy of the Sage of Malmesbury himself. The national legislature was to be empowered to disallow the acts of state legislatures,[24] and the central government was vested, in addition to the powers of the nation under the Articles of Confederation, with plenary authority wherever ". . . the separate States are incompetent or in which the harmony of the United States may be interrupted by the exercise of individual legislation."[25] Finally, just to lock the door against state intrusion, the national Congress was to be given the power to use military force on recalcitrant states.[26] This was Madison's "model" of an ideal national government, though it later received little publicity in *The Federalist*.

The interesting thing was the reaction of the Convention to this militant program for a strong autonomous central government. Some delegates were startled, some obviously leery of so comprehensive a project of reform,[27] but nobody set off any fireworks and nobody walked out. Moreover, in the two weeks that followed, the Virginia Plan received substantial endorsement *en principe;* the initial temper of the gathering can be deduced from the approval "without debate or dissent," on May 31, of the Sixth Resolution which granted Congress the authority to disallow state legislation ". . . contravening *in its opinion* the Articles of Union." Indeed, an amendment was included to bar states from contravening national treaties.[28]

The Virginia Plan may therefore be considered, in ideological terms, as the delegates' Utopia, but as the discussions continued and became more specific, many of those present began to have second thoughts. After all, they were not residents of Utopia or guardians in Plato's Republic who could simply impose a philosophical ideal on subordinate strata of the population. They were practical politicians in a democratic society, and no matter what their private dreams might be, they had to take home an acceptable package and defend it—and their own political futures—against predictable attack. On June 14 the breaking point between dream and reality took place. Apparently realizing that under the Virginia Plan, Massachusetts, Virginia and Pennsylvania could virtually dominate the national

---

tradictory to the general confederation. The states ought to be placed under the control of the general government—at least as much so as they formerly were under the king and British parliament." *Farrand*, I, 471. Forty-six years later, after Yates' "Notes" had been published, Madison tried to explain this statement away as a misinterpretation: he did not flatly deny the authenticity of Yates' record, but attempted a defense that was half justification and half evasion. Madison to W. C. Rives, Oct. 21, 1833. *Farrand*, III, 521–24.

[24] Resolution 6 gave the National Legislature this power subject to review by the Council of Revision proposed in Resolution 8.

[25] Resolution 6.

[26] *Ibid.*

[27] See the discussions on May 30 and 31. "Mr. Charles Pinkney wished to know of Mr. Randolph whether he meant to abolish the State Governts. altogether . . . Mr. Butler said he had not made up his mind on the subject and was open to the light which discussion might throw on it . . . Genl. Pinkney expressed a doubt . . . Mr. Gerry seemed to entertain the same doubt." *Farrand*, I, 33–34. There were no denunciations—though it should perhaps be added that Luther Martin had not yet arrived.

[28] *Farrand*, I, 54. (Italics added.)

government—and probably appreciating that to sell this program to "the folks back home" would be impossible—the delegates from the small states dug in their heels and demanded time for a consideration of alternatives. One gets a graphic sense of the inner politics from John Dickinson's reproach to Madison:

> You see the consequences of pushing things too far. Some of the members from the small States wish for two branches in the General Legislature and are friends to a good National Government; but we would sooner submit to a foreign power than . . . be deprived of an equality of suffrage in both branches of the Legislature, and thereby be thrown under the domination of the large States.[29]

The bare outline of the *Journal* entry for Tuesday, June 14, is suggestive to anyone with extensive experience in deliberative bodies. "It was moved by Mr. Patterson [*sic*, Paterson's name was one of those consistently misspelled by Madison and everybody else] seconded by Mr. Randolph that the further consideration of the report from the Committee of the whole House [endorsing the Virginia Plan] be postponed til tomorrow, and before the question for postponement was taken. It was moved by Mr. Randolph seconded by Mr. Patterson that the House adjourn."[30] The House adjourned by obvious prearrangement of the two principals: since the preceding Saturday when Brearley and Paterson of New Jersey had announced their fundamental discontent with the representational features of the Virginia Plan, the informal pressure had certainly been building up to slow down the steamroller. Doubtless there were extended arguments at the Indian Queen between Madison and Paterson, the latter insisting that events were moving rapidly towards a probably disastrous conclusion, towards a political suicide pact. Now the process of accommodation was put into action smoothly—and wisely, given the character and strength of the doubters. Madison had the votes, but this was one of those situations where the enforcement of mechanical majoritarianism could easily have destroyed the objectives of the majority: the Constitutionalists were in quest of a qualitative as well as a quantitative consensus. This was hardly from deference to local Quaker custom; it was a political imperative if they were to attain ratification.

III

According to the standard script, at this point the "states'-rights" group intervened in force behind the New Jersey Plan, which has been characteristically portrayed as a reversion to the *status quo* under the Articles of Confederation with but minor modifications. A careful examination of the evidence indicates that only in a marginal sense is this an accurate description. It is true that the New Jersey Plan put the states back into the institutional picture, but one could argue that to do so was a recognition of political reality rather than an affirmation of states'-rights. A serious case can be made that the advocates of the New Jersey Plan, far from being

---

[29] *Ibid.*, p. 242. Delaware's delegates had been instructed by their general assembly to maintain in any new system the voting equality of the states. *Farrand*, III, 574.
[30] *Ibid.*, p. 240.

ideological addicts of states'-rights, intended to substitute for the Virginia
Plan a system which would both retain strong national power and have a
chance of adoption in the states. The leading spokesman for the project
asserted quite clearly that his views were based more on counsels of expediency than on principle; said Paterson on June 16: "I came here not to
speak my own sentiments, but the sentiments of those who sent me. Our
object is not such a Governmt. as may be best in itself, but such a one as
our Constituents have authorized us to prepare, and as they will approve."[31]
This is Madison's version; in Yates' transcription, there is a crucial sentence
following the remarks above: "I believe that a little practical virtue is to be
preferred to the finest theoretical principles, which cannot be carried into
effect."[32] In his preliminary speech on June 9, Paterson had stated ". . . to
the public mind we must accommodate ourselves,"[33] and in his notes for
this and his later effort as well, the emphasis is the same. The *structure* of
government under the Articles should be retained:

> 2. Because it accords with the Sentiments of the People
>   [Proof:] 1. Coms. [Commissions from state legislatures defining the juris-
>   diction of the delegates]
>   2. News-papers—Political Barometer. Jersey never would have
>   sent Delegates under the first [Virginia] Plan—
>   Not here to sport Opinions of my own. Wt. [What] can be done. A little
>   practicable Virtue preferable to Theory.[34]

This was a defense of political acumen, not of states'-rights. In fact, Paterson's notes of his speech can easily be construed as an argument for attaining the substantive objectives of the Virginia Plan by a sound political route,
i.e., pouring the new wine in the old bottles. With a shrewd eye, Paterson
queried:

> Will the Operation and Force of the [central] Govt. depend upon the mode
> of Representn.—No—it will depend upon the Quantum of Power lodged in
> the leg. ex. and judy. Departments—Give [the existing] Congress the same
> Powers that you intend to give the two Branches, [under the Virginia Plan]
> and I apprehend they will act with as much Propriety and more Energy . . .[35]

In other words, the advocates of the New Jersey Plan concentrated their
fire on what they held to be the *political liabilities* of the Virginia Plan—
which were matters of institutional structure—rather than on the proposed
scope of national authority. Indeed, the Supremacy Clause of the Constitution first saw the light of day in Paterson's Sixth Resolution; the New Jersey
Plan contemplated the use of military force to secure compliance with
national law; and finally Paterson made clear his view that under either the
Virginia or the New Jersey systems, the general government would ". . .
act on individuals and not on states."[36] From the states'-rights viewpoint, this

---

[31] *Ibid.*, p. 250.
[32] *Ibid.*, p. 258.
[33] *Ibid.*, p. 178.
[34] *Ibid.*, p. 274.
[35] *Ibid.*, pp. 275–76.
[36] "But it is said that this national government is to act on individuals and not on
states; and cannot a federal government be so framed as to operate in the same way? It
surely may." *Ibid.*, pp. 182–83; also *ibid.* at p. 276.

was heresy: the fundament of that doctrine was the proposition that any central government had as its constituents the states, not the people, and could only reach the people through the agency of the state government.

Paterson then reopened the agenda of the Convention, but he did so within a distinctly nationalist framework. Paterson's position was one of favoring a strong central government in principle, but opposing one which in fact *put the big states in the saddle*. (The Virginia Plan, for all its abstract merits, did very well by Virginia.) As evidence for this speculation, there is a curious and intriguing proposal among Paterson's preliminary drafts of the New Jersey Plan:

> Whereas it is necessary in Order to form the People of the U. S. of America in to a Nation, that the States should be consolidated, by which means all the Citizens thereof will become equally intitled to and will equally participate in the same Privileges and Rights . . . it is therefore resolved, that all the Lands contained within the Limits of each state individually, and of the U. S. generally be considered as constituting one Body or Mass, and be divided into thirteen or more integral parts.
>
> Resolved, That such Divisions or integral Parts shall be styled Districts.[37]

This makes it sound as though Paterson was prepared to accept a strong unified central government along the lines of the Virginia Plan if the existing states were eliminated. He may have gotten the idea from his New Jersey colleague Judge David Brearley, who on June 9 had commented that the only remedy to the dilemma over representation was ". . . that a map of the U.S. be spread out, that all the existing boundaries be erased, and that a new partition of the whole be made into 13 equal parts."[38] According to Yates, Brearley added at this point, ". . . then a government on the present [Virginia Plan] system will be just."[39]

This proposition was never pushed—it was patently unrealistic—but one can appreciate its purpose: it would have separated the men from the boys in the large-state delegations. How attached would the Virginians have been to their reform principles if Virginia were to disappear as a component geographical unit (the largest) for representational purposes? Up to this point, the Virginians had been in the happy position of supporting high ideals with that inner confidence born of knowledge that the "public interest" they endorsed would nourish their private interest. Worse, they had shown little willingness to compromise. Now the delegates from the small states announced that they were unprepared to be offered up as sacrificial victims to a "national interest" which reflected Virginia's parochial ambition. Caustic Charles Pinckney was not far off when he remarked sardonically that ". . . the whole [conflict] comes to this": "Give N. Jersey an equal vote, and she will dismiss her scruples, and concur in the Natil. system."[40] What he rather unfairly did not add was that the Jersey delegates were not free agents who could adhere to their private convictions; they had to take back, sponsor and risk their reputations on the reforms approved by the Convention—and in New Jersey, not in Virginia.

[37] *Farrand*, III, 613.
[38] Farrand, I, 177.
[39] *Ibid.*, p. 182.
[40] *Ibid.*, p. 255.

Paterson spoke on Saturday, and one can surmise that over the week-end there was a good deal of consultation, argument, and caucusing among the delegates. One member at least prepared a full length address: on Monday Alexander Hamilton, previously mute, rose and delivered a six-hour oration.[41] It was a remarkably apolitical speech; the gist of his position was that *both* the Virginia and New Jersey Plans were inadequately centralist, and he detailed a reform program which was reminiscent of the Protectorate under the Cromwellian *Instrument of Government* of 1653. It has been suggested that Hamilton did this in the best political tradition to emphasize the moderate character of the Virginia Plan,[42] to give the cautious delegates something *really* to worry about; but this interpretation seems somehow too clever. Particularly since the sentiments Hamilton expressed happened to be completely consistent with those he privately—and sometimes publicly—expressed throughout his life. He wanted, to take a striking phrase from a letter to George Washington, a "strong well mounted government";[43] in essence, the Hamilton Plan contemplated an elected life monarch, virtually free of public control, on the Hobbesian ground that only in this fashion could strength and stability be achieved. The other alternatives, he argued, would put policy-making at the mercy of the passions of the mob; only if the sovereign was beyond the reach of selfish influence would it be possible to have government in the interests of the whole community.[44]

From all accounts, this was a masterful and compelling speech, but (aside from furnishing John Lansing and Luther Martin with ammunition for later use against the Constitution) it made little impact. Hamilton was simply transmitting on a different wave-length from the rest of the delegates; the latter adjourned after this great effort, admired his rhetoric, and then returned to business.[45] It was rather as if they had taken a day off to attend the opera. Hamilton, never a particularly patient man or much of a negotiator, stayed for another ten days and then left, in considerable disgust, for New York.[46] Although he came back to Philadelphia sporadically and attended the last two weeks of the Convention, Hamilton played no part in the laborious task of hammering out the Constitution. His day came later when he led the New York Constitutionalists into the savage imbroglio over ratification—an arena in which his unmatched talent for dirty political infighting may well have won the day. For instance, in the New York Ratifying Convention, Lansing threw back into Hamilton's teeth the sentiments the latter had expressed in his June 18 oration in the Convention. However, having since retreated to the fine defensive positions immortalized in *The Federalist*, the Colonel flatly denied that he had ever been an enemy of the states, or had believed that conflict between states and nation

[41] J. C. Hamilton, cited *ibid.*, p. 293.
[42] See, *e.g.*, Mitchell, *op. cit.*, p. 381.
[43] Hamilton to Washington, July 3, 1787, *Farrand*, III, 53.
[44] A reconstruction of the Hamilton Plan is found in *Farrand*, III, 617–30.
[45] Said William Samuel Johnson on June 21: "A gentleman from New-York, with boldness and decision, proposed a system totally different from both [Virginia and New Jersey]; and though he has been praised by every body, he has been supported by none." *Farrand*, I, 363.
[46] See his letter to Washington cited *supra* note 43.

was inexorable! As Madison's authoritative *Notes* did not appear until 1840, and there had been no press coverage, there was no way to verify his assertions, so in the words of the reporter, ". . . a warm personal altercation between [Lansing and Hamilton] engrossed the remainder of the day [June 28, 1788]."[47]

IV

On Tuesday morning, June 19, the vacation was over. James Madison led off with a long, carefully reasoned speech analyzing the New Jersey Plan which, while intellectually vigorous in its criticisms, was quite conciliatory in mood. "The great difficulty," he observed, "lies in the affair of Representation; and if this could be adjusted, all others would be surmountable."[48] (As events were to demonstrate, this diagnosis was correct.) When he finished, a vote was taken on whether to continue with the Virginia Plan as the nucleus for a new constitution: seven states voted "Yes"; New York, New Jersey, and Delaware voted "No"; and Maryland, whose position often depended on which delegates happened to be on the floor, divided.[49] Paterson, it seems, lost decisively; yet in a fundamental sense he and his allies had achieved their purpose: from that day onward, it could never be forgotten that the state governments loomed ominously in the background and that no verbal incantations could exorcise their power. Moreover, nobody bolted the convention: Paterson and his colleagues took their defeat in stride and set to work to modify the Virginia Plan, particularly with respect to its provisions on representation in the national legislature. Indeed, they won an immediate rhetorical bonus; when Oliver Ellsworth of Connecticut rose to move that the word "national" be expunged from the Third Virginia Resolution ("Resolved that a *national* Government ought to be established consisting of a *supreme* Legislative, Executive and Judiciary"[50]), Randolph agreed and the motion passed unanimously.[51] The process of compromise had begun.

[47] *Farrand*, III, 338.

[48] *Farrand*, I, 321.

[49] Maryland's politics in this period were only a bit less intricate than Rhode Island's: the rural gentry, in much the same fashion that Namier described in England, divided up among families—Chases, Carrolls, Pacas, Lloyds, Tilghmans, etc.—and engaged in what seemed, to the outsider, elaborate political Morris dances. See Philip A. Crowl, *Maryland During and After the Revolution* (Baltimore, 1943). The Maryland General Assembly named five delegates to the Convention and provided that "the said Deputies or such of them as shall attend . . . shall have full Power to represent this State," *Farrand*, III, 586. The interesting circumstance was that three of the delegates were Constitutionalists (Carroll, McHenry and Jenifer), while two were opposed (Martin and Mercer); and this led to an *ad hoc* determination of where Maryland would stand when votes were taken. The vote on equality of representation, to be described *infra*, was an important instance of this eccentricity.

[50] This formulation was voted into the Randolph Plan on May 30, 1787, by a vote of six states to none, with one divided. *Farrand*, I, 30.

[51] *Farrand*, I, 335–36. In agreeing, Randolph stipulated his disagreement with Ellsworth's rationale, but said he did not object to merely changing an "expression." Those who subject the Constitution to minute semantic analysis might do well to keep this instance in mind; if Randolph could so concede the deletion of "national," one may wonder if any word changes can be given much weight.

For the next two weeks, the delegates circled around the problem of legislative representation. The Connecticut delegation appears to have evolved a possible compromise quite early in the debates, but the Virginians and particularly Madison (unaware that he would later be acclaimed as the prophet of "federalism") fought obdurately against providing for equal representation of states in the second chamber. There was a good deal of acrimony and at one point Benjamin Franklin—of all people—proposed the institution of a daily prayer; practical politicians in the gathering, however, were meditating more on the merits of a good committee than on the utility of Divine intervention. On July 2, the ice began to break when through a number of fortuitous events[52]—and one that seems deliberate[53]—the majority against equality of representation was converted into a dead tie. The Convention had reached the stage where it was "ripe" for a solution (presumably all the therapeutic speeches had been made), and the South Carolinians proposed a committee. Madison and James Wilson wanted none of it, but with only Pennsylvania dissenting, the body voted to establish a working party on the problem of representation.

The members of this committee, one from each state, were elected by the delegates—and a very interesting committee it was. Despite the fact that the Virginia Plan had held majority support up to that date, neither Madison nor Randolph was selected (Mason was the Virginian) and Baldwin of Georgia, whose shift in position had resulted in the tie, was chosen. From the composition, it was clear that this was not to be a "fighting" committee: the emphasis in membership was on what might be described as "second-level political entrepreneurs." On the basis of the discussions up to that time, only Luther Martin of Maryland could be described as a "bitter-ender." Admittedly, some divination enters into this sort of analysis, but one does get a sense of the mood of the delegates from these choices—including the interesting selection of Benjamin Franklin, despite his age and intellectual wobbliness, over the brilliant and incisive Wilson or the sharp, polemical Gouverneur Morris, to represent Pennsylvania. His passion for conciliation was more valuable at this juncture than Wilson's logical genius, or Morris' acerbic wit.

There is a common rumor that the Framers divided their time between philosophical discussions of government and reading the classics in political theory. Perhaps this is as good a time as any to note that their concerns were highly practical, that they spent little time canvassing abstractions. A number

---

[52] According to Luther Martin, he was alone on the floor and cast Maryland's vote for equality of representation. Shortly thereafter, Jenifer came on the floor and "Mr. King, from Massachusetts, valuing himself on Mr. Jenifer to divide the State of Maryland on this question . . . requested of the President that the question might be put again; however, the motion was too extraordinary in its nature to meet with success." Cited from "The Genuine Information, . . ." *Farrand*, III, 188.

[53] Namely Baldwin's vote *for* equality of representation which divided Georgia—with Few absent and Pierce in New York fighting a duel, Houston voted against equality and Baldwin shifted to tie the state. Baldwin was originally from Connecticut and attended and tutored at Yale, facts which have led to much speculation about the pressures the Connecticut delegation may have brought on him to save the day (Georgia was the last state to vote) and open the way to compromise. To employ a good Russian phrase, it was certainly not an accident that Baldwin voted the way he did. See *Warren*, p. 262.

of them had some acquaintance with the history of political theory (probably gained from reading John Adams' monumental compilation *A Defense of the Constitutions of Government*,[54] the first volume of which appeared in 1786), and it was a poor rhetorician indeed who could not cite Locke, Montesquieu, or Harrington *in support* of a desired goal. Yet up to this point in the deliberations, no one had expounded a defense of states'-rights or the "separation of powers" on anything resembling a theoretical basis. It should be reiterated that the Madison model had no room either for the states or for the "separation of powers": effectively *all* governmental power was vested in the national legislature. The merits of Montesquieu did not turn up until *The Federalist;* and although a perverse argument could be made that Madison's ideal was truly in the tradition of John Locke's *Second Treatise of Government*,[55] the Locke whom the American rebels treated as an honorary president was a pluralistic defender of vested rights,[56] not of parliamentary supremacy.

It would be tedious to continue a blow-by-blow analysis of the work of the delegates; the critical fight was over representation of the states and once the Connecticut Compromise was adopted on July 17, the Convention was over the hump. Madison, James Wilson, and Gouverneur Morris of New York (who was there representing Pennsylvania!) fought the compromise all the way in a last-ditch effort to get a unitary state with parliamentary supremacy. But their allies deserted them and they demonstrated after their defeat the essentially opportunist character of their objections—using "opportunist" here in a non-pejorative sense, to indicate a willingness to swallow their objections and get on with the business. Moreover, once the compromise had carried (by five states to four, with one state divided), its advocates threw themselves vigorously into the job of strengthening the general government's substantive powers—as might have been predicted, indeed, from Paterson's early statements. It nourishes an increased respect for Madison's devotion to the art of politics, to realize that this dogged fighter could sit down six months later and prepare essays for *The Federalist*

---

[54] For various contemporary comments, see *Warren*, pp. 814–818. On Adams' technique, see Zoltan Haraszti, "The Composition of Adams' *Defense*," in *John Adams and the Prophets of Progress* (Cambridge, 1952), ch. 9. In this connection it is interesting to check the Convention discussions for references to the authority of Locke, Montesquieu and Harrington, the theorists who have been assigned various degrees of paternal responsibility. There are no explicit references to James Harrington; one to John Locke (Luther Martin cited him on the state of nature, *Farrand*, I, 437); and seven to Montesquieu, only one of which related to the "separation of powers" (Madison in an odd speech, which he explained in a footnote was given to help a friend rather than advance his own views, cited Montesquieu on the separation of the executive and legislative branches, *Farrand*, II, 34). This, of course, does not prove that Locke and Co. were without influence; it shifts the burden of proof, however, to those who assert ideological causality. See Benjamin F. Wright, "The Origins of the Separation of Powers in America," *Economica*, Vol. 13 (1933), p. 184.

[55] I share Willmoore Kendall's interpretation of Locke as a supporter of parliamentary supremacy and majoritarianism; see Kendall, *John Locke and the Doctrine of Majority Rule* (Urbana, 1941). Kendall's general position has recently received strong support in the definitive edition and commentary of Peter Laslett, *Locke's Two Treatises of Government* (Cambridge, 1960).

[56] The American Locke is best delineated in Carl Becker, *The Declaration of Independence* (New York, 1948).

in contradiction to his basic convictions about the true course the Convention should have taken.

V

Two tricky issues will serve to illustrate the later process of accommodation. The first was the institutional position of the Executive. Madison argued for an executive chosen by the National Legislature and on May 29 this had been adopted with a provision that after his seven-year term was concluded, the chief magistrate should not be eligible for reelection. In late July this was reopened and for a week the matter was argued from several different points of view. A good deal of desultory speechmaking ensued, but the gist of the problem was the opposition from two sources to election by the legislature. One group felt that the states should have a hand in the process; another small but influential circle urged direct election by the people. There were a number of proposals: election by the people, election by state governors, by electors chosen by state legislatures, by the National Legislature (James Wilson, perhaps ironically, proposed at one point that an Electoral College be chosen by lot from the National Legislature!), and there was some resemblance to three-dimensional chess in the dispute because of the presence of two other variables, length of tenure, and reeligibility. Finally, after opening, reopening, and re-reopening the debate, the thorny problem was consigned to a committee for resolution.

The Brearley Committee on Postponed Matters was a superb aggregation of talent and its compromise on the Executive was a masterpiece of political improvisation. (The Electoral College, its creation, however, had little in its favor as an *institution*—as the delegates well appreciated.) The point of departure for all discussion about the presidency in the Convention was that in immediate terms, the problem was non-existent; in other words, everybody present knew that under any system devised, George Washington would be President. Thus they were dealing in the future tense and to a body of working politicians the merits of the Brearley proposal were obvious: everybody got a piece of cake. (Or to put it more academically, each viewpoint could leave the Convention and argue to its constituents that it had *really* won the day.) First, the state legislatures had the right to determine the mode of selection of the electors; second, the small states received a bonus in the Electoral College in the form of a guaranteed minimum of three votes while the big states got acceptance of the principle of proportional power; third, if the state legislatures agreed (as six did in the first presidential election), the people could be involved directly in the choice of electors; and finally, if no candidate received a majority in the College, the right of decision passed to the National Legislature with each state exercising equal strength. (In the Brearley recommendation, the election went to the Senate, but a motion from the floor substituted the House; this was accepted on the ground that the Senate already had enough authority over the executive in its treaty and appointment powers.)

This compromise was almost too good to be true, and the Framers snapped it up with little debate or controversy. No one seemed to think well of the College as an *institution;* indeed, what evidence there is suggests that there was an assumption that once Washington had finished his tenure as President, the electors would cease to produce majorities and the chief executive would usually be chosen in the House. George Mason observed casually that the selection would be made in the House nineteen times in twenty and no one seriously disputed this point. The vital aspect of the Electoral College was that it got the Convention over the hurdle and protected everybody's interests. The future was left to cope with the problem of what to do with this Rube Goldberg mechanism.

In short, the Framers did not in their wisdom endow the United States with a College of Cardinals—the Electoral College was neither an exercise in applied Platonism nor an experiment in indirect government based on elitist distrust of the masses. It was merely a jerry-rigged improvisation which has subsequently been endowed with a high theoretical content. When an elector from Oklahoma in 1960 refused to cast his vote for Nixon (naming Byrd and Goldwater instead) on the ground that the Founding Fathers intended him to exercise his great independent wisdom, he was indulging in historical fantasy. If one were to indulge in counter-fantasy, he would be tempted to suggest that the Fathers would be startled to find the College still in operation—and perhaps even dismayed at their descendants' lack of judgment or inventiveness.[57]

The second issue on which some substantial practical bargaining took place was slavery. The morality of slavery was, by design, not at issue;[58] but in its other concrete aspects, slavery colored the arguments over taxation, commerce, and representation. The "Three-Fifths Compromise," that three-fifths of the slaves would be counted both for representation and for purposes of direct taxation (which was drawn from the past—it was a formula of Madison's utilized by Congress in 1783 to establish the basis of state contributions to the Confederation treasury) had allayed some Northern fears about Southern over-representation (no one then foresaw the trivial role that direct taxation would play in later federal financial policy), but doubts still remained. The Southerners, on the other hand, were afraid that Congressional control over commerce would lead to the exclusion of slaves or to their excessive taxation as imports. Moreover, the Southerners were disturbed over "navigation acts," i.e., tariffs, or special legislation providing, for example, that exports be carried only in American ships; as a section depending upon exports, they wanted protection from the potential voracity of their commercial brethren of the Eastern states. To achieve this end, Mason and others urged that the Constitution include a proviso that navigation and commercial laws should require a two-thirds vote in Congress.

These problems came to a head in late August and, as usual, were handed to a committee in the hope that, in Gouverneur Morris' words, ".   these things may form a bargain among the Northern and Southern states."[59] The

---

[57] See John P. Roche, "The Electoral College: A Note on American Political Mythology," *Dissent* (Spring, 1961), pp. 197–99. The relevant debates took place July 19–26, 1787, *Farrand*, II, 50–128, and September 5–6, 1787, *ibid.*, pp. 505–31.

[58] See the discussion on August 22, 1787, *Farrand*, II, 366–375; King seems to have expressed the sense of the Convention when he said, "the subject should be considered in a political light only." *Ibid.* at 373.

[59] *Farrand*, II, 374. Randolph echoed his sentiment in different words.

Committee reported its measures of reconciliation on August 25, and on August 29 the package was wrapped up and delivered. What occurred can best be described in George Mason's dour version (he anticipated Calhoun in his conviction that permitting navigation acts to pass by majority vote would put the South in economic bondage to the North—it was mainly on this ground that he refused to sign the Constitution):

> The Constitution as agreed to till a fortnight before the Convention rose was such a one as he would have set his hand and heart to. . . . [Until that time] The 3 New England States were constantly with us in all questions . . . so that it was these three States with the 5 Southern ones against Pennsylvania, Jersey and Delaware. With respect to the importation of slaves, [decision-making] was left to Congress. This disturbed the two Southernmost States who knew that Congress would immediately suppress the importation of slaves. Those two States therefore struck up a bargain with the three New England States. If they would join to admit slaves for some years, the two Southern-most States would join in changing the clause which required the ⅔ of the Legislature in any vote [on navigation acts]. It was done.[60]

On the floor of the Convention there was a virtual love-feast on this happy occasion. Charles Pinckney of South Carolina attempted to overturn the committee's decision, when the compromise was reported to the Convention, by insisting that the South needed protection from the imperialism of the Northern states. But his Southern colleagues were not prepared to rock the boat and General C. C. Pinckney arose to spread oil on the suddenly ruffled water; he admitted that:

> It was in the true interest of the S[outhern] States to have no regulation of commerce; but considering the loss brought on the commerce of the Eastern States by the Revolution, their liberal conduct towards the views of South Carolina [on the regulation of the slave trade] and the interests the weak Southn. States had in being united with the strong Eastern states, he thought it proper that no fetters should be imposed on the power of making commercial regulations; *and that his constituents, though prejudiced against the Eastern States, would be reconciled to this liberality.* He had himself prejudices agst the Eastern States before he came here, but would acknowledge that he had found them as liberal and candid as any men whatever. (Italics added)[61]

Pierce Butler took the same tack, essentially arguing that he was not too happy about the possible consequences, but that a deal was a deal.[62] Many

---

[60] Mason to Jefferson, cited in *Warren*, p. 584.

[61] August 29, 1787, *Farrand*, II, 449–50.

[62] *Ibid.*, p. 451. The plainest statement of the matter was put by the three North Carolina delegates (Blount, Spaight and Williamson) in their report to Governor Caswell, September 18, 1787. After noting that "no exertions have been wanting on our part to guard and promote the particular interest of North Carolina," they went on to explain the basis of the negotiations in cold-blooded fashion: "While we were taking so much care to guard ourselves against being over reached and to form rules of Taxation that might operate in our favour, it is not to be supposed that our Northern Brethren were Inattentive to their particular Interest. A navigation Act or the power to regulate Commerce in the Hands of the National Government . . . is what the Southern States have given in Exchange for the advantages we Mentioned." They concluded by explaining that while the Constitution did deal with other matters besides taxes—"there are

Southern leaders were later—in the wake of the "Tariff of Abominations"—to rue this day of reconciliation; Calhoun's *Disquisition on Government* was little more than an extension of the argument in the Convention against permitting a congressional majority to enact navigation acts.[63]

VI

Drawing on their vast collective political experience, utilizing every weapon in the politician's arsenal, looking constantly over their shoulders at their constituents, the delegates put together a Constitution. It was a make-shift affair; some sticky issues (for example, the qualification of voters) they ducked entirely; others they mastered with that ancient instrument of political sagacity, studied ambiguity (for example, citizenship), and some they just overlooked. In this last category, I suspect, fell the matter of the power of the federal courts to determine the constitutionality of acts of Congress. When the judicial article was formulated (Article III of the Constitution), deliberations were still in the stage where the legislature was endowed with broad power under the Randolph formulation, authority which by its own terms was scarcely amenable to judicial review. In essence, courts could hardly determine when ". . . the separate States are incompetent or . . . the harmony of the United States may be interrupted"; the National Legislature, as critics pointed out, was free to define its own jurisdiction. Later the definition of legislative authority was changed into the form we know, a series of stipulated powers, *but the delegates never seriously reexamined the jurisdiction of the judiciary under this new limited formulation.*[64] All arguments on the intention of the Framers in this matter are thus deductive and *a posteriori*, though some obviously make more sense than others.[65]

The Framers were busy and distinguished men, anxious to get back to

---

other Considerations of great Magnitude involved in the system"—they would not take up valuable time with boring details! *Farrand*, III, 83–84.

[63] See John C. Calhoun, *A Disquisition on Government* (New York, 1943), pp. 21–25, 38. Calhoun differed from Mason, and others in the Convention who urged the two-thirds requirement, by advocating a functional or interest veto rather than some sort of special majority, *i.e.*, he abandoned the search for quantitative checks in favor of a qualitative solution.

[64] The Committee on Detail altered the general grant of legislative power envisioned by the Virginia Plan into a series of specific grants; these were examined closely between August 16 and August 23. One day only was devoted to the Judicial Article, August 27, and since no one raised the question of judicial review of *Federal* statutes, no light was cast on the matter. A number of random comments on the power of the judiciary were scattered throughout the discussions, but there was another variable which deprives them of much probative value: the proposed Council of Revision which would have joined the Executive with the judges in *legislative* review. Madison and Wilson, for example, favored this technique—which had nothing in common with what we think of as judicial review except that judges were involved in the task.

[65] For what it may be worth, I think that judicial review of congressional acts was logically on all fours with review of state enactments and that it was certainly consistent with the view that the Constitution could not be amended by the Congress and President, or by a two-thirds vote of Congress (overriding a veto), without the agreement of three-quarters of the states. *External* evidence from that time supports this view, see Charles Warren, *Congress, the Constitution, and the Supreme Court* (Boston, 1925), pp. 41–128, but the debates *in* the Convention prove nothing.

their families, their positions, and their constituents, not members of the French Academy devoting a lifetime to a dictionary. They were trying to do an important job, and do it in such a fashion that their handiwork would be acceptable to very diverse constituencies. No one was rhapsodic about the final document, but it was a beginning, a move in the right direction, and one they had reason to believe the people would endorse. In addition, since they had modified the impossible amendment provisions of the Articles (the requirement of unanimity which could always be frustrated by "Rogues Island") to one demanding approval by only three-quarters of the states, they seemed confident that gaps in the fabric which experience would reveal could be rewoven without undue difficulty.

So with a neat phrase introduced by Benjamin Franklin (but devised by Gouverneur Morris)[66] which made their decision sound unanimous, and an inspired benediction by the Old Doctor urging doubters to doubt their own infallibility, the Constitution was accepted and signed. Curiously, Edmund Randolph, who had played so vital a role throughout, refused to sign, as did his fellow Virginian George Mason and Elbridge Gerry of Massachusetts. Randolph's behavior was eccentric, to say the least—his excuses for refusing his signature have a factitious ring even at this late date; the best explanation seems to be that he was afraid that the Constitution would prove to be a liability in Virginia politics, where Patrick Henry was burning up the countryside with impassioned denunciations. Presumably, Randolph wanted to check the temper of the populace before he risked his reputation, and perhaps his job, in a fight with both Henry and Richard Henry Lee.[67] Events lend some justification to this speculation: after much temporizing and use of the conditional subjunctive tense, Randolph endorsed ratification in Virginia and ended up getting the best of both worlds.

Madison, despite his reservations about the Constitution, was the campaign manager in ratification. His first task was to get the Congress in New York to light its own funeral pyre by approving the "amendments" to the Articles and sending them on to the state legislatures. Above all, momentum had to be maintained. The anti-Constitutionalists, now thoroughly alarmed and no novices in politics, realized that their best tactic was attrition rather than direct opposition. Thus they settled on a position expressing qualified approval but calling for a second Convention to remedy various defects (the one with the most demagogic appeal was the lack of a Bill of Rights). Madison knew that to accede to this demand would be equivalent to losing the battle, nor would he agree to conditional approval (despite wavering even by Hamilton). This was an all-or-nothing proposition: national salvation or national impotence with no intermediate positions possible. Unable

[66] Or so Madison stated, *Farrand*, II, 643. Wilson too may have contributed; he was close to Franklin and delivered the frail old gentleman's speeches for him.

[67] See a very interesting letter, from an unknown source in Philadelphia, to Jefferson, October 11, 1787: "Randolph wishes it well, & it is thought would have signed it, but he wanted to be on a footing with a popular rival." *Farrand*, III, 104. Madison, writing Jefferson a full account on October 24, 1787, put the matter more delicately—he was working hard on Randolph to win him for ratification: "[Randolph] was not inveterate in his opposition, and grounded his refusal to subscribe pretty much on his unwillingness to commit himself, so as not to be at liberty to be governed by further lights on the subject." *Ibid.*, p. 135.

to get congressional approval, he settled for second best: a unanimous resolution of Congress transmitting the Constitution to the states for whatever action they saw fit to take. The opponents then moved from New York and the Congress, where they had attempted to attach amendments and conditions, to the states for the final battle.[68]

At first the campaign for ratification went beautifully: within eight months after the delegates set their names to the document, eight states had ratified. Only in Massachusetts had the result been close (187–168). Theoretically, a ratification by one more state convention would set the new government in motion, but in fact until Virginia and New York acceded to the new Union, the latter was a fiction. New Hampshire was the next to ratify; Rhode Island was involved in its characteristic political convulsions (the Legislature there sent the Constitution out to the towns for decision by popular vote and it got lost among a series of local issues);[69] North Carolina's convention did not meet until July and then postponed a final decision. This is hardly the place for an extensive analysis of the conventions of New York and Virginia. Suffice it to say that the Constitutionalists clearly outmaneuvered their opponents, forced them into impossible political positions, and won both states narrowly. The Virginia Convention could serve as a classic study in effective floor management: Patrick Henry had to be contained, and a reading of the debates discloses a standard two-stage technique. Henry would give a four- or five-hour speech denouncing some section of the Constitution on every conceivable ground (the federal district, he averred at one point, would become a haven for convicts escaping from state authority!);[70] when Henry subsided, "Mr. Lee of Westmoreland" would rise and literally poleaxe him with sardonic invective (when Henry complained about the militia power, "Lighthorse Harry" really punched below the belt: observing that while the former Governor had been sitting in Richmond during the Revolution, *he* had been out in the trenches with the troops and thus felt better qualified to discuss military affairs).[71] Then the gentlemanly Constitutionalists (Madison, Pendleton and Marshall) would pick up the matters at issue and examine them in the light of reason.

Indeed, modern Americans who tend to think of James Madison as a rather dessicated character should spend some time with this transcript. Probably Madison put on his most spectacular demonstration of nimble rhetoric in what might be called "The Battle of the Absent Authorities." Patrick Henry in the course of one of his harangues alleged that Jefferson was known to be opposed to Virginia's approving the Constitution. This was clever: Henry hated Jefferson, but was prepared to use any weapon that came to hand. Madison's riposte was superb: First, he said that with all

[68] See Edward P. Smith, "The Movement Towards a Second Constitutional Convention in 1788," in J. F. Jameson, ed., *Essays in the Constitutional History of the United States* (Boston, 1889), p. 46–115.

[69] See Bishop, *op. cit., passim.*

[70] See *Elliot's Debates on the Federal Constitution* (Washington, 1836), Vol. 3, pp. 436–438.

[71] This should be quoted to give the full flavor: "Without vanity, I may say I have had different experience of [militia] service from that of [Henry]. It was my fortune to be a soldier of my country. . . . I saw what the honorable gentleman did not see— our men fighting. . . ." *Ibid.*, p. 178.

due respect to the great reputation of Jefferson, he was not in the country and therefore could not formulate an adequate judgment; second, no one should utilize the reputation of an outsider—the Virginia Convention was there to think for itself; third, if there were to be recourse to outsiders, the opinions of George Washington should certainly be taken into consideration; and finally, he knew from privileged personal communications from Jefferson that in fact the latter *strongly favored* the Constitution.[72] To devise an assault route into this rhetorical fortress was literally impossible.

VII

The fight was over; all that remained now was to establish the new frame of government in the spirit of its framers. And who were better qualified for this task than the Framers themselves? Thus victory for the Constitution meant simultaneous victory for the Constitutionalists; the anti-Constitutionalists either capitulated or vanished into limbo—soon Patrick Henry would be offered a seat on the Supreme Court[73] and Luther Martin would be known as the Federalist "bull-dog."[74] And irony of ironies, Alexander Hamilton and James Madison would shortly accumulate a reputation as the formulators of what is often alleged to be our political theory, the concept of "federalism." Also, on the other side of the ledger, the arguments would soon appear over what the Framers "really meant"; while these disputes have assumed the proportions of a big scholarly business in the last century, they began almost before the ink on the Constitution was dry. One of the best early ones featured Hamilton versus Madison on the scope of presidential power, and other Framers characteristically assumed positions in this and other disputes on the basis of their political convictions.

Probably our greatest difficulty is that we know so much more about what the Framers *should have meant* than they themselves did. We are intimately acquainted with the problems that their Constitution should have been designed to master; in short, we have read the mystery story backwards. If we are to get the right "feel" for their time and their circumstances, we must in Maitland's phrase, ". . . think ourselves back into a twilight." Obviously, no one can pretend completely to escape from the solipsistic web of his own environment, but if the effort is made, it is possible to appreciate the past roughly on its own terms. The first step in this process is to abandon the academic premise that because we can ask a question, there must be an answer.

Thus we can ask what the Framers meant when they gave Congress the power to regulate interstate and foreign commerce, and we emerge, reluctantly perhaps, with the reply that (Professor Crosskey to the contrary not-

---

[72] *Ibid.*, p. 329.

[73] Washington offered him the Chief Justiceship in 1796, but he declined; Charles Warren, *The Supreme Court in United States History* (Boston, 1947), Vol. 1, p. 139.

[74] He was a zealous prosecutor of seditions in the period 1798–1800; with Justice Samuel Chase, like himself an alleged "radical" at the time of the Constitutional Convention, Martin hunted down Jeffersonian heretics. See James M. Smith, *Freedom's Fetters* (Ithaca, 1956), pp. 342–43.

withstanding)[75] they may not have known what they meant, that there may not have been any semantic consensus. The Convention was not a seminar in analytic philosophy or linguistic analysis. Commerce was *commerce*—and if different interpretations of the word arose, later generations could worry about the problem of definition. The delegates were in a hurry to get a new government established; when definitional arguments arose, they characteristically took refuge in ambiguity. If different men voted for the same proposition for varying reasons, that was politics (and still is); if later generations were unsettled by this lack of precision, that would be their problem.

There was a good deal of definitional pluralism with respect to the problems the delegates did discuss, but when we move to the question of extrapolated intentions, we enter the realm of spiritualism. When men in our time, for instance, launch into elaborate talmudic exegesis to demonstrate that federal aid to parochial schools is (or is not) in accord with the intentions of the men who established the Republic and endorsed the Bill of Rights, they are engaging in historical Extra-Sensory Perception. (If one were to join this E. S. P. contingent for a minute, he might suggest that the hard-boiled politicians who wrote the Constitution and Bill of Rights would chuckle scornfully at such an invocation of authority: obviously a politician would chart his course on the intentions of the living, not of the dead, and count the number of Catholics in his constituency.)

The Constitution, then, was not an apotheosis of "constitutionalism," a triumph of architectonic genius; it was a patch-work sewn together under the pressure of both time and events by a group of extremely talented democratic politicians. They refused to attempt the establishment of a strong, centralized sovereignty on the principle of legislative supremacy for the excellent reason that the people would not accept it. They risked their political fortunes by opposing the established doctrines of state sovereignty because they were convinced that the existing system was leading to national impotence and probably foreign domination. For two years, they worked to get a convention established. For over three months, in what must have seemed to the faithful participants an endless process of give-and-take, they

[75] Crosskey in his sprawling *Politics and the Constitution* (Chicago, 1953), 2 vols., has developed with almost unbelievable zeal and intricacy the thesis that the Constitution *was* designed to establish a centralized unitary state, but that the political leadership of the Republic in its formative years betrayed this ideal and sold the pass to states'-rights. While he has unearthed some interesting newspaper articles and other material, it is impossible for me to accept his central proposition. Madison and the other delegates, with the exceptions discussed in the text *supra*, did *want* to diminish the power of the states and create a vigorous national government. But they were not fools, and were, I submit, under no illusions when they departed from Philadelphia that this end had been accomplished. The crux of my argument is that *political realities* forced them to water down their objectives and they settled, like the good politicians they were, for half a loaf. The basic difficulty with Crosskey's thesis is that he knows too much—he assumes that the Framers had a perfectly clear idea of the road they were taking; with a semantic machete he cuts blandly through all the confusion on the floor of the meeting to the *real* meanings. Thus, despite all his ornate research apparatus, there is a fundamentally nonempirical quality about Crosskey's work: at crucial points in the argument he falls back on a type of divination which can only be described as Kabbalistic. He may be right, for example, in stating (without any proof) that Richard Henry Lee did *not* write the "Letters from a Federal Farmer," but in this country spectral evidence has not been admissible since the Seventeenth Century.

reasoned, cajoled, threatened, and bargained amongst themselves. The result was a Constitution which the people, in fact, by democratic processes, did accept, and a new and far better national government was established.

Beginning with the inspired propaganda of Hamilton, Madison and Jay, the ideological build-up got under way. *The Federalist* had little impact on the ratification of the Constitution, except perhaps in New York, but this volume had enormous influence on the image of the Constitution in the minds of future generations, particularly on historians and political scientists who have an innate fondness for theoretical symmetry. Yet, while the shades of Locke and Montesquieu *may* have been hovering in the background, and the delegates *may* have been unconscious instruments of a transcendent *telos*, the careful observer of the day-to-day work of the Convention finds no over-arching principles. The "separation of powers" to him seems to be a by-product of suspicion, and "federalism" he views as a *pis aller*, as the farthest point the delegates felt they could go in the destruction of state power without themselves inviting repudiation.

To conclude, the Constitution was neither a victory for abstract theory nor a great practical success. Well over half a million men had to die on the battlefields of the Civil War before certain constitutional principles could be defined—a baleful consideration which is somehow overlooked in our customary tributes to the farsighted genius of the Framers and to the supposed American talent for "constitutionalism." The Constitution was, however, a vivid demonstration of effective democratic political action, and of the forging of a national elite which literally persuaded its countrymen to hoist themselves by their own boot straps. American pro-consuls would be wise not to translate the Constitution into Japanese, or Swahili, or treat it as a work of semi-Divine origin; but when students of comparative politics examine the process of nation-building in countries newly freed from colonial rule, they may find the American experience instructive as a classic example of the potentialities of a democratic elite.

Suggested Reading

The classic but now somewhat discredited work around which revolves so much of the debate over the Constitution is Charles A. Beard's *An Economic Interpretation of the Constitution of the United States** (1913), which still merits reading. Beard found class conflict at the roots of the movement for a new government and represented the Constitution as a conservative counter-revolution. His view was premised in part on a belief in the basic stability of the nation in the 1780s, a view that has been amplified by Merrill Jensen in *The New Nation: A History of the United States During the Confederation, 1781–1789** (1950), and criticized by Richard B. Morris in "The Confederation Period and the Historian," *William and Mary Quarterly*, 3rd Ser., XIII (April 1956), which should be consulted in conjunction with Morris' *The American Revolution Reconsidered** (1967). Jensen's *The Articles of Confederation: The Interpretation of the Social-Constitutional History of the American Revolution, 1774–1781** (1940), also in the same vein, is the best introduction to the history of the first American constitution.

Beard's thesis has been attacked along two lines: (1) that it was internally confused and, (2) that evidence does not bear it out. Among those who charge Beard with faulty argument and poor use of evidence is Robert E. Brown in *Charles Beard and the Constitution** (1956). Forrest McDonald in *We the People: The Economic Origins of the Constitution** (1958) argues conclusively that voting patterns in the Philadelphia Convention did not correlate with economic interests. Besides Jensen, Jackson T. Main in *The Anti-Federalists: Critics of the Constitution, 1781–1788** (1961), and E. James Ferguson in *The Power of the Purse: A History of American Public Finance, 1776–1790** (1961), essentially support the view of economic conflict, although in a different manner than Beard. Part III of Richard Hofstadter's *The Progressive Historians: Turner, Beard, Parrington** (1968) sums up and evaluates most of the controversy.

Much attention has recently been paid to the political and social thought of the leaders in the struggle over a new constitution. Next to Main's study of the antifederalists, the best review of their thought is Cecelia M. Kenyon's "Men of Little Faith: The Anti-Federalists on the Nature of Representative Government," *William and Mary Quarterly*, 3rd Ser., XII (January 1955), recently revised as an introduction to some antifederalist writings in Kenyon, ed., *The Antifederalists** (1966). The federalist ideology, as well as that of the antifederalists, is best explored throughout Wood's *Creation of the American Republic** (1970), not only in the selection reprinted here. Beard laid much emphasis on James Madison's tenth *Federalist* paper, which is discussed more fully and more accurately by Douglass Adair in "The Tenth Federalist Revisited," *William and Mary Quarterly*, 3rd Ser., VIII (January 1951).

On the convention itself, the best narrative is Clinton Rossiter's *1787: The Grand Convention* (1965). The important matter of the state constitutions forms the subject of Benjamin F. Wright's *Consensus and Continuity, 1776–1787** (1958). Robert A. Rutland explores the critical first ten amendments in *The Birth of the Bill of Rights, 1776–1781** (1962).

Some historians have recently tried, not altogether with success, to break out of the traditional formulations of the history of the Constitution. One such attempt is Stanley Elkins and Eric L. McKitrick's "The Founding Fathers: Young Men of the Revolution," *Political Science Quarterly*, LXXVI (June 1961). A provocative effort to go beyond Beard to an explicitly radical commentary on the constitutional conflict is the series of essays by Staughton Lynd, collected in *Class Conflict, Slavery, and the United States Constitution: Ten Essays** (1967).

* Also published in paperback edition.

Politics and Parties
in the Early Republic

President John Adams. Etching, printed and sold by
Amos Doolittle, August 14, 1799 (Library of Congress)

Republican Thought and the Political Violence of the 1790's

John R. Howe

When Americans have thought seriously about violence, they have normally offered two general explanations of its causes. One theory has it that social pathology lies at the roots of violent behavior, that an actual deprivation of physical and spiritual well-being or, as more recent analysts argue, a relative deprivation compared with surrounding and often better off groups impels people to rise in violent protest. The second explanation is that violence arises in ideology, that men rebel because of their commitment to a set of beliefs that explain what is wrong under existing conditions and what might be gained by overturning them.

John R. Howe of the University of Minnesota would have us understand instead that, under some conditions, violence may arise from ideological agreement and conformity. He insists in the essay that follows—an essay that is also noteworthy for dating the revolutionary era as the period from 1765 to 1800 —that an ideology must be examined for its psychological implications as well as its political content. In the revolutionary era there was a "republican set-of-mind" that all men of the 1790s claimed for their own and that seemed at the same time to drive men apart and set them at each other's throats. How, asks the author, are we to make sense of the frenzied discourse and envenomed politics of a generation that had just joined to oust British authority and establish a new republic with a new constitution? Acknowledging the clear differences of policy and program that separated Federalists from Jeffersonians, he believes that such differences fail to explain the tone and depth of the day's political rancor. This is rather to be understood as arising from consensus on basic principles.

In arguing thus, Howe nevertheless distinguishes himself from historians such as Daniel J. Boorstin (*The Genius of American Politics** [1953]), and Louis Hartz (*The Liberal Tradition in America** [1955]) who have explored, and in some cases celebrated, what they claim to be the nonideological character of American thought and politics which has enabled most Americans since the Revolution to remain, comparatively speaking, nonviolent and nonrevolutionary. Howe believes instead—and here he is in company with others—that the political and social thought generated by the revolutionary controversy of the 1760s and 1770s composed a genuine ideology with an integrity and pervasiveness as profound as other major modern ideologies. Moreover, this republican ideology had the capacity to drive men apart and incite to violence—under certain social and political conditions that Howe is at some pains in this essay to specify.

Howe's explanation of the political violence of the 1790s may not supplant more encompassing theories of violence, but it at least raises questions as to their adequacy. However, it still remains unclear precisely how the political violence of which he writes relates to destructive violence against life and property. By political violence does Howe mean violent behavior incited by political passion, or violent electoral combat during which scurrility and libel fill the air? This is a critical question, inasmuch as rhetorical violence (which, one might argue, has been the normal fare of American politics since the Revolution) may very well be a substitute for even more violent behavior.

Furthermore, when are "matters of social and

Republican Thought and the Political Violence of the 1790's. From *American Quarterly*, XIX (Summer 1967), 147–65. Copyright, 1967, Trustees of the University of Pennsylvania. Reprinted by permission of the publisher, the University of Pennsylvania, and the author, John R. Howe.

political ideology" not, in Howe's words, of "paramount importance"? What generation has not "divided sharply in its basic definition of social and political life—particularly over the degree of equality and the proper balance between liberty and authority believed desirable"? Howe himself begins to offer an answer to the question by pointing to the crisis-ridden history of the 1790s everywhere in the Western world. Crises, he believes, bring to the surface the hidden contradictions and illuminate the fragility and difficulties of many theories. Such an explanation helps also to clarify the decline in political violence in other eras—in this case, after Jefferson's election in 1800. But then ideology seems to lose much of its own independent explanatory power and becomes instead one other dimension of human life that is affected by changes in social and political circumstance.

*O*ne of the characteristics of the 1790s that strikes the attention even upon first glance and demands explanation, is the peculiarly violent character of American political life during these years.[1] Throughout our history, politics has not been a notably calm or gentlemanly affair. One need only recall some of the contests of the Jacksonian period, the Populist tactics of the late nineteenth century, the demagogy of Huey Long, or the rough and tumble of Joe McCarthy to realize this. But evidence abounds that the last decade of the eighteenth century constituted a time of peculiar emotion and intensity.

Indication of this is on every hand; for example, in the physical violence, both actual and threatened, which appeared with disturbing regularity. Note the forceful resistance within the several states to the authority of the central government. In Pennsylvania, the flash-point of civil disturbance seemed particularly low, as the Whiskey Rebellion and John Fries' brief rising attest.[2] Or recall the high emotions generated first by such domestic measures as Hamilton's financial program and reinforced by the complex of issues, both foreign and domestic, revolving around the French Revolution and the near-war with France: the Alien and Sedition Acts and the Provisional Army, designed in substantial measure to rid the Federalists of effective political opposition at home; the bands of Jeffersonian militia, formed in the various states and cities from Baltimore to Boston, armed and openly drill-

[1] This paper was first presented to the American Studies Group of Minnesota and the Dakotas, meeting at Minneapolis in the spring of 1966.

[2] Leland Baldwin, *Whiskey Rebels: The Story of a Frontier Uprising* (Pittsburgh, 1939); Harry M. Tinkcom, *Republicans and Federalists in Pennsylvania, 1790–1801* (Harrisburg, Pa., 1950); W. W. H. Davis, *The Fries Rebellion* (Doylestown, Pa., 1899).

ing, preparing to stand against the Federalist army.[3] During the critical days of 1798 and 1799, mobs roamed the streets of Philadelphia inspiring the President of the United States (as John Adams later recalled) to smuggle arms into his home secretly through the back streets.[4]

Events of this sort, however, constituted neither the only nor indeed the most impressive form of violence displayed during the decade. Even more pervasive and ominous was the intensity of spirit and attitude displayed on every hand—and in no place more emphatically than in the political rhetoric of the time. Throughout American political life—in the public press, in speeches, sermons, the private correspondence of individuals—there ran a spirit of intolerance and fearfulness that seems quite amazing. Foreign travelers commented frequently upon it. "The violence of opinion," noted one Frenchman, the "disgraceful and hateful appellations . . . mutually given by the individuals of the parties to each other" were indeed remarkable. Party spirit, he concluded, "infects the most respectable, as well as the meanest of men."[5]

Men in the midst of the political controversy noted the same thing. "You and I have formerly seen warm debates and high political passions," observed Jefferson to Edward Rutledge in 1797. "But gentlemen of different politics would then speak to each other, and separate the business of the Senate from that of society. It is not so now. Men who have been intimate all their lives, cross the streets to avoid meeting, and turn their heads another way, lest they should be obliged to touch their hats. This may do for young men for whom passion is an enjoyment," Jefferson concluded. "But it is afflicting to peaceable minds."[6] Virtually every political figure at some time or another expressed disgust at the abuse to which he was subjected. "I have no very ardent desire to be the butt of party malevolence," complained John Adams to his wife. "Having tasted of that cup, I find it bitter, nauseous, and unwholesome."[7]

Further evidence of the ferocity and passion of political attitudes abounds: in the editorializing of William Cobbett, Benjamin Bache and Philip Freneau; in the acidulous writings of Thomas Paine; in John Quincy Adams' *Publicola* articles. Perhaps most remarkable were the verbal attacks on the

[3] Descriptive accounts can be found, among other places, in Joseph Charles, *The Origins of the American Party System* (Williamsburg, Va., 1956); Stephen Kurtz, *The Presidency of John Adams: The Collapse of Federalism, 1795–1800* (Philadelphia, 1957); Dumas Malone, *Thomas Jefferson and the Ordeal of Liberty, 1791–1801* (Boston, 1962).

[4] John Adams to Thomas Jefferson, June 30, 1813, *The Adams-Jefferson Letters*, ed. Lester Cappon (2 vols.; Chapel Hill, N.C., 1959), II, 346–48. Witness, as well, the burning of John Jay in effigy, the stoning of Alexander Hamilton in the streets of New York and the physical scuffling within the halls of Congress, of which the exchange between Matthew Lyon and Roger Griswold, spittle for fire-tongs, was only the most sensational example. George Gibbs, *The Administrations of Washington and John Adams* (2 vols.; New York, 1846), I, 218–19. Charles Fraser, *Reminiscences of Charleston* (Charleston, S.C., 1854), p. 45. J. F. McLaughlin, *Matthew Lyon, The Hampden of Congress* (New York, 1900), pp. 226–30.

[5] Francis La Rouchefoucauld-Liancourt, *Travels through the United States of North America* (2 vols.; London, 1799), I, 470, 545; II, 514–18.

[6] Thomas Jefferson to Edward Rutledge, June 24, 1797, *The Writings of Thomas Jefferson*, ed. H. A. Washington (9 vols.; Philadelphia, 1871), IV, 191.

[7] John Adams to Abigail Adams, Jan. 20, 1796, *The Life and Works of John Adams*, ed. C. F. Adams (10 vols.; Boston, 1856), I, 485. See also Timothy Pickering to John Clarke, July 22, 1796, Pickering Papers, VI, 207, Massachusetts Historical Society.

venerable Washington which mid-decade brought. In Virginia, men drank the toast: "A speedy Death to General Washington"; and one anti-Federalist propagandist (probably Pennsylvania's John Beckley) composed a series of articles with the express purpose of proving Washington a common thief.[8] Few men (perhaps with the exception of William Cobbett) could surpass Thomas Paine for sheer ferocity of language. Attend to his public comment on Washington's retirement in 1796: "As to you, sir, treacherous in private friendship, and a hypocrite in public life; the world would be puzzled to decide, whether you are an apostate or an imposter; whether you have abandoned good principles, or whether you ever had any."[9]

As one reads the political literature of the time, much of it seems odd and amusing, contrived and exaggerated, heavily larded with satire.[10] But the satire contained venom; it appears amusing to us largely because our own rhetoric of abuse is simply different.

All in all, then, this seems a quite remarkable phenomenon, this brutality both of expression and behavior that marked American political life with such force during these years. Involved were more than disagreements over matters of public policy—though these were real enough. For the political battles of the 1790s were grounded upon a complete distrust of the motives and integrity, the honesty and intentions of one's political opponents. Men were quick to attribute to their enemies the darkest of purposes. Jefferson acknowledged in 1792 his grim distrust of Hamilton. "That I have utterly, in my private conversations, disapproved of the system of the Secretary of the Treasury," he told Washington, "I acknowledge and avow; and this was not merely a speculative difference. His system flowed from principles adverse to liberty, and was calculated to undermine and demolish the republic, by creating an influence of his department over the members of the legislature."[11] James Madison was even more suspicious of Federalist intentions than was Jefferson.[12] And Federalists were quick to find patterns of French Jacobinism in the Republican opposition at home. "I often think that the Jacobin faction will get the administration of our government into their hands ere long," worried Stephen Higginson; "foreign intriguers will unite with the disaffected and disappointed, with Seekers after places, with ambitious popular Demagogues, and the vicious and corrupt of every class; and the combined influence of all these . . . will prove too much for the feeble efforts of the other Citizens."[13] Similarly, John Quincy Adams warned in 1798 that "the antifederalism and servile devotion to a foreign power still

[8] Philip Marsh, "John Beckley: Mystery Man of the Early Jeffersonians," *Pennsylvania Magazine of History and Biography*, LXXII (1948), 59–60.

[9] Thomas Paine to George Washington, July 30, 1796, *The Writings of Thomas Paine*, ed. Moncure D. Conway (4 vols.; New York, 1906–8), III, 213–52.

[10] G. L. Roth, "Verse Satire on Faction, 1790–1794," *William and Mary Quarterly*, XVII (1960), 473–85.

[11] Thomas Jefferson to George Washington, Sept. 9, 1792, *The Writings of Thomas Jefferson*, ed. P. L. Ford (10 vols.; New York, 1892–99), VI, 101–2. See also Jefferson to Philip Mazzei, Apr. 24, 1796, *Writings of Thomas Jefferson*, ed. H. A. Washington, IV, 139–40.

[12] *Letters and Other Writings of James Madison* (4 vols.; Philadelphia, 1865), I, 535–36, 558.

[13] Stephen Higginson to Timothy Pickering, Aug. 29, 1795, "Letters of Stephen Higginson," American Historical Association, *Annual Report, 1896* (Washington, 1897), I, 794.

prevalent in the style of some of our newspapers is a fact that true Americans deplore. The proposal for establishing a Directory in America, like that of France, is no new thing."[14]

By the middle of the decade, American political life had reached the point where no genuine debate, no real dialogue was possible for there no longer existed the toleration of differences which debate requires. Instead there had developed an emotional and psychological climate in which stereotypes stood in the place of reality. In the eyes of Jeffersonians, Federalists became monarchists or aristocrats bent upon destroying America's republican experiment. And Jeffersonians became in Federalist minds social levelers and anarchists, proponents of mob rule. As Joseph Charles has observed, men believed that the primary danger during these years arose not from foreign invaders but from within, from "former comrades-in-arms or fellow legislators."[15] Over the entire decade there hung an ominous sense of crisis, of continuing emergency, of life lived at a turning point when fateful decisions were being made and enemies were poised to do the ultimate evil. "I think the present moment a very critical One with our Country," warned Stephen Higginson, "more so than any one that has passed. . . ."[16]

In sum, American political life during much of the 1790s was gross and distorted, characterized by heated exaggeration and haunted by conspiratorial fantasy. Events were viewed in apocalyptic terms with the very survival of republican liberty riding in the balance. Perhaps most remarkably of all, individuals who had not so long before cooperated closely in the struggle against England and even in the creation of a firmer continental government now found themselves mortal enemies, the bases of their earlier trust somehow worn away.

Now the violent temper of American political life during the 1790s has often been noted by political scientists and historians; indeed, one can scarcely write about these years without remarking upon it. But almost without exception, students of the period have assumed the phenomenon as given and not gone much beyond its description. Professor Marshall Smelser has made the most sustained effort at explanation. The key to an understanding of the decade he finds in differences of political and social principle, and in state and sectional rivalries.[17] Similar explanations are implicit in most other treatments of the period.[18]

[14] John Quincy Adams to Abigail Adams, May 16, 1795, *The Writings of John Quincy Adams*, ed. W. C. Ford (7 vols.; New York, 1913–17), I, 340 n. See also Oliver Wolcott Jr. to Oliver Wolcott, July 11, 1793, George Gibbs, *The Administrations of Washington and John Adams* (2 vols.; New York, 1846), I, 103.

[15] Charles, *Origins of the American Party System*, p. 6.

[16] Stephen Higginson to Timothy Pickering, Aug. 16, 1795, American Historical Association, *Annual Report, 1896* (1897), I, 792–93. See also Timothy Dwight, *The Duty of Americans in the Present Crisis* (New Haven, 1798); Jedediah Morse, *Sermon* (Boston, 1798).

[17] Marshall Smelser, "The Jacobin Phrenzy: Federalism and the Menace of Liberty, Equality, and Fraternity," *Review of Politics*, XIII (1951), 457–82; "The Federalist Period as an Age of Passion," *American Quarterly*, X (1958), 391–419; "Jacobin Phrenzy: The Menace of Monarchy, Plutocracy, and Anglophobia, 1789–1798," *Review of Politics*, XXI (1959), 239–58.

[18] For example, see Charles, *Origins of the American Party System;* Alexander DeConde, *Entangling Alliance; Politics and Diplomacy during the Administrations of George Washington* (Durham, N.C., 1958); John Miller, *The Federalist Era* (New

This argument is certainly to the point, for very real differences of principle and belief did distinguish Federalists from Jeffersonians. As I shall argue more fully in a moment, matters of social and political ideology were of paramount importance to Americans of the late eighteenth century; and this generation divided sharply in its basic definition of social and political life—particularly over the degree of equality and the proper balance between liberty and authority believed desirable. Certainly any explanation of political behavior during the 1790s must take these differences closely into account; nothing in this paper is intended to deny their importance.

I should like, however, to suggest a different approach to the problem; one which emphasizes not the points of opposition between Federalists and Jeffersonians but the peculiar pattern of attitudes and beliefs which most Americans, both Federalists and Jeffersonians, shared—that is, the dominant republican ideology of the time.

Historians have recently claimed that the American people throughout their history have been profoundly nonideological; that they are now and were equally so during the revolutionary era. Daniel Boorstin is at present perhaps the most articulate spokesman of this point of view. The American Revolution, he argues, was a "revolution without dogma." The revolutionary years "did not produce in America a single important treatise on political theory." In fact, during the latter part of the eighteenth century, "a political theory failed to be born." Indeed, Professor Boorstin insists, the revolutionary generation had no "need" for system-building, for their protests were simply "an affirmation of the tradition of British institutions." Missing was any "nationalist philosophy"; the American revolutionaries "were singularly free from most of the philosophical baggage of modern nationalism." In sum,

> the American Revolution was in a very special way conceived as both a vindication of the British past and an affirmation of an American future. The British past was contained in ancient and living institutions rather than in doctrines; and the American future was never to be contained in a theory. The Revolution was thus a prudential decision taken by men of principle rather than the affirmation of a theory. What British institutions meant did not need to be articulated; what America might mean was still to be discovered.[19]

Now this understanding of the revolutionary experience raises numerous

York, 1960). Variations, however, do appear. Charles Beard detects the basis of Federalist-Jeffersonian antagonism in an economic split between commercially oriented capitalists and agrarians (*The Economic Origins of Jeffersonian Democracy* [New York, 1915]). Louis Hartz, on the other hand, explains the tendency of Jeffersonians and Federalists to exaggerate the "monarchical" or "democratic" intentions of their opponents by their common confusion of American and European social systems (*The Liberal Tradition in America* [New York, 1955]). Richard Hofstadter, finally, has identified a "paranoid style" running throughout American political history, but pays only passing attention to the late eighteenth century ("The Paranoid Style of American Politics," *Harper's*, CCXXIX [Nov. 1964]), 47, passim and *Anti-Intellectualism in American Life* (New York, 1963).

[19] Daniel Boorstin, *The Genius of American Politics* (Chicago, 1953), pp. 66, 71, 73, 94–95.

difficulties. For one thing, the Revolution involved quite rash, even pre-sumptuous, decisions. More importantly, the revolutionary generation was profoundly dogmatic, was deeply fascinated with political ideology—the ideology of republicanism. This was a generation of Americans which, per-haps more than any other, viewed the world about them very much through the lens of political ideology, and which found meaning in their own ex-perience largely as republican theory explained it to them. This point emerges clearly enough from examination of early revolutionary tracts written during the 1760s and 1770s, the debates over the new constitutions constructed within the several states, argumentation over the proposed federal constitution, and the political wrangling of the 1790s. Recent studies of the Revolution's political ideology argue much the same point.[20]

The revolutionary break with England and the task of constructing new governments made the American people consciously, indeed self-consciously, republican in loyalty and belief. However lightly royal authority may have rested on the colonies prior to the Revolution, they had then been fully loyal to the idea of monarchy. The English constitutional system they had regarded as the wisest and most benevolent ever devised by man.

With independence, however, they turned their backs willfully not only upon the Crown but upon the whole conception of monarchical govern-ment and became aggressively, even compulsively, republican in orientation. Bernard Bailyn is quite right in suggesting that the break with England forced the American people to sit down and systematically explore political principles for the first time in at least half a century, to come to grips in-tellectually with the political systems which they had already developed, and to decide where their newly embraced republicanism would carry them in the future.[21] Indeed, the whole revolutionary era may be most profitably viewed as a continuing effort by the American people to decide what for them republicanism was to mean.

Republicanism, one quickly finds, is no easy concept to define. Certainly as used within the United States during the late eighteenth century the term remained supple and elusive. Most Americans agreed that republican-ism implied an absence of monarchy and English-like aristocracy, and the establishment of governments directly upon the authority and will of the people. But beyond this, concerning the details of republican political forms, agreement vanished. The concept of republicanism was obviously subject to a variety of readings when individuals as diverse as Alexander Hamilton and Thomas Jefferson, John Adams and John Taylor could each claim allegiance to it.

If the men of this generation differed, however, over the specifics of re-

---

[20] Bernard Bailyn, *Pamphlets of the American Revolution* (Cambridge, 1965) and "Political Experience and Enlightenment Ideas in Eighteenth Century America," *American Historical Review*, LXVII (1962), 339–51; Robert Taylor, *Western Massachu-setts in the Revolution* (Providence, 1954); Cecelia Kenyon, "Men of Little Faith: The Anti-Federalists on the Nature of Representative Government," *William and Mary Quarterly*, XII (1955), 1–43 and "Republicanism and Radicalism in the American Revo-lution: An Old-Fashioned Interpretation," *Wm. & Mary Quarterly*, XIX (1962), 153–82; Gordon Wood, "Rhetoric and Reality in the American Revolution," *Wm. & Mary Quarterly*, XXIII (1966), 3–32.

[21] Bailyn, *American Historical Review*, LXVII, 339–51.

publican theory, most of them shared a common body of assumptions about republican political society—the problems involved in its establishment and the prerequisites for its maintenance and survival—assumptions which together constituted what I would identify as a distinctive world-view, a republican set-of-mind encompassing certain patterns of thought common to both Federalists and Jeffersonians.[22]

One of the fundamental elements of this republican world-view, indeed the most important element for the purposes of this paper, was a widespread belief in the essential frailty and impermanence of republican governments. This notion was founded jointly on the historical assumption that republics had never lasted for long at any time in the past and on the psychological premise that the moral prerequisites of a republican order were difficult if not impossible to maintain.[23]

The men of the revolutionary generation were quite aware that history offered little promise of the success of their republican experiments. From their study of examples both ancient and modern, they knew that the life-span of most republics had been limited. Unlike the English republican theorists of the seventeenth century, they were impressed not with the possibilities of establishing permanent republican orders but with the difficulties of maintaining them at all.[24] Nowhere outside of the United States, with the exception of certain Swiss cantons and scattered European principalities, did republican government prevail by the time of the American Revolution. Of this single, brute historical fact the revolutionary generation was profoundly aware.

For one thing, republics had proved vulnerable historically to hostile threats from the outside, both direct military attack and more subtle forms of influence and subversion. The reasons for this were understood to be several. Republican government, at least by American definition, was described as limited government, carefully restricted in its powers and duties. Republican political society was characterized by a broad permissiveness, by

[22] Let me emphasize once again that I in no way mean to minimize the points of difference between Federalists and Jeffersonians (or to obscure the disagreements within these two political groupings). I agree fully with Joseph Charles that "the fundamental issue of the 1790's [indeed, I would add of the whole revolutionary era] was no other than what form of government and what type of society were to be produced in this country" (*Origins of the American Party System*, p. 7). What I wish to emphasize, however, are certain values and understandings held in common by most Americans during the revolutionary era which contributed importantly to the display of political violence that I am seeking to explain.

[23] The republican persuasion of the American revolutionary generation, compounded of their reading of classical and English republican theory and the writings of the Enlightenment, and of their own unique historical experience has not been adequately elaborated by students of the revolutionary era. Professor Bailyn has recently opened the problem anew; and Gordon Wood's forthcoming study of the political thought of the 1770s and 1780s will carry our understanding of the matter considerably further. For permission to read his manuscript ("The Creation of an American Polity in the Revolutionary Era") in dissertation form, I am most grateful. When completed, it promises to be the most provocative and illuminating study of late-eighteenth-century political thought yet produced.

[24] For the fullest discussion of seventeenth-century English republican thought (which eighteenth-century Americans read with great avidity), see Zera Fink, *The Classical Republicans* (Evanston, Ill., 1945).

the free play of individual liberty, by the absence of any powerful, dominating central authority; in short, by the minimizing of power (that is, the capacity of some individuals to coerce and control others).[25] Thus, republican governments proved particularly susceptible to outright attack (for by definition there should be no standing army, no military machine ready to discourage external foes) and to manipulation by outside powers (the people, after all, could be easily reached and their sensibilities played upon).

To be sure, certain circumstances rendered the United States less vulnerable in this regard than other republics had been: their isolated geographical location, the people's sense of identity with and loyalty to their governments and their willingness to stand in their governments' defense. (The recent struggle against England had demonstrated this.) But still the problem remained, as John Jay took pains to point out in the first numbers of *The Federalist*. In numbers two through five, he warned vigorously against the dangers the American states faced from adequate coordination of their relations with the outside world. The difficulties experienced under the Articles of Confederation, of course, he offered as evidence. Safety against foreign domination, he explained, depended on the states, "placing and continuing themselves in such a situation as not to *invite* hostility or insult. . . ." Nations, he reminded, make war "whenever they have a prospect of getting any thing from it." And such prospects were increased when a people seemed either incapable or unwilling to stand firmly in their own defense. Sensing the continuing suspicion of centralized government, Jay urged upon his readers the importance of learning from past experience and providing their central government with powers adequate to its own preservation. "Let us not forget," he concluded, "how much more easy it is to receive foreign fleets into our ports, and foreign armies into our country, than it is to persuade or compel them to depart."[26] In the late eighteenth century, the American republic stood virtually alone in an overwhelmingly nonrepublican world; in a world, in fact, dominated by monarchies and aristocracies to which the very concept of republicanism was anathema. And the burden of this loneliness was keenly felt.

More importantly, republican governments were deemed frail because of their tendency toward internal decay. If there was one thing upon which virtually the entire revolutionary generation could agree, it was the belief that republican governments were closely dependent upon a broad distribution of virtue among the people. Virtue was one of those marvelously vague yet crucially important concepts that dotted late-eighteenth-century moral and political thought. As used within the United States, it signified the personal virtues of industry, honesty, frugality and so forth. But more importantly, it meant as well a certain disinterestedness, a sense of public responsibility, a willingness to sacrifice personal interest if need be to the public good. Montesquieu had identified virtue as the animating spirit of republican societies; and the American people fully agreed. "The foundation of every government," explained John Adams, "is some principle or

[25] Bailyn, "The Transforming Radicalism of the Revolution," *Pamphlets of the American Revolution.*
[26] *The Federalist*, ed. E. M. Earle, Modern Library edition (New York, nd), pp. 18, 26.

passion in the minds of the people."[27] The informing principle of republican government was virtue. "The only foundation of a free constitution," Adams repeated, "is pure virtue. . . ."[28] To Mercy Warren, he made the same point: "public Virtue is the only Foundation of Republics." There had to be among the people a positive passion for the public good, superior to all private passions. In short, "the only reputable Principle and Doctrine must be that all things must give Way to the public."[29]

Countless Americans echoed Adams' refrain. The problem was that virtue constituted a frail reed upon which to lean. For while men were capable of virtuous behavior, they were also and more often creatures of passion, capable of the most selfish and malicious actions.[30] Americans liked to believe themselves more virtuous than other people, and American behavior during the active years of the revolutionary struggle had convinced many of them of this. The revolution had made extraordinary demands upon their public spiritedness, and they had proved themselves more than adequate to the test. The revolutionary trials had constituted a "furnace of affliction," John Adams believed, testing and refining the American character. The success of the struggle against England had demonstrated virtue's strength among the American people.[31]

By the 1790s, however, the revolutionary crisis was over and it was widely believed that after a period of exhausting moral discipline, men were reverting to their more normal selfish, ambitious and extravagant ways. Evidence was on every hand. The greatest dissolvants of virtue, both private and public, were commonly recognized to be wealth and luxury, for these excited the selfish passions, set men into jealous competition with each other and dimmed their sense of obligation to the larger society. As Thomas Paine remarked in *Common Sense*, "commerce diminishes the spirit both of patriotism and military defence. And history informs us, that the bravest achievements were always accomplished in the non-age of a nation. . . ."[32] "Youth is the seed-time of good habits," he repeated, "as well in nations as in individuals."[33] After an extended period of economic dislocation, brought on by the break with the empire and the war with England, the late 1780s and 1790s witnessed an impressive economic recovery.[34] And this returned prosperity raised powerful questions about American virtue.

[27] "Thoughts on Government," *Life and Works of John Adams*, ed. C. F. Adams, IV, 194.

[28] John Adams to Zabdiel Adams, June 21, 1776, *ibid.*, IX, 401.

[29] John Adams to Mercy Warren, Apr. 16, 1776, "Warren-Adams Letters," Massachusetts Historical Society, *Collections*, LXXII and LXXIII (Boston, 1917 and 1925), LXXII, 222–23.

[30] Concerning the views of human nature held generally by the revolutionary generation, see Clinton Rossiter, *The Political Thought of the Revolution* (New York, 1963), chap. 7 and Stow Persons, *American Minds* (New York, 1958), chap. 7.

[31] John Adams, Diary, July 16, 1786, *The Diary and Autobiography of John Adams*, ed. L. H. Butterfield (4 vols.; Cambridge, 1961), III, 194. See also John Adams to William Gordon, June 23, 1776, Adams Papers Microfilm, Reel 89.

[32] Thomas Paine, *Common Sense, The Political Writings of Thomas Paine* (2 vols.; New York, 1830), I, 53.

[33] *The Complete Writings of Thomas Paine*, ed. Philip Foner (2 vols.; New York, 1945), I, 45.

[34] Stuart Bruchey, *The Roots of American Economic Growth* (New York, 1965),

Throughout the revolutionary era, gloomy observers had wondered if American virtue would prove lasting. "The most virtuous states have become vicious," warned Theophilous Parsons. "The morals of all people, in all ages, have been shockingly corrupted. . . . Shall we alone boast an exemption from the general fate of mankind? Are our private and political virtues to be transmitted untainted from generation to generation, through a course of ages?"[35] Parsons and others had thought it doubtful. The dilemma was compounded by the belief that once begun, the erosion of virtue spiraled downward out of control. When the people grow lax, John Adams had explained, "their deceivers, betrayers, and destroyers press upon them so fast, that there is no resisting afterwards." Designing men forced their attack relentlessly.

> The people grow less steady, spirited, and virtuous, the seekers more numerous and more corrupt, and every day increases the circles of their dependents and expectants, until virtue, integrity, public spirit, simplicity, and frugality, become the objects of ridicule and scorn, and vanity, luxury, foppery, selfishness, meanness, and downright venality swallow up the whole society.[36]

Though written during an earlier year, this reflected the moral and political logic of an entire generation and was the logic of moral and political crisis.

America's economic recovery raised a further problem. Another postulate of republican theory, deriving most clearly from Harrington, declared that republican governments were suitable only for societies which enjoyed a broad distribution of property. "Power follows property," ran the maxim; and republican government presumed the broad distribution of political power among the people. The problem arose from the fact that as wealth increased, its tendency was to consolidate in the hands of a few, thus threatening both the economic and political bases of republicanism. John Taylor in his *Enquiry into the Principles and Tendency of Certain Public Measures* (1794) made precisely these points. "It is evident that exorbitant wealth constitutes the substance and danger of aristocracy," he wrote. "Money in a state of civilization is power. . . . A democratic republic is endangered by an immense disproportion in wealth."[37] J. F. Mercer of Maryland warned the federal Congress of the same thing. "A love and veneration of equality is the vital principle of free Governments," he declared. "It dies when the general wealth is thrown into a few hands."[38] Both Taylor and Mercer found this insidious tendency at work during the 1790s. Indeed Taylor's whole book was aimed directly at Hamilton's financial program and what Taylor conceived to be its effect in promoting the growth of a monied aristocracy. Mercer's comments were uttered in the context of a sustained

chap. 5; Douglass North, *Growth and Welfare in the American Past* (Englewood Cliffs, N.J., 1965), chaps. 4, 5. Other evidence, such as the wholesale price index, registration of patents and charters of incorporation supports this argument. *Historical Statistics of the United States* (Washington, D.C., 1965), pp. 232–33, 313.

[35] Rossiter, *Political Thought of the Revolution*, p. 211.

[36] *Ibid.*, pp. 209–10. For further elaboration on this point, see John Howe, *The Changing Political Thought of John Adams* (Princeton, 1966), chap. 5.

[37] John Taylor, *Enquiry into the Principles and Tendency of Certain Public Measures* (Philadelphia, 1794).

[38] *Annals of Congress, 1791–1793* (Washington, D.C., 1849), pp. 506 ff.

attack upon Hamiltonian "stock-jobbers." Not only Jeffersonians were disturbed about the matter, however; for by the 1790s, John Adams was
warning vigorously against the social and political dangers posed by a growing aristocracy of wealth.[39]

One further element in the dominant republican ideology of these years
contributed to the sense of vulnerability with which it seemed to be en-
veloped. This involved the problem of faction. Few notions were more
widely held by the revolutionary generation than the belief that "faction,"
the internal splintering of society into selfish and competing political groups,
was the chief enemy of republican political society. Republican government, as we have seen, depended essentially upon virtue's broad distribution
among the people. Faction was virtue's opposite; instead of an overriding
concern for the general good, faction presumed the "sacrifice of every national Interest and honour, to private and party Objects."[40] The disruptive
effects of faction increased as a society developed, as wealth increased, as
the people became more numerous and their interests more disparate. Gradually, differences of interest hardened into political divisions, with parties
contesting each other for power. Voters were organized and elections
manipulated, thus destroying both their political independence and integrity.
Permanent party organizations took root, organizations which cared more
for their own survival than for the society as a whole. In their resulting
struggle, passions were further aroused, internal divisions deepened and ultimately civil conflict was brought on. Such was the deadly spiral into which
republican governments too often fell.

Because of republicanism's vulnerability to faction, republican governments were widely believed suitable only for small geographic areas with
essentially homogeneous populations. Even during the 1770s and 1780s, when
the various states had set about constructing their own republican systems,
fears had been voiced that some of them (New York and Virginia were
frequently mentioned) were too large and diverse. The problem was infinitely compounded when talk began of a continental republic encompassing thousands of square miles, sharply opposed economic interests and
radically different ways of life. To attempt a republican government of
such dimensions was to fly in the face both of accepted republican theory
and the clearest lessons of historical experience. This, of course, is what the
anti-federalists repeatedly argued. "The idea of an uncompounded re-
publik," remarked one incredulous observer, "on an average of one thousand
miles in length, and eight hundred in breadth, and containing six millions of
white inhabitants all reduced to the same standard of morals, of habits, and
of laws, is in itself an absurdity, and contrary to the whole experience of
mankind."[41] The argument had a powerful effect upon the whole course
of constitutional debate, as is evidenced by the efforts of Madison and
Hamilton in *The Federalist* to answer it.

[39] Howe, *Changing Political Thought of John Adams*, pp. 140–41.
[40] John Adams to Thomas Jefferson, Nov. 15, 1813, *Adams-Jefferson Letters*, ed. Cappon, II, 401.
[41] The Agrippa Letters, *Essays on the Constitution of the United States*, ed. P. L. Ford
(Brooklyn, 1892), p. 65. Cecelia Kenyon points out how basic this was to the whole antifederalist position (*Wm. & Mary Quarterly*, XII, 12–13).

As the decade of the 1790s progressed, the dangers of faction grew ever more compelling. Acknowledging the political divisions which had sharpened during his second administration, Washington spoke directly to the problem in his Farewell Address, issuing a warning which echoed the fears of the whole society.[42] The latter half of the 1790s witnessed further intensification of the struggle between Federalists and Jeffersonians, bringing ever closer what seemed to many the ultimate danger: a division of the nation into two powerful political parties locked in deadly struggle with each other. In such a setting, it was easy to believe that the familiar pattern of republican collapse was threatening once more.

Again, republican governments were believed frail because liberty, which was peculiarly their product, was under constant attack from power. In this notion lay one of the basic political conceptualizations of the republican generation.[43] History was seen as comprising a continuing struggle between liberty and tyranny, between liberty and power. In this contest, power was the aggressive element, threatening relentlessly through the medium of ambitious and misguided men to encroach upon and narrow liberty's domain. The antagonism between the two was believed inevitable and endless, for by definition they stood unalterably opposed: liberty signifying law or right, the freedom of individuals to determine their own destiny, and power specifying dominion, force, the compulsion of some men by others. The whole course of recorded history displayed the ceaseless antagonism between the two, and America was not to escape the dilemma. "A fondness for power," Alexander Hamilton had declared knowingly, "is implanted in most men, and it is natural to abuse it when acquired."[44] With this belief, most Americans concurred. As Cecelia Kenyon has shown, the anti-federalists of 1787–88 were especially fearful of power's effects upon human nature.[45] But the federalists shared their fears.[46] The reality of this self-interested drive for power, as Professor Kenyon has shown, was "an attitude deeply imbedded and widely dispersed in the political consciousness of the age."[47]

The dilemma posed by power's continuing encroachment upon liberty's domain provided what Edmund Morgan has identified as "the great intellectual challenge" of the revolutionary era: that is, how to devise ways of checking the inevitable operation of depravity in men who sought and

[42] The uneasiness with which both Federalists and Jeffersonians defended their party activities during the 1790s illustrates the force of this pervasive fear. See Noble Cunningham, *The Jeffersonian Republicans: The Formation of Party Organization, 1789–1801* (Chapel Hill, N.C., 1954) and David Fischer, *The Revolution of American Conservatism: The Federalist Party in the Era of Jeffersonian Democracy* (New York, 1965).

[43] Bernard Bailyn has developed this point more fully in the introductory essay to his *Pamphlets of the American Revolution.* The following paragraph draws heavily upon his findings.

[44] *The Works of Alexander Hamilton*, ed. H. C. Lodge (9 vols.; New York, 1885–86), I, 114.

[45] Kenyon, *Wm. & Mary Quarterly*, XII, 13.

[46] See Madison's comments in *Federalist* no. 51.

[47] Kenyon, *Wm. & Mary Quarterly*, XII, 14.

wielded power.[48] The devices most widely, indeed almost universally invoked to achieve this goal were the separation and balance of powers within government.[49] The hope was that in these ways power could be kept under proper restraint by the prevention of its fatal accumulation in the hands of any single individual or group of men.

And yet problems immediately arose, for the American people were by no means in agreement concerning who or what was to be separated from or balanced against each other. Was the proper thing to separate executive, legislative and judicial powers? Or was the more important aim to balance the "constituted bodies" of society against each other: the rich versus the poor, the "aristocracy" versus the "democracy"? Throughout the revolutionary era, there remained substantial disagreement over what the notions of separation and balance really involved.[50]

Moreover, given power's restless and unrelenting character, it was hard to believe that any system of separation or balance could prove permanent. The only hope for liberty's preservation lay in posing power against itself, in setting at balance men's self-interests. And yet given the dynamic character of power's advance, it seemed unlikely that any system of counterpoise could be permanently maintained. This, indeed, was one of the most powerful arguments that critics of the balanced government, such as John Taylor, developed.

A still further consideration contributing to the prevailing belief in the frailty of republican government, one which underlay and informed the notions of virtue and power which we have already examined, involved the revolutionary generation's understanding of the cyclical character of history. In this view, history consisted of the gradual rise and fall of successive empires, each for a period dominating the world and then giving way to another.[51] Over the centuries, there had taken place a constant ebb and flow of ascendant nations, each rising to preeminence and then, after a period of supremacy, entering an era of decline and ultimately giving way to another. This process was often described in terms of a biological analogy; that is, political societies were believed to pursue a natural cycle of infancy, youth, maturity, old age and death. Every nation had unavoidably to pass through the full revolution. Governor James Bowdoin of Massachusetts described with particular clarity the law of cyclical development to which most Americans adhered. "It is very pleasing and instructive," Bowdoin declared,

---

[48] Edmund S. Morgan, "The American Revolution Considered as an Intellectual Movement," *Paths of American Thought*, eds. Arthur Schlesinger Jr. and Morton White (Boston, 1963), p. 26.

[49] John Adams was the most persistent spokesman for the idea of a balanced government, as his three-volume *Defense of the Constitutions of Government of the United States of America*, written during 1786 and 1787, attests.

[50] Francis Wilson, "The Mixed Constitution and the Separation of Powers," *Southwestern Social Science Quarterly*, XV (1934–35), 14–28; Benjamin Wright, "The Origins of the Separation of Powers in America," *Economica*, XIII (1933), 169–85; William Carpenter, "The Separation of Powers in the Eighteen Century," *American Political Science Review*, XXII (1928), 32–44.

[51] This conception has been described in Persons, *American Minds*, chap. 7.

to recur back to the early ages of mankind, and trace the progressive state of nations and empires, from infancy to maturity, to old age and dissolution:— to observe their origin, their growth and improvement . . . to observe the progress of the arts among them . . . to observe the rise and gradual advancement of civilization, of science, of wealth, elegance, and politeness, until they had obtained the summit of their greatness:—to observe at this period the principle of mortality, produced by affluence and luxury, beginning to operate in them . . . and finally terminating in their dissolution. . . . In fine—to observe, after this catastrophe, a new face of things; new kingdoms and empires rising upon the ruins of the old; all of them to undergo like changes, and to suffer a similar dissolution.[52]

Not only did empires wax and wane, but every phase in their life cycle of growth, maturity and decline could be traced out in the character and behavior of their people. David Tappan, Hollis Professor of Divinity at Harvard, explained how this was true. In the early stages of development, he observed, nations were inhabited by men "industrious and frugal, simple in their manners, just and kind in their intercourse, active and hardy, united and brave." Gradually, the practice of such virtues brought the people to a state of manly vigor. They matured and became flourishing in wealth and population, arts and arms. Once they reached a certain point, however, their manners began to change. Prosperity infected their morals, leading them into "pride and avarice, luxury and dissipation, idleness and sensuality, and too often into . . . impiety." These and kindred vices hastened their ruin.[53] A direct correlation existed, then, between national character and the stages of empire.

This cyclical theory of empire provided a perspective within which the events of the 1790s could be viewed, a way of reading their hidden—and ominous—meaning. For if it implied that in contrast to Europe, America was still young—an "Infant Country" it was frequently called—and on the ascent, it implied as well that eventually America must mature and enter its period of decline. And if this cyclical conception of moral and political change allowed success in the revolutionary contest to be interpreted as evidence of youthful virtue, it demanded that the moral decay, personal extravagance and internal bickering of the 1790s be accepted as indication that the American empire had reached its summit and begun its decline far more quickly than anticipated.

Few people, to be sure, jumped immediately to such a gloomy conclusion. The exhilaration of the Revolution continued to work its hopeful effects upon this generation of men. Even the most pessimistic individuals projected America's demise vaguely into the future; some refused to accept the theory's implications at all. Yet the logic of the argument could not be entirely escaped. At the least, it encouraged people to examine with minute care evidences of public and private morality and to search out patterns of significance in them. The doctrine, moreover, had a certain manic quality about it. During moments of hopefulness and success, it acted as a multiplier to expand the future's promise. And yet when the society became troubled,

[52] *Ibid.*, p. 123.
[53] *Ibid.*, p. 125.

when virtue seemed to fade, when internal divisions deepened and the sense of common purpose receded, the cyclical doctrine could work just as powerfully in the opposite direction to enhance the sense of crisis. For the logic of the doctrine was clear: a nation's position in its cycle could be clearly perceived in the behavior of its people. And the downward slide, once begun, could not be reversed.

Finally, this sense of the instability of republican government was heightened still further by the American people's understanding of the critical importance of the historical moment through which they were passing. Few generations of Americans have so self-consciously lived an historical epic as did these men of the late eighteenth century. Virtually every important action they took over a span of more than three decades seemed a turning point of great significance: their defense of basic liberties against England, the declaration of national independence, the establishment of republican governments in the several states, the creation of a new national constitution. This sense of historic grandeur carried into the 1790s. As the first administrative agents of the national government, they found themselves setting precedent with every decision made, every act taken: laying the bases of both foreign and domestic policy, determining by their decisions how the new government would function in practice, how popular or elitist it would be, what powers it would possess and what would be retained by the states. "Many which appear of little importance in themselves and at the beginning," explained Washington, "may have great and durable consequences from their having been established at the commencement of a new general government. It will be much easier," he continued, "to commence the administration, upon a well adjusted system, built on tenable grounds, than to correct errors or alter inconveniences after they shall have been confirmed by habits."[54] Only with this in mind does the intensity of emotion generated by the debate over the use of titles or over President Washington's levees become understandable.

In effect, the American people were carrying further during the 1790s a process upon which they had been embarked for several decades: that is, of defining what republicanism within the United States should in fact mean. Every decision they made loomed as fundamentally important. Their opportunity, they firmly believed, would come but once, and if mishandled could not be recovered. Given the cycle of empire, never again would the American be so competent for the task of understanding or defending liberty. The insidious pressures of power, the perpetual tendency of virtue to decay, the relentless historical cycle of nations promised that.

Their moment, then, was historically unique. "How few of the human race," noted John Adams in wonder, "have ever enjoyed the opportunity of making an election of government, more than of air, soil, or climate for themselves or their children." Throughout history, other peoples had suffered under governments imposed by accident or the wiles of ambitious men. Americans, however, now faced the prospect of modeling their governments anew, "of deliberating upon, and choosing the forms of govern-

---

[54] *The Writings of George Washington*, ed. John C. Fitzpatrick (39 vols.; Washington, D.C., 1931–44), XXX, 321.

ment under which they should live."[55] To blunder in the face of such opportunity would be to compound their disaster.

Moreover, they firmly believed that upon the success of their venture hung the fate of republicanism not only for America but the entire world. "Let us remember that we form a government for millions not yet in existence," reminded one anxious soul. "I have not the act of divination. In the course of four or five hundred years, I do not know how it will work."[56] "I consider the successful administration of the general Government as an object of almost infinite consequence to the present and future happiness of the citizens of the United States," acknowledged Washington.[57]

And yet the success of this momentous undertaking was by no means assured. As late as the 1790s, the American people were painfully aware that theirs was still a political society in process of change; that their political institutions were new, lacking the habit of regularity which only long establishment could provide; that their republican faith was still undergoing definition. The whole venture, as witnesses repeatedly pointed out, remained very much an "experiment." They were embarked directly upon the task of "determining the national character"; of "fixing our national character," as one Jeffersonian remarked, and "determining whether republicanism or aristocracy [the Federalists would say democracy]" would prevail.[58] The society remained malleable, its understanding of "true" republican principles not yet firmly developed, the design of its social and political institutions still unclear.

In sum, the Americans of this generation found themselves living on a balance, at a moment in history given to few men, when decisions they made would determine the whole future of mankind. Surely their reading of their own historic importance was overdrawn; but it seemed not in the least so to them. And altogether it posed at once an exhilarating and yet terrifying responsibility.

These, then, are some of the attitudes, some of the peculiar understandings which informed this republican generation. It was, I submit, a peculiarly volatile and crisis-ridden ideology, one with little resilience, little margin for error, little tradition of success behind it, and one that was vulnerable both psychologically and historically. Within this context, politics was a deadly business, with little room for optimism or leniency, little reason to expect the best rather than suspect the worst of one's political enemies. And in the end, this republican set of mind goes far to make understandable the disturbing violence of American political life during the 1790s.

[55] "Thoughts on Government," *The Life and Works of John Adams*, ed. C. F. Adams, IV, 200.

[56] *Debates in the Several State Conventions on the Adoption of the Federal Constitution*, ed. Jonathan Elliot (2nd ed.; 5 vols.; Philadelphia, 1861), IV, 215.

[57] *The Writings of George Washington*, ed. Fitzpatrick, XXX, 510.

[58] Charles, *Origins of the American Party System*, p. 7, 7n.

The Transit of Power

Richard Hofstadter

Americans take their two-party system so much for granted that we are likely to forget that, like other human institutions, it too has its history. Political scientists remind us that a two-party system is neither inevitable nor essential in the governing of a modern state. Historians, therefore, have recently turned their attention to accounting for the development of party systems in the United States, emphasizing such matters as ideology, party structure, legal rules, and social roles. The late Richard Hofstadter of Columbia University, in his *Idea of a Party System* (1969), asks us also to acknowledge that the very conception of legitimate opposition, from which party competition evolves, has a history inextricably interwoven with the evolution of parties themselves.

In the following selections from that book, Hofstadter is characteristically concerned with the interface between ideas and institutions. How was it, he asks, that the men of the early republic who so feared factional disharmony and the "corruptions" of party came to pioneer in the creation of American party politics? To those acquainted with Hofstadter's historical writings it is no surprise to find his answer filled with the ironies he delighted in unearthing. The first political party in history was headed by a man who wished nothing more than to merge all parties in his ceaseless quest for unanimity. What Jefferson liked to call the "revolution" of 1800 turned out in fact to be a remarkably mild transition between administrations closely bounded by political reality and ideological consensus. Indeed, in Hofstadter's account men who sound as if they are engaged in civil war are actually effecting a peaceful transit of power and establishing an enduring constitutional principle that some nations never succeed in establishing: that a change of government—or, as Americans might better put it, of administration—shall not require a change of constitution.

Thus Hofstadter's underlying theme is that of accommodation. What impresses him is not only the political acumen of so many of the men he examines but also the range of their agreement. Their individual personalities, the nature of existing political institutions, their sense of the fragility of republican society, their shared determination to make the new government work—these and other factors kept their differences within bounds.

Hofstadter was one of a number of American historians writing during the 1950s and 1960s who struggled to make sense of both the ideas and predispositions that most Americans seem to share and the differences that drive them apart. Here he emphasizes the rational understandings that often underlie irrational discourse. The problem remains, however, of explaining the frenzied rhetoric itself; in fact, one wonders whether it was the accommodationist thrust of American political thought or the inability of the disappointed to give their arguments greater relevance and appeal that prevented greater violence. What one misses in this account of Jefferson's taking of command is a sense of the social bases of politics. Under what social conditions do accommodationist politics triumph? Do such politics exist only when social circumstances are agreeable and placid? Or if, as Hofstadter implies, the politics of the time were somehow isolated from the social issues that concern any society, were they in any sense "real" politics?

The Transit of Power. By Richard Hofstadter from *The Idea of a Party System: The Rise of Legitimate Opposition in the United States* (1969), pp. 128–40, 150–69. Originally published by the University of California Press; reprinted by permission of The Regents of the University of California.

II

The election of 1800 was an anomalous election in a double sense: first, in that it was the first election in modern history which, by popular decision, resulted in the quiet and peaceful transition of national power from the hands of one of two embattled parties to another; second, in that it was the first of only two American elections in which, since no candidate had a majority in the Electoral College, the outcome had to be decided in the House of Representatives. The superficial circumstances of the election are quite familiar: the Constitution, written without party tickets in mind, arranged for no separate designation of presidential and vice-presidential candidates before the adoption of the Twelfth Amendment in 1804; in consequence of a lapse in party planning, the two Republican candidates, Jefferson and Burr, turned up with the same number of electoral votes, though it was clearly understood throughout the party that the Virginian was head of the ticket; when the election went to the House, where the states voted as units, the Federalists fell heir to the unhappy luxury of choosing between the two leading Republicans. The resolution of the problem is also a familiar story: how the great majority of the Federalist leaders preferred Burr; how Hamilton repeatedly pleaded that they turn from this dangerous adventurer to the more certain and predictable, as well as endurable, limitations of Jefferson; and how, in the end, under the leadership of James A. Bayard of Delaware, who swallowed Jefferson, as he wrote Adams, "so . . . as not to hazard the Constitution," the necessary portion of them abstained from voting and thus accepted Jefferson, only after an understanding, very delicate and proper and quite indirect, about the character of Jefferson's intentions had been arrived at.[1]

Historians have spent so much effort to unravel the details of this complex election, and in particular to evaluate Burr's role and the character of the tenuous understanding or "bargain" upon which Jefferson's election depended, that some aspects of the situation which we may regard as equally significant have not yet had their due. Since the badly needed definitive account of this election remains to be written, it is necessary to proceed with caution, but it is certainly possible to examine in this event the calculations by which the two party system in the United States took a long and decisive step forward. Here were the Federalists, many of whom, not so many months earlier, had been hoping to finish off the opposition under the pressure of a war with France and through the agency of the Alien and Sedition Acts, now quietly acquiescing in the decision of a few of their fellow partisans to put into office a man whom they had long been portraying as an atheist, a French fanatic, a libertine, a visionary, and a political incompetent. The circumstances give us a rare opportunity to look at the minds of a set of governmental leaders as they faced the loss of power, and

[1] Morton Borden, *The Federalism of James A. Bayard* (1955), 97; I find this the most illuminating of the accounts of this election. See also Cunningham, *The Jeffersonian Republicans*, 239–248, and John S. Pancake, "Aaron Burr: Would-Be Usurper," *William and Mary Quarterly*, 8 (1951), 204–213.

at the interplay between the two sides as they groped for an accommodation.

Abstractly speaking, the choices opened to a defeated governmental party in a new federally organized country where the practice of legitimate opposition is still not wholly certain and where the incoming foes are profoundly suspect are three: *coup d'état,* disunion, or a resigned acceptance of their new operational status. Here we may begin by pointing to the central significance of something that did not happen: *violent resistance was never, at any time, discussed.* Neither was disunion discussed as a serious immediate possibility in 1801, though three years later a small but ineffectual faction of New England Federalists would lay abortive plans to bring it about. Something in the character of the American system was at work to unleash violent language but to inhibit violent solutions, and to reconcile the Federalists to the control of the government by a party they suspected of deep hostility to the Constitution. Somehow we must find a way to explain the rapid shift from the Dionysian rhetoric of American politics during the impassioned years 1795 to 1799[2] to the Apollonian political solution of 1800–1801.

What is observable in a wide range of Federalist letters and memoirs is a basic predisposition among the great majority of them to accept a defeat, fairly administered, even in 1800 before that defeat was a certainty. The whole historical experience of America, as well as the temperament of their class, argued against extreme or violent measures. They were conservative men, and extreme responses that might risk what they sometimes called "the public tranquility" were not to their way of thinking. Even the instrumentalities of force were lacking in the American environment; and a class of intensely political generals, the elite corps of any *coup d'état,* was impressively absent from the American scene.[3] Most Federalists were realistic enough to see that they were not only divided but outvoted; and none of their fulminations against democracy should blind us to the fact that they did not fancy trying to rule without a decent public mandate. Again, the federal system took some of the steam out of their frustration; in New England, where partisan feeling ran strongest among them, the Federalists were, for the time being, still in control of their own affairs at the state

[2] And which would be re-echoed by many in 1803 and after. Although Federalists did not discuss violent resistance, some Republicans talked of such action if the Federalists, in plain violation of the popular will, persisted in snatching the prize from Jefferson. I trust it will be clear that the following discussion is not an attempt to praise the Federalists for their restraint but to pose the problem of their adaptation to the transit of power.

[3] Madison remarked pointedly upon this. Writing to Jefferson February 28, 1801, he said that he had not thought that the "phalanx" of Federalists in the House would hold out against their fellow partisans in the country at large, "and without any military force to abet usurpation. How fortunate that the latter has been withheld: and what a lesson to America and the world is given by the efficacy of the public will where there is no army to be turned against it." *Writings,* VI, 418. Many years afterward, in 1830, Madison still saw the acquiescence of defeated parties in elections as hinging in good part on the absence of force. "As long as the country shall be exempt fom a military force powerful in itself and combined with a powerful faction, liberty and peace will find safeguards in the elective resource and the spirit of people," *Writings,* IX, 370.

level. They had no reason to believe that they would be politically suppressed, and some of them thought that before very long the incompetence
of the Republicans would swing the balance back to their side. Finally, the
nature of the political parties and of political careers in America took some
of the sting out of defeat.

The parties, for all the intensity of their passions and the bombast of their
rhetoric, were new, their organization was rudimentary, and in some parts
of the country partisan loyalties were thinner and more fragile than they
might seem. No one, as Paul Goodman has remarked, had been born a
Federalist or a Republican, and time was to show that switches from side to
side were by no means unthinkable. Also, for many of the top leaders,
politics was far from an exclusive concern. Political leaders were merchants,
planters, lawyers, men of affairs with wide interests and with much capacity for taking pleasure in their private lives. Many of the best of them
looked upon politics as a duty and not a livelihood or a pleasure. "To Bayard," his biographer pointedly observes, "the Senate was a job and not a
career, a position of dignity and respectability rather than a battleground
under observation by the nation." After the first flush of nationalist enthusiasm under Washington, it had become increasingly difficult to find
men willing to accept positions of high responsibility and honor. Offices
were refused or resigned with astonishing frequency, and Jefferson had to
offer the Secretaryship of the Navy on five occasions to four different men
before he had an acceptance. Professional politicians were, to be sure,
emerging—fewer of them among the Federalists than among their foes—but
they were somewhat looked down upon by men of eminence. And professional officeholders were the acknowledged dregs of the political world.[4]

To some degree, the option between Jefferson and Burr distracted the
Federalists from facing the full significance of their loss in 1800 and eased
them into it by stages. The prevailing Federalist preference for Burr, who
was widely regarded as an adventurer without fixed principles and who was
even seen by many as being preferable to Jefferson precisely on this count,
may certainly argue for a spirit of desperation. But here again the party was
divided, and the circumstances of the affair are significant for a reading of
Federalist temperature. What the Federalist leaders had to ponder was not
simply the character of Burr as against that of Jefferson but also whether
there was enough left of the spirit of concord or patriotism after the rancor
of the preceding years to warrant thinking that they could endure Jefferson's possession of power. While it is an interesting question whether there
was a firm, formally concluded "bargain" between the Virginian and some
of his enemies—a question answered by most writers in the negative—it is
still more interesting to note what particular assurances Hamilton suggested
as necessary and that Bayard sought for when Jefferson was subtly and in-

[4] On Bayard, see Borden, *op. cit.*, 159; for some shrewd observations upon the nature
of the political career and party loyalties, see Paul Goodman, "The First American
Party System," in W. N. Chambers and W. D. Burnham, eds., *The American Party Systems: Stages of Development* (1967), especially, 85–89. For some cautions about the
significance of partisan rhetoric, see Noble Cunningham, Jr., *The Jeffersonian Republicans*, 227–229.

directly sounded about his intentions. Hamilton's advice and Bayard's terms shed much light on the practical differences that now separated the parties, and upon the calculations some Federalists were making about the future.

First, as to the terms: Bayard at one point approached a friend of Jefferson suggesting that if certain points of concord could be arrived at, three decisive states would withdraw their opposition to Jefferson's election. The points were enumerated: "First, . . . the subject of the public credit; secondly, the maintenance of the naval system; and lastly, that subordinate public officers employed only in the execution of details established by law shall not be removed from office on the ground of their political character, nor without complaint against their conduct." These points were later reiterated to another intimate of Jefferson's, General Samuel Smith, who then purported to have won Jefferson's assent to them, and so gained Bayard's consent. On the second occasion the names of some of Bayard's friends were submitted, to give substance as it were, to the point about officeholders, and specific assurances involving them were offered in return. What is perhaps most interesting is that Bayard's conditions, in omitting a neutrality policy, deviate on only one count from those Hamilton proposed that the Federalists seek for: "the maintenance of the present system, especially in the cardinal articles of public credit—a navy, neutrality." Later Hamilton added patronage: "The preservation in office of our friends, except in the great departments, in respect to which and in future appointments he ought to be at liberty to appoint his friends."[5]

One is at first disposed to conclude that despite their public ravings about Monocrats and Jacobins, American politicians were beginning to behave like politicians. The patronage question in particular argues for this point of view. But it should be realized too that for the Federalists in 1801 the question, now raised for the first time in national politics, whether an incoming party would make a wholesale sweep of public offices and install everywhere its own partisans, involved more than solicitude for the jobs and livelihoods of their friends. Jefferson's intentions as to removals and replacements were the object of a good deal of discussion in Federalist letters of 1800–1801, whose tenor suggests that, aside from the concern for loaves and fishes which was not a negligible thing for lesser party figures, the patronage issue had two further points of significance. It was, in the first instance, a symbolic matter of decisive importance: if the Federalist followers were to be swept out of all the lesser offices, the act would be a declaration of partisan warfare suggesting that the two parties were incapable of governing in concert, and that the desire of the Jeffersonians to decide the nation's policies was coupled with a gratuitous desire to retaliate and humiliate. A policy of proscription would put an end to the harmony and balance they considered essential to the republican order. Secondly, one must reckon with the Federalists' conviction that by far the larger portion of honest and able men, competent for the public

---

[5] *Ibid.*, 91; Broadus Mitchell, *Alexander Hamilton*, II, 490, 744. Fisher Ames, urging a Federalist bargain with Burr, wanted a clear understanding: that the country be neither "sold, given or lent to France; peace with England, credit and banks left alone"; and that trade "not be tampered with—nor regulated Madison-wise." Welch, *Sedgwick,* 223.

business, were in their ranks; and that hence a wholesale displacement of such men might, quite aside from differences on policies, reduce the level of civic competence to a point at which the new government, established at so much effort and sacrifice, would be ruined. As Fisher Ames put it: "The success of governments depends on the selection of the men who administer them. It seems as if the ruling system would rob the country of all chance, by excluding the only classes proper to make the selection from."[6]

Some historians have been at pains to establish that there was in fact no explicit understanding and hence no "corrupt" bargain between Jefferson and the Federalists; and certainly the way in which he was sounded out through an intermediary, who took it upon himself to tender the desired assurances after exploring Jefferson's mind, leaves Jefferson in the clear. Yet such efforts to acquit our political heroes seem to me somewhat misplaced; we would probably have reason to think less of them if they had been incapable of arriving at some kind of understanding. After all, Jefferson was morally and constitutionally entitled to the presidency, and it was the part of statesmanship, if not indeed of wisdom and morality, to offer the Federalists some assurances about his intentions. The survival of the constitutional system was at stake, and it had become necessary for both sides, in the spirit of practical men, to step back from their partisan embroilments, take a larger look at what they were doing, and try once again to make a fresh estimate of each other.

In this respect, Hamilton's appraisal of Jefferson, expressed in the course of his efforts to persuade other Federalists to accept him rather than choose Burr, becomes most illuminating. It was not many months earlier that Hamilton, trying to persuade Governor John Jay to get New York's electoral procedures changed to increase the chances of the Federalists in the forthcoming presidential election, warned Jay once again that the Republican party was a subversive and revolutionary party, and urged that his "scruples of delicacy and propriety" be set aside: "They ought not to hinder the taking of a *legal* and *constitutional step*, to prevent an *atheist* in Religion and a fanatic in politics from getting possession of the helm of the State."[7]

But in January 1801, faced with the alternative of Burr, Hamilton was pushing this atheist and fanatic as a much safer prospective president and

---

[6] Gibbs, *Memoirs*, II, 457; cf. also 402; cf. Samuel Stanhope Smith: "Good men will be obliged to retire from public affairs; blockheads and villains will soon hold the rein and scourge over us—may the *patricians* yet be able to save the republic, when the *tribunes* shall have urged it to the brink of ruin!" Walter Fee, *The Transition from Aristocracy to Democracy in New Jersey* (1933), 122–123. Cf. Henry M. Wagstaff, ed., "The Harris Letters," *James Sprunt Historical Publications* 14 (1916), 71; H. R. Warfel, ed., *Letters of Noah Webster* (1953), 244; C. R. King, *Life and Correspondence of Rufus King*, III, 353, 409, 475; Henry M. Wagstaff, ed., *The Papers of John Steele*, I, (1924), 215, 445.

[7] Hamilton to Jay, May 7, 1800, H. P. Johnston, *Correspondence and Public Papers of John Jay* (1893), IV, 271. With some men scruple played a part in these proceedings. What Hamilton was proposing—to have the state legislature change the mode of choosing electors so that the people would choose them by districts—corresponded to what was being done elsewhere to their advantage by the Republicans, but Jay would have none of it. With one eye on his scruples, and possibly the other on the verdict of history, he endorsed this letter, "Proposing a measure for party purposes, which I think it would not become me to adopt," and filed it away among his papers. *Ibid.*, 271 n.

portraying him in quite different terms. "I admit," he wrote to Bayard in a remarkable letter,

> that his politics are tinctured with fanaticism; that he is too much in earnest with his democracy; that he has been a mischievous enemy to the principal measures of our past administration; that he is crafty and persevering in his objects; that he is not scrupulous about the means of success, nor very mindful of truth, and that he is a contemptible hypocrite—

thus far as damaging an estimate as any Burrite Federalist could have wished. But, Hamilton went on, Jefferson was really not an enemy to the power of the Executive (this would prove all too true) or an advocate of putting all the powers of government in the House of Representatives. Once he found himself by way of inheriting the executive office, he would be "solicitous to come into the possession of a good estate." And then, prefatory to a long and devastating estimate of Burr's character and talents, there occurs the strategic and prophetic appraisal of Jefferson:

> Nor is it true that Jefferson is zealot enough to do anything in pursuance of his principles, which will contravene his popularity or his interest. He is as likely as any man I know to temporize; to calculate what will be likely to promote his own reputation and advantage, and the probable result of such a temper is the preservation of systems, though originally opposed, which being once established, could not be overturned without danger to the person who did it. To my mind, a true estimate of Mr. Jefferson's character warrants the expectation of a temporizing, rather than a violent system.

Even Jefferson's predilection for France was based more upon the popularity of France in America than upon his own sentiment, and it would cool when that popularity waned. "Add to this, that there is no fair reason to suppose him capable of being corrupted, which is a security that he will not go beyond certain limits." After his scathing dissertation upon Burr, Hamilton reverted to some partisan considerations: if the Republicans got Jefferson, they would be responsible for him; but if the Federalists should install Burr, "they adopt him, and become answerable for him." Moreover, he would doubtless win over many of them, "and the federalists will become a disorganized and contemptible party."[8] Finally, Hamilton repeated to several correspondents his conviction that Burr could not be relied upon to keep any commitment he might make to the Federalists.

In repeated letters to Bayard and others deemed open to his waning influence, Hamilton hammered away at the contrast he had laid down between the temporizing, politic Jefferson, and the dangerous Burr, that "embryo Caesar," "the Catiline of America," the "most unfit man in the United States for the office of President"—a man who, he told Oliver Wolcott in a significant phrase, would call to his side "rogues of all parties, to overrule the good men of all parties."[9] Jefferson would never know how much he owed to Burr for having provided such a chiaroscuro, for throwing him into such high and acceptable relief, if only to a decisive minority of Federalists.

---

[8] Hamilton to Bayard, January 16, 1801, *Works*, J. C. Hamilton ed., (1851), VI, 419–424; the letter is misdated and out of place here, *ibid.*, VI, 520.

[9] For Hamilton's letters on Burr and Jefferson, *ibid.*, VI, 486, 487–489, 495, 497, 499–501, 520–521.

But Hamilton's sense of the situation, his implicit recognition that there were, after all, good men on both sides, casts a powerful shaft of light into the roiled and murky bottoms of Federalist rhetoric. There are moments of supreme illumination in history when the depth of men's belief in their own partisan gabble has to be submitted at last to the rigorous test of practical decision. For about eight years the Federalists had been denouncing Jefferson and his party, and in the last few years their accusations had mounted to the point at which the leader of the opposition, the Vice President of the United States, had been charged with Jacobinism, atheism, fanaticism, unscrupulousness, wanton folly, incompetence, personal treachery, and political treason. Now this atheist in religion and fanatic in politics was to be quietly installed in the new White House, by courtesy of a handful of Federalist Congressmen, and though there was still hardly a man in the Federalist party who trusted him, there was also not a man to raise a hand against him. The Federalists, having failed to install Burr, preferred to risk Jefferson rather than to risk the constitutional system that had been so laboriously built and launched. . . .[10]

IV

It was characteristic of Jefferson that he perceived the keen political conflict of the years just preceding his election not as an opportunity but as a difficulty. Thanks to the efforts both of his detractors and his admirers, his historical reputation has caused us to misread him. In the Federalist tradition, later taken up by so many historians, he was a theorist, a visionary, a radical; and American liberals have praised him for the same qualities the Federalists

[10] The contest of 1800–1801 led to a decisive step, in the form of the Twelfth Amendment, toward constitutional recognition of the role played by parties in the federal government. After 1796, when the election left Jefferson as Adams's Vice President, the Federalists had shown some interest, though without effect, in an electoral change that would give separate designation to the presidential and vice-presidential candidates of each party. After the harrowing experience of 1801, the Republicans took up the idea, and now the Federalists opposed it. By 1803 the Republicans had achieved a sufficiently strong majority to win the required two-thirds vote (22 to 10 in the Senate, 83 to 42 in the House) to adopt the Twelfth Amendment and send it to the states. It was quickly ratified by the necessary number and declared in force by September 25, 1804, in time to govern the presidential election of that year. Resistance in Congress from Federalists was strong—only three Representatives from New England voted for it—and the legislatures of Massachusetts, Connecticut, and Delaware refused to ratify it. "The plan of this amendment," said one Federalist manifesto, "is to bury New England in oblivion and put the reins of Government into the hands of Virginia forever. They, the Democrats, have seized on a moment of delirious enthusiasm to make a dangerous inroad on the Constitution and to prostrate the only mound capable of resisting the headlong influence of the great States and preserving the independence and safety of the small ones." Herman V. Ames, *The Proposed Amendments to the Constitution of the United States during the First Century of Its History*, *Annual Report* of the American Historical Association for 1896 (1897), II, 79 n. One of the most interesting arguments against the Twelfth Amendment was made by Senator James Hillhouse of Connecticut, who wanted to assure that the President and Vice President would indeed always be of different parties "to check and preserve in temper the over-heated zeal of party." "If we cannot destroy party," he urged, "we ought to place every check upon it." Lolabel House, *A Study of the Twelfth Amendment of the Constitution of the United States* (1901), 50. A modern study of the origins of the Twelfth Amendment is badly needed.

abhorred. The modern liberal mind has been bemused by his remarks about the value of a little rebellion now and then, or watering the tree of liberty with the blood of tyrants, or having a complete constitutional revision every twenty or thirty years. But Jefferson's more provocative utterances, it has been too little noticed, were in his private correspondence. His public statements and actions were colored by a relative caution and timidity that reveal a circumspect and calculating mind—or, as so many of his contemporary foes believed, a guileful one. He was not enraptured by the drama of unrestrained political conflict; and with the very important exception of some of his views on foreign policy and war, his approach to public policy was far from utopian. He did not look forward to a vigorously innovative administration—he had seen enough of that. The most stunning achievement of his presidential years, the Louisiana Purchase, was an accident, the outcome of the collapse of Napoleon's ambitions for a Caribbean empire—the inadvertent gift of Toussaint L'Ouverture and the blacks of Haiti to this slaveholding country. Its most stunning disaster was the embargo, and the embargo itself came from Jefferson's penchant, here misapplied, for avoiding conflict. His was, as Hamilton put it in his tardy burst of pragmatic insight, a temporizing and not a violent disposition.

This disposition dictated an initial strategy of conciliation toward the Federalists, which led to a basic acceptance of the Hamiltonian fiscal system, including even the bank, to a patronage policy which Jefferson considered to be fair and compromising and hoped would appease moderate Federalists, and to an early attempt to pursue neutrality and to eschew aggravating signs of that Francophilia and Anglophobia with which the Federalists so obsessively and hyperbolically charged him. But for our concern, it is particularly important to understand that in Jefferson's mind conciliation was not a way of arriving at coexistence or of accommodating a two-party system, but a technique of absorption: he proposed to win over the major part of the amenable Federalists, leaving the intractables an impotent minority faction rather than a full-fledged opposition party. His strategy, which aimed, once again, at a party to end parties, formed another chapter in the quest for unanimity.

"The symptoms of a coalition of parties give me infinite pleasure," wrote Jefferson less than three weeks after delivering his inaugural address.

> Setting aside a few only, I have been ever persuaded that the great bulk of both parties had the same principles fundamentally, and that it was only as to our foreign relations there was any division. These I hope can be so managed as to cease to be a subject of division for us. Nothing shall be spared on my part to obliterate the traces of party and consolidate the nation, if it can be done without abandonment of principle.[11]

His inaugural address itself had been designed to strike the first conciliatory note, and on the key question of party conflict it was a masterpiece of statesmanlike equivocation. It had a number of grace notes that might be calculated to appease opposition sensibilities: a prideful reference to American commerce, a strong hint about sustaining the public credit, an injunction to "pursue our own Federal and Republican principles," the memorable

---

[11] Cunningham, *Jeffersonian Republicans in Power*, 8.

promise of "peace, commerce, and honest friendship with all nations, entangling alliances with none," obeisance to the memory of Washington as "our first and greatest revolutionary character," modest remarks about the fallibility of his own judgment, a promise not only to try to hold the good opinion of his supporters but also "to conciliate that of others by doing them all the good in my power," and finally, that *sine qua non* of inaugural addresses, especially necessary from one widely deemed "an atheist in religion"—an invocation of divine aid.

But it was in speaking of American conflicts that Jefferson achieved his finest subtlety. The acerbity of American political conflict, he suggested, would deceive "strangers unused to think freely and to speak and to write what they think." But now that the issue had been decided, Americans would unite for the common good. "All, too, will bear in mind this sacred principle, that though the will of the majority is in all cases to prevail, that will to be rightful must be reasonable; that the minority possess their equal rights, to violate which could be oppression." Let us restore harmony and affection to our society, he pleaded, and banish political intolerance as we have banished religious intolerance. That the agonies and agitations of Europe should have reached our shores and divided our opinions over proper measures of national safety is hardly surprising, but "every difference of opinion is not a difference of principle. We have called by different names brethren of the same principle. We are all republicans; we are all federalists."[12]

In expressing these healing sentiments, which set a fine precedent for other chief executives taking office after acrimonious campaigns, Jefferson succeeded at a focal moment in reassuring many Federalists. Hamilton thought the address "virtually a candid retraction of past misapprehensions, and a pledge to the community that the new President will not lend himself to dangerous innovations, but in essential points tread in the steps of his predecessors." It contained some foolish but also many good ideas, George Cabot judged. "It is so conciliatory that much hope is derived from it by the Federalists," and he thought it "better liked by our party than his own." Robert Troup, who referred to its "wonderful lullaby effect" also thought it displeasing to the "most violent of the party attached to him," as did James A. Bayard. It was well calculated, Robert Goodloe Harper reported to his constituents, "to afford the hope of such an administration as may conduce to his own glory and the public good." "A fine opening," said Manasseh Cutler.[13]

Yet the Federalists would have been much deceived if they had imagined

---

[12] *Works*, IX, 195. Jefferson also drafted an interesting passage about parties which he did not use in the address: "Wherever there are men there will be parties and wherever there are free men they will make themselves heard. . . . These are the whigs and tories of nature. These mutual jealousies produce mutual security: and while the laws shall be obeyed all will be safe. He alone is your enemy who disobeys them. . . . Let this then be the distinctive mark of an American that in cases of commotion he enlists under no man's banner, enquires for no man's name, but repairs to the standard of the laws. Do this and you need never fear anarchy or tyranny." *Ibid.*, 193 n.

[13] Broadus Mitchell, *Alexander Hamilton*, II, 494. C. R. King, *Rufus King*, III, 407, 408, 461; Hamilton, *Works*, ed. by J. C. Hamilton, VI, 522; Harper, *Speeches*, 324; W. P. and J. P. Cutler, *Manasseh Cutler*, II, 44.

that the striking sentence, "We are all republicans; we are all federalists," implied that Jefferson would put the principles of the two *parties*, and hence the parties themselves, on a nearly equal footing of legitimacy. The context, as well as various private utterances, showed that he meant only that almost all Americans believed both in the federal union and in the general principles of republican government, and that therefore the two parties stood close enough to be not so much reconciled as *merged*, and merged under his own standard. One can only concur here with Henry Adams's remark that Jefferson "wished to soothe the great body of his opponents, and if possible to win them over; but he had no idea of harmony or affection other than that which was to spring from his own further triumph." Jefferson's letters substantiate this interpretation. He had hardly finished the labors of the inauguration before he was writing letters to John Dickinson, James Monroe, and General Horatio Gates in which his hopes were spelled out with great clarity. Large numbers of his fellow citizens had been "hood-winked" from their principles through an extraordinary combination of circumstances, he argued, but it was now possible to enlighten them. An incorrect idea of his own views had got about, but "I am in hopes my inaugural address will in some measure set this to rights, as it will present the leading objects to be conciliation and adherence to sound principle." The leaders of the "late faction" were, of course, "incurables" and need not be courted, but "with the main body of federalists I believe it very practicable." The XYZ affair had created a political delusion among many people, but the uncertainties of the preceding month arising from the presidential election in the House of Representatives, and the alarm over a possible constitutional crisis had produced "a wonderful effect . . . on the mass of federalists." Many wanted only "a decent excuse for coming back" to a party that represented their own deepest views, and others had come over "rather than risk anarchy." Therefore Jefferson's policies, especially as to patronage, would be prudent, and would be so designed as "to give time for a perfect consolidation." In short:

> If we can hit on the true line of conduct which may conciliate the honest part of those who were called federalists, and do justice to those who have so long been excluded from it, I shall hope to be able to obliterate, or rather to unite the names of federalists and republicans. The way to effect it is to preserve principle, but to treat tenderly those who have been estranged from us, and dispose their minds to view our proceedings with candour.[14]

V

Chance plays its part in history. Jefferson's plan of conciliation was favored by a fortunate lull in the European wars, since peace negotiations between France and Great Britain, begun in the month of his inauguration, were concluded a year later in March 1802 when the Treaty of Amiens was at last ratified. For a few years, before war broke out again in May 1803, issues of foreign policy were less exacerbating than they had been at any

[14] Adams, *History of the United States*, I, 201; Jefferson, *Works*, IX, 201–206; cf. 236–237, 282–283.

time since the unwelcome arrival of Citizen Genet. The field was thus left briefly clear for Jefferson's conciliatory strategy on domestic matters to register its effect. The essence of the strategy consisted not in what he did during these first twenty-four months of his administration—for the little he and his party did was provocative enough—but in what he did not do. One could write an alternative scenario for the Jeffersonians, which would call for an all-out attack on the bank charter, a wholesale removal of Federalist officeholders, an inundation of the judiciary with new Republican appointees, an intimate orientation toward France and increasing hostility to England—all things which the most fearful Federalists had reason, by their own lights, to expect. And here some examination of Jefferson's restraint on patronage and the Hamiltonian system is in order.

From the very earliest moment of his administration, Jefferson made it clear to some of his intimates that, however strong the Republican clamor for jobs, restraint in removals was a necessary part of his conciliatory plan. In effect, at an early and vital moment in national development, his patronage policy set the principle that to have been a political opponent of an incoming administration did not necessarily mean the loss of one's job in the civil service. That he found an efficient and respectable body of civil servants when he entered office was a tribute to the administrative practices of his predecessors; that he refused to sweep them out wholesale in response to pressure from office-hungry Republicans was a tribute to him. Rather than clean out Federalist officeholders like a petty chieftain in a partisan vendetta, he tried to arrive at a formula for what might be called civil-service coexistence—a formula that would consider both the needs of his partisans for rewards and the sensibilities of the main body of Federalist officeholders.

Jefferson started from the principle that a difference of opinion on politics is not in itself sufficient ground for removal: "Malconduct is a just ground of removal: mere difference of political opinion is not."[15] Of course he would make no *new* appointments of Federalists, but he expected that retirements, resignations, and occasional removals for incompetence or misconduct would gradually create openings for his partisans. Soon, when it became apparent that this process would not go on fast enough and that Republicans were keenly dissatisfied—few incumbents died, Jefferson said plaintively, and none resigned—he retreated to a new principle: removals of a few especially violent and active Federalist partisans would be necessary to give Republicans a fair share of the jobs. Although it was not acceptable to Federalists, this seems an understandable rule if we remember that Jefferson came in with the entire body of federal officeholders staffed by his opponents, and that, under Republican scruples about frugality, not many new posts would be created. But what would a fair share be? Republicans, he thought, ought to be gradually brought in until they had government jobs proportionate to their numbers in the body politic. This proportion, he once suggested, would be about two-thirds or three-quarters—an awkwardly large part if one considers the number of removals it might require, yet not

[15] *Works*, IX, 225.

a wholly unreasonable estimate if one measures it by the preponderance soon won by the Republicans in Congress.[16]

In this way, the early American regard for quality and continuity in public service, as well as the widespread sense that public office is a species of property right, proved somewhat inhibiting to party warfare. In his eight years Jefferson removed 109 out of 433 men who held office by presidential appointment; and of these 109, 40 were in a special category, the "midnight appointments" of the Adams administration, whose validity he never conceded.[17]

It would be misleading, of course, to suggest that Jefferson's patronage policies mollified the Federalists as much as he might have hoped. They were unable to respect his rejection of their last-minute appointees, whose posts they considered to be based upon impeccable legal and moral foundations. Many of them could see no justice in any removals whatever below the topmost level of Cabinet and diplomatic positions. And at least one local situation, an unfortunate Jeffersonian appointment to the collectorship of New Haven, where a competent last-minute Adams man was replaced by a controversial and allegedly incompetent Republican, stimulated strong protest. Word had reached Connecticut that some kind of understanding had been arrived at over the patronage, and Federalists there considered that Jefferson had violated a firm agreement. In reply to a protest from New Haven merchants, Jefferson pointedly remarked that his own statements about political tolerance, harmony, and affection in social intercourse, and the rights of the minority had been tortured into an inference that the tenure of offices was to be undisturbed. In the preceding administration, only Federalists had been given offices. Now he hardly considered it a violation of the rights of the minority to ask them to share office with the Republican majority who were entitled to "a proportionate share in the direction of public affairs." Some removals were necessary to this end, and he hoped to base them "as much as possible on delinquency, on oppression, on intolerance, on incompetence, on anterevolutionary adherence to our enemies." Once the imbalance had been corrected, he would be happy to arrive at the point where "the only questions concerning a candidate shall be, is he honest, Is he capable? Is he faithful to the Constitution?" This was not a satisfactory formula to the Federalists, but it was at least consistent with the idea of a bipartisan civil service.[18] In any case, the patronage problem illustrated both the possibilities of conciliation and also its limits.

The Hamiltonian system was a less formidable problem. As issues, funding and assumption were dead, killed by the very success of Hamilton's system, and it would have been quixotic in Jefferson to revive them, or to try to reanimate an issue with which William Branch Giles had long before failed to rally Republican forces in Congress. "Some things," Jefferson wrote to Dupont de Nemours in January 1802, "may perhaps be left undone

[16] In the House of Representatives this preponderance varied during Jefferson's eight years from a low of 65 percent (1801–1803) to a high of 83 percent (1807–1809).

[17] Leonard White, *The Jeffersonians*, 379. On patronage policies, see White, chap. 24 and Cunningham, *The Jeffersonian Republicans*, chaps. 2 and 3.

[18] On this affair see Cunningham, *Jeffersonian Republicans in Power*, 19–24; on expectations in Connecticut, S. E. Baldwin, *Life and Letters of Simeon Baldwin* (1919), 434.

from motives of compromise for a time, and not to alarm by too sudden a reformation." As for Hamilton's system, though it might have been avoided in the beginning, it could now no longer be thrown off.

> We can pay his debts in 15 years: but we can never get rid of his financial system. It mortifies me to be strengthening principles which I deem radically vicious, but this vice is entailed on us by the first error. In other parts of our government, I hope we shall be able by degrees to introduce sound principles and make them habitual.

There follows the characteristic sentence: "What is practicable must often control what is pure theory."[19]

Even the Bank, always more objectionable than funding or assumption, would be accepted and retained. Not only was there no attempt to repeal or impair its charter, but under Secretary of the Treasury Gallatin's urgings, its operations were actually extended. To the five banks already existing, the Republicans added three branches, in Washington (1802), Savannah (1802), and New Orleans (1805), the first and last of these on Gallatin's initiative. Jefferson, of course, never gave up his hostility to banks, and he saw in the Bank of the United States, which he still believed to be unconstitutional, a rival political force of great potentiality, one which, "penetrating by its branches every part of the Union, acting by command and in phalanx, may, in a critical moment, upset the government." For the safety of the Constitution, he wrote Gallatin, he was solicitous to "bring this powerful enemy to a perfect subordination under its authorities." And yet he was willing to accept its existence, even its expansion, so long as he could go on grumbling and denouncing it. Gallatin kept assuring him that it was useful, and here again what was practicable was allowed to control pure theory, and Jefferson's relatively sophisticated sense of politics overruled his agrarian economics. Madison was to follow him in approving the Bank's continuance—a matter, he said, of "expediency and almost necessity," a thing confirmed by "deliberate and reiterated precedents." In 1811, when the Bank was permitted to die with the expiration of its twenty-year charter, and at a moment when the country was about to need it most, it had many friends among the agrarian Republicans, who were reluctant to see it go.[20]

It was, of course, the state banks, chartered by Republican legislatures, that multiplied and flourished during the first decade of Republican rule, and toward these Jefferson, without relinquishing his anti-bank prejudices, adopted a most politic attitude. "I am decidedly in favor," he wrote Gallatin in July 1803,

---

[19] *Works*, IX, 344 n. There is an amusing echo of this some years later in a letter of Fisher Ames, of all people, to Josiah Quincy. Laying down tactical principles for the Federalists, Ames wrote: "I confess great prudence and many forbearances are necessary. In almost every case, a popular, or, at least, inoffensive aspect can be given to your argument. . . . The skill of the business is to attempt only what is practicable, and some of the popular tenets are false yet sacred, and therefore respectable." Ames to Josiah Quincy, November 19, 1807, Ames, *Works*, I, 403.

[20] Bray Hammond, *Banks and Politics in America* (1957), 206, 210; on the Republicans and the Bank see chaps. 5, 8, and 9. Charles A. Beard's *Economic Origins of Jeffersonian Democracy* (1915), 440–450, remains a shrewd appraisal of Jefferson's policies on banking.

of making all the banks Republican by sharing deposits among them in proportion to the dispositions they show; if the law now forbids it, we should not let another session of Congress to pass without amending it. It is material to the safety of Republicanism to detach the mercantile interest from its enemies and incorporate them into the body of its friends.[21]

Instead of trying to keep his party purely and dogmatically agrarian—a utopian and surely defeatist course—he was prepared to see it linked to the capitalistic growth of the country, to encourage the development within its ranks of a mercantile-financial-entrepreneurial segment, and thus to have it develop into a heterogeneous coalition, based not only upon geographical but upon economic diversity as well. In this he and his associates succeeded; but in encouraging the further politicization of the banking of the country, and in committing themselves as much as they did to the state banks, they laid the groundwork for the destructive attack on central banking that came with the Jacksonian era.

VI

It hardly needs to be said that Jefferson's middle course did not succeed in appeasing Federalist leaders. At best it can be said that it avoided goading them into violent responses for the brief period during which he consolidated his influence; and when they awoke from the relative torpor into which they receded in 1801, it was only to find, as many of them promptly concluded, that democracy was so much in the ascendant that all hopes of an early return to power had to be given up. By 1803 most of them had decided that Jefferson was as bad as they had ever expected him to be, and some of them were lamenting that the Constitution was dead. They had been infuriated by the Jeffersonian war on the judiciary, which, beginning with the refusal of some of Adams's midnight appointments, went on early in 1802 to the repeal of the Judiciary Act of 1801, and was climaxed by the impeachments of Justices Pickering and Chase in 1804 and 1805. They were intensely discouraged by the Louisiana Purchase in 1803, which not only seemed to cut off all prospects of war with France but added immense western territories out of which they could foresee the Jeffersonians carving many new agrarian states and thus piling further gains on top of the already substantial Republican majorities. By 1804, when a few maddened New England conspirators tried to use Burr's candidacy for the governorship of New York as a pivot upon which to engineer an independent New England–New York confederacy, they were so far out of touch with reality that even some of the most stoutly parochial New England conservatives, whose support they had to have, hung back in discouragement and disapproval. George Cabot, speaking for Chief Justice Theophilus Parsons, Fisher Ames, and Stephen Higginson as well as himself, warned Timothy Pickering that secession was pointless as long as democracy remained such a general creed that even New England was thoroughly infected with it. The best

[21] *Works*, VIII, 252. "It is certainly for the public good to keep all the banks competitors for our favors by a judicious distribution of them, and thus to engage the individuals who belong to them in support of the reformed order of things or at least in an acquiescence under it." *Ibid.*, VIII, 172.

hope for the Federalists, he thought, would be in the public reaction to a gratuitous war with England.[22]

The assault on the judiciary had been, of course, partisan warfare, pure and simple. The federal judiciary was the only one of the three arms of government in which the Federalists remained entrenched in 1801, and some of the federal judges had been outrageously partisan in the trials arising from the Sedition Act. Finally, the lame duck Federalists spurred Republican indignation when in February 1801, less than two weeks before leaving office, they enlarged the federal judiciary by adding sixteen circuit court judges and a battery of attendant marshalls, attorneys, and clerks, thus creating what they expected to be a packet of new jobs for their legal corps and digging themselves even more deeply into the enlarged judicial body. Although the needs of the judicial system gave some good grounds for the measure, the Republicans could see it only in its partisan aspect, and its timing was intensely provocative. The Federalists, Jefferson wrote in December 1801, "have retired into the Judiciary as a stronghold. There the remains of Federalism are to be preserved and fed from the Treasury, and from that battery all the works of Republicanism are to be beaten down and erased."[23]

It is easy to understand the Federalist revulsion over the war on the judiciary. Last-minute or not, the judicial commissions which Madison refused to deliver and which led to the case of *Marbury* v. *Madison* had been authorized in a perfectly legal way. The cutback in the size of the judiciary also seemed to the Federalists a way of dismissing supposedly independent judges simply by dismissing their jobs, and the measure was passed by a partisan Republican vote after a high-pitched debate in Congress which rumbled with threats from the minority of secession and civil war. And finally, the impeachments were candidly political proceedings without any pretension that "high crimes and misdemeanors" were involved. But while we may understand why the Federalists saw the assault on the judiciary as a violent and unendurable provocation, we are not obliged to see it the same way. The prescriptions for the judiciary establishment laid down in the Constitution are extremely vague and permissive. Even under the principles

[22] Henry Adams, *History*, II, 164–166. Cabot's warning to Pickering against premature attempts at secession may be profitably compared with Jefferson's letter to John Taylor, written when the Republicans were fretting under the Alien and Sedition Acts. The caution about extreme remedies is the same, but where Jefferson's was founded upon a buoyant optimism about the possibility of relieving present evils within the Union, Cabot's was founded upon despair over the proposed remedy because of the condition of New England itself. A separation from the Union, he told Pickering, would do no good because as matters now stood the proposed New England Confederation would itself be infected with democracy; the Federalist party had "no energy" and might lose what little it still had in the state if it acted unwisely. Substantial changes in the form of government could come successfully only after further purgatory, only from "the consequences of great suffering or the immediate effects of violence." Separation could come "when our loyalty to the Union is generally perceived to be the instrument of debasement and impoverishment." "We shall go the way of all governments wholly popular,—from bad to worse,—until the evils, no longer tolerable, shall generate their own remedies." Disunion would break up the Federalist party, but "a war with Great Britain manifestly provoked by our rulers" might bring the people of New England to accept dissolution of the Union.

[23] Beveridge, *Marshall*, III, 21.

of strict interpretation, it would have been possible for the Jeffersonians to play fast and loose with the Supreme Court by adding judges—to "pack" it, for example, as Grant later did and F.D.R. proposed to do. The Federalists had already set a precedent for changing its size in 1801, when they cut it back from its original six members to five. On this count E. S. Corwin has observed: "When it came to legislation concerning the Supreme Court, the majority of the Republicans again displayed genuine moderation, for, thrusting aside an obvious temptation to swamp that tribunal with additional judges of their own creed, they merely restored it to its original size under the act of 1789."[24]

Federalist historians like Albert J. Beveridge who have charged that a major Republican reason for reducing the judiciary, the desire to save money, was hypocritical, underestimate the tax-mindedness of early agrarian America. In fact, the Republicans may well have been estopped from drastic action on the judiciary more by their penny-pinching than by their political scruples. Pure considerations of partisan warfare might have dictated not a contraction but an expansion of the judiciary in which the Federalist judges would have been drowned. But Jefferson had called above all for a frugal government, and a frugal government there would be.

Moreover, while John Marshall could have been overpowered by packing the Supreme Court, Federalist entrenchment in the lower federal courts could have been undermined at the same time by a constitutional amendment to change the tenure of judges from life to terms of four or six years; and the activity of the Supreme Court could have been further impaired in a number of ways by modifications of the judiciary acts.[25] The preponderance of the Republicans in Congress and the states after 1802, and certainly after 1804, was such as to make the passage of a constitutional amendment not unduly difficult. Whether their restraint came from scruple, expediency, or ineptitude, the actual response of the Jeffersonians to the Federalist judiciary, when measured against the possibilities open to them, seems relatively moderate—not wholly "temporizing," in Hamilton's language, but certainly not "violent." So far as domestic issues were concerned —patronage, financial policy, and the judicial system—the strain between the two sides was so kept within bounds that it posed no threat to the political order. Once again, as in the 1790's, the acid test was to come with the exacerbations introduced by questions of foreign policy.

As renewed party strife replaced the brief testing period that followed Jefferson's inauguration, his response to the Federalist leaders was as sharp as theirs to him, and while his public stance still invoked the restoration of harmony and affection and left open his bid for the Federalist rank and file, his private correspondence was electric with flashes of impassioned hostility to opposition leaders who would "toll us back to the times when we burnt witches," to the "ravenous crew" of his foes, the "monocrats" who "wish to sap the republic by fraud," "incurables to be taken care of in a mad house," and "heroes of Billingsgate." "I wish nothing but their eternal hatred," he flared out in one of his letters. He could find nothing legitimate

[24] E. S. Corwin, *John Marshall and the Constitution* (1921), 63.
[25] Cf. the judgment of Edward Channing, *The Jeffersonian System* (1906), 22–23.

or useful in the Federalist opposition. "A respectable minority," he explained to Joel Barlow in May 1802, "is useful as censors," but the present minority did not qualify because it was "not respectable, being the bitterest cup of the remains of Federalism rendered desperate and furious with despair."[26] They would not, they should not, survive at all.

If Jefferson was winning over precious few of the Federalist leaders, he had the pleasure at least of taking away much of their following and mobilizing his own to the point of nearly total party victory. To this degree his political optimism was quite justified: he had gauged public sentiment correctly and he was giving the people what they wanted—frugal government, low taxes, fiscal retrenchment, a small army and navy, peace, and the warm sentiments of democratic republicanism. And he had behind him a party far more popular and efficient than anything the Federalists could mobilize against him. He had not been in the White House as much as a year before he was reporting to Dupont de Nemours his immense satisfaction with his efforts at conciliation and unity—by which he meant Republican preponderance. If a presidential election were held a year hence, he ventured on January 18, 1802, solely on grounds of political principle and uncomplicated by personal likes or dislikes, "the federal candidate would not get the vote of a single elector in the U.S." And indeed the Congressional elections of 1802 yielded an overwhelming Republican majority, which, though somewhat weakened later by reactions to the embargo and to the War of 1812, was never substantially endangered. In May Jefferson exulted that Republican advances had reached the point at which "candid federalists acknowledge that their party can never more raise its head." In 1804 he was re-elected with the votes of all New England except Connecticut, and given a party preponderance of four to one in the Senate and five to one in the House. In his second inaugural address he congratulated the country on "the union of sentiment now manifested so generally" and anticipated among the people an "entire union of opinion." In 1807, when the Massachusetts Federalists lost even their governorship, he saw the Federalists as "completely vanquished, and never more to take the field under their own banners."[27] The old dream of national unanimity seemed to be coming true.

As Federalism dwindled away toward virtual impotence, Jefferson seemed to fall victim to a certain inconsistency between his passion for unanimity on one side and on the other to his long-standing philosophical conviction that free men will differ and that differences will engender parties. But he was perhaps less inconsistent than he seemed: to him achieving unanimity meant not establishing a dead level of uniform thought but simply getting rid of the deep and impassioned differences which had arisen only because the extreme Federalists had foisted upon their party a preference for England and for monarchy. Unanimity did not require eliminating various low-keyed and negotiable differences of opinion between different schools of honest republicans. The chief limit to unity now indeed seemed to stem from divisions appearing in the Republican ranks in Congress and from such

[26] *Works*, IX, 241, 242, 268, 284, 290; X, 145; IX, 370.
[27] *Works*, IX, 343 n, 371; X, 135–136, 421.

intrastate factionalism as disturbed the party in Pennsylvania. But none of this worried him unduly. He understood that a party which had no opposition to fight with would develop a centrifugal tendency:

> We shall now be so strong that we shall split again; for freemen thinking differently and speaking and acting as they think, will form into classes of sentiment, but it must be under another name, that of federalism is to become so scouted that no party can rise under it.[28]

On this count we can find him prophetic. Partisan victory seems finally to have brought him back to his original understanding that party differences are founded in human nature. For him the goal of unanimity was satisfied by the elimination of Federalism, the disappearance of fundamental issues; and it may not be too fanciful to see in this some likeness to Burke's satisfaction in the disappearance of "the great parties" which was the very thing Burke thought laid a foundation for moderate party differences and justifiable party loyalties. Jefferson once observed that with "the entire prostration of federalism" the remaining Federalists might form a coalition with the Republican minority; but in this he saw no danger so long as the Republican dissidents were not—here the party obsession raises its head once again—flirting with monarchy. "I had always expected," he wrote to Thomas Cooper in 1807,

> that when the republicans should have put down all things under their feet, they would schismatize among themselves. I always expected, too, that whatever names the parties might bear, the real division would be into moderate and ardent republicanism. In this division there is no great evil,—not even if the minority obtain the ascendency by the accession of federal votes to their candidate; because this gives us one shade only, instead of another, of republicanism.[29]

The notion that the animating principle behind Federalism had been a passion for monarchy, however delusive it had been, led to the comforting conclusion that the last nail had now been driven into the coffin of the hereditary principle, and hence that the country had reached a unanimity deep enough. But in 1807 neither Thomas Jefferson nor George Cabot could possibly have imagined what would come in the next few years: that Jefferson would leave the presidency with a sense of failure and with diminished popularity; that Federalism, for all this, would undergo only a modest resurgence; that a war with Great Britain would finally come under the Republicans, and that, though conducted with consummate incompetence,

---

[28] The new party division, he thought, would be into "whig and tory, as in England formerly," a division founded in the nature of man. *Works*, IX, 371. The understanding that a party enjoying overwhelming preponderance would split was not peculiar to Jefferson. We have seen it in Fisher Ames (p. 145), and in the summer of 1801, Thomas McKean, the Republican governor of Pennsylvania, who would have his own difficulties with party division, had written to Jefferson: "When ever any party are notoriously predominant they will split; this is in nature; it has been the case time immemorial, and will be so until mankind become wiser and better. The Outs envy the Inns. The struggle in such a situation is only for the loaves and the fishes." Cunningham, *Jeffersonian Republicans in Power*, 203.

[29] *Works*, X, 451; he had expressed the same view to Gallatin in 1803, *ibid.*, IX, 456.

it would lead to the complete triumph of Republicanism and the final dis-appearance of the Federalist party.

Suggested Reading

Anyone concerned with the history of the early nineteenth century should read Henry Adams' great *History of the United States of America During the Administrations of Jefferson and Madison*, 9 vols. (1889–1898). A shorter but less compelling treatment of the same era is Marshall Smelser's *The Democratic Republic, 1801–1815* (1968). John C. Miller's *The Federalist Era, 1789–1801** (1960) surveys events in the 1790s.

Few besides Howe and Hofstadter have examined political ideology after the Constitutional Convention of 1787. Daniel J. Boorstin, however, has argued in *The Genius of American Politics** (1953) that the success of American politics stems from the absence of ideological content. William Nisbet Chambers, in *Political Parties in a New Nation: The American Experience, 1776–1809** (1963), analyzes the origins of the first party system from the general perspective of political science. A brilliant and formative short work is Joseph Charles' *The Origins of the American Party System** (1956). The organization and operations of Jefferson's party are authoritatively treated by Noble E. Cunningham, Jr., in two volumes: *The Jeffersonian Republicans: The Formation of Party Organization, 1789–1801** (1957), and *The Jeffersonian Republicans in Power: Party Operations, 1801–1809** (1963). David H. Fischer's *The Revolution of American Conservatism: The Federalist Party in the Era of Jeffersonian Democracy** (1965), though mistitled, is a useful introduction to that party's affairs. Shaw Livermore, Jr.'s *The Twilight of Federalism: The Disintegration of the Federalist Party, 1815–1830* (1962) is one of the few works to deal with the break-up of an American party.

It is often essential to approach political and party history through studies of individual states. Two such studies that might be consulted are Alfred F. Young's *The Democratic Republicans of New York: The Origins, 1763–1797* (1967), which links the emergence of parties to the struggles of the Revolution, and James M. Banner, Jr.'s *To the Hartford Convention: The Federalists and the Origins of Party Politics in Massachusetts, 1789–1815* (1970). An important work that relates politics to the structure of the capital city and the expectations of its inhabitants is James Sterling Young's arresting *The Washington Community, 1800–1828* (1966).

Thomas Jefferson, who helped found modern parties in the United States but wished not to be remembered for his role in doing so, is the subject of countless studies. A lengthy but insightful recent portrait is Merrill D. Peterson's *Thomas Jefferson and the New Nation* (1970). Richard Hofstadter's short essay "Thomas Jefferson: The Aristocrat as Democrat," in his *The American Political Tradition and the Men Who Made It** (1948), pp. 18–43, remains challenging.

* Also published in paperback edition.

Politics and
Public Policy in
Jacksonian America

The Strange Stillbirth of the Whig Party

Lynn L. Marshall

The structure and values of political action are often
shrouded by the normal rounds of party life. A
student of the history of Jacksonian politics reads
about the "spoils system" or the Bank "war" or
nullification and is exposed to interpretations of
Jacksonianism that make of Jackson's triumph in 1828
a victory of democracy over aristocracy, of the
frontier over the older East, of labor over capital, or
of one system of ethnocultural values over another.
In the following essay, Lynn L. Marshall of the
University of California at Santa Barbara reaches
behind the rhetoric of partisan life to offer an
interpretation of Jacksonian politics that is both
congruent with all of the older theses and a sharp
departure from them.

It is Marshall's argument that Jackson's election
marked the emergence of a new ideology of public
service and a new system of organization. Leadership
during the first half-century of the nation's life had
been premised on elite values. Office went to men of
"high" character. The use of authority was governed
by precise rules of precedence and etiquette. And
institutions by and large reflected the canons of life
among the elite: they were small, confidential, and
informal. In Marshall's view, both the federal

301

government and the early political parties were run along these lines.

Jackson's election, in the parlance of modern political science, "modernized" both government and politics. It democratized participation, rationalized authority through greater centralization, and bureaucratized administration. Office now went to men of relative obscurity who valued efficiency and vigor in the prosecution of public affairs. The government now reached out to the average citizen for support, if not guidance. Authority was now defined in such a way as to make the "people" seem sovereign. Administration now became larger, more open, and more systematic. The Jacksonian "revolution" was a transformation in American government and institutional life.

In this essay, Marshall borrows subtly but effectively from the literature on modernization. In so doing he not only clarifies the differences between the parties of Jackson and Webster but also the distinction between Jeffersonian and Jacksonian politics. He implies a significant disjunction between Jeffersonian Democracy and what has so often been taken to be its lineal descendent, Jacksonian Democracy. In this, he joins a growing number of historians who would place Jeffersonianism in the ranks of premodern American ideology and politics. Yet does this not too much underrate the achievement of the earlier generation in party development?

One might further ask how, after all, Jackson's party was able to usher in its new policies with such dramatic force and speed. Was the change dictated primarily by need? Or were there other forces, ideological and social, that would have caused the change even if the Jacksonians had not been around to lead it? That the Jacksonians might have been products or symbols rather than agents of the transformation is suggested by the very evidence that Marshall himself offers concerning the emergence at about the same time of numerous large-scale organizations and the many efforts to establish new kinds of institutions, from interdenominational societies to communitarian settlements.

The Strange Stillbirth of the Whig Party. From *American Historical Review*, LXXII (January 1967), 445–68. Reprinted by permission of the American Historical Association and Lynn L. Marshall.

*T*he Whig party's peculiar birth cannot properly be understood with reference to politics only. In fact, its birth seems to have been integral to concurrent changes in American social organization in a very general sense. Let us entertain the hypothesis that the most significant developments in early nineteenth-century America involved not elevated political ideology (as, for example, states' rights versus national power and laissez faire versus state regulation), but rather changes in the ways Americans organized themselves to solve immediate problems of all sorts, whether public or private. Whig birth coincided with the crest of a ground swell of social change that would shortly reorganize American life around a proliferating series of specialized, large-scale organizations, flexible, functional, and impersonal.

The key element in the formation of the Whig party was party organization, not ideology. There seems sufficient reason to assume that Whig ideology, in early infancy at least, limited itself to opposition to "executive usurpation," the negative issue implied in its choice of name and the focus of its electioneering efforts throughout the mid-1830's.[1] One can hardly find another common ground between John C. Calhoun, prince of nullification, and nationalists like Henry Clay and Daniel Webster, all of whom joined to establish the party. This issue expressed a reaction to threatening changes in party organization and the role of political leadership. How did the Whig party, then, differ from the Jackson party in organizational structure? How did each relate to the structure of society at large? The conditions of Whig birth, seen in this light, may offer some enlightenment on that much-disputed entity, "Jacksonian Democracy."

Part of the obscurity concerning Whig origins has involved its precise date of birth. It has usually been placed somewhere in 1833 or 1834.[2] The name "Whig" was not used formally to designate the party until 1834. If, however, the alignment around the issue of executive usurpation is taken as the effective birth, it may be fixed with precision at a considerably earlier date. It came in July 1832, in direct and explicit reaction to Jackson's veto of the bill rechartering the national bank. Although the anti-Jackson party continued to call itself National Republican through the campaign of 1832, it abruptly and consciously became proto-Whig with the veto message.

On July 11, 1832, Webster rose in the Senate to denounce the Bank veto

[1] The Whig name of course had originated long before in the English parliamentary party opposing usurpations of the king. American colonists during the Revolution had borrowed the name to indicate a similar opposition to the usurpations of George III.

[2] See, e.g., Charles M. Wiltse, *John C. Calhoun: Nullifier, 1829–1839* (New York, 1949), 223; Charles G. Sellers, Jr., *James K. Polk: Jacksonian, 1795–1843* (Princeton, N.J., 1957), 212–13; Glyndon G. Van Deusen, *The Jacksonian Era, 1828–1848* (New York, 1959), 96. The traditional view has attempted to make sense of the Whig party while maintaining primary focus on formal, explicit, ideological main currents running through the full span of American experience, rather than on more explicit, functional ideology. For an example of this, see *id.*, "Some Aspects of Whig Thought and Theory in the Jacksonian Period," *American Historical Review*, LXIII (Jan. 1958), 305–22.

at great length, with all the force of his inimitable voice and commanding presence. Only the day before Jackson had sent his veto message to the Senate, and at the first possible moment Webster sprang to the attack. Webster paid scant attention to the arguments put forth in the veto message. He simply disdained it. He ignored, furthermore, what was ostensibly the principal doctrine of his National Republican party: nationalism versus doctrinaire states' rights. At one point he even noted that the veto's main argument was "little compliment to State sovereignty"—as indeed it was, despite rhetorical flourishes to the contrary. Webster focused instead on "executive usurpation."

> According to the doctrines set forth by the President, although Congress may have passed a law, and although the Supreme Court may have pronounced it constitutional, yet it is, nevertheless, no law at all, if he, in his good pleasure, sees fit to deny it effect; in other words to repeal and annul it.[3]

With this veto, concluded Webster, Jackson had effectively proposed a "pure despotism," and announced, like Louis XIV, " 'I AM THE STATE.' "[4]

On the following day, Henry Clay, the National Republican presidential nominee, delivered similar expressions to his Senate colleagues.[5] This double-barreled display was the more impressive because Webster, Clay, and the other pro-Bank oratorical giants had participated sparingly in the long debate that preceded passage of the bill, knowing that they had sufficient votes to ensure passage. Now, however, they unleashed their full power. Their speeches, moreover, in length, polish, and fluency of delivery, suggested considerable preparation.

Up to that time Webster, Clay, and party had not agitated executive usurpation, but for the remainder of the 1832 campaign it became the main party issue. The *National Intelligencer*, their principal party newspaper, hammered away at it in long series of editorials, calling Jackson a "monarch," "KING OF KINGS," and even "DICTATOR." This campaign originated the "King Andrew" cartoon that would become the Whigs' stock in trade for the next few years. The Bank veto message, the *Intelligencer* warned, had frankly announced "downright Tory doctrines."[6]

By August the accession of Calhoun completed the basic Webster-Clay-Calhoun Whig alignment. Just three weeks after the Bank veto, the *United States Telegraph*, Calhoun's organ in Washington, suddenly began to say pleasant things about Clay. Soon the *Telegraph* printed Clay's Bank veto speech and joined the opposition cacophony about "Executive tyranny."[7] It was odd, on the face of it, that this organ of nullification and ostensible enemy of the Bank should thus abruptly espouse the great hero of tariff and

---

[3] "Speech of Mr. Webster," Washington *National Intelligencer*, Sept. 22, 1832.
[4] *Ibid.*
[5] "Speech of Mr. Clay," *Niles' Weekly Register*, Aug. 11, 1832.
[6] Washington *National Intelligencer*, Sept. 22, 1832; "Review of the Veto," *ibid.*, Oct. 4–18, 1832, in seven numbers; Frances Kemble, *Journal* (2 vols., Philadelphia, 1835), I, 141.
[7] Washington *United States Telegraph*, July 23, August 2, 6, 1832. Calhoun could not bring himself to announce personal, public support of Clay, but the *Telegraph* made his position perfectly clear. Cf. Wiltse, *Calhoun: Nullifier*, 141.

Bank, and strange too that the Webster-Clay-Calhoun alignment would remain intact through the subsequent nullification crisis. A more compelling issue than simple states' rights was at work here.

Prior to July 1832 the National Republicans, an alignment of leaders with strong local identifications, like Clay's to Kentucky and Webster's to Massachusetts, had bent their efforts mainly to showing themselves "national." They had sought to identify themselves with the Bank, internal improvements, and especially the tariff. Executive usurpation had not concerned them. Clay had devoted his campaign efforts mainly to the tariff; he delivered a great tariff speech before the Senate in February, which the party promptly printed and broadcast over the country for political effect.[8] The National Republican "platform"—called the "Address of the National Republican Convention to the People of the United States"—had likewise stressed such "national" issues as the tariff. It too had failed to feature a theme of executive usurpation.[9]

When Webster initiated the charge of executive usurpation so suddenly at the time of the veto, he presented an obviously trumped-up case. The Constitution gave the President an absolute right to veto legislation, *whatever* his reasons or lack of them. The Bank veto message clearly differentiated between the President's legislative and executive functions, just as did the Constitution. Webster, however, advanced the entirely specious argument that Jackson repealed and annulled an established institution, not a mere bill. Jackson, of course, had sought neither to repeal the original charter of the Bank nor to touch the existing institution in any way. For a nationalist, Webster certainly took a novel position. From the outset nationalists had demanded a powerful executive, and, in fact, the plan of the Bank of the United States itself had originated, in 1791, in the executive department. Clearly, something other than the question of nationalism was involved here.

The proto-Whigs calculated and literally forced the issue of executive usurpation, emasculating their ideology in the process. The Jacksonians had struggled to prevent the Bank issue from coming up in that session of Congress. Because Jackson's re-election in 1832 was almost assured without the Bank issue, they would have preferred to avoid anything so potentially dangerous, for Jackson had made known his intent to veto a recharter that did not involve basic changes in the character of the Bank. ". . . If Jackson is to be believed," Clay snidely commented, "he will veto it."[10] The proto-Whigs had to force the veto in order that they might raise their trumped-up issue.[11]

[8] *Niles' Weekly Register*, Feb. 2, 3, 6, Mar. 3, 10, 1832; Clay to Francis Brooke, Mar. 17, 1832, *Works of Henry Clay: Comprising His Life, Correspondence and Speeches*, ed. Calvin Colton (10 vols., New York, 1904), IV, 329.

[9] *Niles' Weekly Register*, Dec. 24, 1831.

[10] Clay to Brooke, June 29, 1832, *Works of Clay*, ed. Colton, IV, 340.

[11] The issue of executive usurpation was strongly voiced in the address of the New York Antimasonic party convention, also timed to coincide almost perfectly with the Bank veto. At that convention prominent National Republicans were placed on the Antimasonic party electoral slate, in spite of their support for the well-known Mason, Clay. The Antimasonic party, meanwhile, continued ostensibly pledged to their own presidential candidate, William Wirt. Wirt represented, incidentally, a classic proto-Whig stance. The Jackson administration, he said, was a "millennium of minnows." Following the Bank veto he wrote: "According to General Jackson's principles, our government is

Why should they have done it? Webster and Clay were shrewd political leaders, not accustomed to raise weak or meaningless issues in the midst of presidential campaigns. There was something substantial behind their actions, although they avoided stating it explicitly, something important enough to throw a nationalist into the arms of a nullifier. The apparent peculiarities of the case indicated changes of a profound nature threatening the customary role of the political leader and the structure of his national political organization. The Bank itself symbolized the type of social structure for which the proto-Whigs stood, and the Jacksonian attack on it a new and challenging alternative.

The following circumstances concerning the Bank veto and the proto-Whig response to it deserve special consideration. Veto and response differed drastically in content, structure, and orientation. The one was aimed directly at voters; the other appealed to members of the political establishment. The veto sought to rally public opinion directly; the replies appealed to the authority of constituted leaders. The Jackson party was immediately voter oriented, and the proto-Whigs, leader oriented. This distinction underlay Ralph Waldo Emerson's epigrammatic characterization of the two parties: "I should say that one has the best cause, and the other contains the best men."[12]

The Bank veto speeches of Webster and Clay addressed fellow political leaders, in fact and in intent. Their style, their choice of language, and the arguments they advanced were not designed for popular consumption. These proto-Whigs sought to show that Jackson had infringed upon the accustomed powers of established, locally based political leaders. They could and did give scant attention to the arguments in the veto message, and none at all to its gist—its rejection of the use of government power to support exclusive private profit-making ventures by a pre-existing social elite—because their chief objection to the veto was its short-circuiting of established political leaders in Congress and Court. They objected to the direct appeal of the veto message to the electorate. The message chose arguments and language with an eye to popular appeal, proposing explicitly that "a new Congress, elected in the midst of such discussion [of the dangerous and unconstitutional features of the Bank], . . . will bear to the Capitol the verdict of public opinion. . . ."[13] Webster replied to this appeal with unconcealed disdain, "[t]he message toils through all the commonplace topics of monopoly, the right of taxation, the suffering of the poor, the arrogance of the rich, with as much painful effort, as if one, or another, or all of them, had something to do with the constitutional questions."[14] The *Intelligencer* likewise coupled its usurpation argument with denunciation of the "infuriate mob" to which the message directed itself, and bitter observations on

---

a despotism. His veto doctrines, as illustrated by his practice, virtually annihilate both Congress and the Supreme Court." (Wirt to Judge [Dabney] Carr, Oct. 25, 1832, John P. Kennedy, *Memoirs of the Life of William Wirt* [2 vols., Philadelphia, 1856], II, 328.)

[12] Ralph Waldo Emerson, *Complete Works of Ralph Waldo Emerson,* ed. Edward Waldo Emerson (12 vols., Boston, 1903–1906), III, 209.

[13] *A Compilation of the Messages and Papers of the Presidents, 1789–1897,* ed. James D. Richardson (10 vols., Washington, D.C., 1899), II, 589.

[14] "Speech of Mr. Webster."

how very little faith could be put in the "virtue and intelligence of the electorate at large.[15]

One of the most striking features of the veto message was indeed its direct orientation to the electorate. It spoke not to the Congress that had passed the bill, nor to the Court that had, years before in the *McCulloch* v. *Maryland* case, ruled a national bank constitutional; it spoke in plain language to voters. And those voters in November would overwhelmingly re-elect Jackson.

Webster and the proto-Whigs all too clearly recognized that the veto message and its direct orientation to voters represented a new approach to politics and new roles for political leaders. It was precisely this that produced their carefully planned proto-Whig alignment. The message was the product, they knew, of that informal board of advisers and organizers whom the anti-Jackson press had begun calling the "Kitchen Cabinet." To Webster, this new brand of political leadership compared invidiously with the old. No one in the Senate supposed, he said, that Jackson had written the veto message himself. This was reprehensible enough, but "whoever may have drawn it up," the President ought at least to have required it to have "passed under the review of professional characters." The matter was one to be decided by elevated, educated, established political leaders. Constituted bodies of such men, the Congress, the Court, even the President's own cabinet, had already decided the matter. How dare "these miserable people" in the "Kitchen Cabinet" presume to argue constitutional doctrine? The proto-Whigs assumed that they need only name the member of the "Kitchen Cabinet" mainly responsible for the authorship of the message to refute the whole of it. The *Intelligencer* demanded simply: "Are the People . . . willing to have AMOS KENDALL to rule over them in the name of ANDREW JACKSON?"[16]

The "Kitchen Cabinet" served as an early version of what would become a national committee. It directed the establishment of an efficient national party structure, beginning with local committees headed by a county superintendent, then district managers to report to state committees, which in turn reported to the central coordinating body in Washington. It built for specialized, functional ends, rather than for such generalized purposes as reinforcing the status system of society at large. It sought to construct out of functionaries recruited without primary regard to extraneous social criteria a faceless party cadre, with well-defined lines of communication and command, designed to perform the special functions of electioneering and channeling of votes. The whole structure was firmly cemented by award of federal offices, especially local postmasterships and local offices connected with the taking of the 1830 census.[17] Into this wide-ranging, efficient struc-

[15] Washington *National Intelligencer*, Aug. 3, 16, 1832.

[16] *Ibid.*, Sept. 4, 1832. Note Richard Longaker, "Was Jackson's Kitchen Cabinet a Cabinet?" *Mississippi Valley Historical Review*, XLIV (June 1957), 94–108, which concludes that the "Kitchen Cabinet" was not a cabinet. The author gives no proper consideration, however, to its participation in noncabinet functions.

[17] See, e.g., Kendall to Francis P. Blair, Jan. 9, Mar. 10, May 24, 1829, Blair-Lee Papers, Princeton University Library. This plan for "an efficient and universal organization of our party" involved the permanent establishment of procedures used for the 1828 Jackson victory in Kentucky, of which Kendall and Blair had been chief architects. For evi-

ture the organizers at Washington fed campaign materials calculated to appeal to the grass roots, and in the Bank veto message they provided a campaign circular par excellence. The proto-Whigs publicly noted that these circulars and the organization distributing them were novel and "a matured system of electioneering."[18]

The Washington *Globe,* the principal Jackson newspaper, had been founded in 1830 as a fundamental part of this new party organization, and as the head of a system of coordinated presses throughout the nation. It so far surpassed its contemporaries in spirit and readability that the proto-Whigs considered its style bad taste. Much of the argument and rhetoric of the veto message had long since appeared in the Jackson press.[19] The Jackson party organization saw to it that special electioneering *Globe* extras and copies of the veto message papered taverns and public places throughout the land. In the remotest counties of the West, voters who had never experienced the last contact with the Bank had begun pressing politicians with detailed inquiries about it.[20]

Some of the most important and innovative features in Jackson party organization were in the roles of its functionaries. It introduced new and lasting types of political leaders. The fact that the party organizer and the party candidate, as redefined in the Jacksonian era, have continued with little change down to the present suggests the long-range significance of these developments. Martin Van Buren, Jackson's chosen successor in the presidency, epitomized the new type of candidate, and Kendall, whom the opposition press called "chief cook and scullion" in the "Kitchen Cabinet," the organizer. Van Buren earned the sobriquet "Little Magician" for political know-how. Wordy, smooth in delivery, practiced in traditional political rhetoric, noncommittal if possible, wise in the ways of voters, Van Buren always kept his finger on the public pulse and studiously avoided wounding anyone's feelings unnecessarily. Although intelligent and successful, he yet suffered from feelings of inferiority because he had never attended college, and he certainly never began to produce any theory of government to match those of John Adams, Alexander Hamilton, or Thomas Jefferson.[21]

---

dence of the extensiveness of party organization on this model, and its uses, consider the remarkably efficient party reaction to the Calhoun defection in 1831. Calhoun's Washington *United States Telegraph* (Mar. 18, 25, 1831) discovered to its dismay that the Jackson party organization produced identical, simultaneous, and shrewdly construed reactions to Calhoun's movements, in such widely separated locations as Ohio, New Hampshire, Kentucky, Washington, D. C., and Tennessee; the unseen hand guiding this "active corps . . . extending from Maine to Missouri" was the "kitchen cabinet."

[18] "The Babbling Politician," *ibid.,* Aug. 2, 1832.

[19] Kendall to Blair, Jan. 9, Mar. 10, May 24, 1829, Aug. 22, Oct. 2, 1830, Blair-Lee Papers. Cf. the anti-Bank editorial printed in the Washington *United States Telegraph,* Dec. 16, 1829, with the Bank veto message, paragraphs 4, 5, 17, 47, *Messages and Papers,* ed. Richardson, II, 576, 577, 581, 591. Cf. also Washington *Globe* editorials of Jan. 19 and Apr. 27, 1831, with paragraph 36 of the veto message *Messages and Papers,* ed. Richardson, II, 586–87.

[20] "Speech of Mr. Clay."

[21] In his *Autobiography* Van Buren was at pains to express his regret at having failed to gain access to what he called the "highest branches of learning." He had often felt his disadvantage "in my conflicts with able and better educated men." He repeatedly expressed this regret at lack of discipline in "mental habits." See *The Autobiography of Martin Van Buren,* ed. John C. Fitzpatrick, *Annual Report, American Historical Association, 1918* (2 vols., Washington, D.C., 1920), II, 12.

Kendall was a former Kentucky newspaper editor rewarded by Jackson with an office in the Treasury. A sallow, tubercular little fellow, painfully shy, he entirely lacked the figure and presence that could attract votes. He nevertheless had abilities. He possessed enormous industry, genius for practical administration, and a remarkable grasp of the principles of organizational efficiency. He could write, moreover, with clarity and effect. At every opportunity he counseled the Jacksonians: "Organize, organize."[22]

How did this party organization differ from the American party previously most highly developed, the Republican party of Jefferson? That party had likewise possessed centralized control and extensive organization—"machinery" and "cadre" of a sort—as well as a coterie of party newspapers. But the national and state caucuses of elected representatives had dominated Jeffersonian party structure. Where the Jeffersonian party had been oriented primarily to established leaders, and only through and by them to popular support, the Jacksonian party went directly to the electorate. The faceless functionaries of the Jackson organization, from socially marginal "Kitchen Cabinet" members like Kendall or *Globe* editor Francis Preston Blair, down to lowly local postmasters and census takers laboring for the party, contrast sharply both with Jeffersonian behind-the-scenes organizers like John Beckley and with party mainstays like Aaron Burr, James Madison, and Alexander Dallas.[23]

Beckley, in contrast to the Jacksonian organizers, was a particular pro-

---

[22] Kendall to Blair, May 10, 1829, Blair-Lee Papers. Among many other productions, Kendall was responsible for the veto message almost in its entirety, although several others did editorial work on it. Historical scholars have subsequently become dreadfully confused about the veto's authorship, but it was known in Washington, well before the message appeared, precisely who was composing it. For a detailed examination of the authorship of the message, see Lynn Marshall, "The Authorship of Jackson's Bank Veto Message," *Mississippi Valley Historical Review*, L (Dec. 1963), 466–77. Research subsequent to the publication of this article, incidentally, has turned up abundant corroborating evidence of Kendall's authorship. For evidence of Kendall's social status, see Alfred Balch to Nicholas Trist [Sept. 1831], Nicholas Trist Papers, Manuscript Division, Library of Congress. This genteel observer and loyal Jacksonian, having seen Kendall at a presidential dinner, thought his "watchfulness and awkwardness" contrasted poorly with "the polished conversation the graceful manner & high tone" of the real elite. "To me he does not look like a Gentleman and therefore I could not talk to him. . . ."

[23] An example of the Jackson party's efficient functionaries was a lowly groceryman in Frankfort, Kentucky. He served also as a very efficient postmaster. (Blair to Van Buren, July 10, 1838, Martin Van Buren Papers, Manuscript Division, Library of Congress.) Among several recently published, provocative studies of party organization in the period 1790–1815, those of Noble Cunningham, Jr., are perhaps the most suggestive: *The Jeffersonian Republicans: The Formation of Party Organization, 1789–1801* (Chapel Hill, N.C., 1957), and *The Jeffersonians in Power: Party Operations, 1801–1809* (Chapel Hill, N.C., 1963). See also William N. Chambers, *Political Parties in a New Nation: The American Experience, 1776–1809* (New York, 1963); Paul Goodman, *The Democratic-Republicans of Massachusetts: Politics in a Young Republic* (Cambridge, Mass., 1964); David H. Fischer, *The Revolution of American Conservatism: The Federalist Party in the Era of Jeffersonian Democracy* (New York, 1965). For the preparation of this paper, furthermore, James Banner made available his thought-provoking unpublished article, "The Federalist Party Organization in Massachusetts, 1800–1815." These studies have pioneered a significant new perspective for viewing American politics. It is the thesis of the present paper that this eminently useful perspective should now be broadened in scope, so as to view party organization in its further development through the Jacksonian era in the context of concurrent development in other large-scale organizations as well as in social structure generally.

tégé and confidant of Virginia's leading gentlemen-politicians of Republican persuasion, Jefferson, Madison, and James Monroe. A polished alumnus of William and Mary, Beckley had been co-opted into politics originally by the local gentry of Henrico County, Virginia, at the age of seventeen and entered national politics by a similar process after his Virginia gentlemen friends had first made him clerk of the House of Burgesses and then clerk of the federal House of Representatives. National organization of the Republican party had begun in Congress, thereafter radiating out to local areas, and in this process Beckley was perfectly placed to play a leading role. The Republican party, first a faction of established leaders aligned around a common ideology, reached out through men like Beckley to other local gentlemen-leaders of similar persuasion. Beckley, Madison, and other Republican organizers, whether operating in Virginia, Pennsylvania, New York, or elsewhere, directed their attention primarily to what they variously described as "respectable persons," "prominent characters," "persons of influence," "suitable characters," or "gentlemen" with "influence among their neighbors."[24] The party operated "particularly by setting on foot expressions of the public mind in important counties, and under the auspices of respectable names."[25]

Contrast this Jeffersonian style of organization with the spirit of the following "Kitchen Cabinet" proposal made in January 1830, and seriously entertained, although seemingly never implemented. The party must organize, it was proposed, in such a way as to circumvent the political dominance of the local gentry established as leading county lawyers, justices in the local courts, and sheriffs. The mass of Jackson voters, "plain farmers and mechanics," should therefore meet in simultaneous local conventions, too numerous for the local establishment to attend all at once, and pass resolutions suggesting candidates for office. "By these means," it was hoped, "the people would take the government into their own hands . . . and an active class of politicians would spring up opposed to them [the local establishment]."[26]

[24] See, e.g., Dallas to Albert Gallatin, Jan. 16, 1805, in Henry Adams, *Life of Albert Gallatin* (Philadelphia, 1879), 327–28; Jefferson to Archibald Stuart, Feb. 13, 1799, *The Works of Thomas Jefferson*, ed. Paul L. Ford (12 vols., New York, 1904–1905), IX, 44; and other correspondence of Jefferson, Monroe, Madison, Burr, and Gallatin in this period. See also, for similar language, Beckley's correspondence with General William Irvine, a respectable gentleman-leader of the Republican party in central Pennsylvania, as extracted in Noble Cunningham, Jr., "John Beckley: An Early American Party Manager," *William and Mary Quarterly*, XIII (Jan. 1956), 40–52. About Beckley, Cunningham concludes: "It is of no little significance that Beckley's efforts were, to a large extent, directed toward winning the support of important citizens who could be counted upon to have influence on their neighbors." (Cunningham, *Jeffersonian Republicans*, 105.)

[25] Monroe to Madison, Oct. 9, 1792, *The Writings of James Monroe*, ed. Stanislaus M. Hamilton (7 vols., New York, 1898–1903), I, 243; Jefferson to Madison, Sept. 1, 1793, *Works of Jefferson*, ed. Ford, VIII, 14; Madison to John Taylor, Sept. 20, 1793, as quoted in Cunningham, *Jeffersonian Republicans*, 57; Madison to Jefferson, Aug. 27, Sept. 2, 1793, *The Writings of James Madison*, ed. Gaillard Hunt (9 vols., New York, 1900–10), VI, 179, 191–93; Madison to Archibald Stuart, Sept. 1, 1793, *ibid.*, 190; see also Cunningham, *Jeffersonian Republicans*, 57–60. Note, incidentally, that Jefferson used the name "Whig" for his new party at this time.

[26] Kendall to Blair, Jan. 28, 1830, Blair-Lee Papers. This too represented a continuation of efforts first begun by Kendall and Blair in Kentucky politics during the 1820's.

Whence came the new Jacksonian mode of party organization? Sophisticated popularly based party structures, on a small scale, had developed in
various states by the 1820's. Although scholarly studies of these parties have
not, for the most part, treated organizational structure per se (preferring to
emphasize ideology and colorful individual careers), it appears that several
state parties, at least, developed in this period a Jacksonian type of impersonal structure by-passing established local elites. The most significant for
the national organization of the Jackson party was the Kentucky Relief
party, which coalesced out of general popular demand for relief laws for
debtors following the panic of 1819. Here, men destined to become important in national Jackson party councils received apprenticeship in popular
politics. *Globe* editor Blair and efficiency expert Kendall simply transferred
Kentucky techniques of the 1820's directly to the national arena.[27] In New
York, moreover, Antimasonic and Van Burenite organizations alike had developed centralized, specialized party apparatus. Antimasons built upon
popular antipathy to a secret elitist group suspected of conspiring to obtain
special privileges, just as the Jacksonians would in the Bank veto message.[28]
The advent of Jackson as a presidential candidate, with his great appeal to
ordinary voters throughout the nation, suggested the viability of political
organization on this model at the national level.

The new approach to politics, however, was part of a general change in
American society. It represented a new approach to social organization for
the accomplishment of any sort of practical purpose. Jacksonian national
party development related very closely to the Jackson administration's development of new organizational principles for the government's executive
departments. These organizational principles, in turn, developed directly
from practical administrative problems that the Jacksonians faced when they
entered office, rather than from any preconceived ideology. When in the
Spring of 1829 the Jacksonians swept in, bent on "reform" as announced in
Jackson's inaugural address, they set forth no new principles of organization.
After a few months in office, however, they proclaimed in Jackson's first
message to Congress their principles of "rotation in office."[29]

It is significant that the Jacksonians did not propose merely to replace
rascals in office with men of honor from their own party, as might well have
been expected had they been interested in "spoils" only. They certainly rewarded friends and punished enemies about as much as they were able in the
award of offices, following the custom in American politics dating from the
inception of party contests. The opposition legitimately screamed "spoils,"
but the moralistic condemnations of the "spoils system" as something peculiarly Jacksonian, which have continued almost without pause ever since,
have obscured profoundly important organizational innovations introduced

[27] Lynn Marshall, "The Genesis of Grass-Roots Democracy in Kentucky," *Mid-
America*, XLVII (Oct. 1965), 269–87; Arndt M. Stickles, *Critical Court Struggle in Kentucky* (Bloomington, Ind., n.d.).

[28] Jabez D. Hammond, *History of Political Parties in the State of New-York* (4th ed.,
2 vols., Cooperstown, N.Y., 1846), II, 384–85; Lee Benson, *The Concept of Jacksonian
Democracy: New York as a Test Case* (Princeton, N.J., 1961), 21–27. Although opportunistic Antimasonic leaders aligned New York Antimasonry against Jackson in 1832,
this does not diminish the essentially "Jacksonian" character of the new mode of organization they represented.

[29] *Messages and Papers*, ed. Richardson, II, 438–49.

by the Jacksonians. In so far as these innovations were concerned, the spoils question was entirely irrelevant.[30] The Jacksonians used the concept of rotation in office as a cloak for organizational changes that might otherwise have appeared revolutionary. By 1829 the idea of rotation in office was neither novel nor did it imply any social change, for it had been proposed on various occasions since the time of the American Revolution, and it was occasionally implemented. South Carolina, doubtless the most conservative and class-controlled state in the Union, provided the leading example of that doctrine in 1830.[31]

Under this cover the Jacksonians proposed to organize the executive department as a rationalized complex of offices, ordered by function, and defined by rules and regulations, so as to be free in so far as possible from irregular custom and individual personalities. In this system individuals could be placed or replaced without upsetting the integrity of the whole. Men were fitted to this system, not it to men.[32] It was the administrative counterpart of the interchangeability of machine parts. Jackson's rotation proposal explicitly denied that office should become "a species of property" or be used to support "the few at the expense of the many." "The duties of all public officers," the message announced, "are, or at least are capable of being made, so plain and simple that men of intelligence may readily qualify themselves for their performance. . . ." In spite of much emphasis on equality of opportunity for all citizens, the Jacksonians justified this system mainly by the "efficiency of Government" that it might bring.[33] The signal organizational insight was this: efficiency lay primarily in the system (rules and regulations) rather than in men (character).

The Jacksonian proposal of rotation in office was never actually put into practice, and the administrative principles it masked were only falteringly applied to the organization of government departments. The post office reorganization of 1836 was its most important product.[34] In part this resulted from opposition to the new system in Congress, which had to provide the basic rules and regulations of office. In part it resulted from opposition within the Jackson party itself, which, after all, was still in a process of de-

[30] Historians seem to have been so mesmerized by the moralistic fervor of the civil service reformers of the late nineteenth century that they continue tirelessly to repeat their righteous condemnations of the Jacksonian spoils system. Leonard D. White, in *The Jacksonians: A Study in Administrative History, 1829–1861* (New York, 1954), has pointed out that the Jacksonians initiated administrative reform. The present paper is not meant to imply that spoils are efficient, but only that there are other more significant issues with which to deal.

[31] Carl Russell Fish, *The Civil Service and the Patronage* (New York, 1905), 79–104. Jefferson himself had proposed that rotation be written into the Constitution of 1787. (Jefferson to Madison, Dec. 20, 1787, *Works of Jefferson*, ed. Ford, V, 372).

[32] This is what the great historian and social analyst Max Weber has called "bureaucratization." See "Bureaucracy" in *From Max Weber: Essays in Sociology*, ed. H. H. Gerth and C. Wright Mills (New York, 1946), 196–244. American "bureaucracy" differed in very important respects from Weber's ideal, however, for Weber emphasized professionalization and life tenure in officeholders. He admired "the apparatus" of administration itself and placed great value on maintaining its integrity. The American variety of "bureaucratic" social organization, as hereafter sketched, essentially the organizational model for the modern industrial world, has defined itself rather differently.

[33] *Messages and Papers*, ed. Richardson, II, 449.

[34] 5 US Statutes at Large 80 (July 2, 1836).

velopment. The new administrative system eventually had its greatest effect outside the realm of government altogether: in large-scale private business. In its "rotation" form, furthermore, the innovative principle of the system—the interchangeability of human parts—was overstated. In any absolute sense it could not work and was not so intended by its authors. Certain offices required expert skills. That did not make them, however, any the less definable by impersonal rules or less subject to later functional redefinition.

It was not that American government had never previously been organized according to rational and functional principles. The government departments had been originally set up on a plan derived from a venerable tradition of bureaucratic structure.[35] Alexander Hamilton, for example, had consciously modeled the new Treasury Department upon its English counterpart. The British Exchequer itself belonged to one of the rationalized bureaucracies long since established during the rise of monarchical national states in Europe. These bureaucracies, however, had established and maintained prestige largely by filling their ranks with careful attention to preexisting social gradations. Thus it had been with Hamilton's system too. The government would gain in respectability, President Washington had agreed, in proportion to the respectability of the officers serving it. Hamilton had therefore chosen men of character and "standing in the community" to fulfill Washington's intent that officials "give dignity and lustre" to their offices.[36]

The application of such social criteria to officeholders rigidified the system and inhibited its efficiency. It was thought that a man once placed in office ought not properly to be removed, except for the grossest misconduct, nor the office changed. The character of the officeholder, once appointed, largely defined the office; his removal or any arbitrary change in his office reflected on his character and was damaging to the whole social system. Consider the case of Federalist Timothy Pickering's clerks in the State Department whose removal, after they had been discovered levying strictly illegal fees from applicants for passports, Pickering greatly regretted because they had "sustained fair characters" in the community at large.[37] Jefferson had acted upon similar premises. Government administration was to him a matter primarily of "virtue and talents." "The whole art of government," he said, "consists in the art of being honest."[38] The Jacksonian alternative, masked in the proposal of rotation in office, offered to increase efficiency by ignoring preexisting social criteria like "character" and "respectability" and defining office impersonally, entirely by rules and regulations.

The Jackson press explicated and justified in various ways the new system announced in the rotation proposal. Throughout 1830 and 1831, and almost down to the moment of the Bank veto, "reform" provided their

[35] Ernest Barker, *The Development of Public Services in Western Europe, 1660–1930* (London, 1944), 1–12; Hans Rosenberg, *Bureaucracy, Aristocracy, and Autocracy: The Prussian Experience, 1660–1815* (Cambridge, Mass., 1958), 1–25, 227–28.

[36] Leonard D. White, *The Federalists: A Study in Administrative History* (New York, 1948), 118, 126, 257–58, and *The Jeffersonians: A Study in Administrative History, 1801–1829* (New York, 1951), 347–68.

[37] *Id., Federalists*, 286–87.

[38] See Jefferson's "A Summary View of the Rights of British America," Aug. 1774, *Works of Jefferson*, ed. Ford, II, 88.

main issue of party agitation. In paper after paper the Jackson organs ran elaborate computations of how much money their administrative reforms had saved the government.[39] These and a multitude of other articles on "reform" made no distinction between general improvements in the efficiency of the system and the money saved by eliminating corruption in officeholders. Any sort of efficiency, as measured by money saved, was equally moral, and any sort of inefficiency, corrupt or otherwise, was equally immoral. While the Jacksonians were exceedingly moralistic and personal in their condemnations of the old administration, they championed a new system to replace it that was remarkably impersonal and strictly regulation. This was to be the officeholder's creed: "I want no discretion. I wish to be able to turn to some law or lawful regulation for every allowance I am called upon to make."[40]

The Jackson press had devoted a considerable proportion of its columns to justifying removals from office. When the opposition shouted "spoils," the Jackson press promptly showed, with remarkable specificity, how the officeholder's books had been in arrears and his accounts carelessly and irregularly drawn, concluding with an exact calculation of the sum lost to the government thereby. The opposition customarily replied with an article ostensibly written by the officeholder himself, but really by some such proto-Whig leader as William Wirt, who condemned the charges as "egregious insolence" and "a pitiful attempt to dishonor the word of a gentleman" by citing "paltry little omissions" (in one case, "that paltry little sum of $3835"). To this the Jacksonians responded in simple, direct, and telling style. Let the regulations of office be strictly obeyed, they said. Books should reflect reality, not false or misleading entries based on customs and justifiable only by appeal to the officeholder's honorable position in the social system. Regulations, not the social status of the officeholder, defined the office. "Property in office," they said, provided the basis for "aristocratic" control of government.[41]

The proto-Whig tacticians faced in an entirely different direction. In the masterful plan of operations they worked out for the campaign of 1832 they sought to gather all respectable political leaders under the "executive usurpation" banner, with the tacit assumption that they would bring with them their local constituencies—precisely the system theretofore traditional in American politics. They forced the recharter bill through, obtained the President's veto, driving thereby a wedge between Jackson and many of his original party leaders, and skillfully developed the Webster-Clay-Calhoun

[39] See, e.g., "The Black List," Washington *United States Telegraph*, Aug. 14–Sept. 24, 1830. The Washington *Globe* reprinted the same series, in corrected and amended form, in June of the following year.

[40] Fourth Auditor's Report, Nov. 30, 1829, Washington *United States Telegraph*, Dec. 10, 1829.

[41] See, e.g., the disputes over Miles King, the removed naval agent at Norfolk, Virginia, and Major William Barney, removed "Superintendent of Light Houses and Buoys." (Washington *United States Telegraph*, July 5, 8, 20, Aug. 24, Sept. 21, 1830; Mary Barney to Jackson, June 13, 1829, *Correspondence of Andrew Jackson*, ed. John Spencer Bassett [7 vols., Washington, D.C., 1926—35], IV, 48; Mary Lane to Mary Barney, Aug. 9, 1830, reprinted from the Laurenceburg *Indiana Palladium* in the Washington *United States Telegraph*, Sept. 21, 1830.)

alignment around the "executive usurpation" position, but they failed utterly to take their principal objective, the presidential election. These battle-proven leaders seemed so rigidly to follow their plan of operations, drawn up according to well-established principles of political warfare, that they failed to comprehend the irresistible power of the new weapon introduced by the Jacksonians. Or perhaps they understood too well, but remained so attached to traditional political modes that they could not give them up without first doing everything in their power to defend them. It is alto-gether remarkable how many respectable political leaders were split away from the Jackson party without apparently impairing its effectiveness at the polls: Samuel Ingham, John M. Berrien, John Branch, John C. Calhoun, John McLean, Louis McLane, Littleton Tazewell, John Tyler, John Eaton, Hugh L. White, to name a few. These men shared common characteristics —stuffiness, social pretension, and great concern for honor, dignity, and decorum. Thus, curiously, from the outset the proto-Whigs methodically maneuvered as if bent on self-destruction, reinforcing their own anachro-nism by publicly eschewing direct popular appeal and gathering into their ranks as many established leaders as possible, while forcing the Jackson party to increase its voter orientation.

This party distinction was not absolute, however, for at least some proto-Whigs were not above trying to organize in the Jacksonian style or apply-ing what was condescendingly called "*ad captandum*" (pleasing to the crowd) techniques. In their own way they had always wooed the electorate anyway. Clay himself, for example, received the plaudits of several of his party cohorts for frankly "*ad captandum*" antiforeign remarks in his widely distributed tariff speech.[42] In his vicious and personal attack on the venerable free trader, Albert Gallatin, whose half century in America could not make him more to Clay than "still at heart an alien," Clay hissed, "Go home to your native Europe."[43]

The proto-Whig alignment, moreover, included the Antimasonic party, a relatively small but highly organized and distinctly voter-oriented party. Some of these proto-Whigs understood the sources of Jacksonian party strength well enough to see clearly the power of the veto message, refusing sometimes even to publicize Webster's speech for fear it would further alienate the electorate. Clay understood the import of the veto at least enough to stop Nicholas Biddle from printing and distributing it generally as a pro-Bank handbill, for that benighted representative of genteel Phila-delphia erudition had thought the message so obviously inappropriate and reprehensible as to make it Bank propaganda. In the midst of the election campaign, furthermore, when proto-Whigs in Virginia seemed ready to give up in despair, Clay counseled fighting fire with fire. "Let our friends or-ganize . . . ," he said, proposing a "central committee" with local commit-tees to "bring the voters to the polls."[44] Even this proposed elaboration of organization, however, retained the flavor of the older model of party struc-

[42] James Barbour to Clay, Mar. 7, 1832, *Works of Clay*, ed. Colton, IV, 328.
[43] Adams, *Gallatin*, 641–42.
[44] Clay to Biddle, Aug. 27, 1832, Nicholas Biddle Papers, Manuscript Division, Library of Congress; Clay to Francis Brooke, Aug. 5, 1832, *Works of Clay*, ed. Colton, IV, 341.

ture, an organization of respectable "friends" who condescended to "bring" in the votes.

The Jackson party, on the other hand, offered no perfect voter orientation either. At Jackson's first inauguration in 1829, that party had offered an alignment of ideologically diverse leaders very similar to the proto-Whigs of 1832. The party arrived at its voter orientation, as expressed in the veto message, haltingly and stumblingly. The 1831 cabinet crisis, revolving around Peggy Eaton, the tavernkeeper's daughter who married the Secretary of War, culminated in an intraparty rash of threatened duels. Such preoccupation with honor and decorum was characteristic of a highly traditional role of leadership. The new 1831 cabinet followed the traditional model of political leadership once more, attempting to weld together a group of socially respectable leaders like Edward Livingston and Louis McLane. Unfortunately the sympathies of these respectables turned out, many times, to lie with the proto-Whigs. McLane, Secretary of the Treasury, offered the prime example of this, becoming a most annoying irritation on the Bank issue. The Jacksonians' attempt to play down that issue in the President's message of December 1831 likewise represented an essentially leader-oriented gambit. They had to be pushed by the opposition, finally, into the Bank issue and frank voter orientation.

Inconsistencies within both parties suggest that each was moving generally in the same direction, in transition from leader orientation to voter orientation, although the Jackson party had advanced further. The Bank issue, however, was perfectly calculated to accelerate the development of the Jackson party and decelerate the opposition, pushing the parties apart until they offered a striking contrast in orientation. The Whigs attempted to exploit their leader orientation to the fullest even after defeat in the election of 1832, achieving their greatest success in 1834 with the Senate censure of Jackson. Their failure in 1832 resulted, they supposed, from Jackson's great popularity as a military hero, not his party organization and electioneering techniques. The decisive defeat in 1836 by less than heroic Van Buren, however, proved without doubt the utility of Jacksonian party organization and techniques. By 1840 the Whigs had adopted these techniques. Even the eminent Webster would brag to voters about his father's log cabin, stumping for such Whig candidates as "Old Tippecanoe," pseudo hero William Henry Harrison.

The two party types represented two distinctly different views of society at large. When the Whigs agitated the question of "spoils," for example, they dealt not so much with technical government administration as with general social values. Government service, in their view, ought to be a function of private social status; it had traditionally been so considered. They looked back to a world in which a gentleman, once appointed to an office, private or public, expected to be continued therein, and the functions of his position fitted to his capabilities. Though not quite "property in office," as the Jacksonians called it, this view emphasized long tenure based on criteria nonfunctional to the operations of the organizations involved, be they government bureaus, private businesses, or even churches. The Whigs were not terribly concerned about "spoils" proper; they objected not to the reward of "friends," but to the social character of the friends rewarded.

The Whiggish view looked back to a society embodying the Lockean liberalism of the eighteenth century. In it, all affairs, political or otherwise, moved under the effective control of sagacious men, each within his own locality sufficiently pre-eminent economically, intellectually, and socially to transcend immediate popular control even if the franchise were widely distributed. Greatest emphasis was placed upon the liberty of the individual to express himself, if he were able and sufficiently educated, in great social theories and high ideals. American constitutions embodied such theories. Hamilton's plan for organization of the Treasury Department likewise exemplified a part of a liberal theory of this sort, as did Gallatin's 1808 scheme for a system of internal improvements, Jefferson's education scheme for Virginia, and the handsome proposals offered by John Quincy Adams in his 1825 inaugural address. Liberal partisans of Republican and Federalist political alignments entertained important ideological differences, but they shared basic assumptions about social structure.

The Jeffersonians envisioned a locally established intellectual elite handing down great humane theories from on high, a conception that differed from the Hamiltonian only in the assumption that the theories would, if worthy, necessarily receive ratification from an enlightened populace. Political parties were defined as like-thinking alignments of sociopolitical leaders; it was always hoped that leaders would reach, through rational discussion, such a consensus as to eliminate the need for parties of any sort. It was quite possible to be both nationalist in ideology, like the Federalists, and to derive social status and the claim to political leadership primarily from membership in a local social establishment.[45]

The Constitution of 1787 perfectly illustrated the proper role of political leadership according to the conception of the eighteenth-century liberal. The Constitution was par excellence a noble theory of government, composed in secret by a group of eminently respectable political leaders representing various local establishments, and handed down to the electorate for ratification. If a majority of the delegates in Philadelphia turned out eventually to be Federalists, a proportion of them became Republicans, including,

---

[45] Cf. Sidney Aronson, *Status and Kinship in the Higher Civil Service: Standards of Selection in the Administrations of John Adams, Thomas Jefferson and Andrew Jackson* (Cambridge, Mass., 1964). This study attempts to compare the higher echelons in the administrations of John Adams, Jefferson, and Jackson, assigning to the Jeffersonians the main responsibility for democratic change, while denying the Jacksonians anything more than a minor and subsidiary role. Although commendable for attempting rigorous quantitative analysis of this distant and difficult area, its results are rendered inconclusive by substantial technical shortcomings. To cite one of several similar weaknesses, the study compares the social status of officeholders in the Jackson administration with those of the Jefferson administration, which preceded it by twenty years, as if this were no different from comparing the Jefferson administration with the Adams administration immediately preceding it. See also another more solid quantitative study, Richard P. McCormick, "New Perspectives on Jacksonian Politics," *American Historical Review*, LXV (Jan. 1960), 288–301. McCormick, however, has concluded from a careful examination of the numbers of voters participating in elections that the advent of Jackson involved no " 'mighty democratic uprising.' " By arbitrarily defining democracy simply as proportion of possible voters participating, however, McCormick ignored the effective power of the electorate as influenced by party structure. See also *id., The Second American Party System: Party Formation in the Jacksonian Era* (Chapel Hill, N.C., 1966), for a view of party formation contrasting with that of the present paper.

of course, the most prominent of them all, Jefferson's hand-picked successor to the presidency, James Madison. Jefferson himself quite approved the process by which the Constitution was drawn up. If he entertained misgivings about some of its provisions, at least until the Bill of Rights was added, he fully approved the leadership role it embodied.[46] That leadership role, mutually respected by Federalists and Republicans, the proto-Whigs sought only to continue.[47]

The proto-Whigs sought to emulate Hamilton and Jefferson and to produce great liberal theories. Clay's "American system" was but a pale reflection, perhaps, but it was nevertheless an effort in this direction. Calhoun's "concurrent majorities," if strained and self-serving, came closer to the mark. Clay's "Ashland" and Calhoun's "Fort Hill" aped "Monticello" and Mount Vernon in emphasizing local attachment to native state and gentry. The Jacksonian reorganization of politics threatened to destroy all this, and the proto-Whigs drew together in a last-ditch effort to defend it. That the two surviving members of the old Republican triumvirate, Madison and Gallatin, should align themselves automatically with the proto-Whigs in 1832 was hardly surprising. Gallatin had long distrusted what would come to be the Jacksonian party type. He had counseled Jefferson in 1801 that they ought greatly to fear "men whose political existence depends on . . . party."[48]

The proto-Whig party alignment ought properly to have been restricted along ideological lines either to like-thinking nationalists, or, alternatively,

---

[46] Jefferson to Madison, Dec. 20, 1787, *Works of Jefferson*, ed. Ford, V, 370–75. It is suggestive that Jefferson here expressed some doubt about the scope of power given the House of Representatives, the most democratically elected body in the proposed government. He approved the executive veto explicitly, moreover, and even suggested that a judicial veto be included as well. Jefferson and Adams, by settling down in their dotage to a long, warm correspondence, showed how akin they really were. "For I agree with you," wrote Jefferson, "that there is a natural aristocracy among men. The grounds of this are virtue and talents . . . ." (Jefferson to Adams, Oct. 28, 1813, *The Adams-Jefferson Letters: The Complete Correspondence between Thomas Jefferson and Abigail and John Adams*, ed. Lester J. Cappon [2 vols., Chapel Hill, N.C., 1959], II, 387–92.

[47] Cf. Chambers, *Political Parties*, 95–109. Chambers has identified a significant change from an elitist, "plebiscitarian," "party of notables" Federalist party, to a truly democratic Republican party, a "party of politicians." He has derived this conceptual framework from Max Weber's essay "Politics as a Vocation." (See *From Max Weber*, ed. Gerth and Mills, 77–128.) These typologies resemble the distinction drawn in the present paper between leader orientation and voter orientation, but Chambers has followed Weber's model too closely and has the full scope of the development too early. Chambers has also suggested the importance of party organization to Jacksonian political developments, in "Party Development and Party Action: The American Origins," *History and Theory*, III (No. 1, 1963), 93, n. 6. Both this and his above-cited book cogently urge the utility of conceptual framework in the study of American party development. On Jacksonian political organization, see also Moisei Ostrogorski, *Democracy and the Organization of Political Parties* (2 vols., New York, 1902), II, 39–79. Weber, in "Politics as a Vocation," evidently based his analysis of American parties on Ostrogorski and Weber too became preoccupied with righteousness about spoils. Note, however, Weber's identification of "bureaucracy" with "*mass democracy*" specifically in American political party development. "In the United States, both parties since Jackson's administration have developed bureaucratically." (*From Max Weber*, ed. Gerth and Mills, 224–25.)

[48] Gallatin to Jefferson, Aug. 10, 1801, Adams, *Gallatin*, 278.

to states' righters. Under the dire threat offered by the Jacksonians, however, the party included all who stood for the traditional leadership role, whatever their ideology. Thus did Calhoun embrace Webster and Clay even while leading the nullification fight. In so doing they looked back longingly to a heroic era when leadership in politics was integral to leadership in society. They reached the *reductio ad absurdum* of their anachronistic localism when, in the 1836 campaign, they put several local presidential candidates into the field simultaneously, to be beaten en masse by Van Buren. Thus was the Whig party born dead in July 1832 and continued in that condition until 1836. Thereafter, however, a total transfusion of Jacksonian blood would miraculously bring it to life.

Alexis de Tocqueville sensed in the United States of 1831–1832 the already half-realized sociopolitical changes against which the proto-Whigs reacted. He saw in a possible "tyranny of the majority" the subversion of the traditional type of locally based, socially secure, political leadership with which he himself identified. Historians have much praised, condemned, or explicated Tocqueville's thought on this point, but have failed to point out that his "tyranny of the majority" was in many respects exactly equivalent to proto-Whig "executive tyranny," including its primary leader orientation. At the very crux of his discussion of the power exercised by the majority over contrary opinions, he noted that, although an individual in the United States may be allowed perfect freedom of expression within certain limits, he absolutely dare not go beyond them. Not that his life would be endangered, but "his political career is closed forever." "You may retain your civil rights," said he, "but they will be useless to you, for you will never be chosen by your fellow citizens if you solicit their votes. . . ." In this way the individual would be "deprived of the rights of mankind."[49]

The Bank of the United States embodied just this leadership ideal championed by Tocqueville and the proto-Whigs. Without denying the obvious economic utility of central control on banking, consider the socially impacted structure of this particular institution. Originally constructed in accordance with a segment of Hamilton's brilliant theory, it represented a grand scheme with which men of honor might reach out imaginatively to secure possibly great benefits for the whole of society. It represented, preeminently, government buttressing of private socioeconomic position. Its enormous economic power was only nominally limited by public opinion, and the only real limitation lay in the honor and intelligence of its essentially dilettante-banker executives. The Bank's structure conformed closely to local social establishments. Each of its many branches had its own board of directors drawn from the local gentry, planters, and merchants, who were generally politicians too, and dilettante bankers all. Only the cashier in each branch represented directly the central institution in a full-time capacity. Obvious social criteria were used in the selection of cashiers, just as they had been used in the selection of Biddle himself as president of the mother bank. For all the banking skill he acquired subsequently, Biddle had been

[49] Alexis de Tocqueville, *Democracy in America* (2 vols., New York, 1945), I, 274–75. For development of related elements in Tocqueville's work, see Seymour Drescher, *Tocqueville and England* (Cambridge, Mass., 1964), 74–104, and "Tocqueville's Two Democracies," *Journal of the History of Ideas*, XXV (Apr.–June 1964), 211–16.

invited into the Bank not on the basis of experience as a banker, in which he was woefully weak, but on his general character, his "virtue and intelligence."[50] The Bank issue in 1832, therefore, was perfectly calculated to point up fundamental social changes then in process.

If the Whiggish ideal seems strange and remote in many respects, the ideal implied in Jacksonian innovations seems familiar by contrast. If the one harked back to the past, the other offered a vision of the future—although usually represented by the Jacksonians themselves as an ideal deriving from a more perfect era in the American past. The Jackson party forever talked of states' rights and paraded Jeffersonian rhetoric, straining to appear traditional. Actually, of course, the Whigs more resembled the Jeffersonians than did the Jacksonians. The Jacksonian ideal, while couched in Jeffersonian shibboleths, involved no great concern for local protection of individual liberty.

Since at least the close of the War of 1812 Americans had been experimenting enthusiastically with new modes of social organization, for purposes spiritual, practical, or merely for amusement. These new alternatives rapidly eroded away the old social order, once so firmly established in New England's townships and Virginia's counties. The new modes of social organization developed directly out of recognition of specific problems and attempts to solve them, as efficiently as possible, in keeping with certain assumptions about the nature of man. It had become obvious to Americans by that date that many things could be done to increase both material and spiritual comforts, things that could never be done by individual efforts of independent yeomen farmers of the Jeffersonian image however dutifully they followed the wise counsels of the rightful *aristoi*. Goods needed to be grown, manufactured, and shipped, messages sent, taxes collected, and souls saved on a grand scale. The situation seemed to demand social reorganization. The resulting American penchant for organization and reorganization, by all classes and for all purposes, startled a sensitive observer like Tocqueville. This period's efflorescence of different types of organizations has been much noted, but here again historians have not concerned themselves with organizational structure so much as with formal ideologies, just as in the case of political parties.

This era's enthusiastic activity in economic affairs—in finance, manufacturing, transportation, and merchandising—involved basic experimentation in modes of social organization as well as advance in economic productivity. These experiments ranged from the Boston Associates' highly successful work force of respectable unmarried farm girls, to Kentucky's ill-fated Lexington Manufacturing Company with its great imported steam engine and cadre of Yankee production "engineers." They ranged from the Erie Canal, to the West's myriad state-chartered banks, to New York City's far-flung new merchandising houses. Apparently not until the 1850's, however, did any really large-scale business organizations develop in the United States, excepting Biddle's Bank and John Jacob Astor's American Fur Company, both of which operated on an earlier organizational model. In the boom

[50] Biddle to John McLean, Jan. 10, 11, 1829, Biddle Papers; Thomas P. Govan, *Nicholas Biddle* (Chicago, 1959), 83–84.

during the mid-1830's there were textile factories in the Philadelphia area employing more than two hundred operatives. Simultaneously, factory workers first organized themselves into large-scale labor unions. That the National Trades' Union crumbled in the panic of 1837, along with many burgeoning factories, detracts nothing from the social significance of such organizational attempts.[51]

The most profound experiments in novel modes of social organization involved affairs other than economic. It seems more than fortuitous, however, that important New York merchants like the Tappan brothers led in establishing a series of new religious-associated organizations for special purposes, broadly Protestant evangelical or moral. Many such groups sprouted in the 1820's. Organized by laymen, each extended over the entire nation. Interdenominational, they were in structure entirely outside either local churches or denominational organizations. The American Sunday School Union, the American Society for Promoting Temperance, the American Home Missionary Society, and several other groups quickly established themselves and grew at a rapid rate. Each soon claimed functionaries numbering in the hundreds, or even thousands, with annual budgets approaching $100,000.[52] Antislavery organization in the 1830's was but one more such effort.

In addition to such specialized organizations, there was an extraordinary variety of attempts at total social reorganization: the familiar communitarian experiments like New Harmony, Brook Farm, and the Mormon communities. These ranged in political structure from Mormon authoritarianism to transcendentalist freedom, from Shakerite celibacy in family relations to Oneidan free love, and, in modes of economic productivity, from foolish bucolic idyl to highly profitable manufacturing enterprise. The widespread expectation, furthermore, among various American Protestant groups during these years that the millennium was at hand seems related to recognition of the passing of accustomed social roles and social order. Jacksonian party development and administrative reform were just one more such experiment in social organization, but they were essentially the system that would ultimately triumph over all others.[53]

The Jacksonians discovered the key to efficiency in an egalitarian ethic, that national principle which Americans generally had come to take for granted in the half century since the Declaration of Independence. The overwhelming triumph of the political party of Jefferson had helped to establish it, and the newness of all social institutions in America had doubtless

---

[51] Alfred D. Chandler, *Strategy and Structure: Chapters in the History of Industrial Enterprise* (Cambridge, Mass., 1962), 19–22. For the Lexington Manufacturing Company, see Ebenezer Stedman's charming recollections, published under the title *Bluegrass Craftsman: Being the Reminiscences of Ebenezer Hiram Stedman, Papermaker, 1808–1885*, ed. Frances L. S. Dugan and Jacqueline P. Bull (Lexington, Ky., 1959), 14–25; see also William A. Sullivan, *The Industrial Worker in Pennsylvania, 1800–1840* (Harrisburg, Pa., 1955), 17–23, 99–118.

[52] William Warren Sweet, *Religion in the Development of American Culture, 1800–1840* (New York, 1952), 188, 262–71.

[53] For an account of one of the most organizationally experimental communitarian groups, see Fawn M. Brodie, *No Man Knows My History: The Life of Joseph Smith* (New York, 1945).

buttressed it at least as much as formal liberal ideology. This egalitarian ethic provided a necessary foundation for Jacksonian changes in social organization. That the Jacksonians connected their "rotation in office" doctrine with egalitarianism was not simply opportunistic. Their recognition that administrative efficiency might be increased by establishing interchangeability of human "parts" required an egalitarian ethic; their faceless, specialized party organization did as well.

By starting with an assumption that, for organizational purposes, individuals could be considered as essentially equivalent, it then became possible to define offices by functional regulations only rather than by the personality or social status of the individuals who occupied them. An organization on this model gained efficiency by its flexibility. It could shift or replace personnel without impairing the integrity of the system as a whole. Offices themselves could be easily redefined so as to perform ever more efficiently the particular organizational function. A national political party should thus efficiently organize to manufacture public support for the administration or channel votes to it. Its principles of organization differed not at all from groups organized to administer the government or to perform economic and other private functions.

A year prior to the Bank veto message, the *Globe* explicitly described this vision. "Government is a *business*. It should be managed by *men of business*." Furthermore, "It is not for *show*; but for *use*." The function of government in society should not be "to make a few men *great*." Therefore, political leaders or officeholders "should not be raised by distinctive marks or unusual incomes, above their fellow-citizens"; nor should they have any "extraordinary dignity . . . attach to their stations." Government ought not to be considered the most important segment of society. In the ideal society, concluded the *Globe*, "In all that belongs to pomp and parade the rich citizen would excell the highest officer of government." Such a government would strictly tend to its business, furthermore, and not use its power to buttress social or economic establishments by granting "monopolies or exclusive privileges," an obvious reference to the Bank of the United States. "Under governments . . . administered by plain, industrious men who would as soon follow any other honest business, how happy would man be!"[54] The Bank veto message alluded to the same vision when it pronounced, with the same emphasis, "Banking . . . is *a business*. . . ."[55] While the proto-Whigs looked back to the role of political leaders like Washington, Hamilton, and Jefferson, this Jacksonian vision anticipated such opportunistic, popularly oriented politicians as Abraham Lincoln as well as such plain business organizers as John D. Rockefeller and Henry Ford. Kendall, architect of Jacksonian administrative reform, performed the same

[54] Washington *Globe*, July 14, 16, 19, 27, 1831. Cf. Weber: "The idea that the bureau activities of the state are intrinsically different in character from the management of private economic offices is a continental European notion and, by way of contrast, is totally foreign to the American way." (*From Max Weber*, ed. Gerth and Mills, 198.)

[55] *Messages and Papers*, ed. Richardson, II, 587. Jefferson had also used the terms "system" and "men of business" in connection with party organization, but clearly meant something quite different by them. (See Jefferson to Caesar A. Rodney, Dec. 31, 1802, as quoted in Cunningham, *Jeffersonians in Power*, 75–76.)

function, following his retirement from politics, for the early telegraph industry. The Jacksonian ideal, in short, envisioned a society made up of just the sorts of flexible, pragmatic organizations that have since become perhaps the most typical products of American culture.

As a political leader Jackson was a transitional figure. No matter how he might try to emulate Washington, the polished military paragon, or Jefferson, the humane political sage, he could not succeed. Jackson developed no elevated rational theory; he reacted directly to events, trusting to his intuitive grasp of immediate practical expedients. Thus he recognized the utility of efficient organization when he saw some particular practical function to be performed. Jackson's character may perhaps best be measured by his choice of chief political lieutenants. In Van Buren and Kendall he demonstrated his taste for the practical, the shrewd, the opportunistic, and the efficient—even though socially obscure.

No change occurred instantaneously in July 1832. The social movement in this period had begun long before and would continue for several decades, but the Age of Jackson, and specifically the veto of the Bank of the United States, was pivotal. Around this point a colonial order made itself over into modern industrial America. Political parties and government departments, especially the post office, were then the largest organizations in the country; the Jacksonian reorganization of them gave the first practical test to innovative techniques of large-scale rational organization on a peculiarly American model. American society would, before long, reorganize itself generally into a series of these great, specialized, flexible, rationally ordered systems, made up of mobile interchangeable operatives. The efficiency and productivity of those devoted to economic affairs would become the envy of the world. There has perhaps been no more sweeping and fundamental change in all of American history. The Whig party in the 1830's recognized it for what it was and fought valiantly against it, until the utter hopelessness of the struggle became too apparent.

Indian Removal and Land Allotment: The Civilized Tribes and Jacksonian Justice

Mary E. Young

The history of Indian-white relations on the American continent, as Mary E. Young of the Ohio State University suggests in the following essay, is as much a chronicle of ignorance, misdirected goodwill, and unanticipated injury as it is of intended evil and simple greed. The interrelationships of peoples are always complex. And, as the cultural anthropologists and sociologists—from whom Young has derived insight —tell us, the meeting of two distinct cultures is bound not only to create friction but also to affect the very structures and values of at least one of the societies.

The "classic" case of Indian removal was that of the Cherokees, in which the state of Georgia extended its jurisdiction over the Cherokee nation despite a Supreme Court decision that it had no authority to do so. We generally find this case cited as an instance of conflict between state and national power and between the courts and the executive branch. Equally compelling, however, is the chronicle of those tribes, like the Cherokees, that were able to adopt many white ways without doing much violence to their own traditions—and who still lost out to the dominant white culture. These Indians were sedentary farmers rather than wandering hunters. Along with the whites, their stock was in the land.

Yet, though Indians and whites together placed a high premium on land, they valued it for different reasons and had different concepts of land use. White Americans respected land ownership and actual farm settlement more for their money value in a market economy than for their suggestion of stability or identification with a community. For their part, the Indians were more concerned with the ancestral roots of their lands than with land values. The key to Jacksonian Indian policy, as Young indicates, lay with exploiting both these differences in relation to the land and the divisions in the native culture between the full-blood and half-breed Indians. The former retained the more or less undiluted values of Indian culture. Full-blood tribal elders thought of themselves as representatives of the entire tribe. They favored the collective ownership of land and, if necessary, its collective sale. The half-breeds, in contrast, not simply because of white blood but chiefly because of association with white culture, had assimilated many values of Western civilization. Out of cultural predisposition as well as self-interest, they preferred fee-simple land ownership and sale. Government agents, few of them venal but most wishing to exclude the Indians from lands coveted by whites, learned to treat with the half-breeds. In this way, they so eroded the solidarity of the tribes and so played on the inexperience of most Indians in "civilized" land dealings that the forced migration of the tribes eventually became possible.

As this essay suggests, the notion of cultural pluralism—the intermixture of cultures each of which is allowed to retain much of its own integrity and identity—is a sophisticated and relatively recent concept that Americans of the 1830s lacked almost to the extent that Americans of the 1970s find it difficult to accept. We must ask if the "solution" to the Indian problem adopted by the generation of the 1830s was any better than the complete assimilation of Indian culture would have been. If government

Indian Removal and Land Allotment: The Civilized Tribes and Jacksonian Justice. From *American Historical Review*, LXIV (October 1958), 31–45. Reprinted by permission of Mary E. Young. This article, in slightly different form, was delivered as a paper at the joint meeting of the Southern Historical Association and the American Historical Association in New York City, December 29, 1957.

agents sent to deal with the Indians were only reflecting the dominant white value system, then where did responsibility for the Indian policy lie? What then was the task of state and national governments in a democratic age: to be the servant of the people, as the Jacksonians claimed, or, in the manner of John Quincy Adams or Henry Clay (both rivals of Andrew Jackson), to direct and educate the people, in this case to their responsibilities toward the Indian? Such a question raises fundamental issues about the nature of democratic society.

*B*y the year 1830, the vanguard of the southern frontier had crossed the Mississippi and was pressing through Louisiana, Arkansas, and Missouri. But the line of settlement was by no means as solid as frontier lines were classically supposed to be. East of the Mississippi, white occupancy was limited by Indian tenure of northeastern Georgia, enclaves in western North Carolina and southern Tennessee, eastern Alabama, and the northern two thirds of Mississippi. In this twenty-five-million-acre domain lived nearly 60,000 Cherokees, Creeks, Choctaws, and Chickasaws.[1]

The Jackson administration sought to correct this anomaly by removing the tribes beyond the reach of white settlements, west of the Mississippi. As the President demanded of Congress in December, 1830:

> What good man would prefer a country covered with forests and ranged by a few thousand savages to our extensive Republic, studded with cities, towns, and prosperous farms, embellished with all the improvements which art can devise or industry execute, occupied by more than 12,000,000 happy people, and filled with all the blessings of liberty, civilization, and religion?[2]

The President's justification of Indian removal was the one usually applied to the displacement of the Indians by newer Americans—the superiority of a farming to a hunting culture, and of Anglo-American "liberty, civilization, and religion" to the strange and barbarous way of the red man. The superior capacity of the farmer to exploit the gifts of nature and of nature's God was one of the principal warranties of the triumph of westward-moving "civilization."[3]

Such a rationalization had one serious weakness as an instrument of policy.

[1] Ellen C. Semple, *American History and Its Geographic Conditions* (Boston, Mass., 1933), p. 160; Charles C. Royce, "Indian Land Cessions in the United States," Bureau of American Ethnology, *Eighteenth Annual Report, 1896–1897* (2 vols., Washington, D.C., 1899), II, Plates 1, 2, 15, 48, 54–56.

[2] James Richardson, *A Compilation of the Messages and Papers of the Presidents of the United States* (New York, 1897), III, 1084.

[3] Roy H. Pearce, *The Savages of America: A Study of the Indian and the Idea of Civilization* (Baltimore, Md., 1953), p. 70; *House Report 227*, 21 Cong., 1 sess., pp. 4–5.

The farmer's right of eminent domain over the lands of the savage could be asserted consistently only so long as the tribes involved were "savage." The southeastern tribes, however, were agriculturists as well as hunters. For two or three generations prior to 1830, farmers among them fenced their plantations and "mixed their labor with the soil," making it their private property according to accepted definitions of natural law. White traders who settled among the Indians in the mid-eighteenth century gave original impetus to this imitation of Anglo-American agricultural methods. Later, agents of the United States encouraged the traders and mechanics, their half-breed descendants, and their fullblood imitators who settled out from the tribal villages, fenced their farms, used the plow, and cultivated cotton and corn for the market. In the decade following the War of 1812, missionaries of various Protestant denominations worked among the Cherokees, Choctaws, and Chickasaws, training hundreds of Indian children in the agricultural, mechanical, and household arts and introducing both children and parents to the further blessings of literacy and Christianity.[4]

The "civilization" of a portion of these tribes embarrassed United States policy in more ways than one. Long-term contact between the southeastern tribes and white traders, missionaries, and government officials created and trained numerous half-breeds. The half-breed men acted as intermediaries between the less sophisticated Indians and the white Americans. Acquiring direct or indirect control of tribal politics, they often determined the outcome of treaty negotiations. Since they proved to be skillful bargainers, it became common practice to win their assistance by thinly veiled bribery. The rise of the half-breed to power, the rewards they received, and their efforts on behalf of tribal reform gave rise to bitter opposition. By the mid-1820's, this opposition made it dangerous for them to sell tribal lands. Furthermore, many of the new leaders had valuable plantations, mills, and trading establishments on these lands. Particularly among the Cherokees and Choctaws, they took pride in their achievements and those of their people in assimilating the trappings of civilization. As "founding Fathers," they prized the political and territorial integrity of the newly organized Indian "nations." These interests and convictions gave birth to a fixed de-

---

[4] Moravian missionaries were in contact with the Cherokees as early as the 1750's. Henry T. Malone, *Cherokees of the Old South: A People in Transition* (Athens, Ga., 1956), p. 92. There is a voluminous literature on the "civilization" of the civilized tribes. Among secondary sources, the following contain especially useful information: Malone, *Cherokees:* Marion Starkey, *The Cherokee Nation* (New York, 1946); Angie Debo, *The Rise and Fall of the Choctaw Republic* (Norman, Okla., 1934) and *The Road to Disappearance* (Norman, Okla., 1941); Grant Foreman, *Indian Removal: The Emigration of the Five Civilized Tribes of Indians* (2d ed., Norman, Okla., 1953); Robert S. Cotterill, *The Southern Indians: The Story of the Civilized Tribes before Removal* (Norman, Okla., 1954); Merrit B. Pound, *Benjamin Hawkins, Indian Agent* (Athens, Ga., 1951). Among the richest source material for tracing the agricultural development of the tribes are the published writings of the Creek agent, Benjamin Hawkins: *Letters of Benjamin Hawkins, 1796–1806* in Georgia Historical Society *Collections,* IX (Savannah, 1916), and *Sketch of the Creek Country in the Years 1798 and 1799* in Georgia Historical Society *Publications,* III (Americus, 1938). For the Choctaws and Cherokees, there is much information in the incoming correspondence of the American Board of Commissioners for Foreign Missions, Houghton Library, Harvard University. On the Chickasaws, see James Hull, "A Brief History of the Mississippi Territory," Mississippi Historical Society *Publications,* IX (Jackson, 1906).

termination, embodied in tribal laws and intertribal agreements, that no more cessions of land should be made. The tribes must be permitted to develop their new way of life in what was left of their ancient domain.[5]

Today it is a commonplace of studies in culture contact that the assimilation of alien habits affects different individuals and social strata in different ways and that their levels of acculturation vary considerably. Among the American Indian tribes, it is most often the families with white or half-breed models who most readily adopt the Anglo-American way of life. It is not surprising that half-breeds and whites living among the Indians should use their position as go-betweens to improve their status and power among the natives. Their access to influence and their efforts toward reform combine with pressures from outside to disturb old life ways, old securities, and established prerogatives. Resistance to their leadership and to the cultural alternatives they espouse is a fertile source of intratribal factions.[6]

To Jacksonian officials, however, the tactics of the half-breeds and the struggles among tribal factions seemed to reflect a diabolical plot. Treaty negotiators saw the poverty and "depravity" of the common Indian, who suffered from the scarcity of game, the missionary attacks on his accustomed habits and ceremonies, and the ravages of "demon rum" and who failed to find solace in the values of Christian and commercial civilization. Not unreasonably, they concluded that it was to the interest of the tribesman to remove west of the Mississippi. There, sheltered from the intruder and the whisky merchant, he could lose his savagery while improving his nobility. Since this seemed so obviously to the Indian's interest, the negotiators conveniently concluded that it was also his desire. What, then, deterred emigration? Only the rapacity of the half-breeds, who were unwilling to give up their extensive properties and their exalted position.[7]

These observers recognized that the government's difficulties were in part of its own making. The United States had pursued an essentially contradictory policy toward the Indians, encouraging both segregation and assimilation. Since Jefferson's administration, the government had tried periodically to secure the emigration of the eastern tribes across the Mississippi. At the same time, it had paid agents and subsidized missionaries who encouraged

[5] Paul W. Gates, "Introduction," *The John Tipton Papers* (3 vols., Indianapolis, Ind., 1942), I, 3–53; A. L. Kroeber, *Cultural and Natural Areas of Native North America* (Berkeley, Calif., 1939), pp. 62–63; John Terrell to General John Coffee, Sept. 15, 1829, Coffee Papers, Alabama Dept. of Archives and History; Campbell and Merriwether to Creek Chiefs, Dec. 9, 1824, *American State Papers: Indian Affairs*, II, 570; Clark, Hinds, and Coffee to James Barbour, Nov. 19, 1826, *ibid.*, p. 709.

[6] See for example, Edward M. Bruner, "Primary Group Experience and the Processes of Acculturation," *American Anthropologist*, LVIII (Aug., 1956), 605–23; SSRC Summer Seminar on Acculturation, "Acculturation: An Exploratory Formulation," *American Anthropologist*, LVI (Dec., 1954), esp. pp. 980–86; Alexander Spoehr, "Changing Kinship Systems: A Study in the Acculturation of the Creeks, Cherokee, and Choctaw," Field Museum of Natural History, *Anthropological Series*, XXXIII, no. 4, esp. pp. 216–26.

[7] Wilson Lumpkin, *The Removal of the Cherokee Indians from Georgia* (2 vols., New York, 1907), I, 61–77; Thomas L. McKenney to James Barbour, Dec. 27, 1826, *House Doc.* 28, 19 Cong., 2 sess., pp. 5–13; Andrew Jackson to Colonel Robert Butler, June 21, 1817, *Correspondence of Andrew Jackson*, ed. John Spencer Bassett (6 vols., Washington, D.C., 1926–28), II, 299.

the Indian to follow the white man's way. Thus it had helped create the class of tribesmen skilled in agriculture, pecuniary accumulation, and political leadership. Furthermore, by encouraging the southeastern Indians to become cultivators and Christians, the government had undermined its own moral claim to eminent domain over tribal lands. The people it now hoped to displace could by no stretch of dialectic be classed as mere wandering savages.[8]

By the time Jackson became President, then, the situation of the United States vis-à-vis the southeastern tribes was superficially that of irresistible force and immovable object. But the President, together with such close advisers as Secretary of War John H. Eaton and General John Coffee, viewed the problem in a more encouraging perspective. They believed that the government faced not the intent of whole tribes to remain near the bones of their ancestors but the selfish determination of a few quasi Indian leaders to retain their riches and their ill-used power. Besides, the moral right of the civilized tribes to their lands was a claim not on their whole domain but rather on the part cultivated by individuals. Both the Indian's natural right to his land and his political capacity for keeping it were products of his imitation of white "civilization." Both might be eliminated by a rigorous application of the principle that to treat an Indian fairly was to treat him like a white man. Treaty negotiations by the tried methods of purchase and selective bribery had failed. The use of naked force without the form of voluntary agreement was forbidden by custom, by conscience, and by fear that the administration's opponents would exploit religious sentiment which cherished the rights of the red man. But within the confines of legality and the formulas of voluntarism it was still possible to acquire the much coveted domain of the civilized tribes.

The technique used to effect this object was simple: the entire population of the tribes was forced to deal with white men on terms familiar only to the most acculturated portion of them. If the Indian is civilized, he can behave like a white man. Then let him take for his own as much land as he can cultivate, become a citizen of the state where he lives, and accept the burdens which citizenship entails. If he is not capable of living like this, he should be liberated from the tyranny of his chiefs and allowed to follow his own best interest by emigrating beyond the farthest frontiers of white settlement. By the restriction of the civilized to the lands they cultivate and by the emigration of the savages millions of acres will be opened to white settlement.

The first step dictated by this line of reasoning was the extension of state laws over the Indian tribes. Beginning soon after Jackson's election, Georgia, Alabama, Mississippi, and Tennessee gradually brought the Indians inside their borders under their jurisdiction. Thus an Indian could be sued for trespass or debt, though only in Mississippi and Tennessee was his testimony invariably acceptable in a court of law. In Mississippi, the tribesmen were

[8] For brief analyses of government policy, see Annie H. Abel, "The History of Events Resulting in Indian Consolidation West of the Mississippi," *Annual Report of the American Historical Association for the Year 1907* (2 vols., Washington, D.C. 1908), I, 233–450; George D. Harmon, *Sixty Years of Indian Affairs, 1789–1850* (Chapel Hill, N. Car., 1941).

further harassed by subjection—or the threat of subjection—to such duties as mustering with the militia, working on roads, and paying taxes. State laws establishing county governments within the tribal domains and, in some cases, giving legal protection to purchasers of Indian improvements encouraged the intrusion of white settlers on Indian lands. The laws nullified the legal force of Indian customs, except those relating to marriage. They provided heavy penalties for anyone who might enact or enforce tribal law. Finally, they threatened punishment to any person who might attempt to deter another from signing a removal treaty or enrolling for emigration. The object of these laws was to destroy the tribal governments and to thrust upon individual Indians the uncongenial alternative of adjusting to the burdens of citizenship or removing beyond state jurisdiction.[9]

The alternative was not offered on the unenlightened supposition that the Indians generally were capable of managing their affairs unaided in a white man's world. Governor Gayle of Alabama, addressing the "former chiefs and headmen of the Creek Indians" in June of 1834 urged them to remove from the state on grounds that

> you speak a different language from ours. You do not understand our laws and from your habits, cannot be brought to understand them. You are ignorant of the arts of civilized life. You have not like your white neighbors been raised in habits of industry and economy, the only means by which anyone can live, in settled countries, in even tolerable comfort. You know nothing of the skill of the white man in trading and making bargains, and cannot be guarded against the artful contrivances which dishonest men will resort to, to obtain your property under forms of contracts. In all these respects you are unequal to the white men, and if your people remain where they are, you will soon behold them in a miserable, degraded, and destitute condition.[10]

The intentions of federal officials who favored the extension of state laws are revealed in a letter written to Jackson by General Coffee. Referring to the Cherokees, Coffee remarked:

> Deprive the chiefs of the power they now possess, take from them their own code of laws, and reduce them to plain citizenship . . . and they will soon determine to move, and then there will be no difficulty in getting the poor Indians to give their consent. All this will be done by the State of Georgia if the U. States do not interfere with her law— . . . This will of course silence those in our country who constantly seek for causes to complain—It may indeed turn them loose upon Georgia, but that matters not, it is Georgia who clamors for the Indian lands, and she alone is entitled to the blame if any there be.[11]

Even before the laws were extended, the threat of state jurisdiction was used in confidential "talks" to the chiefs. After the states had acted, the sec-

[9] Georgia, *Acts*, Dec. 12, 1828; Dec. 19, 1829; Alabama, *Acts*, Jan. 27, 1829; Dec. 31, 1831; Jan. 16, 1832; Dec. 18, 1832; Mississippi, *Acts*, Feb. 4, 1829; Jan. 19, 1830; Feb. 12, 1830; Dec. 9, 1831; Oct. 26, 1832; Tennessee, *Acts*, Nov. 8, 1833; George R. Gilmer to Augustus S. Clayton, June 7, 1830, Governor's Letterbook, 1829–31, p. 36, Georgia Dept. of Archives and History.

[10] Governor John Gayle to former chiefs and headmen of the Creek Indians, June 16, 1834, Miscellaneous Letters to and from Governor Gayle, Alabama Dept. of Archives and History.

[11] Feb. 3, 1830, Jackson Papers, Library of Congress.

retary of war instructed each Indian agent to explain to his charges the meaning of state jurisdiction and to inform them that the President could not protect them against the enforcement of the laws.[12] Although the Supreme Court, in *Worcester* vs. *Georgia*, decided that the state had no right to extend its laws over the Cherokee nation, the Indian tribes being "domestic dependent nations" with limits defined by treaty, the President refused to enforce this decision.[13] There was only one means by which the government might have made "John Marshall's decision" effective—directing federal troops to exclude state officials and other intruders from the Indian domain. In January, 1832, the President informed an Alabama congressman that the United States government no longer assumed the right to remove citizens of Alabama from the Indian country. By this time, the soldiers who had protected the territory of the southeastern tribes against intruders had been withdrawn. In their unwearying efforts to pressure the Indians into ceding their lands, federal negotiators emphasized the terrors of state jurisdiction.[14]

Congress in May, 1830, complemented the efforts of the states by appropriating $500,000 and authorizing the President to negotiate removal treaties with all the tribes east of the Mississippi.[15] The vote on this bill was close in both houses. By skillful use of pamphlets, petitions, and lobbyists, missionary organizations had enlisted leading congressmen in their campaign against the administration's attempt to force the tribes to emigrate.[16] In the congressional debates, opponents of the bill agreed that savage tribes were duty-bound to relinquish their hunting grounds to the agriculturist, but they argued that the southeastern tribes were no longer savage. In any case, such relinquishment must be made in a freely contracted treaty. The extension of state laws over the Indian country was coercion; this made the negotiation of a free contract impossible. Both supporters and opponents of the bill agreed on one cardinal point—the Indian's moral right to keep his land depended on his actual cultivation of it.[17]

A logical corollary of vesting rights in land in proportion to cultivation was the reservation to individuals of as much land as they had improved at the time a treaty was signed. In 1816, Secretary of War William H. Crawford had proposed such reservations, or allotments, as a means of accommo-

[12] John H. Eaton to John Crowell, Mar. 27, 1829, Office of Indian Affairs, Letters Sent, V, 372–73, Records of the Bureau of Indian Affairs, National Archives; Middleton Mackey to John H. Eaton, Nov. 27, 1829, Choctaw Emigration File 111, *ibid.;* Andrew Jackson to Major David Haley, Oct. 10, 1829, Jackson Papers.

[13] 6 *Peters*, 515–97.

[14] Wiley Thompson to Messrs. Drew and Reese, Jan. 18, 1832, Indian Letters, 1782–1839, pp. 173–74, Georgia Dept. of Archives and History; John H. Eaton to Jackson, Feb. 21, 1831, *Sen. Doc. 65*, 21 Cong., 2 sess., p. 6; Cyrus Kingsbury to Jeremiah Evarts, Aug. 11, 1830, American Board of Commissioners for Foreign Missions Manuscripts; Tuskeneha to the President, May 21, 1831, Creek File 176, Records of the Bureau of Indian Affairs; Journal of the Commissioners for the Treaty of Dancing Rabbit Creek, *Sen. Doc.* 512, 23 Cong., 1 sess., p. 257.

[15] 4 *Statutes-at-Large*, 411–12.

[16] J. Orin Oliphant, ed., *Through the South and West with Jeremiah Evarts in 1826* (Lewisburg, Pa., 1956), pp. 47–61; Jeremiah Evarts to Rev. William Weisner, Nov. 27, 1829, American Board of Commissioners for Foreign Missions Manuscripts; *Sen. Docs.* 56, 59, 66, 73, 74, 76, 77, 92, 96, 21 Cong., 1 sess.

[17] Gales and Seaton, *Register of Debates in Congress, VI*, 311, 312, 320, 357, 361, 1022, 1024, 1039, 1061, 1110, 1135.

dating the removal policy to the program of assimilation. According to Crawford's plan, individual Indians who had demonstrated their capacity for civilization by establishing farms and who were willing to become citizens should be given the option of keeping their cultivated lands, by fee simple title, rather than emigrating. This offer was expected to reconcile the property-loving half-breeds to the policy of emigration. It also recognized their superior claim, as cultivators, on the regard and generosity of the government. The proposal was based on the assumption that few of the Indians were sufficiently civilized to want to become full-time farmers or state citizens.[18]

The Crawford policy was applied in the Cherokee treaties of 1817 and 1819 and the Choctaw treaty of 1820. These agreements offered fee simple allotments to heads of Indian families having improved lands within the areas ceded to the government. Only 311 Cherokees and eight Choctaws took advantage of the offer. This seemed to bear out the assumption that only a minority of the tribesmen would care to take allotments. Actually, these experiments were not reliable. In both cases, the tribes ceded only a fraction of their holdings. Comparatively few took allotments; but on the other hand, few emigrated. The majority simply remained within the diminished tribal territories east of the Mississippi.[19]

The offer of fee simple allotments was an important feature of the negotiations with the tribes in the 1820's. When the extension of state laws made removal of the tribes imperative, it was to be expected that allotments would comprise part of the consideration offered for the ceded lands. Both the ideology which rationalized the removal policy and the conclusions erroneously drawn from experience with the earlier allotment treaties led government negotiators to assume that a few hundred allotments at most would be required.

The Choctaws were the first to cede their eastern lands. The treaty of Dancing Rabbit Creek, signed in September, 1830, provided for several types of allotment. Special reservations were given to the chiefs and their numerous family connections; a possible 1,600 allotments of 80 to 480 acres, in proportion to the size of the beneficiary's farm, were offered others who intended to emigrate. These were intended for sale to private persons or to the government, so that the Indian might get the maximum price for his improvements. The fourteenth article of the treaty offered any head of an Indian family who did not plan to emigrate the right to take up a quantity of land proportional to the number of his dependents. At the end of five years' residence those who received these allotments were to have fee simple title to their lands and become citizens. It was expected that approximately two hundred persons would take land under this article.[20]

[18] *American State Papers: Indian Affairs*, II, 27. A general history of the allotment policy is Jay P. Kinney, *A Continent Lost—A Civilization Won: Indian Land Tenure in America* (Baltimore, Md., 1937).

[19] 7 *Statutes-at-Large*, 156–60, 195–200, 210–14; Cherokee Reservation Book, Records of the Bureau of Indian Affairs; Special Reserve Book A, *ibid.*; James Barbour to the Speaker of the House, Jan. 23, 1828, *American State Papers: Public Lands*, V, 396–97.

[20] 7 *Statutes-at-Large*, 334–41; manuscript records of negotiations are in Choctaw File 112, Records of the Bureau of Indian Affairs.

The Creeks refused to sign any agreements promising to emigrate, but their chiefs were persuaded that the only way to put an end to intrusions on their lands was to sign an allotment treaty.[21] In March, 1832, a Creek delegation in Washington signed a treaty calling for the allotment of 320 acres to each head of a family, the granting of certain supplementary lands to the chiefs and to orphans, and the cession of the remaining territory to the United States. If the Indian owners remained on their allotments for five years, they were to receive fee simple titles and become citizens.[22] Returning to Alabama, the chiefs informed their people that they had not actually sold the tribal lands but "had only made each individual their own guardian, that they might take care of their own possessions, and act as agents for themselves."[23]

Unlike the Creeks, the Chickasaws were willing to admit the inevitability of removal. But they needed land east of the Mississippi on which they might live until they acquired a home in the west. The Chickasaw treaty of May, 1832, therefore, provided generous allotments for heads of families, ranging from 640 to 3,200 acres, depending on the size of the family and the number of its slaves. These allotments were to be auctioned publicly when the tribe emigrated and the owners compensated for their improvements out of the proceeds.[24] Although the fullblood Chickasaws apparently approved of the plan for a collective sale of the allotments, the half-breeds, abetted by white traders and planters, persuaded the government to allow those who held allotments to sell them individually.[25] An amended treaty of 1834 complied with the half-breeds' proposals. It further stipulated that leading half-breeds and the old chiefs of the tribe comprise a committee to determine the competence of individual Chickasaws to manage their property. Since the committee itself disposed of the lands of the "incompetents," this gave both protection to the unsophisticated and additional advantage to the half-breeds.[26]

Widespread intrusion on Indian lands began with the extension of state laws over the tribal domains. In the treaties of cession, the government promised to remove intruders, but its policy in this respect was vacillating and ineffective. Indians whose allotments covered valuable plantations proved anxious to promote the sale of their property by allowing buyers to enter the ceded territory as soon as possible. Once this group of whites was admitted, it became difficult to discriminate against others. Thus a large number of intruders settled among the Indians with the passive connivance

[21] John Crowell to Lewis Cass, Jan. 25, 1832, Creek File 178, Records of the Bureau of Indian Affairs.

[22] 7 *Statutes-at-Large*, 366–68.

[23] John Scott to Lewis Cass, Nov. 12, 1835, Creek File 193, Records of the Bureau of Indian Affairs.

[24] 7 *Statutes-at-large*, 381–89.

[25] John Terrell to Henry Cook, Oct. 29, 1832 (copy), John D. Terrell Papers, Alabama Dept. of Archives and History; Benjamin Reynolds to John Coffee, Dec. 12, 1832, Chickasaw File 83, Records of the Bureau of Indian Affairs; Terrell to John Tyler, Feb. 26, 1841 (draft), Terrell Papers; G. W. Long to John Coffee, Dec. 15, 1832, Coffee Papers; Rev. T. C. Stuart to Daniel Green, Oct. 14, 1833, American Board of Commissioners for Foreign Missions Manuscripts.

[26] 7 *Statutes-at-Large*, 450–57.

of the War Department and the tribal leaders. The task of removing them was so formidable that after making a few gestures the government generally evaded its obligation. The misery of the common Indians, surrounded by intruders and confused by the disruption of tribal authority, was so acute that any method for securing their removal seemed worth trying. Furthermore, their emigration would serve the interest of white settlers, land speculators, and their representatives in Washington. The government therefore chose to facilitate the sale of allotments even before the Indians received fee simple title to them.[27]

The right to sell his allotment was useful to the sophisticated tribesman with a large plantation. Such men were accustomed to selling their crops and hiring labor. Through their experience in treaty negotiations, they had learned to bargain over the price of lands. Many of them received handsome payment for their allotments. Some kept part of their holdings and remained in Alabama and Mississippi as planters—like other planters, practicing as land speculators on the side.[28] Nearly all the Indians had some experience in trade, but to most of them the conception of land as a salable commodity was foreign. They had little notion of the exact meaning of an "acre" or the probable value of their allotments.[29] The government confused them still further by parceling out the lands according to Anglo-American, rather than aboriginal notions of the family structure and land ownership. Officials insisted, for example, that the "father" rather than the "mother" must be defined as head of the family and righteously refused to take cognizance of the fact that many "fathers" had "a plurality of wives."[30]

[27] William Ward to Secretary of War, Oct. 22, 1831, Choctaw Reserve File 133; Mushulatubbee to Lewis Cass, Feb. 9, 1832, Choctaw File 113; W. S. Colquhoun to General George S. Gibson, Apr. 20, 1832, Choctaw Emigration File 121; A. Campbell to Secretary of War, Aug. 5, 1832, Choctaw File 113; John Kurtz to Benjamin Reynolds, Aug. 9, 1833, Office of Indian Affairs, Letters Sent, XI, 74; S. C. Barton to Elbert Herring, Nov. 11, 1833, Choctaw File 113; William M. Gwin to Lewis Cass, Apr. 8, 1834, Choctaw File 84, Records of the Bureau of Indian Affairs; Mary E. Young, "The Creek Frauds: A Study in Conscience and Corruption," *Mississippi Valley Historical Review*, XLVII (Dec., 1955), 415–19.

[28] Benjamin Reynolds to Lewis Cass, Dec. 9, 1832, Apr. 29, 1835, Chickasaw File 83 85, Records of the Bureau of Indian Affairs; David Haley to Jackson, Apr. 15, 1831, *Sen. Doc.* 512, 23 Cong., 1 sess., p. 426; Elbert Herring to George W. Elliott, Jan. 23, 1833, Office of Indian Affairs, Letters Sent, IX, 516, Records of the Bureau of Indian Affairs; J. J. Abert to J. R. Poinsett, July 19, 1839, Creek File 220, *ibid*. See Special Reserve Books and Special Reserve Files A and C, and William Carroll's List of Certified Contracts for the Sale of Chickasaw Reservations, Special File, Chickasaw, Records of the Bureau of Indian Affairs, and compare Chickasaw Location Book, Records of the Bureau of Land Management, National Archives.

[29] George S. Snyderman, "Concepts of Land Ownership among the Iroquois and their Neighbors," in *Symposium on Local Variations in Iroquois Culture*, ed. William N. Fenton, Bureau of American Ethnology *Bulletin 149* (Washington, D.C., 1951), pp. 16–26; Petition of Choctaw Chiefs and Headmen, Mar. 2, 1832, Choctaw Reserve File 133; James Colbert to Lewis Cass, June 5, 1835, Chickasaw File 84; Benjamin Reynolds to Elbert Herring, Mar. 11, 1835, Chickasaw File 85, Records of the Bureau of Indian Affairs.

[30] Memorial of Chickasaw Chiefs to the President, Nov. 25, 1835, Chickasaw File 84; Thomas J. Abbott and E. Parsons, Sept. 7, 1832, *Sen Doc.* 512, 23 Cong., 1 sess., pp. 443–44; Elbert Herring to E. Parsons, B. S. Parsons, and John Crowell, Oct. 10, 1832, *ibid.*, p. 524; Leonard Tarrant to E. Herring, May 15, 1833, Creek File 202, Records of the

Under these conditions, it is not surprising that the common Indian's legal freedom of contract in selling his allotment did not necessarily lead him to make the best bargain possible in terms of his pecuniary interests. Nor did the proceeds of the sales transform each seller into an emigrant of large independent means. A right of property and freedom to contract for its sale did not automatically invest the Indian owner with the habits, values, and skills of a sober land speculator. His acquisition of property and freedom actually increased his dependence on those who traditionally mediated for him in contractual relations with white Americans.

Prominent among these mediators were white men with Indian wives who made their living as planters and traders in the Indian nations, men from nearby settlements who traded with the leading Indians or performed legal services for them, and interpreters. In the past, such individuals had been appropriately compensated for using their influence in favor of land cessions. It is likely that their speculative foresight was in part responsible for the allotment features in the treaties of the 1830's. When the process of allotting lands to individuals began, these speculative gentlemen made loans of whisky, muslin, horses, slaves, and other useful commodities to the new property-owner. They received in return the Indian's written promise to sell his allotment to them as soon as its boundaries were defined. Generally they were on hand to help him locate it on "desirable" lands. They, in turn, sold their "interest" in the lands to men of capital. Government agents encouraged the enterprising investor, since it was in the Indian's interest and the government's policy that the lands be sold and the tribes emigrate.[31] Unfortunately, the community of interest among the government, the speculator, and the Indian proved largely fictitious. The speculator's interest in Indian lands led to frauds which impoverished the Indians, soiled the reputation of the government, and retarded the emigration of the tribes.

An important factor in this series of complications was the government's fallacious assumption that most of the "real Indians" were anxious to emigrate. Under the Choctaw treaty, for example, registration for fee simple allotments was optional, the government expecting no more than two hundred registrants. When several full-bloods applied for lands, the Choctaw agent assumed that they were being led astray by "designing men" and told them they must emigrate. Attorneys took up the Choctaw claims, located thousands of allotments in hopes that Congress would confirm them,

Bureau of Indian Affairs; Alexander Spoehr, "Kinship Systems," pp. 201–31; John R. Swanton, *Indians of the Southeastern United States*, Bureau of American Ethnology *Bulletin 137* (Washington, D.C., 1946).

[31] John Coffee to Andrew Jackson, July 10, 1830, Creek File 192, Records of the Bureau of Indian Affairs; John Crowell to John H. Eaton, Aug. 8, 1830, Creek File 175, *ibid.*; John H. Brodnax to Lewis Cass, Mar. 12, 1832, *Sen. Doc.* 512, 23 Cong., 1 sess., III, 258–59; John Terrell to General John Coffee, Sept. 15, 1829, Coffee Papers; J. J. Abert to [Lewis Cass], June 13, 1833, Creek File 202, Records of the Bureau of Indian Affairs; contract between Daniel Wright and Mingo Mushulatubbee, Oct. 7, 1830, *American State Papers: Public Lands*, VII, 19; W. S. Colquhoun to Lewis Cass, Sept. 20, 1833, *ibid.*, p .13; Chapman Levy to Joel R. Poinsett, June 19, 1837, Choctaw Reserve File 139, Records of the Bureau of Indian Affairs; James Colbert to Lewis Cass, June 5, 1835, Chickasaw File 84, *ibid.*; Chancery Court, Northern District of Mississippi, Final Record A, 111, M, 235–37, Courthouse, Holly Springs, Mississippi.

and supported their clients in Mississippi for twelve to fifteen years while the government debated and acted on the validity of the claims. There was good reason for this delay. Settlers and rival speculators, opposing confirmation of the claims, advanced numerous depositions asserting that the attorneys, in their enterprising search for clients, had materially increased the number of claimants.[32] Among the Creeks, the Upper Towns, traditionally the conservative faction of the tribe, refused to sell their allotments. Since the Lower Towns proved more compliant, speculators hired willing Indians from the Lower Towns to impersonate the unwilling owners. They then bought the land from the impersonators. The government judiciously conducted several investigations of these frauds, but in the end the speculators outmaneuvered the investigators. Meanwhile, the speculators kept the Indians from emigrating until their contracts were approved. Only the outbreak of fighting between starving Creeks and their settler neighbors enabled the government, under pretext of a pacification, to remove the tribe.[33]

Besides embarrassing the government, the speculators contributed to the demoralization of the Indians. Universal complaint held that after paying the tribesman for his land they often borrowed back the money without serious intent of repaying it, or recovered it in return for overpriced goods, of which a popular article was whisky. Apprised of this situation, Secretary of War Lewis Cass replied that once the Indian had been paid for his land, the War Department had no authority to circumscribe his freedom to do what he wished with the proceeds.[34]

Nevertheless, within their conception of the proper role of government, officials who dealt with the tribes tried to be helpful. Although the Indian must be left free to contract for the sale of his lands, the United States sent agents to determine the validity of the contracts. These agents sometimes refused to approve a contract that did not specify a fair price for the land in question. They also refused official sanction when it could not be shown that the Indian owner had at some time been in possession of the sum stipulated.[35] This protective action on the part of the government, together with its several investigations into frauds in the sale of Indian lands, apparently did secure the payment of more money than the tribesmen might otherwise have had. But the effort was seriously hampered by the near impossibility of obtaining disinterested testimony.

In dealing with the Chickasaws, the government managed to avoid most of the vexing problems which had arisen in executing the allotment pro-

[32] Mary E. Young, "Indian Land Allotments in Alabama and Mississippi, 1830–1860" (manuscript doctoral dissertation, Cornell University, 1955), pp. 70–82; Franklin L. Riley, "The Choctaw Land Claims," Mississippi Historical Society *Publications*, VIII (1904), 370–82; Harmon, *Indian Affairs*, pp. 226–59.

[33] Young, "Creek Frauds," pp. 411–37.

[34] Lewis Cass to Return J. Meigs, Oct. 31, 1834, *Sen. Doc.* 428, 24 Cong., 1 sess., p. 23.

[35] Lewis Cass, "Regulations," for certifying Creek contracts, Nov. 28, 1833, *Sen. Doc.* 276, 24 Cong., 1 sess., pp. 88–89; *id.*, "Regulations," Feb. 8, 1836, Chickasaw Letterbook A, 76–78, Records of the Bureau of Indian Affairs; Secretary of War to the President, June 27, 1836, Choctaw Reserve File 136, *ibid.* For adjudications based on the above regulations, see Special Reserve Files A and C and Choctaw, Creek, and Chickasaw Reserve Files, Records of the Bureau of Indian Affairs, *passim.*

gram among their southeastern neighbors. This was due in part to the improvement of administrative procedures, in part to the methods adopted by speculators in Chickasaw allotments, and probably most of all to the inflated value of cotton lands during the period in which the Chickasaw territory was sold. Both the government and the Chickasaws recognized that the lands granted individuals under the treaty were generally to be sold, not settled. They therefore concentrated on provisions for supervising sales and safeguarding the proceeds.[36] Speculators in Chickasaw lands, having abundant resources, paid an average price of $1.70 per acre. The Chickasaws thereby received a better return than the government did at its own auctions. The buyers' generosity may be attributed to their belief that the Chickasaw lands represented the last first-rate cotton country within what were then the boundaries of the public domain. In their pursuit of a secure title, untainted by fraud, the capitalists operating in the Chickasaw cession established a speculators' claim association which settled disputes among rival purchasers. Thus they avoided the plots, counterplots, and mutual recriminations which had hampered both speculators and government in their dealings with the Creeks and Choctaws.[37]

A superficially ironic consequence of the allotment policy as a method of acquiring land for white settlers was the fact that it facilitated the engrossment of land by speculators. With their superior command of capital and the influence it would buy, speculators acquired 80 to 90 per cent of the lands allotted to the southeastern tribesmen.[38]

For most of the Indian beneficiaries of the policy, its most important consequence was to leave them landless. After selling their allotment, or a claim to it, they might take to the swamp, live for a while on the bounty of a still hopeful speculator, or scavenge on their settler neighbors. But ultimately most of them faced the alternative of emigration or destitution, and chose to emigrate. The machinations of the speculators and the hopes they nurtured that the Indians might somehow be able to keep a part of their allotted lands made the timing of removals less predictable than it might otherwise have been. This unpredictability compounded the evils inherent in a mass migration managed by a government committed to economy and unversed in the arts of economic planning. The result was the "Trail of Tears."[39]

The spectacular frauds committed among the Choctaws and Creeks, the administrative complications they created and the impression they gave that

[36] "Memorial of the Creek Nation . . . ," Jan. 29, 1883, *House Misc. Doc.* 18, 47 Cong., 2 sess.

[37] Average price paid for Chickasaw lands computed from William Carroll's List of Certified Contracts, Special Reserve File, Chickasaw, Records of the Bureau of Indian Affairs; Young, "Indian Allotments," 154–67.

[38] See calculations in Young, "Indian Allotments," 141–42, 163–64. No system of estimating percentages of land purchased for speculation from figures of sales is foolproof. The assumption used in this estimate was that all those who bought 2,000 acres or more might be defined as speculators. Compare James W. Silver, "Land Speculation Profits in the Chickasaw Cession," *Journal of Southern History,* X (Feb., 1944), 84–92.

[39] For the story of emigration, see Foreman, *Indian Removal;* Debo, *Road to Disappearance,* pp. 103–107 and *Choctaw Republic,* pp. 55–57. Relations between speculation and emigration can be traced in the Creek, Choctaw, and Chickasaw Emigration and Reserve Files, Records of the Bureau of Indian Affairs.

certain self-styled champions of the people were consorting with the avaricious speculator gave the allotment policy a bad reputation. The administration rejected it in dealing with the Cherokees,[40] and the policy was not revived on any considerable scale until 1854, when it was applied, with similar consequences, to the Indians of Kansas.[41] In the 1880's, when allotment in severalty became a basic feature of American Indian policy, the "civilized tribes," then in Oklahoma, strenuously resisted its application to them. They cited their memories of the 1830's as an important reason for their intransigence.[42]

The allotment treaties of the 1830's represent an attempt to apply Anglo-American notions of justice, which enshrined private property in land and freedom of contract as virtually absolute values, to Indian tribes whose tastes and traditions were otherwise. Their history illustrates the limitations of intercultural application of the Golden Rule. In a more practical sense, the treaties typified an effort to force on the Indians the alternative of complete assimilation or complete segregation by placing individuals of varying levels of sophistication in situations where they must use the skills of businessmen or lose their means of livelihood. This policy secured tribal lands while preserving the forms of respect for property rights and freedom of contract, but it proved costly to both the government and the Indians.

How lightly that cost was reckoned, and how enduring the motives and rationalizations that gave rise to it, may be gathered from the subsequent experience of the southeastern tribes in Oklahoma. There, early in the twentieth century, the allotment policy was again enforced, with safeguards hardly more helpful to the unsophisticated than those of the 1830's. Once more, tribal land changed owners for the greater glory of liberty, civilization, and profit.[43]

Suggested Reading

Two classic and continually fresh analyses of American society in the 1830s are those of two French visitors, Alexis de Tocqueville, who wrote the more analytical *Democracy in America*,* ed. by Phillips Bradley, 2 vols. (1945), and Michael Chevalier, who wrote the more casual *Society, Manners, and Politics in the United States** (1961). The best recent overview of the era of Jackson, which incorporates most of the current scholarship, is Edward Pessen's *Jacksonian*

[40] Hon. R. Chapman to Lewis Cass, Jan. 25, 1835, Cherokee File 7, Records of the Bureau of Indian Affairs; Lewis Cass to Commissioners Carroll and Schermerhorn, Apr. 2, 1835, Office of Indian Affairs, Letters Sent, XV, 261, *ibid.*; "Journal of the Proceedings at the Council held at New Echota . . . ," Cherokee File 7, *ibid.*, Joint Memorial of the Legislature of the State of Alabama . . . , Jan. 9, 1836, *ibid.*; William Gilmer to Andrew Jackson, Feb. 9, 1835, Jackson Papers; 7 *Statutes-at-Large*, 483–84, 488–89.

[41] Paul W. Gates, *Fifty Million Acres: Conflicts over Kansas Land Policy, 1854–1890* (Ithaca, N.Y., 1954), pp. 11–48.

[42] Memorial of the Creek Nation on the Subject of Lands in Severalty Among the Several Indian Tribes," Jan. 29, 1883, *House Misc. Doc.* 18, 47 Cong., 2 sess.

[43] Compare Angie Debo, *The Five Civilized Tribes of Oklahoma: Report on Social and Economic Conditions* (Philadelphia, Pa., 1951) and Kinney, *Indian Land Tenure*, pp. 243–44.

America: Society, Personality, and Politics* (1969). A thoughtful and distinctive study of public issues between the War of 1812 and the time of Jackson's election is George Dangerfield's *The Awakening of American Nationalism, 1815–1828** (1965).

The modern debate over Jackson's politics commenced with Arthur M. Schlesinger, Jr.'s *The Age of Jackson** (1945), which still repays careful attention. Two differing and provocative interpretations are Richard Hofstadter's "Andrew Jackson and the Rise of Liberal Capitalism," in his *The American Political Tradition and the Men Who Made It** (1948), pp. 44–66, and Bray Hammond's *Banks and Politics in America: From the Revolution to the Civil War** (1957), chapters 11–15, who argues that Jacksonianism was the politics of expectant capitalists. Marvin Meyers in *The Jacksonian Persuasion** (1957) depicts Jackson and his adherents as trying to restore the older verities rather than to create a new order. The role of Jackson himself as a man for his season is explored by John William Ward in *Andrew Jackson: Symbol for an Age** (1955). Lee Benson in *The Concept of Jacksonian Democracy: New York as a Test Case** (1961) distinguishes the politics of the era on the basis of distinct ethno-cultural value systems and questions whether Jacksonian Democracy existed. A path-breaking essay, which places in sharp perspective the electoral achievements of Jacksonian "democracy," is Richard P. McCormick's "New Perspectives on Jacksonian Politics," *American Historical Review*, LXV (January 1960).

The fullest, but not the most integrated, survey of the party structure of the 1830s is Richard P. McCormick's *The Second American Party System: Party Formation in the Jacksonian Era** (1966), which McCormick has usefully compressed in "Political Development and the Second Party System," in William Nisbet Chambers and Walter Dean Burnham, eds., *The American Party Systems: Stages of Political Development** (1967). The two major episodes of Jackson's presidency, nullification and the Bank War, are treated in William W. Freehling's *Prelude to Civil War: The Nullification Controversy in South Carolina, 1816–1836** (1965), and Robert V. Remini's *Andrew Jackson and the Bank War** (1967). Most of the conflicting interpretations and differing approaches to Jacksonian democracy are usefully brought together in Edward Pessen, ed., *New Perspectives on Jacksonian Parties and Politics** (1969).

* Also published in paperback edition.

Society and Reform
at Mid-Century

The Dimensions
of Occupational Mobility

Stephan Thernstrom

The "rags-to-riches" myth has exerted a profound
influence on American thought and expectations since
the onset of colonization. Like all myths, this one
had a basis in reality. At least some men of humble
origins moved rapidly up the scale of wealth and
status—rapidly enough at least to draw attention to
their good fortune and make others believe that such
ascent was within their grasp. Also like all myths, this
one contained exaggeration and created a false and
sometimes tragic sense of reality.

Historians have long explored the contents of the
myth through the lives of exceptional individuals
—like Andrew Carnegie—and through imaginative
literature—such as the stories of Horatio Alger. But
not until recently have they begun systematically to
examine the reality of past social mobility in the
United States, with which sociologists have dealt
concretely for some time. The selection that follows
(taken from a longer study, as occasional references
will suggest) represents not only this new historical
concern but also the result of the exploitation of often
ignored historical sources. In it, Stephan Thernstrom of
Harvard University selects Newburyport,
Massachusetts, as a case study and seeks to discover

343

the measurable incidence of social mobility in one mid-nineteenth-century city.

This essay is an example of what has come to be called the "new" social history. Its practitioners turn for information to records of births and deaths, census files, tax rolls, cemetery registers, and business directories. They are more interested—though not exclusively so, as Thernstrom's essay indicates—in the composition and activities of large populations than in individual lives. Through techniques of statistical inference and sophisticated computer calculations, they deal with concepts of percentage and probability.

As Thernstrom suggests, the results can be of great significance. He finds in nineteenth-century Newburyport, among other things, a large, anonymous, floating population of unskilled workers whose upward mobility, if it ever existed, is almost impossible to measure due to their constant motion in and out of town. He is able to demonstrate greater mobility among semiskilled and skilled workers than among the unskilled; among the native-born than the immigrant workers; between generations than within them. Even so, upward mobility was slight in all categories and infrequent between manual and nonmanual trades. The resulting picture is that of a spatially fluid society with a relatively low incidence of social mobility—by no means what the rags-to-riches myth would have us believe.

Not only do Thernstrom's discoveries throw into question the reputedly great economic mobility of Americans; they also create wonder that, given the lack of mobility and the existence of actual deprivation, radical social movements never gained much force in the United States. It may be, of course, that Newburyport and the other industrial cities of New England at the time were exceptional in their low level of opportunity, that higher social mobility existed elsewhere. The vast migration of the least well off also helped prevent the coming together of stable unskilled working-class populations who might have provided the tinder of revolution. What is more, the very belief in mobility reduced social pressures: though failure was at hand, success might still lie just ahead.

The Dimensions of Occupational Mobility. Reprinted by permission of the publishers from Stephan Thernstrom, *Poverty and Progress: Social Mobility in a Nineteenth-Century City*, pp. 80–114, Cambridge, Mass.: Harvard University Press, Copyright, 1964, by the President and Fellows of Harvard College.

But, of course, an explanation for the relative
placidity of the working population might lie
elsewhere. How did workers value their own capacity
to effect change? Had they become fatalists? It may
be that the "rags-to-riches" myth never penetrated to
the most needy working families, that it was a myth
held primarily by the venturesome and somewhat
more secure lower middle classes.

*J*ohn R. Fowle was an ordinary workman of Newburyport, nothing more. Born in New Hampshire in 1802, Fowle was listed
variously as "laborer," "gardener," and "porter" in the census schedules and
local city directories of the 1850–1880 period. Nor did he display any great
talent for saving money; the census and tax assessor's records show him
without any property holdings during these years. Fowle had five daughters and four sons; none of them received much education. Two of the
sons left Newburyport while still youths. A third started work as a common
laborer, but after a few years of unskilled labor, and a few more as an operative in a shoe factory, he was able to open a small grocery; the shop was
rented, and his inventory was valued at $300.

John Fowle's youngest son, Stephen, had a more striking career. Where he
obtained the capital for his first venture into business is unknown. In 1856,
a lad of twenty-two, he paid only a poll tax. Two years later tax records
show him the owner of a house and lot valued at $1100, and the city direc-
tory lists him as a "newsdealer." His news agency prospered, and Stephen
was willing to take risks. He sold the house for $1250 in 1862, and looked
for new possibilities. Not long after, with the aid of $4500 borrowed from
the Institution for Savings, he entered into a series of transactions which
gained him a home just off the best residential street (High) and a shop on
the main business thoroughfare (State). His real estate holdings reached
$8000 by the time of the Census of 1870; his inventories of periodicals,
fruit, and sundries approached $2000. The Fowle store is still doing well on
the same site after ninety years, though the family itself has disappeared
from the city.

Michael Lowry, born in Ireland in 1815, came to the New World in the
great exodus following the famine. Lowry settled in Newburyport in the
late forties, and worked there as a day laborer the rest of his life. His eight
sons were put to work as soon as they were able, but the family remained
propertyless, living in rented quarters along the waterfront. One son, James,
had a minor success; he saved $450 out of his wages as a mariner to purchase
a house. None of the other children appear to have advanced in the slight-
est; all were unskilled laborers or seamen in 1880, lacking property holdings
or savings accounts. Thomas Lowry did embark on certain ventures which

might have produced a considerable income, but his brief career as a house-breaker ended with five years behind bars.

Pat Moylan was one of the few laborers in Newburyport who owned his own home in 1850. Moylan too was Irish, but he had immigrated to America well before the Great Famine, and had married a native-born girl. His successes over this thirty-year period were moderate, but they were sufficient to allow his children greater career opportunities than was common at this social level. Sometime in the 1850's Moylan found the job he was to hold until his death—night watchman at a textile mill. If his daily wages were not much higher than they had been as a common laborer, he was now sure of steady employment. His Olive Street home, valued at $700, made it unnecessary to pay out a large portion of his income in rent; he reported an additional $300 in personal property on the Census of 1870. Moylan's children were freer than most of their companions from compelling pressure to enter the labor market at the earliest possible age. Two of his five daughters graduated from the Female High School, a rare achievement for a working class girl at this time. Moylan's eldest son became a factory operative at sixteen, but during the Civil War decade acquired the skills of a blacksmith. Albert and James entered more promising situations; one was employed as a clerk in a cotton mill in 1880, while the other was still studying at Brown High School.

William Hardy, like John Fowle, was a native-born day laborer; like Fowle, Hardy never succeeded in accumulating any property. Hardy's two eldest sons did little better; one became a seaman, the other a factory operative. His two younger boys, however, were able to move into a skilled manual calling. Neither James, a machinist, nor Frank, a molder, could claim any property holdings in 1880, but each had entered occupations with earning opportunities well above those for unskilled labor.

The families of Michael and Jeremiah Haley achieved impressive property mobility without any occupational mobility at all. Michael and Jeremiah were recorded as common laborers in the Eighth, Ninth, and Tenth United States Censuses. In 1860 Michael owned property on Monroe Street worth $700; Jeremiah had none. In 1864 Jeremiah, who had three young children working to supplement his income, bought a half share in the Monroe Street house for $400; Michael used this sum to purchase another lot. Michael added steadily to his holdings; by 1880 he paid taxes on $1700 in real estate. In 1870 Jeremiah sold his half share back to Michael, and invested in a larger place on Dove Street, valued at $900 in 1880. The two brothers between them had five sons, none of whom entered any skilled or nonmanual occupation. One of Jeremiah's sons, Pat, did save enough money to build a small house next door to his father's, but he too remained but an ordinary unskilled manual laborer.[1]

These few sketches make one thing quite clear. The situation of the hundreds of Newburyport residents ranked common laborers on the United

---

[1] Information for these cases was drawn from the following sources: manuscript schedules of the Seventh, Eighth, Ninth and Tenth U.S. Censuses; Newburyport Assessor's Valuation Lists, 1850–1880; local city directories; newspapers; a series of manuscript volumes of registrations for the Putnam, Brown, and Female high schools for this period (scattered years). The school registration records are stored in the office of the Superintendent of Schools at the Newburyport High School.

States Census of 1850, 1860, and 1870 had seemed bleak: these men and their families shared a common plight as members of the lowest social stratum in the community. As these cases reveal, however, not all of these families remained at the very bottom of the Newburyport social ladder. Some, like the Lowrys, were trapped in poverty and illiteracy; others were socially mobile in a variety of ways. This much can be established by examining the life histories of a few families. But a handful of instances cannot reveal what *proportion* of the laboring population of Newburyport reaped the benefits of social mobility, nor can it indicate what *avenues* of social advance were of particular significance to the working class. Perhaps the Lowry family was typical, and the Fowles a curious exception; perhaps the embittered editor of the Boston *Pilot* was right that 95 out of 100 workmen in America were fated to "live and die in the condition in which they were born."[2] Or was Stephen Fowle a representative man, an example of the opportunities open to a wide segment of the working class? To answer the question requires a statistical analysis of social mobility.

Social mobility refers to the process by which individuals alter their social position. But to say this, unhappily, is to say nothing until social position has been defined. The terms social status and social class raise perilously complex and disputed problems of definition. A brief comment at this point will clarify the approach taken here; the subject will be considered further in a later chapter. One major sociological school—represented by W. Lloyd Warner and his followers—emphasizes the prestige dimension of class; the study of social mobility becomes the study of the subtle "climbing" tactics by which the ambitious manipulate others in an effort to improve their prestige rank. Status is measured by polling the community social elite; great emphasis is placed on the intricacies of etiquette. Whatever the merits of this subjective approach to social class and social mobility, it is of little value to the historian, for historical records rarely yield the information necessary to apply prestige categories systematically to societies of the past.

The historical study of social mobility requires the use of objective criteria of social status. The most convenient of these is occupation. Occupation may be only one variable in a comprehensive theory of class, but it is the variable which includes more, which sets more limits on the other variables than any other criterion of status.[3] An analysis of the occupational mobility of unskilled laborers and their sons in Newburyport, therefore, is an appropriate starting point.[4] But such an analysis must take into consideration the changing composition of the Newburyport laboring class.

[2] *Pilot*, Jan. 6, 1855.

[3] Gösta Carlsson, *Social Mobility and Class Structure* (Lund, Sweden, 1958), pp. 44–45. Virtually every significant theorist of class sees occupation as a central determinant. Cf. Leonard Reissman, *Class in American Society* (Glencoe, Ill., 1959), p. 158.

[4] The primary source of data for this analysis was the manuscript schedules of the U.S. Census for 1850, 1860, 1870, and 1880. The sample consisted of all Newburyport residents who listed their occupation as "laborer" on the Census of 1850, 1860, or 1870, and all male children of these men. Errors undoubtedly were made in tracing the careers of these hundreds of individuals. For a variety of reasons such errors are most likely to have led to some overestimation of the extent of migration out of the community and perhaps some underestimation of the frequency of upward occupational mobility. However a cross check against the Newburyport Assessor's lists revealed few mistakes and suggests that the margin of error in gathering data was relatively small. One obvious source of possible error is that some of these individuals may have changed

Observers of cities have too often treated the modern community as a self-contained entity with a stable population core. A city like Newburyport, whose total population has varied little in the past century, is particularly conducive to such illusions. It is hardly surprising that Lloyd Warner's volumes on Newburyport social life miss the significance of migration in and out of the community and view social mobility exclusively as a reshuffling of its inhabitants into different social classes.

A careful scrutiny of the composition of the Newburyport laboring class in the 1850–1880 period suggests how misleading the myth of stability can be. The most common, if most easily overlooked, form of mobility experienced by the ordinary laborers of nineteenth century Newburyport was mobility out of the city. Slightly less than 40 percent of all the unskilled laborers and their children living in the community at mid-century were still listed there in the Census of 1860; of the 454 men in this class in 1860, but 35 percent were to be found in the city a decade later; the comparable figure for 1870–1880 was 47 percent. (Local health records indicate that deaths accounted for few of these departures.) The first generalization to make about the "typical" Newburyport laborer of this period, it appears, is that he did not live in Newburyport very long! Contemporary observers were correct in characterizing the new working class as floating. For a majority of these permanent transients, Newburyport provided no soil in which to sink roots. It was only one more place in which to carry on the struggle for existence for a few years, until driven onward again.

Even before the effects of occupational and property mobility are taken into account, therefore, it is evident that Newburyport did not develop a degraded proletarian class with fixed membership in the 1850–1880 period. The founders of Lowell had thought of the factory labor force as being made up of "a succession of learners"; to a striking extent this was true of the lowest stratum in Newburyport. A large and steady stream of working class men poured out of the community during these years. Their places were taken by masses of newcomers. Ireland was a continuing source of fresh and unskilled labor throughout this period; a smaller but still important group came from the stagnant farms of Vermont, New Hampshire, and Maine. These streams of migration in and out of the community resulted in a turnover of more than half of the local unskilled labor force each decade.

Two of the chief social trends of nineteenth century America—the mass influx of immigrants from the Old World, and the drift of population from country to city—thus appear on our small stage. This volatile society made a hero of the man on the road, heading for the Great West or the Great

---

their names during the period of the study, a common tactic of socially ambitious ethnics. I doubt that this was a factor of much significance for this group, though. None of my laborers are recorded on the *List of Persons Whose Names Have Been Changed in Massachusetts, 1780–1883* put out by the Secretary of the Commonwealth (Boston, 1885). Some may have changed their names without legal formalities, of course. But the device itself made most sense for the geographically mobile individuals; a new name was most useful in a new place (or a different neighborhood in a great metropolis), where people did not know the old one. This subject, unhappily, cannot be explored within the confines of a community study like the present one.

City.[5] And American folklore equated movement with success—the hero was on the make as well as on the move. A few shreds of evidence from recent sociological inquiries support this old belief that geographical mobility and upward social mobility are positively related, but whether the myth had any foundation in fact in nineteenth century America is unknown.[6]

This whets our curiosity about the subsequent career patterns of the hundreds of laborers who worked in Newburyport for a short time in the 1850–1880 period and then moved on. It is quite impossible, let it be said immediately, to trace these individuals and thereby to provide a certain answer as to how many of them later won fame and fortune. Without a magical electronic device capable of sifting through tens of millions of names and locating a few hundred, there is no way of picking out former residents of Newburyport on later national censuses. We do know something, however, about the experiences of these men in Newburyport, about the circumstances in which they departed from the community, and about the New England labor market at this time. On the basis of this information we may venture certain inferences about their future with a degree of confidence.

In only a handful of all these cases was the laborer migrating from Newburyport in a particularly strategic position to take advantage of new opportunities in another community. For instance, if the son of a laborer, unencumbered as yet with family responsibilities, was fortunate enough to possess a substantial savings account and perhaps a high school education or

[5] The volatility of the population in nineteenth century America has not received the scholarly attention it deserves. A few recent studies report exceptionally high rates of population turnover in various kinds of communities. Curti found that less than 50 percent of each occupational group remained resident in Trempealeau County, Wisconsin, for as long as a decade in the 1850–1880 period (*The Making of an American Community*, pp. 65–77). The population of Rochester, New York, appears to have been even less stable at this time: only 47 percent of a sample of 500 names drawn from the 1849 city directory could be located in the 1855 edition, and the figure fell to 20 percent in 1859 (Blake McKelvey, *Rochester, the Flower City, 1855–1890*, Cambridge, Mass., 1949, p. 3). For statistical data on the rapid turnover of workers in the textile mills of Holyoke, Massachusetts, in the 1850's, see Ray Ginger, "Labor in a Massachusetts Cotton Mill, 1853–1860," *The Business History Review*, 28 (1954): 67–91. The whole question requires systematic study by social and economic historians. For some valuable methodological suggestions see Eric E. Lampard, "Urbanization and Social Change: on Broadening the Scope and Relevance of Urban History," in Oscar Handlin and John Burchard, ed., *The Historian and the City* (Cambridge, Mass., 1963), pp. 225–247. Cf. Rowland T. Berthoff, "The American Social Order: A Conservative Hypothesis," *American Historical Review*, 65 (1960): 495–514.

[6] Richard Scudder and C. Arnold Anderson, "Migration and Vertical Occupational Mobility," *American Sociological Review* 19 (1954): 329–334; Ronald Freeman and Amos Hawley, "Migration and Occupational Mobility during the Depression," *American Journal of Sociology*, 55 (1950): 171–177; Lipset and Bendix, *Social Mobility in Industrial Society*, pp. 206–218. A close study of population mobility in Norristown, Pennsylvania, however, shows that a majority of migrants to the community experienced no change in occupational status as an accompaniment of the migration process. And among those who did shift occupational level, a higher proportion were mobile in a downward direction! See Sidney Goldstein, *Patterns of Mobility, 1910–1950: The Norristown Study; A Method of Measuring Migration and Occupational Mobility in the Community* (Philadelphia, 1958), p. 53.

some experience in a skilled or nonmanual occupation, his employment prospects after migration were obviously excellent. Such cases, however, were rare. The great majority of laborers who left Newburyport departed under less auspicious circumstances. Without financial resources, occupational skill, or education, frequently with heavy family responsibilities, the range of alternatives open to these men in their new destination was slender. Laborers like these were not lured to leave Newburyport by the prospect of investing their savings and skills more profitably elsewhere; they left the city when the depressed state of the local labor market made it impossible for them to subsist where they were. As a result of the collapse of 1857, for example, Newburyport suffered a population decline estimated by the *Herald* at "more than one thousand." Most of these departures, it was thought, were cases of workers moving to "locations where work is more abundant."[7]

That the geographical mobility of such laborers dramatically improved their opportunities for upward social mobility seems highly unlikely. The telling objection which has been advanced against the famous "safety valve" theory of the frontier applies here.[8] Migrant laborers from the city rarely had the capital or the knowledge necessary to reap the benefits of the supply of "free land" at the frontier. It seems to have been largely artisans, schoolteachers, farmers, and unsuccessful businessmen who sought their fortunes in Illinois wheat or California gold. The Newburyport newspapers of the 1850–1880 period reported but a single instance of a local laborer who successfully settled in the West, and his was not a case of which Horace Greeley could be proud. The *Herald* of June 22, 1878, carried news of a letter from one Michael Welch, then in Nevada. Welch, the son of a local laborer, had been the treasurer of one of Newburyport's volunteer fire companies; when he left for the frontier he took the treasury with him! Welch advised his parents that he was doing very well in Nevada, and would soon repay the stolen funds. Few workmen in the city, needless to say, found capital to finance a trip west so readily available.[9]

Neither were laborers migrating from Newburyport likely to discover acres

---

[7] *Herald*, May 28, 1858.

[8] Carter Goodrich and Sol Davison, "The Wage Earner in the Westward Movement," *Political Science Quarterly*, 50 (1935): 161–185 and 51 (1936): 61–110; Fred A. Shannon, "A Post Mortem on the Labor Safety Valve Theory," *Agricultural History*, 19 (1945): 31–37; Clarence H. Danhof, "Farm-Making Costs and the 'Safety Valve'; 1850–1860" *Journal of Political Economy*, 49 (1941): 317–359.

[9] *Herald*, June 22, 1878. Cf. Cole, *Immigrant City*, pp. 132–133. Cole believes that the frontier was somehow a source of hope for the ordinary workman of Lawrence in this period: "For those whose future seemed completely hopeless there was the possibility of moving west." He does not, however, produce any evidence demonstrating that significant numbers of manual laborers from the community actually moved west. It is impressive that sample surveys conducted in Saskatchewan and Alberta in 1930–31 revealed that a significant number of the farm operators of the prairie provinces had some previous experience in unskilled or semiskilled employment; see C. A. Dawson and Eva R. Younge, *Pioneering in the Prairie Provinces: The Social Side of the Settlement Process* (Toronto, 1940), pp. 120–123, 318. But many of these men had been born and raised on farms, and it is probable that relatively few of them had ever worked as laborers in cities hundreds of miles from the frontier. For other negative evidence on this point, see Handlin, *Boston's Immigrants*, p. 159, and the literature cited there.

of diamonds on the urban frontier. The community fell within the orbit of Boston, which became a great industrial center in the middle decades of the century partly because of the vast reservoir of cheap labor provided by immigration. The unskilled labor market which was centered in Boston included Lowell, Lawrence, Lynn, and smaller cities like Newburyport and Chicopee. There was a high rate of labor mobility from city to city within this market, the flow varying with local fluctuations in the demand for unskilled workers.[10] In these circumstances, differences not only in wages and working conditions but in promotion opportunities as well probably were marginal. Certainly it is doubtful that a workman without capital or skills would have found it markedly easier to advance himself in Boston than in Newburyport. The great metropolis offered alluring opportunities at the top to those with the proper requisites, but to the common laborer who drifted there from Newburyport it probably meant only more of the same. Indeed, occupational opportunities for the unskilled may have been somewhat less in a great city like Boston, where many of the most helpless and destitute members of the working class tended to cluster.

The social mobility study described below necessarily gives disproportionate attention to the settled minority of workmen who remained within the community for a decade or more and whose careers could therefore be traced. It is highly improbable, however, that our lack of precise knowledge of the later careers of migrants from Newburyport has led to an underestimation of the upward mobility eventually achieved by laborers in the sample. The circumstances in which they departed and the character of the unskilled labor market in New England make it unlikely that large numbers of these workmen were more successful in their new places of residence than were their counterparts who remained in Newburyport.

An inquiry of this kind, in fact, is biased to some degree in the opposite direction. To analyze the social adjustment of workmen who settled in a particular city long enough to be recorded on two or more censuses is to concentrate on laborers who were most resistant to pressures to migrate, and these tended to be men who had already attained a modicum of economic security in the community. Thus four fifths of the local unskilled laborers who owned real property in 1850 were still living in Newburyport in 1860, a persistence rate of 80 percent; the comparable figure for propertyless laborers in this decade was 31 percent. Migration was, in this sense, a selective process. Masses of unskilled newcomers—from rural areas and from abroad—streamed into the nineteenth century city. Large numbers of these men were unable to establish a secure place for themselves in the community. Unemployment was always a possibility, and all too often a grim reality. When jobs were too few to go around, the rumor of work in Lawrence, or Lynn, or Holyoke was enough to draw these men on. Workmen who remained in Newburyport for any length of time were therefore a somewhat select group, because to find sufficiently stable employment to maintain a settled residence in a community was itself success of a kind to

[10] Cf. Handlin, *Boston's Immigrants*, chap. iii, esp. pp. 70–71; Percy Wells Bidwell, "Rural Economy in New England at the Beginning of the Nineteenth Century," *Transactions of the Connecticut Academy of Arts and Sciences*, 20 (1916): 383–391; Shlakman, *Economic History of a Factory Town*, chap. iii, v, and vi.

the laborer. In tracing the changing social position of groups of Newbury-port workmen we must keep this relationship between geographical mobility and social mobility clearly in mind. The process of internal migration within the unskilled labor market removed many of the least successful laborers from the community; the following analysis of occupational and property mobility in Newburyport applies primarily to a settled minority from the total unskilled laboring population which passed through the community between 1850 and 1880.

The Nature of the Occupational Hierarchy

To speak of occupational mobility presupposes the social gradation of occupations, a gradation implied in such phrases as the social ladder and the occupational pyramid. The question we should now turn to is, in effect, how to justify the use of these metaphors in a specific historical context. The sociologist is able to go about this task more directly than the historian; by various polling devices he may ask the members of the society he studies how they rank various occupations.[11] While the historian may extrapolate certain of these findings back into the past, he must rely chiefly on indirect evidence to support his judgments as to the nature of the occupational hierarchy.

The occupational classification scheme used in this study is simple, designed to make possible some immediate generalizations from the census data. Occupational mobility is defined as a move from one to another of the four broad categories: unskilled manual occupations, semiskilled manual occupations, skilled manual occupations, and nonmanual occupations. Moves within these categories, involving more subtle changes in status, will be ignored for the present; they will receive some attention at a later point.

The superior ranking of nonmanual occupations seems incontestable. Status differences between manual and nonmanual callings have narrowed somewhat in recent years, with some overlapping between highly skilled manual jobs and certain routine nonmanual occupations. In the nineteenth century, however, the gulf between the two was wide. The annual income of the ordinary white collar worker was at least twice that of the typical laborer.[12] Newburyport papers of the period spoke of "the general belief" that manual work was undesirable; it was often complained that far too many young men were irrationally eager to become clerks and professionals, that not enough were willing to learn a secure manual trade.[13]

Within the broad category of manual labor, three levels of occupational status must be distinguished. If the social distance between these three was less than that between manual and nonmanual occupations as a group, status

[11] For a useful guide to the abundant sociological literature on this matter, see Albert J. Reiss, Jr., *Occupations and Social Status* (Glencoe, Ill., 1961).

[12] Robert K. Burn estimates that in 1890 the average white collar wage was twice the wage for manual labor; see "The Comparative Economic Position of Manual and White Collar Employees," *Journal of Business*, 27 (1954): 257–267.

[13] *Union*, Oct. 30, 1849; *Herald*, April 15, 1856, Sept. 16, 1857, Oct. 29, 1870. Cf. Bureau of Labor, *Fourth Annual Report*, pp. 393–394.

distinctions within the working class occupational world were nonetheless important. At the top of the manual laboring group stood the skilled crafts-men, artisans, and mechanics—carpenters, caulkers, sailmakers, master mari-ners, tailors, butchers, and so forth. (Some Newburyport artisans in this period were self-employed and owned significant amounts of capital; these were considered small businessmen and placed in the nonmanual category.) Certain of these trades were prospering during these years, while others were declining from changes in technology and market structure. Even the stagnating trades, however, remained markedly superior to other sources of manual employment. The artisan possessed a special skill; he had a "voca-tion," a "calling," rather than a mere "job." His earnings, as Tables 1 and 2 clearly show, were much higher than those of the semiskilled or unskilled workman; his wife and children were under much less pressure to enter the labor market themselves to supplement the family income.

Status differences between unskilled and semiskilled occupations were less dramatic, but they did exist. . . . The common laborer was, to an extreme degree, at the mercy of the harsh uncertainties of the casual labor market. Without a specific economic function to perform regularly for a pre-dictable reward, he was forced to take his chances daily in the competition for temporary employment. His wages were invariably below those of his fellow workmen in other occupations, and his children were the first to be forced to seek work to keep the family going.

TABLE 1   Occupational Differences in Employment and Annual Earnings, Essex County, Massachusetts, 1875[a]

	Number in Sample	Days Worked[b]	Mean Annual Earnings
Skilled occupations			
machinist	135	272.4	$601.94
blacksmith	68	260.0	567.60
carpenter	359	218.0	534.40
mason	101	177.6	524.02
cotton spinner (male)	14	280.5	523.75
shoecutter (male)	254	243.1	521.05
painter	108	207.8	474.79
Semiskilled occupations			
shoecutter, undesignated	883	234.3	418.68
factory operative, undesignated (male)	191	249.6	379.62
Unskilled occupations			
common laborer	412	230.6	358.68

[a] Compiled from the Massachusetts Bureau of Statistics of Labor, *Seventh Annual Re-port*, pp. 122–199.

[b] On the basis of a six-day week, without considering holidays, the number of possible work days in a year is 312.

By the criteria of earnings, skilled required, and definiteness of function, semiskilled jobs were a cut above this. The ordinary operative in a shoe factory or textile mill, the gardener, or the night watchman did not perform as complex a task as the spinner, shoecutter, or mason, and his wages were correspondingly lower.[14] But it would be a mistake to suppose that such jobs required no "skill" at all, and that they were in no way superior to common laboring positions. The semiskilled workmen of Newburyport had a somewhat more secure and respected position than the general laborers. Their function was more clearly defined, their wages were a bit higher and a bit more regular, and they were better able to support their families on their own income.[15]

One further question about the Newburyport occupational hierarchy must be considered. The shape of a community's occupational structure is obviously a prime determinant of the range of occupational mobility opportunities there. Consider an extreme case—a city in which 95 percent of the labor force holds unskilled jobs, with only 5 percent in the higher occupational categories. Even if the occupants of these few high status positions were continually recruited from the bottom class, the majority of men in this community would remain laborers all their lives. The opposite polar type would be a city with only a small fraction of its residents in lowly occupations; here a much slower turnover of personnel in high status jobs

[14] It should be noted that the shoemakers of the community—a very large group—were ranked as semiskilled rather than skilled workmen. The old-fashioned master of the bench has often been portrayed as the archetypal skilled craftsman, but by 1850 the traditional artisan had largely disappeared from the Newburyport shoe industry. A few independent masters still made entire shoes in their shops at mid-century, but the bulk of production was carried on through a putting-out system. The mobile laborers who became "shoemakers" in the fifties, sixties, and seventies seem not to have served any apprenticeship at all. Their task was to perform simple, semiskilled operations on leather farmed out to them by Lynn entrepreneurs. The status of these men, judging from their wages, working conditions, and training, must have been essentially the same as operatives in the textile mills and comb factory, rather than carpenters, masons, and similar artisans. By the 1870's, the local shoe industry had moved into the factory, and most "shoemakers" were simply operatives, except for a skilled minority who did specialized tasks—shoecutting, for example. Such specialized workmen have been ranked in the skilled class, of course. For the shoe industry in Newburyport, see J. D. Parsons, *Newburyport: Its Industries* (Newburyport, 1887), pp. 20–21; *Union*, Jan. 12, Jan. 14, 1853. On the evolution of American shoe manufacture, see Blanche Hazard, *The Organization of the Boot and Shoe Industry in Massachusetts before 1875* (Cambridge, Mass., 1921); John R. Commons, "American Shoemakers, 1648–1895," *Quarterly Journal of Economics*, 24 (1909): 39–84. Warner and Low, *The Social System of the Modern Factory* is a fanciful account of the changing status of the Newburyport shoemaker.

[15] Tables 1 and 2 indicate these differences clearly. For comparative evidence supporting this line of argument, see Wilbert E. Moore, *Industrialization and Labor: Social Aspects of Economic Development* (Ithaca, 1951), esp. chap. iv; Charles Booth, *Life and Labour of the People in London* (9 vol. ed., London, 1892–1897), vol. VIII; R. Dahrendorf, "Unskilled Labor in British Industry" (unpubl. diss., London School of Economics, 1956). The only occupational prestige poll which has included a broad range of manual laboring jobs ranked casual laborers, farm laborers, and laundry workers well below ordinary factory operatives; Raymond B. Cattell, "The Concept of Social Status," *Journal of Social Psychology*, 15 (1942): 293–308. See also Michael Young and Peter Willmott, "Social Grading by Manual Laborers," *British Journal of Sociology*, 7 (1956): 337–345.

TABLE 2   Occupational Differences in Annual Wages and Proportion of Family
Income Earned by Family Head, Massachusetts, 1874[a]

	Number in Sample	Mean Annual Wage of Family Head	Percent of Total Family Income
Skilled occupations			
machinist	41	$746.54	89.5
carpenter	44	716.57	86.6
teamster	6	646.67	86.2
Semiskilled occupations			
mill hand	13	594.31	71.9
shoemaker	22	527.41	68.4
Unskilled occupations			
laborer	43	414.42	56.8

[a] Compiled from the Massachusetts Bureau of Statistics of Labor, *Sixth Annual Report*, pp. 221–354. The wage levels here, it will be noted, are consistently higher than those reported for Essex County a year later (Table 1). This is largely because the 1874 sample was gathered in a way which biased the findings toward the more prosperous representatives of each occupation. We are interested in relative differentials here, so the bias is unimportant.

would mean relatively greater mobility opportunities for lower class persons. The significance of data about occupational mobility in a given community cannot be grasped without some sense of the range of mobility which could be "expected" within that community.[16]

The Newburyport occupational structure at mid-century resembled the second polar type more closely than the first. Only about 8 percent of the labor force held unskilled jobs; three times as many occupied nonmanual positions of some kind. Approximately one quarter of the employed males of the city were semiskilled workers, while almost 40 percent were skilled laborers. The diversity of skilled trades was striking—thirty-nine varieties of artisan could be counted on the local census schedules for 1850. It is misleading to classify mid-century Newburyport a "mill town"; its occupational structure was not heavily weighted toward unskilled and semiskilled callings. The community had a highly diversified craft economy, with almost two thirds of its labor force in the top two occupational categories and less than a tenth at the very bottom.

Between 1850 and 1880 the main outlines of the Newburyport occupa-

[16] Sociologists have developed elaborate statistical techniques for distinguishing "pure mobility" from mobility caused by overall changes in the occupational structure. Typical applications of contingency analysis to this problem are found in Natalie Rogoff, *Recent Trends in Occupational Mobility* (Glencoe, Ill., 1953); David V. Glass, ed., *Social Mobility in Britain* (London, 1954); Joseph A. Kahl, *The American Class Structure* (New York, 1957). It was not appropriate to utilize these techniques in the present study, both because of the smallness of the sample and because there were no major changes in the Newburyport occupational structure between 1850 and 1880.

TABLE 3   Occupational and Geographical Mobility of Three Groups of Laborers, 1850–1880

Year	Occupational Status Attained				Rate of Persist-ence[a]	Number in Sample
	Unskilled	Semiskilled	Skilled	Nonmanual		
1850 Census Group						
1860	64%	16%	15%	5%	32%	55
1870	36	39	9	15	64	35
1880	57	21	7	14	40	14
1860 Census Group						
1870	74	12	8	5	33	74
1880	69	19	6	6	65	48
1870 Census Group						
1880	79	6	10	5	41	102

[a] This column provides a measure of the geographical mobility of workmen in the
sample. The rate of persistence of a group for a particular decade is defined as that proportion of the group recorded on the census at the start of the decade that is still present in the community at the end of the decade. Thus 32 percent of the unskilled laborers of 1850 still lived in Newburyport in 1860; 64 percent of the men in this group
as of 1860 still lived in Newburyport in 1870, and so forth.

tional structure did not change drastically. A distinct shrinking of employment in the skilled trades did occur, matched by a moderate expansion of
both semiskilled and nonmanual callings. But the local economy, which had
reached a plateau after the rapid growth of the 1840's, did not undergo
large-scale technological changes which fundamentally altered the opportunity structure. The declining proportion of skilled positions in the city,
and the expansion of semiskilled and white collar occupations reflect national trends of the period, but in Newburyport these tendencies manifested
themselves more slowly than in other more dynamic nineteenth century
cities.[17] The local occupational structure offered a relative abundance of
high status positions in 1850; its general shape seemed equally favorable to
upward occupational mobility in 1880.

Intra-generational Occupational Mobility, 1850–1880

The career patterns of hundreds of unskilled laborers of nineteenth century Newburyport are summed up in Table 3. A simple generalization
immediately suggests itself: less than half of the unskilled laborers listed in
the city on the Census of 1850, 1860, or 1870 remained there for as much as a
decade, and only a minority of those who did attained a higher status occu-

[17] These observations about the Newburyport occupational structure are based on
my tabulation of the occupations of all Newburyport males listed in the manuscript
schedules of the U.S. Census of 1850, and a summary of the occupations of Newburyport citizens in 1875; see the Commonwealth of Massachusetts, *The Census of Massachusetts, 1875: Population and Social Statistics* (Boston, 1875), I, 502.

pation.* The experiences of these obscure workmen, however, were sufficiently varied and complex to merit closer scrutiny.[18]

Of the 171 common laborers employed in Newburyport in 1850, fully two thirds had disappeared from the city by 1860. A few of these had died; most had moved away. Of those who remained, almost two thirds were still ordinary unskilled laborers after a decade. Only 5 percent had risen into a nonmanual calling. Upward mobility was restricted almost entirely to the skilled and semiskilled occupations; a sixth of these men acquired semiskilled positions by 1860, a slightly smaller proportion found skilled employment.

During the Civil War decade, however, this group fared better. Its members were older, and more securely settled in the community; the persistence rate of the group for 1860–1870 was twice that for 1850–1860. Their occupational adjustment improved markedly in one respect. While two thirds of them had made no occupational gains at all between 1850 and 1860, by 1870 only one third of the group still held completely unskilled laboring jobs.

Almost all of the upward mobility attained by these men in the Civil War decade involved one small step up the occupational ladder. The dramatic shift out of the unskilled occupations was accompanied by only a small expansion of the nonmanual category and by an actual decrease in the skilled category. By far the most widespread form of upward mobility was into positions of only slightly higher status than unskilled labor—semiskilled jobs of various kinds.

Occupational opportunities for the immigrants from rural New England and abroad who arrived in Newburyport *after* 1850 were somewhat less favorable. The laborers first listed in Newburyport in the Census of 1860 remained more heavily concentrated in unskilled jobs ten and twenty years later than the men of the 1850 group. Three quarters of them attained no occupational mobility after a decade in the community, and nearly 70 percent were still common laborers after two decades. One laborer in twenty from those who stayed throughout the Civil War decade obtained a nonmanual position of some kind by 1870; no further gains of significance were made in this category during the seventies. The prospects of moving into a skilled manual job were also remote: only 8 percent held skilled positions after a decade in the city, and the proportion fell to 6 percent by 1880. The most marked difference between the attainments of the 1850 and 1860 groups, however, was in the semiskilled occupations. The unskilled laborer

---

* A word of warning is in order here. The discussion which follows is based on a series of tables which display in percentages the changing occupational distribution of several groups of men and boys. Scrutiny of the absolute numbers from which these percentages were calculated will reveal that, in some instances, occupational shifts by relatively few men appear as a rather dramatic percentage change. These changes in the occupational adjustment of even a small group of individuals are suggestive, but the reader must recall that this is an interpretative essay based on fragmentary data, not a large-scale, definitive statistical study.

[18] The career patterns of three groups of laborers are traced here. The first of these groups consists of Newburyport residents listed as unskilled laborers on the manuscript schedules of the U.S. Census of 1850. The second consists of men first listed as laborers in Newburyport on the Census of 1860, and the third of unskilled workmen new to the community in 1870.

who came to Newburyport after 1850 had fewer prospects of attaining the very modest advance in status involved in becoming a fisherman, a factory operative, a gardener, a night watchman.

The shrinkage of semiskilled opportunities is even more evident from the experiences of the laborers first listed in the Census of 1870. Some two thirds of the men in the 1850 group remained trapped in the unskilled category after a decade; the comparable figure for the 1860 group was three fourths; in the case of the 1870 group, four out of five men remained laborers for at least a decade. This unfavorable trend, however, did not mean the appearance of new barriers against movement into the skilled and nonmanual occupations. The prospects of becoming a grocer or a mason were quite similar for members of all three groups. The chief advantage of the more successful group was that they enjoyed superior access to jobs of a semiskilled character.

It is tempting to conclude flatly that a change somewhat unfavorable to common laborers occurred in the Newburyport occupational structure during these years. But a different explanation of the pattern of declining opportunities can be conceived. We know that the industrial transformation of the Newburyport economy coincided with the arrival of masses of impoverished Irish peasants, and that the proportion of foreign-born men in the local working class rose steadily through the 1850–1880 period. It is possible that foreign laborers had fewer opportunities than their native counterparts throughout this period and that the two later groups had a larger proportion of immigrants than the 1850 group.

Did Yankee workmen climb into higher status occupations more easily than immigrant laborers in these years, as many observers believed, or were ethnic differences in mobility opportunities actually negligible? The relationship between occupational mobility and ethnicity is displayed in Table 4; while the absolute numbers from which these distributions were calculated were tiny in some instances, the uniformity of the pattern which emerges is impressive. The immigrant workman in Newburyport was markedly less successful than his native counterpart in climbing out of the ranks of the unskilled in the 1850–1880 period. In each of the three groups at each census disproportionately high numbers of the foreign-born remained concentrated at the bottom of the occupational scale. The disadvantages of the newcomers were reflected, to some extent, in their underrepresentation in the skilled and nonmanual callings. But the sharpest difference in mobility opportunities was not in the two highest occupational categories but in the semiskilled field. The distribution of the 1850 group in 1870—with 77 percent of its native-born members and 14 percent of its immigrants holding semiskilled jobs—is only the most dramatic illustration of a tendency evident throughout Table 4. Evidently many local employers shared Francis Bowen's belief that "the rude labor" to which the newcomers had become accustomed had "so incapacitated them for higher tasks" that a factory could not be profitably run if more than a third of its labor force was made up of immigrants. "Foreigners generally, and the Irish in particular," wrote Bowen, "cannot be employed at all" in the factory, "except in that small proportion to the total number of hands which will make it pos-

TABLE 4 Ethnic Differences in Intra-Generational Occupational Mobility

Year	Occupational Status Attained								Number in Sample	
	Unskilled		Semiskilled		Skilled		Nonmanual			
	Native	Foreign	Native	Foreign	Native	Foreign	Native	Foreign	Native	Foreign
	1850 Census Group									
1860	47%	72%	32%	8%	15%	14%	5%	6%	19	36
1870	15	55	77	14	0	14	8	18	13	22
1880	25	70	25	20	25	0	25	10	4	10
	1860 Census Group									
1870	50	83	30	5	5	10	15	2	20	54
1880	50	74	30	15	10	5	10	5	10	38
	1870 Census Group									
1880	60	84	15	4	15	9	10	4	20	82

sible to restrict them to the lower or less difficult tasks."[19] In the Newbury-port factories of this period the proportion of immigrant workmen on the payroll was kept well below that supposedly dangerous level.

The shrinking of opportunities in the semiskilled occupations, therefore, was intimately connected with the changing ethnic composition of the Newburyport laboring class. The proportion of foreign-born men in the community labor force was steadily rising, and in these years the immigrants had particularly restricted access to employment in the occupations most open to the ambitious common laborer. It is noteworthy, however, that the special handicaps of immigrant laborers do not fully account for the inferior showing of the 1860 and 1870 groups. When the occupational experiences of native and foreign laborers are tabulated separately—as in Table 4—the pattern of declining mobility shows up in the figures for both groups.

A few general conclusions about the mobility patterns of common laborers in Newburyport in the 1850–1880 period can now be suggested. The composition of the community's unskilled laboring force was extremely fluid: a majority of the men registered as laborers on a United States Census in these years left the city before a second census was taken. These high rates of migration from the community significantly affected occupational adjustment; the improved occupational distribution of the three groups was partly due to the simple fact that unsuccessful laborers were quicker to leave Newburyport than successful ones.

Surprisingly, however, variations in the flow of migrants from the city were not closely related to variations in occupational opportunities there. The persistence rates of the 1850 and 1860 groups (Table 3) were almost identical—32 and 33 percent respectively the first decade, 64 and 65 percent respectively in the second decade—even though the occupational gains of the two were not. The 1870 group departed somewhat from the pattern; 41 percent of its members remained in Newburyport for at least a decade. This instance hints at a mild negative relationship between group persistence and occupational mobility, since the most stable of the three groups was also the least mobile occupationally. Ethnic differences in migration seem to have followed no consistent pattern. Foreign-born laborers were less successful occupationally than their native competitors throughout these three decades; the persistence rates of the newcomers, however, were lower in 1860 and 1870 and much higher in 1880. The rate of emigration, therefore, was an independent variable which strongly influenced the occupational adjustment of unskilled laborers; it did not vary in response to changes in occupational mobility opportunities in the community.

The common workman who remained in Newburyport in these years had only a slight chance of rising into a middle class occupation, even if "middle class" is generously defined to include the ownership of a subsistence farm. Only one laborer in twenty succeeded in making this advance during his first decade in the city. In the case of the 1850 group this proportion increased to three in twenty after two decades, but the two-decade figure

[19] Bowen, *Principles of Political Economy*, pp. 86–87.

for the 1860 group remained one in twenty. Moreover, neither politics nor religion, often assumed to have been important channels of upward mobility for immigrant groups, provided any opportunities for these men. Not one instance of ascent of this kind was recorded in the 1850–1880 period. The climb into a nonmanual occupation was not impossible for the unskilled workman, but it was achieved by only a tiny minority.

It is perhaps not very surprising that men without capital, education, or special training of any sort should have had limited access to nonmanual occupations. More noteworthy is the fact that these laborers found so little opportunity to enter skilled manual occupations. Approximately a third of the total Newburyport labor force in this period was made up of artisans and craftsmen of various sorts, but few laborers found openings here.

In none of the groups of laborers did as much as a quarter of the men succeed in obtaining either skilled or nonmanual positions in the period studied. From 75 to 85 percent of them remained near the bottom of the social ladder in the low-skill, low-pay occupational universe. The great majority continued to work as day laborers; most of those who did change occupations became semiskilled workmen, performing simple manual tasks at slightly higher wages and with somewhat more regular employment than they had previously enjoyed.

The opportunity to take this very modest step upward into the semiskilled category varied in two significant ways—according to the laborer's nativity and to his time of arrival in the community. Compared to the Yankee, the foreign-born workman was generally underrepresented at all occupational levels above unskilled labor, but his chief disadvantage was not at the top of the occupational ladder but at the second rung. Similarly, the growing tendency of laborers who arrived in Newburyport after 1850 to remain fixed in unskilled occupations involved a relatively small reduction in mobility into skilled and nonmanual positions; most of the change was due to the restriction of employment opportunities in the semiskilled category.

Inter-generational Occupational Mobility, 1850–1880

If nineteenth century Americans were optimistic about the laborer's chances of "pulling himself up by his own bootstraps," they were more optimistic still about his children's prospects for success. The following analysis of career patterns of sons of Newburyport laborers will help to determine to what extent such optimism was justified.

Intra-generational mobility is computed by comparing men's occupations at two or more points in their career, but the task of estimating inter-generational mobility is rather more complicated. A comparison of the status of two different individuals—father and son—is sought. At what point in the careers of the two is it appropriate to make the comparison? Half of this problem has been solved here by arranging the data on sons' occupations by age group, so that the occupational status of sons at varying stages of their careers is displayed (Table 5). Control for age is particularly important in this case because most boys entered the labor market in their early teens, and there is good reason to doubt that the jobs they held at that tender age

TABLE 5 Occupational and Geographical Mobility of Sons of Laborers, 1850–1880[a]

Year	Occupational Status Attained				Rate of Persistence	Number in Sample
	Unskilled	Semiskilled	Skilled	Nonmanual		
Youths Born 1830–1839						
1850	39%	56%	6%	0%	—	18
1860	10	76	7	7	29%	41
1870	11	48	30	11	56	27
1880	11	42	37	11	63	19
Youths Born 1840–1849						
1860	11	84	2	4	54	57
1870	28	45	17	10	32	58
1880	21	46	17	17	33	24
Youths Born 1850–1859						
1870	23	59	11	7	54	95
1880	33	40	20	8	44	76
Youths Born 1860–1869						
1880	25	60	7	8	56	73

[a] The reader may be surprised to see the number of youths in a group increasing from decade to decade in some instances, at the same time that the persistence rate figure indicates that half to two thirds of the group members left Newburyport each decade. The explanation is that large numbers of youths were coming *into* the city during these years as well, and that these have been included in the analysis.

provide a reasonable measure of inter-generational mobility. It is obviously important to determine how closely the adult occupations of these sons corresponded to the occupations they held while in their teens. One recent study revealed that well over half of a sample of white collar and professional workers in Oakland, California, had worked in a manual laboring position at some point in their early career, persuasive evidence of the dangers of ignoring intra-generational mobility in a study of inter-generational mobility.[20] By utilizing age groups in analyzing the career patterns of laborers' sons this danger can be avoided.

There remains the difficulty that not all of the fathers of these men continued to be unskilled laborers through the entire period of the study. Some, we have seen, moved up the occupational ladder themselves. How did a father's mobility or lack of mobility influence his son's prospects for occupational advance? This question will be considered at a later point. For the present it will simplify matters to ignore occupational advances made by the father and to consider all fathers laborers. Most of them did in fact remain laborers, and, as we shall see later, those who did climb a notch or two upwards had little success in passing on their advantage to their offspring.

Perhaps the most important question to ask about the hundreds of laborers' sons whose careers are recorded in Table 5 is whether or not they customarily inherited the occupation of their fathers and themselves became unskilled day laborers. The answer is apparent in a glance. In none of the age groups at any of the four censuses between 1850 and 1880 did a majority of sons hold unskilled jobs. The most frequently chosen occupation in every instance was in the semiskilled manual category. More often than not, it has been shown, the unskilled Newburyport workman remained an unskilled laborer throughout this period; more often than not the son of such a man became a semiskilled worker.

The really dramatic opening up of semiskilled employment opportunities to laborers' sons occurred in the 1850's. Even in 1850 a slight majority of the handful of sons old enough to be employed held semiskilled positions, but the extent of direct occupational inheritance was still quite high for this group—close to 40 percent. A decade later the situation was strikingly different: almost 85 percent of the boys in the teen-age group held semiskilled jobs, and 75 percent of the youths aged 20–29; only a tenth of the members of either group were mere common laborers! Very few, on the other hand, had climbed more than one rung up the status ladder. Barely 5 percent of the teen-agers working in 1860 had entered skilled or nonmanual callings. The comparable figure for youths in their twenties was higher, but even this meant no more than that one in thirteen held a skilled job and one in thirteen a nonmanual job. By far the most common form of inter-generational mobility evident by 1860 was into semiskilled occupations.

After 1860 there continued to be a heavy concentration of laborers' sons in semiskilled callings, but a significant tightening up occurred. Eighty-five percent of the teenagers in 1860 held semiskilled jobs, less than 60 percent of the teen-agers in 1870. For the group aged 20–29 in 1860 the drop was from 76 percent to 45 percent. A great wave of working class children entered

[20] Lipset and Bendix, *Social Mobility*, p. 168.

the labor market during the Civil War decade, and the local employers hiring semiskilled labor did not expand their activity sufficiently to absorb all of them. Indeed, one major source of semiskilled employment began to dry up during this decade. Almost half of the laborers' sons who held semiskilled jobs at the time of the Census of 1860 listed themselves as "fisherman" or "seaman." Both the fishing industry and the coasting trade carried on out of Newburyport experienced a sharp decline during the sixties; by 1870 the maritime industries accounted for only a quarter of the semiskilled jobs held by these youths and by 1880, less than 15 percent. Semiskilled employment was coming increasingly to mean factory employment.

What happened to the boys for whom the cotton mills and shoe factories of Newburyport had no room? The narrowing of semiskilled opportunities in the sixties forced increasing numbers of the fathers of these youths to remain common laborers. This happened to some extent to the sons as well; the 1870 Census showed a rise in the concentration of sons in unskilled positions. It is striking, however, that this decade also saw a corresponding increase in mobility into the two higher occupational classes. In the case of the two younger groups in 1870, the increase in direct occupational inheritance was approximately equal to the increase in the skilled and nonmanual category. For men in the 30–39 age bracket in 1870 the constriction of semiskilled opportunities during the Civil War decade resulted in a substantial rise in the proportion holding high status jobs, but virtually no increase at all in the unskilled category.

A certain number of laborers' sons gained a foothold in the white collar world after 1860—ten members of the group became clerks between 1860 and 1870, for example. But the skilled crafts were a more important source of upward mobility. The 1870 and 1880 figures show that it was uncommon for more than one in ten to cross the barrier dividing manual from nonmanual occupations, while two to three times as many youths characteristically found skilled employment. No single craft or group of crafts appears to have been unusually open to penetration from below; there was a broad scattering of upwardly mobile sons throughout the trades. The 1870 group, for example, included four blacksmiths, two carpenters, two machinists, two painters, two iron molders, a tailor, a baker, and a mason.

Two other aspects of the process of inter-generational mobility require comment—the role of ethnic differences and the influence of geographical mobility. It has already been demonstrated that the immigrant workman was markedly less successful than his native counterpart in climbing up the occupational ladder. Did the children of immigrant laborers face similar handicaps, or did ethnic barriers to mobility affect only the first generation immigrant? A comparison of the occupational distribution of native and foreign sons in 1850, 1860, 1870, and 1880 is presented in Table 6. The conclusion to be drawn from it is obvious: sons of Yankee laborers obtained high status employment in Newburyport much more easily than sons of foreign-born workmen in these years. The proportion of native youths in skilled and nonmanual positions was consistently higher than the proportion of foreign sons; the latter clustered heavily near the bottom of the occupational scale. But, unlike their fathers, immigrant children were not thought "incapacitated" for factory employment. The upper levels of the factory

TABLE 6 Occupational Distribution of Sons of Native and Foreign-born Laborers, 1850–1880

Occupational category	1850		1860		1870		1880	
	Native	Foreign	Native	Foreign	Native	Foreign	Native	Foreign
Number in sample	19	14	34	76	37	148	37	158
Unskilled	26%	71%	12%	8%	8%	27%	19%	27%
Semiskilled	53	21	53	88	38	55	38	50
Skilled	21	7	18	3	27	14	24	15
Nonmanual	0	0	18	1	27	5	19	8

hierarchy were completely closed to them, but a high proportion found semiskilled positions in local factories.[21]

These ethnic differences in mobility opportunities narrowed somewhat in the post–Civil War years. The censuses of 1870 and 1880 showed gains for foreign sons in both the skilled and nonmanual categories. The popular belief that second-generation Americans labored under no special handicaps in the race for occupational status was excessively optimistic, but the evidence of Table 6 hints at the beginning of a trend toward some equalization of opportunities. It is interesting to note, however, that by 1880 none of these youths had advanced through the mobility channels so often stressed in impressionistic accounts of immigrant life—politics and religion. To become a priest required education; to become a ward boss required some education too, and a well-organized, politically conscious constituency. The Irish of Newburyport, and later immigrant groups as well, eventually attained these requisites, but only after long years of struggle.

Like their fathers, these youths tended to be transient members of the community, and migration seems to have influenced their occupational adjustment in much the same way. A certain number of working class youths who had already attained some occupational mobility in the community left Newburyport during these years, but the net effect of emigration was to improve the occupational distribution of the group as a whole by removing a disproportionately large number of the least successful. The persistence of these laborers' sons (Table 5) varied roughly by age: very young children and men above thirty tended to be relatively stable members of the community; boys in their teens and twenties were most likely to move on. The persistence rates of sons of native-born laborers were generally, but not uniformly, higher than those of immigrant children. None of these variations can be clearly attributed to changes in the occupational structure.

Fathers and Sons

This survey of the career patterns of Newburyport laborers and their sons in the 1850–1880 period suggests the following conclusions.*

1) Unskilled manual laborers characteristically remained common laborers; the odds that an unskilled laborer living in Newburyport would hold

---

[21] Cf. the assertion of Warner and Srole that in these years "openings created by the general expansion of the economic system, particularly the establishment of large factories, were filled almost entirely by natives . . . . Only unskilled occupations were available to the Irish as farm laborers, stevedores, carters, hod carriers, and domestics" (*The Social Systems of American Ethnic Groups*, p. 31). This is a mistaken judgment for the Irish immigrants of Newburyport, and a grossly mistaken one for the children of such immigrants. Warner's error may in part be attributed to the fact that he based his opinion on an analysis of data drawn from local city directories, and these provide no information on the occupations of young men still living with their parents.

* It must be remembered, of course, that these conclusions refer not to the entire working class population of the community but to *unskilled* laborers and their sons. Recent mobility research suggests the likelihood that an investigation of the career patterns of *skilled* families would have revealed substantially greater movement into nonmanual occupations. Presumably it would also have disclosed evidence of downward occupational mobility, since skilled workmen (unlike common laborers) have status to lose.

the same lowly position ten years later were at least two to one throughout this period. The sons of these laborers, by contrast, typically became semi-skilled workmen; no more than one in four inherited the exact occupation of his father and remained in it.

2) Relatively few of the adult laborers studied worked their way up into a position in a skilled craft—approximately one in ten. The sons of these men were considerably more successful in penetrating the skilled trades, at least after 1860; the 1870 and 1880 figures for sons in their twenties or older holding skilled jobs range from 17 to 37 percent.

3) The contrast between generations was less sharp at the top of the occupational scale. Entry into a nonmanual occupation was almost as difficult for the son of a common laborer as for his father. Since working class families frequently found education for their children a luxury, this is not surprising. The possibility of purchasing a farm or opening a small business existed for both generations; approximately one laborer in ten was able to do this in the three decades studied.

4) The composition of the Newburyport working class was highly unstable. Large numbers of unskilled workmen drifted into the community, but only a minority remained for long. Migration was an important mechanism of occupational adjustment in that it was selective; the successful were less likely to leave than the unsuccessful.

5) Foreign-born workmen and their sons were handicapped in the occupational competition. The sons, however, experienced fewer obstacles to occupational mobility than their fathers; ethnic differences in inter-generational occupational mobility were narrowing somewhat by 1880.

6) Adult laborers employed in Newburyport in 1850 had somewhat greater prospects for occupational advance than those who arrived after 1850. In the case of the sons of these men, however, the trend was in the opposite direction. Some four fifths of the laborers' sons who entered the labor market during the 1850's found semiskilled positions; while the shrinking of semiskilled opportunities after 1860 forced some of these youths back into unskilled jobs, an equally large group rose into skilled and nonmanual callings.

Thus we can conclude that while these laborers and their sons experienced a good deal of occupational mobility, only in rare cases was it mobility very far up the social ladder. The occupational structure was fluid to some degree, but the barriers against moving more than one notch upward were fairly high. Success of the kind achieved by Stephen Fowle was attainable, but only the few were able to grasp it.

Romantic Reform in America, 1815-1865

John L. Thomas

Attempts to alleviate social ills and to purify the individual spirit have long histories in the United States. Indeed, reform is older than the republic itself. And yet historians generally agree that the first great wave of reform—the first reform movement —commenced in the third decade of the nineteenth century. In the following essay, John L. Thomas of Brown University joins a growing number of historians who are attempting to explain the causes and significance of the antebellum reformist impulse. Thomas' interest lies primarily with the intellectual, rather than the social, origins.

    Although he believes that perfectionism was central to this reform movement, Thomas also carefully delineates the movement's complex origins and ramifications. What he calls "Romantic" reform was rooted in a conservative religious impulse that aimed at individual moral redemption and that sought to prevent infidelity, disorder, and vice. But as so often occurs, a conservative, preventive impulse gave birth to radical departures—in moral sentiment, political ideology, and social action. Yet, as Thomas is at some pains to make clear, the Romantic reformers by and large sought social regeneration through education. Their radical prescriptions for change did not vent themselves through political activity. In fact—and here

Thomas is at one with many recent historians of reform most of the reformers were positively anti-institutional. Even their most striking institutional achievements—the communitarian settlements premised on utopian goals—were "anti-institutional" institutions.

Thomas lays less stress than some on the interests of reformers in disciplining and controlling the democratic masses, although many of the reform leaders he singles out possessed elitist values and assumed an obligation to aid those less fortunate than they. The irony, of course, is that they turned in their reform work to a reliance on the most "democratic" of reformist methods: individual conversion. This was the link between reform and the Protestant religion and romanticism of the age. This also, in part, accounted for its appeal in an era that sought the restoration of older and simpler values in its politics and that produced literary masterpieces that were largely conceived as pastoral adventures.

The Civil War, in Thomas's view, put an end to Romantic reform. But as others have argued (see especially George Frederickson, *The Inner Civil War** [1965]), many of the major intellects of the prewar decades, including some of whom Thomas writes, were attracted, once the war broke out, to the institutional and ordering requirements of war-making. This leads one to ask if Thomas has not too much slighted those who had faith in institutional action and who retained associations with institutions of all kinds (and about whom David Rothman writes in *The Discovery of the Asylum** [1971]). Moreover, could the connected forces of perfectionism, humanitarianism, and transcendentalism alone have so disrupted American institutions as to help bring on the Civil War? Did not other more directly "social" forces, such as economic stress, industrialization, and slavery also bring on the division of the Union?

Readers should also bear in mind that the North had no monopoly on romanticism. The Southern contemporaries of these Northern reformers were nurtured on Scott and Byron and produced such figures as Edgar Allen Poe, John Pendleton Kennedy, and William Gilmore Sims. In the South, however,

Romantic Reform in America, 1815–1865. From *American Quarterly*, XVII (Winter 1965), 656–81. Copyright, 1965, Trustees of the University of Pennsylvania. Reprinted by permission of the publisher, the University of Pennsylvania, and the author, John L. Thomas.

romanticism gave birth more to the "Cavalier," rather than to the Yankee reformer, mentality. And in this difference lies another dimension of the history of antebellum America.

*C*onfronted by the bewildering variety of projects for regenerating American society, Emerson concluded his survey of humanitarian reform in 1844 with the observation that "the Church, or religious party, is falling away from the Church nominal, and . . . appearing in temperance and nonresistance societies; in movements of abolitionists and of socialists . . . of seekers, of all the soul of the soldiery of dissent." Common to all these planners and prophets, he noted, was the conviction of an "infinite worthiness" in man and the belief that reform simply meant removing "impediments" to natural perfection.[1]

Emerson was defining, both as participant and observer, a romantic revolution which T. E. Hulme once described as "spilt religion."[2] A romantic faith in perfectibility, originally confined by religious institutions, overflows these barriers and spreads across the surface of society, seeping into politics and culture. Perfectibility—the essentially religious notion of the individual as a "reservoir" of possibilities—fosters a revolutionary assurance "that if you can so rearrange society by the destruction of oppressive order then these possibilities will have a chance and you will get Progress." Hulme had in mind the destructive forces of the French Revolution, but his phrase is also a particularly accurate description of the surge of social reform which swept across Emerson's America in the three decades before the Civil War. Out of a seemingly conservative religious revival there flowed a spate of perfectionist ideas for the improvement and rearrangement of American society. Rising rapidly in the years after 1830, the flood of social reform reached its crest at midcentury only to be checked by political crisis and the counterforces of the Civil War. Reform after the Civil War, though still concerned with individual perfectibility, proceeded from new and different assumptions as to the nature of individualism and its preservation in an urban industrial society. Romantic reform ended with the Civil War and an intellectual counterrevolution which discredited the concept of the irreducible self and eventually redirected reform energies.

Romantic reform in America traced its origins to a religious impulse which was both politically and socially conservative. With the consolidation of independence and the arrival of democratic politics the new nineteenth-century generation of American churchmen faced a seeming crisis. Egalitarianism and rising demands for church disestablishment suddenly appeared

---

[1] Ralph Waldo Emerson, "The New England Reformers," *Works* (Centenary ed.), III, 251; "*Man the Reformer*," Works, I, 248–49.

[2] T. E. Hulme, "Romanticism and Classicism," *Speculations: Essays on Humanism and the Philosophy of Art*, ed. Herbert Read (London, 1924), reprinted in *Critiques and Essays in Criticism, 1920–1948*, ed. Robert Wooster Stallman (New York, 1949), pp. 3–16.

to threaten an inherited Christian order and along with it the preferred status of the clergy. Lyman Beecher spoke the fears of more than one of the clerical party when he warned that Americans were fast becoming "another people." When the attempted alliance between sound religion and correct politics failed to prevent disestablishment or improve waning Federalist fortunes at the polls, the evangelicals, assuming a defensive posture, organized voluntary benevolent associations to strengthen the Christian character of Americans and save the country from infidelity and ruin. Between 1815 and 1830 nearly a dozen moral reform societies were established to counter the threats to social equilibrium posed by irreligious democrats. Their intense religious concern could be read in the titles of the benevolent societies which the evangelicals founded: the American Bible Society, the American Sunday School Union, the American Home Missionary Society, the American Tract Society. By the time of the election of Andrew Jackson the benevolent associations formed a vast if loosely coordinated network of conservative reform enterprises staffed with clergy and wealthy laymen who served as self-appointed guardians of American morals.[3]

The clerical diagnosticians had little difficulty in identifying the symptoms of democratic disease. Infidelity flourished on the frontier and licentiousness bred openly in seaboard cities; intemperance sapped the strength of American workingmen and the saving word was denied their children. Soon atheism would destroy the vital organs of the republic unless drastic moral therapy prevented. The evangelicals' prescription followed logically from their diagnosis: large doses of morality injected into the body politic under the supervision of Christian stewards. No more Sunday mails or pleasure excursions, no more grog-shops or profane pleasures, no family without a Bible and no community without a minister of the gospel. Accepting for the moment their political liabilities, the moral reformers relied on the homeopathic strategy of fighting democratic excess with democratic remedies. The Tract Society set up three separate printing presses which cranked out hundreds of thousands of pamphlets for mass distribution. The Home Missionary Society subsidized seminarians in carrying religion into the backcountry. The Temperance Union staged popular conventions; the Peace Society sponsored public debates; the Bible Society hired hundreds of agents to spread its propaganda.

The initial thrust of religious reform, then, was moral rather than social, preventive rather than curative. Nominally rejecting politics and parties, the evangelicals looked to a general reformation of the American character achieved through a revival of piety and morals in the individual. By probing his conscience, by convincing him of his sinful ways and converting him to right conduct they hoped to engineer a Christian revolution which would leave the foundations of the social order undisturbed. The realization of their dream of a nonpolitical "Christian party" in America would ensure a one-party system open to moral talent and the natural superiority of Christian leadership. Until their work was completed, the evangelicals stood

---

[3] For discussions of evangelical reform see John R. Bodo, *The Protestant Clergy and Public Issues, 1812–1848* (Princeton, 1954) and Clifford S. Griffin, *Their Brothers' Keepers* (New Brunswick, N.J., 1960).

ready as servants of the Lord to manage their huge reformational apparatus in behalf of order and sobriety.

But the moral reformers inherited a theological revolution which in undermining their conservative defenses completely reversed their expectations for a Christian America. The transformation of American theology in the first quarter of the nineteenth century released the very forces of romantic perfectionism that conservatives most feared. This religious revolution advanced along three major fronts: first, the concentrated antitheocratic assault of Robert Owen and his secular utopian followers, attacks purportedly atheistic and environmentalist but in reality Christian in spirit and perfectionist in method; second, the revolt of liberal theology beginning with Unitarianism and culminating in transcendentalism; third, the containment operation of the "new divinity" in adapting orthodoxy to the criticism of liberal dissent. The central fact in the romantic reorientation of American theology was the rejection of determinism. Salvation, however variously defined, lay open to everyone. Sin was voluntary: men were not helpless and depraved by nature but free agents and potential powers for good. Sin could be reduced to the selfish preferences of individuals, and social evils, in turn, to collective sins which, once acknowledged, could be rooted out. Perfectionism spread rapidly across the whole spectrum of American Protestantism as different denominations and sects elaborated their own versions of salvation. If man was a truly free agent, then his improvement became a matter of immediate consequence. The progress of the country suddenly seemed to depend upon the regeneration of the individual and the contagion of example.

As it spread, perfectionism swept across denominational barriers and penetrated even secular thought. Perfection was presented as Christian striving for holiness in the "new heart" sermons of Charles Grandison Finney and as an immediately attainable goal in the come-outer prophecies of John Humphrey Noyes. It was described as an escape from outworn dogma by Robert Owen and as the final union of the soul with nature by Emerson. The important fact for most Americans in the first half of the nineteenth century was that it was readily available. A romantic religious faith had changed an Enlightenment doctrine of progress into a dynamic principle of reform.

For the Founding Fathers' belief in perfectability had been wholly compatible with a pessimistic appraisal of the present state of mankind. Progress, in the view of John Adams or James Madison, resulted from the planned operation of mechanical checks within the framework of government which balanced conflicting selfish interests and neutralized private passions. Thus a properly constructed governmental machine might achieve by artifact what men, left to their own devices, could not—gradual improvement of social institutions and a measure of progress. Perfectionism, on the contrary, as an optative mood demanded total commitment and immediate action. A latent revolutionary force lay in its demand for immediate reform and its promise to release the new American from the restraints of institutions and precedent. In appealing to the liberated individual, perfectionism reinforced the Jacksonian attack on institutions, whether a "Monster Bank," or a secret Masonic order, entrenched monopolies or the Catholic Church. But in emphasizing the unfettered will as the proper vehicle for reform it provided a millenarian alternative to Jacksonian politics. Since social evils were simply individual acts of selfishness compounded, and since Americans could attempt the perfect society any time they were so inclined, it followed that the duty of the true reformer consisted in educating them and making them models of good behavior. As the sum of individual sins social wrong would disappear when enough people had been converted and rededicated to right conduct. Deep and lasting reform, therefore, meant an educational crusade based on the assumption that when a sufficient number of individual Americans had seen the light, they would automatically solve the country's social problems. Thus formulated, perfectionist reform offered a program of mass conversion achieved through educational rather than political means. In the opinion of the romantic reformers the regeneration of American society began, not in legislative enactments or political manipulation, but in a calculated appeal to the American urge for individual self-improvement.

Perfectionism radically altered the moral reform movement by shattering the benevolent societies themselves. Typical of these organizations was the American Peace Society founded in 1828 as a forum for clerical discussions of the gospel of peace. Its founders, hoping to turn American attention from the pursuit of wealth to the prevention of war, debated the question of defensive war, constructed hypothetical leagues of amity, and in a general way sought to direct American foreign policy into pacific channels. Perfectionism, however, soon split the Peace Society into warring factions as radical nonresistants, led by the Christian prefectionist Henry C. Wright, denounced all use of force and demanded the instant creation of an American society modeled on the precepts of Jesus. Not only war but all governmental coercion fell under the ban of the nonresistants who refused military service and political office along with the right to vote. After a series of skirmishes the nonresistants seceded in 1838 to form their own New England Non-Resistant Society; and by 1840 the institutional strength of the peace movement had been completely broken.

The same power of perfectionism disrupted the temperance movement. The founders of the temperance crusade had considered their reform an integral part of the program of moral stewardship and had directed their campaign against "ardent spirits" which could be banished "by a correct and efficient public sentiment." Until 1833 there was no general agreement on a pledge of total abstinence: some local societies required it, others did not. At the first national convention held in that year, however, the radical advocates of temperance, following their perfectionist proclivities, demanded a pledge of total abstinence and hurried on to denounce the liquor traffic as "morally wrong." Soon both the national society and local and state auxiliaries were split between moderates content to preach to the consumer and radicals bent on extending moral suasion to public pressure on the seller. After 1836 the national movement disintegrated into scattered local societies which attempted with no uniform program and no permanent success to establish a cold-water America.

By far the most profound change wrought by perfectionism was the sudden emergence of abolition. The American Colonization Society, founded in 1817 as another key agency in the moral reform complex, aimed at strength-

ening republican institutions by deporting an inferior and therefore undesirable Negro population. The cooperation of Southerners hoping to
strengthen the institution of slavery gave Northern colonizationists pause,
but they succeeded in repressing their doubts until a perfectionist ethic
totally discredited their program. The abolitionist pioneers were former
colonizationists who took sin and redemption seriously and insisted that
slavery constituted a flat denial of perfectibility to both Negroes and whites.
They found in immediate emancipation a perfectionist formula for casting
off the guilt of slavery and bringing the Negro to Christian freedom. Destroying slavery, the abolitionists argued, depended first of all on recognizing it as sin; and to this recognition they bent their efforts. Their method
was direct and intensely personal. Slaveholding they considered a deliberate
flouting of the divine will for which there was no remedy but repentance.
Since slavery was sustained by a system of interlocking personal sins, their
task was to teach Americans to stop sinning. "We shall send forth agents to
lift up the voice of remonstrance, of warning, of entreaty, and of rebuke,"
the Declaration of Sentiments of the American Anti-Slavery Society announced. Agents, tracts, petitions and conventions—all the techniques of the
moral reformers—were brought to bear on the consciences of Americans to
convince them of their sin.

From the beginning, then, the abolitionists mounted a moral crusade
rather than an engine of limited reform. For seven years, from 1833 to 1840,
their society functioned as a loosely coordinated enterprise—a national directory of antislavery opinion. Perfectionist individualism made effective organization difficult and often impossible. Antislavery delegates from state
and local societies gathered at annual conventions to frame denunciatory
resolutions, listen to endless rounds of speeches and go through the motions
of electing officers. Nominal leadership but very little power was vested in
a self-perpetuating executive committee. Until its disruption in 1840 the
national society was riddled with controversy as moderates, disillusioned by
the failure of moral suasion, gradually turned to politics, and ultras,
equally disenchanted by public hostility, abandoned American institutions altogether. Faced with the resistance of Northern churches and state
legislatures, the perfectionists, led by William Lloyd Garrison, deserted
politics for the principle of secession. The come-outer abolitionists, who
eventually took for their motto "No Union with Slaveholders," sought an
alternative to politics in the command to cast off church and state for a holy
fraternity which would convert the nation by the power of example. The
American Anti-Slavery Society quickly succumbed to the strain of conflicting philosophies and warring personalities. In 1840 the Garrisonians seized
control of the society and drove their moderate opponents out. Thereafter
neither ultras nor moderates were able to maintain an effective national organization.

Thus romantic perfectionism altered the course of the reform enterprise
by appealing directly to the individual conscience. Its power stemmed from
a millennial expectation which proved too powerful a moral explosive for
the reform agencies. In one way or another almost all of the benevolent
societies felt the force of perfectionism. Moderates, attempting political
solutions, scored temporary gains only to receive sharp setbacks. Local

option laws passed one year were repealed the next. Despite repeated attempts the Sunday School Union failed to secure permanent adoption of its texts in the public schools. The Liberty Party succeeded only in electing a Democratic president in 1844. Generally, direct political action failed to furnish reformers with the moral leverage they believed necessary to perfect American society. The conviction spread accordingly that politicians and legislators, as Albert Brisbane put it, were engaged in "superficial controversies and quarrels, which lead to no practical results."[4] Political results, a growing number of social reformers were convinced, would be forthcoming only when the reformation of society at large had been accomplished through education and example.

The immediate effects of perfectionism, therefore, were felt outside politics in humanitarian reforms. With its confidence in the liberated individual perfectionism tended to be anti-institutional and exclusivist; but at the same time it posited an ideal society in which this same individual could discover his power for good and exploit it. Such a society would tolerate neither poverty nor suffering; it would contain no condemned classes or deprived citizens, no criminals or forgotten men. Impressed with the necessity for saving these neglected elements of American society, the humanitarian reformers in the years after 1830 undertook a huge rescue operation.

Almost to a man the humanitarians came from moral reform backgrounds. Samuel Gridley Howe was a product of Old Colony religious zeal and a Baptist education at Brown; Thomas Gallaudet a graduate of Andover and an ordained minister; Dorothea Dix a daughter of an itinerant Methodist minister, school mistress and Sunday school teacher-turned-reformer; E. M. P. Wells, founder of the reform school, a pastor of a Congregational church in Boston. Louis Dwight, the prison reformer, had been trained for the ministry at Yale and began his reform career as a traveling agent for the American Tract Society. Robert Hartley, for thirty years the secretary of the New York Association for Improving the Condition of the Poor, started as a tract distributor and temperance lecturer. Charles Loring Brace served as a missionary on Blackwell's Island before founding the Children's Aid Society.

In each of these cases of conversion to humanitarian reform there was a dramatic disclosure of deprivation and suffering which did not tally with preconceived notions of perfectibility—Dorothea Dix's discovery of the conditions in the Charlestown reformatory, Robert Hartley's inspection of contaminated milk in New York slums, Samuel Gridley Howe's chance conversation with Dr. Fisher in Boston. Something very much like a conversion experience seems to have forged the decisions of the humanitarians to take up their causes, a kind of revelation which furnished them with a ready-made role outside politics and opened a new career with which they could become completely identified. With the sudden transference of a vague perfectionist faith in self-improvement to urgent social problems there emerged a new type of professional reformer whose whole life became identified with the reform process.

---

[4] Arthur Brisbane, *Social Destiny of Man: or, Association and Reorganization of Industry* (Philadelphia, 1840), introduction, p. vi.

Such, for example, was the conversion of Dorothea Dix from a lonely and afflicted schoolteacher who composed meditational studies of the life of Jesus into "D. L. Dix," the militant advocate of the helpless and forgotten. In a very real sense Miss Dix's crusade for better treatment of the insane and the criminal was one long self-imposed subjection to suffering. Her reports, which recorded cases of unbelievable mistreatment, completed a kind of purgative rite in which she assumed the burden of innocent suffering and passed it on as guilt to the American people. The source of her extraordinary energy lay in just this repeated submission of herself to human misery until she felt qualified to speak out against it. Both an exhausting schedule and the almost daily renewal of scenes of suffering seemed to give her new energies for playing her romantic reform role in an effective and intensely personal way. Intense but not flexible: there was little room for exchange and growth in the mood of atonement with which she approached her work. Nor was her peculiarly personal identification with the victims of American indifference easily matched in reform circles. Where other reformers like the abolitionists often made abstract pleas for "bleeding humanity" and "suffering millions," hers was the real thing—a perfectionist fervor which strengthened her will at the cost of psychological isolation. Throughout her career she preferred to work alone, deploring the tendency to multiply reform agencies and ignoring those that existed either because she disagreed with their principles, as in the case of Louis Dwight's Boston Prison Discipline Society, or because she chose the more direct method of personal appeal. In all her work, even the unhappy and frustrating last years as superintendent of nurses in the Union Army, she saw herself as a solitary spokesman for the deprived and personal healer of the suffering.

Another reform role supplied by perfectionism was Bronson Alcott's educator-prophet, the "true reformer" who "studied man as he is from the hand of the Creator, and not as he is made by the errors of the world." Convinced that the self sprang from divine origins in nature, Alcott naturally concluded that children were more susceptible to good than people imagined and set out to develop a method for uncovering that goodness. With the power to shape personality the teacher, Alcott was sure, held the key to illimitable progress and the eventual regeneration of the world. The teacher might literally make society over by teaching men as children to discover their own divine natures. Thus true education for Alcott consisted of the process of self-discovery guided by the educator-prophet. He sharply criticized his contemporaries for their fatal mistake of imposing partial and therefore false standards on their charges. Shades of the prison house obscured the child's search for perfection, and character was lost forever. "Instead of following it in the path pointed out by its Maker, instead of learning by observation, and guiding it in that path; we unthinkingly attempt to shape its course to our particular wishes. . . ."[5]

To help children avoid the traps set by their elders Alcott based his whole system on the cultivation of self-awareness through self-examination. His pupils kept journals in which they scrutinized their behavior and analyzed

[5] For a careful analysis of Alcott's educational theories see Dorothy McCuskey, *Bronson Alcott, Teacher* (New York, 1940), particularly pp. 25–40 from which these quotations are taken.

their motives. Ethical problems were the subject of frequent and earnest debate at the Temple School as the children were urged to discover the hidden springs of perfectibility in themselves. No mechanical methods of rote learning could bring on the moment of revelation; each child was unique and would find himself in his own way. The real meaning of education as reform, Alcott realized, came with an increased social sense that resulted from individual self-discovery. As the creator of social personality Alcott's teacher was bound by no external rules of pedagogy: as the primary social reformer he had to cast off "the shackles of form, of mode, and ceremony" in order to play the required roles in the educational process.

Alcott's modernity lay principally in his concept of the interchangeability of roles—both teacher and pupils acquired self-knowledge in an exciting give-and-take. Thus defined, education became a way of life, a continuing process through which individuals learned to obey the laws of their own natures and in so doing to discover the laws of the good society. This identification of individual development with true social unity was crucial for Alcott, as for the other perfectionist communitarians, because it provided the bridge over which they passed from self to society. The keystone in Alcott's construction was supplied by the individual conscience which connected with the "common conscience" of mankind. This fundamental identity, he was convinced, could be demonstrated by the learning process itself which he defined as "sympathy and imitation, the moral action of the teacher upon the children, of the children upon him, and each other." He saw in the school, therefore, a model of the good community where self-discovery led to a social exchange culminating in the recognition of universal dependency and brotherhood. The ideal society—the society he hoped to create—was one in which individuals could be totally free to follow their own natures because such pursuit would inevitably end in social harmony. For Alcott the community was the product rather than the creator of the good life.

Fruitlands, Alcott's attempt to apply the lessons of the Temple School on a larger scale, was designed to prove that perfectionist educational reform affected the "economies of life." In this realization lay the real import of Alcott's reform ideas; for education, seen as a way of life, meant the communitarian experiment as an educative model. Pushed to its limits, the perfectionist assault on institutions logically ended in the attempt to make new and better societies as examples for Americans to follow. Communitarianism, as Alcott envisioned it, was the social extensi n of his perfectionist belief in education as an alternative to politics.

In the case of other humanitarian reformers like Samuel Gridley Howe perfectionism determined even more precisely both the role and intellectual content of their proposals. Howe's ideal of the good society seems to have derived from his experiences in Greece where, during his last year, he promoted a communitarian plan for resettling exiles on the Gulf of Corinth. With government support he established his colony, "Washingtonia," on two thousand acres of arable land, selected the colonists himself, bought cattle and tools, managed its business affairs, and supervised a Lancastrian school. By his own admission these were the happiest days of his life: "I laboured here day & night in season & out; & was governor, legislator, clerk, constable, & everything but patriarch."[6] When the government withdrew its support and brigands overran the colony, Howe was forced to abandon the project and return home. Still, the idea of an entire community under the care of a "patriarch" shouldering its collective burden and absorbing all its dependents in a cooperative life continued to dominate the "Doctor's" reform thinking and to determine his methods.

The ethical imperatives in Howe's philosophy of reform remained constant. "Humanity demands that every creature in human shape should command our respect; we should recognise as a brother every being upon whom God has stamped the human impress." Progress he likened to the American road. Christian individualism required that each man walk separately and at his own pace, but "the rear should not be left too far behind . . . none should be allowed to perish in their helplessness . . . the strong should help the weak, so that the whole should advance as a band of brethren." It was the duty of society itself to care for its disabled or mentally deficient members rather than to shut them up in asylums which were "offsprings of a low order of feeling." "The more I reflect upon the subject the more I see objections in principle and practice to asylums," he once wrote to a fellow-reformer. "What right have we to pack off the poor, the old, the blind into asylums? They are of us, our brothers, our sisters—they belong in families. . . ."[7]

In Howe's ideal society, then, the handicapped, criminals and defectives would not be walled off but accepted as part of the community and perfected by constant contact with it. Two years of experimenting with education for the feeble-minded convinced him that even "idiots" could be redeemed from what he called spiritual death. "How far they can be elevated, and to what extent they may be educated, can only be shown by the experience of the future," he admitted in his report to the Massachusetts legislature but predicted confidently that "each succeeding year will show even more progress than any preceding one."[8] He always acted on his conviction that "we shall avail ourselves of special institutions less and the common schools more" and never stopped hoping that eventually all blind children after proper training might be returned to families and public schools for their real education. He also opposed the establishment of reformatories with the argument that they only collected the refractory and vicious and made them worse. Nature mingled the defective in common families, he insisted, and any departure from her standards stunted moral growth. He took as his model for reform the Belgian town of Geel where mentally ill patients were boarded at public expense with private families and allowed maximum freedom. As soon as the building funds were available he introduced the cottage system at Perkins, a plan he also wanted to apply to reformatories. No artificial and unnatural institution could replace

[6] Letter from Howe to Horace Mann, 1857, quoted in Harold Schwartz, *Samuel Gridley Howe* (Cambridge, 1956), p. 37.

[7] Letter from Howe to William Chapin, 1857, quoted in Laura E. Richards, *Letters and Journals of Samuel Gridley Howe* (2 vols.; New York, 1909), II, 48.

[8] Second Report of the Commissioners on Idiocy to the Massachusetts Legislature (1849), quoted in Richards, *Howe*, II, 214.

the family which Howe considered the primary agency in the perfection of the individual.

Howe shared his bias against institutions and a preference for the family unit with other humanitarian reformers like Robert Hartley and Charles Loring Brace. Hartley's "friendly visitors" were dispatched to New York's poor with instructions to bring the gospel of self-help home to every member of the family. Agents of the AICP dispensed advice and improving literature along with the coal and groceries. Only gradually did the organization incorporate "incidental labors"—legislative programs for housing reform, health regulations and child labor—into its system of reform. Hartley's real hope for the new urban poor lay in their removal to the country where a bootstrap operation might lift them to sufficiency and selfhood. "Escape then from the city," he told them, "—for escape is your only recourse against the terrible ills of beggary; and the further you go, the better."[9] In Hartley's formula the perfectionist doctrine of the salvation of the individual combined with the conservative appeal of the safety-valve.

A pronounced hostility to cities also marked the program of Charles Loring Brace's Children's Aid Society, the central feature of which was the plan for relocating children of the "squalid poor" on upstate New York farms for "moral disinfection." The Society's placement service resettled thousands of slum children in the years before the Civil War in the belief that a proper family environment and a rural setting would release the naturally good tendencies in young people so that under the supervision of independent and hard-working farmers they would save themselves.[10]

There was thus a high nostalgic content in the plans of humanitarians who emphasized pastoral virtues and the perfectionist values inherent in country living. Their celebration of the restorative powers of nature followed logically from their assumption that the perfected individual—the truly free American—could be created only by the reunification of mental and physical labor. The rural life, it was assumed, could revive and sustain the unified sensibility threatened by the city. A second assumption concerned the importance of the family as the primary unit in the reconstruction of society. As the great debate among social reformers proceeded it centered on the question of the limits to which the natural family could be extended. Could an entire society, as the more radical communitarians argued, be reorganized as one huge family? Or were there natural boundaries necessary for preserving order and morality? On the whole, the more conservative humanitarians agreed with Howe in rejecting those communal plans which, like Fourier's, stemmed from too high an estimate of "the capacity of mankind for family affections."[11]

[9] New York A.I.C.P., *The Mistake* (New York, 1850), p. 4, quoted in Robert H. Bremner, *From the Depths: the Discovery of Poverty in the United States* (New York, 1956), p. 38.

[10] Brace's views are set forth in his *The Dangerous Classes of New York and Twenty Years Among Them* (New York, 1872). For a brief treatment of his relation to the moral reform movement see Bremner, *From the Depths*, chap. iii.

[11] Letter from Howe to Charles Sumner, Apr. 8, 1847, quoted in Richards, *Howe*, II, 255–56.

That intensive education held the key to illimitable progress, however, few humanitarian reformers denied. They were strengthened in their certainty by the absolutes inherited from moral reform. Thus Howe, for example, considered his work a "new field" of "practical religion." The mental defective, he was convinced, was the product of sin—both the sin of the parents and the sin of society in allowing the offspring to languish in mental and moral darkness. Yet the social evils incident to sin were not inevitable; they were not "inherent in the very constitution of man" but the "chastisements sent by a loving Father to bring his children to obedience to his beneficent laws."[12] These laws—infinite perfectibility and social responsibility—reinforced each other in the truly progressive society. The present condition of the dependent classes in America was proof of "the immense space through which society has yet to advance before it even approaches the perfection of civilization which is attainable."[13] Education, both the thorough training of the deprived and the larger education of American society to its obligations, would meet the moral challenge.

The perfectionist uses of education as an alternative to political reform were most thoroughly explored by Horace Mann. Mann's initial investment in public school education was dictated by his fear that American democracy, lacking institutional checks and restraints, was fast degenerating into "the spectacle of gladiatorial contests" conducted at the expense of the people. Could laws save American society? Mann thought not.

> With us, the very idea of legislation is reversed. Once, the law prescribed the actions and shaped the wills of the multitude; here the wills of the multitude prescribe and shape the law . . . . now when the law is weak, the passions of the multitude have gathered irresistible strength, it is fallacious and insane to look for security in the moral force of law. Government and law . . . will here be moulded into the similitude of the public mind. . . .[14]

In offering public school education as the only effective countervailing force in a democracy Mann seemingly was giving vent to a conservative dread of unregulated change in a society where, as he admitted, the momentum of hereditary opinion was spent. Where there was no "surgical code of laws" reason, conscience and benevolence would have to be provided by education. "The whole mass of mind must be instructed in regard to its comprehensive and enduring interests." In a republican government, however, compulsion was theoretically undesirable and practically unavailable. People could not be driven up a "dark avenue" even though it were the right one. Mann, like his evangelical predecessors, found his solution in an educational crusade.

> Let the intelligent visit the ignorant, day by day, as the oculist visits the blind mind, and detaches the scales from his eyes, until the living sense leaps to light. . . . Let the love of beautiful reason, the admonitions of conscience, the sense of religious responsibility, be plied, in mingled tenderness

[12] First Report of the Commissioners on Idiocy (1848), quoted in Richards, *Howe*, II, 210–11.

[13] *Ibid.*, pp. 210–11.

[14] Horace Mann, "The Necessity of Education in a Republican Government," *Lectures on Education* (Boston, 1845), pp. 152, 158.

and earnestness, until the obdurate and dark mass of avarice and ignorance and prejudice shall be dissipated by their blended light and heat.[15]

Here in Mann's rhetorical recasting was what appeared to be the old evangelical prescription for tempering democratic excess. The chief problem admittedly was avoiding the "disturbing forces of party and sect and faction and clan." To make sure that education remained nonpartisan the common schools should teach on the *"exhibitory"* method, "by an actual exhibition of the principle we would inculcate."

Insofar as the exhibitory method operated to regulate or direct public opinion, it was conservative. But implicit in Mann's theory was a commitment to perfectionism which gradually altered his aims until in the twelfth and final report education emerges as a near-utopian device for making American politics simple, clean and, eventually, superfluous. In the Twelfth Report Mann noted that although a public school system might someday guarantee "sufficiency, comfort, competence" to every American, as yet "imperfect practice" had not matched "perfect theory." Then in an extended analysis of social trends which foreshadowed Henry George's classification he singled out "poverty" and "profusion" as the two most disturbing facts in American development. "With every generation, fortunes increase on the one hand, and some new privation is added to poverty on the other. We are verging toward those extremes of opulence and penury, each of which unhumanizes the mind."[16] A new feudalism threatened; and unless a drastic remedy was discovered, the "hideous evils" of unequal distribution of wealth would cause class war.

Mann's alternative to class conflict proved to be nothing less than universal education based on the exhibitory model of the common school. Diffusion of education, he pointed out, meant wiping out class lines and with them the possibility of conflict. As the great equalizer of condition it would supply the balance-wheel in the society of the future. Lest his readers confuse his suggestions with the fantasies of communitarians Mann hastened to point out that education would perfect society through the individual by creating new private resources. Given full play in a democracy, education gave each man the "independence and the means by which he can resist the selfishness of other men."

Once Mann had established education as an alternative to political action, it remained to uncover its utopian possibilities. By enlarging the "cultivated class" it would widen the area of social feelings—"if this education should be universal and complete, it would do more than all things else to obliterate factitious distinctions in society." Political reformers and revolutionaries based their schemes on the false assumption that the amount of wealth in America was fixed by fraud and force, and that the few were rich because

[15] "An Historical View of Education; Showing Its Dignity and Its Degradation," *Lectures on Education,* pp. 260, 262.

[16] This quotation and the ones from Mann that follow are taken from the central section of the *Twelfth Report* entitled "Intellectual Education as a Means of Removing Poverty, and Securing Abundance," Mary Peabody Mann, *Life of Horace Mann* (4 vols.; Boston, 1891), IV, 245–68. See also the perceptive comments on Mann in Rush Welter, *Popular Education and Democratic Thought in America* (New York, 1962), pp. 97–102, from which I have drawn.

the many were poor. By demanding a redistribution of wealth by legislative fiat they overlooked the power of education to obviate political action through the creation of new and immense sources of wealth.

Thus in Mann's theory as in the programs of the other humanitarians the perfection of the individual through education guaranteed illimitable progress. The constantly expanding powers of the free individual ensured the steady improvement of society until the educative process finally achieved a harmonious, self-regulating community. "And will not the community that gains its wealth in this way . . . be a model and a pattern for nations, a type of excellence to be admired and followed by the world?" The fate of free society, Mann concluded, depended upon the conversion of individuals from puppets and automatons to thinking men who were aware of the strength of the irreducible self and determined to foster it in others.

As romantic perfectionism spread across Jacksonian society it acquired an unofficial and only partly acceptable philosophy in the "systematic subjectivism" of transcendental theory.[17] Transcendentalism, as its official historian noted, claimed for all men what a more restrictive Christian perfectionism extended only to the redeemed. Seen in this light, self-culture —Emerson's "perfect unfolding of our individual nature"—appeared as a secular amplification of the doctrine of personal holiness. In the transcendentalist definition, true reform proceeded from the individual and worked outward through the family, the neighborhood and ultimately into the social and political life of the community. The transcendentalist, Frothingham noted in retrospect, "was less a reformer of human circumstances than a regenerator of the human spirit. . . . With movements that did not start from this primary assumption of individual dignity, and come back to that as their goal, he had nothing to do."[18] Emerson's followers, like the moral reformers and the humanitarians, looked to individuals rather than to institutions, to "high heroic example" rather than to political programs. The Brook-Farmer John Sullivan Dwight summed up their position when he protested that "men are anterior to systems. Great doctrines are not the origins, but the product of great lives."[19]

Accordingly the transcendentalists considered institutions—parties, churches, organizations—so many arbitrarily constructed barriers on the road to self-culture. They were lonely men, Emerson admitted, who repelled influences. "They are not good citizens; not good members of society. . . ."[20] A longing for solitude led them out of society, Emerson to the woods where he found no Jacksonian placards on the trees, Thoreau to his reclusive leadership of a majority of one. Accepting for the most part Emerson's dictum that one man was a counterpoise to a city, the

[17] The phrase is Santayana's in "The Genteel Tradition in American Philosophy." For an analysis of the anti-institutional aspects of transcendentalism and reform see Stanley Elkins, *Slavery* (Chicago, 1959), chap. iii.

[18] Octavius Brooks Frothingham, *Transcendentalism in New England* (Harper Torchbooks ed.: New York, 1959), p. 155.

[19] John Sullivan Dwight as quoted in Frothingham, *Transcendentalism*, p. 147.

[20] "The Transcendentalist," *Works*, I, 347–48.

transcendentalists turned inward to examine the divine self and find there the material with which to rebuild society. They wanted to avoid at all costs the mistake of their Jacksonian contemporaries who in order to be useful accommodated themselves to institutions without realizing the resultant loss of power and integrity.

The most immediate effect of perfectionism on the transcendentalists, as on the humanitarians, was the development of a set of concepts which, in stressing reform by example, opened up new roles for the alienated intellectual. In the first place, self-culture accounted for their ambivalence toward reform politics. It was not simply Emerson's reluctance to raise the siege on his hencoop that kept him apart, but a genuine confusion as to the proper role for the reformer. If government was simply a "job" and American society the senseless competition of the marketplace, how could the transcendentalist accept either as working premises? The transcendentalist difficulty in coming to terms with democratic politics could be read in Emerson's confused remark that of the two parties contending for the presidency in 1840 one had the better principles, the other the better men. Driven by their profound distaste for manipulation and chicanery, many of Emerson's followers took on the role of a prophet standing aloof from elections, campaigns and party caucuses and dispensing wisdom (often in oblique Emersonian terminology) out of the vast private resources of the self. In this sense transcendentalism, like Christian perfectionism, represented a distinct break with the prevailing Jacksonian views of democratic leadership and the politics of compromise and adjustment.

One of the more appealing versions of the transcendental role was the hero or genius to whom everything was permitted, as Emerson said, because "genius is the character of illimitable freedom." The heroes of the world, Margaret Fuller announced, were the true theocratic kings: "The hearts of men make music at their approach; the mind of the age is like the historian of their passing; and only men of destiny like themselves shall be permitted to write their eulogies, or fill their vacancies."[21] Margaret Fuller herself spent her transcendentalist years stalking the American hero, which she somehow confused with Emerson, before she joined the Roman Revolution in 1849 and discovered the authentic article in the mystic nationalist Mazzini.

Carlyle complained to Emerson of the "perilous altitudes" to which the transcendentalists' search for the hero led them. Despite his own penchant for hero-worship he came away from reading the *Dial* "with a kind of shudder." In their pursuit of the self-contained hero they seemed to separate themselves from "this same cotton-spinning, dollar-hunting, canting and shrieking, very wretched generation of ours."[22] The transcendentalists, however, were not trying to escape the Jacksonian world of fact, only to find a foothold for their perfectionist individualism in it. They sought a way of implementing their ideas of self-culture without corrupting them with

[21] Such was her description of Lamennais and Beranger as quoted in Mason Wade, *Margaret Fuller* (New York, 1940), 195.
[22] Quoted in Wade, *Margaret Fuller*, pp. 88–89.

the false values of materialism. They saw a day coming when parties and politicians would be obsolescent. By the 1850s Walt Whitman thought that day had already arrived and that America had outgrown parties.

> What right has any one political party, no matter which, to wield the American government? No right at all . . . . and every American young man must have sense enough to comprehend this. I have said the old parties are defunct; but there remains of them empty flesh, putrid mouths, mumbling and speaking the tones of these conventions, the politicians standing back in shadow, telling lies, trying to delude and frighten the people. . . .[23]

Whitman's romantic alternative was a "love of comrades" cementing an American brotherhood and upholding a redeemer president.

A somewhat similar faith in the mystical fraternity informed Theodore Parker's plan for spiritual revolution. Like the other perfectionists, Parker began by reducing society to its basic components—individuals, the "monads" or "primitive atoms" of the social order—and judged it by its tendency to promote or inhibit individualism. "Destroy the individuality of those atoms, . . . all is gone. To mar the atoms is to mar the mass. To preserve itself, therefore, society is to preserve the individuality of the individual."[24] In Parker's theology perfectionist Christianity and transcendentalist method merged to form a loving brotherhood united by the capacity to apprehend primary truths directly. A shared sense of the divinity of individual man held society together; without it no true community was possible. Looking around him at ante-bellum America, Parker found only the wrong kind of individualism, the kind that said, "I am as good as you, so get out of my way." The right kind, the individualism whose motto was "You are as good as I, and let us help one another,"[25] was to be the work of Parker's spiritual revolution. He explained the method of revolution as one of *"intellectual, moral,* and *religious* education—everywhere and for all men."* Until universal education had done its work Parker had little hope for political stability in the United States. He called instead for a new "party" to be formed in society at large, a party built on the idea that "God still inspires men as much as ever; that he is immanent in spirit as in space." Such a party required no church, tradition or scripture. "It believes God is near the soul as matter to the sense. . . . It calls God father and mother, not king; Jesus, brother, not redeemer, heaven home, religion nature."[26]

Parker believed that this "philosophical party in politics," as he called it, was already at work in the 1850s on a code of universal laws from which to deduce specific legislation "so that each statute in the code shall represent a fact in the universe, a point of thought in God; so . . . that legislation shall be divine in the same sense that a true system of astronomy be divine."

---

[23] Walt Whitman, "The Eighteenth Presidency," an essay unpublished in Whitman's lifetime, in *Walt Whitman's Workshop,* ed. Clifton Joseph Furness (Cambridge, 1928), pp. 104–5.

[24] Quoted in Daniel Aaron, *Men of Good Hope* (Oxford paperback ed.: New York, 1961), p. 35.

[25] Theodore Parker, "The Political Destination of America and the Signs of the Times" (1848) excerpted in *The Transcendentalists,* ed. Perry Miller (Anchor ed.: Garden City, N.Y., 1957), p. 357.

[26] Quoted in R. W. B. Lewis, *The American Adam* (Chicago, 1955), p. 182.

Parker's holy band represented the full fruition of the perfectionist idea of a "Christian party" in America, a party of no strict political or sectarian definition, but a true reform movement, apostolic in its beginnings but growing with the truths it preached until it encompassed all Americans in a huge brotherhood of divine average men. Party members, unlike time-serving Whigs and Democrats, followed ideas and intuitions rather than prejudice and precedent, and these ideas led them to question authority, oppose legal injustice and tear down rotten institutions. The philosophical party was not to be bound by accepted notions of political conduct or traditional attitudes toward law. When unjust laws interpose barriers to progress, reformers must demolish them.

So Parker himself reasoned when he organized the Vigilance Committee in Boston to defeat the Fugitive Slave Law. His reasoning epitomized perfectionist logic: every man may safely trust his conscience, properly informed, because it is the repository for divine truth. When men learn to trust their consciences and act on them, they naturally encourage others to do the same with the certainty that they will reach the same conclusions. Individual conscience thus creates a social conscience and a collective will to right action. Concerted right action means moral revolution. The fact that moral revolution, in its turn, might mean political revolt was a risk Parker and his perfectionist followers were willing to take.

Both transcendentalism and perfectionist moral reform, then, were marked by an individualist fervor that was disruptive of American institutions. Both made heavy moral demands on church and state; and when neither proved equal to the task of supporting their intensely personal demands, the transcendentalists and the moral reformers became increasingly alienated. The perfectionist temperament bred a come-outer spirit. An insistence on individual moral accountability and direct appeal to the irreducible self, the faith in self-reliance and distrust of compromise, and a substitution of universal education for partial reform measures, all meant that normal political and institutional reform channels were closed to the perfectionists. Alternate routes to the millennium had to be found. One of these was discovered by a new leadership which made reform a branch of prophecy. Another was opened by the idea of a universal reawakening of the great god self. But there was a third possibility, also deeply involved with the educational process, an attempt to build the experimental community as a reform model. With an increasing number of reformers after 1840 perfectionist anti-institutionalism led to heavy investments in the communitarian movement.

The attraction that drew the perfectionists to communitarianism came from their conviction that the good society should be simple. Since American society was both complicated and corrupt, it was necessary to come out from it; but at the same time the challenge of the simple life had to be met. Once the true principles of social life had been discovered they had to be applied, some way found to harness individual perfectibility to a social engine. This urge to form the good community, as John Humphrey Noyes experienced it himself and perceived it in other reformers, provided the connection between perfectionism and communitarianism, or, as Noyes put it, between "Revivalism" and "Socialism." Perfectionist energies directed initially against institutions were diverted to the creation of small self-contained communities as educational models. In New England two come-outer abolitionists, Adin Ballou and George Benson, founded cooperative societies at Hopedale and Northampton, while a third Garrisonian lieutenant, John Collins, settled his followers on a farm in Skaneateles, New York. Brook Farm, Fruitlands and the North American Phalanx at Redbank acquired notoriety in their own day; but equally significant, both in terms of origins and personnel, were the experiments at Raritan Bay under the guidance of Marcus Spring, the Marlboro Association in Ohio, the Prairie Home Community of former Hicksite Quakers, and the Swedenborgian Brocton Community. In these and other experimental communities could be seen the various guises of perfectionism.

Communitarianism promised drastic social reform without violence. Artificiality and corruption could not be wiped out by partial improvements and piecemeal measures but demanded a total change which, as Robert Owen once explained, "could make an immediate, and almost instantaneous, revolution in the minds and manners of society in which it shall be introduced." Communitarians agreed in rejecting class struggle which set interest against interest instead of uniting them through association. "Whoever will examine the question of social ameliorations," Albert Brisbane argued in support of Fourier, "must be convinced that *the gradual perfecting of Civilization* is useless as a remedy for present social evils, and that the only effectual means of doing away with indigence, idleness and the dislike for labor is to do away with civilization itself, and organize Association . . . in its place."[27] Like the redemptive moment in conversion or the experience of self-discovery in transcendentalist thought, the communitarian ideal pointed to a sharp break with existing society and a commitment to root-and-branch reform. On the other hand, the community was seen as a controlled experiment in which profound but peaceful change might be effected without disturbing the larger social order. Massive change, according to communitarian theory, could also be gradual and harmonious if determined by the model.

Perfectionist religious and moral reform shaded into communitarianism, in the case of a number of social reformers, with the recognition that the conversion of the individual was a necessary preparation for and logically required communal experimentation. Such was John Humphrey Noyes' observation that in the years after 1815

> the line of socialistic excitement lies parallel with the line of religious Revivals. . . . The Revivalists had for their one great idea the regeneration of the soul. The great idea of the Socialists was the regeneration of society, which is the soul's environment. These ideas belong together and are the complements of each other.[28]

So it seemed to Noyes' colleagues in the communitarian movement. The course from extreme individualism to communitarianism can be traced in

27 Albert Brisbane, *Social Destiny of Man*, p. 286, quoted in Arthur Eugene Bestor, *Backwoods Utopias: The Sectarian and Owenite Phases of Communitarian Socialism in America: 1663–1829* (Philadelphia, 1950), p. 9.
28 John Humphrey Noyes, *History of American Socialism* (Philadelphia, 1870), p. 26.

George Ripley's decision to found Brook Farm. Trying to win Emerson to his new cause, he explained that his own personal tastes and habits would have led him away from plans and projects.

> I have a passion for being independent of the world, and of every man in it. This I could do easily on the estate which is now offered. . . . I should have a city of God, on a small scale of my own. . . . But I feel bound to sacrifice this private feeling, in the hope of the great social good.

That good Ripley had no difficulty in defining in perfectionist terms:

> . . . to insure a more natural union between intellectual and manual labor than now exists; to combine the thinker and the worker, as far as possible, in the same individual; to guarantee the highest mental freedom, by providing all with labor, adapted to their tastes and talents, and securing to them the fruits of their industry; to do away with the necessity of menial services, by opening the benefits of education and the profits of labor to all; and thus to prepare a society of liberal, intelligent, and cultivated persons, whose relations with each other would permit a more simple and wholesome life, than can be led amidst the pressure of our competitive institutions.[29]

However varied their actual experiences with social planning, all the communitarians echoed Ripley's call for translating perfectionism into concerted action and adapting the ethics of individualism to larger social units. Just as the moral reformers appealed to right conduct and conscience in individuals the communitarians sought to erect models of a collective conscience to educate Americans. Seen in this light, the communitarian faith in the model was simply an extension of the belief in individual perfectibility. Even the sense of urgency characterizing moral reform was carried over into the communities where a millennial expectation flourished. The time to launch their projects, the social planners believed, was the immediate present when habits and attitudes were still fluid, before entrenched institutions had hardened the American heart and closed the American mind. To wait for a full quota of useful members or an adequate supply of funds might be to miss the single chance to make the country perfect. The whole future of America seemed to them to hinge on the fate of their enterprises.

Some of the projects were joint-stock corporations betraying a middle-class origin; others were strictly communistic. Some, like the Shaker communities, were pietistic and rigid; others, like Oneida and Hopedale, open and frankly experimental. Communitarians took a lively interest in each others' projects and often joined one or another of them for a season before moving on to try utopia on their own. The division between religious and secular attempts was by no means absolute: both types of communities advertised an essentially religious brand of perfectionism. Nor was economic organization always an accurate means of distinguishing the various experiments, most of which were subjected to periodic constitutional overhauling and frequent readjustment, now in the direction of social controls and now toward relaxation of those controls in favor of individual initiative.

The most striking characteristic of the communitarian movement was

[29] Letter from Ripley to Ralph Waldo Emerson, Nov. 9, 1840, in *Autobiography of Brook Farm*, ed. Henry W. Sams (Englewood Cliffs, N.J., 1958), pp. 5–8.

not its apparent diversity but the fundamental similarity of educational purpose. The common denominator or "main idea" Noyes correctly identified as *"the enlargement of home—the extension of family union beyond the little man-and-wife circle to large corporations."*[30] Communities as different as Fruitlands and Hopedale, Brook Farm and Northampton, Owenite villages and Fourier phalanstaeries were all, in one way or another, attempting to expand and apply self-culture to groups. Thus the problem for radical communitarians was to solve the conflict between the family and society. In commenting on the failure of the Brook Farmers to achieve a real community, Charles Lane, Alcott's associate at Fruitlands, identified what he considered the basic social question of the day—"whether the existence of the marital family is compatible with that of the universal family, which the term 'Community' signifies."[31] A few of the communitarians, recognizing this conflict, attempted to solve it by changing or destroying the institution of marriage. For the most part, the perfectionist communitarians shied away from any such radical alteration of the family structure and instead sought a law of association by which the apparently antagonistic claims of private and universal love could be harmonized. Once this law was known and explained, they believed, then the perfect society was possible—a self-adjusting mechanism constructed in accordance with their recently discovered law of human nature.

Inevitably communitarianism developed a "science of society," either the elaborate social mathematics of Fourier or the constitutional mechanics of native American perfectionists. The appeal of the blueprint grew overwhelming: in one way or another almost all the communitarians succumbed to the myth of the mathematically precise arrangement, searching for the perfect number or the exact size, plotting the precise disposition of working forces and living space, and combining these estimates in a formula which would ensure perfect concord. The appeal of Fourierism stemmed from its promise to reconcile productive industry with "passional attractions." "Could this be done," John Sullivan Dwight announced, "the word 'necessity' would acquire an altogether new and pleasanter meaning; the outward necessity and the inward prompting for every human being would be one and identical, and his life a living harmony."[32] Association fostered true individuality which, in turn, guaranteed collective accord. In an intricate calculation involving ascending and descending wings and a central point of social balance where attractions equalled destinies the converts to Fourierism contrived a utopian alternative to politics. The phalanx represented a self-perpetuating system for neutralizing conflict and ensuring perfection. The power factor—politics—had been dropped out; attraction alone provided the stimulants necessary to production and progress. Here in the mathematical model was the culmination of the "peaceful revolution" which was to transform America.

[30] Noyes, *American Socialisms*, p. 23.

[31] Charles Lane, "Brook Farm," *Dial*, IV (Jan. 1844), 351–57, reprinted in Sams, *Brook Farm*, pp. 87–92.

[32] John Sullivan Dwight, "Association in its Connection with Education," a lecture delivered before the New England Fourier Society, in Boston, Feb. 29, 1844. Excerpted in Sams, *Brook Farm*, pp. 104–5.

The communitarian experiments in effect were anti-institutional institutions. In abandoning political and religious institutions the communitarians were driven to create perfect societies of their own which conformed to their perfectionist definition of the free individual. Their communities veered erratically between the poles of anarchism and collectivism as they hunted feverishly for a way of eliminating friction without employing coercion, sure that once they had found it, they could apply it in a federation of model societies throughout the country. In a limited sense, perhaps, their plans constituted an escape from urban complexity and the loneliness of alienation. But beneath the nostalgia there lay a vital reform impulse and a driving determination to make American society over through the power of education.

The immediate causes of the collapse of the communities ranged from loss of funds and mismanagement to declining interest and disillusionment with imperfect human material. Behind these apparent reasons, however, stood the real cause in the person of the perfectionist self, Margaret Fuller's "mountainous me," that proved too powerful a disruptive force for even the anti-institutional institutions it had created. It was the perfectionist ego which allowed the communitarian reformers to be almost wholly nonselective in recruiting their membership and to put their trust in the operation of an atomistic general will. Constitution-making and paper bonds, as it turned out, were not enough to unite divine egoists in a satisfactory system for the free expression of the personality. Perfectionist individualism did not make the consociate family. The result by the 1850s was a profound disillusionment with the principle of association which, significantly, coincided with the political crisis over slavery. Adin Ballou, his experiment at Hopedale in shambles, summarized the perfectionist mood of despair when he added that "few people are near enough right in heart, head and habits to live in close social intimacy."[33] Another way would have to be found to carry divine principles into social arrangements, one that took proper account of the individual.

The collapse of the communitarian movement in the 1850s left a vacuum in social reform which was filled by the slavery crisis. At first their failure to consolidate alternative social and educational institutions threw the reformers back on their old perfectionist individualism for support. It was hardly fortuitous that Garrison, Mann, Thoreau, Howe, Parker, Channing, Ripley and Emerson himself responded to John Brown's raid with a defense of the liberated conscience. But slavery, as a denial of freedom and individual responsibility, had to be destroyed by institutional forces which could be made to sustain these values. The antislavery cause during the secession crisis and throughout the Civil War offered reformers an escape from alienation by providing a new identity with the very political institutions which they had so vigorously assailed.

The effects of the Civil War as an intellectual counterrevolution were felt both in a revival of institutions and a renewal of an organic theory of society. The war brought with it a widespread reaction against the seeming sentimentality and illusions of perfectionism. It saw the establishment of new

[33] Letter from Ballou to Theodore Weld, Dec. 23, 1856, quoted in Benjamin P. Thomas, *Theodore Weld: Crusader for Freedom* (New Brunswick, N.J., 1950), p. 229.

organizations like the Sanitary and the Christian Commissions run on principles of efficiency and professionalism totally alien to perfectionist methods.
Accompanying the wartime revival of institutions was a theological reorientation directed by Horace Bushnell and other conservative churchmen
whose longstanding opposition to perfectionism seemed justified by the war.
The extreme individualism of the ante-bellum reformers was swallowed up
in a Northern war effort that made private conscience less important than
saving the Union. Some of the abolitionists actually substituted national
unity for freedom for the slave as the primary war aim. Those reformers
who contributed to the war effort through the Sanitary Commission or the
Christian Commission found a new sense of order and efficiency indispensable. Older perfectionists, like Dorothea Dix, unable to adjust to new demands, found their usefulness drastically confined. Young Emersonians
returned from combat convinced that professionalism, discipline and subordination, dubious virtues by perfectionist standards, were essential in a
healthy society. A new emphasis on leadership and performance was replacing the benevolent amateurism of the perfectionists.

Popular education and ethical agitation continued to hold the post-war
stage, but the setting for them had changed. The three principal theorists
of social reform in post-war industrial America—Henry George, Henry
Demarest Lloyd and Edward Bellamy—denounced class conflict, minimized
the importance of purely political reform, and, like their perfectionist pre-
cursors, called for moral revolution. The moral revolution which they
demanded, however, was not the work of individuals in whom social responsibility developed as a by-product of self-discovery but the ethical
revival of an entire society made possible by the natural development of
social forces. Their organic view of society required new theories of personality and new concepts of role-playing, definitions which appeared variously in George's law of integration, Lloyd's religion of love, and Bellamy's
economy of happiness. And whereas Nemesis in the perfectionist imagination had assumed the shape of personal guilt and estrangement from a
pre-established divine order, for the post-war reformers it took on the social
dimensions of a terrifying relapse into barbarism. Finally, the attitudes of
the reformers toward individualism itself began to change as Darwinism
with the aid of a false analogy twisted the pre-war doctrine of self-reliance
into a weapon against reform. It was to protest against a Darwinian psychology of individual isolation that Lloyd wrote his final chapter of *Wealth
Against Commonwealth*, declaring that the regeneration of the individual
was only a half-truth and that "the reorganization of the society which he
makes and which makes him is the other half."

> We can become individual only by submitting to be bound to others. We
> extend our freedom only by finding new laws to obey. . . . The isolated
> man is a mere rudiment of an individual. But he who has become citizen,
> neighbor, friend, brother, son, husband, father, fellow-member, in one is just
> so many times individualized.[34]

Lloyd's plea for a new individualism could also be read as an obituary for
perfectionist romantic reform.

[34] Henry Demarest Lloyd, *Wealth Against Commonwealth* (Spectrum paperback ed.:
Englewood Cliffs, N.J., 1963), pp. 174, 178.

The Origins
of American Feminism

William L. O'Neill

William L. O'Neill of Rutgers University is the most
recent historian to essay an interpretation of American
feminism from its inception in the early nineteenth
century. In the following selection from a larger
work, he takes up the rise of the women's movement
and attempts to relate its development to the social
circumstances of mid-nineteenth-century women.

Modern feminism, he believes, traces its origins to
the "emergence" of the conjugal family and the
dislocations in the life and expectations of women that
ensued. Neither industrialization nor the ideology of
the Declaration of Independence will explain the onset
of feminism in the 1830s. The mid-Victorian ethos
tried to spiritualize women and succeeded in defining
their nature in negative reference to men's. The result
—almost foreordained, a student of social movement
might conclude—was irresoluble tensions that gave
birth to new modes of expression, new ideologies, and
novel protest.

Historians may fault O'Neill's analysis on various
grounds. The women's organizations that O'Neill
believes were such a sharp departure from earlier
efforts were characteristic of American institutional
development generally since the 1820s. Moreover, the
role of Victorian attitudes was at best ambivalent.
They tried to suppress a part of women's—and men's

—nature. But they also glorified women and gave to some of them a heightened sense of worth and efficacy. The legacy of Victorianism may therefore have been more complex than O'Neill believes.

One wonders also about an explanation tied to a rigid dating of the general spread of the conjugal family. If feminism was "one reaction to the great pressures that accompanied the emergence of the nuclear family," then its rise might have been expected earlier; for historians now think that the nuclear family was common, at least in Britain and America, from as early as the seventeenth century. And even if its triumph did occur in the nineteenth century, then why should this not help explain the departures of Jacksonian Democracy, the abolitionist movement, and territorial expansion? Perhaps it can, but one suspects that O'Neill has too quickly banished from his explanatory scheme the congruent emergence of other social forces, such as the city and the periodical press, that deeply affected women.

*W*e know very little about the causes of social change, a process always easier to describe than explain, and this is especially true where our domestic institutions are concerned. For a long time scholars believed that the Victorian family (always known to its critics as the patriarchal family) was of ancient lineage predating the Christian era. But now, thanks especially to Philippe Ariés' pioneering work *Centuries of Childhood*, it appears that the modern conjugal family emerged quite recently. If so, the origins of feminism are easier to understand.[1] When it was thought that the conjugal family, with its emphasis on privacy and domesticity, and its preoccupation with the training of children, went far back in time, it was difficult to explain why women suddenly began to press against its limitations in the 1830's. If in truth women had been abused for centuries, why did they wait so long before rebelling? Generally, Americans advanced two arguments in explanation—one economic and the other ideological. The economic argument was most concisely expressed by Walter Lippmann who observed in 1914 that "the mere withdrawal of industries from the home has drawn millions of women out of the home, and left millions idle within

The Origins of American Feminism. Reprinted by permission of Quadrangle Books from *Everyone Was Brave*, pp. 3–24, by William L. O'Neill, copyright © 1969, 1971 by William L. O'Neill.

[1] Philippe Ariés, *Centuries of Childhood: A Social History of Family Life* (New York, 1962).

it."[2] The industrial revolution forced women to alter their styles of life and inevitably brought them into conflict with customs and institutions based on obsolete economic factors. Alternatively, it was often argued that women were belatedly responding to the libertarian ideologies fostered by the French and American revolutions, that they were demanding equal rights denied them by prejudices, superstitions, and tyrannies incompatible with the enlightened social and political ideals of the nineteenth century.

There is something to be said for both these contentions, but they leave much untold. The industrial revolution is a catchall often used to explain everything for which we do not have a better answer. The sociologist William J. Goode points out that there is nothing in the industrial process itself which determines how families will be organized, and that industrialism has shown itself compatible with a variety of family systems.[3] Similarly, knowing that libertarianism is infectious does not help us appreciate why specific groups make certain responses at particular times. Why, for example, did women wait for more than half a century after the American Revolution before asking that the Declaration of Independence be applied to them as well as to men?

If we assume, however, that the conjugal family system with its great demands upon women was a fairly recent development and became general only in the nineteenth century, then the feminist response becomes explicable. In completing the transformation of the family from a loosely organized, if indispensable, adjunct of Western society into a strictly defined nuclear unit at the very center of social life, the Victorians laid a burden on women which many of them could or would not bear. The Victorians had attempted, moreover, to compensate women for their increased domestic and pedagogic responsibilities by enveloping them in a mystique which asserted their higher status while at the same time guaranteeing their actual inferiority. Hence the endless polemics on the moral purity and spiritual genius of woman which found their highest expression in the home, but which had to be safeguarded at all costs from the corrupting effects of the man-made world beyond the domestic circle. Unfortunately for the Victorians, this rationale was ultimately self-defeating, as William R. Taylor and Christopher Lasch have suggested.

> The cult of women and the Home contained contradictions that tended to undermine the very things they were supposed to safeguard. Implicit in the myth was a repudiation not only of heterosexuality but of domesticity itself. It was her purity, contrasted with the coarseness of men, that made woman the head of the Home (though not of the family) and the guardian of public morality. But the same purity made intercourse between men and women at last almost literally impossible and drove women to retreat almost exclusively into the society of their own sex, to abandon the very Home which it was their appointed mission to preserve.[4]

---

[2] Walter Lippmann, *Drift and Mastery* (New York, 1914), p. 214.

[3] See especially his *World Revolution and Family Patterns* (Glencoe, Ill., 1963).

[4] William R. Taylor and Christopher Lasch, "Two 'Kindred Spirits': Sorority and Family in New England, 1839–1846," *New England Quarterly*, XXXVI (March 1963), 35.

The libertarian rhetoric of the early feminists masked, therefore, separatist and sororital impulses which affected vast numbers. Discontented women first expressed themselves, as Taylor and Lasch point out, in literary pursuits and church work. By the end of the nineteenth century these small shoots had flowered into great national organizations like the National American Woman Suffrage Association (NAWSA), the Woman's Christian Temperance Union (WCTU), and the General Federation of Women's Clubs (GFWC), which took millions of women outside the home.

Feminism is, then, perhaps best understood as one reaction to the great pressures that accompanied the emergence of the nuclear family. It was not a rebellion born of ancient slavery but part of a collective response to the sexual awareness deliberately inspired by Victorian society in an attempt to foster what the twentieth century would consider an oppressive domesticity. The Victorians taught women to think of themselves as a special class. Having become conscious of their unique sexual identity, however—a consciousness heightened by the common experiences forced upon them by the cult of purity—they could no longer accept uncritically those role definitions drawn up for them by the alien male. Victorian society created The Woman, where before there had been only women. Yet the alternatives were even less agreeable. The worst thing about the situation of women in the nineteenth century was, as Ronald V. Sampson has pointed out, that because they were denied liberty they sought power, and, especially, power over their children. "The Victorian family as depicted by [Samuel] Butler is essentially an unholy alliance between an overbearing but petty patriarch and a vain adulatory consort for the purpose of deceiving their offspring as to the real nature of their parents and a society composed of them and their like"[5]

Every society learns to endure a certain discrepancy between its professed aims and its real ones—ideology and actuality never correspond exactly. But every so often, for reasons no one really knows, the gap becomes too great to be papered over with pious assurances. If the chasm is wide enough it may lead to rebellion or civil war, as was the case when slavery could no longer be reconciled with republican principles; if the distance is not so great, less drastic responses become possible. Feminism exploited one such weak point. It was disquieting because its very existence was a contradiction in terms for the Victorians, who believed they had accorded women a higher and more honorable estate than had any previous generation. That so many women failed to agree with them called into question the whole system of values which revolved around the home and the chaste Mother-Priestess who made it possible. In this very special sense, therefore, feminism was a radical movement. On the face of it, equal rights for women was not a demand likely to compromise the essential Victorian institutions. In fact, it threatened to do so because the Victorians had given the nuclear family a transcendent significance all out of proportion to its functional value. In the process they created a social problem which threatened to undo a patiently constructed domestic system and, what was worse, by its very existence undermined the animating principles of the Victorian ethos.

[5] Ronald V. Sampson, *The Psychology of Power* (New York, 1966), p. 104.

It is hard for us now to appreciate the strength and courage of the early feminists who set themselves against the network of ideas, prejudices, and almost religious emotionalism that simultaneously degraded and elevated women—"the cult of true womanhood," as one historian calls it, which made central virtues of piety, purity, submissiveness, and domesticity. Almost the only form of activity permitted women was religious work, because it did not take them away from their true "sphere." "From her home woman performed her great task of bringing men back to God."[6] Woman, it was believed, was morally and spiritually superior to man because of her highly developed intuition, refined sensibilities, and especially because of her life-giving maternal powers which defied man's comprehension. But woman was also physically weaker than man, inferior to him in cognitive ability, and wholly unsuited to the rough world outside the home. This was just as well, because women were largely responsible for The Family—the principal adornment of Christian civilization and the bedrock upon which society rested.[7]

While the Victorian conception of women as wan, ethereal, spiritualized creatures bore little relation to the real world where women operated machines, worked the fields, hand-washed clothing, and toiled over great kitchen stoves, it was endorsed by both science and religion. Physicians, clergymen, and journalists churned out a stream of polemical literature in support of this thesis. Even fashion conspired to the same end, for the bustles and hoops, the corsets and trailing skirts in which women were encased throughout much of the nineteenth century seemed designed to prevent all but the desperate from entering the vigorous world of men. The weight of metal, cloth, and bone which women were expected to bear as a matter of course should itself have disproved the notion that they were peculiarly delicate creatures, but, of course, it did not. Feminine delicacy was considered visible evidence of their superior sensibilities, the "finer clay" of which they were made. Women who were not delicate by nature became so by design. In the end, the fashion was self-defeating, for it aroused fears that women would become incapable of discharging their essential functions. The Civil War helped wake middle-class women from "their dream of a lady-like uselessness," and when Vassar College was founded its trustees put physical education at the head of their list of objectives.[8]

The cult of delicacy was an extreme and transient expression of an enduring conviction that feminists had to deal with if they were to win equality. They could not admit that the differences between the sexes were so marked as to make women inherently and eternally inferior; neither could they escape the fact that women everywhere were subordinate to men. Moreover, the weight of opinion against them was so great that it was hard for even the most talented women to free themselves of the invidious assumptions that kept them in their place. Margaret Fuller, who pressed with exceptional

[6] Barbara Welter, "The Cult of True Womanhood: 1820–1860," *American Quarterly*, XVIII (Summer 1966), 162.

[7] For a more elaborate survey of these ideas, see William L. O'Neill, *Divorce in the Progressive Era* (New Haven, 1967), Ch. 3.

[8] Amy Louise Reed, "Female Delicacy in the Sixties," *Century*, LXVIII (October 1915), 863.

vigor against the binding conventions of her day, consistently fell back on transcendental clichés like "the especial genius of Woman I believe to be electrical in movement, intuitive in function, spiritual in tendency," thereby denigrating her own intellectual capacities while struggling for recognition as a social philosopher.[9] Of course, her career belied her words, for throughout her life she attacked (with little apparent success) a whole range of important topics. At bottom she must have felt that intuition was not entirely a substitute for reason. Although Miss Fuller was the most intellectually ambitious American woman of her generation, she was certainly not alone, for the acute Englishwoman Harriet Martineau observed at the end of the 1830's that "in my progress through the country I met with a greater variety and extent of female pedantry than the experience of a lifetime in Europe would afford." But, she hastened to add, pedantry was not to be despised in an oppressed class, as it "indicates the first struggle of intellect with its restraints; and it is therefore a hopeful symptom."[10]

Underneath the cheerful cant (which was to grow rather than diminish with time) about women's superior morality and intuitive genius, we can sense the first uncertain efforts of intelligent American women to find their true selves. The most alert feminists did not accept the prevailing sentiments as final, or worry about their inherent nature. They took the inferiority of women as an existential reality and concerned themselves with bringing women to an awareness of it. The great suffragist Elizabeth Cady Stanton, in a characteristic letter to her colleague Lucy Stone in 1856, asked why woman put up with her degraded state, and answered herself by saying:

> She patiently bears all this because in her blindness she sees no way of escape. Her bondage, though it differs from that of the negro slave, frets and chafes her just the same. She too sighs and groans in her chains; and lives but in the hope of better things to come. She looks to heaven; whilst the more philosophical slave sets out for Canada.[11]

Feminists were willing to concede that social disabilities had produced an inferior woman, but they did not see this as a good reason for perpetuating the order responsible for her condition. In 1878 Joslyn Gage, corresponding secretary of the National Woman's Suffrage Association, told a committee of the New York Senate that the argument that women should not be given their freedom until they had become fit for it reminded her of Macauley's statement that "if men [or women] are to wait for liberty till they have become good and wise in slavery, they may indeed wait forever."[12]

[9] Sarah Margaret Fuller Ossoli, *Woman in the Nineteenth Century* (Boston, 1855), p. 115.

[10] Harriet Martineau, *Society in America*, III (London, 1837), 107.

[11] Elizabeth Cady Stanton, Susan B. Anthony, and Matilda Joslyn Gage, eds., *History of Woman Suffrage, 1848–61* (New York, 1881), p. 860. This rich collection of letters, speeches, newspaper cuttings, and the like extended into six volumes as follows: Volumes II, *1861–76* (New York, 1882) and III, *1876–85* (Rochester, 1887) were edited as above. Volume IV, *1885–1900* (Rochester, 1902) was edited by Susan B. Anthony (who also published Volumes III and IV) and Ida Husted Harper. Volumes V and VI, *1900–1920* (New York, 1922) were edited by Ida Husted Harper and published by the National American Woman Suffrage Association.

[12] *Ibid.*, III, 94.

The parallel with slavery which the early feminists drew again and again was, on the face of it, strained and unreal. Yet, even though *feeling* enslaved is clearly not the same as *being* enslaved, there were real similarities between the women's rights and anti-slavery movements. Not only were women, and usually the same women, active in both causes, but the causes themselves were in many respects alike. Both aimed at removing unconscionable handicaps imposed by law and custom on specific groups in American society. Harriet Martineau summed up the whole case for woman suffrage in these words: "One of the fundamental principles announced in the Declaration of Independence is, that governments derive their just powers from the consent of the governed. How can the political condition of women be reconciled with this?"[13] But while efforts to extend the rights and opportunities already enjoyed by white males to the rest of society were consistent with the essential premises of the American system, and therefore conservative, such attempts violated conventions and beliefs which, however much they compromised the spirit of the Constitution, were venerated equally with it. Thus, both abolitionists and feminists found themselves in the ironic but characteristically American position of those who put themselves outside the national consensus by a too literal rendering of its sacred texts.

If women were not slaves, to be at once patronized and discriminated against was bad enough.

> While woman's intellect is confined, her morals crushed, her health ruined, her weaknesses encouraged, and her strength punished, she is told that her lot is cast in the paradise of women: and there is no country in the world where there is so much boasting of the 'chivalrous' treatment she enjoys.

In brief, "indulgence is given her as a substitute for justice."[14] Since most Americans seemed ignorant of womankind's degraded state, the first tasks confronting feminists were relatively uncomplicated. They had, on the one hand, to agitate and propagandize against the prevailing system of ideas, and on the other to seize whatever private advantages they could for themselves. Religion formed the cornerstone of the case against feminine equality, and consequently the first major work by an American feminist, Sarah Grimké's *Letters on the Equality of the Sexes and the Condition of Women* (1838), was directed against those clergymen who believed God had ordained women's inferior state. Miss Grimké took the offensive because she and her sister Angelina had come under fire for their anti-slavery lectures. In a pastoral letter, the General Association of Congregational Ministers of Massachusetts denounced such activities and urged women to refrain from any public works save only leading souls to pastors for instruction. This was bad advice indeed, according to Miss Grimké. "I have suffered too keenly from the teaching of man to lead any one to him for instruction. More souls have probably been lost . . . by trusting in man in the early stages of religious experience, than by any other error."[15]

Miss Grimké made no concessions whatever to masculine complacency.

[13] Martineau, *Society in America*, I, 199.

[14] *Ibid.*, III, 105–106.

[15] Sarah M. Grimké, *Letters on the Equality of the Sexes and the Condition of Women* (Boston, 1838), p. 17.

Man "has done all he could to debase and enslave her mind; and now he looks triumphantly on the ruin he has wrought and says, the being he has thus deeply injured is his inferior."[16] The burden of Miss Grimké's arguments was, however, scriptural. She insisted that false translations and perverse interpretations of the sacred writings had obscured God's true intent. It was perfectly clear to her that "whatsoever it is morally right for a man to do, it is morally right for a woman to do." This forceful, dignified, and lucid exposition did not immediately lay waste the enemy clerics. Nonetheless, Miss Grimké deserves some credit for the changes that finally made the Protestant clergy more sympathetic to woman's emancipation than any other professional group.

Less successful was the direct assault on Christian doctrine launched by Elizabeth Cady Stanton. Ardently skeptical from the time when as a girl she had suffered a nervous collapse on hearing the great revivalist Charles G. Finney preach, Mrs. Stanton missed no opportunities to slam the churches. She was responsible for the anti-clerical resolutions passed by the National Woman Suffrage Association, which described woman as the victim of "priestcraft and superstitution." Mrs. Stanton capped her long campaign with the *Woman's Bible*, a two volume reinterpretation so embarrassing to orthodox feminists that it was officially disowned by her own suffrage association. One of her last communications to the association was a defiant letter indicating the canon law as "more responsible for woman's slavery today than the civil code."

While bold women were calling attention to the human record as a "history of repeated injuries and usurpations on the part of man toward woman, having in direct object the establishment of an absolute tyranny over her," and demanding for women "immediate admission to all the rights and privileges which belong to them as citizens of the United States," more were finding self-help and self-culture useful to their private emancipation.[17] Gradually their thirst for knowledge found expression in female seminaries and colleges (beginning with Emma Willard's Troy Female Seminary in 1821), in the admissions of women to regular colleges and universities, and in the opening of professional training on a limited scale. Few women secured a good education before the Civil War, but by 1870 eleven thousand women were enrolled in some 582 institutions of higher learning, while many more had obtained enough formal schooling to become teachers themselves. Equally if not more important was the growth of women's clubs and societies which gave married women in particular outlets for their frustrated energies and sororital aspirations.[18]

By 1860 the emancipation of women was proceeding apace on two distinct levels. Privately, as students, teachers, and in a few cases professionals, and as members of small, often informal societies, middle-class women were enlarging their "sphere" and reaching out for wider oppor-

---

[16] *Ibid.*, p. 11.

[17] From the "Declaration of Sentiments" adopted by the first Woman's Rights Convention at Seneca Falls, New York, in 1848. *History of Woman Suffrage*, I, 70–71.

[18] Mildred White Wells, *Unity in Diverity* (Washington, D.C., 1953), pp. 9–17. Some of these still exist, e.g., the Ladies Association for Educating Females of Jacksonville, Illinois, founded in 1833.

tunities beyond the domestic circle. Publicly, in their still-limited women's rights movement, in temperance work, and most strikingly of all as abolitionists, they were challenging Victorian stereotypes and laying the groundwork for that empire of women's organizations soon to be born. Although the fortitude required for these novel efforts ought not to be minimized, neither level demanded complex intellectual rationales. Self-culture and education were hard to fault in an age of progress and enlightenment. Moreover, the pioneers of female education were principally concerned with making women better wives, mothers, and teachers of the young. Catherine Beecher, the most prolific advocate of educated women, saw education as the cure for every social ill, but she was specifically concerned with training women in "domestic economy" for their true profession as housewives, and providing spinsters like herself with useful employment. She flatly disagreed with the feminist demand for equality in all things. The bible clearly stipulated that man was to be the "chief magistrate" of the home, and she believed this was in no way demeaning to woman who acquired certain compensations in the process.[19]

The case for women's rights, although far more offensive to Victorian sensibilities, was equally simple. It was based largely on the Declaration of Independence and the republican and egalitarian principles advanced since 1776. The force of an argument so framed could hardly be denied in America, and Victorians were forced to combat its lucid precepts with biblical citations of decreasing weight, and confused references to psychological, physiological, and anthropological principles of uncertain value. Democratic Americans did concede much of the feminist case in fact, however much they resisted it in principle, as the substantial number of legal reforms enacted from the 1830's on showed. The country held firm on woman suffrage, but otherwise reformers found it possible to improve property and marriage laws in state after state. The early feminists were thus encouraged to believe that equality could be won in their lifetimes.

The Civil War had a powerful effect on the fortunes of women. Having acquired some practical experience and some education outside the home, they were able for the first time to participate actively in a national enterprise. The Union's Sanitary Commission and other relief agencies, although controlled largely by men, gave vast numbers of women public work to do. Thousands served as nurses, and daring individuals such as Clara Barton, Mary Livermore, and Louisa May Alcott, not to mention the eccentric few who became spies, soldiers, and the like, distinguished themselves.[20] On the ideological front, Elizabeth Cady Stanton and Susan B. Anthony formed the National Woman's Loyal League to inspire patriotism, support the Thirteenth Amendment, and secure for women an honorable role in the war effort. Most importantly, perhaps, the war gave Union women a heroic myth which echoed down the generations. Their considerable services lost

[19] Catherine Beecher, *Woman's Profession as Mother and Educator* (Philadelphia, 1872). See also her *The True Remedy for the Wrongs of Woman* (Boston, 1851), and *The Duty of American Women to Their Country* (New York, 1845).

[20] The range of feminine activities is described in Mary Elizabeth Massey, *Bonnet Brigades: American Women and the Civil War* (New York, 1966).

nothing in the retelling. It quickly became a fixed principle that when the war ended "woman was at least fifty years in advance of the normal position which continued peace would have assigned her."[21] Women understandably needed to believe that large benefits had flowed from their large contribution to a long and horrid war, but in reality they had gained little of permanent use from it. The improvement in their educational opportunities was well under way by 1860, and the war only slightly increased the demand for women teachers and, in a few cases, women undergraduates in colleges depleted by the Army.[22] A few women became government clerks, and after the war some hung on to their ill-paying jobs, but government service did not become an attractive or important occupation for women until the next century. Perhaps an additional hundred thousand women found jobs in industry after 1861, but an army of overworked and underpaid female operatives already existed, and the war had little effect on industry's long-range employment patterns. The war enhanced women's self-confidence, and to some extent it stimulated them organizationally, but the mobilization of women on a national scale did not begin until the 1880's.

For women the most important consequence of the war was not masculine recognition of their services, or (mostly) the lack of it. Rather, it was the passage of the 13th Amendment which crowned the labors of female abolitionists and at the same time touched off a crisis in the women's rights movement with far-reaching consequences. Quickened by their fruitful labors during the war, and certain that the Negro's hour must be theirs also, suffragists assumed in the flush of Union victory that they would soon win the vote. At the first postwar women's rights convention, Theodore Tilton, a liberal journalist, spoke for many when he asked, "Are we only a handful? We are more than formed the Anti-slavery Society . . . which grew into a force that shook the nation. Who knows but that tonight we are laying the cornerstone of an equally grand movement." The aged Sojourner Truth, ex-slave and a beloved figure in the movement, called for woman's immediate enfranchisement. "I want it done very quick. It can be done in a few years." The youthful Frances Gage assured her listeners that in speaking for temperance around the country she had found her audiences alive to the need for women's votes. "They are ready for this work."[23]

But if the cry of votes for women no longer seemed as bizarre in 1866 as it had in 1848, suffragists were still badly out of step with the rest of America. It soon became apparent that the 14th Amendment would apply to men only, and in 1867, despite great efforts, a woman suffrage referendum was overwhelmingly defeated in Kansas. These two setbacks embittered the

[21] *Ibid.*, p. 339. A statement made by Clara Barton in 1888. Confederate women performed more traditional services during the war, and suffered in ways that Union women did not, but in time they also idealized these experiences. By the end of the century their shared memories were an important unifying force making it possible for Northern and Southern women to work together in organizations like the General Federation of Women's Clubs.

[22] Coeducation came into being at the University of Wisconsin, for example, largely because there were not enough male students left to assure its continuation during the war. See the unpublished master's thesis by Jean Rasmusen Droste, "Women at Wisconsin" (University of Wisconsin, 1967), p. 28.

[23] *History of Woman Suffrage*, II, 177–198.

more extreme feminists, who concluded after Kansas that men could not be trusted. Years later the authors of *The History of Woman Suffrage* recalled that after their humiliation, "we repudiated man's counsels forevermore; and solemnly vowed that there should never be another season of silence until woman had the same rights everywhere on this green earth, as man." Man could be of little help in the great work, because while he regarded woman as "his subject, his inferior, his slave, their interests must be antagonistic." Also in 1867 feminists attempted to have the word "male" struck from the New York State constitution, with the word "white," over the objections of Horace Greeley who felt with most reformers that it was the Negro's hour and that feminists should wait to press their claims until black suffrage was secured. To which Mrs. Stanton and her friends replied:

> No, no, this is the hour to press woman's claims; we have stood with the black man in the Constitution over half a century, and it is fitting now that the constitutional door is open that we should enter with him into the political kingdom of equality. Through all these years he has been the only decent compeer we have had. Enfranchise him, and we are left outside with lunatics, idiots and criminals for another twenty years.[24]

Their shocked disbelief that men would so humiliate them by supporting votes for Negroes but not for women demonstrated the limits of their sympathy for black men, even as it drove these former allies further apart. Early in 1869 Elizabeth Cady Stanton observed that at a recent suffrage convention in Washington several Negroes had said men should always dominate women, and that white women were the Negro's worst enemy. Mrs. Stanton complained that this "republican cry of 'manhood suffrage' creates an antagonism between black men and all women . . ." This trend, she warned, in language as ominous as it was unfortunate, "will culminate in fearful outrages on womanhood, especially in the southern states."[25] Additional evidence of the suffragists' hardening attitudes came when Mrs. Stanton and Miss Anthony aligned themselves with a notorious speculator and bigot, George F. Train, who campaigned with them for woman suffrage and provided financing for their weekly journal, *Revolution*. With his usual delicacy, Garrison described Train as a "crack-brained harlequin and semi-lunatic," a "ranting egotist and low blackguard," and a "nigger-baiter."[26] Train may not have been all that bad, but he was bad enough to antagonize those friends of woman suffrage who had not already been put off by the women's fight against the 14th Amendment. The Stantonites candidly admitted to judging every man solely on his views toward immediate woman suffrage, and Train was the only man they knew who did not worry about the effects of equal suffrage on the Negro's chances. All he asked in return was that *Revolution* carry news of his financial schemes. Not even Wendell Phillips, a good friend of the suffragists' cause, was pardoned for thinking that black men needed the vote more than white women. "Mr. Phillips, with his cry, 'this is the negro's hour,' has done more to delay justice for

[24] *Ibid.*, II, 267–270.

[25] Elizabeth Cady Stanton, "Women and Black Men," *Revolution*, February 4, 1869, p. 88.

[26] William Lloyd Garrison, "Letter to Editor," *Revolution*, January 20, 1868, p. 149.

woman, and to paralyze her efforts for her own enfranchisement, than any man in the nation," Mrs. Stanton declared.[27]

By 1869 the Stanton-Anthony forces had worked themselves into an untenable position. Their policies of simultaneously advancing a wide range of reforms while taking a hard and narrow line on woman suffrage exerted unbearable strain on the suffrage movement as a whole. Feminists divided, therefore, into two groups, with the radical New Yorkers becoming the National Woman Suffrage Association, and the more conservative Bostonians, led by Henry B. Blackwell, Lucy Stone, Julia Ward Howe, and T. W. Higginson, among others, forming the rival American Woman Suffrage Association. The AWSA conceded that this was indeed "the Negro's hour," but mainly it confined itself to the woman question. Its position on black suffrage notwithstanding, the National has generally been admired by historians for the large, generous approach it took to contemporary social questions. *Revolution* did have a good word to say about every good cause, but its general strategy remained hopelessly confused and obscure. The journal's first issue announced modestly that

> we shall show that the ballot will secure for woman equal place and equal wages in the world of work; that it will open to her the schools, colleges, professions and all the opportunities and advantages of life; that in her hand it will be a moral power to stay the tide of crime and misery on every side.[28]

Obviously, if the vote would do all this the Stantonites had good reason to go as far as they did in pursuit of it. But, of course, it would not, and there were those in the group who understood the suffrage's limitations and the importance of advancing other reforms as well. When Boston suffragists (in their own organ, the *Woman's Journal*) attacked *Revolution's* policy of backing every worthy cause, the radicals pointed out that they wanted to vote:

> But we are not dreamers or fanatics; and we know that the ballot when we get it, will achieve for woman no more than it has achieved for man. And to drop all other demands for the sake of uniting to demand the ballot only, may seem the whole duty of the *Woman's Journal*, but is only a very small part of the mission of the REVOLUTION. The ballot is not even half the loaf; it is only a crust—a crumb. The ballot touches only those interests, either of women or men, which take their root in political questions. But woman's chief discontent is not with her political, but with her social, and particularly her marital bondage. The solemn and profound question of marriage . . . is of more vital consequence to woman's welfare, reaches down to a deeper depth in woman's heart, and more thoroughly constitutes the core of the woman's movement, than any such superficial and fragmentary question as woman's suffrage.[29]

How splendidly put, how true—how confusing to loyal readers whom *Revolution* had previously urged to labor for a right which would of itself secure their emancipation.

Suffragists could not have it both ways. Either the vote was central to

[27] Elizabeth Cady Stanton, "A Pronunciamento," *Revolution*, July 15, 1869, p. 24.
[28] "The Ballot—Bread, Virtue, Power," *Revolution*, January 8, 1868, p. 1.
[29] Laura Bullard, "What Flag Shall We Fly?," *Revolution*, October 27, 1870, p. 264.

woman's freedom, in which case the American was pursuing a proper course, or it was but one of many necessary items, and the National was fully justified in casting a broad net. Time was to show that the Stantonites had reached, however imperfectly, the appropriate conclusions. But their diagnosis was obscured by a habit of using every available argument for woman suffrage, even when they contradicted one another, and by the organization's congenital inability to make those compromises essential to a struggling movement which could ill afford to alienate its friends. Having already lost their allies in the old anti-slavery camp, the radicals quickly proceeded to offend the nascent labor movement. Susan B. Anthony encouraged working women to form trade unions and was a delegate to one of the early National Labor Congresses. Meanwhile, *Revolution* was being printed in a "rat office" (one paying less than the union scale), and Miss Anthony was urging women to better themselves by acting as strikebreakers. Still, when the National Labor Congress refused to readmit Miss Anthony as a delegate in 1869, the radical feminists could see this only as another example of male chauvinism. Elizabeth Cady Stanton concluded that the incident "proved what THE REVOLUTION has said again and again, that the worst enemies of Woman's Suffrage will ever be the laboring classes of men."[30] Having previously consigned Negroes and reformers to that same category, *Revolution* by its own admission had no friends at all and no reason for believing that women would ever get the vote.

All this having been said, it remains true that the National possessed something of value, the loss of which was greatly to affect the future of American women. Alone of the major women's groups in this period, the NWSA admitted, however fitfully, that the heart of the woman question was domestic and not legal or political; that woman's place in the family system was the source from which her other inequities derived. Marriage, its members believed, was organized exclusively to gratify man's selfish needs and wants, and consequently was "opposed to all God's laws." Mrs. Stanton declared: "For what man can honestly deny that he has not a secret feeling that where his pleasure and woman's seem to conflict, the woman must be sacrificed; and what is worse, woman herself has come to think so too."[31]

Mrs. Stanton insisted that she and her friends were not against marriage as such, "only against the present form that makes man master, woman slave. The only revolution that we would inaugurate is to make woman a self-supporting, dignified, independent, equal partner with man in the state, the church, the home."[32] Of course, this is so far from being the case even today that Victorians may be excused for thinking her proposals quite revolutionary enough. Apart from easy divorce, the radical feminists had few other specific proposals to offer. Sex education for boys appealed to some women as one way of insuring a more tender regard for wives, as well as a

[30] Elizabeth Cady Stanton, "National Labor Congress," *Revolution*, August 26, 1869, p. 120.

[31] Elizabeth Cady Stanton to Lucy Stone, November 24, 1856, *History of Woman Suffrage*, I, 860.

[32] Elizabeth Cady Stanton, "Anniversary of the National Woman Suffrage Association," *Revolution*, May 19, 1870, p. 306.

deterrent to "solitary vice."[33] But these suggestions were bound to seem feeble, perhaps even disingenuous, in view of the impassioned language used to denounce the prevailing sexual norms. Rape appeared to Mrs. Stanton as merely another expression of the general malaise. Citing a recent case, she explained in 1869 that the statutes which "make woman man's chattel slave; theologies that make her his subject, owing obedience; cutoms that make her his toy and drudge, his inferior and dependent, will ever be expressed by the lower orders of men in such disgusting outrages."[34]

These repeated charges amply warrant our belief that Victorian women generally entertained a low opinion of the sexual act. Yet clearly it does not follow from this that marriage in the nineteenth century was considered a satisfactory expression of sexual refinement, or an adequate defense of female gentility. By today's standards marital sex was perhaps infrequent and decorous, but the double standard of morality and the cult of true womanhood had the curious effect of making such high demands on male continence that few normal men could exhibit the self-control women demanded of them. When the dangers of childbirth were added to the horrors of "conjugal commerce," we ought not to be surprised that sex was something a great many women could readily do without, and that they viewed as loathsome and perverse a system which forced it on them. This was especially true of advanced women, and while most suffragists were married, they tended to marry later, have fewer children, and to be much more divorce-prone than the average woman. Mrs. Stanton did not conform to this pattern. She had five children and only one husband. But in her memoirs she tells us that her life began at fifty when her children could take care of themselves.

It would be wrong to think that Mrs. Stanton was prudish or unreasonable on sexual matters. She was, in fact, one of the very few women reformers who thought that women's willingness to identify chastity with moral worth was a sign of their slave mentality. She never believed, as most other women did, that purity was essential to greatness in either men or women. When in the 1890's the brilliant Irish leader Charles Parnell was driven out of British politics for living in sin with a married woman, she remarked dryly that "if the women of England take up the position there can be no true patriotism without chastity, they will rob some of the most illustrious rulers of their own sex of any reputation for ability in public affairs."[35] She ardently championed the brightest female spirits of her own day, who often led unconventional sex lives. Most American women were scandalized by George Sand; even those like Margaret Fuller who admired her were forced to lament that "a woman of Sand's genius—as free, as bold, and pure from even the suspicion of error might have filled an apostolic station among her people."[36] Others like Harriet Beecher Stowe were less charitable, inspiring

[33] Mrs. L. B. Chandler, "Motherhood," *Woodhull and Claflin's Weekly*, April 29, 1871, p. 6. Isabella Beecher Hooker expressed the same thoughts in a more unbalanced way. See Robert E. Riegel, *American Feminists* (Lawrence, Kans., 1963), pp. 142–143.

[34] Elizabeth Cady Stanton, "Woman's Protectors," *Revolution*, January 21, 1869, p. 40.

[35] Elizabeth Cady Stanton, "Patriotism and Chastity," *Westminster Review*, CXXXV (January 1891), 2.

[36] Fuller, *Women in the Nineteenth Century*, p. 233.

Mrs. Stanton on one occasion to declare flatly that "George Sand has done a grander work for women in her pure life and bold utterances of truth, than any woman of her day and generation; while Mrs. Stowe has been vacillating over every demand for her sex, timidly watching the weathercock of public sentiment and ridiculing the advance guard."[37] But few women agreed with Mrs. Stanton. Frances Willard surely represented the great majority when she said, rightly no doubt, that Parnell's disgrace showed the growth of women's influence. With a characteristic disregard for the facts of the case, she cried out, "God be thanked that we live in an age when men as a class have risen to such an appreciation of women as a class, that the mighty tide of their public sentiment will drown out any man's reputation who is false to woman and the home."[38]

Thus, while the Stanton group's position on marriage was not really very radical, and reflected much the same fear and suspicion of sex which animated most feminists, the fact that it recognized the existence of a marriage question was itself enough to put it beyond the pale. The last serious effort to reunite the suffrage movement failed in 1870, despite the best efforts of Theodore Tilton, when Mrs. Stanton's views on marriage and divorce were strongly condemned at the American Woman Suffrage Association's convention. The split which was originally caused by the Stantonites' refusal to accept Negro suffrage, was now being sustained, personalities apart, by their critique of Victorian marriage. . . .

Suggested Reading

An imaginative, if overstated, interpretation of American social history, which highlights the nineteenth century, is Rowland Berthoff's "The American Social Order," *American Historical Review*, LXV (April 1960). Daniel J. Boorstin's *The Americans: The National Experience** (1965) is a brilliant delineation of many aspects of the century's social life which also wrong-headedly slights the role of ideas and expectations.

On the complex history of the frontier thesis of Frederick Jackson Turner, which has so deeply affected American social history, Ray A. Billington's *America's Frontier Heritage** (1966) provides the fullest review and makes some contributions of its own. A detailed study of the development and structure of a western farming community, somewhat along the lines of Thernstrom's for Newburyport, is Merle Curti's *The Making of An American Community: A Case Study of Democracy in a Frontier County** (1959). In *The Plain People of Boston, 1830–1860: A Study in City Growth* (1971), Peter R. Knights tries to unearth—and, with a superabundance of statistics, present—the history of the lives of one city's simple folk. The immigrant's life in America is brilliantly captured in two works of Oscar Handlin: *Boston's Immigrants: A Study in Acculturation,** rev. ed. (1959), and *The Uprooted: The Epic Story of the Great Migrations that Made the American People** (1951).

[37] Elizabeth Cady Stanton, "A Word About George Sand," *Revolution*, September 15, 1870, p. 169.
[38] In Rachel Foster Avery, ed., *Transactions of the National Council of Women of the United States* (Philadelphia, 1891), p. 38.

A handy review of American social and reform movements, devoid, however, of all interpretation, is Alice Felt Tyler's *Freedom's Ferment: Phases of American Social History from the Colonial Period to the Outbreak of the Civil War** (1944). The entire concept of "reform" is sharply called into question by David J. Rothman in *The Discovery of the Asylum: Social Order and Disorder in the New Republic** (1971). The social and class interests of the reformers is the subject of many fine recent studies, including Michael B. Katz's *The Irony of Early School Reform: Educational Innovation in Mid-Nineteenth Century Massachusetts** (1968), Joseph R. Gusfield's *Symbolic Crusade: Status Politics and the American Temperance Movement** (1963), and David Donald's "Toward a Reconsideration of Abolitionists," in his *Lincoln Reconsidered: Essays on the Civil War Era,** 2nd ed. (1956). Donald is sharply rebutted by Martin Duberman in "The Abolitionists and Psychology," *The Journal of Negro History*, XLVII (July 1962), and by Aileen Kraditor in *Means and Ends in American Abolitionism: Garrison and His Critics on Strategy and Tactics, 1834–1850** (1969). The leading abolitionist is the subject of John L. Thomas's fine study, *The Liberator: William Lloyd Garrison* (1963).

* Also published in paperback edition.

The Tragic Flaw: Slavery

From Day Clean to First Dark

Kenneth Stampp

Scholars no longer argue about whether slavery was good or bad. That question was settled over a hundred years ago, and settled so decisively that one cannot find a white Southerner in the late nineteenth century defending the institution of slavery even during the most acrimonious flare-ups of sectional animosities. Nevertheless, some of the more insidious assumptions of the old proslavery rationalizations remained operative, especially the assumptions that slaves deserved enslavement and benefited from slavery.

According to one line of argument, though slavery was an indefensible human relationship in theory and as a legal institution, it was not so uniformly harsh as the abolitionist propaganda would have one believe. Far from fostering a life of unrelieved horror and degradation, slavery was a relatively benign arrangement for the management of a labor force, and the planters displayed considerable paternalism in their regard for the welfare of "their people." According to Ulrich B. Phillips, the most distinguished historian of this point of view whose scholarship dominated the field throughout the first half of the twentieth century, slavery was a schoolhouse of civilization in which primitive Africans were exposed

Cotton plantation (Yale University Art Gallery, Mabel Brady Garvan Collection)

to Christianity, absorbed civilized ways of thinking and acting, and learned advanced economic skills. Working primarily from the records of large plantations, Phillips insisted that slaves in general were happy and docile. They benefited from slavery, and the degree of benefit was limited more by the nature of the slave than by the nature of slavery. To Phillips, slavery was less a business than a way of life. It was simply one method of controlling labor so as to make possible an aristocratic class with a clear code of public duty and private honor. The plantation, in Phillips' view (which is pointedly not the same as the slave's), was a patriarchal community dominated by the paternalistic master.

The view of slavery set forth by Phillips, principally in *American Negro Slavery* (1918) and in *Life and Labor in the Old South* (1929) was first comprehensively challenged by Kenneth Stampp in 1956 in his book, *The Peculiar Institution: Slavery in the Ante-Bellum South.* That Stampp's self-assigned task was the destruction of Phillips' interpretation is clearly revealed by the identical organization of his book to that of *American Negro Slavery.* The difference was that in each chapter Stampp reached conclusions strikingly different from those of Phillips. Using similar sources in an exhaustive and imaginative way, Stampp destroyed the myth of the happy slave. In his portrait, though the varieties of slavery were many, they were all harsh, and the slave himself, whatever his situation, was full of rebelliousness.

It is not surprising that Stampp reached conclusions different from Phillips because he started with very different assumptions. "I have assumed," he wrote in the Preface to *The Peculiar Institution*, "that the slaves were merely ordinary human beings, that innately Negroes *are*, after all, only white men with black skins, nothing more, nothing less." Such a frank statement of preconceptions is rare and is to be welcomed, but it has been held up to various degrees of ridicule as we have increasingly come to appreciate the distinctiveness of Afro-American culture since Stampp wrote. Eugene Genovese, for instance, claims we have learned much more about the Afro-American experience from racists such as Phillips than from liberal assimilationists of Stampp's persuasion. The racists at least described what they perceived as the "peculiarities" of black behavior, and thus revealed much about black personality, religion, language, music and society. White liberals, with a few exceptions, have denied by implication that blacks have a culture and a history of their own.

This echoes the charge brought by black intellectuals that white historians always treat blacks as the objects of history and seldom as the subjects. That is, because black sources have been nonexistent or underutilized, and because of frequently subconscious racist assumptions, blacks are not seen as taking an active part in the events of their own lives. They are instead passive pebbles being washed about by the waves of white historical forces.

In the selections that follow, Kenneth Stampp describes the lives of slaves in the American South. The reader should notice the variety and complexity of the slave system, which makes it difficult to talk about the "typical" slave experience, and remember that slightly over half of the slaves in the United States in 1860 lived on plantations employing twenty or more slaves. On this basis Stampp may be less than convincing in his argument that the life of the slave was harsh, whatever its setting. However, one must conclude that there were many inhumane features of slavery: the physical treatment of slaves, the forced separation of blacks from their African heritage, the mere fact of being owned by, or subject to the will of, another human being, and the poor self-image that was the result of immersion in a racist society that considered some humans to be mere property.

3

For the owner of a few slaves, labor management was a problem of direct personal relationships between individuals. For the owner of many, the problem was more difficult and required greater ingenuity. Both classes of masters desired a steady and efficient performance of the work assigned each day. They could not expect much cooperation from their slaves, who had little reason to care how much was produced. Masters measured the success of their methods by the extent to which their interest in a maximum of work of good quality prevailed over the slaves' predilection for a minimum of work of indifferent quality. Often neither side won a clear victory.

Slaveowners developed numerous variations of two basic methods of managing their laborers: the "gang system" and the "task system." Under the first of these systems, which was the one most commonly used, the field-hands were divided into gangs commanded by drivers who were to work them at a brisk pace. Competent masters gave some thought to the capacities of individual slaves and to the amount of labor that a gang could reasonably be expected to perform in one day. But the purpose of the gang system was to force every hand to continue his labor until all were discharged from the field in the evening.

Under the task system, each hand was given a specific daily work assignment. He could then set his own pace and quit when his task was completed. The driver's job was to inspect the work and see that it was performed satisfactorily before the slave left the field. "The advantages of this system," according to a Georgia rice planter, "are encouragement to the laborers, by equalizing the work of each agreeable to strength, and the avoidance of watchful superintendence and incessant driving. As . . . the task of each [slave] is separate, imperfect work can readily be traced to the neglectful worker."[1]

The task system was best adapted to the rice plantation, with its fields divided into small segments by the network of drainage ditches. Outside the Low Country of South Carolina and Georgia planters occasionally used this system or at least experimented with it, but many of them found it to be unsatisfactory. For one thing, they could get no more work out of their stronger slaves than out of their weaker ones, since the tasks were usually standardized. The planters also found that the eagerness of slaves to finish their tasks as early as possible led to careless work. After using the task system for twenty years, an Alabama planter abandoned it because of evils "too numerous to mention." A South Carolina cotton planter, who also gave it up, noted with satisfaction that under the gang system his slaves did "much more" and were "not so apt to strain themselves."[2]

Actually, most planters used a combination of the two systems. Cotton planters often worked plow-hands in gangs but gave hoe-hands specific tasks of a certain number of cotton rows to hoe each day. Each hand was expected to pick as much cotton as he could, but he might be given a minimum quota that had to be met. Sugar, rice, and tobacco planters applied the task system to their coopers, and hemp growers used it with hands engaged in breaking or hackling hemp. Masters generally tasked their hands for digging ditches, cutting wood, or mauling rails.

Thus most slaves probably had some experience with both systems. From their point of view each system doubtless had its advantages and drawbacks. A strong hand might have preferred to be tasked if he was given an opportunity to finish early. But many slaves must have been appalled at the ease with which they could be held responsible for the quality of their work. The gang system had the disadvantages of severe regimentation and of hard driving which was especially onerous for the weaker hands. But there was less chance that a slave might be detected and held individually responsible for indifferent work. In the long run, however, the rigors of either system were determined by the demands of masters and overseers.

The number of acres a slaveholder expected each of his field-hands to cul-

---

[1] *Southern Agriculturist*, VI (1833), p. 576.
[2] Sellers, *Slavery in Alabama*, p. 67; Hammond Diary, entry for May 16, 1838.

tivate depended in part upon how hard he wished to work them. It also depended upon the nature of the soil, the quality of the tools, and the general efficiency of the agricultural enterprise. Finally, it depended upon the crop. Cotton growers on flat prairies and river bottoms planted as many as ten acres per hand but rarely more than that. Those on hilly or rolling lands planted from three to eight acres per hand. Since a slave could ordinarily cultivate more cotton than he could pick, acreage was limited by the size of the available picking force. By the 1850's each hand was expected to work from nine to ten acres of sugar but seldom more than five acres of rice or three of tobacco, plus six or more of corn and other food crops.[3] The yield per acre and per hand varied with the fertility of the soil, the care in cultivation, the damage of insects, and the whims of the weather.

When calculating his yield per field-hand a slaveholder was not calculating his yield per slave, for he almost always owned fewer field-hands than slaves. Some of his slaves performed other types of work, and the very young and the very old could not be used in the fields. The master's diseased, convalescing, and partially disabled slaves, his "breeding women" and "sucklers," his children just beginning to work in the fields, and his slaves of advanced years were incapable of laboring as long and as hard as full-time hands.

Most masters had systems of rating such slaves as fractional hands. Children often began as "quarter hands" and advanced to "half-hands," "three-quarter hands," and then "full hands." As mature slaves grew older they started down this scale. "Breeding women" and "sucklers" were rated as "half hands." Some planters organized these slaves into separate gangs, for example, into a "sucklers gang." Children sometimes received their training in a "trash gang," or "children's squad," which pulled weeds, cleaned the yard, hoed, wormed tobacco, or picked cotton. Seldom were many more than half of a master's slaves listed in his records as field-hands, and always some of the hands were classified as fractional. Olmstead described a typical situation on a Mississippi cotton plantation: "There were 135 slaves, big and little, of which 67 went to the field regularly—equal, the overseer thought, to 60 able-bodied hands."[4]

The master, not the parents, decided at what age slave children should be put to work in the fields. Until they were five or six years old children were "useless articles on a plantation." Then many received "their first lessons in the elementary part of their education" through serving as "water-toters" or going into the fields alongside their mothers.[5] Between the ages of ten and twelve the children became fractional hands, with a regular routine of field labor. By the time they were eighteen they had reached the age when they could be classified as "prime field-hands."

[3] These are generalized figures from a survey of many plantation records. See also *De Bow's Review*, II (1846), pp. 134, 138; X (1851), p. 625; Sydnor, *Slavery in Mississippi*, pp. 13–14; Gray, *History of Agriculture*, II, pp. 707–708; Sitterson, *Sugar Country*, pp. 127–28; Robert, *Tobacco Kingdom*, p. 18.

[4] Olmsted, *Back Country*, p. 47; id., *Seaboard*, p. 433; *Southern Agriculturist*, VI (1833), pp. 571–73; Sydnor, *Slavery in Mississippi*, pp. 18–20; Sellers, *Slavery in Alabama*, p. 66.

[5] [Joseph H. Ingraham], *The South-West. By a Yankee* (New York, 1835), II, p. 126; Charles S. Davis, *The Cotton Kingdom in Alabama* (Montgomery, 1939), p. 58.

Mature slaves who did not work in the fields (unless they were totally disabled or extremely old) performed other kinds of valuable and productive labor. Old women cooked for the rest of the slaves, cared for small children, fed the poultry, mended and washed clothes, and nursed the sick. Old men gardened, minded stock, and cleaned the stable and the yard.

Old or partially disabled slaves might also be put to spinning and weaving in the loom houses of the more efficient planters. The printed instructions in a popular plantation record book advised overseers to adopt this policy:

> Few instances of good management will better please an employer, than that of having all the winter clothing spun and woven on the place. By having a room devoted to that purpose . . . where those who may be complaining a little, or convalescent after sickness, may be employed in some light work, and where all of the women may be sent in wet weather, more than enough of both cotton and woolen yarn can be spun for the supply of the place.[6]

One planter reported that he had his spinning jenny "going at a round rate[.] Old Charles[is] Spinning and Esther reeling the thread. . . . Charles will in this way be one of my most productive laborers and so will several of the women[.]"[7] Thus a master's productive slaves were by no means limited to those listed as field-hands.

The bondsmen who were valued most highly were those who had acquired special skills which usually exempted them from field work entirely. This select group of slave craftsmen included engineers, coopers, carpenters, blacksmiths, brickmakers, stone masons, mechanics, shoemakers, weavers, millers, and landscapers. The excellence of the work performed by some of them caused slaveowners to make invidious comparisons between them and the free artisans they sometimes employed. An Englishman recalled an interview with the overseer on a Louisiana sugar plantation:

> It would have been amusing, had not the subject been so grave, to hear the overseer's praises of the intelligence and skill of these workmen, and his boast that they did all the work of skilled laborers on the estate, and then to listen to him, in a few minutes, expatiating on the utter helplessness and ignorance of the black race, their incapacity to do any good, or even to take care of themselves.[8]

Domestic servants were prized almost as much as craftsmen. The number and variety of domestics in a household depended upon the size of the establishment and the wealth of the master. They served as hostlers, coachmen, laundresses, seamstresses, cooks, footmen, butlers, housemaids, chambermaids, children's nurses, and personal servants. On a large plantation specialization was complete:

> The cook never enters the house, and the nurse is never seen in the kitchen; the wash-woman is never put to ironing, nor the woman who has charge of the ironing-room ever put to washing. Each one rules supreme in her wash-

---

[6] Thomas Affleck, *The Cotton Plantation Record and Account Book* (Louisville and New Orleans, 1847–).

[7] Gustavus A. Henry to his wife, December 3, 1846, Gustavus A. Henry Papers; Herbert A. Kellar (ed.), *Solon Robinson, Pioneer and Agriculturist* (Indianapolis, 1936), II, p. 203.

[8] William H. Russell, *My Diary North and South* (Boston, 1863), p. 273.

house, her ironing-room, her kitchen, her nursery, her house-keeper's room; and thus . . . a complete system of domesticdom is established to the amazing comfort and luxury of all who enjoy its advantages.[9]

But the field-hands remained fundamental in the slave economy. Though their work was classified as unskilled labor, this of course was a relative term. Some visitors described the "rude" or "slovenly" manner in which slaves cultivated the crops, how "awkwardly, slowly, and undecidedly" they moved through the fields.[10] But other observers were impressed with the success of many masters in training field-hands to be efficient workers, impressed also by the skill these workers showed in certain crucial operations in the production of staple crops. Inexperienced hands had their troubles in sugar houses and rice fields, in breaking and hackling hemp, and in topping, suckering, sorting, and prizing tobacco. Even the neophyte cotton picker soon wondered whether this was unskilled labor, as one former slave testified: "While others used both hands, snatching the cotton and depositing it in the mouth of the sack, with a precision and dexterity that was incomprehensible to me, I had to seize the boll with one hand, and deliberately draw out the white, gushing blossom with the other." On his first day he managed to gather "not half the quantity required of the poorest picker."[11]

Field workers kept up a ceaseless struggle to make the lands fruitful, against the contrary efforts of the insects and the elements. The battle seemed at times to be of absorbing interest to some of the slaves, conscripts though they were. In a strange and uneasy kind of alliance, they and their masters combatted the foes that could have destroyed them both.

4

In 1860, probably a half million bondsmen lived in southern cities and towns, or were engaged in work not directly or indirectly connected with agriculture. Some farmers and planters found it profitable, either temporarily or permanently, to employ part of their hands in non-agricultural occupations. Along the rivers slaves cut wood to provide fuel for steamboats and for sale in neighboring towns. In swamplands filled with juniper, oak, and cypress trees they produced shingles, barrel and hogshead staves, pickets, posts, and rails. In North Carolina's Dismal Swamp slave gangs labored as lumberjacks.[12] In the eastern Carolina pine belt several thousand slaves worked in the turpentine industry. An owner of one hundred and fifty slaves in Brunswick County, North Carolina, raised just enough food to supply his force; he made his profits from the annual sale of thousands of barrels of turpentine. Many smaller operators also combined turpentine production with subsistence farming.[13]

[9] Ingraham (ed.), *Sunny South*, pp. 179–81.

[10] Henry Watson, Jr., to Theodore Watson, March 3, 1831, Watson Papers; Olmsted, *Seaboard*, pp. 18–19.

[11] Solomon Northup, *Twelve Years a Slave* (Buffalo, 1853), pp. 178–79.

[12] Gustavus A. Henry to his wife, December 12, 1848, Henry Papers; John Nevitt Ms. Plantation Journal; William S. Pettigrew to James C. Johnston, January 24, 1856, Pettigrew Family Papers; Olmsted, *Seaboard*, pp. 153–55.

[13] Olmsted, *Seaboard*, pp. 339–42; Guion G. Johnson, *Ante-Bellum North Carolina* (Chapel Hill, 1937), pp. 487–88.

Elsewhere in the South bondsmen worked in sawmills, gristmills, quarries, and fisheries. They mined gold in North Carolina, coal and salt in Virginia, iron in Kentucky and Tennessee, and lead in Missouri. On river boats they were used as deck hands and firemen. Slave stokers on a Mississippi River steamer bound for New Orleans, who sang as they fed wood to the boiler fires, intrigued a European traveler: "It was a fantastic and grand sight to see these energetic black athletes lit up by the wildly flashing flames . . . while they, amid their equally fantastic song, keeping time most exquisitely, hurled one piece of firewood after another into the yawning fiery gulf."[14]

Other slaves were employed in the construction and maintenance of internal improvements. They worked on the public roads several days each year in states which required owners to put them to such use. For many years slaves owned by the state of Louisiana built roads and cleared obstructions from the bayous. Slaves also worked for private internal improvements companies, such as the builders of the Brunswick and Altamaha Canal in Georgia and the Cape Fear and Deep River Navigation Company in North Carolina. In Mississippi a hundred were owned by a firm of bridge contractors, the Weldon brothers.[15]

Railroad companies employed bondsmen in both construction and maintenance work. As early as 1836 the Richmond, Fredericksburg, and Potomac Railroad Company advertised for "a large number" of slave laborers. In the same year the Alabama, Florida, and Georgia Railroad Company announced a need for five hundred "able-bodied negro men . . . to be employed in felling, cutting, and hewing timber, and in forming the excavations and embankments upon the route of said Rail Road." During the 1850's southern newspapers carried the constant pleas of railroad builders for slaves. Almost every railroad in the ante-bellum South was built at least in part by bondsmen; in Georgia they constructed more than a thousand miles of roadbed. In 1858, a Louisiana newspaper concluded: "Negro labor is fast taking the place of white labor in the construction of southern railroads."[16]

Bondsmen in southern cities and towns, in spite of the protests of free laborers, worked in virtually every skilled and unskilled occupation. They nearly monopolized the domestic services, for most free whites shunned them to avoid being degraded to the level of slaves. Many of the Southerners who owned just one or two slaves were urban dwellers who used them as cooks, housekeepers, and gardeners. The wealthier townspeople often had staffs of domestic servants as large as those of rural planters. Other domestics found employment in hotels and at watering places.

Town slaves worked in cotton presses, tanneries, shipyards, bakehouses, and laundries, as dock laborers and stevedores, and as clerks in stores. Masters who owned skilled artisans such as barbers, blacksmiths, cabinet makers, and shoemakers often provided them with shops to make their services avail-

14 Fredrika Bremer, *The Homes of the New World* (New York, 1853), II, p. 174.

15 Joe Gray Taylor, "Negro Slavery in Louisiana" (unpublished doctoral dissertation, Louisiana State University, 1951), pp. 43–44, 115–17; Raleigh *North Carolina Standard*, June 6, 1855; August 13, 1859; Horace S. Fulkerson, *Random Recollections of Early Days in Mississippi* (Vicksburg, 1885), pp. 130–31.

16 Richmond *Enquirer*, August 2, 1836; Sellers, *Slavery in Alabama*, pp. 200–201; Flanders, *Plantation Slavery in Georgia*, pp. 197–98; Taylor, "Negro Slavery in Louisiana," pp. 112–13.

able to all who might wish to employ them. Many white mechanics used slave assistants. In short, as a visitor to Natchez observed, town slaves included

> mechanics, draymen, hostlers, labourers, hucksters, and washwomen, and the heterogeneous multitude of every other occupation, who fill the streets of a busy city—for slaves are trained to every kind of manual labour. The blacksmith, cabinet-maker, carpenter, builder, wheelwright,—all have one or more slaves labouring at their trades. The negro is a third arm to every working man, who can possibly save money enough to purchase one. He is emphatically the 'right-hand man' of every man.[17]

The quality of the work of slave artisans had won favorable comment as early as the eighteenth century. Among them were "many ingenious Mechanicks," wrote a colonial Georgian, "and as far as they have had opportunity of being instructed, have discovered as good abilities, as are usually found among people of our colony."[18]

Some Southerners were enthusiastic crusaders for the development of factories which would employ slaves. They were convinced that bondsmen could be trained in all the necessary skills and would provide a cheaper and more manageable form of labor than free whites. "When the channels of agriculture are choked," predicted an industrial promoter, "the manufacturing of our own productions will open new channels of profitable employment in our slaves." Others thought that slavery was one of the South's "natural advantages" in its effort to build industries to free it from "the incessant and vexatious attacks of the North."[19] They believed that industrialization and slavery could proceed hand in hand.

Southern factory owners gave evidence that this was more than idle speculation. Every slave state had industrial establishments which made some use of slave labor. In Kentucky, the "ropewalks" which manufactured cordage and the hemp factories which produced cotton bagging and "Kentucky jeans" employed slaves extensively.[20] Almost all of the thirteen thousand workers in the tobacco factories of the Virginia District were bondsmen. The majority of them were employed in the three leading tobacco manufacturing cities—Richmond, Petersburg, and Lynchburg. These slave workers were not only a vital part of this industry but also a curiously paradoxical element in the society of the tobacco towns.[21]

From its earliest beginnings the southern iron industry depended upon skilled and unskilled slaves. Negro iron workers were employed in Bath County, Kentucky, and along the Cumberland River in Tennessee. In the Cumberland country the majority of laborers at the iron furnaces were slaves. Montgomery Bell, owner of the Cumberland Iron Works, engaged

---

[17] [Ingraham], *South-West*, II, p. 249.

[18] Quoted in Flanders, *Plantation Slavery in Georgia*, p. 47. See also Leonard P. Stavisky, "Negro Craftsmanship in Early America," *American Historical Review*, IV (1949), 315–25.

[19] *De Bow's Review*, VIII (1850), p. 76; IX (1850), pp. 432–33.

[20] Hopkins, *Hemp Industry*, pp. 135–37; J. Winston Coleman, Jr., *Slavery Times in Kentucky* (Chapel Hill, 1940), pp. 81–82.

[21] Robert, *Tobacco Kingdom*, pp. 197–203; Alexander MacKay, *The Western World; or Travels in the United States in 1846–47* (London, 1849), II, p. 74.

his own three hundred slaves and many others in every task connected with the operation of forge and furnace.[22] In the Great Valley of Virginia, where the southern industry was centered during the early nineteenth century, slaves constituted the chief labor supply.

Until the 1840's, the famed Tredegar Iron Company in Richmond used free labor almost exclusively. But in 1842, Joseph R. Anderson, then commercial agent of the company, proposed to employ slaves as a means of cutting labor costs. The board of directors approved of his plan, and within two years Anderson was satisfied with "the practicability of the scheme." In 1847, the increasing use of slaves caused the remaining free laborers to go out on strike, until they were threatened with prosecution for forming an illegal combination. After this protest failed, Anderson vowed that he would show his workers that they could not dictate his labor policies: he refused to re-employ any of the strikers. Thereafter, as Anderson noted, Tredegar used "almost exclusively slave labor except as the Boss men. This enables me, of course, to compete with other manufacturers."[23]

But it was upon the idea of bringing textile mills to the cotton fields that southern advocates of industrialization with slave labor pinned most of their hopes. In cotton factories women and children were needed most, and hence it was often argued that they would provide profitable employment for the least productive workers in agriculture. Though the majority of southern textile workers were free whites, and though some believed that this work ought to be reserved for them, a small number of slaves were nevertheless employed in southern mills.

Occasionally mill owners managed to work slaves and free whites together with a minimum of friction. A visitor found equal numbers of the two groups employed in a cotton factory near Athens, Georgia: "There is no difficulty among them on account of colour, the white girls working in the same room and at the same loom with the black girls; and boys of each colour, as well as men and women, working together without apparent repugnance or objection."[24] But even if some white workers would tolerate this, slaveowners ordinarily looked upon it as a dangerous practice.

The southern press gave full reports of cotton mills which used slave labor and ecstatic accounts of their success. A Pensacola newspaper cited the local Arcadia Cotton Factory, which employed only slaves, to prove that "with the native skill and ingenuity of mere labor—the labor of the hands— the negro is just as richly endowed as the white." The Saluda mill, near Columbia, South Carolina, operated on the "slave-labor, or anti free-soil system." The white managers testified to the "equal efficiency, and great superiority in many respects" of slaves over free workers.[25] During the 1830's and 1840's, a half dozen other cotton mills in South Carolina's Middle and Low Country employed bondsmen. Most other southern states could point to one or more mills which used this type of labor. To many observers

---

[22] Coleman, *Slavery Times in Kentucky*, p. 64; Robert E. Corlew, "Some Aspects of Slavery in Dickson County," *Tennessee Historical Quarterly*, X (1951), pp. 226–29.

[23] Kathleen Bruce, *Virginia Iron Manufacture in the Slave Era* (New York, 1931), pp. 231–38.

[24] James S. Buckingham, *The Slave States of America* (London, [1842]), II, p. 112.

[25] Pensacola *Gazette*, April 8, 1848; *De Bow's Review*, IX (1850), pp. 432–33.

the enterprises of Daniel Pratt at Prattsville, near Montgomery, Alabama, provided models for other Southerners to copy. Pratt worked slaves not only in his cotton mill but also in his cotton gin factory, iron foundry, sash and door factory, machine shop, and carriage and wagon shop.[26]

Actually, the ante-bellum South had relatively few cotton mills, and most of them were small enterprises manufacturing only the coarser grades of cloth. In 1860, the fifteen slave states together had only 198 mills each employing an average of 71 workers, whereas Massachusetts alone had 217 mills each employing an average of 177 workers. Many of the southern factories resembled the one owned by a small manufacturer in East Tennessee which contained only three hundred spindles operated by fourteen slave hands.[27]

Still, in these textile mills and in what little other industry existed in the Old South there was abundant evidence that slaves could be trained to be competent factory workers. The evidence was sufficient to raise serious doubts that slavery was tied to agriculture, as some defenders and some critics of the institution believed.

·   ·   ·

6

Mammy Harriet had nostalgic memories of slavery days: "Oh, no, we was nebber hurried. Marster nebber once said, 'Get up an' go to work,' an' no oberseer ebber said it, neither. Ef some on 'em did not git up when de odders went out to work, marster nebber said a word. Oh, no, we was nebber hurried."[28] Mammy Harriet had been a domestic at "Burleigh," the Hinds County, Mississippi, estate of Thomas S. Dabney. She related her story of slave life there to one of Dabney's daughters who wrote a loving volume about her father and his cotton plantation.

Another slave found life less leisurely on a plantation on the Red River in Louisiana:

> The hands are required to be in the cotton field as soon as it is light in the morning, and, with the exception of ten or fifteen minutes, which is given them at noon to swallow their allowance of cold bacon, they are not permitted to be a moment idle until it is too dark to see, and when the moon is full, they often times labor till the middle of the night.

Work did not end when the slaves left the fields. "Each one must attend to his respective chores. One feeds the mules, another the swine—another cuts the wood, and so forth; besides the packing [of cotton] is all done by candle light. Finally, at a late hour, they reach the quarters, sleepy and overcome with the long day's toil."[29] These were the bitter memories of

[26] E. M. Lander, Jr., "Slave Labor in South Carolina Cotton Mills," *Journal of Negro History*, XXXVIII (1953), pp. 161–73; Charles H. Wesley, *Negro Labor in the United States, 1850–1925* (New York, 1927), pp. 15–20; *American Cotton Planter and Soil of the South*, I (1857), pp. 156–57.

[27] William B. Lenoir to William Lenoir, May 18, 1833, Lenoir Family Papers.

[28] Susan Dabney Smedes, *Memorials of a Southern Planter* (Baltimore, 1887), p. 57.

[29] Northup, *Twelve Years a Slave*, pp. 166–68.

Solomon Northup, a free Negro who had been kidnapped and held in bondage for twelve years. Northup described his experiences to a Northerner who helped him prepare his autobiography for publication.

Mammy Harriet's and Solomon Northup's disparate accounts of the work regimen imposed upon slaves suggest the difficulty of determining the truth from witnesses, Negro and white, whose candor was rarely uncompromised by internal emotions or external pressures. Did Dabney's allegedly unhurried field-hands (who somehow produced much cotton and one of whom once tried to kill the overseer) feel the same nostalgia for slavery days? How much was Northup's book influenced by his amanuensis and by the preconceptions of his potential northern readers?

And yet there is nothing in the narratives of either of these ex-slaves that renders them entirely implausible. The question of their complete accuracy is perhaps less important than the fact that both conditions actually did exist in the South. Distortion results from exaggerating the frequency of either condition or from dwelling upon one and ignoring the other.

No sweeping generalization about the amount of labor extracted from bondsmen could possibly be valid, even when they are classified by regions, or by occupations, or by the size of the holdings upon which they lived. For the personal factor transcended everything else. How hard the slaves were worked depended upon the demands of individual masters and their ability to enforce them. These demands were always more or less tempered by the inclination of most slaves to minimize their unpaid toil. Here was a clash of interests in which the master usually, but not always, enjoyed the advantage of superior weapons.

Not only must glib generalizations be avoided but a standard must be fixed by which the slave's burden of labor can be judged. Surely a slave was overworked when his toil impaired his health or endangered his life. Short of this extreme there are several useful standards upon which judgments are based. If, for example, the quantity of labor were compared with the compensation the inevitable conclusion would be that most slaves were overworked. Also by present-day labor standards the demands generally made upon them were excessive. These, of course, were not the standards of the nineteenth century.

Another standard of comparison—though not an altogether satisfactory one—is the amount of work performed by contemporary free laborers in similar occupations. Independent farmers and artisans set their own pace and planned their work to fit their own convenience and interests, but they nevertheless often worked from dawn to dusk. Northern factory workers commonly labored twelve hours a day. This was arduous toil even for free laborers who enjoyed the advantages of greater incentives and compensation. Yet contemporaries did not think that slaves were overworked when their masters respected the normal standards of their day. Some slaveowners did respect them, and some did not.

Unquestionably there were slaves who escaped doing what was then regarded as a "good day's work," and there were masters who never demanded it of them. The aphorism that took two slaves to help one to do nothing was not without its illustrations. After lands and slaves had remained in the hands of a single family for several generations, planters sometimes developed a patriarchal attitude toward their "people" and took pride in treating them indulgently. Such masters had lost the competitive spirit and the urge to increase their worldly possessions which had characterized their ancestors. To live gracefully on their declining estates, to smile tolerantly at the listless labor of their field-hands, and to be surrounded by a horde of pampered domestics were all parts of their code.

In Virginia, the easygoing manner of the patricians was proverbial. But Virginia had no monopoly of them; they were scattered throughout the South. Olmsted visited a South Carolina rice plantation where the tasks were light enough to enable reasonably industrious hands to leave the fields early in the afternoon. Slaves on several sea-island cotton plantations much of the time did not labor more than five or six hours a day.[30]

The production records of some of the small slaveholding farmers indicated that neither they nor their slaves exerted themselves unduly. These masters, especially when they lived in isolated areas, seemed content to produce little more than a bare subsistence. In addition, part of the town slaves who hired their own time took advantage of the opportunity to enjoy a maximum of leisure. The domestics of some wealthy urban families willingly helped to maintain the tradition that masters with social standing did not examine too closely into the quantity or efficiency of their work.

From these models proslavery writers drew their sentimental pictures of slave life. The specific cases they cited were often valid ones; their profound error was in generalizing from them. For this leisurely life was the experience of only a small fraction of the bondsmen. Whether they lived in the Upper South or Deep South, in rural or urban communities, on plantations or farms, the labor of the vast majority of slaves ranged from what was normally expected of free labor in that period to levels that were clearly excessive.

It would not be too much to say that masters usually demanded from their slaves a long day of hard work and managed by some means or other to get it. The evidence does not sustain the belief that free laborers generally worked longer hours and at a brisker pace than the unfree. During the months when crops were being cultivated or harvested the slaves commonly were in the fields fifteen or sixteen hours a day, including time allowed for meals and rest.[31] By ante-bellum standards this may not have been excessive, but it was not a light work routine by the standards of that or any other day.

In instructions to overseers, planters almost always cautioned against overwork, yet insisted that the hands be made to labor vigorously as many hours as there was daylight. Overseers who could not accomplish this were discharged. An Arkansas master described a work day that was in no sense unusual on the plantations of the Deep South:

> We get up before day every morning and eat breakfast before day and have everybody at work before day dawns. I am never caught in bed after day light nor is any body else on the place, and we continue in the cotton fields

[30] Olmsted, *Seaboard*, pp. 434–36; Guion G. Johnson, *A Social History of the Sea Islands* (Chapel Hill, 1930), pp. 124–25; E. Merton Coulter, *Thomas Spalding of Sapelo* (Baton Rouge, 1940), p. 85.

[31] Gray, *History of Agriculture*, I, pp. 556–57.

when we can have fair weather till it is so dark we cant see to work, and this history of one day is the history of every day.[32]

Planters who contributed articles on the management of slaves to southern periodicals took this routine for granted. "It is expected," one of them wrote,

> that servants should rise early enough to be at work by the time it is light. . . . While at work, they should be brisk. . . . I have no objection to their whistling or singing some lively tune, but no *drawling* tunes are allowed in the field, for their motions are almost certain to keep time with the music.[33]

These planters had the businessman's interest in maximum production without injury to their capital.

The work schedule was not strikingly different on the plantations of the Upper South. Here too it was a common practice to regulate the hours of labor in accordance with the amount of daylight. A former slave on a Missouri tobacco and hemp plantation recalled that the field-hands began their work at half past four in the morning. Such rules were far more common on Virginia plantations than were the customs of languid patricians. An ex-slave in Hanover County, Virginia, remembered seeing slave women hurrying to their work in the early morning "with their shoes and stockings in their hands, and a petticoat wrapped over their shoulders to dress in the field the best way they could."[34] The bulk of the Virginia planters were businessmen too.

Planters who were concerned about the physical condition of their slaves permitted them to rest at noon after eating their dinners in the fields. "In the Winter," advised one expert on slave management, "a hand may be pressed all day, but not so in Summer. . . . In May, from one and a half to two hours; in June, two and a half; in July and August, three hours rest [should be given] at noon."[35] Except for certain essential chores, Sunday work was uncommon but not unheard of if the crops required it. On Saturdays slaves were often permitted to quit the fields at noon. They were also given holidays, most commonly at Christmas and after the crops were laid by.

But a holiday was not always a time for rest and relaxation. Many planters encouraged their bondsmen to cultivate small crops during their "leisure" to provide some of their own food. Thus a North Carolina planter instructed his overseer: "As soon as you have laid by the crop give the people 2 days but . . . they must work their own crops." Another planter gave his slaves a "holiday to plant their potatoes," and another "holiday to get in their potatoes." James H. Hammond once wrote in disgust: "Holiday for the negroes who fenced in their gardens. Lazy devils they did nothing after 12 o'clock." In addition, slave women had to devote part of their time when

---

[32] Gustavus A. Henry to his wife, November 27, 1860, Henry Papers.

[33] *Southern Cultivator*, VIII (1850), p. 163.

[34] William W. Brown, *Narrative of William W. Brown, a Fugitive Slave* (Boston, 1847), p. 14; Olmsted, *Seaboard*, p. 109; *De Bow's Review*, XIV (1853), pp. 176–78; Benjamin Drew, *The Refugee: or the Narratives of Fugitive Slaves in Canada* (Boston, 1856), p. 162.

[35] *Southern Cultivator*, VIII (1850), p. 163.

they were not in the fields to washing clothes, cooking, and cleaning their cabins. An Alabama planter wrote: "I always give them half of each Saturday, and often the whole day, at which time . . . the women do their household work; therefore they are never idle."[36]

Planters avoided night work as much as they felt they could, but slaves rarely escaped it entirely. Night work was almost universal on sugar plantations during the grinding season, and on cotton plantations when the crop was being picked, ginned, and packed. A Mississippi planter did not hesitate to keep his hands hauling fodder until ten o'clock at night when the hours of daylight were not sufficient for his work schedule.[37]

Occasionally a planter hired free laborers for such heavy work as ditching in order to protect his slave property. But, contrary to the legend, this was not a common practice. Most planters used their own field-hands for ditching and for clearing new ground. Moreover, they often assigned slave women to this type of labor as well as to plowing. On one plantation Olmsted saw twenty women operating heavy plows with double teams: "They were superintended by a male negro driver, who carried a whip, which he frequently cracked at them, permitting no dawdling or delay at the turning."[38]

Among the smaller planters and slaveholding farmers there was generally no appreciable relaxation of this normal labor routine. Their production records, their diaries and farm journals, and the testimony of their slaves all suggest the same dawn-to-dusk regimen that prevailed on the large plantations.[39] This was also the experience of most slaves engaged in nonagricultural occupations. Everywhere, then, masters normally expected from their slaves, in accordance with the standards of their time, a full stint of labor from "day clean" to "first dark."

Some, however, demanded more than this. Continuously, or at least for long intervals, they drove their slaves at a pace that was bound, sooner or later, to injure their health. Such hard driving seldom occurred on the smaller plantations and farms or in urban centers; it was decidedly a phenomenon of the large plantations. Though the majority of planters did not sanction it, more of them tolerated excessively heavy labor routines than is generally realized. The records of the plantation regime clearly indicate that slaves were more frequently overworked by calloused tyrants than overindulged by mellowed patriarchs.

That a large number of southern bondsmen were worked severely during the colonial period is beyond dispute. The South Carolina code of 1740 charged that "many owners . . . do confine them so closely to hard labor, that they have not sufficient time for natural rest."[40] In the nineteenth cen-

[36] Henry K. Burgwyn to Arthur Souter, August 6, 1843, Henry King Burgwyn Papers; John C. Jenkins Diary, entries for November 15, 1845; April 22, 1854; Hammond Diary, entry for May 12, 1832; De Bow's Review, XIII (1852), pp. 193–94.

[37] Jenkins Diary, entry for August 7, 1843.

[38] Olmsted, Back Country, p. 81; Sydnor, Slavery in Mississippi, p. 12.

[39] See, for example, Marston Papers; Torbert Plantation Diary; De Bow's Review, XI (1851), pp. 369–72; Drew, Refugee; Douglass, My Bondage, p. 215; Trexler, Slavery in Missouri, pp. 97–98.

[40] Hurd, Law of Freedom and Bondage, I, p. 307; Flanders, Plantation Slavery in Georgia, p. 42.

tury conditions seemed to have improved, especially in the older regions of the South. Unquestionably the ante-bellum planter who coveted a high rank in society responded to subtle pressures that others did not feel. The closing of the African slave trade and the steady rise of slave prices were additional restraining influences. "The time has been," wrote a planter in 1849, "that the farmer could kill up and wear out one Negro to buy another; but it is not so now. Negroes are too high in proportion to the price of cotton, and it behooves those who own them to make them last as long as possible."[41]

But neither public opinion nor high prices prevented some of the bondsmen from suffering physical breakdowns and early deaths because of overwork. The abolitionists never proved their claim that many sugar and cotton growers deliberately worked their slaves to death every seven years with the intention of replacing them from profits. Yet some of the great planters came close to accomplishing that result without designing it. In the "race for wealth" in which, according to one Louisiana planter, all were enlisted, few proprietors managed their estates according to the code of the patricians.[42] They were sometimes remarkably shortsighted in the use of their investments.

Irresponsible overseers, who had no permanent interest in slave property, were frequently blamed for the overworking of slaves. Since this was a common complaint, it is important to remember that nearly half of the slaves lived on plantations of the size that ordinarily employed overseers. But planters could not escape responsibility for these conditions simply because their written instructions usually prohibited excessive driving. For they often demanded crop yields that could be achieved by no other method.

Most overseers believed (with good reason) that their success was measured by how much they produced, and that merely having the slave force in good condition at the end of the year would not guarantee re-employment. A Mississippi overseer with sixteen years of experience confirmed this belief in defending his profession: "When I came to Mississippi, I found that the overseer who could have the most cotton bales ready for market by Christmas, was considered best qualified for the business—consequently, every overseer gave his whole attention to cotton bales, to the exclusion of everything else."[43]

More than a few planters agreed that this was true. A committee of an Alabama agricultural society reported:

> It is too commonly the case that masters look only to the yearly products of their farms, and praise or condemn their overseers by this standard alone, without ever once troubling themselves to inquire into the manner in which things are managed on their plantations, and whether he may have lost more in the diminished value of his slaves by over-work than he has gained by his large crop.

This being the case, it was understandably of no consequence to the overseer that the old hands were "worked down" and the young ones "over-

[41] *Southern Cultivator*, VII (1849), p. 69.
[42] Kenneth M. Clark to Lewis Thompson, December 29, 1859. Thompson Papers.
[43] *American Cotton Planter and Soil of the South*, II (1858), pp. 112–13.

strained," that the "breeding women" miscarried, and that the "sucklers" lost their children. "So that he has the requisite number of cotton bags, all is overlooked; he is re-employed at an advanced salary, and his reputation increased."[44]

Some planters, unintentionally perhaps, gave overseers a special incentive for overworking slaves by making their compensation depend in part upon the amount they produced. Though this practice was repeatedly denounced in the ante-bellum period, many masters continued to follow it nevertheless. Cotton growers offered overseers bonuses of from one to five dollars for each bale above a specified minimum, or a higher salary if they produced a fixed quota. A Louisiana planter hired an overseer on a straight commission basis of $2.75 per bale of cotton and four cents per bushel of corn. A South Carolina rice planter gave his overseer ten per cent of the net proceeds. And a Virginian offered his overseer "the seventh part of the good grain, tobacco, cotton and flax" that was harvested on his estate. "Soon as I hear [of] such a bargain," wrote a southern critic, "I fancy that the overseer, determined to save his salary, adopts the song of 'drive, drive, drive.' "[45]

Masters who hired their slaves to others also helped to create conditions favoring ruthless exploitation. The overworking of hired slaves by employers with only a temporary interest in their welfare was as notorious as the harsh practices of overseers. Slaves hired to mine owners or railroad contractors were fortunate if they were not driven to the point where their health was impaired. The same danger confronted slaves hired to sugar planters during the grinding season or to cotton planters at picking time. Few Southerners familiar with these conditions would have challenged the assertion made before a South Carolina court that hired slaves were "commonly treated more harshly . . . than those in possession of their owner[s]."[46]

But the master was as responsible for the conduct of those who hired his slaves as he was for the conduct of the overseers he employed. Overworked slaves were not always the innocent victims of forces beyond his control; there were remedies which he sometimes failed to apply. A staunch defender of slavery described a set of avaricious planters whom he labeled "Cotton Snobs," or "Southern Yankees." In their frantic quest for wealth, he wrote indignantly, the crack of the whip was heard early and late, until their bondsmen were "bowed to the ground with over-tasking and over-toil."[47] A southern physician who practiced on many cotton plantations complained, in 1847, that some masters still regarded "their sole interest to consist in large crops, leaving out of view altogether the value of negro property and its possible deterioration." During the economic depression of the 1840's, a planter accused certain cotton growers of trying to save themselves by increasing their cotton acreage and by driving their slaves harder, with the result that slaves broke down from overwork. An Alabama news-

[44] *American Farmer*, II (1846), p. 78; *Southern Cultivator*, II (1844), pp. 97, 107.

[45] *North Carolina Farmer*, I (1845), pp. 122–23. Agreements of this kind with overseers are in the records of numerous planters.

[46] Catterall, *Judicial Cases*, II, p. 374.

[47] Hundley, *Social Relations*, pp. 132, 187–88.

paper attributed conditions such as these to "avarice, the desire of growing rich."[48]

On the sugar plantations, during the months of the harvest, slaves were driven to the point of complete exhaustion. They were, in the normal routine, worked from sixteen to eighteen hours a day, seven days a week.[49] Cotton planters who boasted about making ten bales per hand were unconsciously testifying that their slaves were overworked. An overseer on an Arkansas plantation set his goal at twelve bales to the hand and indicated that this was what his employer desired. On a North Carolina plantation a temporary overseer assured the owner that he was a "hole hog man rain or shine" and boasted that the slaves had not been working like men but "like horses." "I'd ruther be dead than be a nigger on one of these big plantations," a white Mississippian told Olmsted.[50]

Sooner or later excessive labor was bound to take its toll. In the heat of mid-summer, slaves who could not bear hard driving without sufficient rest at noon simply collapsed in the fields. In Mississippi a planter reported "numerous cases" of sunstroke in his neighborhood during a spell of extreme heat. His own slaves "gave out." On a Florida plantation a number of hands "fainted in the field" one hot August day. Even in Virginia hot weather and heavy labor caused "the death of many negroes in the harvest field."[51]

What else was there in the lives of slaves besides work, sleep, and procreation? What filled their idle hours? What occupied their minds? What distinguished them from domestic animals? Much will never be known, for surviving records provide only brief glimpses into the private life of the slave quarters. But much can be learned from Negro songs and folklore, from the recollections of former slaves, and from the observations of the more perceptive and sensitive whites.

The average bondsman, it would appear, lived more or less aimlessly in a bleak and narrow world. He lived in a world without schools, without books, without learned men; he knew less of the fine arts and of aesthetic values than he had known in Africa; and he found few ways to break the monotonous sameness of all his days. His world was the few square miles of earth surrounding his cabin—a familiar island beyond which were strange places (up North where people like him were not slaves), frightening places ("down the river" where overseers were devils), and dead places (across the ocean where his ancestors had lived and where he had no desire to go). His world was full of mysteries which he could not solve, full of forces

[48] De Bow's Review, I (1846), pp. 434–36; III (1847), p. 419; Selma Free Press, quoted in Tuscaloosa Independent Monitor, July 14, 1846.

[49] This is apparent from the records of sugar planters. See also Sitterson, Sugar Country, pp. 133–36; Olmsted, Seaboard, pp. 650, 667–68.

[50] P. Weeks to James Sheppard, September 20, 1854, James Sheppard Papers; Doctrine Davenport to Ebenezer Pettigrew, April 24, 1836, Pettigrew Family Papers; Olmsted, Back Country, pp. 55–57, 202.

[51] Jenkins Diary, entries for August 9, 1844; July 7, 1846; June 30, 1854; Ulrich B. Phillips and James D. Glunt (eds.), Florida Plantation Records from the Papers of George Noble Jones (St. Louis, 1927), p. 90; John B. Garrett Ms. Farm Journal, entry for July 19, 1830.

which he could not control. And so he tended to be a fatalist and futilitarian, for nothing else could reconcile him to his life.

When they left Africa the Negroes carried with them a knowledge of their own complex cultures. Some elements of their cultures—or at least some adaptations or variations of them—they planted somewhat insecurely in America. These surviving "Africanisms" were evident in their speech, in their dances, in their music, in their folklore, and in their religion. The amount of their African heritage that remained varied with time and place. More of it was evident in the eighteenth century when a large proportion of the slaves were native Africans, than in the mid-nineteenth century when the great majority were second- and third-generation Americans. Fieldhands living on large plantations in isolated areas, such as the South Carolina and Georgia sea islands, doubtless preserved more "Africanisms" than slaves who were widely dispersed in relatively small holdings or who lived in their master's houses as domestics. How substantial and how durable the African heritage was is a question over which students of the American Negro have long disagreed.[52]

But the disagreement has been over the size of what was admittedly a fragment; few would deny that by the ante-bellum period slaves everywhere in the South had lost most of their African culture. In bondage, the Negroes lacked cultural autonomy—the authority to apply rigorous sanctions against those who violated or repudiated their own traditions. Instead, they were exposed to considerable pressure to learn and accept whichever of the white man's customs would help them to exist with a minimum of friction in a biracial society. Before the Civil War, American Negroes developed no cultural nationalism, no conscious pride in African ways. At most they unconsciously preserved some of their old culture when it had a direct relevance to their new lives, or they fused it with things taken from the whites.

If anything, most ante-bellum slaves showed a desire to forget their African past and to embrace as much of white civilization as they could. They often looked with contemptuous amusement upon newly imported Africans. When a Tennessean attempted to teach a group of slaves a dance he had witnessed on the Guinea coast, he was astonished by their lack of aptitude and lack of interest. In fact, the feelings of these slaves were "hurt by the insinuation which his effort conveyed."[53] Thus the "Africanisms" of the slaves—even of the Gullah Negroes of South Carolina sea islands—were mere vestiges of their old cultures. For example, a few African words remained in their speech; the rest was the crude and ungrammatical English of an illiterate folk.

There was an element of tragedy in this. The slaves, having lost the bulk of their African heritage, were prevented from sharing in much of the best southern white culture. There were exceptions, of course. Occasionally a

---

[52] The literature on this subject is vast, but for the two points of view see Robert E. Park, "The Conflict and Fusion of Cultures with Special Reference to the Negro," *Journal of Negro History*, IV (1919), pp. 111–33; Melville J. Herskovits, "On the Provenience of New World Negroes," *Social Forces*, XII (1933), pp. 247–62.

[53] Ingraham (ed.), *Sunny South*, pp. 146–47.

gifted slave overcame all obstacles and without formal education became a brilliant mathematician or a remarkable linguist. A few showed artistic talents of a high order. Others learned to read and write, or, in the case of house servants, manifested polite breeding which matched—and sometimes surpassed—that of their masters. But the life of the generality of slaves, as a visitor to South Carolina observed, was "far removed from [white] civilization"; it was "mere animal existence, passed in physical exertion or enjoyment." Fanny Kemble saw grown slaves "rolling, tumbling, kicking, and wallowing in the dust, regardless alike of decency, and incapable of any more rational amusement; or lolling, with half-closed eyes, like so many cats and dogs, against a wall, or upon a bank in the sun, dozing away their short leisure hour."[54]

This was essentially the way it had to be as long as the Negro was held in bondage. So far from slavery acting as a civilizing force, it merely took away from the African his native culture and gave him, in exchange, little more than vocational training. So far from the plantation serving as a school to educate a "backward" people, its prime function in this respect was to train each new generation of slaves. In slavery the Negro existed in a kind of cultural void. He lived in a twilight zone between two ways of life and was unable to obtain from either many of the attributes which distinguish man from beast. Olmsted noted that slaves acquired, by example or compulsion, some of the external forms of white civilization; but this was poor compensation for "the systematic withdrawal from them of all the usual influences which tend to nourish the moral nature and develop the intellectual faculties, in savages as well as in civilized free men."[55]

What, then, filled the leisure hours of the slaves? The answer, in part, is that these culturally rootless people devoted much of this time to the sheer pleasure of being idle. Such activities as they did engage in were the simple diversions of a poor, untutored folk—activities that gave them physical pleasure or emotional release. Slaves probably found it more difficult to find satisfying amusements on the small farms where they had few comrades, than in the cities and on the plantations where they could mix freely with their own people.

"I have no desire to represent the life of slavery as an experience of nothing but misery," wrote a former bondsman. In addition to the unpleasant things, he also remembered "jolly Christmas times, dances before old massa's door for the first drink of egg-nog, extra meat at holiday times, midnight visits to apple orchards, broiling stray chickens, and first-rate tricks to dodge work." Feasting, as this account suggested, was one of the slave's chief pleasures, one of his "principle sources of comfort." The feast was what he looked forward to not only at Christmas but when crops were laid by, when there was a wedding, or when the master gave a reward for good behavior. "Only the slave who has lived all the year on his scanty allowance of meal and bacon, can appreciate such suppers," recalled another ex-bondsman. Then his problems were forgotten as he gave himself up "to the intoxication of pleasurable amusements." Indeed he might when, for

[54] Harrison, *Gospel Among the Slaves*, p. 245; [Ingraham], *South-West*, II, p. 194; Kemble, *Journal*, p. 66.
[55] Olmstead, *Back Country*, pp. 70–71.

example, a Tennessee master provided a feast such as this: "They Barbecue *half* a small Beef and two fat shoats and some Chickens—have peach pies— Chicken pies, beets[,] Roasting Ears and potatoes in profusion."[56]

Occasions such as Christmas or a corn-shucking were times not only for feasting but also for visiting with slaves on nearby establishments. In Virginia a visitor observed that many bondsmen spent Sundays "strolling about the fields and streets" finding joy in their relative freedom of movement. They dressed in bright-colored holiday clothes, which contrasted pleasantly with their drab everyday apparel. The slaves seemed to welcome each holiday with great fervor, for they found in it an enormous relief from the boredom of their daily lives. "All are brushing up, putting on their best rigging, and with boisterous joy hailing the approach of the Holy days," noted an Arkansas master at the start of the Christmas season.[57]

Dancing was one of the favorite pastimes of the slaves, not only on special holidays but on Saturday nights as well. A few pious masters prohibited this diversion, as did a Virginian who was shocked when neighborhood slaves attended a dancing party: "God forbid that one of my Family either white or colored should ever be caught at such an abominable and adulterous place." But most masters, too wise to enforce a regime so austere, permitted a shuffle at least occasionally. "This is Saturday night," wrote a Louisianian, "and I hear the fiddle going in the Quarter. We have two parties here among the Negroes. One is a dancing party and the other a Praying party. The dancers have it tonight, and the other party will hold forth tomorrow."[58]

The kinds of jigs and double shuffles that slaves indulged in were once described as "dancing all over"; they revealed an apparent capacity to "agitate every part of the body at the same time." Such dances were physical and emotional orgies. Fanny Kemble found it impossible to describe "all the contortions, and springs, and flings, and kicks, and capers" the slaves accomplished as they danced "Jim Crow." A visitor at a "shake-down" in a Louisiana sugar house found the dancers in a "thumping ecstacy, with loose elbows, pendulous paws, angulated knees, heads thrown back, and backs arched inwards—a glazed eye, intense solemnity of mien."[59] Slaves danced to the music of the fiddle or banjo, or they beat out their rhythm with sticks on tin pans or by clapping their hands or tapping their feet. These ancestors of twentieth-century "jitterbugs" developed their own peculiar jargon too. In Virginia a skilled dancer could "put his foot good"; he was a "ring-clipper," a "snow-belcher," and a "drag-out"; he was no "bug-eater," for he could "carry a broad row," "hoe de corn," and "dig de taters."[60]

Other holiday amusements included hunting, trapping, and fishing. In

[56] Henson, *Story*, pp. 19–20, 56; Northup, *Twelve Years a Slave*, pp. 213–16; Steward, *Twenty-Two Years a Slave*, pp. 28–31; Bills Diary, entry for July 24, 1858.

[57] Emerson Journal, entry for September 19, 1841; John W. Brown Diary, entry for December 25, 1853.

[58] Walker Diary, entry for February 13, 1841; H. W. Poynor to William G. Harding, March 22, 1850, Harding-Jackson Papers.

[59] *De Bow's Review*, XI (1851), p. 66; Kemble, *Journal*, pp. 96–97; Russell, *Diary*, pp. 258–59.

[60] *Farmers' Register*, VI (1838), pp. 59–61.

spite of legal interdictions, slaves gambled with each other and with "disso-lute" whites. But some found both pleasure and profit in using their leisure to pursue a handicraft; they made brooms, mats, horse collars, baskets, boats, and canoes. These "sober, thinking and industrious" bondsmen scorned those who wasted time in frivolities or picked up the white man's vices.[61]

A few things in the lives of slaves belonged to them in a more intimate and personal way; these were things which illustrated peculiarly well the blending of African traditions with new experiences in America. For in-stance, folklore was important to them as it has always been to illiterate people. Some of it preserved legends of their own past; some explained nat-ural phenomena or described a world of the spirits; and some told with charming symbolism the story of the endless warfare between black and white men. The tales of Br'er Rabbit, in all their variations, made virtues of such qualities as wit, strategy, and deceit—the weapons of the weak in their battles with the strong. Br'er Bear had great physical power but was a hap-less bumbler; Br'er Fox was shrewd and crafty as well as strong but, none-theless, was never quite a match for Br'er Rabbit. This was a scheme of things which the slave found delightful to contemplate.[62]

The bondsmen had ceremonial occasions of their own, and they devised special ways of commemorating the white man's holidays. At Christmas in eastern North Carolina, they begged pennies from the whites as they went "John Canoeing" (or "John Cunering") along the roads, wearing masks and outlandish costumes, blowing horns, tinkling tambourines, danc-ing, and chanting

> Hah! Low! Here we go!
> Hah! Low! Here we go!
> Hah! Low! Here we go!
> Kuners come from Denby!

Virginia slaves had persimmon parties where they interspersed dancing with draughts of persimmon beer and slices of persimmon bread. At one of these parties the banjo player sat in a chair on the beer barrel: "A long white cowtaïl, queued with red ribbon ornamented his head, and hung gracefully down his back; over this he wore a three-cocked hat, decorated with pea-cock feathers, a rose cockade, a bunch of ripe persimmons, and . . . three pods of red pepper as a top-knot." On some Louisiana sugar plantations, when the cutters reached the last row of cane they left the tallest cane standing and tied a blue ribbon to it. In a ceremony which marked the end of the harvest, one of the laborers waved his cane knife in the air, "sang to the cane as if it were a person, and danced around it several times before cutting it." Then the workers mounted their carts and triumphantly carried the last cane to the master's house where they were given a drink.[63]

Rarely did a contemporary write about slaves without mentioning their music, for this was their most splendid vehicle of self-expression. Slave

[61] Johnson, *Ante-Bellum North Carolina*, pp. 555–57; Douglass, *My Bondage*, pp. 251–52.

[62] Crum, *Gullah*, p. 120; Benjamin A. Botkin (ed.), *Lay My Burden Down*, p. 2.

[63] Johnson, *Ante-Bellum North Carolina*, p. 553; *Farmers' Register*, VI (1838), pp. 59–61; Moody, "Slavery on Louisiana Sugar Plantations," *loc. cit.*, p. 277 n.

music was a unique blend of "Africanisms," of Protestant hymns and revival songs, and of the feelings and emotions that were a part of life in servitude.[64] The Negroes had a repertory of songs for almost every occasion, and they not only sang them with innumerable variations but constantly improvised new ones besides. They sang spirituals which revealed their conceptions of Christianity and professed their religious faith. They sang work songs (usually slow in tempo) to break the monotony of toil in the tobacco factories, in the sugar houses, on the river boats, and in the fields. They sang whimsical songs which told little stories or ridiculed human frailties. They sang nonsense songs, such as "Who-zen-John, Who-za" sung by a group of Virginia slaves as they "clapped juber" to a dance:

> Old black bull come down de hollow,
> He shake hi' tail, you hear him bellow;
> When he bellow he jar de river,
> He paw de yearth, he make it quiver.
> Who-zen-John, who-za.[65]

Above all, they sang plaintive songs about the sorrows and the yearnings which they dared not, or could not, more than half express. Music of this kind could hardly have come from an altogether carefree and contented people. "The singing of a man cast away on a desolate island," wrote Frederick Douglass, "might be as appropriately considered an evidence of his contentment and happiness, as the singing of a slave. Sorrow and desolation have their songs, as well as joy and peace."[66] In their somber and mournful moods the bondsmen voiced sentiments such as these: "O Lord, O my Lord! O my good Lord keep me from sinking down"; "Got nowhere to lay my weary head"; "My trouble is hard"; "Nobody knows the trouble I've seen"; and "Lawd, I can't help from cryin' somctime." The Gullah Negroes of South Carolina sang:

> I know moon-rise, I know star-rise,
>   Lay dis body down.
> I walk in de moonlight, I walk in de starlight,
>   To lay dis body down.
> I'll walk in de graveyard, I'll walk through de graveyard,
>   To lay dis body down.
> I'll lie in de grave and stretch out my arms;
>   Lay dis body down;
> I go to de judgment in de evenin' of de day,
>   When I lay dis body down;
> And my soul and your soul will meet in de day
>   When I lay dis body down.[67]

One final ingredient helped to make pleasant the leisure hours of numerous slave men and women: alcohol in its crudest but cheapest and most con-

---

[64] The most recent collection of slave songs is Miles Mark Fisher, *Negro Slave Songs in the United States* (Ithaca, 1953).

[65] *Farmers' Register*, VI, (1838), pp. 59–61.

[66] Douglass, *My Bondage*, pp. 99–100.

[67] Thomas Wentworth Higginson, *Army Life in a Black Regiment* (Boston, 1870), p. 209.

centrated forms. To be sure, these bibulous bondsmen merely indulged in a common vice of an age of hard liquor and heavy drinkers; but they, more than their masters, made the periodic solace of the bottle a necessity of life. In preparing for Christmas, slaves somehow managed to smuggle "fresh bottles of rum or whisky into their cabins," for many thought of each holiday as a time for a bacchanalian spree. Indeed, recalled a former bondsman, to be sober during the holidays was "disgraceful; and he was esteemed a lazy and improvident man, who could not afford to drink whisky during Christmas."[68] No law, no threat of the master, ever kept liquor out of the hands of slaves or stopped the illicit trade between them and "unscrupulous" whites. Some masters themselves furnished a supply of whisky for holiday occasions, or winked at violations of state laws and of their own rules.

There was little truth in the abolitionist charge that masters gave liquor to their slaves in order to befuddle their minds and keep them in bondage. On the other hand, many bondsmen used intoxicants for a good deal more than an occasional pleasant stimulant, a mere conviviality of festive occasions. They found that liquor provided their only satisfactory escape from the indignities, the frustrations, the emptiness, the oppressive boredom of slavery. Hence, when they had the chance, they resorted to places that catered to the Negro trade or found sanctuaries where they could tipple undisturbed. What filled their alcoholic dreams one can only guess, for the dreams at least were theirs alone.

·   ·   ·

[68] Hundley, *Social Relations*, pp. 359–60; Olmsted, *Seaboard*, pp. 75, 101–102; Adams Diary, entry for December 29, 1857; Douglass, *My Bondage*, pp. 251–52.

American Slaves
and Their History

Eugene Genovese

Though his findings were fresh, the problems that
Kenneth Stampp was pursuing in the book from
which the previous selections were taken were
traditional. He was fundamentally concerned with
slavery as a moral problem for whites, both in the
antebellum period and now. He described the ways in
which the system operated and in which slaves were
treated and was interested in the response of the
slaves primarily in order to know whether they
accepted their slavery or whether they resisted.
Stampp carried the interpretation of the evidence
along those lines about as far as it can be pursued.
Because he wrote within the existing conceptual
framework, his book teeters on the margin of
diminishing returns.

   The conceptual logjam was exploded in 1959 by
the appearance of Stanley Elkins' *Slavery*, which
posed the question, what did slavery do to the slave?
Assuming the actual existence of Sambo, the shuffling,
childish, happy-go-lucky stereotype so frequently
found in the accounts of whites who observed slavery
firsthand, Elkins reasoned that Sambo was the result
of a process of infantilization analogous to that
experienced by many inmates of Nazi concentration

camps. Caught in a no-exit situation in which the slave was totally powerless and the master totally powerful, the slave adapted by reverting to child-like behavior, even to the point of identifying with his oppressor.

Fruitful and stimulating as the concentration camp analogy has been, it has failed to convince most professional historians. Among other things, they point to the admittedly imperfect nature of the comparison between a concentration camp and a plantation, to the difficulty of being certain how common Sambo was, to the impossibility of knowing whether the Sambo personality was a thoroughly internalized pattern of behavior or whether it was a role consciously adopted and lightly shed, and to the speculative nature of any judgment as to the precise kind of psychological mechanism that gave rise to the pattern of behavior. Other historians do concede, however, that Elkins asked the right question: how did the institution of slavery affect the slave?

Eugene Genovese, though disagreeing sharply with Elkins' conclusions, is one of a group of scholars that includes anthropologists and sociologists as well as historians that has taken this question seriously and has begun to explore the extent to which slaves created for themselves areas of life in which they were capable of being autonomous. This kind of study requires, as Genovese points out in the following essay, a history of life in the quarters, a history seen from the bottom up. The focus must be on the slave himself as an actor. What did he do in those hours of time and areas of life that did not affect the master's primary interests and thus were not closely supervised by the master or his agent? Those hours and areas became the crucible in which the African past and the slave present were fused into a new culture.

It would be very difficult to understand the rapid emergence after the Civil War of talented blacks without understanding the complex nature of slave society, the variety of experiences it provided, and the existence within it of a limited but real amount of psychological living space for blacks. More subtly, as Genovese argues, one must grasp the mutuality of the relationship between slave and master. It was not a simple one-way relationship of dominance and submission, but a relationship governed by an

American Slaves and Their History. From *In Red and Black,* pp. 102–28, by Eugene Genovese. Copyright © 1971 by Eugene Genovese. Reprinted by permission of Pantheon Books, a Division of Random House, Inc.

implicit contract that prescribed rights and obligations on both sides. It would be both foolish and immoral to think the bargain was a fair one, but it would be myopic not to recognize that both sides held expectations about the behavior of the other and felt limitations on their own freedom of action. Both master and slave recognized that they were linked together in a social system.

It is from this perspective that George Frederickson and Christopher Lasch ("Resistance to Slavery," *Civil War History*, XIII [December 1967]), have suggested that a better analogy for the plantation than the concentration camp is the penitentiary. An understanding of prison culture, in which the custodians maintain a tenuous control over the institution through a constant tug-of-war with the inmate social structure, makes it possible to understand how slaves could recognize the master's legitimacy but not the obligation to obey him. Like prisoners, slaves came to terms with their slavery in a variety of ways. They played Sambo. They were loyal to the master and competed for recognition by the master and by their fellows as excellent slaves. They engaged in sabotage, malingering, stealing, running away, and even murder. They apparently acquiesced and did what they had to do to get along.

Given this variety of responses of the slaves to their conditioning, say Frederickson and Lasch, it is useless to get involved in the confrontation between Phillips and Stampp about whether slaves were happy and docile or angry and rebellious. Slaves frequently engaged in noncooperation of different kinds, but not to the extent of the sort of political resistance that clearly implies a recognition of the system's illegitimacy and a vision of an achievable alternative. Though insurrections were not unknown and certainly were feared by southern whites, they were much less frequent or significant than in the Caribbean or in South America. Slaves in the American South lacked the awareness of collective victimization that would have impelled them to organize sustained assaults against the system. Like modern penitentiary inmates, Frederickson and Lasch urge, each individual slave followed a shifting set of personal strategies for coping with his situation.

In the essay that follows, Genovese goes to some pains to assure the reader that he is not trying to whitewash the slave system by attributing to slaves some control over it and some insulation from the

power of the master. One might wonder if he
succeeds in giving the reader a more sophisticated
understanding of what slavery was like from the point
of view of the slave without making it seem less
horrible than Kenneth Stampp maintains it was.
Furthermore, Genovese's point of view has great
implications for contemporary black nationalist
ideologies. One might think Genovese's view detracts
from such ideologies because it deemphasizes
victimization and revolutionary heroes, but it also
enhances those ideologies by explaining how a
separate black culture could have survived and grown
despite the impact of slavery.

*T*he history of the lower classes has yet to be written.
The ideological impact of the New Left, the intellectual exigencies of the
black liberation movement, and the developing academic concern for the
cultural dimension of politics and history have converged to produce the expectation that it will be. If one per cent of the hosannas heaped upon E. P.
Thompson's *The Making of the English Working Class* could be translated
into disciplined effort to extend its achievement, the future would be bright.
And indeed, good work is finally being done, although precious little of it
by those who regularly pontificate on the need to rewrite history "from the
bottom up."

History written from the bottom up is neither more nor less than history
written from the top down: It is not and cannot be good history. To write
the story of a nation without taking into consideration the vicissitudes of a
majority of its people is simply not a serious undertaking. And yet, it is
preposterous to suggest that there could conceivably be anything wrong
with writing a book about the ruling class alone, or about one or another
elite, or about any segment of society no matter how small. No subject is
too small to treat. But a good historian writes well on a small subject
while taking account (if only implicitly and without a single direct reference) of the whole, whereas an inferior one confuses the need to isolate
a small portion of the whole with the license to assume that that portion
thought and acted in isolation. One may, for example, write Southern history by focusing on either blacks or whites, slaves or masters, tenant farmers or landlords; it will be good or bad history if, among other things, the
author knows that the one cannot be discussed without a deep understanding of the other. The fate of master and slave was historically intertwined
and formed part of a single social process; each in his own way struggled for
autonomy—struggled to end his dependence upon the other—but neither
could ever wholly succeed. The first problem in the writing of social history
lies in this organic antagonism: We tend to see the masters in their own

terms, without acknowledgment of their dependence upon the slaves; we also tend to see the slaves in the masters' terms, without acknowledgment of the extent to which the slaves freed themselves from domination.

There cannot be, therefore, any such thing as "history from the bottom up." A good study of plantation architecture, apart from its contribution to aesthetics, would be one that grasped the social link between the culture of the Big House and that of both the slave quarters and small nonslaveholding farmhouses, for the Big House, whatever else it did, served to impress the humbler men in and out of its orbit. Such a study need never mention the quarters or the farmhouses, but if the essential insight fails or remains undeveloped and abstract, then the entire effort must remain limited. Should it succeed, then it must be ranked as a valuable contribution to the history of Southern society and its constituent races and classes. To consider such a study "elitist" because it concerns itself with upper-class life or eschews moralistic pronouncements is a modern form of absurdity.

There is much to be said for the current notion that blacks will have to write their own history: Black people in the United States have strong claims to separate nationality, and every people must interpret its own history in the light of its own traditions and experience. At the same time, the history of every people must be written from without, if only to provide a necessary corrective in perspective; sooner or later the history of every people must flow from the clash of viewpoints and sensibilities that accompanies both external and internal confrontation. But for the South there is a more compelling reason for black and white scholars to have to live with each other. There is simply no way of learning about either blacks or whites without learning about the other. If it is true, as I suspect, that the next generations of black scholars will bring a special viewpoint to Southern history, then their success or failure will rest, in part, on their willingness to teach us something new about the masters as well as the slaves. He who says the one, is condemned to say the other.

I should like to consider some debilitating assumptions often brought by social historians to the study of the lower classes, and to suggest a way of avoiding the twin elitist notions that the lower classes are generally passive or generally on the brink of insurrection. We have so many books on slavery in the Old South that specialists need to devote full time merely to keeping abreast of the literature. Yet, there is not a single book and only a few scattered articles on life in the quarters—except of course for such primary and undigested sources as the slave narratives and plantation memoirs. A good student might readily be able to answer questions about the economics of the plantation, the life of the planters, the politics of slavery expansionism, or a host of other matters, but he is not likely to know much about slave life, about the relationship of field to house slaves, or about the relationship between the slave driver or foreman and other slaves. To make matters worse, he may well think he knows a good deal, for the literature abounds in undocumented assertions and plausible legends.

The fact remains that there has not been a single study of the driver—the most important slave on the larger plantations—and only a few sketchy and misleading studies of house slaves. So far as the life of the quarters is concerned, it is enough to note that the notion persists, in the face of abundant

but

ves had no family life to speak of. Historians and sociolo-
nd black, have been guilty of reasoning deductively from
nce—slave marriages were not recognized by law in the
have done little actual research.

to discuss the family in detail here, nor house slaves and
tter, but I should like to touch on all three in order to
int. We have made a great error in the way in which we
..ewed slave life, and this error has been perpetuated by both whites
and blacks, racists and antiracists. The traditional proslavery view and that
of such later apologists for white supremacy as U. B. Phillips have treated
the blacks as objects of white benevolence and fear—as people who needed
both protection and control—and devoted attention to the ways in which
black slaves adjusted to the demands of the master class. Abolitionist propaganda and the later, and now dominant, liberal viewpoint have insisted that
the slave regime was so brutal and dehumanizing that blacks should be seen
primarily as victims. Both these viewpoints treat black people almost wholly
as objects, never as creative participants in a social process, never as half of a
two-part subject.

True, abolitionist and liberal views have taken account of the ways in
which slaves resisted their masters by shirking their work, breaking tools, or
even rebelling, but the proslavery view generally noted that much too, even
if within the context of a different interpretation. Neither has ever stopped
to consider, for example, that the evidence might reflect less a deliberate
attempt at sabotage or alleged Negro inferiority than a set of attitudes
toward time, work, and leisure which black people developed partly in
Africa and partly in the slave quarters—a set of attitudes which constituted
a special case in a general pattern of behavior associated with preindustrial
cultures. Preindustrial peoples knew all about hard work and discipline, but
their standards were those of neither the factory nor the plantation and
were embedded in a radically different culture. Yet, even such sympathetic
historians as Kenneth Stampp who give some attention to slaves as subjects
and actors, have merely tried to show that slaves exercised some degree of
autonomy in their responses to the blows or cajoling of their masters. We
have yet to receive a respectful treatment—apart from some brief but suggestive passages in the work of W. E. B. Du Bois, C. L. R. James and perhaps one or two others—of their attempts to achieve an autonomous life
within the narrow limits of the slave plantation.[1] We have yet to have a
synthetic record of their incessant struggle to escape from the culture as
well as the psychological domination of the master class.

In commenting briefly on certain features of family life, house slaves, and
drivers, I should like to suggest some of the rich possibilities inherent in an
approach that asks much more than "What was done to the slaves?" and, in
particular, asks, "What did the slaves do for themselves and how did they
do it?" In a more leisurely presentation it would be possible and, indeed,

[1] See, e.g., C. L. R. James, "The Atlantic Slave Trade and Slavery: Some Interpretations of Their Significance in the Development of the United States and the Western
World," *Amistad*, #1 (Vintage Books, 1970). Du Bois's writings are full of important
ideas and hypotheses. See especially *Black Reconstruction in America* and *Souls of Black
Folk*.

necessary to discuss slave religion, entertainment, songs and dances, and many other things. But perhaps we may settle for a moment on one observation about slave religion.

We are told a great deal about the religious instruction of the slaves, by which is meant the attempt to inculcate a version of Protestant Christianity. Sometimes this instruction is interpreted as a good thing in itself and sometimes as a kind of brainwashing, but we may leave this question aside. Recently, Vincent Harding, following the suggestive probing in Du Bois's work, has offered a different perspective and suggested that the slaves had their own way of taking up Christianity and forging it into a weapon of active resistance.[2] Certainly, we must be struck by the appearance of one or another kind of messianic preacher in almost every slave revolt on record. Professor Harding therefore asks that we look at the slaves as active participants in their own religious experience and not merely as objects being worked on by slaveholding ideologues. This argument may be carried further to suggest that a distinctly black religion, at least in embryo, appeared in the quarters and played a role—the extent and precise content of which we have yet to evaluate—in shaping the daily lives of the slaves. In other words, quite apart from the problem of religion as a factor in overt resistance to slavery, we need to know how the slaves developed a religious life that enabled them to survive as autonomous human beings with a culture of their own within the white master's world.

One of the reasons we know so little about this side of the story—and about all lower-class life—is that it is undramatic. Historians, white and black, conservative, liberal, and radical, have a tendency to look for the heroic moments, either to praise or to excoriate them, and to consider ordinary life as so much trivia. Yet, if a slave helped to keep himself psychologically intact by breaking his master's hoe, he might also have achieved the same result by a special effort to come to terms with his God, or by loving a woman who shared his burdens, or even by aspiring to be the best worker on the plantation. We normally think of someone who aspires to be a good slave as an Uncle Tom, and maybe we should. But human beings are not so simple. If a slave aspires to a certain excellence within the system, and if his implicit trust in the generous response of the master is betrayed—as often it must be in such a system—then he is likely to be transformed into a rebel. And if so, he is likely to become the most dangerous kind of rebel, first because of his smashed illusions and second because of the skills and self-control he taught himself while appearing on the scene as an Uncle Tom. The historical record of slavery is full of people who were model slaves right up until the moment they killed their overseer, ran away, burned down the Big House, or joined an insurrection.

So what can be said about the decidedly non-Christian element in the religion of the slave quarters? The planters tell us repeatedly that every plantation had its conjurer, its voodoo man, its witch doctor. To the planters this means a residue of African superstition, and it is, of course, possible

[2] Vincent Harding, "Religion and Resistance Among Ante-Bellum Negroes, 1800–1860," August Meier and Elliott Rudwick, eds., *The Making of Black America* 1 (New York, 1969), 179–197.

that by the 1830s all that remained in the slave quarters were local superstitions rather than a continuation of the highly sophisticated religions originally brought from Africa. But the evidence suggests the emergence of an indigenous and unique combination of African and European religious notions, adapted to the specific conditions of slave life by talented and imaginative individuals, which represented an attempt to establish a spiritual life adequate to the task of linking the slaves with the powerful culture of the masters and yet providing them with a high degree of separation and autonomy.

When we know enough of this story we shall know a good deal about the way in which the culture of an oppressed people develops. We often hear the expression "defenseless slaves," but, although any individual at any given moment may be defenseless, a whole people rarely, if ever, is. It may be on the defensive and dangerously exposed, but it almost invariably finds its own ways to survive and fight back. The trouble is that we keep looking for overt rebellious actions—the strike, the revolt, the murder, the arson, the tool-breaking—and often fail to realize that, in given conditions and at particular times, the wisdom of a people and their experience in struggle dictates a different course and an emphasis on holding together both individually and collectively. From this point of view, the most ignorant of the field slaves who followed the conjurer on the plantation was saying no to the boss and seeking an autonomous existence. That the conjurer may, in any one case, have been a fraud and even a kind of extortionist and, in another case, a genuine popular religious leader is, from this point of view, of little importance.

Let us take the family as an illustration. Slave law refused to recognize slave marriages and family ties. In this respect United States slavery was far worse than Spanish American or Luso-Brazilian. In those Catholic cultures the Church demanded and tried to guarantee that slaves be permitted to marry and that the sanctity of the slave family be upheld. As a result, generations of American historians have concluded that American slaves had no family life and that Cuban and Brazilian slaves did. This judgment will not bear examination. The slave trade to the United States was closed early: no later than 1808, except for statistically insignificant smuggling, and, in fact, for most states it ended decades earlier. The rise of the Cotton Kingdom and the great period of slavery expansion followed the closing of the slave trade. Slavery, in the numbers we are accustomed to thinking of, was a product of the period following the end of African importations. The slave force that was liberated during and after the War for Southern Independence was overwhelmingly a slave force born and raised in this country. We have good statistics on the rate of increase of that slave population, and there can be no doubt that it compared roughly to that of the whites—apart from the fact of immigration—and that furthermore, it was unique among New World slave classes. An early end to the slave trade, followed by a boom in cotton and plantation slavery, dictated a policy of encouraging slave births. In contrast, the slave trade remained open to Cuba and to Brazil until the second half of the nineteenth century; as a result, there was little economic pressure to encourage family life and slave-breeding. In Brazil and Cuba, far more men than women were imported from Africa until late in the history of the respective slave regimes; in the Old South, a rough sexual parity was established fairly early. If, therefore, religion and law militated in favor of slave families in Cuba and Brazil and against them in the Old South, economic pressure worked in reverse. The result was a self-reproducing slave force in the United States and nowhere else, so far as the statistics reveal.

It may immediately be objected that the outcome could have reflected selective breeding rather than family stability. But selective breeding was tried in the Caribbean and elsewhere and never worked; there is no evidence that it was ever tried on a large scale in the South. Abolitionists charged that Virginia and Maryland deliberately raised slaves—not merely encouraged, but actually fostered slave-breeding. There is no evidence. If slave-raising farms existed and if the planters were not complete fools they would have concentrated on recruiting women of childbearing age and used a relatively small number of studs. Sample studies of major slave-exporting counties in Virginia and Maryland show no significant deviations from the parallel patterns in Mississippi or other slave-buying regions.

Now, it is clear that Virginia and Maryland—and other states as well—exported their natural increase for some decades before the war. But this was a process, not a policy; it reflected the economic pressures to supplement a waning income from agriculture by occasional slave sales; it was not incompatible with the encouragement of slave families and, in fact, reinforced it. Similarly, planters in the cotton states could not work their slaves to death and then buy fresh ones, for prices were too high. They had been too high from the very moment the Cotton Kingdom began its westward march, and therefore a tradition of slave-killing never did take root. As time went on, the pressures mounted to provide slaves with enough material and even psychological satisfaction to guarantee the minimum morale needed for reproduction. These standards of treatment—so much food, living space, time off, etc.—became part of the prevailing standard of decency, not easily violated by greedy slaveholders. In some respects the American slave system may have been the worst in the world, as so many writers insist But in purely material terms, it was probably the best. American slaves were generally fed, clothed, housed, and worked better than those of Cuba, Jamaica, or Brazil.

But the important thing here is that the prevailing standard of decency was not easily violated because the slaves had come to understand their own position. If a master wished to keep his plantation going, he had to learn the limits of his slaves' endurance. If, for example, he decided to ignore the prevailing custom of giving Sunday off or of giving an extended Christmas holiday, his slaves would feel sorely tried and would certainly pay him back with one or another form of wrecking. The slaves remained in a weak position, but they were rarely completely helpless, and by guile, brute courage and a variety of other devices they taught every master just where the line was he dared not cross if he wanted a crop. In precisely this way, slaves took up the masters' interest in their family life and turned it to account. The typical plantation in the South was organized by family unit. Man and wife lived together with children, and within a considerable sphere the man was in fact the man in the house.

Whites violated black family life in several ways. Many families were disrupted by sales, especially in the upper South, where economic pressures were strong. White men on the plantations could and often did violate black women. Nothing can minimize these injustices. The frequency of sales is extremely hard to measure. Many slaves were troublesome and sold many times over; this inflated the total number of sales but obscured the incidence of individual transfers. The crimes against these black people are a matter of record, and no qualifications can soften their impact. But it is not at all certain that most slaves did not live stable, married lives in the quarters despite the pressures of the market. I do not wish to get into the vexing question of the violation of black women here, but certainly there was enough of it to justify the anger of those who condemned the slave regime on this ground alone. The evidence, however, does not warrant the assumption that a large percentage of black plantation women were so violated. In other words, for a judgment on the moral quality of the regime, this subject is extremely important; for an assessment of the moral life of the slaves, it is much less so.

What the sources show—both the plantation books and letters of the masters, and also the reports of runaway slaves and ex-slaves—is that the average plantation slave lived in a family setting, developed strong family ties, and held the nuclear family as the proper social norm. Planters who often had to excuse others, or even themselves, for breaking up families by sale, would sometimes argue that blacks did not really form deep and lasting attachments, that they lacked strong family sense, that they were naturally promiscuous, and so forth. Abolitionists and ex-slaves would reinforce the prevalent notion by saying that slavery was so horrible, no real family tie could be maintained. Since planters, abolitionists, and ex-slaves all said the same thing, it has usually been taken as the truth. Only it was not.

In the first place, these various sources also say opposite things, which we rarely notice. Planters agonized over the breakup of families and repeatedly expressed regrets and dismay. Often, they went to great lengths to keep families together at considerable expense, for they knew how painful it was to enforce separations. Whether they were motivated by such material considerations as the maintenance of plantation morale or more lofty sentiment is neither here nor there. They often demonstrated that they knew very well how strong the family ties were in the quarters. Planters did everything possible to encourage the slaves to live together in stable units; they recognized that a man was easier to control if he had a wife and children to worry about. The slaves, on their side, behaved variously, of course. Many were, indeed, promiscuous although much of the charge of promiscuity stemmed not so much from actual promiscuity as from sequential polygamy. They did change partners more often than Victorian whites could stomach. (In this respect, they might be considered the great forerunners of the white, middle-class sexual morality of the 1960s.) I stress this side of things—the interest of the master in slave family stability and the effort of the slave to protect his stake in a home, however impoverished—because it is now fashionable to believe that black people came out of slavery with little or no sense of family life. But if so, then we need to know why, during early Reconstruction, so many thousands wandered over the South looking for their spouse or children. We do not know just how many slaves lived as a family or were willing and able to maintain a stable family life during slavery. But the number was certainly great, whatever the percentage, and as a result, the social norm that black people carried from slavery to freedom was that of the nuclear family. If it is true that the black family has disintegrated in the ghettos—and we have yet to see conclusive evidence—then the source will have to be found in the conditions of economic and social oppression imposed upon blacks during recent decades. The slave experience, for all its tragic disruptions, pointed toward a stable postslavery family life, and recent scholarship demonstrates conclusively that the Reconstruction and post-Reconstruction black experience carried forward the acceptance of the nuclear family norm.[3]

Let us consider the role of the male and the legend of the matriarchy. Almost all writers on slavery describe the slave man as "a guest in the house" who could have no role beyond the purely sexual. The slave narratives and the diaries and letters of white plantation owners tell us something else. His position was undeniably precarious and frustrating. If his wife was to be whipped, he had to stand by and watch; he could not fully control his own children; he was not a breadwinner in the usual sense; and, in a word, there were severe restrictions imposed upon the manifestations of what we somewhat erroneously call manliness. But, both masters and ex-slaves tell us about some plantations on which certain women were not easily or often punished because it was readily understood that, to punish the woman, it would be necessary to kill her man first. These cases were the exception, but they tell us at the start that the man felt a duty to protect his woman. If circumstances conspired to prevent his fulfilling that duty, those circumstances often included his woman's not expecting it and, indeed, consoling him about the futility of such a gesture. We cannot know what was said between a man and a woman when they lay down together at night after such outrages, but there are enough hints in the slave narratives to suggest that both knew what a man could do, as well as what he "should" do, especially when there were children to consider. Many scholars suggest that black women treated their men with contempt for not doing what circumstances made impossible. This is a deduction from tenuous assumptions; it is not a demonstrated fact.

Beyond that, the man of the house did do various things. He trapped and hunted animals to supplement the diet in the quarters, and in this small but important and symbolic way he was a breadwinner. He organized the garden plot and presided over the division of labor with his wife. He disciplined his children—or divided that function with his wife as people in other circumstances do—and generally was the source of authority in the cabin. This relationship within the family was not always idyllic. In many instances, his authority over both wife and children was imposed by force. Masters forbade men to hit their wives and children and whipped them for it; but they did it anyway and often. And there is not much evidence that women readily ran to the master to ask that her husband be whipped for

---

[3] Herbert Gutman has presented several papers to scholarly meetings and is close to completing a major book on the historical development of the black family from slavery to World War I. I am indebted to him for allowing me to see the manuscript in progress and for discussing the data with me.

striking her. The evidence on these matters is fragmentary, but it suggests that the men asserted their authority as best they could; the women expected to have to defer to their husbands in certain matters; and that both tried hard to keep the master out of their lives. The conditions were unfavorable, and perhaps many men did succumb and in one way or another became emasculated. But we might also reflect on the ways in which black men and women conspired to maintain their own sense of dignity and their own autonomy by settling things among themselves and thereby asserting their own personalities.

Black women have often been praised—and justly so—for their strength and determination in holding their families together during slavery, when the man was supposedly put aside or rendered irrelevant. It is time, I think, to praise them for another thing they seem to have been able to do in large numbers: to support a man they loved in ways deep enough and varied enough to help him resist the mighty forces for dehumanization and emasculation. Without the support of their women, not many black men could have survived; but with it—and there is plenty of testimony that they often had it—many could and did.

If our failure to see the plantation from the vantage point of the slave quarters has led us to substitute abstractions for research on the slave family, so has it saddled us with unsubstantiated and erroneous ideas on house slaves. According to the legend, house slaves were the Uncle Toms of the system—a privileged caste apart, contemptuous of the field hands, jealous of their place in the affection or at least eye of the white master and mistress, and generally speaking, finks, sellouts, and white man's niggers. Like most stereotypes, this one has its kernel of truth. There were, indeed, many house slaves who fit the description. But we might begin by considering a small fact. Half the slaves in the rural South lived on farms of twenty or fewer slaves; another twenty-five per cent lived on plantations with twenty to fifty slaves. Only twenty-five per cent, in other words, lived on plantations of fifty or more, and of those, the overwhelming majority lived on units of less than one hundred—that is, on units of less than twenty slave families. In short, the typical house slave serviced either a small farm or, at best, a moderate plantation. Only a few lived and worked on plantations large enough to permit the formation of a separate group of house slaves—of enough house slaves to form a caste unto themselves.

Our idea of the fancy-dressed, uppity, self-inflated house slave who despised the field blacks and identified with the whites is a product of the relatively small group who lived in the towns and cities like Charleston, New Orleans, and Richmond. These townhouse slaves and a tiny group of privileged house slaves on huge plantations could and sometimes did form a separate caste with the attributes described in the literature. Certainly, the great planters and their families, who left most of the white-family records that have been relied on as the major source, would most likely have remembered precisely these slaves. Even these blacks deserve a more careful look than they have received, for they were much more complicated people than we have been led to believe. But, the important point is that the typical house slave was far removed from this condition. He, or more likely she, worked with perhaps one to three or four others on an estate too small to permit any such caste formation.

If the typical house slave was an Uncle Tom and a spoiled child of the whites, then we need to be told just why so many of them turn up in the records of runaways. There is abundant evidence from the war years. We hear much about the faithful retainers who held the Yankees off from the Big House, or protected young missus, or hid the family silver. Such types existed and were not at all rare. But they do not appear to have been nearly so numerous as those house slaves who joined the field slaves in fleeing to the Yankee lines when the opportunity arose. The best source on this point is the planters themselves, who were shocked at the defection of their favorite slaves. They could readily understand the defection of the field hands, whom they considered stupid and easily led, but they were unable to account for the flight, sometimes with expressions of regret and sometimes with expressions of anger and hatred, of their house slaves. They had always thought they knew these blacks, loved them, were loved by them, and they considered them part of the family. One day they learned that they had been deceiving themselves and living intimately with people they did not know at all. The house slaves, when the opportunity presented itself, responded with the same range of behavior as did the field slaves. They proved themselves just as often rebellious and independent as they did docile and loyal.

This display of independence really was nothing new. If it is true that house slaves were often regarded as traitors to the black cause during slave rebellions, it is also true that their appearance in those rebellions was not as rare as we are led to believe. A black rebel leader told Denmark Vesey and his followers not to trust the house slaves because they were too tied to the whites, but we ought also note that some of the toughest and most devoted of those leaders in Charleston in 1822 were themselves house slaves. In particular, the great scandal of the event in Charleston was the role played by the most trusted slaves, of the governor of South Carolina. Certainly, the role of the house slave was always ambiguous and often treacherous. But if many house slaves betrayed their fellows, many others collected information in the Big House and passed it on to the quarters. We know how well-informed the field slaves were about movements of Yankee troops during the war; we know that these field slaves fled to the Yankee lines with uncanny accuracy in timing and direction. Probably no group was more influential in providing the necessary information than those very house slaves who are so often denigrated.

The decision of slaves, whether house slaves or not, to protect whites during slave insurrections or other catastrophes, hardly proves them to have been Toms. The master-slave relationship, especially when it occurred in the intimacies of the Big House, was always profoundly ambivalent. Many of the same slaves who protected their masters and mistresses from harm and thereby asserted their own humanity were anything but docile creatures of the whites.

Since most house slaves worked on estates too small for a separate existence, their social life was normally down in the quarters and not apart or with the whites. The sexes were rarely evenly matched in the house, where women predominated, and even when they were, the group was too small for natural pairing off. A large number of house slaves married field hands or, more likely, the more skilled artisans or workers. Under such circumstances, the line between house slaves and field hands was not sharp for most slaves. Except on the really large units, house slaves were expected to help out in the fields during picking season and during emergencies. The average house slave got periodic tastes of field work and had little opportunity to cultivate airs.

There are two general features to the question of house slaves that deserve comment: first, there is the ambiguity of their situation and its resultant ambivalence toward whites; the other is the significance of the house slave in the formation of a distinctly Afro-American culture. The one point I should insist upon in any analysis of the house slave is ambivalence. People, black and white, slave and master, thrown together in the intimacy of the Big House, had to emerge loving and hating each other. Life together meant sharing each other's pains and problems, confiding secrets, having company when no one else would do, being forced to help one another in a multitude of ways. It also meant jointly experiencing, but in tragically opposite ways, the full force of lordship and bondage: that is, the full force of petty tyranny imposed by one woman on another; of expecting someone to be at your beck and call regardless of her own feelings and wishes; of being able to take out one's frustrations and disappointments on an innocent bystander, who would no doubt be guilty enough of something since servants are always falling short of the expectations.

To illustrate the complexity of black slave behavior in the Big House, let us take a single illustration. It is typical in the one sense that it catches the condition of ambiguity and of entwined, yet hostile, lives. Beyond that, it is of course unique, as are all individual experiences. Eliza L. Magruder was the niece of a deceased planter and politician from the Natchez, Mississippi, region and went to live with her aunt Olivia, who managed the old plantation herself. Miss Eliza kept a diary for the years 1846 and 1847 and then again for 1854 and 1857.[4] Possibly, she kept a diary for the intermittent years which has been lost. In any case, she has a number of references to a slave girl, Annica, and a few to another, Lavinia. We have here four women, two white and two black, two mistresses and two servants, thrown together in a single house and forced on each other's company all year long, year after year.

On April 17, 1846, Miss Eliza wrote in her diary more or less in passing, "Aunt Olivia whipped Annica for obstinacy." This unladylike chastisement had followed incidents in which Annica had been "impudent." About a month later, on September 11, Annica took another whipping—for "obstinacy." Miss Eliza appears to have been a bit squeamish, for her tone, if we read it correctly, suggests that she was not accustomed to witnessing such unpleasantness. On January 24, 1847, she confided to her diary, "I feel badly. Got very angry and whipped Lavinia. O! for government over my temper." But the world progresses, and so did Miss Eliza's fortitude in the

<hr />

[4] Ms. diary in Louisiana State University library, Baton Rouge, La.

face of other people's adversity. When her diary resumed in 1854, she had changed slightly: the squeamishness had diminished. Annica had not changed: she had remained her old, saucy self. October 26, 1854: "Boxed Annica's ears for impertinence."

Punctuated by this war of wills, daily life went on. Annica's mother lived in Jackson, Mississippi, and mother and daughter kept in touch. Since Annica could neither read nor write, Miss Eliza served as her helpmate and confidant. December 5, 1854: "I wrote for Annica to her mother." Mamma wrote back in due time, no doubt to Annica's satisfaction, but also to her discomfiture. As Miss Eliza observed on January 25, 1855, "Annica got a letter from her mammy which detected her in a lie. O! that negroes generally were more truthful." So, we ought not to be surprised that Miss Eliza could write without a trace of the old squeamishness on July 1, 1855, "I whipt Annica."

The impertinent Annica remained undaunted. November 29, 1855: "Aunt Olivia gave Annica a good scolding and made her ask my pardon and will punish her otherwise." Perhaps we should conclude that Annica's atrocious behavior had earned the undying enmity of the austere white ladies, but some doubts may be permitted. On July 24, 1856, several of their neighbors set out on a trip to Jackson, Mississippi, where, it will be recalled, Annica's mother lived. Aunt Olivia, with Miss Eliza's concurrence, sent Annica along for a two-week holiday and provided ten dollars for her expenses. On August 3, Annica returned home in time for breakfast. In the interim Miss Eliza had Lavinia as an object of wrath, for Lavinia had "very much provoked" her by lying and by being impertinent. "Aunt Olivia boxed her ears for it." Lavinia's day of glory did not last; it was not long before Annica reclaimed full possession of the title of the most impudent nigger in the Big House. On September 4, 1856, "Annica was very impertinent, and I boxed her ears." Three days later, wrote Miss Eliza, "I kept Annica in in the afternoon for impudence." The next day (September 8) Miss Eliza told Aunt Olivia about Annica's misconduct. "She reproved her for it and will I suppose punish her in some way." Life traveled on into November, when on the tenth day of the month, "Aunt Olivia whipt Annica for impertinence."

At this point, after a decade of impudence, impertinence, obstinacy, whipping, and ear-boxing, one might expect that Annica would have been dispatched to the cotton fields by women who could not abide her. But she remained in the Big House. And what shall we make of such incidents as that which occurred on the night of December 29, 1856, when poor Annica was ill and in pain? It is not so much that Miss Eliza sat up with her, doing what she could; it is rather that she seemed both concerned and conscious of performing a simple duty. On the assumption that the illness left Annica weak for a while, Miss Eliza of course still had Lavinia. January 30, 1857: "I boxed Lavinia's ears for coming up late when I told her not."

On April 23, 1857, Annica greatly pleased Miss Eliza by making her a white bonnet. But by April 26, Annica was once again making trouble: "Aunt Olivia punished Annica by keeping her in her room all afternoon." And the next day: "Aunt Olivia had had Annica locked up in the garret all day. I pray it may humble her and make further punishment unnecessary."

On August 18, 1857, "Aunt Olivia held a court of enquiry, but didn't find out who ripped my pattern." There is no proof that Annica did it; still one wonders. Two weeks later in Miss Eliza's Sunday school, "Annica was strongly tempted to misbehave. I brought her in however." The entries end there.

Let us suppose the ladies had carried their household into the war years: What then? It would take little imagination to see Annica's face and to hear her tone as she marched into the kitchen to announce her departure for the federal lines. It would not even take much imagination to see her burning the house down. Yet, she had never been violent, and we should not be too quick to assume that she would easily have left the only home she had known as an adult and the women who wrote letters to her mamma, exchanged confidences, and stayed up with her on feverish nights. The only thing we can be sure of is that she remained impudent to the day she died.

What I think this anecdote demonstrates above all is the ambivalence inherent in the Big House relationship and the stubborn struggle for individuality that house slaves, whip or no whip, were capable of. Yet it may also hint at another side and thereby help explain why so many black militants, like so many historians before them, are quick to condemn the whole house-slave legacy as one to be exorcized. The house slaves were, indeed, close to the whites, and of all the black groups they exhibited the most direct adherence to certain white cultural standards. In their religious practices, their dress, their manners, and their prejudices they were undoubtedly the black group most influenced by Euro-American culture. But this kind of cultural accommodation was by no means the same thing as docility or Uncle Tomism. Even a relatively assimilated house slave could and normally did strike back, assert independence, and resist arbitrariness and oppression. We are today accustomed to thinking of black nationalists as "militants" and civil rights integrationists as "moderates," "conservatives," or something worse. Yet, Dr. Martin Luther King, Jr., and his followers were and are militant integrationists, prepared to give up their lives for their people; on the other hand, there are plenty of black nationalists who are anything but militant. The tension between integration and separatism has always rent the black community, but now it has led us to confuse questions of militancy with those of nationalism. In fact, the combinations vary; there is no straight identification of either integrationists or separatists with either militancy or accommodation. Field hands or house slaves could be either docile, "accommodating," or rebellious, and in all probability most were all at once.

If today the house slaves have a bad press, it is largely because of their cultural assimilationism, from which it is erroneously deduced that they were docile. The first point may be valid; the second is not. LeRoi Jones, for example, in his brilliant book, *Blues People*, argues convincingly that field slaves had forged the rudiments of a distinct Afro-American culture whereas the house slaves largely took over the culture of the whites. He writes primarily about black music, but he might easily extend his analysis to language and other fields. There are clearly two ways of looking at this side of the house-slave experience. On the one hand, the house slaves reinforced white culture in the slave quarters; they were one of the Americanizing elements in the black community. On the other hand, they wittingly or unwittingly served as agents of white repression of an indigenous Afro-

American national culture. Of course, both these statements are really the same; it is merely that they differ in their implicit value judgments. But we ought to remember that this role did not reduce the house slave to Uncle Tomism. Rather, it was played out by house slaves who were in their own way often quite rebellious and independent in their behavior. And therefore, even these slaves, notwithstanding their assimilationist outlook and action, also contributed in no small degree to the tradition of survival and resistance to oppression that today inspires the black liberation movement.

If today we are inclined to accept uncritically the contemptuous attitude that some critics have toward the house slave, we might ponder the reflections of the great black pianist, Cecil Taylor. Taylor was speaking in the mid-1960's—a century after slavery—but he was speaking of his own father in a way that I think applies to what might be said of house slaves. Taylor was talking to A. B. Spellman, as reported in Spellman's book, *Four Lives in the Bebop Business:*

> Music to me was in a way holding on to Negro culture, because there wasn't much of it around. My father has a great store of knowledge about black folklore. He could talk about how it was with the slaves in the 1860s, about the field shouts and hollers, about myths of black people . . . . He worked out in Long Island for a State Senator. He was a house servant and a chef at the Senator's sanatorium for wealthy mental wrecks. And actually it was my father more than the Senator himself who raised the Senator's children . . . .
>
> And I really used to get dragged at my father for taking such shit off these people. I didn't dig his being a house servant. I really didn't understand my old man; well, you're my generation and you know the difference between us and our fathers. Like, they had to be strong men to take what they took. But of course we didn't see it that way. So that I feel now that I really didn't understand my father, who was a really lovely cat. He used to tell me to stay cool, not to get excited. He had a way of letting other people display their emotions while keeping control of his own. People used to say to me, 'Cecil, you'll never be the gentleman you father was.' That's true. My father was quite a gentleman . . . . I wish that I had taken down more about all that he knew about black folklore, because that's lost too; he died in 1961.[5]

We may end with another misunderstood group of slaves—the drivers. These black slave foremen were chosen by the master to work under his direction or that of an overseer and to keep the hands moving. They would rouse the field slaves in the morning and check their cabins at night; would take responsibility for their performance; and often, would be the ones to lay the whip across their backs. In the literature the drivers appear as ogres, monsters, betrayers, and sadists. Sometimes they were. Yet, Mrs. Willie Lee Rose, in her book, *Rehearsal for Reconstruction*, notes that it was the drivers in the Sea Islands who kept the plantations together after the masters had fled the approach of the Yankees, who kept up discipline, and who led the blacks during those difficult days. Now, it is obvious that if the drivers were what they have been reported as having been, they would have had their throats cut as soon as their white protectors had left. In my own research for the war years I have found repeatedly, almost monotonously, that when

[5] A. B. Spellman, *Four Lives in the Bebop Business* (New York, 1966), pp. 49-50.

the slaves fled the plantations or else took over plantations deserted by the whites, the drivers emerged as the leaders. Moreover, the runaway records from the North and from Canada reveal that a number of drivers were among those who successfully escaped the South.

One clue to the actual state of affairs may be found in the agricultural journals for which many planters and overseers wrote about plantation matters. Overseers often complained bitterly that masters trusted their drivers more than they trusted them. They charged that quite often overseers would be fired at the driver's instigation and that, in general, masters were too close to their drivers and too hostile and suspicious toward their white overseers. The planters did not deny the charges; rather, they admitted them and defended themselves by arguing that the drivers were slaves who had earned their trust and that they had to have some kind of check on their overseers. Overseers were changed every two or three years on most plantations whereas drivers remained in their jobs endlessly. The normal state of affairs was for any given driver to remain in his position while a parade of overseers came and went.

It had to be so. The slaves had to be controlled if production was to be on schedule, but only romantics could think that a whip alone could effect that result. The actual amount of work done and the quality of life on the plantation was the result of a compromise between masters and slaves. It was a grossly unfair and one-sided compromise, with the master holding a big edge, but the slaves did not simply lie down and take whatever came. They had their own ways of foot-dragging, dissembling, delaying, and sabotaging. The role of the driver was to minimize the friction by mediating between the Big House and the quarters. On the one hand he was the master's man: he obeyed orders, inflicted punishments, and stood for authority and discipline. On the other hand, he could and did tell the master that the overseer was too harsh, too irregular; that he was incapable of holding the respect of the hands; that he was a bungler. The slaves generally knew just how much they had to put up with under a barbarous labor system but they also knew what even that system regarded as going too far. The driver was their voice in the Big House as well as the master's voice in the quarters.

Former slaves tell us of drivers who were sadistic monsters, but they also tell us of drivers who did everything possible to soften punishments and to protect the slaves as best they could. It was an impossible situation, but there is little evidence that drivers were generally hated by the field hands. The selection of a driver was a difficult matter for a master. First, the driver had to be a strong man, capable of bullying rather than being bullied. Second, he had to be uncommonly intelligent and capable of understanding a good deal about plantation management. A driver had to command respect in the quarters. It would be possible to get along for a while with a brutal driver who could rule by fear, but generally, planters understood that respect and acquiescence were as important as fear, and that a driver had to do more than make others afraid of him. It was then necessary to pick a man who had leadership qualities in the eyes of the slaves.

The drivers commanded respect in various ways. Sometimes they became preachers among the slaves and got added prestige that way. Sometimes, possibly quite often, they acted as judge and jury in the quarters.

Disputes among slaves arose often, generally about women and family matters. If there were fights or bitter quarrels, and if they were called to the attention of the overseer or the master, the end would be a whipping for one or more participants. Under such circumstances, the driver was the natural choice of the slaves themselves to arbitrate knotty problems. With such roles in and out of the quarters, it is no wonder that so many drivers remained leaders during and after the war when the blacks had the choice of discarding them and following others.

Every plantation had two kinds of so-called "bad niggers." The first kind were those so designated by the masters because they were recalcitrant. The second kind were those so designated by the slaves themselves. These were slaves who may or may not have troubled the master directly but who were a problem to their fellow slaves because they stole, or bullied, or abused other men's women. The drivers were in a position to know what was happening in the quarters and to intervene to protect weaker or more timid slaves against these bullies. In short, the drivers' position was highly ambiguous and on balance was probably more often than not positive from the slave point of view. Whatever the intentions of the master, even in the selection of his own foremen—his own men, as it were—the slaves generally were not passive, not objects, but active agents who helped shape events, even if within narrow limits and with great difficulty.

We know that there were not many slave revolts in the South, and that those that did occur were small and local affairs. There were good reasons for the low incidence of rebellion: In general, the balance of forces was such that revolt was suicide. Under such conditions, black slaves struggled to live and to make some kind of life for themselves. If their actions were less bombastic and heroic than romantic historians would like us to believe, they were nonetheless impressive in their assertion of resourcefulness, dignity, and a strong sense of self and community. Had they not been, the fate of black America after emancipation would have been even grimmer than it was. For the most part the best that the slaves could do was live, not merely physically but with as much inner autonomy as was humanly possible.

Every man has his own judgment of heroism, but we might reflect on the kind of heroism alluded to by Cecil Taylor in his moving tribute to his father. There are moments in the history of every people—and sometimes these historical moments are centuries—in which they cannot do more than succeed in keeping themselves together and maintaining themselves as human beings with a sense of individual dignity and collective identity. Slavery was such a moment for black people in America, and their performance during it bequeathed a legacy that combined many negative elements to be exorcized[6] and repudiated with decisive elements of community self-discipline.

[6] I have discussed some of these negative features in "The Legacy of Slavery and the Roots of Black Nationalism," *Studies on the Left*, 6 (Nov.–Dec., 1966), 3–26. I stand by much of what I wrote there, but the essay is doubtless greatly weakened by a failure to appreciate black slave culture and its political implications. As a result, the political story I tried to tell is dangerously distorted. Still, that legacy of slavishness remains an important part of the story, and I think I identified some of its features correctly. I am indebted to many colleagues and friends for their criticism, without which I could not have arrived at the reconsiderations on which the present essay is based; in particular, the criticism of George Rawick has been indispensable.

If one were to tax even the privileged house slaves or drivers with the question, "Where were you when your people were groaning under the lash," they could, if they chose, answer with a paraphrase of the Abbé Sieyès, but proudly and without his cynicism, "We were with our people, and together we survived."

Suggested Reading

The starting point for the student of American slavery is the scholarship of Ulrich B. Phillips, especially *American Negro Slavery** (1918) and *Life and Labor in the Old South** (1928). The most thorough reexamination and refutation of Phillips is to be found in Kenneth Stampp's *The Peculiar Institution** (1956), though Herbert Aptheker's *American Negro Slave Revolts** (1943) helped to undermine Phillip's assumption that slaves were happy. More recently, Gerald W. Mullin has examined the evidence on docility in *Flight and Rebellion: Slave Resistance in Eighteenth Century Virginia* (1972).

Those who wish to begin at the beginning with specialized studies should consult Daniel P. Mannix and Malcolm Cowley's *Black Cargoes: A History of the Atlantic Slave Trade, 1518–1865* (1962) and *The African Slave Trade** (1961, originally published as *Black Mother*), by Basil Davidson. A careful quantitative analysis with revisionist implications is Philip D. Curtin's *The Atlantic Slave Trade: A Census* (1969). Two monumental and exciting pieces of scholarship deal with the question of white racial attitudes in the colonial era: David B. Davis's *The Problem of Slavery in Western Culture* (1966) and Winthrop Jordan's *White Over Black** (1968). George M. Frederickson has analyzed a similar set of questions in *The Black Image in the White Mind: The Debate on Afro-American Character and Destiny, 1817–1914** (1971). Attitudes toward slavery of the revolutionary generation are the subjects of Robert McColley's study, *Slavery in Jeffersonian Virginia* (1964).

A number of studies with specialized foci have added perspective to our understanding of the institution of slavery. Richard C. Wade in *Slavery in the Cities** (1964) has examined an important but numerically small part of the slavery experience as has Robert Starobin in his book *Industrial Slavery in the Old South** (1970). Valuable comprehensive surveys include John Hope Franklin's *From Slavery to Freedom: A History of Negro Americans*, 3rd ed. (1967), and Clement Eaton's *The Growth of Southern Civilization, 1790–1860** (1961). Probably the best collection of articles and essays is that by Allen Weinstein and Frank Otto Gatell, eds., *American Negro Slavery** (1968).

In addition to these books, the reader might wish to refer to works that place a sharper focus on slavery as experienced by Afro-Americans themselves. The best general introduction to Afro-American history is the highly interpretive survey by August Meier and Elliot Ruduick, *From Plantation to Ghetto** (1966). A useful selection of articles that place needed emphasis on the black perspective has been compiled by Robert V. Haynes, ed., *Blacks in White America Before 1865** (1972). The most comprehensive collection of documents is Leslie Fishel and Benjamin Quarles' *The Black American: A Documentary History** (1967). Charles H. Nichols has imaginatively reconstructed the slavery experience from the bottom up in *Many Thousand Gone: The Ex-Slaves' Account of Their Bondage and Freedom* (1963), and Gilbert Osofsky's *Puttin' On Ole Massa* (1969) is in the same vein.

Comparative approaches have recently been particularly fruitful for historians of slavery. The pathbreaker was Frank Tannenbaum, in *Slave and Citizen: The Negro in the Americas** (1946). The field exploded following the publication of *Slavery: A Problem in American Institutional and Intellectual Life** (1959, 2nd ed., 1968), ed. by Stanley M. Elkins. Many of the results of that explosion can be traced in the essays in Ann J. Lane, ed., *The Debate Over Slavery: Stanley Elkins and His Critics** (1971). Some of the best works on comparative slavery are found in Laura Foner and Eugene D. Genovese, eds., *Slavery in the New World: A Reader in Comparative History** (1969). An especially provocative comparative attack on the problem of the origins of the different systems of postslavery racial attitudes found in the United States and Brazil is Carl Degler's *Neither White Nor Black** (1971).

* Also published in paperback edition.

A Nation Divided

The Slave South:
An Interpretation

Eugene Genovese

W. J. Cash begins his popular interpretation *The Mind of the South* by observing, "There exists among us by ordinary—both North and South—a profound conviction that the South is another land, sharply differentiated from the rest of the American nation, and exhibiting within itself a remarkable homogeneity." Observers still generally believe that the South is an exception to most of the generalizations that can be made about American history and national character, but there is considerable disagreement about how the old South is best described and best understood. It used to be the fashion to write about the South as if it were governed by an oligarchy of slave owners with all the accoutrements and pretensions of an aristocracy, a practice that was cheered by adherents of the Lost Cause and worshipers of the cult of the Cavalier. After a long era of debunking in the twentieth century, of which Cash's book was a part, our image of the Cavalier South has been fragmented.

Frank L. Owsley and historians who follow his lead emphasize the fact that the typical Southerner before the Civil War was not a planter but a yeoman farmer. Only one white family out of four owned

457

slaves and less than 5 percent of the southern white population could be classified as planters. The Owsley school considered the old South the land of the plain folk. A variant of this point of view has been offered by David Potter, who suggests that the South was a folk culture. According to Potter, in folk society, the land-to-man relationship was more direct and primal and the man-to-man relationship was more personal than in self-conscious modern society. Whereas Owsley emphasizes the frontier experience and democratic leanings which produced the sort of unruly "hell of a fellow" Southerner described by W. J. Cash and David Donald, Potter tries to take into account the embarrassingly dominant position of planters in social, economic, and political life by using as a defining characteristic the common values and codes of behavior that were shared throughout the social structure.

Today, however, the dominant view of the old South among historians would probably go under the rubric of "planter capitalism," a view in which slave owners are pictured as hard working capitalists who differed from capitalists in the North only in that they were turning out an agricultural product rather than a manufactured one. According to this line of argument the capitalistic nature of the system was revealed in the fact that it produced a staple crop for a distant market, responded to supply and demand, vested capital in land and slaves, and operated with funds borrowed from banks and factors.

Recently, the pendulum has swung back with the work of a Marxist scholar, Eugene Genovese of the University of Rochester, who is currently developing a large scale reinterpretation of antebellum southern history. Genovese maintains that we must see slavery not only as a moral problem, or as simply another way in which capitalists can squeeze surplus value out of labor, but as an institution that made possible a social system very different from the one that existed in the North at the same time. It was a society dominated by a class of precapitalistic planters.

In support of his point of view, Genovese indicates several sources of economic irrationality in the southern economic system and concludes that therefore slavery could not have been a capitalistic institution. But the main thrust of Genovese's critique is that slavery made possible an aristocracy, and though this aristocracy was tied to the capitalistic world by bonds of commodity production and marketing, it behaved as an aristocracy rather than as a capitalistic bourgeoisie. Because of the planters' tendency toward conspicuous consumption and their pattern of reinvestment in land and slaves which militated against industrialization, because slave labor was inefficient, and because southern agrarianism prevented the growth of a home market, industrialism was retarded and the South found itself in political and economic conflict with the more advanced North.

The South quickly discovered that its economic system was in danger of collapsing. The conflict between North and South became centered on competition for western land when it became obvious that fresh lands were needed in order for slavery to survive. Staple crop agriculture had depleted the lands on the eastern seaboard, and they could be reclaimed only through extensive and expensive agricultural reform. Agricultural reform—that is, more careful cultivation—required financing, and this was possible only by the sale of surplus slaves to the lower South and the West. Consequently, western lands were needed for the survival of the social system. It might have been more rational to let the system of slavery die a natural death, but that course was not taken because the slave-owning class was in control of southern society and made every effort to perpetuate itself. Note that Genovese portrays the planters as acting not from economic self-interest, but from class interests, and these are very different. Note also that Genovese's scheme of southern society and history requires that the planter aristocracy be seen as unified and generally conscious of its class interests.

It is in emphasizing the class motives of the southern planters that Genovese has made his most solid contribution. There is abundant evidence that the South, despite its democratic institutions, was dominated by its economic elite, the planters, even though there were also serious divisions within the elite, and planters divided over political parties and candidates. One must wonder, however, if it helps to understand the behavior of the planters to think of them as premodern, or as "the closest things to feudal lords imaginable in a nineteenth-century

bourgeois republic." In the essay that follows,
Genovese's criteria for modernization are difficult to
determine and may not be adequate. The
irrationalities of the slave system to which
Genovese refers may not be so irrational. What would
happen to Genovese's rationale if one viewed the slave
as a capital investment rather than as a laborer?
There may be a flaw in the logic of Genovese's
argument that the southern economy was inefficient
because the South was developing more slowly than
the North, and it is possible that the South as a region
was using its resources to its best comparative
advantage. Some economic historians argue that this
indeed was the case. There is currently a great debate
raging about the facts of the matter. Recently
collected data indicate that per capita income in the
South was not much lower than per capita income in
the North in 1860 and that in the previous few decades
it had been rising, even if the gap between North and
South was growing larger. If plantations were so
inefficient, one would have difficulty in explaining
why they were absorbing more and more of the land
in the South to the detriment of small land holdings.

The Problem

The uniqueness of the antebellum South continues to challenge the imagination of Americans, who, despite persistent attempts, cannot divert their
attention from slavery. Nor should they, for slavery provided the foundation on which the South rose and grew. The master-slave relationship permeated Southern life and influenced relationships among free men. A full
history would have to treat the impact of the Negro slave and of slaveless
as well as slaveholding whites, but a first approximation, necessarily concerned with essentials, must focus on the slaveholders, who most directly
exercised power over men and events. The hegemony of the slaveholders,
presupposing the social and economic preponderance of great slave plantations, determined the character of the South. These men rose to power in a
region embedded in a capitalist country, and their social system emerged as
part of a capitalist world. Yet, a nonslaveholding European past and a
shared experience in a new republic notwithstanding, they imparted to
Southern life a special social, economic, political, ideological, and psychological content.

To dissolve that special content into an ill-defined agrarianism or an elusive planter capitalism would mean to sacrifice concern with the essential for
concern with the transitional and peripheral. Neither of the two leading
interpretations, which for many years have contended in a hazy and unreal
battle, offers consistent and plausible answers to recurring questions, espe-

cially those bearing on the origins of the War for Southern Independence. The first of these interpretations considers the antebellum South an agrarian society fighting against the encroachments of industrial capitalism; the second considers the slave plantation merely a form of capitalist enterprise and suggests that the material differences between Northern and Southern capitalism were more apparent than real. These two views, which one would think contradictory, sometimes combine in the thesis that the agrarian nature of planter capitalism, for some reason, made coexistence with industrial capitalism difficult.[1]

The first view cannot explain why some agrarian societies give rise to industrialization and some do not. A prosperous agricultural hinterland has generally served as a basis for industrial development by providing a home market for manufactures and a source of capital accumulation, and the prosperity of farmers has largely depended on the growth of industrial centers as markets for foodstuffs. In a capitalist society agriculture is one industry, or one set of industries, among many, and its conflict with manufacturing is one of many competitive rivalries. There must have been something unusual about an agriculture that generated violent opposition to the agrarian West as well as the industrial Northeast.

The second view, which is the more widely held, emphasizes that the plantation system produced for a distant market, responded to supply and demand, invested capital in land and slaves, and operated with funds borrowed from banks and factors. This, the more sophisticated of the two interpretations, cannot begin to explain the origins of the conflict with the North and does violence to elementary facts of antebellum Southern history.

Slavery and the Expansion of Capitalism

The proponents of the idea of planter capitalism draw heavily, willingly or not, on Lewis C. Gray's theory of the genesis of the plantation system. Gray defines the plantation as a "capitalistic type of agricultural organization in which a considerable number of unfree laborers were employed under a unified direction and control in the production of a staple crop."[2] Gray considers the plantation system inseparably linked with the international development of capitalism. He notes the plantation's need for large outlays of capital, its strong tendency toward specialization in a single crop, and its commercialism and argues that these appeared with the industrial revolution.

In modern times the plantation often rose under bourgeois auspices to provide industry with cheap raw materials, but the consequences were not always harmonious with bourgeois society. Colonial expansion produced three sometimes overlapping patterns: (1) the capitalists of the advanced country simply invested in colonial land—as illustrated even today by the

---

[1] For a succinct statement of the first view see Frank L. Owsley, "The Irrepressible Conflict," in Twelve Southerners, *I'll Take My Stand* (New York, 1930), p. 74. One of the clearest statements of the second view is that of Thomas P. Govan, "Was the Old South Different?" *JSH*, XXI (Nov. 1955), 448.

[2] *History of Agriculture in the Southern United States to 1860* (2 vols.; Gloucester, Mass., 1958), I, 302.

practice of the United Fruit Company in the Caribbean; (2) the colonial planters were largely subservient to the advanced countries—as illustrated by the British West Indies before the abolition of slavery; and (3) the planters were able to win independence and build a society under their own direction—as illustrated by the Southern United States.

In alliance with the North, the planter-dominated South broke away from England, and political conditions in the new republic allowed it considerable freedom for self-development. The plantation society that had begun as an appendage of British capitalism ended as a powerful, largely autonomous civilization with aristocratic pretensions and possibilities, although it remained tied to the capitalist world by bonds of commodity production. The essential element in this distinct civilization was the slaveholders' domination, made possible by their command of labor. Slavery provided the basis for a special Southern economic and social life, special problems and tensions, and special laws of development.

The Rationality and Irrationality of Slave Society

Slave economies normally manifest irrational tendencies that inhibit economic development and endanger social stability. Max Weber, among the many scholars who have discussed the problem, has noted four important irrational features.[3] First, the master cannot adjust the size of his labor force in accordance with business fluctuations. In particular, efficiency cannot readily be attained through the manipulation of the labor force if sentiment, custom, or community pressure makes separation of families difficult. Second, the capital outlay is much greater and riskier for slave labor than for free.[4] Third, the domination of society by a planter class increases the risk of political influence in the market. Fourth, the sources of cheap labor usually dry up rather quickly, and beyond a certain point costs become excessively burdensome. Weber's remarks could be extended. Planters, for example, have little opportunity to select specifically trained workers for special tasks as they arise.

There are other telling features of this irrationality. Under capitalism the pressure of the competitive struggle and the bourgeois spirit of accumulation direct the greater part of profits back into production. The competitive side of Southern slavery produced a similar result, but one that was modified by the pronounced tendency to heavy consumption. Economic historians and sociologists have long noted the high propensity to consume among landed aristocracies. No doubt this difference has been one of degree. The greater

---

[3] *The Theory of Social and Economic Organization* (New York, 1947), pp. 276 ff. The term "rational" is used in its strictly economic sense to indicate that production is proceeding in accordance with the most advanced methods to maximize profits.

[4] This simple observation has come under curious attack. Kenneth M. Stampp insists that the cost of purchasing a slave forms the equivalent of the free worker's wage bill. See *The Peculiar Institution* (New York, 1956), pp. 403 ff. The initial outlay is the equivalent of part of the capitalist's investment in fixed capital and constitutes what Ulrich B. Phillips called the "overcapitalization of labor" under slavery. The cost of maintaining a slave is only a small part of the free worker's wage bill, but the difference in their productivity is probably greater than the difference in their cost under most conditions.

part of slavery's profits also find their way back into production, but the method of reinvestment in the two systems is substantially different. Capitalism largely directs its profits into an expansion of plant and equipment, not labor; that is, economic progress is qualitative. Slavery, for economic reasons as well as for those of social prestige, directs its reinvestments along the same lines as the original investment—in slaves and land; that is, economic progress is quantitative.

In the South this weakness proved fatal for the slaveholders. They found themselves engaged in a growing conflict with Northern farmers and businessmen over such issues as tariffs, homesteads, internal improvements, and the decisive question of the balance of political power in the Union. The slow pace of their economic progress, in contrast to the long strides of their rivals to the north, threatened to undermine their political parity and result in a Southern defeat on all major issues of the day. The qualitative leaps in the Northern economy manifested themselves in a rapidly increasing population, an expanding productive plant, and growing political, ideological, and social boldness. The slaveholders' voice grew shriller and harsher as they contemplated impending disaster and sought solace in complaints of Northern aggression and exploitation.

Just as Southern slavery directed reinvestment along a path that led to economic stagnation, so too did it limit the volume of capital accumulated for investment of any kind. We need not reopen the tedious argument about the chronology of the plantation, the one-crop system, and slavery. While slavery existed, the South had to be bound to a plantation system and an agricultural economy based on a few crops. As a result, the South depended on Northern facilities, with inevitably mounting middlemen's charges. Less obvious was the capital drain occasioned by the importation of industrial goods. While the home market remained backward, Southern manufacturers had difficulty producing in sufficient quantities to keep costs and prices at levels competitive with Northerners. The attendant dependence on Northern and British imports intensified the outward flow of badly needed funds.

Most of the elements of irrationality were irrational only from a capitalist standpoint. The high propensity to consume luxuries, for example, has always been functional (socially if not economically rational) in aristocratic societies, for it has provided the ruling class with the façade necessary to control the middle and lower classes. Thomas R. Dew knew what he was doing when he defended the high personal expenditures of Southerners as proof of the superiority of the slave system.[5] Few Southerners, even few slaveholders, could afford to spend lavishly and effect an aristocratic standard of living, but those few set the social tone for society. One wealthy planter with a great house and a reputation for living and entertaining on a grand scale could impress a whole community and keep before its humbler men the shining ideal of plantation magnificence. Consider Pascal's observation that the habit of seeing the king accompanied by guards, pomp, and all the paraphernalia designed to command respect and inspire awe will produce those reactions even when he appears alone and informally. In the popular

[5] *The Pro-Slavery Argument* (Charleston, S.C., 1852), p. 488.

mind he is assumed to be naturally an awe-inspiring being.[6] In this manner, every dollar spent by the planters for elegant clothes, a college education for their children, or a lavish barbecue contributed to the political and social domination of their class. We may speak of the slave system's irrationality only in a strictly economic sense and then only to indicate the inability of the South to compete with Northern capitalism on the latter's grounds. The slaveholders, fighting for political power in an essentially capitalist Union, had to do just that.

Capitalist and Pseudo-Capitalist Features of the Slave Economy

The slave economy developed within, and was in a sense exploited by, the capitalist world market; consequently, slavery developed many ostensibly capitalist features, such as banking, commerce, and credit. These played a fundamentally different role in the South than in the North. Capitalism has absorbed and even encouraged many kinds of precapitalist social systems: serfdom, slavery, Oriental state enterprises, and others. It has introduced credit, finance, banking, and similar institutions where they did not previously exist. It is pointless to suggest that therefore nineteenth-century India and twentieth-century Saudi Arabia should be classified as capitalist countries. We need to analyze a few of the more important capitalist and pseudo-capitalist features of Southern slavery and especially to review the barriers to industrialization in order to appreciate the peculiar qualities of this remarkable and anachronistic society.[7]

The defenders of the "planter-capitalism" thesis have noted the extensive commercial links between the plantation and the world market and the modest commercial bourgeoisie in the South and have concluded that there is no reason to predicate an antagonism between cotton producers and cotton merchants. However valid as a reply to the naive arguments of the proponents of the agrarianism-versus-industrialism thesis, this criticism has unjustifiably been twisted to suggest that the presence of commercial activity proves the predominance of capitalism in the South.[8] Many precapitalist economic systems have had well-developed commercial relations, but if every commercial society is to be considered capitalist, the word loses all meaning. In general, commercial classes have supported the existing system of production. As Maurice Dobb observes,[9] their fortunes are bound up with those of the dominant producers, and merchants are more likely to seek an extension of their middlemen's profits than to try to reshape the economic order.

---

[6] Blaise Pascal, *Pensées* (Modern Library ed.; New York, 1941), p. 105.

[7] This colonial dependence on the British and Northern markets did not end when slavery ended. Sharecropping and tenantry produced similar results. Since abolition occurred under Northern guns and under the program of a victorious, predatory outside bourgeoisie, instead of under internal bourgeois auspices, the colonial bondage of the economy was preserved, but the South's political independence was lost.

[8] Govan, *JSH*, XXI (Nov. 1955), 448.

[9] *Studies in the Development of Capitalism* (New York, 1947), pp. 17 f. In the words of Gunnar Myrdal: "Trade by itself . . . rather tends to have backwash effects and to strengthen the forces maintaining stagnation or regression." *Rich Lands and Poor* (New York, 1957), p. 53.

We must concern ourselves primarily with capitalism as a social system, not merely with evidence of typically capitalistic economic practices. In the South extensive and complicated commercial relations with the world market permitted the growth of a small commercial bourgeoisie. The resultant fortunes flowed into slaveholding, which offered prestige and economic and social security in a planter-dominated society. Independent merchants found their businesses dependent on the patronage of the slaveholders. The merchants either became planters themselves or assumed a servile attitude toward the planters. The commercial bourgeoisie, such as it was, remained tied to the slaveholding interest, had little desire or opportunity to invest capital in industrial expansion, and adopted the prevailing aristocratic attitudes.

The Southern industrialists were in an analogous position, although one that was potentially subversive of the political power and ideological unity of the planters. The preponderance of planters and slaves on the countryside retarded the home market. The Southern yeomanry, unlike the Western, lacked the purchasing power to sustain rapid industrial development.[10] The planters spent much of their money abroad for luxuries. The plantation market consisted primarily of the demand for cheap slave clothing and cheap agricultural implements for use or misuse by the slaves. Southern industrialism needed a sweeping agrarian revolution to provide it with cheap labor and a substantial rural market, but the Southern industrialists depended on the existing, limited, plantation market. Leading industrialists like William Gregg and Daniel Pratt were plantation-oriented and proslavery. They could hardly have been other.

The banking system of the South serves as an excellent illustration of an ostensibly capitalist institution that worked to augment the power of the planters and retard the development of the bourgeoisie. Southern banks functioned much as did those which the British introduced into Latin America, India, and Egypt during the nineteenth century. Although the British banks fostered dependence on British capital, they did not directly and willingly generate internal capitalist development. They were not sources of industrial capital but "large-scale clearing houses of mercantile finance vying in their interest charges with the local usurers."[11]

The difference between the banking practices of the South and those of the West reflects the difference between slavery and agrarian capitalism. In the West, as in the Northeast, banks and credit facilities promoted a vigorous economic expansion. During the period of loose Western banking (1830–1844) credit flowed liberally into industrial development as well as into land purchases and internal improvements. Manufacturers and merchants dominated the boards of directors of Western banks, and landowners played a minor role. Undoubtedly, many urban businessmen speculated in land and had special interests in underwriting agricultural exports, but they

---

[10] An attempt was made by Frank L. Owsley and his students to prove that the Southern yeomanry was strong and prosperous. For a summary treatment see *Plain Folk of the Old South* (Baton Rouge, La., 1949). This view was convincingly refuted by Fabian Linden, "Economic Democracy in the Slave South: An Appraisal of Some Recent Views," *JNH*, XXXI (April 1946), 140–89.

[11] Paul A. Baran, *The Political Economy of Growth* (New York, 1957), p. 194.

gave attention to building up agricultural processing industries and urban enterprises, which guaranteed the region a many-sided economy.[12]

The slave states paid considerable attention to the development of a conservative, stable banking system, which could guarantee the movement of staple crops and the extension of credit to the planters. Southern banks were primarily designed to lend the planters money for outlays that were economically feasible and socially acceptable in a slave society: the movement of crops, the purchase of land and slaves, and little else.

Whenever Southerners pursued easy-credit policies, the damage done outweighed the advantages of increased production. This imbalance probably did not occur in the West, for easy credit made possible agricultural and industrial expansion of a diverse nature and, despite acute crises, established a firm basis for long-range prosperity. Easy credit in the South led to expansion of cotton production with concomitant over-production and low prices; simultaneously, it increased the price of slaves.

Planters wanted their banks only to facilitate cotton shipments and maintain sound money. They purchased large quantities of foodstuffs from the West and, since they shipped little in return, had to pay in bank notes. For five years following the bank failures of 1837 the bank notes of New Orleans moved at a discount of from 10 to 25 per cent. This disaster could not be allowed to recur. Sound money and sound banking became the cries of the slaveholders as a class.

Southern banking tied the planters to the banks, but more important, tied the bankers to the plantations. The banks often found it necessary to add prominent planters to their boards of directors and were closely supervised by the planter-dominated state legislatures. In this relationship the bankers could not emerge as a middle-class counterweight to the planters but could merely serve as their auxiliaries.

The bankers of the free states also allied themselves closely with the dominant producers, but society and economy took on a bourgeois quality provided by the rising industrialists, the urban middle classes, and the farmers who increasingly depended on urban markets. The expansion of credit, which in the West financed manufacturing, mining, transportation, agricultural diversification, and the numerous branches of a capitalist economy, in the South bolstered the economic position of the planters, inhibited the rise of alternative industries, and guaranteed the extension and consolidation of the plantation system.

If for a moment we accept the designation of the planters as capitalists and the slave system as a form of capitalism, we are then confronted by a captialist society that impeded the development of every normal feature of capitalism. The planters were not mere capitalists; they were precapitalist, quasi-aristocratic landowners who had to adjust their economy and ways of thinking to a capitalist world market. Their society, in its spirit and fundamental direction, represented the antithesis of capitalism, however many compromises it had to make. The fact of slave ownership is central to our

---

[12] The best introduction to this period of Western banking is the unpublished doctoral dissertation of Carter H. Golembe, "State Banks and the Economic Development of the West, 1830–1844," Columbia University, 1952, esp. pp. 10, 82–91. *Cf.* Bray Hammond, "Long and Short Term Credit in Early American Banking," *QJE*, XLIX (Nov. 1934), esp. p. 87.

problem. This seemingly formal question of whether the owners of the means of production command labor or purchase the labor power of free workers contains in itself the content of Southern life. The essential features of Southern particularity, as well as of Southern backwardness, can be traced to the relationship of master to slave.

The Barriers to Industrialization

If the planters were losing their economic and political cold war with Northern capitalism, the failure of the South to develop sufficient industry provided the most striking immediate cause. Its inability to develop adequate manufactures is usually attributed to the inefficiency of its labor force. No doubt slaves did not easily adjust to industrial employment, and the indirect effects of the slave system impeded the employment of whites.[13] Slaves did work effectively in hemp, tobacco, iron, and cotton factories but only under socially dangerous conditions. They received a wide variety of privileges and approached an elite status. Planters generally appreciated the potentially subversive quality of these arrangements and looked askance at their extension.

Slavery led to the rapid concentration of land and wealth and prevented slaveholding class hostile to industrialism. The slaveholders feared a strong urban bourgeoisie, which might make common cause with its Northern counterpart. They feared a white urban working class of unpredictable social tendencies. In general, they distrusted the city and saw in it something incongruous with their local power and status arrangements.[14] The small slaveholders, as well as the planters, resisted the assumption of a heavy tax burden to assist manufacturers, and as the South fell further behind the North in industrial development more state aid was required to help industry offset the Northern advantages of scale, efficiency, credit relations, and business reputation.

Slavery led to the rapid concentration of land and wealth and prevented the expansion of a Southern home market. Instead of providing a basis for industrial growth, the Southern countryside, economically dominated by a few large estates, provided only a limited market for industry. Data on the cotton textile factories almost always reveal that Southern producers aimed at supplying slaves with the cheapest and coarsest kind of cotton goods. Even so, local industry had to compete with Northern firms, which sometimes shipped direct and sometimes established Southern branches.

William Gregg, the South's foremost industrialist, understood the modest proportions of the Southern market and warned manufacturers against trying to produce exclusively for their local areas. His own company at Graniteville, South Carolina, produced fine cotton goods that sold much better

[13] Slavery impeded white immigration by presenting Europeans with an aristocratic, caste-ridden society that scarcely disguised its contempt for the working classes. The economic opportunities in the North were, in most respects, far greater. When white labor was used in Southern factories, it was not always superior to slave labor. The incentives offered by the Northern economic and social system were largely missing; opportunities for acquiring skills were fewer; in general, productivity was much lower than in the North.

[14] Richard C. Wade's recent *Slavery in the Cities* (New York, 1964) provides new support for these conclusions.

in the North than in the South. Gregg was an unusually able man, and his success in selling to the North was a personal triumph. When he had to evaluate the general position of Southern manufacturers, he asserted that he was willing to stake his reputation on their ability to compete with Northerners in the production of *"coarse cotton fabrics."*[15]

Some Southern businessmen, especially those in the border states, did good business in the North. Louisville tobacco and hemp manufacturers sold much of their output in Ohio. Some producers of iron and agricultural implements sold in nearby Northern cities. This kind of market was precarious. As Northern competitors rose and the market shrank, Southern producers had to rely on the narrow and undependable Southern market.[16] Well before 1840 iron-manufacturing establishments in the Northwest provided local farmers with excellent markets for grain, vegetables, molasses, and work animals. During the antebellum period and after, the grain growers of America found their market at home. America's rapid industrial development offered farmers a magnificently expanding urban market, and not until much later did they come to depend to any important extent on exports.

To a small degree the South benefited in this way. By 1840 the tobacco-manufacturing industry began to absorb more tobacco than was being exported, and the South's few industrial centers provided markets for local grain and vegetable growers. Since the South could not undertake a general industrialization, few urban centers rose to provide substantial markets for farmers and planters. Southern grain growers, except for those close to the cities of the free states, had to be content with the market offered by planters who preferred to specialize in cotton or sugar and buy foodstuffs. The restricted rations of the slaves limited this market, which inadequate transportation further narrowed. It did not pay the planters to appropriate state funds to build a transportation system into the back country, and any measure to increase the economic strength of the back-country farmers seemed politically dangerous to the aristocracy of the Black Belt. The farmers of the back country remained isolated, self-sufficient, and politically, economically, and socially backward. Those grain-growing farmers who could compete with producers in the Upper South and the Northwest for the plantation market lived within the Black Belt. Since the planters did not have to buy from these local producers, the economic relationship greatly strengthened the political hand of the planters.

The General Features of Southern Agriculture

The South's greatest economic weakness was the low productivity of its labor force. The slaves worked indifferently. They could be made to work

[15] William Gregg, *Essays on Domestic Industry* (first published in 1845; Graniteville, S.C., 1941), p. 4. Original emphasis.

[16] Consider the experience of the locomotive, paper, and cotton manufacturers as reported in: Carrol H. Quenzel, "The Manufacture of Locomotives and Cars in Alexandria in the 1850's," *VMHB*, LXII (April 1954), 182 ff; Ernest M. Lander, Jr., "Paper Manufacturing in South Carolina before the Civil War," *NCHR*, XXIX (April 1952), 225 ff; Adelaide L. Fries, "One Hundred Years of Textiles in Salem," *NCHR*, XXVII (Jan. 1950), 13.

reasonably well under close supervision in the cotton fields, but the cost of supervising them in more than one or two operations at a time was prohibitive. Slavery prevented the significant technological progress that could have raised productivity substantially. Of greatest relevance, the impediments to technological progress damaged Southern agriculture, for improved implements and machines largely accounted for the big increases in crop yields per acre in the Northern states during the nineteenth century.

Slavery and the plantation system led to agricultural methods that depleted the soil. The frontier methods of the free states yielded similar results, but slavery forced the South into continued dependence upon exploitative methods after the frontier had passed further west. It prevented reclamation of worn-out lands. The plantations were much too large to fertilize easily. Lack of markets and poor care of animals by slaves made it impossible to accumulate sufficient manure. The low level of capital accumulation made the purchase of adequate quantities of commercial fertilizer unthinkable. Planters could not practice proper crop rotation, for the pressure of the credit system kept most available land in cotton, and the labor force could not easily be assigned to the required tasks without excessive costs of supervision. The general inefficiency of labor thwarted most attempts at improvement of agricultural methods.

The South, unable to feed itself, faced a series of dilemmas in its attempts to increase production of nonstaple crops and to improve its livestock. An inefficient labor force and the backward business practices of the dominant planters hurt. When planters did succeed in raising their own food, they also succeeded in depriving local livestock raisers and grain growers of their only markets. The planters had little capital with which to buy improved breeds and could not guarantee the care necessary to make such investments worth while. Livestock raisers also lacked the capital, and without adequate urban markets they could not make good use of the capital they had.

Thoughtful Southerners, deeply distressed by the condition of their agriculture, made a determined effort to remedy it. In Maryland and Virginia significant progress occurred in crop diversification and livestock improvement, but this progress was contingent on the sale of surplus slaves to the Lower South. These sales provided the income that offset agricultural losses and made possible investment in fertilizers, equipment, and livestock. The concomitant reduction in the size of the slave force facilitated supervision and increased labor productivity and versatility. Even so, the income from slave sales remained an important part of the gross income of the planters of the Upper South. The reform remained incomplete and could not free agriculture from the destructive effects of the continued reliance on slave labor.

The reform process had several contradictions, the most important of which was the dependence on slave sales. Surplus slaves could be sold only while gang-labor methods continued to be used in other areas. By the 1850s the deficiencies of slavery that had forced innovations in the Upper South were making themselves felt in the Lower South. Increasingly, planters in the Lower South explored the possibilities of reform. If the deterioration of agriculture in the Cotton Belt had proceeded much further, the planters would have had to stop buying slaves from Maryland and Virginia and look for markets for their own surplus slaves. Without the acquisition of fresh lands there could be no general reform of Southern agriculture. The Southern economy was moving steadily into an insoluble crisis.

The Ideology of the Master Class

The planters commanded Southern politics and set the tone of social life. Theirs was an aristocratic, antibourgeois spirit with values and mores emphasizing family and status, a strong code of honor, and aspirations to luxury, ease, and accomplishment. In the planters' community, paternalism provided the standard of human relationships, and politics and statecraft were the duties and responsibilities of gentlemen. The gentleman lived for politics, not, like the bourgeois politician, off politics.

The planter typically recoiled at the notions that profit should be the goal of life; that the approach to production and exchange should be internally rational and uncomplicated by social values; that thrift and hard work should be the great virtues; and that the test of the wholesomeness of a community should be the vigor with which its citizens expand the economy. The planter was no less acquisitive than the bourgeois, but an acquisitive spirit is compatible with values antithetical to capitalism. The aristocratic spirit of the planters absorbed acquisitiveness and directed it into channels that were socially desirable to a slave society: the accumulation of slaves and land and the achievement of military and political honors. Whereas in the North people followed the lure of business and money for their own sake, in the South specific forms of property carried the badges of honor, prestige, and power. Even the rough parvenu planters of the Southwestern frontier—the "Southern Yankees"—strove to accumulate wealth in the modes acceptable to plantation society. Only in their crudeness and naked avarice did they differ from the Virginia gentlemen. They were a generation removed from the refinement that follows accumulation.

Slavery established the basis of the planter's position and power. It measured his affluence, marked his status, and supplied leisure for social graces and aristocratic duties. The older bourgeoisie of New England in its own way struck an aristocratic pose, but its wealth was rooted in commercial and industrial enterprises that were being pushed into the background by the newer heavy industries arising in the West, where upstarts took advantage of the more lucrative ventures like the iron industry. In the South few such opportunities were opening. The parvenu differed from the established planter only in being cruder and perhaps sharper in his business dealings. The road to power lay through the plantation. The older aristocracy kept its leadership or made room for men following the same road. An aristocratic stance was no mere compensation for a decline in power; it was the soul and content of a rising power.

Many travelers commented on the difference in material conditions from one side of the Ohio River to the other, but the difference in sentiment was seen most clearly by Tocqueville. Writing before the slavery issue had inflamed the nation, he remarked that slavery was attacking the Union "indirectly in its manners." The Ohioan "was tormented by wealth," and would turn to any kind of enterprise or endeavor to make a fortune. The Kentuckian coveted wealth "much less than pleasure or excitement," and money had "lost a portion of its value in his eyes."[17]

Achille Murat joined Tocqueville in admiration for Southern ways. Compared with Northerners, Southerners were frank, clever, charming, generous, and liberal.[18] They paid a price for these advantages. As one Southerner put it, the North led the South in almost everything because the Yankees had quiet perseverance over the long haul, whereas the Southerners had talent and brilliance but no taste for sustained labor. Southern projects came with a flash and died just as suddenly.[19] Despite such criticisms from within the ranks, the leaders of the South clung to their ideals, their faults, and their conviction of superiority. Farmers, said Edmund Ruffin, could not expect to achieve a cultural level above that of the "boors who reap rich harvests from the fat soil of Belgium." In the Northern states, he added with some justification, a farmer could rarely achieve the ease, culture, intellect, and refinement that slavery made possible.[20] The prevailing attitude of the aristocratic South toward itself and its Northern rival was ably summed up by William Henry Holcombe of Natchez: "The Northerner loves to make money, the Southerner to spend it."[21]

At their best, Southern ideals constituted a rejection of the crass, vulgar, inhumane elements of capitalist society. The slaveholders simply could not accept the idea that the cash nexus offered a permissible basis for human relations. Even the vulgar parvenu of the Southwest embraced the plantation myth and refused to make a virtue of necessity by glorifying the competitive side of slavery as civilization's highest achievement. The slaveholders generally, and the planters in particular, did identify their own ideals with the essence of civilization and, given their sense of honor, were prepared to defend them at any cost.

This civilization and its ideals were antinational in a double sense. The plantation offered virtually the only market for the small nonstaple-producing farmers and provided the center of necessary services for the small cotton growers. Thus, the paternalism of the planters toward their slaves was reinforced by the semipaternal relationship between the planters and their neighbors. The planters, in truth, grew into the closest thing to feudal lords imaginable in a nineteenth-century bourgeois republic. The planters' protestations of love for the Union were not so much a desire to use the Union to protect slavery as a strong commitment to localism as the highest form of liberty. They genuinely loved the Union so long as it alone among the great states of the world recognized that localism had a wide variety of rights. The Southerners' source of pride was not the Union, nor the nonexistent Southern nation; it was the plantation, which they raised to a political principle.

[17] Alexis de Tocqueville, *Democracy in America* (2 vols.; New York, 1945), I, 364.
[18] Achille Murat, *America and the Americans* (Buffalo, 1851), pp. 19, 75.
[19] J. W. D. in the *Southern Eclectic*, II (Sept. 1853), 63–66.
[20] *Address to the Virginia State Agricultural Society* (Richmond, Va., 1853), p. 9.
[21] Diary dated Aug. 25, 1855, but clearly written later. Ms. in the University of North Carolina.

The Inner Reality of Slaveholding

The Southern slaveholder had "extraordinary force." In the eyes of an admirer his independence was "not as at the North, the effect of a conflict with the too stern pressure of society, but the legitimate outgrowth of a sturdy love of liberty."[22] This independence, so distinctive in the slaveholders' psychology, divided them politically from agrarian Westerners as well as from urban Easterners. Commonly, both friendly and hostile contemporaries agreed that the Southerner appeared rash, unstable, often irrational, and that he turned away from bourgeois habits toward an aristocratic pose.

Americans, with a pronounced Jeffersonian bias, often attribute this spirit to agrarians of all types, although their judgment seems almost bizarre. A farmer may be called "independent" because he works for himself and owns property; like any grocer or tailor he functions as a petty bourgeois. In Jefferson's time, when agriculture had not yet been wholly subjected to the commanding influences of the market, the American farmer perhaps had a considerable amount of independence, if we choose to call self-sufficient isolation by that name, but in subsequent days he has had to depend on the market like any manufacturer, if not more so. Whereas manufacturers combine to protect their economic interests, such arrangements have proved much more difficult, and until recently almost impossible, to effect among farmers. In general, if we contrast farmers with urban capitalists, the latter emerge as relatively the more independent. The farmer yields constantly to the primacy of nature, to a direct, external force acting on him regardless of his personal worth; his independence is therefore rigorously circumscribed. The capitalist is limited by the force of the market, which operates indirectly and selectively. Many capitalists go under in a crisis, but some emerge stronger and surer of their own excellence. Those who survive the catastrophe do so (or so it seems) because of superior ability, strength, and management, not because of an Act of God.

The slaveholder, as distinct from the farmer, had a private source of character making and mythmaking—his slave. Most obviously, he had the habit of command, but there was more than despotic authority in this master-slave relationship. The slave stood interposed between his master and the object his master desired (that which was produced); thus, the master related to the object only mediately, through the slave. The slaveholder commanded the products of another's labor, but by the same process was forced into dependence upon this other.[23]

Thoughtful Southerners such as Ruffin, Fitzhugh, and Hammond understood this dependence and saw it as arising from the general relationship of labor to capital, rather than from the specific relationship of master to slave. They did not grasp that the capitalist's dependence upon his laborers remains obscured by the process of exchange in the capitalist market. Although all commodities are products of social relationships and contain human labor, they face each other in the market not as the embodiment of

---

[22] William M. Sanford (?), Southern Dial, I (Nov. 1857), 9.
[23] Cf. G. W. F. Hegel, The Phenomenology of Mind (2 vols.; London, 1910), I, 183 ff.

human qualities but as things with a seemingly independent existence. Similarly, the laborer sells his labor-power in the way in which the capitalist sells his goods—by bringing it to market, where it is subject to the fluctuations of supply and demand. A "commodity fetishism" clouds the social relationship of labor to capital, and the worker and capitalist appear as mere observers of a process over which they have little control.[24] Southerners correctly viewed the relationship as a general one of labor to capital but failed to realize that the capitalist's dependence on his laborers is hidden, whereas that of master on slave is naked. As a Mississippi planter noted:

> I intend to be henceforth stingy as far as unnecessary expenditure—as a man should not squander what another accumulates with the exposure of health and the wearing out of the physical powers, and is not that the case with the man who needlessly parts with that which the negro by the hardest labor and often undergoing what we in like situation would call the greatest deprivation . . .[25]

This simultaneous dependence and independence contributed to that peculiar combination of the admirable and the frightening in the slaveholder's nature: his strength, graciousness, and gentility; his impulsiveness, violence, and unsteadiness. The sense of independence and the habit of command developed his poise, grace, and dignity, but the less obvious sense of dependence on a despised other made him violently intolerant of anyone and anything threatening to expose the full nature of his relationship to his slave. Thus, he had a far deeper conservatism than that usually attributed to agrarians. His independence stood out as his most prized possession, but the instability of its base produced personal rashness and directed that rashness against any alteration in the status quo. Any attempt, no matter how well meaning, indirect, or harmless, to question the slave system appeared not only as an attack on his material interests but as an attack on his self-esteem at its most vulnerable point. To question either the morality or the practicality of slavery meant to expose the root of the slaveholder's dependence in independence.

The General Crisis of the Slave South

The South's slave civilization could not forever coexist with an increasingly hostile, powerful, and aggressive Northern capitalism. On the one hand, the special economic conditions arising from the dependence on slave labor bound the South, in a colonial manner, to the world market. The concentration of landholding and slaveholding prevented the rise of a prosperous yeomanry and of urban centers. The inability to build urban centers restricted the market for agricultural produce, weakened the rural producers, and dimmed hopes for agricultural diversification. On the other hand, the same concentration of wealth, the isolated, rural nature of the plantation system, the special psychology engendered by slave ownership, and the political opportunity presented by the separation from England,

---

[24] Cf. Karl Marx, *Capital* (3 vols.; New York, 1947), I, 41–55.
[25] Everard Green Baker Diary, Feb. 13, 1849, in the University of North Carolina. The entry was unfinished.

converged to give the South considerable political and social independence. This independence was primarily the contribution of the slaveholding class, and especially of the planters. Slavery, while it bound the South economically, granted it the privilege of developing an aristocratic tradition, a disciplined and cohesive ruling class, and a mythology of its own.

Aristocratic tradition and ideology intensified the South's attachment to economic backwardness. Paternalism and the habit of command made the slaveholders tough stock, determined to defend their Southern heritage. The more economically debilitating their way of life, the more they clung to it. It was this side of things—the political hegemony and aristocratic ideology of the ruling class—rather than economic factors that prevented the South from relinquishing slavery voluntarily.

As the free states stepped up their industrialization and as the westward movement assumed its remarkable momentum, the South's economic and political allies in the North were steadily isolated. Years of abolitionist and free-soil agitation bore fruit as the South's opposition to homesteads, tariffs, and internal improvements clashed more and more dangerously with the North's economic needs. To protect their institutions and to try to lessen their economic bondage, the slaveholders slid into violent collision with Northern interests and sentiments. The economic deficiencies of slavery threatened to undermine the planters' wealth and power. Such relief measures as cheap labor and more land for slave states (reopening the slave trade and territorial expansion) conflicted with Northern material needs, aspirations, and morality.[26] The planters faced a steady deterioration of their political and social power. Even if the relative prosperity of the 1850s had continued indefinitely, the slave states would have been at the mercy of the free, which steadily forged ahead in population growth, capital accumulation, and economic development. Any economic slump threatened to bring with it an internal political disaster, for the slaveholders could not rely on their middle and lower classes to remain permanently loyal.[27]

When we understand that the slave South developed neither a strange form of capitalism nor an undefinable agrarianism but a special civilization built on the relationship of master to slave, we expose the root of its conflict with the North. The internal contradictions in the South and the external conflict with the North placed the slaveholders hopelessly on the defensive with little to look forward to except slow strangulation. Their only hope lay in a bold stroke to complete their political independence and to use it to provide an expansionist solution for their economic and social problems. The ideology and psychology of the proud slaveholding class made surrender or resignation to gradual defeat unthinkable, for its fate, in its own eyes at least, was the fate of everything worth while in Western civilization.

---

[26] These measures met opposition from powerful sections of the slaveholding class for reasons that cannot be discussed here. The independence of the South would only have brought the latent intraclass antagonisms to the surface.

[27] The loyalty of these classes was real but unstable. For our present purposes let us merely note that Lincoln's election and federal patronage would, if Southern fears were justified, have led to the formation of an antiplanter party in the South.

Slavery and the Republican Ideology

Eric Foner

Almost every historian now agrees that the Civil War would not have happened if there had been no slavery. Yet, the exact relationship of slavery to the war remains something of a problem. One question that has intrigued historians since the appearance of Leon Litwack's *North of Slavery* in 1961, which documented the pervasive racial discrimination in the North, is how antislavery sentiment won so much support in a section permeated with racism. Lee Benson, in *Toward the Scientific Study of History* (1972), has estimated that no more than 5 percent of Northerners in 1860 would have favored immediate abolition of slavery. Although part of the answer to this apparent paradox is that there were individuals who were at the same time antislavery and antiblack, a more complete explanation is to be found in the ideology that the Republican Party extracted from the public mind and made its own.

Through a perceptive analysis of what the Republicans said, Eric Foner of Columbia University in his book *Free Soil, Free Labor, and Free Men* (1970) has reconstructed the Republican world view. He believes that *the concept of "free labor" lay at the heart of the Republican ideology, and expressed a coherent social outlook, a model of the good society. Political anti-slavery was not merely a negative doctrine, an attack on southern slavery and the society built upon it; it was an affirmation of the superiority of the social system of the North—a dynamic, expanding capitalist society, whose achievements and destiny were almost wholly the result of the dignity and opportunities which it offered the average laboring man.*

When North and South argued about slavery, at issue were competing value systems and not simply the matter of the morality of slavery. As a way of understanding the complexities of the period, Foner's interpretation is a great advance over the older assumption that antislavery sentiment was the result of moral fervor or the slightly cynical thought that the antislavery cause became the symbol that cloaked the operation of a host of more mundane material and political interests.

Analyzing the place of antislavery sentiment within the Republican ideology is Foner's major purpose. He finds that the antislavery stance arose from an amalgam of different, often poorly articulated, ideas. It helped to focus feelings of resentment of southern political power, whether they derived from revulsion at the thought of the aristocratic life style of the South or from the fear that agrarian political interests were blocking policies that were needed for progress. It derived from a devotion to the Union, especially because unity was a precious commodity in a society that was constantly undergoing fragmentation and reintegration and because the democratic messianism of a revolutionary society could only be demonstrated by the visible success of the Union. It expressed an axiomatic faith in the superiority of free labor and the immorality of slavery as a form of relationship among fellow human beings. At the same time, it served to mask and implement some racist antipathy toward blacks by keeping blacks as well as slaves out of western lands, while it served to translate a generalized commitment to the northern social order. Barrington Moore, in *Social Origins of Dictatorship and Democracy* (1966), puts forth much the same idea although his emphasis differs from Foner's: "The conclusion reached after much uncertainty amounts to the statement that the American Civil War was the last revolutionary offensive on the part of what one may legitimately call urban or bourgeois capitalist democracy. . . . Slavery was an obstacle to a political and social democracy."

Genovese and Foner have examined opposite sides of a conflict and have arrived at conclusions that complement each other. In their views, both North and South assumed that expansion was necessary in order for their respective social systems to survive. The perception that the social systems were different and antagonistic produced the conflict over the western territories. It is important to note, as Genovese and Foner substantiate, that slavery was not merely the symbol of sectional conflict but the real basis for it. Southern society was very different from that of the North because slavery made possible the existence of a dominant class that diverged sharply in material interests and values from the dominant class in the North. Furthermore, for both Genovese and Foner, secession was not a blunder or a wildly romantic gesture. It was the rational realization that the inability to expand meant the destruction of the planter class and that Lincoln's election was a real threat not only to the expansion of slavery but in the long run to the very existence of the southern society. The South correctly understood the Republican ideology.

*O*f the American Civil War," James Ford Rhodes wrote over a half a century ago, "it may safely be asserted that there was a single cause, slavery." In this opinion, Rhodes was merely echoing a view which seemed self-evident to Abraham Lincoln and many other participants in the sectional conflict. Their interpretation implicitly assumes that the ante-bellum Republican party was primarily a vehicle for anti-slavery sentiment. Yet partly because historians are skeptical of explanations made by partici-pants of their own behavior, Rhodes' view quickly fell under attack. Even before Rhodes wrote, John R. Commons had characterized the Republicans as primarily a homestead party, and Charles and Mary Beard later added the tariff as one of its fundamental concerns. More recently, historians have stressed aversion to the presence of blacks—free or slave—in the western territories as the Republicans' motive for opposing the extension of slavery. Because the Republicans disavowed the intention of attacking slavery in states where it already existed by direct federal action, their anti-slavery declarations have been dismissed by some historians as hypocritical.[1] And recently, a political analyst, not a professional historian, revealed how commonplace a cynical attitude toward the early Republican party has become when he wrote: "The Republican Party succeeded by soft-pedalling the issue of slavery altogether and concentrating on economic issues which would attract Northern businessmen and Western farmers."[2]

Controversy over the proper place of anti-slavery in the Republican ideology is hardly new. During the 1850's, considerable debate occurred within abolitionist circles on the proper attitude toward Republicanism. In part, this was simply an extension of the traditional schism between political and non-political abolitionists, and it is not surprising that William Lloyd Garrison and his followers should have wasted little enthusiasm on the Republicans. Yet many abolitionists who had no objection on principle to political involvements considered the anti-slavery commitment of the Republican party insufficient to merit their support. Gerrit Smith and William Goodell, for example, who had been instrumental in organizing the Liberty party in New York State, declared that they could not support a party which recognized the constitutionality of slavery anywhere in the Union. The Republican party, Smith charged, "refuses to oppose slavery where it is, and opposes it only where it is not," and he continuously urged radicals like Chase and Giddings to take an abolitionist stance.[3] Theodore Parker made the same criticism. When Chase declared in the Senate that the federal government would not interfere with slavery in the states, Parker wrote that while he did not object to attacking slavery one step at a time, he "would not promise *not to take other steps.*"[4]

Yet it is important to remember that despite their criticisms of the Republican party, leading abolitionists maintained close personal relations with Republican leaders, particularly the radicals. The flow of letters between Chase and Smith, cordial even while each criticized the attitude of the other, is one example of this. Similarly, Parker kept up a correspondence with Henry Wilson, Charles Sumner, and William Seward as well as Chase.[5] And

[1] James Ford Rhodes, *Lectures on the American Civil War* (New York, 1913), 2; Roy F. Basler *et al.*, eds., *The Collected Works of Abraham Lincoln* (9 vols.: New Brunswick, 1953–55), VII, 332; John R. Commons, "Horace Greeley and the Working Class Origins of the Republican Party," *PSQ*, XXIV (September 1909), 488; Charles A. Beard and Mary R. Beard, *The Rise of American Civilization* (2 vols.: New York, 1933 ed.), II, 39; Eugene H. Berwanger, *The Frontier Against Slavery* (Urbana, 1967); Milton Viorst, *Fall From Grace* (New York, 1968), 39; Bernard Mandel, *Labor: Free and Slave* (New York, 1955), 147.

[2] I. F. Stone, "Party of the Rich and Well-Born," *New York Review of Books*, June 20, 1968, 34. Cf. George H. Mayer, *The Republican Party 1854–1966* (New York, 1967 ed.), 75.

[3] Margaret L. Plunkett, "A History of the Liberty Party with Emphasis on Its Activities in the Northeastern States" (unpublished doctoral dissertation, Cornell University, 1930), 173n. Cf. Gerrit Smith to Salmon P. Chase, April 15, 1855, March 1, August 13, 1856, January 26, 1857, Salmon P. Chase Papers, HSPa; William Goodell to George W. Julian, June 18, 1857, Giddings-Julian Papers, LC.

[4] John Weiss, *Life and Correspondence of Theodore Parker* (2 vols.: New York, 1864), II, 228. Cf. II, 208, 223.

[5] Hans L. Trefousse, *The Radical Republicans, Lincoln's Vanguard for Racial Justice* (New York, 1969), 15–19; Henry Steele Commager, *Theodore Parker* (Boston, 1936),

he and Wendell Phillips, both experts at the art of political agitation, recognized the complex interrelationship between abolitionist attempts to create a public sentiment hostile to slavery, and the political anti-slavery espoused by Republicans. "Our agitation, you know, helps keep yours alive in the rank and file," was the way Wendell Phillips expressed it to Sumner. And Seward agreed that the abolitionists played a vital role in awakening the public conscience—"open[ing] the way where the masses can follow." For their part, abolitionists like Theodore Parker were happy to borrow statistics and arguments from the anti-slavery speeches of politicians.[6]

The evidence strongly suggests that outside of Garrison's immediate circle, most abolitionists voted with the Republican party despite their wish that the party adopt a more aggressive anti-slavery position. Indeed, abolitionist societies experienced financial difficulties in the late 1850's, as former contributors began giving their money to the Republicans. Even Gerrit Smith, who insisted he could "never vote for any person who recognizes a law for slavery," contributed five hundred dollars to the Frémont campaign. The attitude of many abolitionists was summed up by Elizur Wright, a proponent of Smith and Goodell's brand of political anti-slavery who nonetheless voted for Lincoln in 1860. While Wright criticized the Republicans for their shortcomings on slavery, he acknowledged that "the greatest recommendation of the Republican Party is, that its enemies do not quite believe its disclaimers, while they do believe that [it is] sincerely opposed to slavery as far as it goes." Prophetically, he added: "Woe to the slave power under a Republican President if it strikes the first blow."[7]

The fact that so many abolitionists, not to mention radical Republicans, supported the Republican party, is an indication that anti-slavery formed no small part of the Republican ideology. Recent historians have concluded, moreover, that writers like Beard greatly overestimated the importance of economic issues in the elections of 1856, 1858, and 1860. We have already seen how tentative was the Republican commitment to the tariff. As for the homestead issue, Don E. Fehrenbacher has pointed out that the Republicans carried most of the Northwest in 1856 when free land was not a political issue, and that in 1860, Douglas Democrats supported the measure as ardently as Republicans.[8] More important, it would have been suicidal for the

---

254–61. For Chase's high regard for Smith, see Chase to Smith, October 18, 1852, December 15, 1854, Salmon P. Chase Papers, LC; Chase to Charles D. Cleveland, May 27, 1853, Chase to Smith, March 4, 1857, Chase Papers, HSPa.

[6] Wendell Phillips to Charles Sumner, March 7, 1853, Charles Sumner Papers, Houghton Library, Harvard University; Frederick W. Seward, ed., *Seward at Washington* (2 vols.: New York, 1891), I, 208. Parker is quoted in George Sumner to Chase, February 14, 1854, Chase Papers, HSPa.

[7] Irving H. Bartlett, *Wendell Phillips, Brahmin Radical* (Boston, 1961), 206; Aileen S. Kraditor, "A Note on Elkins and the Abolitionists," *CWH*, XIII (December 1967), 333; Betty Fladeland, *James Gillespie Birney: Slaveholder to Abolitionist* (Ithaca, 1955), 292; H. Warren to Zebina Eastman, December 24, 1856, Zebina Eastman Papers, ChicHS; New York *Tribune*, February 25, 1857; Gerrit Smith to Horace Greeley, October 25, 1856, Horace Greeley Papers, LC; Ralph V. Harlow, *Gerrit Smith, Philanthropist and Reformer* (New York, 1939), 364; Elizur Wright, *An Eye-Opener for the Wide Awakes* (Boston, 1860), 47, 53–54.

[8] George H. Knoles, ed., *The Crisis of the Union* (Baton Rouge, 1965), 18, 27; Allan Nevins, *The Emergence of Lincoln* (2 vols.: New York, 1950), II, 302.

Republicans to have put their emphasis on economic policies, particularly the neo-Whiggism described by Beard. If one thing is evident after analyzing the various elements which made up the party, it is that anti-slavery was one of the few policies which united all Republican factions. For political reasons, if for no other, the Republicans were virtually obliged to make anti-slavery the main focus of their political appeal. Such questions as the tariff, nativism, and race were too divisive to be stressed, while the homestead issue could be advanced precisely because it was so non-controversial in the North.

Conservative Republicans and radicals, ex-Democrats and former Whigs, all agreed that slavery was the major issue of the 1850's. It was not surprising that Giddings should insist that "there is but one real issue between the Republican party and those factions that stand opposed to it. That is the question of slavery," or that Salmon P. Chase should declare that the election of 1860 had not turned on "subordinate questions of local and temporary character," but had vindicated the principle of "the restriction of slavery within State limits."[9] But Orville H. Browning, as conservative as Giddings and Chase were radical, appraised the politics of 1860 in much the same way. "It is manifest to all," he declared, "that there is an unusual degree of political interest pervading the country—that the people, everywhere, are excited, . . . and yet, from one extremity of the Republic to the other, scarcely any other subject is mentioned, or any other question discussed . . . save the question of negro slavery. . . ." Ex-Democrats in the Republican party fully agreed. Both Francis Spinner and Preston King rejected suggestions that Democratic economic policies be engrafted onto the Republican platform, on the ground that these must await settlement until the slavery issue had been decided. As Spinner tersely put it, "Statesmen cannot make issues for the people. As live men we must take the issues as they present themselves." The potency of the slavery issue, and the way in which it subordinated or absorbed all other political questions, was noted by the anti-Lecompton Democrat from New York, Horace Clark, on the eve of the 1860 campaign: "It is not to be controverted that the slavery agitation is not at rest. It has absorbed and destroyed our national politics. It has overrun State politics. It has even invaded our municipalities; and now, in some form or other, everywhere controls the elections of the people."[10]

In a recent study of Civil War historiography, Roy F. Nichols observed that we still do not know whether either section had reached its own consensus on major issues by 1861. Some historians have interpreted the strong showing of Stephen A. Douglas in the free states as proof that a substantial

[9] George W. Julian, *The Life of Joshua R. Giddings* (Chicago, 1892), 379; L. E. Chittenden, *A Report of the Debates and Proceedings in the Secret Sessions of the Conference Convention . . . Held at Washington, D.C., in February A.D. 1861* (New York, 1864), 428. Cf. 131–32, 327; [James Russell Lowell], "The Election of November," *Atlantic Monthly*, VI (October 1860), 499; Thomas Richmond to Lyman Trumbull, December 14, 1860, Lyman Trumbull Papers, LC.

[10] *Speech of Hon. O. H. Browning, Delivered at the Republican Mass Meeting, Springfield, Ill., August 8th, 1860* (Quincy, 1860), 3; John Bigelow, *Retrospections of an Active Life* (5 vols.: New York, 1909–13), I, 179–80; Sarah J. Day, *The Man on a Hill Top* (Philadelphia, 1931), 223–24; *Congressional Globe*, 36 Congress, 1 Session, 23. Cf. 120; Robert L. Bloom, "Newspaper Opinion in the State Election of 1860," *PaH*, XXVIII (October 1961), 352–53; New York *Tribune*, November 9, 1860.

portion of the electorate rejected the Republican brand of anti-slavery.[11] Though there is some truth in this view, it is important to remember that by 1860 the Douglas Democrats shared a good many of the Republicans' attitudes toward the South. One of the most striking aspects of the Democratic debate over the Lecompton constitution was the way in which the Douglasites echoed so many of the anti-southern views which anti-Nebraska Democrats had expressed only a few years earlier. There is a supreme irony in the fact that the same methods which Douglas had used against dissident Democrats in 1854 were now turned against him and his supporters. Buchanan applied the patronage whip ruthlessly, and anti-Lecompton Democrats complained that a new, pro-slavery test had suddenly been imposed upon the party. And like the anti-Nebraska Democrats, who were now members of the Republican party, the Douglasites insisted that they commanded the support of most northern Democrats. Historians have tended to agree with them. Roy Nichols suggests that the enthusiasm Douglas's anti-southern stand aroused among rank and file Democrats was one reason why he refused to accept the compromise English bill to settle the Lecompton controversy, and recent students of Pennsylvania and Indiana politics agree that the vast majority of the Democracy in those states favored Douglas against the administration.[12]

The bitterness of Douglas Democrats against the South did not abate between 1858 and 1860. They believed that the South had embarked upon a crusade to force slavery into all the territories, and protested that endorsement of such a goal would destroy the northern Democracy. "We have confided in their honor, their love of justice, their detestation of what is wrong," Henry Payne, a prominent Ohio Democrat, said of his southern colleagues in 1858, *"but we can do it no more."*[13] And many Republicans believed that, even if Douglas made his peace with the Democratic organization, many of his followers had acquired "a feeling against Slavery and its arrogant demands which *if cherished* will prevent their going back. . . ." A few Democrats did defect to the Republican party in 1858, 1859, and 1860,

[11] Roy F. Nichols, "A Hundred Years Later: Perspectives on the Civil War," *JSH*, XXXIII (May 1967), 157; Mary Scrugham, *The Peaceable Americans of 1860–1861* (New York, 1921), 23, 51, 69; Elbert B. Smith, *The Death of Slavery* (Chicago, 1967), 166.

[12] Roy F. Nichols, *The Disruption of American Democracy* (New York, 1948), 165, 173; *Congressional Globe*, 35 Congress, 1 Session, 1055, Appendix, 322, 2 Session, Appendix, 171, 36 Congress, 1 Session, 119; Philadelphia *Press*, cited in New York *Times*, March 15, 1858; Elmer D. Elbert, "Southern Indiana Politics on the Eve of the Civil War 1858–1861" (unpublished doctoral dissertation, Indiana University, 1967), 95; Michael F. Holt, "Forging a Majority: The Formation of the Republican Party in Pittsburgh, Pennsylvania, 1848–1860" (unpublished doctoral dissertation, Johns Hopkins University, 1967), 375. Cf. J. Robert Lane, *A Political History of Connecticut During the Civil War* (Washington, 1941), 98.

[13] Cincinnati *Gazette*, March 3, 1858. Cf. Don E. Fehrenbacher, *Prelude to Greatness, Lincoln in the 1850's* (New York, 1964 ed.), 57; Howard C. Perkins, ed., *Northern Editorials on Secession* (2 vols.: New York, 1942), I, 47, 49; *Congressional Globe*, 35 Congress, 1 Session, 474, 1239, 1354, 1905, Appendix, 321. The resentment expressed by the anti-Lecompton Congressman from New York, Horace Clark, was typical: "I am one of that Democratic party of the North which has been often beaten and torn in its struggle for the maintenance of the constitutional rights of the South, until we have been, as it were, driven to take refuge within the walls of our northern cities." *Congressional Globe*, 35 Congress, 1 Session, 1307.

including a former chairman of the Iowa Democracy, several anti-Lecompton Congressmen, and F. P. Stanton, the former Democratic governor of Kansas.[14] That there were not more defections largely reflected the continuation into 1860 of Douglas's contest with the administration, which increasingly took on what one historian calls "a semi-free-soil" tone. And when the 1860 Democratic national convention broke up over the South's insistence on a platform guaranteeing slavery in the territories, the bitterness of the Douglasites knew no bounds. The reporter Murat Halstead observed that he had "never heard Abolitionists talk more rancorously of the people of the South than the Douglas men here." For their part, southerners insisted they would not accept popular sovereignty since this would be as effective as the Wilmot Proviso in barring slavery from the territories.[15]

There were, of course, many important differences between the Douglasites and Republicans. Douglas still insisted in 1860 that the slavery question was not important enough to risk the disruption of the Union, he was much more inclined to use racism as a political weapon, and, as one Republican newspaper put it, in words echoed by several recent scholars, Douglas "does not recognize the moral element in politics. . . ."[16] Yet in their devotion to the Union and their bitter opposition to southern domination of the government, Republicans and Douglasites stood close together in 1860. There was much truth in the observation of one Republican that "the rupture between the northern and southern wing of the democracy, is permanent with the masses . . . ," and the experiences of the Douglas Democrats in the years preceding the Civil War go a long way toward explaining the unanimity of the North's response to the attack on Fort Sumter.[17]

II

The attitude of the Douglasites toward the South on the eve of the Civil War partially reflected their assessment of northern opinion regarding slavery. Politicians of all parties agreed that northerners opposed slavery as an

[14] A. H. Reeder to Wayne MacVeagh, August 20, 1858, Wayne MacVeagh Papers, HSPa; Morton M. Rosenberg, "The Election of 1859 in Iowa," *IJH*, LVII (January 1959), 2–3; *Wisconsin State Journal*, July 28, 1860; Charles Francis Adams Diary, December 15, 1859, Adams Papers, MHS. Cf. Lyman Trumbull to Chase, June 17, 1858, Chase Papers, HSPa.

[15] Henry C. Hubbart, *The Older Middle West 1840–1880* (New York, 1936), 133–38; Wilfred E. Binkley, *American Political Parties* (2nd ed.: New York, 1947), 203; Nevins, *Emergence of Lincoln*, II, 227; Knoles, ed., *Crisis of the Union*, 56–57. Republicans were quite annoyed at the Douglas Democrats' attempts to portray themselves as the "real" anti-southern, anti-slavery party. Chicago *Press and Tribune*, August 12, 1858; James G. Blaine, *Political Discussions* (Norwich, Conn., 1887), 12; James R. Doolittle to Hannibal Hamlin, September 18, 1859, Hannibal Hamlin Papers, University of Maine, Orono; *Speech of Carl Schurz, of Wisconsin, at the Cooper Institute . . .* (Washington, 1860), 1.

[16] Springfield *Republican*, April 14, 1860; *Congressional Globe*, 36 Congress, 1 Session, 733; Robert W. Johannsen, "Stephen A. Douglas, Popular Sovereignty and the Territories," *Historian*, XXII (August 1960), 379; Nevins, *Ordeal*, II, 107–9.

[17] Ralston Skinner to Chase, June 7, 1860, Chase Papers, LC; Robert W. Johannsen, "The Douglas Democracy and the Crisis of Disunion," *CWH*, IX, (September 1963), 229–47. Cf. Preston King to Azariah C. Flagg, May 7, 1860, Azariah C. Flagg Papers, Columbia University; Cincinnati *Gazette*, March 12, 1858.

abstract principle, although they disagreed on the intensity of this sentiment. John C. Calhoun had estimated in 1847 that while only 5 per cent of northerners supported the abolitionists, more than 66 per cent viewed slavery as an evil, and were willing to oppose its extension constitutionally. Similarly, a conservative Republican declared in 1858, "There is no man [in the North] who is an advocate of slavery. There is no man from that section of the country who will go before his constituents and advocate the extension of slavery." Northern Democrats had the same perception of northern sentiments. Even the Hunkers of New York, who consistently opposed the Wilmot Proviso, refused to say "that they are not opposed to slavery." For as William L. Marcy declared in 1849, "In truth we all are."[18]

Anti-slavery as an abstract feeling had long existed in the North. It had not, however, prevented abolitionists from being mobbed, nor anti-slavery parties from going down to defeat. Democrats and Whigs had long been able to appeal to devotion to the Union, racism, and economic issues, to neutralize anti-slavery as a political force. "The anti-slavery sentiment," Hamilton Fish explained in 1854, "is inborn, and almost universal at the North . . . but it is only as a *sentiment* that it generally pervades; it has not and cannot be inspired with the activity that even a very slight interest excites."[19] But Fish failed to foresee the fundamental achievement of the Republican party before the Civil War: the creation and articulation of an ideology which blended personal and sectional interest with morality so perfectly that it became the most potent political force in the nation. The free labor assault upon slavery and southern society, coupled with the idea that an aggressive Slave Power was threatening the most fundamental values and interests of the free states, hammered the slavery issue home to the northern public more emphatically than an appeal to morality alone could ever have done.

To agree with Rhodes that slavery was ultimately the cause of the Civil War, therefore, is not to accept the corollary that the basis of the Republican opposition to slavery was simple moral fervor. In a speech to the Senate in 1848, John M. Niles listed a dozen different reasons for his support of the Wilmot Proviso—but only once did he mention his belief that slavery was morally repugnant. And thirteen years later, George William Curtis observed that "there is very little moral mixture in the 'Anti-Slavery' feeling of this country. A great deal is abstract philanthropy; part is hatred of slaveholders; a great part is jealousy for white labor, very little is consciousness of wrong done and the wish to right it." The Republican ideology included all these elements, and much more. Rhodes argued that northerners wished to preserve the Union as a first step toward abolition. A more accurate formulation would reverse the equation and say that many Republicans were anti-slavery from the conviction that slavery threatened the Union.

[18] Richard K. Crallé, ed., *The Works of John C. Calhoun* (6 vols.: Charleston and New York, 1851–56), IV, 387–88; *Congressional Globe*, 35 Congress, 1 Session, 1312; Alto Lee Whitehurst, "Martin Van Buren and the Free Soil Movement" (unpublished doctoral dissertation, University of Chicago, 1932), 189. Cf. J. Franklin Jameson, ed., "Correspondence of John C. Calhoun," *Annual Report* of AHA, 1899, II, 1143; Chicago *Democratic Press*, July 18, 1854; Chittenden, ed., *Peace Conference Proceedings*, 199–200.

[19] Hamilton Fish to John M. Bradford, December 16, 1854, Letterbook, Hamilton Fish Papers, LC.

Aside from some radicals, who occasionally flirted with disunion, most Republicans were united by the twin principles of free soil and Unionism. Cassius M. Clay even suggested that the Free-Soilers in 1851 adopt the name "Liberty and Union" party, in order to impress their essential goals upon the electorate. The New York *Times* emphasized this aspect of Republican thought in 1857: "The barbaric institution of slavery will become more and more odious to the northern people because it will become more and more plain . . . that the States which cling to Slavery thrust back the American idea, and reject the influences of the Union."[20]

Still, Unionism, despite its importance to the mass of northerners, and obviously crucial to any explanation of the Republicans' decision to resist secession, was only one aspect of the Republican ideology. It would have been just as logical to compromise on the slavery question if the preservation of the Union were the paramount goal of Republican politics. Nor should Republicanism be seen merely as the expression of the northern drive toward political power. We have seen, to be sure, that resentment of southern power played its part, that many Democratic-Republicans had watched with growing jealousy the South's domination of the Democratic party and the national government, and that many former Whigs were convinced that the South was blocking economic programs essential for national economic development. But there is more to the coming of the Civil War than the rivalry of sections for political power. (New England, after all, could accept its own decline in political power without secession.)

In short, none of these elements can stand separately; they dissolve into one another, and the total product emerges as ideology. Resentment of southern political power, devotion to the Union, anti-slavery based upon the free labor argument, moral revulsion to the peculiar institution, racial prejudice, a commitment to the northern social order and its development and expansion—all these elements were intertwined in the Republican world-view. What they added up to was the conviction that North and South represented two social systems whose values, interests, and future prospects were in sharp, perhaps mortal, conflict with one another. The sense of difference, of estrangement, and of growing hostility with which Republicans viewed the South, cannot be overemphasized. Theodore Sedgwick of New York perhaps expressed it best when he declared during the secession crisis: "The policy and aims of slavery, its institutions and civilization, and the character of its people, are all at variance with the policy, aims, institutions, education, and character of the North. There is an irreconcilable difference in our interests, institutions, and pursuits; in our sentiments and feelings." Greeley's *Tribune* said the same thing more succinctly: "We are not one people. We are two peoples. We are a people for Freedom and a people for Slavery. Between the two, conflict is inevitable." An attack not simply on the institution of slavery, but upon southern society itself, was thus at the heart of the Republican mentality. Of all historians, I think Avery Craven caught this feature best: "By 1860, slavery had become the symbol and car-

[20] *Congressional Globe*, 30 Congress, 1 Session, 1199–1200; Gordon Milne, *George William Curtis and the Genteel Tradition* (Bloomington, 1956), 112; Rhodes, *Lectures*, 5–6; Cassius M. Clay to Chase, August 12, 1851, Chase Papers, HSPa; New York *Times*, May 16, 1857.

rier of *all* sectional differences and conflicts."[21] Here and elsewhere, Craven describes the symbolic nature of the slavery controversy, reflected as it was in the widespread acceptance among Republicans of the Slave Power idea—a metaphor for all the fears and resentments they harbored toward the South. But Craven did leave out something crucial. Slavery was not only the symbol, but also the real basis of sectional conflict, for it was the foundation of the South's economy, social structure, aspirations, and ideology.

"Why do we Meddle with Slavery?" the New York *Times* asked in an 1857 editorial. The answer gives us a penetrating insight into the Republican mind on the eve of Civil War:

> The great States of the North are not peopled exclusively by quidnuncs and agitators. . . . Nevertheless, we do give ourselves great and increasing concern about the existence of Slavery in States over whose internal economy we have no right and no wish to exercise any control whatever. Nevertheless, we do feel, and the feeling is growing deeper in the northern heart with every passing year, that our character, our prosperity, and our destiny are most seriously involved in the question of the perpetuation or extinction of slavery in those States.

What is striking about this statement is a concern directed not only against the extension of slavery, but against its very existence. Lincoln put the same concern even more succinctly to a Chicago audience in 1859, "Never forget," he said, "that we have before us this whole matter of the right or wrong of slavery in this Union, though the immediate question is as to its spreading out into new Territories and States."[22]

Lincoln and the editors of the *Times* thus made explicit that there was more to the contest over the extension of slavery than whether the institution should spread to the West. As Don E. Fehrenbacher puts it, the territorial question was the "skirmish line of a more extensive struggle."[23] Only by a comprehension of this total conflict between North and South, between Republican and southern ideologies, can the meaning of the territorial issue be fully grasped. Its importance went even beyond the belief shared widely in both sections that slavery required expansion to survive, and that confinement to the states where it already existed would kill it. For in each ideology was the conviction that its own social system must expand, not only to insure its own survival but to prevent the expansion of all the evils the other represented. We have already seen how Republicans believed that free society, with its promise of social mobility for the laborer, required territorial expansion, and how this was combined with a messianic desire to spread the benefits of free society to other areas and peoples. Southerners had their own grandiose design. "They had a magnificent dream of empire," a Republican recalled after the war, and such recent writers as C. Stanley Urban and Eugene Genovese have emphasized how essential expansionism was in the southern ideology. The struggle for the West

---

[21] *Congressional Globe*, 36 Congress, 2 Session, 797; New York *Tribune*, April 12, 1855; Avery Craven, *An Historian and the Civil War* (Chicago, 1964), 163. Cf. Avery Craven, *The Repressible Conflict* (Baton Rouge, 1939), 76.

[22] New York *Times*, May 16, 1857; Basler, ed., *Lincoln Works*, III, 369.

[23] Knoles, ed., *Crisis of the Union*, 22–23.

represented a contest between two expansive societies, only one of whose aspirations could prevail. The conflict was epitomized by two statements which appeared in the Philadelphia *North American* in 1856. Slavery, the *North American* argued, could not be allowed to expand, because it would bring upon the West "a blight whose fatal influence will be felt for centuries." Two weeks later the same paper quoted a southern journal, which, in urging slavery expansionism, used precisely this logic in reverse. Such expansion, the southern paper argued, would "forbid the extension of the evils of free society to new people and coming generations."[24]

Here then was a basic reason why the South could not accept the verdict of 1860. In 1848, Martin Van Buren had said that the South opposed the principle of free soil because "the prohibition carries with it a reproach to the slaveholding states, and . . . submission to it would degrade them." Eight years later, the Richmond *Enquirer* explained that for the South to abandon the idea of extending slavery while accepting Republican assurances of non-interference in the states would be "pregnant with the admission that slavery is wrong, and but for the constitution should be abolished." To agree to the containment of slavery, the South would have had to abandon its whole ideology, which had come to view the institution as a positive good, the basis of an enlightened form of social organization.[25]

III

Although it has not been the purpose of this study to examine in any detailed way the southern mind in 1860, what has been said about the Republican ideology does help to explain the rationale for secession. The political wars of the 1850's, centering on the issue of slavery extension, had done much to erode whatever good feeling existed between the sections. The abolitionist Elihu Burrit suggested in 1857 that a foreigner observing American politics would probably conclude "that the North and South were wholly occupied in gloating upon each others' faults and failings." During the 1856 campaign, Burrit went on, sectional antagonisms had been brought "to a pitch of rancor, never reached before" in American politics. This was precisely the reason that Union-loving conservatives like Hamilton Fish dreaded the mounting agitation. "I cannot close my eyes to the fact which all history shows," Fish wrote Thurlow Weed in 1855, "that every physical revolution (of governments) is preceded by a moral revolution. [Slavery agitation] leads to estrangement first, and next to hostility and hatred which end inevitably in separation." By the time of the secession crisis another former

[24] Roeliff Brinkerhoff, *Recollections of a Lifetime* (Cincinnati, 1904), 42; C. Stanley Urban, "The Ideology of Southern Imperialism: New Orleans and the Caribbean, 1845–1860," *Louisiana Historical Quarterly*, XXXIX (January 1956), 48–73; Eugene D. Genovese, *The Political Economy of Slavery* (New York, 1965), 243–49; Philadelphia *North American and United States Gazette*, September 10, 1856; Richmond *Enquirer*, cited in Philadelphia *North American and United States Gazette*, September 25, 1856. Cf. *National Era*, March 10, 1859.

[25] O. C. Gardiner, *The Great Issue* (New York, 1848), 146; Richmond *Enquirer*, June 16, 1856, clipping, scrapbook, Giddings Papers; Genovese, *Political Economy*, 250. Cf. Robert R. Russel, "The Issues in the Congressional Struggle Over the Kansas-Nebraska Bill, 1854," *JSH*, XXIX (May 1963), 190; Chaplain W. Morrison, *Democratic Politics and Sectionalism* (Chapel Hill, 1967), 65–66.

Whig could observe that "the people of the North and of the South have come to hate each other worse than the hatred between any two nations in the world. In a word the moral basis on which the government is founded is all destroyed."[26]

It is thus no mystery that southerners could not seriously entertain Republican assurances that they would not attack slavery in the states. For one thing, in opposing its extension, Republicans had been logically forced to attack the institution itself. This, indeed, was one of the reasons why radicals accepted the emphasis on non-extension. "We are disposed to select this single point," Sumner explained to Chase, "because it has a peculiar practical issue at the present moment, while its discussion would, of course, raise the whole question of slavery." Frederick Douglass agreed that agitation for the Wilmot Proviso served "to keep the subject before the people—to deepen their hatred of the system—and to break up the harmony between the Northern white people and the Southern slaveholders. . . ."[27] As we have seen, many Republicans, both radicals and moderates, explicitly stated that non-extension was simply the first step, that there would come a day when slavery would cease to exist.

As southerners viewed the Republican party's rise to power in one northern state after another, and witnessed the increasingly anti-southern tone of the northern Democrats, they could hardly be blamed for feeling apprehensive about the future. Late in 1859, after a long talk with the moderate Unionist Senator from Virginia, R. M. T. Hunter, Senator James Dixon of Connecticut reported that the Virginian was deeply worried. "What seems to alarm Hunter is the *growth* of the Anti-slavery feeling at the North."[28] Southerners did not believe that this anti-slavery sentiment would be satisfied with the prohibition of slavery in the territories, although even that would be bad enough. They also feared that a Republican administration would adopt the radicals' program of indirect action against slavery. This is why continued Democratic control of Congress was not very reassuring, for executive action could implement much of the radicals' program. Slavery was notoriously weak in the states of Missouri, Maryland, and Delaware. With federal patronage, a successful emancipation movement there might well be organized. And what was more dangerous, Lincoln might successfully arouse the poor whites in other states against the slaveholders. "Cohorts of Federal office-holders, Abolitionists, may be sent into [our] midst," a southern Senator warned in January 1861; ". . . Postmasters . . . controlling the mails, and loading them down with incendiary documents," would be appointed in every town. One southern newspaper declared that

[26] Cleveland *Leader*, August 27, 1857; Hamilton Fish to Thurlow Weed, November 18, 1855, Letterbook, Fish Papers; L. B. Hamlin, ed., "Selections From the William Greene Papers, II," *Quarterly Publications* of Historical and Philosophical Society of Ohio, XIV (January–March 1919), 26.

[27] Sumner to Chase, February 7, 1848, Chase Papers, LC; Philip S. Foner, ed., *The Life and Writings of Frederick Douglass* (4 vols.: New York, 1950–55), II, 70. Cf. Craven, *Historian and the Civil War*, 41; Helen M. Cavenaugh, "Anti-Slavery Sentiment and Politics in the Northwest, 1844–1860," (unpublished doctoral dissertation, University of Chicago, 1938), 140–41; N. J. Tenney to Chase, July 28, 1848, Chase Papers, LC.

[28] James Dixon to Gideon Welles, December 17, 1859, Gideon Welles Papers, LC. Cf. Chittenden, *Peace Conference Proceedings*, 93.

"the great lever by which the abolitionists hope to extirpate slavery in the states, is the aid of the non-slaveholding citizens of the South." The reply of Republicans to these warnings was hardly reassuring. Commenting on one southern editorial, the Cincinnati *Commercial* declared that the spread of anti-slavery sentiment among southern poor whites was "an eventuality against which no precautions can avail." And by December 1860, Republican Congressmen were already receiving applications for office from within the slave states.[29]

For many reasons, therefore, southerners believed that slavery would not be permanently safe under a Republican administration. Had not William H. Seward announced in 1858, "I know, and you know, that a revolution has begun. I know, and all the world knows, that revolutions never go backward." Did not Republican Congressmen openly express their conviction that "slavery must die"? The Republican policy of preventing the spread of slavery, one southerner wrote to William T. Sherman, "was but the entering wedge to overthrow it in the States."[30]

The delegates to South Carolina's secession convention, in their address to the people of the state, explained why they had dissolved the state's connection with the Union:

> If it is right to preclude or abolish slavery in a Territory, why should it be allowed to remain in the States? . . . In spite of all disclaimers and professions, there can be but one end by the submission of the South to the rule of a sectional anti-slavery government at Washington; and that end, directly or indirectly, must be—the emancipation of the slaves of the South.

Emancipation might come in a decade, it might take fifty years. But North and South alike knew that the election of 1860 had marked a turning point in the history of slavery in the United States. To remain in the Union, the South would have had to accept the verdict of "ultimate extinction" which Lincoln and the Republicans had passed on the peculiar institution.[31]

The decision for civil war in 1860–61 can be resolved into two questions —why did the South secede, and why did the North refuse to let the South secede? As I have indicated, I believe secession should be viewed as a total and logical response by the South to the situation which confronted it in the election of Lincoln—logical in the sense that it was the only action consistent with its ideology. In the same way, the Republicans' decision to maintain the

[29] Nevins, *Emergence of Lincoln,* II, 469; *Congressional Globe,* 36 Congress, 2 Session, 357; Dwight L. Dumond, ed., *Southern Editorials on Secession* (New York, 1931), 173–74; Perkins, ed., *Northern Editorials,* I, 55–56; Herman Cox to Trumbull, November 27, 1860, William Gayle to Trumbull, December 9, 1860, Trumbull Papers; Nichols, *Disruption,* 352–53. Cf. Robert R. Russel, "The Economic History of Negro Slavery," *AgH,* XI (October 1937), 320–21; *Congressional Globe,* 36 Congress, 2 Session, 49.

[30] George E. Baker, ed., *The Works of William H. Seward* (5 vols.: Boston, 1853–84), IV, 302; *Congressional Globe,* 36 Congress, 2 Session, Appendix, 69; Walter L. Fleming, ed., *General W. T. Sherman As College President* (Cleveland, 1912), 287. Cf. Henry R. Selden to James R. Doolittle, May 14, 1858, James R. Doolittle Papers, NYPL.

[31] John Amasa May and Joan Reynolds Faust, *South Carolina Secedes* (Columbia, 1960), 88–89; Genovese, *Political Economy,* 266–69. I am greatly indebted in my understanding of the secession crisis to conversations with William W. Freehling of the University of Michigan. Professor Freehling's forthcoming study of the South in the 1850's will undoubtedly be a major contribution to Civil War historiography.

Union was inherent in their ideology. For the integrity of the Union, important as an end in itself, was also a prerequisite to the national greatness Republicans felt the United States was destined to achieve. With his faith in progress, material growth, and the spread of both democratic institutions and American influence throughout the world, William Seward brought the Republican ideology to a kind of culmination. Although few Republicans held as coherent and far-reaching a world view as he, most accepted Lincoln's more modest view that the American nation had a special place in the world, and a responsibility to prove that democratic institutions were self-sustaining. Much of the messianic zeal which characterized political anti-slavery derived from this faith in the superiority of the political, social, and economic institutions of the North, and a desire to spread these to their ultimate limits.

When a leading historian says, therefore, that the Republican party in 1860 was bound together "by a common enmity rather than a common loyalty," he is, I believe, only half right.[32] For the Republicans' enmity toward the South was intimately bound up with their loyalty to the society of small-scale capitalism which they perceived in the North. It was its identification with the aspirations of the farmers, small entrepreneurs, and craftsmen of northern society which gave the Republican ideology much of its dynamic, progressive, and optimistic quality. Yet paradoxically, at the time of its greatest success, the seeds of the later failure of that ideology were already present. Fundamental changes were at work in the social and economic structure of the North, transforming and undermining many of its free-labor assumptions. And the flawed attitude of the Republicans toward race, and the limitations of the free labor outlook in regard to the Negro, foreshadowed the mistakes and failures of the post-emancipation years.

Suggested Reading

A convenient guide to the extremely rich historical literature on the Old South is Arthur Link and Rembert Patrick's collection *Writing Southern History* (1965). A recent distinguished addition to this literature is *Prelude to Civil War: The Nullification Controversy in South Carolina, 1816–1836* (1966) by William W. Freehling, which leads in directions other than those taken by Genovese. No serious student should miss the craftsmanship and scholarship of the essays by David Potter collected as *The South and the Sectional Conflict* (1968), where still other lines of interpretation are pursued.

William R. Taylor, in *Cavalier and Yankee: The Old South and American National Character** (1961), analyzes the myths and literary themes associated with the plantation as responses of Northerners and Southerners to rapid social change. *Romanticism and Nationalism in the Old South* (1949) by Rollin G. Osterweis offers a similar portrait of the southern temperament. Frank Lawrence Owsley in *Plain Folks of the Old South** (1949) stressed, and perhaps over-emphasized, the middle-class and democratic nature of the agrarian South. Wilbur J. Cash's synthesis of southern character, *The Mind of the South** (1941),

---

[32] William B. Hesseltine, *Lincoln and the War Governors* (New York, 1948), 4.

ingeniously melds the aristocratic and plebeian interpretations. The social history of the back country is most pleasantly approached through Everett Dick's book *The Dixie Frontier** (1948), and the status of women in southern culture is analyzed extensively for the first time by Anne F. Scott in *The Southern Lady: From Pedestal to Politics, 1830–1930* (1970). The standard text is Clement Eaton's *The Mind of the Old South,** rev. ed. (1967). The pre-Revolutionary South is most succinctly captured by Charles Sydnor in *Gentlemen Freeholders: Political Practices in Washington's Virginia* (1952) and by Carl Bridenbaugh in *Myths and Realities: Societies of the Colonial South* (1952).

Over the years, one of the most heatedly contested areas of scholarship has been the economics of slavery and the plantation system. The original master of the field was Lewis C. Gray, whose study *History of Agriculture in the Southern United States to 1860* (2 vols., 1933) can still be read with profit and should be read in order to understand the distinctiveness of Genovese's approach. The current debate got under way with a paper first published in 1958 by Alfred H. Conrad and John R. Meyer, available now in their book *The Economics of Slavery and Other Studies in Econometric History* (1964), which used modern principles of economic analysis to conclude that slavery was not dying out of its own inefficiency as had been argued by such historians as Charles W. Ramsdell and U. B. Phillips. The ensuing debate is intelligently assessed and sampled by Harold Woodman in *Slavery and the Southern Economy** (1966). The most recent, if not the final, words can be found in Robert W. Fogel and Stanley L. Engerman, eds., *The Reinterpretation of American Economic History* (1971).

The beginning point for the scholar of the antislavery movement should be the two general works: Gilbert H. Barnes's *The Anti-Slavery Impulse, 1830–1844* (1933), and Louis Filler's *The Crusade Against Slavery, 1830–1860** (1960). Benjamin Quarles' study *Black Abolitionists** (1969) filled a large void in the literature. There is an extensive biographical literature on individual abolitionists. Some of the best studies include John L. Thomas' *The Liberator, William Lloyd Garrison* (1963), Stephen B. Oates's *To Purge This Land With Blood: A Biography of John Brown** (1970), Bertram Wyatt-Brown's *Lewis Tappan and the Evangelical War Against Slavery** (1969), and Edward Magdol's *Owen Lovejoy: Abolitionist in Congress* (1967).

Arthur Zilversmit, in *The First Emancipation: The Abolition of Negro Slavery in the North* (1967), finds humane ideals operating in this section of the country, although some of the most recent literature on the subject of race relations and abolitionism has tended to detract from the claims of the moral superiority of the North. This is certainly true of the essay by David Donald in his *Lincoln Reconsidered** (1956), which argued that abolitionists tended to be men whose declining social status in a changing world led them to reform as a means of recapturing the past. Eugene Berwanger in *The Frontier Against Slavery: Western Anti-Negro Prejudice and the Slavery Extension Controversy* (1967) uncovered some unlovely motives behind western anti-slavery sentiment. Leon Litwack's *North of Slavery: The Negro in the Free States, 1790–1860** (1961) locates the origins of Jim Crow practices in the homeland of the abolition movement. Larry Gara in *The Liberty Line: The Story of the Underground Railroad* (1961) found the underground railroad less extensive and less welcome in the North than the oral tradition suggests. But the abolitionists are also defended on many points, even by the authors mentioned above. The best single source of proabolitionist historiography is the collection of essays edited by Martin Duberman, *The Antislavery Vanguard* (1965). One of its contributors, James M. McPherson, elaborated his defense in *The Struggle for Equality: Abolitionists and the Negro in the Civil War and Reconstruction* (1964).

In *The Black Image in the White Mind** (1971), George M. Fredrickson insightfully surveys nineteenth-century racism in both North and South. A standard text is William S. Jenkins' *Pro-Slavery Thought in the Old South* (1935). Eugene Genovese's *The World the Slaveholders Made* (1969) is a cultural analysis of the southern planter and in particular of the writings of George Fitzhugh.

The beginnings of sectional controversy can be studied in Glover Moore's book *The Missouri Controversy, 1819–1821* (1953). John R. Alden believes that sectional consciousness was complete at the time of the Revolution and argues his case in *The First South* (1961) and *The South in the Revolution, 1763–1789* (1957). Support for this point of view and its more far-reaching implications is supplied by Staughton Lynd in an essay in a collection of his essays, *Class Conflict, Slavery, and the United States Constitution** (1967). William Freehling's excellent study of the nullification controversy in South Carolina, *Prelude to Civil War* (1966), examines the developing sectional crisis in its embryonic stages.

Two recent quantitative studies of roll call behavior in Congress, Thomas B. Alexander's *Sectional Stress and Party Strength* (1967), and Joel Silbey's *The Shrine of Party* (1967), illustrate that the party system, new as it was, was strong enough to contain the pressures of the anti-slavery impulse. Roy F. Nichols, in *The Disruption of American Democracy** (1948), claims that when the Democratic party finally burst, secession and Civil War quickly followed. The closest study of the secession crisis itself is David Potter's *Lincoln and his Party in the Secession Crisis** (1942), but one should also see Richard N. Current's *Lincoln and the First Shot** (1963). Allan Nevins provides a magnificent narrative of the developing crisis in *The Emergence of Lincoln* (2 vols., 1950). A less grand account with a different point of view is Avery Craven's *The Coming of the Civil War* (1942) and *The Growth of Southern Nationalism* (1953). William and Bruce Catton's *Two Roads to Sumter** (1963) is readable but accurate. For a comprehensive historiographical synthesis of the literature on the coming of secession, one should read Thomas J. Pressly, *Americans Interpret Their Civil War** (1954).

* Also published in paperback edition.